# PHARMACY DEPARTMENT COMPLIANCE MANUAL

## 2003 Edition

### Highlights

- Medicare prescription drug coverage
- OIG Advisory Opinion information on pharmacy and drug arrangements
- Elements of an effective hospital based compliance program
- Corporate Integrity Agreements
- Antitrust and retail pharmacy networks
- FDA stance on retail pharmacy compounding
- Postmarket surveillance for devices
- OTC drug labeling requirements
- The pediatric rule for drug labels
- Patient rights and Medicare Conditions of participation
- Appropriate activities for nuclear pharmacists
- Employee safety under OSHA
- OSHA reporting requirements
- Joint Commission position on automated dispensing
- Medical error and the pharmacist role in prevention and detection
- Joint Commission standard impacting medical error
- Medical error reduction techniques
- The pharmacy department and emergency preparedness
- New Hospital Accreditation Standards Analysis of proposed modifications to existing medication use standards, to be implemented in January 2004

Aspen Publishers
Health Law and Compliance Series

# Pharmacy Department Compliance Manual 2003 Edition

# Aspen Publishers
# Health Law and Compliance Series

Emergency Department
Compliance Manual

The Health Care Compliance
Professional's Manual

Home Care
Compliance Manual

Hospital Perinatal
Compliance Manual

Long Term Care Compliance
Resource Manual

Pharmacy Department
Compliance Manual

Radiology Department
Compliance Manual

Aspen Publishers
Health Law and Compliance Series

# Pharmacy Department Compliance Manual 2003 Edition


Aspen Publishers

**Consulting Editor**
Karl G. Williams, RPh, Esq.

**Contributing Editors**
Elizabeth Mohre, JD
Jane L. Conley, MS
Ann H. Nevers, JD
Kathleen McGuire Gilbert

1185 Avenue of the Americas
New York, NY 10036
www.aspenpublishers.com

All forms, checklists, guidelines, and policies and procedures are presented as examples and should never be used as the basis for a legal document. They are intended as resources that can be selectively used and adapted—with the advice of the facility attorney—to meet state, local, individual hospital, and specific department needs and requirements.



Library of Congress Cataloging-in-Publication Data

Pharmacy department compliance manual / Aspen Health Law and Compliance Center;
Karl G. Williams, consulting editor;
contributing editors, Elizabeth H. Mohre, Jane L. Conley, Ann H. Nevers,
Kathleen McGuire Gilbert—6th ed.
p. cm.—(AHLCC compliance series)
Includes index.
ISBN 0-7355-3341-5
1. Hospital pharmacies—Standards—United States.
2. Hospital pharmacies—United States—Quality control. I. Williams, Karl G.
II. Series. III. Aspen Health Law and Compliance Center compliance series.

RA975.5.P5 P49 2001
362.1′782′021873—dc21
2001022380



Orders: (800) 638-8437
Customer Service: (800) 234-1660

Editorial Services: Amy Frevert
Printing and Manufacturing: Terri Miner

Library of Congress Catalog Card Number: 2001022380
ISBN: 0-7355-4160-4

*Printed in the United States of America*

1 2 3 4 5

# About Aspen Publishers

Aspen Publishers, headquartered in New York City, is a leading information provider for attorneys, business professionals, and law students. Written by preeminent authorities, our products consist of analytical and practical information covering both U.S. and international topics. We publish in the full range of formats, including updated manuals, books, periodicals, CDs, and online products.

Our proprietary content is complemented by 2,500 legal databases, containing over 11 million documents, available through our Loislaw division. Aspen Publishers also offers a wide range of topical legal and business databases, linked to Loislaw's primary material. Our mission is to provide accurate, timely, and authoritative content in easily accessible formats, supported by unmatched customer care.

To order any Aspen Publishers title, go to *www.aspenpublishers.com* or call 1-800-638-8437.

To reinstate your manual update service, call 1-800-638-8437.

For more information on Loislaw products, go to *www.loislaw.com* or call 1-800-364-2512.

For Customer Care issues, e-mail CustomerCare@aspenpublishers.com; call 1-800-234-1660; or fax 1-800-901-9075.

**Aspen Publishers**
**A Wolters Kluwer Company**

# SUBSCRIPTION NOTICE

This Aspen Publishers product is updated on a periodic basis with supplements to reflect important changes in the subject matter. If you purchased this product directly from Aspen Publishers we have already recorded your subscription for the update service.

If, however, you purchased this product from a bookstore and wish to receive future updates and revised or related volumes billed separately with a 30-day examination review, please contact our Customer Care Department at 1-800-234-1660, or send your name, company name (if applicable), address, and the title of the product to:

Aspen Publishers
7201 McKinney Circle
Frederick, MD 21704

# Table of Contents

# Editorial Board

# Introduction

Pharmacy department compliance issues can be overwhelming. Federal laws, state laws, liability concerns, and Joint Commission on Accreditation of Healthcare Organizations (Joint Commission) requirements affect nearly all aspects of patient care and departmental management. Managers must balance their compliance obligations against both patient care concerns and limited resources. This manual is an effort to assist pharmacy department managers in finding that balance by providing urgently needed information in a current, comprehensive, and easy-to-use compliance tool.

## FEATURES OF THIS MANUAL

### Legal Compliance Questions and Answers

This section of the manual is aimed at providing an easy reference to legal issues commonly encountered in hospital pharmacy departments. A list of questions at the front of this section will enable you to quickly locate helpful and current information in a variety of difficult legal areas such as fraud and abuse laws, Medicare reimbursement, tax issues, Health Insurance Portability and Accountability Act (HIPAA), the Controlled Substances Act, worker safety and environmental issues, prescription and medication order screening, substitution, patient counseling, and patient records. Citations to laws, regulations, and cases are provided for guiding additional research.

### Joint Commission Survey Questions and Answers

This section contains valuable advice from staff members at hospitals that have successfully navigated a Joint Commission survey. Interviewees provide frank and detailed information on what surveyors looked for, how to prepare staff for the survey, and how to demonstrate participation in performance improvement activities. This section is organized by topic to allow you to readily compare the experiences of different hospitals across the country.

## Hospital Accreditation Standards Analysis

This section analyzes the Joint Commission standards that apply to the pharmacy department. The Joint Commission emphasizes a hospitalwide, function-based approach to evaluating compliance, making it difficult for department managers to know precisely what is expected of them. This section boils down the standards, in an accessible grid format, and designates the responsibilities of pharmacy managers with regard to demonstrating compliance with the standards *in the pharmacy department.*

Managers should also make efforts to participate in hospitalwide compliance activities (such as performance improvement initiatives) because evaluation of interdepartmental activities is an important part of the survey process. These activities are not emphasized in this section of the manual, however, as they are usually coordinated by someone outside of the pharmacy with facilitywide responsibilities.

The applicable standards are presented one at a time, along with the following categories of guidance:

- *Comment:* This column describes the relationship between pharmacy and hospital responsibility for demonstrating compliance with the standard and indicates what the standard assesses.
- *Evidence:* This column lists the types of evidence that might be used to show compliance with the standard. Special emphasis is paid to documents that are developed or maintained in the pharmacy.
- *Staff Questions:* This column lists questions that the Joint Commission surveyor might ask the pharmacy director, pharmacy staff members, and others to assess compliance with the standard.
- *Reference:* This column provides cross references to the forms included in this manual that correlate with the standard.

## Reference Materials for Pharmacy Department Compliance

This section of the manual provides documentation that hospitals across the country have used to show compliance with Joint Commission standards, as well as documentation used to meet legal requirements discussed in Legal Compliance Questions and Answers. Sample documentation includes forms and policies crucial to accreditation compliance, including Pharmacist Scope of Assessment, Pharmaceutical Care Plan, Pharmaceutical Care Transfer Form, New Pharmacy Associate Orientation, and pharmacy staff competencies.

## CMS and Joint Commission Standards Checklist

This tool allows customers to cross reference the Medicare Conditions of Participation to the Joint Commission Standards, and also provides a place for them to note any deviations in their own state law requirements. This checklist will simplify compliance efforts by highlighting duplications and inconsistencies in the many standards that pharmacy departments must follow.

# Acknowledgments

Development of the *Pharmacy Department Compliance Manual* was a unique project, requiring the participation of many individuals. We are especially grateful to Consulting Editor Karl G. Williams, Seton Health, Troy, New York, who shared his expertise and knowledge regarding preparing for the Joint Commission surveys, as well as reviewing the manuscript and providing many sample materials from his organization. We also applaud the group of professionals who graciously consented to interviews about their recent Joint Commission survey experiences. Their candid comments bring a personal touch to the manual.

Appreciation is also due to the dedication and talent of Aspen staff without whom our efforts would not have come to fruition, especially Terri Miner, Production Manager, Production; and Amy Frevert, Editorial Services.

Cynthia Conner
Editorial Director
Aspen Publishers

# Acknowledgements

# Part 1

# Legal Compliance Questions and Answers

## Part 1 Contents

## INTRODUCTION TO COMPLIANCE

The emphasis on establishing corporate compliance programs for hospitals and other health care facilities is the direct result of the government's aggressive efforts over the last five years to enforce legislative provisions governing health care fraud and abuse. Corporate compliance programs have been imposed on numerous providers by the government as part of settlements following fraud and abuse investigations, and many health care organizations have voluntarily implemented such programs to protect themselves from sanctions under fraud and abuse laws. As a result, compliance efforts have been closely linked with the subject of fraud and abuse legislation, even though an effective compliance program is much broader in scope and covers many other types of legislative requirements and prohibitions. In fact, compliance efforts should be directed at establishing a culture within a hospital that promotes prevention, detection, and resolution of all instances of conduct that do not conform to all federal and state laws, private payer health program requirements, as well as the hospital's ethical and business policies. [Department of Health and Human Services, Office of Inspector General, Compliance Program Guidance for Hospitals, Feb. 23, 1998]

The Model Compliance Guidance for Hospitals of the Office of Inspector General (OIG) sets forth the basic elements of an effective hospital compliance program and lists a number of risk areas that are of particular concern to hospitals. While many of these risk areas focus on practices that could implicate fraud and abuse laws, other legal issues that should be addressed in an effective compliance program include

- medical records documentation practices
- patient confidentiality
- employment, licensure, and staffing issues
- environmental compliance issues
- informed consent issues
- quality of care issues
- antitrust issues
- tax exempt status issues [Department of Health and Human Services, Office of Inspector General, Compliance Program Guidance for Hospitals, Feb. 23, 1998]

In the pharmacy department, a plethora of additional compliance considerations come into play, largely as a result of the materials handled and the commensurate risk to staff and patients. For example, regulations concerning radioactive materials, hazardous waste, and drug distribution systems are paramount in any compliance review. The chart entitled "How Hospital Pharmacies Are Regulated," beginning on page 1:2, illustrates the scope and application of pharmacy regulation.

## HOW HOSPITAL PHARMACIES ARE REGULATED

| Regulatory Area | Sources Of Law | Enforcement Entities | Inspection Authority | Penalties/Remedies | Hospital Applicability |
|---|---|---|---|---|---|
| Food and drug law | Federal Food, Drug, and Cosmetic Act (FDCA), state drug laws | Federal Food and Drug Administration (FDA), analogous state agencies | FDA and state authorities may inspect pharmacies to assess compliance, or in response to a complaint. | Written warnings, cease and desist order, seizure of goods, criminal charges (resulting in fines or imprisonment), civil monetary penalties | Although the FDA's enforcement activities are focused primarily on drug manufacturers, certain areas of FDA regulation are of great importance to hospital pharmacy practice, including regulation of compounding and distribution of investigational drugs. |
| Controlled substances law | Federal Controlled Substances Act (CSA), state laws governing narcotics and other controlled substances | Federal Drug Enforcement Administration (DEA, a division of the Department of Justice), analogous state agencies | The DEA may inspect a pharmacy with an administrative warrant, or with consent. If consent is refused, the DEA must obtain an administrative inspection warrant, although probable cause is not required. In an emergency, or where there is an imminent danger to public health, the warrant is not required. | Imprisonment, severe fines, loss of DEA registration, loss of state license | Although a drug order for inpatient use does not constitute a "prescription" under the CSA, hospital pharmacies must comply with a complex scheme of recordkeeping and controlled distribution requirements. |
| Medicare Conditions of Participation | Social Security Act (SSA) | Centers for Medicare and Medicaid Services (CMS) and state agencies under contract to CMS (usually a state health department) | Medicare surveys are usually conducted annually by a state agency under contract to CMS. CMS conducts validation surveys on a small percentage of hospitals that received deemed status due to Joint Commission on Accreditation of Healthcare Organizations (Joint Commission) or American Osteopathic Association (AOA) accreditation. A validation survey is usually conducted shortly after a Joint Commission or AOA survey. | Hospitals that do not meet the Medicare Conditions of Participation or receive deemed status cannot participate in Medicare. | Most hospitals comply with the Medicare Conditions of Participation, either by receiving certification from HCFA, or obtaining deemed status through accreditation by AOA or the Joint Commission. |

*continues*

**How Hospital Pharmacies are Regulated** continued

| Regulatory Area | Sources Of Law | Enforcement Entities | Inspection Authority | Penalties/Remedies | Hospital Applicability |
|---|---|---|---|---|---|
| Occupational health | Occupational Safety and Health Act (OSHA), and broad range of implementing federal regulations, applicable state and local regulations | The OSHA and analogous state agencies | OSHA has broad powers to enter and inspect place of employment on a periodic basis, and to conduct investigations in response to employee complaints. | Written warning citations, criminal charges (resulting in fines or imprisonment), and other penalty fines | Pharmacy staff must not only be familiar with OSHA issues that apply throughout the hospital, such as hazards associated with bloodborne pathogens, but also with special hazards encountered in the pharmacy department, such as hazardous medications. |
| Environmental laws | Broad range of federal environmental statutes including those governing safe disposal of hazardous waste, licensing requirements for facilities disposing of radioactive waste, and state and local regulations | The Environmental Protection Agency (EPA) and analogous state agencies | EPA has broad powers to require sources of hazardous waste to submit reports, monitor hazardous waste disposal, and certify compliance with EPA regulations. | Written warning citations, criminal charges (resulting in fines or imprisonment), and other civil and criminal penalties | The pharmacy department is a key site for the preparation, handling, and disposal of hazardous substances and hazardous waste, including hazardous chemicals and drugs, infectious waste, and radioactive waste. |
| Reimbursement | SSA, FDA statutes and regulations, state law | CMS, FDA, state agencies | See Fraud and Abuse. | Loss of reimbursement, loss of state license, professional disciplinary action, exclusion from Medicare and Medicaid, termination by health plan | Many reimbursement requirements are governed by state law; hospital pharmacies should check both federal and state law. |
| Fraud and abuse | Fraud and abuse provisions in SSA, civil False Claims Act, Stark law, state laws and regulations governing same topics | Health and Human Services Office of Inspector General (OIG), Department of Justice, CMS, state Medicaid Fraud Control Units | The OIG has subpoena power, the right to immediate access of documents necessary to the performance of its statutory duties, and conducts most of its investigative duties through the FBI. | Criminal penalties, civil monetary penalties, exclusion from Medicare | Many hospitals are developing corporate compliance plans based on the OIG model plan in an effort to avoid fraud and abuse violations. Pharmacy billing should be a component of the plan. |

*continues*

**How Hospital Pharmacies are Regulated** continued

| Regulatory Area | Sources Of Law | Enforcement Entities | Inspection Authority | Penalties/Remedies | Hospital Applicability |
|---|---|---|---|---|---|
| Antitrust laws | Robinson-Patman Act, Prescription Drug Marketing Act, and state laws prohibiting discriminatory pricing, and/or requiring unitary pricing | The Antitrust Division of the U.S. Department of Justice, the Federal Trade Commission, and analogous state agencies | Not applicable | Criminal prosecution, fines, and civil monetary penalties under both federal and state antitrust laws | Under some state laws, hospital pharmacy directors are responsible for hospital drug purchasing decisions, and therefore should be familiar with federal and state antitrust laws pertaining to the purchase, transfer, or resale of such drugs. |
| Hospital pharmacy practice | Hospital licensure laws and regulations, pharmacist and pharmacy licensure laws and regulations | State departments of health, boards of pharmacy | State licensing boards generally have authority to make periodic inspections, as well as investigations in response to complaints. | Loss of license, ban from participation in state funded programs, professional disciplinary action, civil liability | State hospital licensing and board of pharmacy regulations govern pharmacy activities in detail and must be fully understood by pharmacy staff. |

## PAYMENT AND PRICING ISSUES

In addition to the federal laws that address the handling of drugs and other substances, hospital pharmacy directors must be familiar with federal regulation of the transactional aspects of practice. Pharmacy departments must understand the legal issues surrounding reimbursement so they can obtain the revenue that they are due and avoid severe penalties under the fraud and abuse laws, such as exclusion from the Medicare program. Pharmacy departments must also comply with federal and state antitrust laws that affect drug pricing when making drug purchasing and formulary decisions. (The ethical responsibilities associated with pharmacy transactions are discussed in Standards RI.1 through RI.2 in Part 3 of this Manual.)

### Reimbursement

#### Does Medicare provide coverage for prescription drugs?

Medicare Part A provides coverage for drugs and biologicals that are used in the hospital and that are ordinarily furnished by the hospital for the care and treatment of inpatients. [Medicare Intermediary Manual 155.2 & 3101.3] Drugs and biologicals used outside of the hospital are in general not covered by Medicare Part A. However, Medicare Part A will pay for a limited supply of drugs and biologicals if they are medically necessary to permit the patient's discharge from the hospital and a limited supply is required until the patient can obtain a continuing supply. [Medicare Intermediary Manual 3103.3 & 42 C.F.R. 409.13]

In general, Medicare Part B does not cover prescription drugs and biologicals for outpatients or inpatients who have exhausted their Part A benefits. There are many exceptions to this general rule, however, including the following:

- A drug or biological that is not usually self-administered, is provided incident to a physician's service, is reasonable and necessary for the diagnosis or treatment of the illness or injury, is not excluded as an immunization, and has not been determined by the Food and Drug Administration (FDA) to be less than effective is covered. The presumption is that intravenous and intramuscular drugs are not usually self-administered, but subcutaneous drugs are. Non-injectable drugs such as oral, suppository, or topical medications are excluded from coverage. The Medicare carrier is to review each indication for a drug to determine if the drug is usually self-administered for that indication. [*See* Program Memorandum AB-02-072 (May 15, 2002) and Program Memorandum AB-02-139 (Oct. 11, 2002).]
- A reasonable supply of antigens prepared by a physician who has examined the patient and has determined a treatment plan and dosage regimen is covered. [Medicare Carriers Manual 2049.4]
- Immunizations are excluded, unless they are directly related to the treatment of an injury or direct exposure to a disease or condition, such as anti-rabies treatment, tetanus antitoxin or booster vaccine, or immune globulin.

In addition, pneumococcal, hepatitis B, and influenza virus vaccines are covered even in the absence of injury or direct exposure.

- Unlabeled use of anticancer drugs, if a number of conditions are met, is covered.
- Immunosuppressive drugs for up to 44 months following discharge from a hospital for a Medicare-covered organ transplant are covered.
- Erythropoietin is covered for the treatment of anemia for patients with chronic renal failure who are on dialysis.
- Certain oral anticancer drugs meeting a number of conditions are covered.
- Blood clotting factors for hemophilia patients are covered. [Medicare Carrier's Manual 2049 through 2049.5]
- Supplies that are necessary for the effective use of durable medical equipment, such as oxygen, tumor chemotherapy agents used with an infusion pump, or heparin used with a home dialysis system are covered. [Medicare Carrier's Manual 2100.5]
- Blood glucose monitoring, under certain circumstances, is covered. [The Centers for Medicare and Medicaid Services (CMS) (formerly Health Care Financing Administration (HCFA)) Program Memorandum, Transmittal AB-00–99, issued Oct. 24, 2000]

---

**How does Medicare reimburse prescription drugs that are covered?**

When outpatient prescription drugs are covered by Medicare, they are reimbursed based on 95% of the average wholesale price (AWP). However, Medicare research has found a number of drugs available in the marketplace at lower than AWP. It has been recommended that Medicare establish payment rates based on actual market transactions that reflect acquisition costs. [*Medicare Outpatient Drugs: Program Payments Should Better Reflect Market Prices,* Testimony before Senate Subcommittee on Health, U.S. GAO-02-531T (Mar. 14, 2002), *see also Reimbursement for Prescription Drugs,* DHHS OIG Testimony before Senate Committee on Finance (Mar. 14, 2002).]

---

**How do Medicare HMOs cover prescription drugs?**

In 1997, the Medicare+Choice program was established by the Balanced Budget Act. Under the Medicare+Choice program, CMS contracts with health plans who provide Medicare benefits to beneficiaries through an HMO delivery model. HMOs participating in the Medicare+Choice program are free to provide additional Medicare benefits to beneficiaries including outpatient prescription drugs. When a drug benefit is offered, the plan may choose to limit coverage by placing a dollar limit on prescription drug coverage, by charging coinsurance or copayments to beneficiaries, by covering only certain types of drugs (only brand name or generic), or by only covering drugs on a formulary. The pharmacy should check with the HMO administrator to determine the Medicare HMO prescription drug coverage for an individual since coverage can vary between HMOs. In

2001, 87% of HMOs had a dollar limit on the prescription drug coverage. [*Medicare HMO Rx Drug Benefit: Information Available to Beneficiaries on Dollar Limits,* OEI 03-00-00430 (May 17, 2002).]

---

**What is the Medicare-endorsed Prescription Drug Card Initiative?**

The Medicare-endorsed Prescription Drug Card initiative is a Medicare effort to assist beneficiaries to obtain lower prescription drug costs by recognizing drug discount programs that offer drug discounts through use of formularies, generic drugs, or rebates. Even though the Medicare benefit generally does not cover prescription drugs, Medicare will endorse sponsors that secure rebates or discounts from drug manufacturers on name brand and generic drugs. Cost savings must be shared with beneficiaries. It is hoped that cost savings will eliminate medication noncompliance such as unfilled prescriptions, skipped medication doses, or partial doses.

In order to qualify for endorsement, the sponsor must offer rebates or discounts, have stable prices, have three years experience, agree to enroll only Medicare beneficiaries in the program, have good retail access, provide customer service support for beneficiaries, and protect beneficiary privacy. Programs interested in being endorsed will submit an application within 60 days of solicitation by Medicare. Endorsed entities will have six months to implement the program. The endorsed entity can charge a one-time enrollment fee that does not exceed $25 to the beneficiary. Medicare intends to establish a Gold Star designation for those who offer price concessions and high levels or rebates. [67 Fed. Reg. 56618 (Sept. 4, 2002).]

---

**What is the prospective payment system for hospital outpatient services?**

The outpatient prospective payment system is a new payment system for hospital outpatient services, including emergency services and urgent care. Payment for hospital outpatient services will be made under recently developed rates for Ambulatory Payment Classification (APC) groups, similar in concept to diagnosis-related groups (DRGs), with which pharmacists are familiar. The Centers for Medicare and Medicaid Services (CMS) [formerly Health Care Financing Administration (HCFA)] has classified outpatient services and procedures into 451 groups that are comparable clinically and use similar resource amounts. CMS has assigned each APC a weight based on the median costs for the services within the APC group. The payment rate is the product of a conversion factor and the APC rate. The prospective payment system applies to nearly all hospitals, including those hospitals that are excluded from the inpatient prospective payment system and community mental health centers, but it does not apply to critical access hospitals and Maryland hospitals. [65 Fed. Reg. 18,434 (2000), codified at 42 C.F.R. Parts 409 through 413, 419, 424, 489, 498, & 1003. For detailed information on billing procedures and rates, consult http://www.hcfa.gov.]

### What services are excluded from the outpatient prospective payment system?

The following services are not paid for under the outpatient prospective payment system:

- services provided by certain providers, including: physicians, nurse practitioners, physician assistants, certified nurse midwives, psychologists, anesthetists, and clinical social workers, which will continue to be paid for under the Medicare fee schedule
- rehabilitation services
- ambulance services
- prosthetics, prosthetic supplies, devices, and implants (except for intraocular lenses), and orthotic devices
- durable medical equipment, except implantable durable medical equipment
- clinical diagnostic laboratory services
- services provided to patients with end-stage renal disease (ESRD) that are paid under the ESRD composite rate, and drugs and supplies furnished during dialysis
- services and procedures that cannot be safely furnished in an outpatient setting or that require inpatient care
- services provided to persons who are inpatients of a skilled nursing facility (SNF) and that are covered under the SNF prospective payment system
- services not covered by Medicare, including services that are not medically necessary

### What are transitional pass-through drugs?

By law, certain drugs will be reimbursed outside of the APC groups. These drugs are included on a list of transitional pass-through drugs and will be reimbursed at a higher rate. The items designated by the law are the following:

1. Current orphan drugs, as designated under section 526 of the Federal Food, Drug, and Cosmetic Act
2. Current cancer therapy drugs, biologicals, and brachytherapy devices. These items are those drugs or biologicals that are used in cancer therapy, including (but not limited to) chemotherapeutic agents, antiemetics, hematopoietic growth factors, colony-stimulating factors, biological response modifiers, bisphosphonates, and brachytherapy devices.
3. Current radiopharmaceutical drugs and biological products used for diagnostic, monitoring, or therapeutic purposes.
4. New drugs, biologicals, or medical devices

CMS has established a process for requesting additions to the transitional pass-through list. For details, and the most current list, consult http://www.hcfa.gov. [For the criteria for establishing new categories of medical devices eligible for transitional pass-through payments, *see* 66 Fed. Reg. 55850 (Nov. 2, 2001), codified at 42 C.F.R. Part 419 and *Process and Information Required to Determine Eligibility of Drugs and Biologicals for Transitional Pass-Through Payment* (Oct. 10, 2002 at http://www.cms.hhs.gov/medlearn/refopps.asp).]

---

**Does Medicaid provide reimbursement for prescription drugs?**

Medicaid covers inpatient prescription drugs and, unlike Medicare, provides outpatient prescription drug coverage as an optional service. [42 U.S.C. 1396d(a)] Currently, all states cover outpatient prescription drugs. In an effort to contain costs, encourage the use of generic drugs, and make the drug benefit more uniform across the country, the government created the maximum allowable cost for drugs (MAC) program in 1975. Pursuant to the MAC program, a pharmacist's reimbursement varies depending on whether the drug is a multiple source drug for which CMS has established a specific upper limit or another drug. [42 C.F.R. 447.331]

---

**How are multiple source drugs reimbursed?**

CMS (formerly HCFA) publishes listings that identify and set federal upper limits (FUL) for certain commonly used multiple source drugs. The reimbursement for these drugs is calculated at 150 percent of the published price for the least costly therapeutic equivalent. Pharmacies dispensing these drugs are reimbursed the listed price of the drug plus a reasonable dispensing fee. [42 C.F.R. 447.332] The payment limit for brand name drugs does not apply if a physician certifies in his or her own handwriting that a specific brand is medically necessary for a particular recipient. Each state Medicaid agency decides what certification form and procedure are used. The regulations provide that a check-off box on a form is not acceptable but a notation like "brand necessary" is permitted. [42 C.F.R. 447.331]

---

**How are drugs that are not on the multiple source drug list reimbursed?**

Drugs that are not multiple source drugs or are not on CMS's (formerly HCFA's) reimbursement schedule for commonly used multiple source drugs are reimbursed at the lower of the estimated acquisition costs plus reasonable dispensing fees or the usual and customary charge for the drug. [42 C.F.R. 447.331]

An audit report on Medicaid Pharmacy acquisition costs found wide variation in discounts from average wholesale prices (AWP) for pharmacy purchasers. The report found the following fluctuations in actual discounts. Pharmacies were found to purchase single source innovator drugs at 17.2% below AWP, all drugs without FULs were discounted 27.2% below AWP, multiple source drugs without FULs were discounted an estimated 44.2% below AWP, and multiple source drugs with FULs were discounted about 72.1% below AWP. Because of the variation in price discounts, the report recommended that states use a four-tier reimbursement methodology based on AWP. Tier-one would be for single source brand name drugs to be paid as a percentage discount off AWP. Tier-two, for innovator multiple source drugs without FULs would be paid as a percentage discount off AWP. Tier-three, for non-innovator multiple source drugs without FULs would be paid a percentage discount off AWP. Tier-four for FUL multiple source drugs would be paid at FUL price. This would allow the state to reimburse the prescription drugs more in line with actual acquisition costs. CMS agreed with the report and planned to share the recommendations with state Medicaid programs. [*Medicaid Pharmacy—Additional Analyses of the Actual Acquisition Cost of Prescription Drug Products,* A-06-02-00041 (Sept. 16, 2002)].

**How do Medicaid formularies work?**

Federal law allows states to establish Medicaid drug formularies that identify pharmaceuticals for which Medicaid will pay. A state formulary must be established by a committee that includes physicians and pharmacists. A drug may be excluded from the formulary if, based on the labeling, it does not have a significant, clinically meaningful therapeutic advantage over other drugs in the formulary. The goal of the formulary is to achieve savings, as well as protect the health of people covered by Medicaid. Drugs not included in the formulary may be covered on a prior authorization basis. [42 U.S.C. 1396r-8(d)]

**Are there other state laws that affect reimbursement for prescription drugs?**

Many states have begun to enact laws that allow seniors and other eligible beneficiaries to purchase drugs at reduced prices. For example, a 1999 California law requires pharmacists to give Medicaid discounts to all Medicare-eligible individuals. (CAL. BUS. & PROF. CODE § 4425 and CAL. HEALTH & SAFETY CODE § 130401) In Iowa, effective January 2002, a prescription drug discount program will allow Medicare-eligible individuals to negotiate discounts for a small annual membership fee. New Jersey has two plans that allow lower-income seniors to buy prescription drugs from participating pharmacies: (1) Pharmaceutical Assistance to the Aged and Disabled (PAAD) that provides for an out-of-pocket cost of $5 per prescription and (2) Senior Gold Prescription Discount Program that covers prescriptions for $15 plus one-half the remaining cost of the drug. (N.J. CODE § 30:4D-44, 30:4D-45) A Florida law passed in 2001 allows the state to negotiate discounts on "preferred" drugs that are greater than the Medicaid rebate rates. A 2002 law establishes a "Ron Silver Senior Drug Program" to provide prescription drugs for low-income elderly (FLA. STAT. § 409.065, 409.066).

In Maine, legislation permits residents who are not Medicaid-eligible or covered under any other prescription drug benefit program to enroll in the "Maine Rx" program and then buy prescription drugs from participating pharmacies at the discounted Medicaid rates; the pharmacies are then reimbursed from a state fund created with negotiated rebate payments from participating drug manufacturers, similar to Medicaid.

A pharmaceutical industry challenge to Maine's program was initially upheld; however, on appeal the case was dismissed until the Secretary of Health and Human Services (HHS) could review the Maine program to determine whether or not it should be approved. [*See Pharmaceutical Research and Manufacturers of America v. Thompson,* 191 F. Supp. 2d 48 (D.D.C. 2002), 313 F.3d 600 (D.C. App. 2002) and *Pennsylvania Pharmacy Assn. v. Houston,* 283 F.3d 531 (3d. Cir. 2001), *cert. denied,* 2002 U.S. LEXIS 6003 (U.S. Oct. 7, 2002) where the court found that the pharmacy association had no right to challenge Medicaid reimbursement rates.] In a similar case, with a different result, a federal appeals court has preliminarily enjoined the state of Vermont from implementing a law that would have allowed it to expand its Medicaid prescription drug program to include certain higher-income elderly and other non–Medicaid-eligible citizens. [*See Pharmaceutical Research and Manufacturers of America v. U.S.,* 251 F. 3d 219 (2001), reversing the lower court at 135 F. Supp. 2d 1 (D.D.C. 2001).]

If the Maine and Vermont drug benefit programs are upheld it is likely that other states will follow and develop similar programs. Pharmacy directors and benefit managers should be aware of the developing laws in their state that affect prescription drug benefits and reimbursement.

---

**Are there any legal restrictions on charges for investigational drugs?**

The FDA allows charges to be imposed on investigational drugs as long as sponsors or investigators meet certain requirements. [21 C.F.R. 312.7] However, most payers exclude investigational drugs from coverage, because they are very expensive and have not been proven effective. Health plans have developed a variety of strategies for excluding experimental drugs. The experimental exclusion may be a separate contract clause or may be set forth in a definition of "medically necessary" treatments covered by the plan. Subscriber contracts may or may not differentiate between experimental and investigational procedures. Many health plans link drug product coverage to FDA approval, as that is based on scientific proof of safety and efficacy and usually establishes a conservative standard. Other plans cover an unapproved medication if studies reported in medical literature sufficiently establish the usefulness of the drug. Pharmacists dispensing investigational drugs should advise patients that their insurer or health plan may not pay for the treatment.

In response to reported denials of coverage for cutting-edge care, some states have attempted to increase the availability of experimental treatments through regulation. California requires an external review mechanism for denials of experimental procedures and treatments, under some circumstances. The law applies to both health care service plans and insurers, in cases in which an enrollee has a life-threatening or seriously debilitating condition and the enrollee's physician certifies that standard treatment would not be appropriate or effective. [Cal. Health & Safety Code 1370.4; Cal. Ins. Code 10145.3] Other states have adopted guidelines for coverage that might otherwise be excluded. In Rhode Island, insurers and health maintenance organizations (HMOs) must cover unapproved cancer therapies if the patient is enrolled in a clinical trial, there is not superior approved therapy, and data provide a "reasonable expectation" that the unapproved therapy will be at least equally as effective as the approved alternative. [R.I. GEN. LAWS 27–18–36.2, 27–19–32.2, 27–20–27.2, & 27–41–41.2] In Maryland, insurers, nonprofit health service plans, and HMOs are required to cover the cost of treatment in clinical trials for treatment provided for a life-threatening condition or for patients with cancer. [MD. CODE ANN., Ins. 15–827] Finally, some states have legislatively mandated coverage for specific treatments. One example of a treatment for which coverage was mandated after litigation concerning its experimental status is high-dose chemotherapy with autologous bone marrow transplant for breast cancer, considered experimental by some plans. [MINN. STAT. 62A.309]

---

**Does Medicare cover investigational drugs administered in clinical trials?**

In 2000, CMS released a policy on what items and services will be covered in connection with clinical trials. Medicare covers (1) the routine costs of qualifying clinical trials as well as (2) reasonable and necessary items and services used to diagnose and treat complications arising from participation in all clinical trials. Routine costs of a clinical trial include all items and services that are provided in either the experimental or the control arms of a trial except those listed below as not covered. Services provided to Medicare beneficiaries in both the experimental group and the control group are eligible for coverage provided that all other criteria in this instruction are met. Covered routine costs include

- items or services that are typically provided absent a clinical trial (e.g., medically necessary conventional care)
- items and services required for the provision of the investigational item or service (e.g., administration of a noncovered chemotherapeutic agent)
- items and services required for the clinically appropriate monitoring of the effects of the item or service, or the prevention of complications
- items and services that are medically necessary for the diagnosis or treatment of complications arising from the provision of an investigational item or service

Covered routine costs do not include

- the investigational item or service itself
- items and services
  - for which there is no Medicare benefit category, or
  - that are statutorily excluded, or
  - that fall under a national noncoverage policy
- items and services furnished solely to satisfy data collection and analysis needs that are not used in the direct clinical management of the patient (e.g., monthly computed tomographic scans for a condition usually requiring only a single scan)

- items and services customarily provided by the research sponsors free of charge for any enrollee in the trial
- items and services provided solely to determine trial eligibility [Medicare Coverage Policy—Clinical Trials, available on the Internet at http:/www.cms.hhs.gov]

---

**What are the reimbursement implications of off-label uses?**

States can exclude from Medicaid coverage outpatient drugs when they are prescribed for a use other than a "medically accepted indication," based on the approved labeling and officially recognized compendia. [42 U.S.C. 1396r-8(d)] Most private insurers also restrict reimbursement for off-label uses.

A growing number of states are enacting legislation requiring coverage of off-label uses, however. Some state laws require coverage of certain off-label uses, such as off-label uses for cancer. A Rhode Island law provides that no health insurer that provides coverage for prescription drugs shall exclude coverage of any drug used for the treatment of cancer because the drug has not been approved by the FDA for that indication. This use of the drug must, however, be recognized in one of the standard reference compendia or in the medical literature. [R.I. GEN. LAWS 27–55–2] Several other states do not restrict off-label use to the treatment of a particular condition. For example, in Alabama no insurance policy that provides coverage for drugs can exclude coverage for off-label use of a drug, if the off-label use is recognized for treatment in one of the standard reference compendia, in the medical literature, or by the Commissioner of Insurance. [ALA. CODE 27–1–10.1; *see also* OHIO REV. CODE ANN. 3923.60 & TENN. CODE ANN. 56–7–2352]

---

**Can pharmacists receive reimbursement for providing disease management services?**

The Balanced Budget Act of 1997 provides that a physician or any other individual or entity designated by the Secretary of the Department of Health and Human Services can furnish diabetes self-management education. [42 U.S.C. 1395x (qq)] CMS has issued a final rule implementing the Balanced Budget Act provision. Under the rule, a physician or qualified nonphysician provider would receive payment for educational and training services furnished in an outpatient setting to a Medicare beneficiary with diabetes. Any provider furnishing diabetes education would have to employ at least a registered dietitian and a certified diabetic educator to provide education services. A licensed pharmacist who was a Medicare supplier of durable medical equipment could qualify for payment under the rule if the pharmacist met payment and quality standards. A diabetes education program must be accredited by an appropriate accrediting organization or approved by CMS [65 Fed. Reg. 83130 (Dec. 19, 2000), confirmed at 66 Fed. Reg. 14861 (Mar. 14, 2001) and codified at 42 C.F.R. 410.140-410.146].

### Can pharmacists obtain reimbursement for pharmaceutical care activities?

Pharmacists in many states are attempting to obtain payment for patient care activities and have begun to make legislative and regulatory inroads. In some states, pharmacists have gained the authority to perform diagnostic tests, prescribe certain drugs, and otherwise follow patients, without specific payment legislation. (For further discussion of this issue, refer to Pharmaceutical Care Legislation, under **State Regulation of Pharmacy Activities.**) Mississippi was the first state to allow reimbursement for pharmacists who provide certain disease management services to Medicaid beneficiaries. Pharmacists can provide services to patients in the areas of diabetes, asthma, hyperlipidemia, and anticoagulation. In order to provide disease management services, a pharmacist must be registered to practice pharmacy in the state of Mississippi and be certified to provide disease management services by the state's board of pharmacy. [MISS. REG. 13–010–022]

## Fraud and Abuse

### What types of activities are governed by health care fraud and abuse legislation?

Both at the state and federal levels, statutory fraud and abuse prohibitions apply to the following categories of health care provider activities:

- false claims or other fraudulent billing activities
- bribes or kickbacks, including a complex array of discounts, rebates, profit-sharing agreements, or other business relationships
- illegal referrals, prohibiting physicians or other types of health care providers from referring patients for health care services to entities in which the physician has a financial interest

### What state and federal laws sanction fraudulent activity in the provision of pharmaceutical services?

At the federal level, fraud and abuse prohibitions are largely defined in the Medicare/Medicaid statute [in particular 42 U.S.C. 1320a-7a and 1320a-7b] and the Stark laws [42 U.S.C. 1395nn] and enforced under these statutes as well as the civil False Claims Act [31 U.S.C. 3729 through 3733] and Health Insurance Portability and Accountability Act (HIPAA) [42 U.S.C. 1128A(a)(5)]. The Medicare/Medicaid statute contains prohibitions relating to false claims and fraudulent billing practices and also prohibits specific categories of referral payments, including kickbacks, bribes, or rebates. The Stark law bans a more specific type of referral between a physician and entities in which the physician has a financial interest, including entities that provide outpatient prescription and inpatient and outpatient hospital services. Later in this section is a discussion of program guidelines for the pharmaceutical industry.

At the state level, many jurisdictions have illegal remuneration laws similar to the federal statute [*See, e.g.,* MICH. COMP. LAWS ANN. 752.1004] as well as false claims legislation. [MICH. COMP. LAWS. ANN. 752.1001] The majority of states have also enacted some form of self-referral legislation, although these statutes vary widely from jurisdiction to jurisdiction and frequently bear little resemblance to their federal counterpart, the Stark law. In addition, many states have professional practice statutes that prohibit the receipt of rebates or discounts for prescribing a particular drug or, more generally, the practice of prescribing drugs for financial gain. [*See* LA. REV. STAT. ANN. 37:1285] Finally, both state unfair trade laws and state consumer protection laws have been applied in cases involving alleged fraudulent practices within the pharmacy industry. [*See, e.g., Sullivan's Wholesale Drug Co. v. Faryl's Pharmacy, Inc.,* 573 N.E. 2d 1370 (Ill. App. Ct. 1991), *appeal denied,* 580 N.E.2d 136 (1991).]

---

**What types of pharmacy practices can constitute fraud under federal and state laws?**

As the preceding answer indicates, the broad language of many of the fraud and abuse prohibitions in federal law and in numerous state statutes makes these provisions applicable to a very wide range of potentially illegal activity. Examples of fraudulent conduct in the provision of pharmaceutical services include the following:

*Submitting claims for payment for drugs that were never prescribed or dispensed.* If the prosecutor has evidence that the error was intentional, this might well be the subject of the most serious crime in this regulatory scheme: fraud. Likewise, double billing, or submitting more than one claim for the same prescription, is abhorred and would be treated aggressively. The presence of some indication that the claim was made intentionally is pivotal in determining whether the crime is fraud, which might result in jail time, or abuse, which carries the more pedestrian penalties of monetary fines and perhaps exclusion from participation in Medicare/Medicaid.

*Submitting claims for payment for items that are nonreimbursable.* It is a violation of the False Claims Act to knowingly seek federal reimbursement for drugs or devices that are considered nonreimbursable. This may result in either fraud allegations or civil monetary penalties. In a recent case, seven hospitals in Arizona, Florida, and California agreed to pay $5.5 million to settle charges that they unlawfully billed Medicare and TRICARE, the military health care program, for surgical procedures using experimental cardiac devices that had not been approved for marketing by the FDA. Although reimbursement policy for experimental devices has changed since the lawsuit was filed, when the procedures involved were performed, Medicare considered them to be nonreimbursable.

*Dispensing a generic but billing for the cost of the equivalent brand name prescription drug.* This might well result in fraud but has been equally likely to result in civil monetary penalties. In fact there have been numerous cases in which a malfunction in the computer system, automatically billing for brand regardless of what was dispensed, resulted in this improper practice. Because the label is printed correctly, the dispensing pharmacist is unable to detect any error and has no reason to suspect it might be billed to Medicaid improperly. This scenario supplies sufficient evidence to conclude that there is no intent on the part of the pharmacy to commit this wrongful act and a fraud charge/conviction is highly unlikely. A charge of abuse, an unnecessary increase in charges to the Medicaid or Medicare program, with significant monetary penalties and the possibility of exclusion, is the probable result. Also, one should pay particular attention to ensuring that the proper National Drug Code (NDC) number is used. If a larger package size is purchased or a new generic is added to the formulary, the NDC number of the more expensive product could carelessly be reported to the payer, resulting in wrongfully high costs. A systematic approach should be taken to assuring that the correct NDC is entered into the computer when new products are added or different multiple-source products may be used. Likewise, the product cost should be verified on a routine basis.

*Partially filling prescriptions while billing for the full amount.* An area that has been the subject of concern in recent years involves partial fills. That is, when there is an inadequate supply of medication for a particular order, such that it will require the remainder to be supplied on a different day, Medicaid should be billed only once for this as it pays only one dispensing fee per prescription. Billing the fee a second time when the remaining quantity is supplied would be considered a false claim. Also, if the patient never returns to obtain the remainder and it is retained in stock, the pharmacy should issue a credit accounting for the portion that is not delivered.

*Submitting claims that lack adequate supporting documentation.* If there is an inadequate paper trail to support claims, in the exact format demanded by CMS (formerly HCFA), this could be a trouble area. Medication administration, not only the order or the dispensing, must be charted. Inconsistencies between the dosage actually administered and the dosage that corresponds to a billing code are a major concern. Emergency department medication claims may be particularly likely to suffer from inadequate documentation.

*Using the wrong pricing formula.* Pricing formulas are another thorny area for pharmacy managers. The formula employed for Medicaid prescriptions, for example, varies from state to state. A significant number of states use the lower of the pharmacy's "usual and customary charge" or the average wholesale price (AWP) minus a fixed percentage plus a dispensing fee. Virginia, for example uses the AWP of the medication – 9% + $4.25 with co-pays of $1 for generic medication and $2 for brand. Problems may arise when pharmacies either do not know the formula or seek a higher reimbursement and hope the state Medicaid office does not take note. This practice, because it is marginal in nature, is not likely to be prosecuted under the felony fraud provisions but would certainly be characterized as abuse of the system resulting in monetary penalties and possibly exclusion. Also, many states demand that the pharmacy be reimbursed only the amount that is equal to the "'best price'" for a given medication. Problems can arise when discounts are offered to certain customers to the exclusion of Medicaid.

*Charging for sample medications.* Another pricing issue may arise in connection with the use of sample medications. Although the Prescription Drug Marketing Act (PDMA), discussed below, prohibits the dispensing of samples without exception in retail practice, there is a limited exception carved out for institutional practice. When samples are dispensed to inpatients it is unlawful to charge any amount, even a handling fee, for these medications. Not only is this a violation of the PDMA but it also may be characterized as fraud or abuse because of the unnecessary increase in costs to the program. A recent example of this type of fraudulent practice involved a federal investigation in Massachusetts that resulted in the pharmaceutical manufacturer of the prostate cancer drug Lupron pleading guilty to criminal fraud and being assessed fines of $875 million for fraudulent pricing and marketing and for giving free samples to physicians and advising them to bill Medicare for them. Several physicians were also indicted in the investigation, and pled guilty to fraud in connection with billing for free Lupron samples. Further, if samples are provided to the pharmacy in an effort to increase prescribing to Medicare or Medicaid patients, the antikickback statute is implicated. Note, however, that any violation of the PDMA is a felony and, unlike the antikickback statute, the government need not prove that the defendant acted willfully (that is, with a specific intent to violate the law). It is enough to show that the defendant knew that the drug he or she sold was a sample. Institutions should have a policy concerning the use of samples and record of actual usage to answer any charges of impropriety in this practice.

*Inducements and marketing from drug manufacturers.* If the purpose of a pharmaceutical marketing initiative is to induce the prescribing or dispensing of a prescription drug payable under Medicare or Medicaid, then the criminal antikickback law will come into play. Three examples are discussed in OIG Special Fraud Alert of August 25, 1994. The first of these is characterized as a "product conversion" program where the participant pharmacy is given a cash payment by Company A every time it causes conversion to its generic equivalent product from Company B's product. The second scheme is characterized as a "frequent flier" program in which physicians are given credit air travel each time they fill out a questionnaire for a new patient placed on its product. The third program involves a "research grant" in which physicians are given substantial cash awards for nominal recordkeeping tasks associated with the patient's medication therapy.

In general the OIG would be suspicious about any prize, gift, or cash payments offered to providers (physicians, pharmacists, mail order companies, managed care organizations) in exchange for prescribing or providing specific products. Such practices are particularly suspicious when the awards are based on volume. Scientific grants must include a substantial "scientific value" and include "actual scientific pursuit."

The concern of the OIG in this area is pharmaceutical marketing programs that cross a line from the traditional advertising and educational activities into activities that induce utilization based on anything other than the patient's best interest. Offering a financial incentive to prescribe or dispense a given product causes interference with the relationship between the physician and the patient or the pharmacist and the patient. This is exactly the kind of activity the antikickback law was designed to prevent. In addition, where the patient is a Medicaid beneficiary, these programs may tend to increase cost from unnecessary utilization and result in abuse charges. [U.S. Department of Health and Human Services, Office of Inspector General, *Special Fraud Alert: Prescription Drug Marketing Schemes,* OIG 94–18 (Aug. 1994), available on the Internet at http://www.oig.hhs.gov/fraud/docs/alertsandbulletins/121994.html]

*Routine waiver of co-payments.* OIG advisory opinions, though not directly addressing pharmacy practice, have consistently stated that the routine waiver of co-payments under Medicare Part B (outpatient), results in an unnecessary increase in costs to the program. In addition, the waiver of co-payments or deductibles may be construed as a kickback. Though very few outpatient medications are covered under Medicare Part B (post-transplant immunosuppressants, diabetic test strips and supplies, oral chemotherapeutics, and bronchodilator solutions), the list may be expanding in the near future. Also, the Part B program covers many kinds of durable medical equipment in which pharmacists are often involved. For these reasons a review of the OIG concern is warranted. [U.S. Department of Health and Human Services, Office of the Inspector General, *Special Fraud Alert Regarding Waivers of Co-Insurance and Deductible Amounts Under Medicare Part B,* OIG-91–23 (May 1991), available on the Internet at http://www.oig.hhs.gov/fraud/docs/alertsandbulletins/121994.html]

The Medicare Part B deductible is currently $100 per year and the co-payment for Part B services is 20%. For example, if an outpatient receives product worth $100, the co-payment will be $20 and the Part B covered amount $80. The position of OIG is two-pronged. The first prong involves abuse, the unnecessary increase in costs to the program. OIG assumes that if the $20 co-payment is routinely waived, the actual cost is only $80 in the above example and the amount the supplier should be reimbursed $80 × 80% or $64. The $16 difference is inflation of cost to the program.

The second prong of the analysis of OIG concerns the inducement of referrals. As one recalls from the antikickback provisions (above), it is illegal to offer any form of remuneration to generate business payable by Medicare or Medicaid. The OIG argues that the waiver would have the effect of encouraging beneficiaries to do business with them and result in excessive utilization.

This waiver of co-payment deductibles might seem to be an innocuous thing that in fact would serve those covered by the programs. The logic is that any unnecessary utilization might deprive another recipient of truly necessary products and services. It is useful to focus on the phrase "routine waiver" in this context. OIG has stated in this advisory that waiver of co-pay and/or deductible in the case of legitimate financial hardship is permissible.

*Ambulance restocking arrangements.* Agreements between hospitals and ambulance suppliers under which hospitals restock drugs and medical supplies used during emergency runs at no charge could technically violate the antikickback statute if this practice is intended to induce ambulance personnel to steer patients to a particular hospital. If in fact all the hospitals within a geographic area served by the same emergency medical services (EMS) council participate in ambulance restocking programs, it is unlikely that free ambulance restocking could influence the referral process, however. A new safe harbor to the antikickback statute was implemented by the OIG in December 2001 that provides broad protection for restocking arrangements in which the ambulance provider pays the facility fair market value for replenished drugs or supplies used in connection with the transport, or in which free or discounted restocking is provided by the hospital, as long as the restocking arrangement is not conditioned on the volume or value of any referrals between the hospital and the ambulance service. [66 Fed. Reg. 62979]

*Gifts and Other Inducements to Beneficiaries.* Offering gifts to Medicare and Medicaid providers to influence their choice of provider raises quality and cost concerns. A Special Advisory Bulletin has indicated the following principles will be used to determine whether a gift is appropriate.

- Inexpensive gifts, with a retail value of less than $10 individually and aggregate annual value of less than $50 are permissible.
- More expensive items can be offered if they fall within five statutory waivers: (1) nonroutine, unadvertised waivers of copayments or deductibles based on individual determination or financial need or exhaustion of collection; (2) disclosed differentials in health insurance copayments or deductibles; (3) incentives to promote preventive care as long as not disproportionate to the value of care provided; (4) practices permitted under any antikickback safe harbor such as approved discounts or cost-sharing amounts; and (5) waivers of copayments in excess of the minimum copayments based on the Medicare hospital outpatient fee schedule.
- Consideration is underway for potential exceptions for complimentary local transportation and free goods in connection with certain clinical studies.
- Items offered after approval in an OIG advisory opinion. (*OIG Special Advisory Bulletin: Offering Gifts and Other Inducements to Beneficiaries,* Aug. 2002).

---

**What specific types of contract provisions should be reviewed carefully to ensure compliance with fraud and abuse laws and other federal health program requirements?**

Pharmacy departments are likely to have many contracts, such as contracts with suppliers, equipment providers, or temporary staff. Department heads should carefully consider with whom they contract to ensure that they are not involved or implicated in a fraud and abuse investigation. In addition, department heads should consult with legal counsel and the business office before entering into a contract. Department heads, hospitals, and legal counsel should carefully consider whether the following contract provisions are contained in the contract and in compliance with applicable federal laws and regulations:

*Identification of the parties.* Ensure that the contract properly identifies the entity or person with whom the hospital is contracting. The Balanced Budget Act of 1997 imposes civil monetary penalties against any provider who contracts with an individual or entity that the facility knows or should know is excluded from federal health care programs. The hospital should also identify the principals in the contracting organization, and be sure they are not excluded persons. [42 U.S.C. 1320a-7a(a)]

*Representation of nonexclusion.* The other party should represent that it is not excluded from federal health plan participation at the time of the contract, that it will not do anything that will cause it to be excluded during the term of the agreement, and that if it is excluded, it will promptly notify the hospital. The party should also represent that it will not arrange or contract with any employee, contractor, or agent it knows or should know is excluded to provide items or services under the contract. [42 U.S.C. 1320a-7a(a)]

*Access to books and records.* Where appropriate, the contract should provide for access to books and records, as required by federal regulations. Hospitals should require immediate notification of the nature and scope of any request for access and also seek copies of any books, records, or documents proposed to be provided to the government to give the hospital an opportunity to lawfully oppose the production of documents. [42 U.S.C. 1395x (v)(1)(I)]

*Compliance plan participation.* The contract should recognize the hospital's compliance program and require the other provider to cooperate, including such things as making employees available for training, providing access to necessary billing documentation, and participating in audits upon request. The contract should also require the other party to notify the hospital immediately (if the hospital is involved or merely a witness) of any violation of any applicable law, regulation, third-party reimbursement, or breach of ethics program. The hospital should also consider whether to require the other party to maintain a compliance plan.

*Compliance with applicable law.* The contract should require the other party to comply with all federal, state, and local laws, regulations, and governmental orders in providing items or services under the contract. The other party should also be required to comply, where applicable, with requirements of the Joint Commission on Accreditation of Healthcare Organizations (Joint Commission) or national professional ethical guidelines. Finally, the party should be obliged to comply with the hospital's internal rules, regulations, and policies, which the hospital must then make available to the other party.

*Investigations and reviews.* The other party should be obliged, during the term of the contract and perhaps also for a period of time afterward, to notify the hospital of any complaint, investigation, inquiry, or review by any governmental agency or third-party payer regarding any of the items or services provided under the contract. The hospital should also consider whether to reserve the right to terminate the contract if an investigation or inquiry proceeds beyond a designated level.

*Termination due to changes in the environment or breach of law.* The hospital should retain the right to terminate or modify the contract in the event that a significant change occurs in any applicable health law or its interpretation; in a significant payer's payment methodology that affect the continuing viability or legality of the method of doing business under the contract; in the ability of either party to be reimbursed for services or items provided; or in the ability to make referrals. The contract should also give the hospital the right to terminate the contract when the other party has breached any compliance plan, or if a breach has a potential to threaten the licensure or Medicare/Medicaid certification of the hospital or may subject the hospital to a fine, to a civil, administrative, or criminal penalty, or to other sanction. [Adapted from Wolin & McAdams, *Focus on Fraud and Abuse*, vol. 3, no. 3 (May 1999)]

---

**What compliance program recommendations have been made for pharmacy manufacturers?**

The draft OIG Compliance Program Guidance for Pharmaceutical Manufacturers was published October 3, 2002. Originally, the OIG intended to publish guidance for the entire pharmaceutical industry, but has since decided to focus this guidance on manufacturers and to treat retail pharmacies separately. However, retail pharmacies should be aware of the voluntary guidelines for pharmacy manufacturers.

Three main risk areas have been identified for pharmaceutical manufacturers.

(1) *Integrity of data used to establish government reimbursement*—Many government programs establish reimbursement rates based on price and sales information provided by pharmaceutical manufacturers. A knowing submission of false, fraudulent, or misleading information could lead to liability under the False Claims Act or antikickback statute. Prices reported by manufacturers should reflect price reductions, rebates, up-front payments, coupons, goods in kind, free or reduced price services, grants, or other price concessions.

(2) *Kickbacks and other illegal remuneration*—Concerns about illegal remuneration occur in relationships with purchasers such as wholesale pharmacies, physicians and other health care providers, or sales agents in the following ways.

- If discounts or price concessions are made to purchasers in order to induce the wholesaler, pharmacy benefit manager (PBM), or other entity to recommend the product, then this would raise antikickback concerns. While the antikickback statute allows discounts to customers under an exception, the exception only applies when there is a price reduction of the product. Thus, other kinds of price concessions such as other product discounts, free or reduced priced goods, education grants, conversion payments, signing bonuses, or up-front rebates would not qualify for the discount exception. Further, any other remuneration as part of the sale may also be considered illegal remuneration. For example, manufacturers sometimes offer product-related billing assistance, reimbursement consultation, free or below market rate goods or services that may be considered an inducement to make a referral.
- Average Wholesale Price (AWP) is the benchmark that is frequently used to establish reimbursement rates for prescription drugs. Thus if the manufacturer were to manipulate AWP to increase purchaser profits, it could be considered an illegal kickback.
- Switching arrangements occur, when a manufacturer offers pharmacies or other health care providers cash payments or other benefits when a

patient's prescription is changed to the manufacturer's product. Switching arrangements are suspect under the antikickback statute.

- Consulting arrangement can raise concerns when the manufacturer engages the physician or other health care professional as a consultant, advisor, or researcher as part of marketing or research activity. The arrangements pose a risk of fraud and abuse when the arrangement is a token activity to disguise otherwise improper payments.
- Other activities that offer benefits to physicians or others in a position to make referrals may include things like entertainment, recreation, travel, or meals associated with marketing presentations, sponsorships to conferences in order to generate referrals, grants for research and education, gifts or other gratuities. It is recommended that manufacturers comply with the Pharmaceutical Research and Manufacturers of America (PhRMA) Marketing Code on Interactions with Health Care Professionals available at http://www.phrma.org. However, compliance with the code is not a guarantee that illegal conduct will be avoided. Each arrangement should be analyzed for possible illegal conduct.
- Manufacturers can be liable for improper activities by sales agents who engage in improper marketing or promotional activities.

(3) *Drug Samples*—Because drug samples may have monetary value to the recipient, it is important that manufacturers take measures to prevent the sale or billing of samples. This could include sales training, clear labeling, and packaging of individual samples as not for sale.

---

**What have Office of Inspector General (OIG) Advisory Opinions concluded about various pharmacy or drug arrangements?**

The Office of Inspector General (OIG) issues advisory opinions upon request to health care providers interested in learning whether the OIG would consider a proposed activity as illegal. While advisory opinions are only binding on the entity requesting the opinion, they can provide insight into fraud and abuse analysis that the OIG may make. Because fraud and abuse laws can be highly complex, it is important to consult with legal counsel before putting a pharmacy or drug arrangement in place.

For example, in reviewing whether an Internet-based chronic disease management business that enrolled health plan members in an on-line clinical compliance program that sold advertising to pharmacies and pharmaceutical companies, the OIG determined that it would not impose sanctions on the program. A factor that impacted the decision was the fact that points awarded to program members were only redeemable for goods and services not reimbursable by any federal health care program. [*See OIG Advisory Opinion* No. 02-12 (Aug. 21, 2002)]

However, in another opinion, the OIG determined that a program would violate the antikickback statute when a nonprofit foundation established and funded by a pharmaceutical company to subsidize cost-sharing amounts incurred by financially needy patients using its drug. Because there were alternative options such as providing free drugs without billing federal health care programs or establishing an independent foundation with contributions from several drug manufacturers to make grants based on need, the OIG refused to sanction the program. [*See OIG Advisory Opinion* No.02-13 (Sept. 27,2002).]

In another opinion, the OIG reviewed a program to provide free equipment to hemophilia patients as well as free electronic pagers to the parents of pediatric hemophilia patients. The OIG determined that this program would violate the antikickback statute because the value of the benefit provided was not limited to $10 per item or $50 per year. [*See OIG Advisory Opinion* 02-14 (Sept. 30, 2002).]

---

**What are the elements of an effective hospital-based compliance program?**

A hospital-based compliance program should include the following elements.

- written standards of conduct and policies and procedures that promote compliance
- designation of a Chief Compliance Officer (COO) who reports to the CEO and governing body
- development of regular, effective training and education for all employees effective communication including a complaint hotline
- establishing a system to respond to allegations of illegal activities
- use of audits and evaluation to monitor compliance and reduce problems
- investigation and remediation of systemic problems (OIG Compliance Program for Hospitals, (63 Fed Reg. 8987)

The pharmacy department should be prepared to assist the corporate COO with compliance efforts.

---

**If a pharmacy violates a fraud and abuse law resulting in a corporate integrity agreement (CIA), what kind of obligations may arise under the agreement?**

Each corporate integrity agreement (CIA) is determined by the Office of Inspector General (OIG) in efforts to ensure that in the future there will be compliance with fraud and abuse requirements. A corporate integrity agreement may include a requirement that a Corporate Compliance Officer and Committee be in place; written codes of conduct and policies and procedures, training and education take place; an independent review organization (IRO) consultation to review compliance activities; and regular reporting of compliance and other efforts to the OIG. Any elements of the compliance plan that were lacking at the time of the fraud and abuse will be required as part of the CIA. The OIG can also exclude the provider from participation in the Medicare and Medicaid program.

## Antitrust

### How do hospital drug-purchasing decisions involving the selection of drug manufacturers-suppliers potentially trigger antitrust concerns?

Hospitals and other institutional buyers (e.g., HMOs, nursing homes, etc.) usually purchase drugs at much lower prices than independent and chain pharmacies because of strong buying cooperatives, nonprofit status, and restrictive formularies. The legality of the drug manufacturer's business practice of selling its products at different prices to different buyers, known as differential pricing, has been challenged under the Robinson-Patman Act. This statute makes it unlawful for sellers to discriminate in price between purchasers of similar products when discriminating may substantially injure competition.

The Act applies not only to the manufacturer or seller setting the prices but also applies to any person who "knowingly receives the benefits of" the discriminatory pricing practices. [15 U.S.C. 13(a)] Thus, an injured competitor (such as a retail pharmacy) may sue both the seller who discriminated and the hospital-buyer who knowingly purchased products at a discriminatory price. It is important to note, however, that the hospital-buyer cannot be held liable if an injured competitor's claim against the seller cannot be established, or if the seller has a valid affirmative defense. [*See Great Atlantic & Pacific Tea Co. v. Federal Trade Comm'n*, 440 U.S. 69 (1979)]

### Are there limits to when the Robinson-Patman Act applies to a hospital's purchase of drugs at discounted prices?

For several reasons, drug manufacturers' longstanding practice of selling their products at discounted prices to hospitals has not often resulted in antitrust liability for hospitals. First, the Robinson-Patman Act often does not apply in the context of drug purchasing by hospitals. The Act applies only if the price discrimination occurs between competing buyers; thus, when an independent retail pharmacy purchases prescription drugs at a higher cost than that charged to a hospital in the same area for the drugs it purchases for inpatient use, this differential pricing does not violate the Act because the independent pharmacy does not compete with the hospital for inpatients.

Second, the differential pricing practices of drug manufacturers to high-volume purchasers, such as hospitals, may fall within a well-recognized defense to Robinson-Patman claims known as the cost-justification defense. As applied to hospital drug purchasing, savings to the manufacturer through economies of manufacture, sale, or delivery (e.g., large-quantity purchases to health care institutions) may be viewed as a valid justification for the price difference granted to hospital buyers. A federal trial judge relied on this defense in dismissing Robinson-Patman claims in a major class action brought against drug manufacturers by retail pharmacists. The court ruled that the retail pharmacists did not have the same ability to "move market share" through formularies as did the HMOs that received deep discounts on drug products. [*In re Brand Name Prescription Drugs Antitrust Litigation,* 94 C 897, MDL 997 (N.D. Ill. Jan. 19, 1999). *See also In re Brand Name Prescription Drugs Antitrust Litig.*, 186 F.3d 781 (7th Cir. 1999); *In re Brand Name Prescription Drugs Antitrust Litig.,* 94 C 897, MDL 997 (N.D. Ill. Feb. 10, 2000)]

Third, nonprofit status brings many hospitals' drug purchases within the scope of the Nonprofit Institutions Act. [15 U.S.C. 13c] This Act, a statutory amendment to the Robinson-Patman Act, provides that nonprofit charitable institutions, including nonprofit hospitals, are exempt from the Robinson-Patman Act with respect to such institutions' purchase of goods (i.e., drugs and other supplies) at a discount for their "own use."

---

**What does "own use" mean?**

The U.S. Supreme Court has defined "own use" as it applies to nonprofit hospital pharmacies as "what may reasonably be regarded as use by the hospital in the sense that such use is a part of and promotes the hospital's intended institutional operation in the care of persons who are its patients." The Court further elaborated upon this definition by outlining how hospitals may use discounted drugs without violating antitrust laws. "Exempt" sales include drugs that are dispensed to the following groups:

- inpatients, emergency department patients, and outpatients (i.e., non-inpatient, nonemergency patients that received treatment on the premises) for use on hospital premises
- inpatients or emergency department patients upon discharge and for personal use away from hospital premises
- outpatients for personal use away from hospital premises
- hospital employees and their dependents, students at the hospital and their dependents, and medical staff and their dependents, all for their own personal use

Sales to the following groups are not covered by the "own use" exemption:

- former patients of the hospital renewing prescriptions originally dispensed when patients were discharged from the hospital
- nondependents (e.g., friends of employees or medical staff members)
- walk-in customers with no connection to the hospital (e.g., patrons of a physician's office building)

For drugs sold to customers in these three categories, the nonprofit hospital must purchase the drugs at the supplier's usual (not discounted) rate and must account separately for the sales, or it will lose its "own use" exemption and thus can be scrutinized for violating the Robinson-Patman Act. [*See, e.g., Abbott Laboratories v. Portland Retail Druggists Ass'n, Inc.*, 425 U.S. 1 (1976)]

**Does a nonprofit entity's transfer of drugs at cost to affiliated facilities or entities fall within the "own use" exemption?**

Whether a nonprofit hospital may share the benefit of discount drug prices by transferring such drugs at cost to affiliated facilities is an unsettled area of antitrust law, and the answer to this question depends upon the particular facts and circumstances of each case. Accordingly, nonprofit hospital pharmacies should always seek legal counsel prior to sharing the benefits of discounted drug purchases through transferring such drugs at cost to affiliated entities. There is some legal authority on this question, however. The Federal Trade Commission (FTC), one of the two federal antitrust enforcement agencies, has issued several advisory opinions that provide some guidance. The FTC has indicated that it would not find a violation based on the sales of prescription drugs under the following circumstances:

- Sales by a hospital association comprised of nonprofit hospitals to retired employees in accordance with retirees' pension plan. [*Connecticut Hospital Association,* Dec. 20, 2001 superceding *North Mississippi Health Servs.,* Oct. 3, 1996]
- Sales by a nonprofit multispecialty medical clinic to patients treated by physicians in the clinic by pharmacies located in the clinics where physicians practice. [*Harvard Vanguard Medical Associates, Inc.,* Dec. 18, 2001]
- Sales of drugs bought by a nonprofit hospital through primary care clinics operated by the same nonprofit health system to health system employees and to patients covered by a risk contract between the system and a for-profit HMO. The FTC also found transfers to the hospital's nonprofit home care subsidiary permissible. [*BJC Health Sys.,* Nov. 9, 1999]
- Sales by a nonprofit skilled nursing facility to volunteers working at the facility [*Wesley Health Care Center, Inc,* Apr. 29, 1999]
- Sales by a nonprofit medical center to patients of a hospital cancer center funded by an affiliated charitable trust. [*North Mississippi Health Servs.,* Jan. 7, 1998]
- Sales by a nonprofit hospital to an unaffiliated nonprofit hospice, with caveats on the price calculation. [*North Ottawa Comm. Hosp.,* Oct. 22, 1996]
- Sales by a nonprofit medical center to clinics operated by the medical center. [*Valley Baptist Med. Ctr.,* Sept. 19, 1996]
- Sales by a nonprofit hospital to related nonprofit clinics. [*William W. Backus Hosp.,* June 11, 1996]
- Sales by a nonprofit hospital to a hospital-operated home health program. [*Elkhart Gen. Hosp.,* June 13, 1994]
- Sales by nonprofit hospitals to related nonprofit long-term care facilities. [*Presentation Health Sys.,* Dec. 21, 1993]

However, the Federal Trade Commission (FTC) found that the following sales of prescription drugs were not protected by the nonprofit institution exemption:

- sales of drugs by a nonprofit hospital to patients of the physician-hospital organization to which the hospital belongs [*Henry County Mem'l Hosp.,* Apr. 10, 1997]

These advisory opinions should give practitioners some guidance to consider when a novel resale practice is proposed. However, there are several caveats to be made in connection with another organization's reliance on these advisory opinions. First, the opinions rendered are based on specific situations. One should proceed deliberately before relying on a particular advisory's relevance to a situation even though there seems to be congruence. Second, the FTC expressly reserves the right to change its opinion for any of numerous reasons, including change in law, changed circumstances, or misrepresentation. Third, remember that private parties are privileged to sue under these laws. Though the FTC advisory may be persuasive, a civil court judge is under no obligation to follow the agency's opinion in a lawsuit brought by a community pharmacy over an institution's "own use" sales. For these reasons, it is always sound practice to seek advice of legal counsel before making a significant change in business practice concerning resale policy. [FTC advisory opinions are available on the Internet at http://www.ftc.gov]

---

**Are there any questions about the continued validity of the "own use" exemption?**

With so many institutions involved in purchasing alliances with both for-profit and not-for-profit partners, the question about the continuing relevance of the Nonprofit Institutions Act often comes up. In other words, the discriminatory price received by most facilities is based *not* on its not-for-profit status but on its ability to commit to purchasing (in conjunction with many other organizations) a large volume. This brings the institution, the group purchasing organization (GPO), and the manufacturer within the "cost justification" exception to the Robinson-Patman Act described above. It is logical to conclude that, because the discriminatory prices obtained are not based on not-for-profit status, the "own use" limitations should *not* apply. This is supported by the Robinson-Patman jurisprudence: a lower cost of doing business (due to the economies of scale) permits a discriminatory price. Indeed, the cost justification exception satisfies the primary goals of the antitrust law of greater commercial efficiency and lower prices discussed above. In spite of this apparent loophole, the "own use" guidelines should be followed. The same restrictions rendered by the Abbott decisions are generally included in the agreements negotiated by GPOs at the *request* of the manufacturers. When an institution violates the agreement, it is in breach of the contract, *not* the antitrust law. The manufacturer or the GPO, but not the FTC, may sue the institution.

---

**What federal law specifically prohibits hospitals from attempting to make a profit by reselling drugs purchased at a discount?**

The Prescription Drug Marketing Act (PDMA), enacted in 1988, forbids hospitals and other health care entities to resell prescription drug products. [21 U.S.C. 353] Importantly, dispensing pursuant to a prescription is not "reselling" under the PDMA. The law addresses the problem of prescription drug products becoming misbranded and adulterated under the Food, Drug, and Cosmetic Act (FDCA) as a result of diversion from the normal stream of distribution. Resale schemes can also create antitrust problems; unfair competition may result when pharmacies that purchase drugs in a diversionary market obtain a price advantage over those that do not participate in resale transactions.

There are exceptions, however. The PDMA does not apply to

- the sale or dispensing of a drug pursuant to a valid prescription
- the purchase of drugs for a provider's "own use" from a group purchasing organization of which it is a member
- the temporary transfer of drugs to a retail pharmacy for a medical emergency
- sales among facilities under common control
- sales between nonprofit affiliates
- properly conducted drug returns by hospitals, health care entities, and charitable institutions [21 U.S.C. 353(c)(3)(B); 21 C.F.R. 205.3]

The PDMA also prohibits the sale, purchase, and trade of prescription drug samples. [21 U.S.C. 353(c)(1)]

---

**What types of prescription drug sales are permitted under the PDMA?**

Regulations clarifying the limitations on prescription drug distribution under the PDMA were issued in December 1999. Under the regulations, the following distribution by hospitals and health care entities do not implicate the PDMA:

- sales for emergency medical reasons
- sales pursuant to valid prescriptions
- sales of blood or blood components intended for transfusion [21 C.F.R. 203.22]

By permitting sales pursuant to valid prescriptions, the regulations allow sales to walk-in customers, former patients, and other individuals who are not hospital patients or employees. Hospital pharmacies are cautioned, however, that the Nonprofit Institutions Act continues to limit exemption from the Robinson-Patman Act's prohibitions on sales of prescription drugs purchased at a discount to the hospital's or nonprofit health system's "own use."

---

**Does the PDMA address drug distributions within a health care organization?**

The December 1999 federal regulations implementing the PDMA enumerate the following exemptions to the ban on redistribution of prescription drugs sold to hospitals and charitable organizations:

- purchases of drugs for its own use by a hospital or other health care entity that is a member of a group purchasing organization or from other hospitals or health care entities that are members of the organization

- sales by a charitable organization to a nonprofit affiliate of the organization to the extent otherwise permitted by law
- sales among hospitals or other health care entities that are under common control
- sales by hospitals or health care entities owned or operated by federal or state governments to other government hospitals or health care entities [21 C.F.R. 203.22]

To the extent that these allowances in some respects might be broader than what is considered under Robinson-Patman (as interpreted through the FTC advisory opinions described above), hospital leaders are cautioned that compliance with the stricter standard is well advised.

---

**When does the PDMA not apply to drug returns?**

To be exempt from the PDMA, drug returns by hospitals, health care entities, and charitable institutions must meet certain requirements. [21 C.F.R. 205.3] The hospital, health care entity, or charitable institution must document the return by completing a credit memo that specifies the following:

- the name and address of the institution or health care entity
- the name and address of the manufacturer or wholesale distributor from which the institution or health care entity acquired the drug
- the product name and lot or control number
- the quantity of the drug returned
- the date of the return

The institution or health care entity must keep a copy of the credit memo for its records and forward a copy to the drug's manufacturer. Finally, the institution or health care entity must provide documentation to the manufacturer or wholesale distributor showing that the returned drugs were kept under proper conditions for storage, handling, and shipping. [21 C.F.R. 203.23]

---

**Do any state laws address drug manufacturers' differential pricing practices?**

More than 20 states currently have an antidiscriminatory pricing provision in their antitrust statutes; such provisions typically mirror the Robinson-Patman Act's broad prohibition on price discrimination that results in substantial lessening of competition. [*See, e.g.*, CAL. BUS. & PROF. CODE ANN. 17045; FLA. STAT. ANN. 540.01; 740 ILCS 10/3]

In addition, several states (including Maine, Minnesota, North Carolina, and Wisconsin) have enacted unitary pricing statutes. These statutes generally require that all parties receive the same price as the party receiving the best price, but exempt state or federal purchasers, hospitals, and nonprofit organizations from the best price provision, allowing those entities to continue receiving discounts. In Maine and Wisconsin, for example, the statutes essentially require the drug manufacturer to offer rebates, free merchandise, samples, and similar trade concessions to every purchaser and the wholesaler on terms equal to its offer to the most favored purchaser, but exempts discounts for volume purchases if the discounts are justified by economies or efficiencies resulting from the volume purchases and the discounts are made available to all purchasers and wholesalers on proportionally equal terms. [*See, e.g.*, 22 ME. REV. STAT. ANN. 2681; WIS. STAT. 100.31]

### What is the role of pharmacy benefit managers (PBMs)?

PBMs administer and manage prescription drug benefits on behalf of plan sponsors, such as self-insured employers, insurance companies, and HMOs. Like other medical care organizations (MCOs), the PBM's objective is to provide high-quality care (i.e., pharmaceutical care) at the lowest possible cost. Although PBMs are relatively new entities, they have become a major market force in the managed care environment. The number of PBMs has grown rapidly in recent years.

In addition to providing prescription claims services or mail-order pharmacy services on behalf of insurers, many PBMs have expanded their services to include formulary development and management, pharmacy network development to serve health plan enrollees, generic substitution, and drug utilization review. Also, PBMs represent health plans and their enrollees in dealing with other participants in the prescription drug market. For example, PBMs typically negotiate with drug manufacturers to obtain rebates for a plan sponsor. Most PBMs also negotiate with retail pharmacies to obtain discounts on prescription drug prices and dispensing fees for health plan enrollees.

Many PBMs use the formulary approach to manage prescription drug costs. They provide physicians and others with printed formularies and encourage these physicians to prescribe lower cost formulary drugs over both nonformulary drugs and higher cost formulary drugs. Because of the potential effect on drug sales, manufacturers offer PBMs rebates in exchange for including certain drugs on a formulary and for designating those drugs as low cost.

### What antitrust concerns are raised by PBM practices?

A recent trend of large drug manufacturers' merging with some of the largest PBMs has led to concerns about whether these ventures will reduce competition in markets for pharmaceuticals and PBM services, and thereby violate antitrust laws. The FTC has been actively involved in reviewing PBM/drug manufacturer mergers to determine their potential impact on competition in the markets involved. One of the first PBM/drug manufacturer mergers was the purchase by Merck & Co., Inc., of a large PBM, Medco Containment Services, Inc., in November 1993. Although declining to challenge the merger, the FTC stated that it would continue to monitor the Merck/Medco venture, as well as other mergers between drug manufacturers and PBMs. [*See* U.S. Government Accounting Office, *Pharmacy Benefit Managers; Early Results on Ventures with Drug Manufacturers,* Pub. No. GAO/HEHS-96-45 (Nov. 1995)]

After investigating the merger between Eli Lilly & Co. and a large PBM, PCS Health Systems, the FTC challenged the venture on the grounds of its potential anticompetitive effects. Ultimately, the FTC entered into a consent agreement with the drug manufacturer that established safeguards to ensure that the manufacturer and the PBM maintain a competitive process for determining which drugs to include on the PBM's formulary. Among other safeguards, the consent decree requires that the PBM maintain an open formulary and that Lilly ensure that the PBM accepts all discounts, rebates, or other concessions offered by Lilly's competitors for drugs that are accepted for listing on the open formulary. [*In re Lilly & Co.,* FTC No. 941 0102 (July 31, 1995)]

---

### Can retail pharmacies combine into pharmacy networks without violating antitrust laws?

Pharmacy networks may be established to provide health education and monitoring services to diabetes, asthma, or other chronic disease patients. These networks can take a variety of forms in order to attempt to meet the market demand for disease management. As a general rule, the Health Care Antitrust Statements set forth jointly by the Department of Justice (DOJ)/Federal Trade Commission (FTC) indicate that "naked agreements" among competitors to fix prices are illegal per se under antitrust laws. However, when a joint venture significantly integrates competitors, the venture will be reviewed under the rule of reason to determine if the venture is reasonably necessary and creates pro competitive efficiencies. If the venture creates market efficiencies it will be allowed to continue. Further, the Statements indicate that financial risk sharing between providers may justify application of the rule of reason to analysis of venture. As with other antitrust issues, it is important to consult with legal counsel in order to ensure antitrust law compliance when network arrangements are put into place. [*Statements of Antitrust Enforcement Policy and Analytical Principles Relating to Health Care Antitrust,* Department of Justice (DOJ) /Federal Trade Commission (FTC), Statement 9 (1996)]

The FTC has reviewed several proposed pharmacy networks under the rule of reason analysis and found them to be acceptable. A Pharmacists Association set up two pharmacist service networks to offer health education services to diabetes and asthma patients. One network was to provide asthma self-management education and the other network was to provide diabetes education. The services were not connected to the dispensing of prescription drugs and would result in several visits for each patient who needed services as assessed by a physician. Pharmacists desiring to enroll in the network had to complete state education requirements. It was estimated that less than 20% of licensed pharmacists would take the courses needed to join the network. Contracts between the network and payers were to either be on a capitated basis or with a shared risk reward agreement. The program was nonexclusive since network members could participate in other networks that competed in the marketplace. The FTC found that the benefits to competition offered by the pharmaceutical network outweighed the risks. [FTC Advisory Opinion: *New Jersey Pharmacists Association,* Aug. 12,1997.]

Similarly, an open pharmacy network that included both drug product distribution and disease management services was found to be acceptable under the rule of reason analysis. The pharmacies in the network comprised 40% to 45% of the pharmacies in the county, but dispensed less than 20% of the volume of prescription pharmaceuticals for the county. Because sufficient information was not provided about subcontractor relationships, the FTC refused to comment on subcontract relationships indicating that inclusion of chain drug stores or supermarket chain pharmacies in the network might impair market competition so that the arrangement would raise antitrust concerns. [FTC Advisory Opinion: *Orange Pharmacy Equitable Network,* May 19, 1999).]

Another pharmacy network was developed to provide a package of medication and patient care services such as disease management, avoiding adverse drug interactions, condition assessment, review of drug compliance, recommending drug substitutions or generic substitutes. The exclusive network would develop standard disease management programs, medication protocols, and education programs. The network pharmacists agreed to share financial risk through the network. The FTC found that the network would include less than 5% of all pharmacies in the two-state region it covered. The network was found acceptable because there were sufficient competitive alternatives to keep market competition intact. [FTC Advisory Opinion: *Northeast Pharmacy Service Corporation,* July 27, 2000.]

## Tax Implications

### How can selling pharmaceuticals to the public trigger tax consequences for a hospital?

Many hospitals are exempt from corporate income taxation under Section 501(c)3 ("Subchapter C") of the Internal Revenue Code of 1954. Congress carved out this exception for hospitals and other businesses "organized and operated exclusively for religious, charitable, scientific, testing for public safety, literary or educational purposes." As long as the business activities are conducted to further the nonprofit purpose of the organization, they will be exempt from taxation. If the activities are determined to be in competition with outside providers (such as community pharmacies), the Internal Revenue Service (IRS) is empowered to levy and collect the corporate *tax and penalties* for "unrelated business taxable income" ("UBTI") resulting from the improper sales. This provision is not a prohibition against resale of pharmaceuticals but a penalty to be enforced when the pharmacy department violates the code by engaging in an "unrelated trade or business."

The Internal Revenue Code defines "unrelated trade or business" as "any trade or business the conduct of which is not substantially related to the exercise or performance by such organization of its charitable, educational or other purpose constituting the basis for its exemption." [26 U.S.C. 513]

In other words, the activities of the organization are diverging from the activities related to the nonprofit exemption and taking on a competitive flavor. The IRS analysis for hospital pharmacies will include considerations of factors such as satellite pharmacies in medical office buildings, advertisements for competitive nonexempt services, hospital policies concerning the promotion of resales, and departmental records. Realizing that it could not consider every possibility, Congress carved out an exception to the rule. Section 513(a)(2) allows for the occasional situation in which the resale is for "any trade or business . . . which is carried on . . . for the convenience of its . . . patients."

The Income Tax Regulations (written by the IRS) further define the nature of an activity engaged in for the convenience of an organization's patients as one in which the organization engages "only discontinuously or periodically" and which does not incorporate the competitive and promotional activities typical of commercial endeavors. As long as these sales are occasional and not promoted, they will not be subject to UBTI. [26 C.F.R. 1.513-1]

The federal courts provide two examples in which the IRS found income from nonprofit hospital pharmacy sales subject to corporate tax as unrelated business taxable income. Instead of disputing the IRS directly in the tax court, the hospitals chose instead to pay the tax and sue for a refund in the local federal district court. The hospitals argued that their resales are in fact related to their nonprofit activities and should be exempt. These cases operate as examples of the interpretation of the UBTI law by the federal courts.

In *Carle Foundation v. United States*, the Seventh Circuit Court of Appeals reversed the lower court's decision, which, in effect, validated the position of the IRS. The IRS maintained that sales by a hospital pharmacy to a nonexempt clinic were substantially unrelated to the hospital's tax-exempt purpose and therefore subject to the UBTI provisions. The appellate court agreed with the IRS. In this case the hospital rented out office space to a private clinic run by physicians engaged in the practice of medicine on a for-profit basis. The hospital's business interest in the clinic was limited to collecting rents; there was no other business association with the clinic. As a courtesy the pharmacy resold pharmaceuticals to the clinic for office use. The court found that while the hospital and clinic were closely related in their activities, they were separate legal entities and that the sales of pharmaceuticals to the clinic was not primarily for the benefit of the hospital's patients, the nonprofit purpose of the hospital. [*Carle Foundation v. United States*, 611 F.2d 1192 (7th Cir. 1979), *cert. denied* 449 U.S. 824 (1980).]

The Fifth Circuit Court of Appeals reached a different conclusion in *Hi-Plains Hospital v. United States*. The court found that sales of pharmaceuticals to nonhospital patients for the convenience of the prescribing physicians was indeed related to the business of the hospital and for the benefit of its patients. The hospital argued and the court adopted the position that the sales in question were part of a package of incentives to attract and retain physicians in their rural community. That is, allowing the physician's office patients to fill their prescriptions at the hospital pharmacy was beneficial to the physicians. To the extent that this "benefit" was successful in keeping practitioners in the rural community, it redounded to the (perhaps indirect) benefit of the institution in being able to retain staff physicians and continue to offer acute care services, its nonprofit purpose. [*Hi-Plains Hospital v. United States,* 670 F.2d 528 (5th Cir. 1982)]

## FOOD, DRUG, AND COSMETIC ACT

The FDCA is of great importance to the pharmaceutical industry. [21 U.S.C. 301–394] This federal statute regulates food products, medications, medical devices, and cosmetics in the United States. With regard to drugs and devices, the FDCA is directed at protecting consumers by establishing standards for safety and effectiveness. The FDCA and its implementing regulations are broad, extending to clinical research, approval, manufacture, storage, marketing, labeling, recordkeeping, and sales of drugs. Considering the breadth of the FDCA, a limited part of the statute is of special interest to hospital pharmacists, as discussed in this section. (Joint Commission standards relating to FDCA compliance are primarily discussed in **Care of Patients: Medication** in Part 3 of this Manual.)

### What does the FDCA prohibit?

Although many FDCA provisions are directed at manufacturers, the following prohibited acts are of interest to pharmacists. It is a violation of the federal law to

- commit any act with respect to a drug or device in interstate commerce that results in the article being adulterated or misbranded
- introduce, receive, or deliver in interstate commerce any drug or device that is adulterated or misbranded
- refuse to permit access to, verification, or copying of records required by the FDCA, or fail to establish or maintain any record or report required by the FDCA
- refuse to permit entry or inspection authorized by the FDCA
- fail to comply with FDCA device and investigational device requirements
- fail to maintain and transmit copies of all printed matter required to be included in the drug's package to any licensed practitioner who requests it [21 U.S.C. 331]

### What is misbranding?

Misbranding is a legal term defined in the FDCA that encompasses a variety of failures to comply with FDCA labeling requirements. Examples of misbranding include false or misleading labels, labels lacking required information or warnings, labels without adequate directions for use, and illegible labels. [21 U.S.C. 352]

### What is adulteration?

Adulteration describes a drug or device that fails to satisfy the FDA's purity standards. The broadly applicable definition encompasses even pure drugs and devices, under certain conditions. Specifically, the statute deems a drug adulterated not only if the drug itself is impure, but also if

- it has been prepared, packed, or held under unsanitary conditions whereby it may have been contaminated; or
- the drug is labeled as a drug recognized in an official compendium, but the drug's strength differs from, or its quality or purity falls below, the standard set forth in the compendium; or
- the drug is not listed in an official compendium, and its strength differs from, or its purity or quality falls below, what is represented on the label; or
- any substance has been mixed or packed with the drug to reduce the drug's strength, or any substance has been substituted for the drug [21 U.S.C. 351]

Similarly, a device is adulterated not only if the device itself does not conform to standards, but if it has been prepared, packed, or held under unsanitary conditions where it may have been contaminated. [21 U.S.C. 351]

## Compounding Drugs

### Why is the distinction between compounding and manufacturing important?

Certain FDCA provisions apply to manufacturers but not to compounding pharmacists. For example, the FDCA requires drug manufacturers to register with the FDA and submit to inspection every two years. Manufacturers must also comply with Current Good Manufacturing Practice regulations. If compounding or manufacturing results in a new drug, extensive statutory requirements for new drugs apply. State boards of pharmacy may also take administrative action against pharmacists who manufacture, rather than merely compound, drugs. Thus, hospital pharmacists who wish to avoid enforcement must remain within the bounds of compounding, as it is defined by federal and state agencies, and not become manufacturers on the basis of their drug production activities.

### How does the FDCA define the limits of compounding?

The FDA Modernization Act of 1997 (FDAMA) attempted to resolve, at least in part, the longstanding conflict between traditional pharmacy compounding practices and the FDA's position on what constitutes manufacturing. Under the Act, licensed pharmacists and pharmacies are exempt from having to comply with the adulteration, misbranding, and "new drug" statutes and regulations, as long as they do not advertise or promote specific compounded drugs. A licensed pharmacist may compound a drug for an individual patient based on the unsolicited receipt of a valid prescription, when the prescription (or a notation on the prescription approved by the prescriber) states that a compounded drug is necessary. Compounding may be performed by a licensed pharmacist or licensed physician and may be done in advance of a prescription, if a drug is prepared in a limited quantity for a particular patient, based on the patient's treatment or physician's ordering history with the pharmacist. Under the FDAMA, a pharmacist may not compound a drug under consideration for FDA approval and must comply with published standards (if they exist), using approved substances for compounding. Further, a compounding pharmacist must not essentially copy a commercially available drug product, unless the prescriber has determined that the compounded version produces a "significant difference" for an individual patient. The pharmacist must keep a record of the substances used for compounding, including manufacturer names and lot numbers. This compounding definition does not apply to positron emission tomography drugs or radiopharmaceuticals. [FDAMA, § 127, codified at 21 U.S.C. 353a]

In 2000, the FDA issued a concept paper exploring the criteria for identifying drug products that are "demonstrably difficult to compound," for which compounding would not be permitted under the FDAMA allowance described above. The preliminary list of these products includes all sterile products, transdermal delivery systems, metered-dose inhaler products, and dry powder inhaler products. [FDA Concept Paper: Drug Products that Present Demonstrable Difficulties for Compounding Because of Reasons of Safety or Effectiveness, June 2000, available on the Internet at http://www.fda.gov]

**What is the impact of the Supreme Court on the FDA Modernization Act (FDAMA)?**

The legality of the FDAMA, however, has been successfully challenged. A federal appeals court found in 2001 that the provisions of the Act that prohibit pharmacists from advertising drugs they compound for prescriptions from licensed physicians are an unlawful restriction on commercial speech, and therefore the entire Act is invalid. The Supreme Court upheld this decision finding that the advertising restriction which stated that providers "not advertise or promote the compounding of any particular drug, class of drug, or type of drug" was unconstitutional. [21 U.S.C. 353a] The statute restricted free commercial speech.

Even if the ban on advertising advanced a government interest, the government failed to demonstrate that the restriction on commercial speech was not more extensive than necessary to serve the government interest. The advertising ban was too broad because it restricted speech that would be beneficial such as advising a physician of the availability of a compounded drug for special medical needs. The court found that there were other means to achieve the government goal without restricting free speech such as regulation of large scale manufacture, prohibition of wholesale sales, or limitation of manufacturing to prescriptions received. [*Thompson v. Western States Medical Center,* 122 S. Ct. 1497 (2002), *affirming* 238 F.3d 1090 (9th Cir. 2001).]

**What is the current FDA policy regarding retail pharmacy compounding?**

The FDA has issued guidance to staff and industry in regard to retail pharmacy compounding and enforcement policies. The FDA has indicated that retail pharmacies that compound drugs from a prescription for an individual patient from a licensed practitioner are not subject to review for compounding practices. However, some retail pharmacies have developed practices more like drug manufacturers and wholesalers in that they order large quantities of unapproved drugs, they prepare compounded drugs in advance of valid prescriptions for them, and sell to physicians and patients when there is only a remote professional relationship. When the retailer acts like the manufacturer and distributor in these instances, then the retail pharmacy can be held to comply with the same provisions of the statute as the manufacturer.

When the retail pharmacy compounding activity is not in significant violation of the FDA requirements for manufacturers, then the FDA will defer to state authority in which coordinated efforts between the state and the FDA result in investigation, referrals, and follow-up action by the state.

When the retail pharmacy compounding activity results in significant violations of the new drug, adulteration, or misbranding provisions of the statute, the FDA will consider its own enforcement action. [*See Guidance for FDA Staff and Industry,* 4 Compliance Policy Guides Manual 460.200, Pharmacy Compounding (June 7, 2002)]

---

**What factors will the FDA consider to decide whether to take enforcement action for compounding activity that violates adulteration or misbranding provisions of the statute?**

The FDA will consider whether the pharmacy has been involved in the following activities when deciding whether to take enforcement action.

- Compounding drugs in anticipation of receiving prescriptions except in limited quantities related to drugs compounded after receiving a valid prescription
- Compounding drugs removed from the market for safety reasons
- Compounding finished drugs from bulk active ingredients that are not components of FDA-approved drugs without an FDA investigational new drug application (IND)
- Receiving or storing drug substances without written assurance that the drug was made in an FDA-registered facility
- Receiving, storing, or using drugs not guaranteed to meet official compendia requirements
- Using commercial-scale manufacturing or testing equipment to compound drug products
- Compounding drugs for third parties who resell to individual patients or offering compounded drug products at wholesale
- Compounding drug products that are commercially available in the marketplace
- Failing to operate in compliance with state law regarding the practice of pharmacy

[*See Guidance for FDA Staff and Industry,* 4 Compliance Policy Guides Manual 460.200, Pharmacy Compounding (June 7, 2002), *Appendix A* contains a list of drugs removed from the market for safety reasons]

## ADR Reporting

### What is MedWatch?

MedWatch is the voluntary reporting system that the FDA has established for health care professionals, including pharmacists, to report adverse drug reactions (ADRs). The FDCA does not require ADR reporting, but the FDA encourages it, as the agency relies on postmarketing reports to revise labeling. According to the FDA, health professionals should report serious adverse events, such as when the patient outcome is

- death
- life-threatening condition
- condition requiring hospitalization
- significant, persistent, or permanent disability
- congenital anomaly, or
- condition requiring intervention to prevent permanent impairment or damage

The FDA advises health professionals to report ADRs even in the absence of details, or when it is not certain that the product caused the ADR. Pharmacists should also contact the FDA to report suspected drug quality problems such as contamination, questionable stability, defective components, and poor packaging and labeling. [FDA, *MedWatch: The FDA Medical Products Reporting Program,* FDA Form 3500 (1993). Detailed information on the MedWatch Program is available on the Internet at http://www.fda.gov]

### Why should pharmacists report ADRs?

Although federal law does not require individual practitioners to report serious ADRs, the importance of doing so is clear, as health professionals serve as the primary source of information on the effects of drugs once they have been approved for marketing. State laws often require ADR monitoring, if not reporting. State laws differ from FDA provisions in that the goal is improving patient care, not manufacturer labeling. For example, state provisions may require documentation of ADRs, ongoing monitoring, and staff education. These provisions may be found in hospital licensing statutes, hospital pharmacy laws and regulations, pharmacist practice acts, and medical record laws and regulations. [*See e.g.,* So. Car. Code Ann § 40-43-99 requiring documentation of adverse reactions in a patient profile, New York Con. Law § 369-bb requiring monitoring and educational information regarding ADRs, and Utah Code Ann. § 26-18-103 requiring staff education regarding ADR.]

In addition, the Joint Commission requires hospitals to track ADRs as part of the performance improvement process. (*See* **Care of Patients: Medication** in Part 3 of this Manual.) As the result of the review of ADR reports, the Joint Commission may identify specific medication-related sentinel events in a Sentinel Event Alert, describing their common underlying causes and suggesting steps to prevent future occurrences, in order to assist hospitals in improving performance. A recent alert, for example, warned of medication errors related to potentially dangerous abbreviations and dose expressions in prescription orders and other medication information communications. [Joint Commission, Sentinel Event Alert, Issue 23, Sept. 2001, available on the Internet at http://www. jcaho.org/edu_pub/sealert/sea23.html]

Further, the American Society of Health-System Pharmacists (ASHP) has issued a guideline stating that "it is the pharmacist's responsibility and professional obligation to report any suspected ADRs." [*ASHP Guidelines, Adverse Drug Reaction Monitoring and Reporting,* ASHP, AM. J. HEALTH-SYS. PHARM. 1995; 52:417-9, available on the Internet at http://www.ashp.org/bestpractices] (For materials related to ADR reporting, see Part 4 of this Manual, under **Care of Patients.**)

---

### What are the ASHP guidelines for reporting ADRs?

ASHP calls for pharmacists in organized health care settings to develop ADR monitoring and reporting programs with mechanisms for monitoring, detecting, evaluating, documenting, and reporting ADRs, as well as providing feedback and education to health care practitioners and patients. The program should incorporate a concurrent ADR surveillance system, as well as prospective ADR surveillance for high-risk drugs or high-risk patients. ASHP defines ADR more broadly than the FDA, including less serious unexpected drug responses that require discontinuing the drug, changing drug therapy, or modifying the dose, or that negatively affect prognosis. The ASHP guideline makes detailed recommendations regarding the ADR monitoring processes and the pharmacist's role. [*ASHP Guidelines, Adverse Drug Reaction Monitoring and Reporting,* ASHP, issued 1994, is available on the Internet at http://www.ashp.org/bestpractices]

---

### How should a pharmacist file an ADR report with the FDA?

Pharmacists can file a report in the following four ways:

1. faxing a report to 1–800-FDA-0178
2. calling 1-800-FDA-1088
3. mailing a MedWatch voluntary reporting form to MedWatch, Food and Drug Administration, HF-2, 5600 Fishers Lane, Rockville, MD 20852-9787
4. via the Internet at http://www.fda.gov/medwatch/report/hcp.htm

---

### Are there any confidentiality protections for ADR reporters and patients?

The FDA has issued a regulation preventing disclosure of information identifying individuals who voluntarily report an adverse drug or device event to the agency, as well as any other individuals named in a MedWatch report. The regulation, directed at drug and device manufacturers and FDA officials, seeks to encourage adverse event reporting by protecting the anonymity of reporters.

The rule makes confidential the name, address, institution, and other information related to the identity of the reporter and any other person named in the adverse event report. Exceptions to the rule allow disclosure if the reporter and the patient identified in the report both consent, if a court orders disclosure in the course of a medical malpractice suit, or if the patient identified in the report requests information. The regulation states that it overrides state and local laws and regulations that either permit or deny disclosure of the identities of individuals identified in adverse event reports. [21 C.F.R. 20.63]

## Device Reporting and Tracking

### How does device reporting differ from ADR reporting under the FDCA?

Medical device reporting is mandatory under the FDCA. In addition, there is a regulatory scheme for tracking the distribution of medical devices. Medical device reporting and tracking requirements apply to manufacturers, distributors, and device user facilities, which include hospitals, ambulatory surgical facilities, nursing homes, and outpatient treatment facilities. [21 U.S.C. 360i]

### When is a device event report required?

When a facility becomes aware that a device may have caused or contributed to a patient's death or serious injury, the facility must report the information, using the mandatory MedWatch form, within 10 days. Facilities must submit reports of device-related *injuries* to the manufacturer, if known; otherwise, to the FDA. Reports of device-related *deaths* must be submitted to the FDA and the manufacturer. Facilities must also submit an annual report containing a summary of reports made by the facility, due January 1 each year. [21 U.S.C. 360i]

To some extent, device-reporting requirements will be simplified by the FDAMA, however. Within the next few years, adverse device event reporting will not be required for all facilities but will be limited to a representative subset, to be identified through regulation. Once the representative program is implemented, hospitals will not be required by law to report device-related deaths and injuries, unless they are a "sentinel" facility required to report. Hospitals should consider continuing device monitoring, however, for accreditation, quality improvement, risk management, and other purposes. [FDAMA, § 213, codified at 21 U.S.C. 360i. For more detailed information on the evolving device reporting and tracking requirements, consult the FDA's Center for Devices and Radiological Health Web site at http://www.fda.gov/cdrh]

### How does device tracking work?

The FDAMA has changed the device tracking responsibilities of "final distributors" such as hospitals. Formerly, after purchasing or acquiring a tracked device, the final distributor of a device in a covered category was required to promptly provide the manufacturer with certain information to assist the manufacturer in tracking the device and contacting the patient. Now, hospitals are only required to track devices when the FDA has specifically ordered the manufacturer to institute a tracking program for that device. At this time, there are 16 categories of devices subject to tracking orders. For example, tracking orders are in place for mechanical replacement heart valves, electromechanical infusion pumps used outside device user facilities, breathing frequency monitors, continuous ventilators, dura mater, and abdominal aortic aneurysm stent grafts. The criteria to determine whether a device will be tracked is based on: (1) the likelihood of sudden catastrophic failure; (2) the likelihood of significant adverse clinical outcomes; and (3) the need for prompt professional intervention. [*See* Medical Tracking at http://www.fda.gov/cdrh/devadvice/353.html and 64 Fed. Reg. 29 (Feb. 12,1999)]

---

**What must a hospital do to comply with FDA device tracking requirements?**

The manufacturer bears responsibility for establishing the tracking method, but the following information must be maintained by hospitals and other entities that serve as final distributors of medical devices to patients:

- the distributor's (hospital's) name and address
- the lot, batch, model, serial number, or other device identifier
- name, address, telephone number, and social security number of the patient who received the device
- date the device was provided to the patient
- name, mailing address, and telephone number of the prescribing physician, as well as of the physician who regularly follows the patient
- when applicable, the date the device was explanted (with contact information for the explanting physician), date of patient death, date device was returned to the manufacturer, or date device was permanently retired or disposed of

Because device-tracking information must be made available to the device manufacturer for inspection upon request, tracking information may be kept separate from other files. Further, patients may refuse to have their devices tracked. The refusal must be documented by the product, model, and serial number, and the information provided to the manufacturer. Patients need not, however, consent in writing to have a device tracked or to have their identity released to a manufacturer. [FDAMA, §§ 211 & 212, codified at 21 U.S.C. 360i & 3601; 21 C.F.R. 821.30; *Guidance on Medical Device Tracking,* FDA, Center for Devices and Radiological Health, Office of Compliance, revised January 2000, is available on the Internet at http://www.fda.gov]

---

**What postmarket surveillance is required for devices?**

Postmarket surveillance is the collection, analysis, and interpretation of information about a marketed device in a systematic, scientifically valid way. Postmarket surveillance can be required of class II and class III devices that: (1) upon failure of the device would cause serious and adverse health consequences; (2) when the device is intended to be implanted for more than one year; or (3) when the device is intended to be used to support or sustain life. Failure to comply with postmarket surveillance when required can result in the product being misbranded.

The FDA has issued guidance criteria and approaches for postmarket surveillance. While not binding, the guidance sets forth the agency's thinking on the subject. Criteria the FDA would consider to determine whether postmarket surveillance is appropriate include: whether there are important and unanswered questions about the device such as a new or expanded use; changes in the device characteristics; long-term evaluation of rare events; or public health concerns that arise. The FDA will also consider how well public health concerns are handled, the practicality of postmarket surveillance strategies, and the magnitude of the risk to public health from the question.

Once it has been determined that postmarket surveillance will take place, the FDA will meet with manufacturers prior to submission of the first order for surveillance for a device. The required surveillance may then involve conducting a detailed review of complaint history and scientific literature, nonclinical testing of the device, patient follow-up, analysis of data or registries, case-control studies of implanted patients, or studies such as consecutive enrollment, cross-sectional, nonrandomized controlled cohort, or randomized controlled trials. [*Postmarket Surveillance Final Rule,* 67 Fed. Reg. 38878 (June 6, 2002) and *Guidance on Criteria and Approaches for Post Market Surveillance* available at http://www.fda.gov/cdrh/modact/critappr.pdf]

## Recalls

### What is the FDA's authority to recall drugs and devices?

Although the FDA does not have statutory authority to require a recall, federal regulations describe the manner in which a manufacturer may voluntarily recall a defective drug product or device. The regulations note that a recall offers broader consumer protection from an illegal product than an FDA action, cautioning that a manufacturer that refuses to recall a product at the FDA's request may face seizure or other enforcement action. The FDA may request a recall when a product presents a risk of illness, injury, or gross consumer deception; the manufacturer has not initiated a recall; and the FDA action is necessary to protect the public health. [21 C.F.R. 7.40–7.59]

There are three classes of recalls, each triggering different procedures:

1. A Class I recall applies to products that are reasonably likely to cause either serious adverse effects on health or death.
2. A Class II recall applies to products that may cause reversible adverse effects on health or pose only a remote risk of serious adverse effects.

3. A Class III recall applies to products not likely to cause adverse effects on health. [21 C.F.R. 7.3]

### What other entities require pharmacies to prepare for recalls?

State laws and regulations typically require hospital pharmacies to establish procedures for implementing recalls. In Washington, for example, the pharmacy director must "develop and implement a recall procedure to assure that potential harm to patients within the hospital is prevented and that all drugs included on the recall are returned to the pharmacy for proper disposition." [WASH. ADMIN. CODE 246–873–080] ASHP, in its minimum standards for hospital pharmacies, requires pharmacies to maintain a written procedure for how to respond to a recall notice. [*ASHP Guidelines, Minimum Standard for Pharmacies in Hospitals,* ASHP, issued 1995, is available on the Internet at http://www.ashp.org/bestpractices] (For Joint Commission requirements, see Standard TX.3.5.6 in Part 3 of this Manual. For sample materials, see Part 4 of this Manual, under **Care of Patients.**)

### What is a hospital pharmacist's responsibility once a recall has been issued?

A pharmacist who receives a recall notice should immediately follow the instructions in the recall notice. Recall strategies require varying "levels" of notification (e.g., notifying retail outlets, notifying consumers), so pharmacists should carefully determine their scope of responsibility and act accordingly. For a pharmacy to implement a recall that requires notification of patients and/or return of drugs, pharmacy records must include the information necessary to track the products that have been recalled. Thus, drug distribution systems should anticipate the possibility of a recall and incorporate appropriate recordkeeping procedures.

## Drug Samples

### How does the FDCA affect the distribution of drug samples?

A drug sample is a unit of a prescription drug that is not intended for sale but rather to promote the sale of the drug. Under the FDCA, no person may sell, purchase, or trade, or offer to sell, purchase, or trade, a drug sample. Manufacturers may only provide drug samples to prescribers and institutional pharmacies at the written request of a licensed prescriber. The recipient must sign a receipt that will be returned to the manufacturer. The manufacturer must maintain records of drug sample distributions for three years and report any thefts or significant losses. Only licensed health care professionals with prescribing authority and institutional pharmacies (including hospital and HMO pharmacies) may distribute drug samples to patients. [21 U.S.C. 353]

### Are there other federal laws that regulate the distribution of drug samples?

The PDMA (discussed in detail in the section on Antitrust) also regulates the distribution of drug samples. The statute, which is aimed at preventing prescription drug diversion to unauthorized individuals, largely regulates manufacturers and distributors, rather than hospitals. The PDMA regulations do not apply to hospital pharmacies providing drug samples to patients in accordance with the directions of a licensed prescriber, however, as long as the pharmacy lawfully received the sample. [21 U.S.C. 353; 21 C.F.R. Part 203.1]

### Do state laws address the distribution of drug samples?

Some states take the same approach as ASHP, discouraging distribution of drug samples but requiring a controlled distribution system where samples are used. [IOWA ADMIN. CODE r. 657–7.8] Some states are more permissive, merely stating that drug samples must be received and distributed under the purview of the pharmacy department. [ARIZ. ADMIN. CODE 4–23–661] Other states prohibit distribution of samples outright. In New Jersey, for example, licensing rules for pharmaceutical services in rehabilitation hospitals state, "drug samples shall not be accepted, placed or maintained in stock, distributed, or used in the facility." [N.J. ADMIN. CODE tit. 8:43H-10.4] Hospital pharmacists must ensure compliance with state law, as well as weigh the risks and benefits of drug samples when developing drug distribution procedures.

### What does ASHP recommend with regard to controlling drug samples?

Presumably due to the difficulty of tracking the distribution of drug samples, ASHP directs that use of drug samples be eliminated "to the extent possible." Where samples are permitted, however, ASHP's minimum standards for hospital pharmacies require the pharmacy to ensure the proper storage and integrity of drug samples, as well as to maintain appropriate records. [*ASHP Guidelines, Minimum Standard for Pharmacies in Hospitals,* ASHP, issued 1995, is available on the Internet at http://www.ashp.org/bestpractices] (For a drug sample inventory form, see Part 4 of this Manual, under **Care of Patients.**)

## Drug Labels under the FDCA

### What information should appear on the label of a prescription drug dispensed to a consumer?

Under the FDCA, a drug dispensed to a patient pursuant to a prescription (written or oral) must be labeled with

- name and address of the dispenser
- serial number
- date when the prescription was written or filled
- name of the prescriber
- name of the patient (if stated in the prescription)
- directions for use
- cautionary statements contained in the prescription [21 U.S.C. 353(b)(2)]

A final rule amends prescription drug labeling requirements by removing the requirement that prescription drugs be labeled with "Caution: Federal law prohibits dispensing without prescription" and adding in its place a requirement that prescription drugs be labeled with "Rx only" or "n only." [67 Fed. Reg. 4904 (Feb. 2, 2002).]

In 2000, the United States Pharmacopeia (USP) revised product dating specifications, requiring pharmacists to affix a "beyond use" date, rather than an expiration date, to prescription containers. [Claudia C. Okeke et al., *Revised USP standards for product dating, packaging, and temperature monitoring,* 57 AM. J. HEALTH-SYST PHARM 1441 (Aug. 1, 2000)]

**How do labeling requirements apply to unit dose packaging?**

The FDA has acknowledged that it may not be practical to require the same label information for unit doses of drugs dispensed in hospitals as for drugs dispensed for outpatient use. According to FDA guidance, the label on a unit dose of a drug must set forth the following:

- established name of the drug, or of each active ingredient, if there is more than one active ingredient
- quantity of each active ingredient
- expiration date (beyond use date, according to USP standards)
- lot number or control number
- name and place of business of the manufacturer, packer, or distributor
- statements required by official compendia
- number of dosage units in the container, and the strength per dosage unit
- statement "Warning: may be habit-forming," if applicable ["Unit Dose Labeling for Solid and Liquid Dosage Forms," CPG 7132b.10]

**What other guidance exists for unit dose labels?**

State laws and regulations may address either expressly or by implication the labeling of drugs dispensed to inpatients, including unit dose packaging. Under Georgia hospital pharmacy regulations, for example, all drugs dispensed by hospital pharmacies (including for ward inventory) must be in "appropriate containers" and be labeled to include, at a minimum, brand or generic name, strength, lot number, and expiration date. [GA. COMP. R. & REGS. r. 480–13-.06] In Oregon, retail pharmacies must include on labels of prescription drug containers, other than unit dose packaging, a physical description of the medication. [OR. ADMIN. R. 855–041–0065]

According to ASHP, a unit dose label should include nonproprietary name, dosage form (if special or other than oral), strength of dose and total contents delivered, special notes (on storage, preparation, and administration), expiration date, and control number. [*ASHP Technical Assistance Bulletin, Single Unit and Unit Dose Packages of Drugs*, ASHP, issued 1985, is available on the Internet at http://www.ashp.org/bestpractices] (For a sample labeling policy and procedure, see Part 4 of this Manual, under **Care of Patients.**)

---

**What are the requirements for Over-The-Counter (OTC) drug labeling?**

FDA regulations require OTC drugs to have clear and readable labeling. The OTC format includes standardized headings and subheadings, simple language to communicate information, and writing in easy-to-read print. The label must include the product's active ingredients and dose, medication purpose and use, specific warnings, dosage instructions and inactive ingredients. A drug that requires the labeling and does not include it will be considered misbranded. [*See* 21 C.F.R. 201.66]

---

**What is a patient package insert (PPI)?**

For more than 40 drugs, the FDA has mandated that specific language regarding use and hazards be displayed on the packaging and labeling. For a small group of pharmaceuticals, the FDA has expanded this concept from specific warnings on the container label to more detailed information provided to the patient in pamphlet form. A "patient package insert" is the popular name for this type of handout. PPIs were first provided to patients receiving oral contraceptives but are now also included with intrauterine devices and estrogen-containing drugs. [21 C.F.R. 310.501, 310.502, 310.515] Other drugs must be distributed with a PPI, not by regulation, but as part of the approved labeling for the drug. Examples include Nicorette, Rogaine, Halcion, and Norplant System. When a PPI is required, the drug manufacturer must supply the pharmacist with an adequate number of PPIs. The pharmacist is then responsible for delivering the PPI to the patient each time the drug is dispensed.

---

**Are there special rules for PPIs in hospitals?**

There are exceptions to PPI requirements for hospital inpatients. PPIs need not be provided to hospitalized patients with each administration of an estrogen-containing drug, for example. Rather, the patient may be given the insert only before the first administration of the drug and every 30 days thereafter. [21 C.F.R. 310.515(b)(3)]

At least one court has held that a hospital inpatient may sue a hospital for failing to provide the PPI directly to the patient, and not only to the patient's attending physician. A physician prescribed an estrogen-containing drug to an inpatient who had undergone surgery. When the drug was dispensed to the patient, she did not receive a PPI. She later sued the hospital for negligently failing to provide the PPI. The hospital argued that it had no duty to provide the PPI directly to the patient, as hospital policy made the prescribing physician responsible for PPI distribution. The court allowed the lawsuit to go forward, reasoning that the regulations require that the PPI be given to the patient (not the physician) and do not indicate that distribution may be left to the physician. [*Schlieter v. Carlos,* Nos. 97–0955 SC – 1592 SC (D.N.M. Aug. 31, 1989)]

---

### What is the status of the MedGuide initiative?

MedGuide is the moniker for an FDA initiative to improve the written information about prescription drugs for consumers. In 1995, the agency proposed a regulation that would require manufacturers to produce written medication guides for certain drugs, if the industry did not meet targets for voluntarily providing written prescription drug information by the year 2000. [60 Fed. Reg. 44,182] The FDA later withdrew its proposed regulations. Federal appropriations legislation requires that the goals of the original MedGuide regulation be met, not through regulation, but by a voluntary private sector process. [104 Pub. Laws 180, § 601]

The FDA, however, maintains that the appropriations legislation did not affect the agency's authority to implement mandatory information distribution for the small number of drug products that the agency deems pose a "serious and significant concern." For these products, the FDA has issued a final rule regarding the distribution of medication guides. [21 C.F.R. Part 208, 63 Fed. Reg. 66,378 (Dec. 1, 1998).] The agency will identify drug products that pose such a concern and will require additional patient information to be distributed with these products when they are dispensed on an outpatient basis. The FDA estimates that only 5 to 10 products a year will require medication guides, which will be approved by the agency and distributed by the manufacturer through other entities in the distribution chain. The dispenser will bear responsibility to provide the information directly to the patient. Drug labeling is especially important when: (1) the drug label would prevent serious adverse effects; (2) the drug product is one that has serious risk that is effected by patient use; and (3) the drug product is important to health and patient adherence to directions for use is crucial to the drug's effectiveness. In 2000, the first medication guide was required, for Lotronex, used to treat irritable bowel syndrome.

---

### What is the pediatric rule?

In December 1998, the FDA issued the final pediatric rule requiring drug manufacturers to assess the safety and effectiveness of certain human drugs and biological products in pediatric patients. The pediatric rule requires new drug applications as well as applications for new active ingredients, indications, dosages, dosing regimes, or route of administration to include data to assess whether the drug or biologic agent is safe and effective for pediatric patients. Adequate pediatric studies are required to provide information for this. The FDA can also require data submission on pediatric safety even if the company has not submitted an application for change in use.

In January 2002, the Best Pharmaceuticals for Children Act (BPCA) became law. The BPCA authorizes the National Institutes of Health (NIH) to fund studies for drugs when the manufacturer has declined to conduct the requested pediatric studies and other conditions are met. Information from these studies can then be included on the label of pediatric products. In anticipation of future rulemaking in this area, the FDA has requested comments on appropriate ways to update the pediatric rule to effectively address the need for pediatric studies and labeling. [67 Fed. Reg. 20070 (Apr. 24, 2002).]

## Investigational Drugs

### What are the duties of an investigator participating in a clinical trial?

Federal regulations contain detailed requirements for investigators conducting clinical trials. The investigator is responsible for ensuring that the investigation is conducted in compliance with federal regulations, protecting the safety of the patients, obtaining signed informed consent forms, and controlling the investigational drugs. Investigational drugs may only be administered to subjects under the personal supervision of the investigator or a subinvestigator responsible to the investigator. The investigator must retain records of the disposition of the investigational drug, including dates, quantity, and use by subjects. Investigators must also file financial disclosure reports, make reports to the drug's sponsor, ensure that the Institutional Review Board (IRB) complies with federal regulations, report any changes in protocol to the IRB, and comply with federal requirements for storing controlled substances. Investigators must also permit FDA officials to inspect records. [21 C.F.R. 312.50 through 312.70] (For a discussion of billing for investigational drugs, see **Reimbursement**.) (For more on investigational drug studies, see the discussion of **Patient Rights and Organizational Ethics** as well as Standard TX.3.8 in Part 3 of this Manual.)

### Do pharmacists dispensing investigational drugs have special duties?

Although the federal regulations impose detailed requirements for informed consent and other patient protections on investigators, pharmacists play an important role in complying with those requirements. For example, the pharmacy dispensing investigational drugs to clinical trial subjects might maintain a separate logbook for each clinical trial to record important information such as:

- patients enrolled
- drug preparation instructions

- dosing information
- labeling
- authorized prescribers
- ordering, dispensing, and administration records
- information relevant to the IRB-approved protocol

Pharmacists must also be aware of labeling obligations unique to investigational drugs. In blind clinical trials that employ a placebo, the label should reflect the possibility that either the investigational drug or the placebo has been dispensed. The label may state "Neurosurgery Study Drug," for example. Federal regulations require that investigational drugs be labeled "Caution: New Drug—Limited by Federal Law to Investigational Use." The label must not bear any false or misleading statement and must not represent that the drug is safe or effective. [21 C.F.R. 312.6] (For sample materials on investigational drugs, see Part 4 of this Manual, under **Care of Patients**.)

---

**How do state laws address investigational drug studies?**

State laws may require hospitals to adopt policies and procedures for investigational drug use, direct hospital pharmacies to assume control of investigational drugs distribution, or establish more detailed requirements. In California, for example, hospital licensing regulations state that investigational drugs must be used only under the direct supervision of the principal clinical investigator, who must be a medical staff member and ensure patient informed consent. Information about the investigational drug (including dosage form, route of administration, strength, actions, uses, side effects, adverse effects, interactions, and symptoms of toxicity) must be available both in the pharmacy and at the nursing station from which the drug is administered. The pharmacist is responsible for labeling, storage, and distribution of investigational drugs. [Cal. Code Regs. tit. 22, § 70263] Other state regulations address the administration of investigational drugs, permitting nurses to administer investigational drugs after they have been trained by the physician-investigator or pharmacist regarding the effects of the drug. [N.D. Admin. Code 61–07–01–12]

---

**Has ASHP addressed the duties of pharmacists with regard to research?**

According to ASHP, pharmacists should support a hospital's research activities. The minimum standards for hospitals include the following guidelines.

- A pharmacist ensures that policies and procedures for safe use of investigational drugs are followed.
- The pharmacy oversees the distribution and control of all investigational drugs, which are approved for use by an IRB and dispensed and administered to consenting patients according to an approved protocol.
- A pharmacist is included on the IRB.
- A pharmacist has access to information on all studies and research projects involving medications and medication-related devices used in the hospital.

- A pharmacist provides written information about the safe and proper use of investigational drugs (where known), including adverse effects and ADRs, to health care providers responsible for prescribing, dispensing, and administering investigational drugs. [*ASHP Guidelines, Minimum Standard for Pharmacies in Hospitals,* ASHP, issued 1995, is available on the Internet at http://www.ashp.org/bestpractices]

### May investigational drugs be dispensed outside of clinical trials?

The FDA has issued regulations that make investigational drugs available to very ill patients earlier in the drug development process. The Treatment IND, for example, is a procedure that allows investigational new drugs (INDs) to be administered outside of a controlled clinical trial. The drug's sponsor submits a treatment protocol to the FDA, explaining how the drug will be used and providing data on safety and effectiveness. Individual physicians may also request authorization to use an investigational drug to treat patients, under certain circumstances. [21 C.F.R. 312.34]

Investigational drugs are made available to cancer patients under a mechanism similar to the Treatment IND called Group C. The Group C protocols are similar to the Treatment IND protocols, the primary difference being that the National Cancer Institute, rather than the FDA, administrates the use of the investigational cancer drugs. Pharmacists should note that drugs dispensed under these programs retain their investigational status, which triggers patient safeguards such as informed consent requirements, IRB approval, and safety reports.

## Off-Label Use

### What is the FDA's approach to off-label uses of FDA-approved medications?

An off-label use, also known as an unapproved or unlabeled use, refers to treatment with an FDA-approved drug of a condition not covered by the approved labeling, or under conditions not included on the labeling. Off-label uses are particularly common in cancer treatment. In a 1972 FDA interpretive ruling, the agency clearly pronounced that off-label uses are legal under the FDCA, because the FDCA is not intended to interfere with the practice of medicine. The ruling states

> If an approved new drug is shipped in interstate commerce with the approved package insert, and neither the shipper nor the recipient intends that it be used for an unapproved purpose, the requirements of the [FDCA] are satisfied. Once the new drug is in a local pharmacy after interstate shipment, the physician may, as part of the practice of medicine, lawfully prescribe a different dosage for his patient, or may otherwise vary the conditions of use from those approved in the package insert, without informing or obtaining the approval of the Food and Drug Administration. [37 Fed. Reg. 16,503 (1972)]

The agency has generally initiated enforcement as a result of promotion of unapproved uses against the manufacturer, rather than against the physician prescribing or pharmacist dispensing for unapproved uses. However, the FDA's authority to limit manufacturer dissemination of information on unapproved uses has been the subject of regulation and ongoing constitutional challenges. Regardless of the disposition of this controversy, pharmacists dispensing drugs for off-label uses should consider whether the prescriber and patient have received appropriate information about the drug therapy (informed consent). (For further discussion of a pharmacist's responsibility when presented with a prescription order for an off-label use, see **State Regulation of Pharmacy Activities, Prescription and Medication Order Screening**, below.)

## CONTROLLED SUBSTANCES ACT

The objective of the Controlled Substances Act (CSA) [21 U.S.C. 801–971] is to limit the use of certain chemical substances to legitimate medical purposes. The legislative means to achieving this goal involves a multifaceted approach that includes the classification of drugs; registration by those who manufacture, distribute, prescribe, or dispense controlled substances; documentation of the manufacture, distribution, and dispensing of all controlled substances; specific labeling for lawfully dispensed controlled substances; and regulation for the transfer and disposal of controlled substances. The federal Drug Enforcement Administration (DEA) is the organization primarily responsible for promulgating the regulations that interpret and enforce the CSA. Because the CSA is integral to the day-to-day practice of pharmacy, hospital-based or otherwise, pharmacists should thoroughly understand what this law requires. Further, states have enacted their own controlled substances protections, often with additional requirements. Pharmacists must comply with both federal and state laws, meeting whichever overlapping provisions are stricter. (For a discussion of Joint Commission compliance with regard to controlled substances, see **Care of Patients: Medication** in Part 3 of this Manual.)

### What is a controlled substance?

Most drugs that require a physician's prescription are not controlled substances. At the federal level, a drug becomes a controlled substance by designation of the Attorney General of the United States, who relies on the recommendation of the Secretary of Health and Human Services. Factors taken into consideration when determining whether a substance should be classified as a controlled substance include the potential for abuse, the pharmacological effect of the drug, and the likelihood of drug dependence. [21 U.S.C. 811(c)]

Controlled substances are divided into five categories, called "schedules." The schedule in which a drug is placed determines which regulations must be followed when preparing, storing, and distributing the drug. When placing a controlled substance into one of the five schedules, the Attorney General weighs the drug's potential for abuse, which may lead to physical or psychological dependency, against the drug's potential medical benefits. Briefly, the characteristics of each schedule are as follows:

1. Schedule I includes drugs that have a high potential for abuse, have no currently accepted medical treatment use in the United States, and lack accepted safety for use under medical supervision. These substances are not normally handled by practicing pharmacists. Examples of Schedule I substances are heroin, marijuana, and mescaline.
2. Schedule II includes drugs that have a high potential for abuse but have a currently accepted medical treatment use in the United States. Schedule II substances, when abused, may lead to severe psychological or physical dependence. Examples of Schedule II drugs are amphetamine, codeine, Hydromorphone, meperidine, morphine, oxycodone.
3. Schedule III includes drugs that have less potential for abuse than the substances in Schedules I and II and have a currently accepted medical use. Abuse may lead to moderate to low physical dependence or high psychological dependence. Examples of Schedule III drugs are anabolic steroids, phendimetrazine, and products containing small amounts of certain Schedule II drugs, such as codeine, in combination with noncontrolled ingredients, such as aspirin.
4. Schedule IV includes drugs that have a lower potential for abuse than Schedule III substances and a currently accepted medical use. Abuse may lead to more limited physical dependence or psychological dependence. Examples are Alprazolam (Xanax), diazepam (Valium), phenobarbital, phentermine.
5. Schedule V includes drugs that have a lower potential for abuse than Schedule IV substances and a currently accepted medical use. Abuse may lead to more limited physical dependence or psychological dependence than Schedule IV substances. [21 U.S.C. 812(b)] Examples are Buprenorphine and many cough preparations that contain a limited amount of codeine.

---

### What are the basic requirements for pharmacists for prescribing, dispensing, and importing controlled substances?

Pharmacies filling prescriptions for controlled substances must be registered with DEA and licensed to dispense controlled substances in the state in which they operate. A prescription not issued in the usual course of professional practice, or not for legitimate and authorized research, is not considered valid. Both practitioners and pharmacies are responsible for ensuring that only legitimate prescriptions are written and filled. Pharmacists must receive written and manually signed prescriptions for Schedule II substances. They may receive oral or faxed prescriptions for Schedules III–V substances, provided they confirm the legitimacy of the prescription and the practitioner. Prescriptions for Schedule II substances may not be refilled. Prescriptions for Schedules III–V substances may be refilled up to five times, but no prescriptions may be filled or refilled more than six months after the date the prescription was issued. Only persons registered with DEA as importers and who are in compliance with DEA requirements may have controlled substances shipped into the jurisdiction of the United States from a foreign country.

## Registration

### What is registration?

Individuals and entities may only prescribe and handle controlled substances under a valid Drug Enforcement Administration (DEA) registration number, issued by the agency to individuals and entities that complete the agency's registration process. The DEA registration number that is issued to prescribers helps pharmacists to determine the validity of prescriptions that are presented for filling. Pharmacies and practitioners are usually required to register every three years. [*See* application process for pharmacies, 21 C.F.R. 1301.17(a)]

### What activities trigger the DEA registration requirement?

Under the CSA and its regulations, activities that require registration if they involve controlled substances include:

- manufacturing
- distributing
- dispensing
- conducting research or instructional activities
- conducting narcotic treatment programs
- conducting chemical analysis
- compounding, under limited circumstances [21 U.S.C. 823; 21 C.F.R. 1301.13(e)]

### What is a coincident activity?

Ordinarily, each activity listed in the previous answer requires a separate DEA registration. A coincident activity, however, is an activity that is integral to a registered activity so that it does not require a separate registration. If an activity is necessary to a registered activity and takes place at the same physical location as the registered activity, registration for the coincident activity generally is not required. For example, a hospital registered as a dispenser may provide a limited quantity of controlled substances to physicians registered under the CSA without triggering the distribution registration requirement. [21 C.F.R. 1301.13(e)]

### What activities trigger the dispensing registration requirement?

Dispensing has a broader meaning under the CSA than under state pharmacy practice acts. The CSA defines dispensing as delivering a controlled substance to the ultimate user, either by, or pursuant to the order of, a practitioner. Dispensing includes the prescribing, administering, packaging, labeling, and compounding necessary to prepare the substance for delivery. Thus, physicians, nurse practitioners, or physicians' assistants who prescribe controlled substances and pharmacists who prepare controlled substances must do so under a valid DEA registration number. Hospital-based nurses administering mediations to inpatients do not need a DEA number. The regulations specifically exclude orders dispensed for immediate administration such as drugs given to a bed-bound hospital patient from the definition of prescription. In a narcotic treatment program, controlled substances can be given to the patient by the physician or prescribing practitioner or by the licensed or registered nurse or pharmacist under the direction of the prescribing practitioner. [21 U.S.C. 802(10), 21 C.F.R. 1300.01(35), 21 C.F.R. 1301.74]

### Can nurse practitioners and physician assistants register as dispensers?

Federal regulations specifically allow midlevel practitioners, such as nurse practitioners, physician assistants, and midwives to register as dispensers, if state law grants them prescriptive authority. [21 C.F.R. 1300.01(b)(28)]

### Does each employee of a registered entity need to register?

A valid registration extends to any bona fide agent or employee of the registered dispenser, distributor, or dispenser (unless the registrant is a midlevel practitioner) if the employee is acting in the usual course of business or employment. Specifically, hospital employees who dispense controlled substances in the course of their official duties are exempt from registration. Thus, individual pharmacists employed by registered hospitals need not individually register to prepare and dispense controlled substances. [21 C.F.R. 1301.22]

### Do hospital employees need a separate registration to prescribe controlled substances?

In the past, practitioners authorized by state law to prescribe controlled substances could not prescribe controlled substances for *outpatients* under the hospital's registration but were permitted to order controlled substances for *inpatients* under the hospital's registration. In 1995, however, the CSA regulations were amended to allow practitioners to prescribe (for *both* inpatients and outpatients) under the hospital's DEA registration number when

- the prescribing is in the usual course of the practitioner's professional practice;
- the practitioner is authorized by state law to prescribe;
- the hospital has verified that the practitioner is authorized to prescribe;
- the practitioner is acting within the scope of his or her employment in the hospital;
- the hospital has authorized the practitioner to prescribe under the hospital registration and has designated a specific internal code number for that practitioner;

- the internal code number must consist of numbers, letters, or a combination of both, and must be a suffix to the institution's DEA registration number, preceded by a hyphen; and
- the hospital keeps a current list of internal codes and corresponding practitioners, available to other registrants and law enforcement authorities to verify the prescribing practitioner's authority [21 C.F.R. 1301.22(c)]

---

**When must a practitioner obtain a separate registration?**

Practitioners who wish to conduct research concerning Schedule I substances, and those who treat substance dependence through maintenance or detoxification programs, generally must register separately for these activities. There is an exception for practitioners dispensing narcotics in Schedules III, IV, or V in connection with ancillary services. [21 U.S.C. 823(f) & (g)]

---

**How does the CSA define manufacturing?**

Manufacturing refers to the production, preparation, propagation, compounding, or processing of a controlled substance, by extraction from natural origin, and/or by chemical synthesis, including packaging, repackaging, labeling, or relabeling. Manufacturing does not include the preparation, compounding, packaging, or labeling of a controlled substance by a practitioner incident to administration or dispensing in the course of professional practice. [21 U.S.C. 802(15)]

Just as under the FDCA, pharmacists should be aware that engaging in compounding activities that exceed regulatory limits may trigger the manufacturer's registration requirement. Compounding is permitted if the controlled substance is distributed to a practitioner who is also registered to dispense the controlled substance. The distribution must be recorded by both practitioners in accordance with regulatory requirements. If the substance is a Schedule I or II substance, a designated order form must be used. Finally, the total number of dosage units that a pharmacy manufactures each year may not exceed five percent of the pharmacy's total controlled substances distribution for that year. [21 C.F.R. 1307.11]

---

**When must a hospital register as a distributor?**

Distributing, which requires separate registration with the DEA, is defined as delivering, other than by administering or dispensing, a controlled substance. [21 U.S.C. 802(11)] A practitioner (including a hospital) registered as a dispenser may provide controlled substances to health professionals without registering separately as a distributor, provided that the following three conditions are met:

1. the controlled substance is distributed only to other registrants, such as practitioners;

2. distribution of controlled substances to other registrants does not exceed five percent of the total dosages dispensed and distributed by the practitioner during any 12-month period; and
3. the required order forms for Schedule I and II drugs are maintained [21 C.F.R. 1307.11(a)]

## Recordkeeping under the CSA

### What types of records must registered hospitals keep?

Under the CSA and its regulations, hospital pharmacies must keep an inventory of controlled substances, records of controlled substances received, and records of controlled substances disposition. Records of Schedule I and II controlled substances must be maintained separately from all other pharmacy records. Records of substances in Schedules III through V may either be kept separate from all other records, or in a manner that makes them "readily retrievable." The records must be kept available for at least two years. [21 C.F.R. 1304.04(h)] Readily retrievable means that the records are kept in an electronic or mechanized system so that they can be separated from all other records in a reasonable time, or that the records are visually identifiable from other items by being asterisked, redlined, or marked in some other manner. [21 C.F.R. 1300.01(b)(38)]

### Can controlled substance records be kept on a computer?

If the computerized recordkeeping system complies with CSA regulations, controlled substance records may be kept in an electronic format. The registrant need not notify the DEA that the records are maintained on an in-house computer system. If the records are maintained off site, however, the regulations for centralized records apply. When controlled substance records are centralized, the registrant must notify the DEA 14 days before centralizing the records. The notification must identify the names and DEA numbers of the registrants that are centralizing records, the exact location of the records, the nature of the records being centralized, and whether the records will be kept in computerized form. If the records rely on a code system, the registrant must provide the DEA with the key. Even when controlled substance records are centralized, executed order forms, prescriptions, and inventory records must be maintained on the registered site. [21 C.F.R. 1304.04(a), 1304.04(b)(2)]

### What information must be kept in a controlled substances inventory?

The CSA requires a written inventory of all controlled substances every two years (although state law might require a perpetual inventory, and ASHP recommends it). Registered dispensers must record the following information in an inventory for all controlled substances kept on hand in finished form:

- the name of the controlled substance
- the finished form and number of units or volume of each finished form
- the number of commercial containers of each finished form

For Schedule I and II substances, an exact count or measure must be made. For Schedule III, IV, and V substances, an estimate is satisfactory, unless the container holds more than 1,000 units, in which case an exact count must be made. [21 C.F.R. 1304.11(e)]

For controlled substances that are awaiting disposal, maintained for quality control, or maintained for extemporaneous compounding, required inventory information consists of

- the name of the substance
- the total quantity, to the nearest metric unit weight or the total number of units of finished form, and
- the reason for maintaining the substance and whether it is capable for manufacturing a controlled substance in finished form [21 C.F.R. 1304.11(e)]

Hospital pharmacies must retain each inventory for two years for inspection by the DEA. As new items are classified as controlled substances, they must be added to the inventory.

---

**What does "on hand" mean?**

Controlled substances are "on hand" if they are in the possession of the registrant, including

- substances returned by a patient (if state law allows returns)
- ordered substances that have not been invoiced
- stored substances, and
- substances in possession of employees of the registrant intended for distribution as complimentary samples [21 C.F.R. 1304.11(a)] (For a discussion of FDCA rules on samples, see Drug Samples under the **Food, Drug, and Cosmetic Act.**)

---

**What is required for records of receipt of controlled substances?**

Dispensers (including hospital pharmacies) must maintain complete and accurate records of the receipt of all controlled substances. The records must include the name of the substance received; a description of the finished form; the number of commercial containers received from other persons; the date of receipt; the number of containers in each receipt; and the name, address, and registration number of the person who provided the containers. [21 C.F.R. 1304.22(c)]

### What records must be kept for controlled substances dispensed?

Dispensers must also record the number of units or volume of controlled substance in finished form dispensed, including the name and address of the person to whom it was dispensed, the date of dispensing, and the written or typewritten name or initials of the person who dispensed or administered the controlled substance. [21 C.F.R. 1304.22(c)]

### How must records of refills be kept?

Refills of Schedule III and IV prescriptions must be recorded on the back of the original prescription, or on another readily retrievable document. The notation must include the name and dosage of the controlled substance, the quantity dispensed, the initials of the pharmacist dispensing the refill, the total number of refills for the prescription, and the date of the refill. No such prescription may be refilled more than six months after the prescription was issued or refilled more than five times. [21 C.F.R. 1306.22(a)]

A second alternative is to maintain refill records on a computer. Computerized records of Schedule III and IV controlled substance refills must meet the following criteria:

- The system must permit on-line retrieval of the original prescription order information, including prescription number; date of original prescription; name and address of the patient; name, address, and DEA number of the prescriber; name, strength, dosage form, and quantity of the prescribed substance; quantity dispensed; and the total number of refills authorized.
- The system must permit on-line retrieval of the current refill history.
- If the system provides a daily printout of refill information, each pharmacist who refilled Schedule III or IV controlled substances during that day must verify, date, and sign the printout within 72 hours. The daily log must be maintained in a separate file for two years.
- If the system does not provide a daily printout, the pharmacy must maintain a bound log book or separate file in which each pharmacist who dispensed a refill of a Schedule III or IV substance verifies, by signature, that the information is correct. This type of record must also be retained for two years.
- The system must be able to print, within 48 hours, a refill-by-refill audit trail for any Schedule III or IV controlled substance, including the name of the prescriber; name and address of the patient; quantities dispensed; date of refills; identity of dispensing pharmacist; and the number of the original prescription order.
- The system must provide for a backup method for authorizing and documenting refills during computer down-time. [21 C.F.R. 1306.22(b)]

**Has ASHP addressed how hospitals should keep controlled substance dispersal records?**

ASHP recommends that, for inpatients, hospitals maintain drug administration records derived from, but separate from, the patient chart to make controlled substance records more accessible. ASHP suggests the following three ways of isolating controlled substance dispersal records:

1. a medication administration record, included in a separate section of the patient's chart, apart from physicians' and nurses' notes
2. computer records, designed so that records of Schedule II controlled substances can be retrieved separately from records of substances in Schedules III through V, or
3. certificates of disposition or proof-of-use sheets that require institutional personnel to make an entry on paper or in an automated system, confirming that a controlled substance was administered. [*ASHP Technical Assistance Bulletin, Use of Controlled Substances in Organized Health Care Setting,* ASHP, issued 1993.]

**What should a pharmacy do if DEA order forms are lost or stolen?**

DEA Form 222 is the official federal order form for controlled substances in Schedules I and II. The form is issued only to controlled substance registrants and is imprinted with identifying information, such as the name, address, and DEA number of the registrant. If even a single order form is lost or stolen, the registrant must immediately notify the DEA. [21 C.F.R. 1305.12(b)]

**How should sales of nonprescription controlled substances be recorded?**

Controlled substances may be nonprescription drugs. Nonetheless, the DEA restricts the dispensing of these medications as follows:

- Only a pharmacist or pharmacy intern may dispense nonprescription controlled substances.
- Purchasers must be at least 18 years old.
- The pharmacist must know the purchaser or obtain suitable identification.
- For opium-containing substances, no more than eight ounces or 48 dosage units may be dispensed to the same purchaser within a 48-hour period.
- For all other nonprescription controlled substances, no more than four ounces or 24 dosage units may be dispensed to the same purchaser within a 48-hour period.
- The pharmacist must record, in a bound record book, the name and address of the purchaser, the name and quantity of the substance purchased, the date of purchase, and the name or initials of the dispensing pharmacist. [21 C.F.R. 1306.26]

### How should the theft or loss of controlled substances be documented?

Upon discovering that a controlled substance has been stolen or lost, a pharmacy must notify the DEA and local police. The pharmacy must file a report with the DEA on Form 106. The form requires the pharmacy to provide a list of controlled substances stolen, as well as information concerning the type of theft and subsequent security measures. [21 C.F.R. 1301.74 & 1301.76]

### What is the procedure for disposing of controlled substances?

A pharmacy may not dispose of unused controlled substances without requesting DEA permission and instructions. The pharmacy must complete DEA Form 41, an inventory of drugs "surrendered," and forward it to the agency. The DEA will then advise the pharmacy which of the following alternatives to follow to dispose of the drug:

- transfer to a person authorized to possess the substance
- delivery to a DEA agent or nearest office
- destruction in the presence of a DEA agent or other authorized person, or
- other means to ensure the substance will not be available to an unauthorized person. [21 C.F.R. 1307.21(b)]

If a pharmacy must regularly dispose of controlled substances, the DEA may authorize disposal without prior approval upon conditions indicated by the DEA. Pharmacists considering the destruction of controlled substances should also observe hazardous waste regulations issued by the Environmental Protection Agency (EPA). (For further discussion, see Disposal of Hazardous Waste, under **Occupational Safety and Environment of Care.**)

### What records are required when a pharmacy returns controlled substances to a supplier?

A hospital returning a controlled substance to the manufacturer or supplier must keep a written record of the date of the return; the name, form, and quantity of the substance; the name, address, and registration number of the hospital; and the name, address, and registration of the supplier or manufacturer, if known. If the substance being returned is in Schedule I or II, DEA order Form 222 must be completed and maintained as a record of the transaction. [21 C.F.R. 1307.12]

### What are the penalties for failing to keep records as required by the CSA?

The penalties for noncompliance with the CSA and DEA regulations include monetary fines, loss of registration, and criminal sanctions. Imprisonment is also possible for intentional recordkeeping violations. [21 U.S.C. 842(c)]

### Are there penalties for inadvertent recordkeeping mistakes?

For civil charges to apply, no knowledge or intent is needed. The courts have held that a strict liability standard of care applies in actions for controlled substance recordkeeping violations. That is, even an inadvertent error can be the basis for civil action by the DEA [*United States v. Green Drugs*, 905 F.2d 694 (3d Cir.), *cert. denied*, 498 U.S. 985 (1990)] and can subject a pharmacy or pharmacist to significant monetary penalties. Pharmacists have been charged with violations of controlled substance regulations in cases involving dating a prescription in the wrong place and failing to complete a box on a federal form, and for filing controlled substance prescription issued by a hospital resident physician who used his supervising physician's DEA number instead of the hospital's number. [N.C. Board of Pharmacy Newsletter, Vol. 20, No. 2, Oct. 1998] Because even small infractions might lead to substantial penalties, pharmacies must follow strict standards in complying with the CSA.

## Prescriptions

### When is a controlled substance prescription valid?

Federal regulations state that, although responsibility for proper prescribing and dispensing of controlled substances falls on the prescriber, the pharmacist bears a "corresponding responsibility" to ensure that controlled substance prescriptions are issued for a legitimate medical purpose by an individual practitioner in the usual course of professional practice. [21 C.F.R. 1306.04(a)] (For additional discussion of prescription requirements, see Prescription and Medication Order Screening, under **State Regulation of Pharmacy Activities.**)

### Who may prescribe controlled substances?

Because the CSA defers to state law to establish prescribing authority, the classes of health care providers who may prescribe controlled substances varies from state to state. For example, nurse practitioners, chiropractors, and pharmacists may be permitted to prescribe in some states, but not others. To ascertain whether prescriptions are valid, pharmacists must be familiar with prescribing authority laws in the states in which they practice. (*See also* "Should pharmacists screen drug orders and prescriptions for prescriptive authority?" under Prescription and Medication Order Screening.) (For related materials, see Part 4 of this Manual, under **Care of Patients.**)

### What information must appear on a prescription?

Controlled substances intended for outpatient use must be dispensed pursuant to a valid prescription. Controlled substance prescriptions must contain the date the prescription was issued; the full name and address of the patient; the drug name, strength, dosage form, quantity prescribed, directions for use; name, address, and DEA registration number of the prescriber; and the prescriber's signature. Prescriptions must be issued in ink, indelible pencil, or be typewritten. [21 C.F.R. 1306.05(a)]

---

### Are oral medication orders for Schedule II drugs permissible in a hospital setting?

Schedule II controlled substances have special limitations, including a specific requirement that a prescription for a Schedule II drug be in writing. However, oral medication orders for Schedule II controlled substances are permissible for hospitalized patients, as long as the drug is dispensed for immediate administration to a patient. This permits a physician to ask a nurse to give an injection of Demerol stat, for example, without first writing the order. When controlled substances ordered for hospital patients are not for immediate administration, a written order is required before the drugs are dispensed. [21 C.F.R. 1306.11(c)] (For a related discussion, see **Patient Record Documentation and Confidentiality.**)

---

### Does a faxed prescription satisfy recordkeeping requirements?

A pharmacist may dispense a controlled substance in Schedules III, IV, or V on the basis of a facsimile of a written, signed prescription (or based on an oral prescription reduced to writing by the pharmacist). Generally, a faxed prescription for a Schedule II controlled substance is only permitted if the pharmacist receives the original prescription before dispensing the substance. However, pharmacists may dispense Schedule II drugs without the original if the prescription

- is for a narcotic Schedule II substance to be compounded for the direct administration to a patient by parenteral, intravenous, intramuscular, subcutaneous, or intraspinal infusion
- is for a Schedule II substance for a resident of a long-term care facility
- is for a Schedule II narcotic substance for a patient in a licensed or Medicare certified or state licensed hospice [21 C.F.R. 1306.11]

---

### Is partial filling of a Schedule II drug permissible in an institutional setting?

Strict limitations on partial filling of prescriptions are some of the additional precautions imposed on Schedule II substances. In long-term care facilities or for a patient with a terminal illness, however, the balance of a partially filled prescription for a Schedule II controlled substance need not be filled within 72 hours. Instead, the pharmacist may partially fill the prescription, in individual doses, for up to 60 days. The quantity dispensed, remaining quantity authorized to be dispensed, each dispensing date, and the identity of each dispensing pharmacist must be recorded. [21 C.F.R. 1306.13(b)]

### Do state laws address dispensing of controlled substances to outpatients?

State laws generally distinguish between inpatient and outpatient dispensing of controlled substances in the following ways:

- requiring written prescriptions for controlled substances dispensed to outpatients
- requiring more detailed labeling on drugs dispensed to outpatients
- requiring controlled substance prescriptions for outpatients to be dispensed only from the pharmacy

## Labels

### What should appear on the label of a controlled substance dispensed to a consumer?

When dispensed to an outpatient or retail customer pursuant to a valid prescription, a container holding controlled substances must be labeled with

- the date the prescription was initially filled
- name and address of the pharmacy
- names of the patient and prescriber
- prescription number
- directions for use and cautionary statements
- the warning, "Caution: Federal law prohibits the transfer of this drug to any person other than the patient to whom it was prescribed" (unless the drug is a nonprescription drug or is dispensed in a blinded investigational study). [21 C.F.R. 290.5, 1306.14 (a), 1306.24(a)] (For a sample outpatient prescription labeling policy, see Part 4 of this Manual, under **Care of Patients.**)

A proposed regulation would remove the requirement that certain habit-forming drugs bear the statement "Warning—May be habit forming." [65 Fed. Reg. 18934, corrected at 65 Fed. Reg. 21378]

### How do controlled substance labeling rules apply in an institutional setting?

A medication order for immediate administration to an inpatient is not a prescription, as defined by controlled substance regulations. Because the labeling requirements discussed in the previous question apply to prescriptions, they do not apply when dispensing pursuant to a medication order for immediate administration to an inpatient. Even when drugs are dispensed to an inpatient pursuant to a prescription, the labeling requirements in the previous question do not apply if

- not more than a 7-day supply of a Schedule II medication, or not more than a 34-day supply or 100 dosage units (whichever is less) of a Schedule III, IV, or V medication, is dispensed at a time
- the controlled medication is not in the patient's possession prior to use, and
- the institution maintains proper security and appropriate records concerning the medication

The responsible pharmacist not only must employ a system that adequately identifies the supplier, product, and patient but also must explain the medication's use and the necessary precautions. [21 C.F.R. 1306.21, 1306.14(b), 1306.24(b)] (For a sample labeling policy, see Part 4 of this Manual under **Care of Patients.**)

## Security

### What security must a pharmacy provide for controlled substances?

Federal regulations establish security requirements that apply to all practitioners registered to possess or handle controlled substances. The level of security that is appropriate in a particular hospital depends on a number of factors, including the location of the institution, the general characteristics of the building, and the adequacy of supervision over employees. In all facilities, controlled substances must be stored in a securely locked and substantially constructed cabinet. As an alternative, pharmacies and institutional practitioners may disperse controlled substances in Schedules II through V on pharmacy shelves among noncontrolled substances in a manner that deters theft. Certain extremely potent narcotics must be stored in a safe or steel cabinet equivalent to a U.S. Government Classification V security container. [21 C.F.R. 1301.75] State law or regulation may require double locks for all controlled substances. [UTAH ADMIN. CODE 432–100–24]

### How should controlled substances be kept in areas of the hospital outside the pharmacy?

Controlled substances kept outside the pharmacy in other hospital units (e.g., nursing and surgical units) remain the responsibility of the director of pharmacy and must be kept in physically secure locations. According to ASHP, controlled substances kept as floor stock should be maintained in a securely locked, substantially constructed storage unit. In surgical, delivery, or special procedure areas, security procedures should emphasize managing wasted drugs. Precautions might include providing the same physical security, documenting beginning and end of shift inventories, and recording administration used for floor stock; maintaining no controlled substances in the area (instead requiring an anesthesiologist or anesthetist to bring the controlled substances to the area and maintain appropriate records); and instituting a satellite pharmacy in the immediate area of the operating rooms. [*ASHP Technical Assistance Bulletin, Use of Controlled Substances in Organized Health Care Setting,* ASHP, issued 1993]

State laws may require all or some of these precautions. Washington state hospital pharmacy regulations require an actual count at each change of shift of Schedule II and III controlled substances kept as floor stock. [WASH. ADMIN. CODE 246–873–080] In California, drugs maintained on nursing units must be inspected by a pharmacist at least monthly. [CAL. REGS. tit. 22, 70263] In New York, pharmacy "substock" of controlled substances must be tracked with administration sheets indicating the date and hour of administration, patient name, prescriber name, and other information. [10 N.Y.C.R.R. 80.46] Hospital policies and procedures for drugs maintained outside the pharmacy should be designed to comply with applicable state law. (For a sample policy, see Part 4 of this Manual, under **Care of Patients.**)

### Do state regulations address waste of controlled substances?

State laws may require documentation of waste. In New Jersey, for example, hospital policies must address what to do when controlled substances are lost, contaminated, unintentionally wasted, or destroyed. The policy must require a written report, signed by the individuals involved and any witnesses. Where drugs are intentionally wasted (such as when only a partial dose is administered) hospital policy must require documentation including the signature of a second person who witnessed the disposition. [N.J. ADMIN. CODE 8:43H-10.4]

In Washington, when a nurse administers a partial dose of a controlled substance, a second nurse must witness the wasting of the remaining controlled substance and countersign a record of destruction. Destruction of larger amounts of controlled substances must comply with hospital policy, a copy of which must be on file with the DEA and the state board of pharmacy. The policy must provide for ensuring that all destructions make the controlled substance unrecoverable, destruction is performed by a pharmacist and one other licensed health professional, records are maintained by the pharmacy for two years, and quarterly summaries are sent to the DEA and state board of pharmacy. [WASH. ADMIN. CODE 246–873–080]

### Do controlled substance security requirements address pharmacy personnel?

Registrants may be subject to DEA enforcement for failing to properly screen employees before hiring. Practitioners must not employ a person in a position with access to controlled substances if that person has been convicted of a felony offense relating to controlled substances, the person's own DEA registration was revoked or surrendered for cause, or the person's registration application was denied. [21 C.F.R. 1301.76(a)]

The DEA assumes that employers will use the following two questions to screen employees who will have access to controlled substances:

1. Have you been convicted of any felony within the past five years or of any misdemeanor within the past two years, or are you presently formally charged with committing a criminal offense? (Do not include traffic violations, juvenile offenses, or military convictions, except by general court-martial.) If the answer is yes, furnish details of conviction, offense, location, date, and sentence.
2. In the past three years, have you ever knowingly used any narcotics, amphetamines, or barbiturates, other than those prescribed to you by a physician? If the answer is yes, furnish details of conviction, offense, location, date, and sentence. [21 C.F.R. 1301.90]

## MEDICARE CONDITIONS OF PARTICIPATION

Hospitals must meet a detailed list of requirements, known as the Conditions of Participation, to be reimbursed under the Medicare and Medicaid programs. [42 C.F.R. Parts 416, 482, 485, and 489] These regulations set out the standards hospitals must meet in a variety of operational and strategic areas. Each condition of participation contains one or more standards that outline the condition's requirements. A hospital must comply with all conditions before it can qualify for payment for services provided to Medicare and Medicaid beneficiaries. One condition of participation governs pharmaceutical services and is discussed in this section.

### What requirements are contained in the condition of participation for pharmaceutical services?

The condition of participation for pharmaceutical services contains two standards. The first standard governs pharmacy management and administration, requiring that the pharmacy or drug storage area be administered in accordance with accepted professional principles. The standard requires the following:

- The hospital must employ a full-time, part-time, or consulting pharmacist to develop, supervise, and coordinate the pharmacy department's activities.
- There must be an adequate number of personnel working in the pharmacy department to ensure that quality services are provided.
- Pharmacy department employees must keep current and accurate records showing the receipt and disposition of all scheduled drugs. [42 C.F.R. 482.25(a)]

The second standard requires that drugs and biologicals be distributed in accordance with pharmacy practice standards and federal and state law. This standard requires the following:

- A pharmacist must supervise all compounding, packaging, and dispensing of drugs.
- The pharmacy must keep drugs in a locked storage area.

- Outdated, mislabeled, or otherwise unusable drugs must be made unavailable for patient use.
- When the pharmacist is unavailable, only personnel designated by medical staff and pharmaceutical policies may remove drugs from the pharmacy or storage area.
- The medical staff must have a policy specifying when drugs that are not specifically prescribed as to time or number of doses must automatically be stopped.
- Drug administration errors, ADRs, and incompatibilities must be immediately reported to the attending physician and, if appropriate, to the hospitalwide quality assurance program.
- Abuses and losses of controlled substances must be reported to the individual responsible for the pharmaceutical services and to the chief executive officer, as appropriate.
- The professional staff must have access to information about drug interactions, drug therapy, side effects, toxicology, dosage, indications for use, and routes of administration.
- The medical staff must establish a formulary system to ensure quality pharmaceuticals at reasonable costs. [42 C.F.R. 482.25(b)]

---

**How does the proposed condition of participation for pharmaceutical services differ from the condition of participation currently in effect?**

CMS issued a proposed rule revising the hospital conditions of participation on December 19, 1997. [62 Fed. Reg. 66,726, to be codified at 42 C.F.R. Parts 416, 482, 485, and 489] Two aspects of the proposed rule impact hospital pharmacists. The proposed rule removes almost all references to pharmacists contained in the current condition of participation for pharmaceutical services. Thus, the condition of participation will no longer contain a requirement that a pharmacist develop, supervise, and coordinate the pharmacy department's activities. In addition, the proposed rule requires a nurse, medical doctor, or osteopath to review medication orders but does not include pharmacists on the medication review team.

The focus of the proposed rule is to integrate care through a focus on patient rights, patient assessment, care planning and coordination of services, and quality assessment and performance improvement. The proposed requirements for pharmaceutical services focus on: adverse drug event monitoring to keep medical error rate below two percent, drug management procedures, and limitations on discharge orders for psychopharmacological drugs.

---

**What effect will the proposed condition of participation have on pharmacy practice?**

The proposed condition of participation eliminating all references to pharmacists likely will have little impact on actual pharmacy practice. Current Joint Commission standards and many state laws list requirements applicable to pharmacists. The Joint Commission requires pharmacists to conduct medication review. [TX.3.5.2] In addition, many state laws require hospital pharmacies to be directed by a licensed pharmacist. [*See, e.g.*, Ariz. Admin. Code R4–23–653; Iowa Admin. Code 657–7.6; Wash. Admin. Code 246–873–040]

---

**What patients' rights are established in the conditions of participation?**

The conditions of participation for hospitals establish the following rights for patients.

- The right to participate in the development of his or her plan of care
- The right to make informed decisions about his or her care
- The right to formulate advanced directives
- The right to have a family member or other person notified of his or her admission to the hospital
- The right to personal privacy
- The right to receive care in a safe setting
- The right to be free from abuse or harassment
- The right to confidentiality of his or her clinical records
- The right to access information in the clinical records
- The right to be free from restraints that are not medically necessary
- The right to be free from seclusion or restraint for behavior management.

In addition, patients should be given notice of their rights and have a process for prompt resolution of patient grievances. [42 C.F.R. 482.13]

---

**Do the conditions of participation address chemical restraints?**

In 2000, the Medicare Conditions of Participation were amended to incorporate a patients' bill of rights, which set standards for the use of restraint and seclusion of hospital patients. The regulations establish patients' right to be free from both physical restraints and drugs that are used as a restraint that are not medically necessary or are used as a means of coercion, discipline, convenience, or retaliation by staff. The standards distinguish between the use of restraint for medical and surgical care, and the use of restraint or seclusion for behavior management, setting forth separate criteria for each. [42 C.F.R. 482.13]

---

**What constitutes a restraint?**

Under the regulations, a restraint is any manual method, physical device, mechanical device, material, or equipment attached or adjacent to the patient's body that he or she cannot easily remove, if it restricts freedom of movement or access to one's body. A drug constitutes a restraint if it is a medication used to control behavior or to restrict the patient's freedom of movement and is not a standard treatment for the patient's medical or psychiatric condition. [42 C.F.R. 482.13]

### How do the patients' rights standards limit the use of restraints for medical and surgical care?

The standards, which have generated much controversy in the hospital community,

- limit restraint use to those situations in which less restrictive interventions have been determined to be ineffective to protect the patient or others from harm
- require the order of a physician or qualified licensed independent practitioner
- prohibit the use of standing or PRN (as needed) orders for restraints
- require consultation with the patient's treating physician as soon as possible (if the physician did not personally write the order)
- necessitate a written amendment of the patient's plan of care
- mandate that restraints be implemented in the least restrictive manner possible and in accordance with safe and appropriate restraining techniques
- require the withdrawal of restraints at the earliest possible time
- establish that restraint use must be continually assessed, monitored, and reevaluated
- impose ongoing staff training requirements [42 C.F.R. 482.13]

### What documentation is necessary with regard to restraint orders and evaluations?

The guidance states that the rationale that a patient might fall is an inadequate basis for using a restraint. Each individual patient's history of falls, medical condition, and symptoms must be evaluated on a case-by-case basis—restraints are not a substitute for adequate staffing and monitoring, according to the guidelines. The guidelines emphasize the importance of documentation of continual reevaluation of patients in restraints, the rationale for ordering a restraint, the rationale for the time frame for the order, and the fact that other, less restricting alternatives were considered. Consistency with hospital policy and reliance on current standards of safety and technique are also factors in evaluating whether restraint use is appropriate. [CMS, *Interpretive Guidelines, Hospital Conditions of Participation for Patients' Rights,* May 2000]

## OCCUPATIONAL SAFETY AND ENVIRONMENT OF CARE

This section discusses the federal and state regulations, as well as ASHP guidelines, that are particularly relevant to hospital pharmacy departments in the areas of infection control, handling and storage of hazardous materials such as cytotoxic drugs, and disposal of hazardous substances. The two federal agencies with enforcement authority over federal laws governing these matters are the Occupational Safety and Health Administration (OSHA) and the Environmental Protection Agency (EPA). Analogous state agencies also play an important role.

OSHA and the Joint Commission have formed a successful partnership to promote safety and health for health care workers. The joint program, initiated in 1996, was originally developed as a three-year venture but has been extended in recognition of the benefits gained from the partnership. OSHA and the Joint Commission have worked together to help hospitals and other health care facilities understand how to meet the requirements of both the federal agency and the accreditation organization. As part of that effort, OSHA and the Joint Commission have jointly developed training materials and publications for health care facilities, and provided specific examples in Joint Commission accreditation manuals to illustrate how compliance with OSHA standards also satisfies Joint Commission standards. In addition, the partnership has enabled OSHA and the Joint Commission to minimize duplicative compliance activities. [*See OSHA and Joint Commission Extend Efforts To Promote Health and Safety for Health Care Workers*, OSHA Trade News Release (June 8, 2000), available on the Internet at http://www.osha.gov] (Joint Commission standards relating to environmental issues are discussed under **Management of the Environment of Care** in Part 3 of this Manual.)

## Bloodborne Pathogens

### What is OSHA's bloodborne pathogen standard?

The OSHA bloodborne pathogen standard applies primarily to the health care industry. The standard was recently revised by the Needlestick Safety and Prevention Act [Pub. L. No.106-430, 66 Fed. Reg. 5317], which was passed in November 2000 and became effective in April 2001, and contains the following key provisions:

- exposure control plan
- engineering and work practice controls
- personal protective equipment
- disposal of waste and cleaning of workplace
- employer-provided hepatitis B vaccinations
- postexposure evaluation
- notice of hazards to employees
- recordkeeping [29 C.F.R. 1910.1030]

Policies and procedures aimed at satisfying requirements in these areas will be developed at the institutional level and reviewed annually. Some requirements, discussed below, have direct application in the pharmacy department. (For sample procedures for administering prophylaxis prescriptions after exposure to human immunodeficiency virus (HIV), see Part 4 of this Manual under **Surveillance, Prevention, and Control of Infection.**)

**What kinds of equipment or engineering controls must be used in the pharmacy department to help prevent the spread of bloodborne pathogens?**

Hospitals must implement engineering controls such as puncture-resistant containers for used sharps, self-sheathing sharps and needles, protective shields, safer medical devices such as sharps with engineered sharps injury protections and needleless systems, and biosafety cabinets. The standard requires employers to regularly inspect and repair engineering controls. [29 C.F.R. 1910.1030(b) & (d)] In an annual review of their exposure control plan, hospitals must consider safer needle devices as part of the reevaluation of appropriate engineering controls, and must involve frontline (i.e., nonmanagerial) employees in the identification and selection of safer devices. The revised standard also mandates that in the exposure control plan employers document how they received input from the employees, either by listing the employees involved and describing the process by which input was requested, or by presenting other documentation, including reference to minutes of meetings, copies of requests for employee participation, or records of employees' responses.

In addition, the National Institute of Occupational Safety and Health (NIOSH) has issued an alert on preventing needlestick injuries in health care settings. The alert contains detailed recommendations for employers and employees. [NIOSH Alert, *Preventing Needlestick Injuries in Health Care Settings,* NIOSH Pub. No. 2000–108 (1999), available on the Internet at http://www.cdc.gov/niosh]

**What kinds of work practice controls must be used in the pharmacy department to prevent the spread of bloodborne pathogens?**

Employees are prohibited from eating, drinking, and storing food in areas where there is potential for exposure to bloodborne pathogens or where blood, body fluids, or both are stored (e.g., refrigerators and cabinets, medication carts). [29 C.F.R. 1910.1030(d)(2)(ix) & (x)] In addition, handwashing must be performed as soon as feasible after exposure to blood or other potentially infectious materials (including potentially contaminated inanimate objects) and after removal of gloves or other personal protective equipment. [29 C.F.R. 1910.1030(d)(2)(iii) through (vi)]

Because handwashing may be the single most important procedure for preventing nosocomial infections, the hospital and its pharmacy staff must use an appropriate handwashing technique on a routine basis. Such procedures should include handwashing at the beginning of the pharmacist's shift, after visiting the restroom, before and after eating, and prior to beginning the preparation of sterile products. [For more information, *see* Centers for Disease Control and Prevention, *Draft Guideline for Infection Control in Health Care Personnel, 1997,* reprinted at 62 Fed. Reg. 47276]

### Does OSHA's bloodborne pathogens standard contain specific requirements regarding the handling of sharps?

OSHA's bloodborne pathogens standard prohibits employees from shearing, breaking, recapping, removing, or bending contaminated sharps and other sharps such as razor blades and broken ampuls; from picking up potentially contaminated glassware by hand; and from reaching by hand into a container that may contain contaminated reusable sharps. [29 C.F.R. 1910.1030(d)(2)(vii) & (d)(4)(ii)(D) and (E). For recommendations on preventing needlestick injuries in health care settings, *see* NIOSH Alert, *Preventing Needlestick Injuries in Health Care Settings,* NIOSH Pub. No. 2000–108 (1999), available on the Internet at http://www.cdc.gov/niosh] (For a more detailed discussion of regulatory requirements governing disposal of sharps, see questions under **Disposal of Hazardous Waste.**)

### What measures does OSHA's bloodborne pathogen standard require hospitals to take in cleaning the work site and disposing of contaminated waste?

Requirements for cleaning the work site and disposing of contaminated waste include

- implementing a written plan that describes the method and frequency of cleaning
- performing regular inspection and decontamination of reusable garbage bins and pails that hold potentially contaminated medical waste
- ensuring that blood specimens and other potentially infectious materials are placed in properly labeled containers that will prevent leakage during handling, storage, and transport
- requiring employees who have contact with potentially contaminated inanimate objects to wear appropriate personal protective equipment such as gloves and gowns [29 C.F.R. 1910.1030(d)(4)]

(For a more detailed discussion of OSHA's bloodborne pathogen standard as it relates to disposal of contaminated waste, see questions under **Disposal of Hazardous Waste.**)

### What must employers do to communicate the hazards of bloodborne pathogens to employees?

Employers are required to communicate the hazards of bloodborne pathogens to employees through proper placement of written warnings and labels [29 C.F.R. 1910.1030(g)(1)], and employee training and education. [29 C.F.R. 1910.1030(g)(2)] Employers must provide training when the employee is first assigned to a job in which there is occupational exposure and then provide additional training on an annual basis or any time changes in work tasks affect the employee's risk of exposure. [29 C.F.R. 1910.1030(g)]

### What kinds of records must employers keep regarding occupational exposure?

Employers must maintain medical records for each employee with occupational exposure for the duration of the employee's employment plus 30 years. The records must be kept confidential by the employer during this period, and the employer may not disclose contents of the records without the employee's express written consent. The standard also requires employers to maintain training records for a period of three years from the date of training but does not require that they be kept confidential. [29 C.F.R. 1910.1030(h)] Hospitals must keep a log to track *all* needlesticks, not only those cuts or sticks that actually lead to illness, and must maintain the privacy of employees who have suffered those injuries. At a minimum the log must contain a description of the incident, the type and brand of device involved in the incident, and the location of the incident (i.e., department or work area). The sharps injury log may include additional information as long as an employee's privacy is protected. [66 Fed. Reg. 5317]

### What will OSHA compliance investigators look for with respect to bloodborne pathogens?

In recognition of technological advances and new research, OSHA has issued guidance for compliance investigators who enforce the bloodborne pathogen standard. Since the standard itself was revised by the Needlestick Safety and Prevention Act in 2000, OSHA has updated its compliance directive to conform with the revised standard. The new compliance directive can be found on the Internet at http://www.osha-slc.gov/OshDoc/Directive_data/CPL_2-2_69.html. The enforcement procedures do not carry the force of law or regulation, but health care employers are well advised to become familiar with the revised guidance because it will direct agency officials during compliance inspections. The Instruction requires investigators to assess whether employers perform the following:

- The employer has conducted an annual review of the exposure control plan. The plan should reflect consideration and use of the safer medical devices that are now commercially available.
- Engineering controls, including safer medical devices, needle devices, work practices, administrative controls, and personal protective equipment, are used to reduce occupational exposure to the lowest feasible level. The guidance emphasizes the importance of needleless systems and sharps with engineered sharps injury protection and provides detailed guidance on what constitutes sufficient use of engineering controls.
- The employer has established a log to track all needlesticks, maintaining the privacy of employees who have suffered needlestick injuries.
- The employer has relied on relevant evidence (beyond FDA approval) to ensure effectiveness of devices designed to prevent employee exposure to bloodborne pathogens.

- Employees are solicited to give input in identifying and selecting safer devices for implementation.
- Employees receive effective training when safer devices are implemented. The Instruction highlights the value of interactive training sessions that provide the opportunity for discussion with a qualified trainer.
- The most recent Centers for Disease Control and Prevention (CDC) guidelines on hepatitis B vaccines and postexposure evaluation and follow-up for HIV and hepatitis C are followed.

The directive also addresses the compliance responsibilities of several types of "employers." Where companies provide services on an independent contractor basis, both the company and the "host employer" are responsible for all provisions of the bloodborne pathogen standard. Part-time, temporary, and per diem employees are covered by the standard also.

Finally, OSHA has replaced and updated its sample documentation and other appendices. The agency has provided examples of committees, sample engineering control evaluation forms, a sample exposure control plan, an Internet resource list, and CDC guidelines. [OSHA Instruction CPL 2–2.44D, *Enforcement Procedures for the Occupational Exposure to Bloodborne Pathogens* (Nov. 5, 1999), is available on the Internet at http://www.osha.gov]

---

**Do any state laws address the control of bloodborne pathogens in the health care setting?**

As of June 2002, 21 states and 2 territories have enacted some type of legislation related to health care worker bloodborne pathogen exposures. These state laws, which are OSHA-approved, typically require that state health departments or labor departments develop administrative regulations to implement the laws. State laws are aimed at adding additional safeguards for health care workers, creating broader protections than the federal OSHA standard and/or covering public employees not covered by OSHA.

Although the state laws vary in their scope and coverage, they commonly include requirements for:

- listing of safety devices as engineering controls
- developing a list of available safety devices by the state that employers can use
- developing a written exposure plan by employers, with periodic review
- developing protocols for identifying and selecting safety devices and involving frontline employees in the process
- using a sharps injury log to report needlestick injuries
- developing methods to increase use of vaccines and personal protective equipment
- waiving or exempting from safety device use under certain circumstances (including patient and/or worker safety issues, market unavailability, etc.)
- placing sharps containers in accessible positions

- training for workers in the use of safety devices [National Institute of Occupational Safety & Health, "Overview of State Needle Safety Legislation," available on the Internet at http://www.cdc.gov/niosh/ndl-law.html]

Many of the state laws contain more unique requirements such as surveillance programs, strict requirements for safety device use, and the use of statewide advisory boards.

Since the revisions to the OSHA bloodborne pathogens standard, those states and territories with individual, OSHA-approved needlestick requirements were required to comply with the new federal standards or adopt a more stringent amendment to their existing standard, by October 18, 2001.

## PARENTERAL AND STERILE PRODUCTS

### What health risks are associated with the preparation, handling, and storage of parenteral and sterile products?

The preparation and storage of parenteral and sterile products may create a risk of microbial growth. To maximize the stability of these products, hospital pharmacy departments must strictly adhere to infection control policies and procedures in this area, including staff training regarding the proper preparation techniques and safety precautions related to storage. According to ASHP, hospital pharmacy departments should consider preparation and handling of sterile products "of paramount importance" in establishing internal pharmacy policies, procedures, and quality improvement programs. [*ASHP Statement, Pharmacist's Role in Infection Control,* ASHP, issued 1998, is available at http://www.ashp.org/bestpractices]

### Do federal and state laws regulate the preparation, handling, and storage of parenteral and sterile products by hospital pharmacy departments?

Although there are no specific federal laws regulating the preparation, handling, and storage of parenteral and sterile products by hospital pharmacy departments, the CDC has published guidelines relevant to this area; for example, the CDC has issued guidelines for hand hygiene in health care settings and prevention of intravascular catheter-related infections as well as specific guidelines for hospital environmental control, infection control, and prevention of intravascular infections. [*See* CDC, *Guideline for Hand Hygiene in Health-Care Setting* 51 MMWR RR-16 (Oct. 25,2002), *Guidelines for the Prevention of Intravascular Catheter-Related Infections* 51 MMWR RR-10 (Aug. 16, 2002), available online at http://www.cec.gov/mmwr and CDC, *Guideline for Handwashing and Hospital Environmental Control,* updated Nov. 18, 2000. CDC, *Guideline for Infection Control for Hospital Personnel,* 1998; *Guideline for Prevention of Intravascular Infections,* updated Nov. 18, 2000, guidelines are available on the Internet at -http://www.cdc.gov/ncidod/hip/guide/overview.htm]

Several states have regulations requiring hospitals to implement specific policies and procedures to ensure the proper preparation, handling, and storage of parenteral and sterile products. In some states, these regulations simply provide a brief list of minimum standards that hospital pharmacy departments must meet in preparing, labeling, and distributing parenteral and sterile products, but also either require the director of pharmacy to establish detailed written policies and procedures in this area or mandate compliance with more specific standards established by the Joint Commission or ASHP. [*See, e.g.*, Utah Admin. Code R156–17a-618; Vt. Code R. 04–030–230, § 4.411] Other states' regulations are quite specific, outlining in detail measures that hospital pharmacy departments must take to ensure the following: preparation of sterile drug products in a physical environment suitable for use of aseptic technique; proper maintenance of equipment (e.g., cleaning and certification procedures for laminar airflow hoods); related recordkeeping policies and procedures (e.g., documentation of refrigerator and freezer temperatures); and an ongoing quality assurance control program to monitor personnel performance, equipment, and facilities. [*See, e.g.*, N.M. Admin. Code tit. 16, 19.6.11(1) & 19.7.9 (9.6); Wis. Admin. Code ch. Phar. 15, 15.03–15.07, 15.09–15.11] In addition, some states have specific pharmacy practice requirements pertaining to the relabeling and dispensing of parenteral and sterile medications in hospitals. [*See, e.g.*, Conn. Gen. Stat. 20–621]

### What are some typical infection control policies and procedures regarding the preparation of parenteral and sterile products?

Hospital pharmacy departments usually designate areas for preparing parenteral and sterile products, and these areas should minimize opportunities for particulate and microbial contamination of products. Some hospital pharmacy departments devote a separate room to preparing sterile products, but in hospitals where this is not possible, sterile medications should be prepared and handled in a clean, well-lighted area with minimal potential for contamination of products (e.g., an area of the pharmacy away from traffic that allows for product preparation without interruptions).

Although the Joint Commission does not require the use of laminar airflow hoods, hospital pharmacy departments using this equipment in preparing sterile products must ensure its proper maintenance. The hoods should be cleaned once each shift with a cleaning agent approved by the infection control committee, and such cleaning should be documented (e.g., in a hood cleaning log). In addition, routine maintenance of the hoods, such as cleaning and replacing filters, should be performed on a regular basis (e.g., monthly or quarterly). The pharmacy department also must make arrangements for a qualified inspector to annually inspect this equipment and certify that it is operationally efficient. (For a sample hood cleaning log, see Part 4 of this Manual under **Surveillance, Prevention, and Control of Infection.**)

Some hospital infection control committees also may require microbiological monitoring or "culturing" of the sterile products or laminar airflow hoods used in preparing these products. If the infection control committee does require such cultures, the pharmacy department must comply with these requirements, even though the Joint Commission's infection control standards do not require cultures of sterile products, personnel, or the facility's environment. [For detailed recommendations on policies and procedures pertaining to the preparation of parenteral and sterile products, *see ASHP Guidelines on Quality Assurance for Pharmacy-Prepared Sterile Products,* ASHP, issued 2000, available on the Internet at http://www.ashp.org/bestpractices.] (For sample infection control materials, see Part 4 of this Manual under **Surveillance, Prevention, and Control of Infection.**)

---

**What should an infection control training program cover with respect to preparation and handling of parenteral and sterile products?**

Hospital pharmacy departments should educate their staff members who prepare parenteral and sterile products as to the importance of handwashing, the use of aseptic technique, and the proper use of laminar airflow hoods (if required by hospital policy). In addition, a training program in this area should address the necessity of complete and accurate labeling of sterile products, with particular emphasis on policies and procedures for assigning expiration dates to compounded solutions based on stability of the product and potential for microbial growth. Policies and procedures should be very specific regarding the actual preparation of these products (e.g., avoiding incompatibilities, labeling intravenous admixtures, compounding procedures). [For detailed recommendations pertaining to personnel education and training in these areas, *see ASHP Guidelines on Quality Assurance for Pharmacy-Prepared Sterile Products,* ASHP, issued 2000, available on the Internet at http://www.ashp.org/bestpractices.]

Hospital pharmacy departments should also make their staffs aware of all requirements regarding the visual inspection of sterile-product containers and contents (before and after preparation). Pharmacy infection control policies and procedures regarding such inspections typically require the pharmacist to check for defective containers, cloudiness, or other indicators of incompatibilities or particulate matter, as well as for incomplete or inaccurate labels, and to properly destroy all products suspected of defects. Also, pharmacists must carefully inspect sterile products prior to their release from the pharmacy and, from that inspection, should verify that the product is suitable for administration (e.g., has been prepared accurately and demonstrates no signs of microbial growth).

---

**What are some typical infection control policies and procedures regarding the proper storage of parenteral and sterile products?**

Hospital pharmacy departments usually have detailed policies and procedures for the storage of sterile products because properly storing these products is often an effective way to minimize microbial growth. In determining how a particular sterile product should be stored, pharmacists should carefully check product information and literature regarding information on the product's stability and guidance on proper storage. Some products are light sensitive, for example, and thus must be stored in the dark. Some products can be stored at room temperature for a period of hours or days, while other products must be refrigerated or frozen to maintain their stability over longer periods of time. Pharmacists also must regularly monitor the shelf life of sterile products and discard those that have passed their assigned expiration dates. [For detailed recommendations pertaining to proper storage and expiration dating of parenteral and sterile products, *see ASHP Guidelines on Quality Assurance for Pharmacy-Prepared Sterile Products,* ASHP, issued 2000, available on the Internet at http://www.ashp.org/bestpractices.] (For a sample refrigerator temperature log, see Part 4 of this Manual under **Surveillance, Prevention, and Control of Infection.**)

In addition, policies and procedures should address proper storage of multiple-dose sterile product containers (if used). Although the ASHP has recommended that pharmacists encourage the use of single-dose packages of sterile drugs instead of multiple-dose containers, for some hospitals completely eliminating the use of multiple-dose containers is not feasible. Policies and procedures in this area should be very specific and should include provisions for recording initial use of a multiple-dose container and for defining the time periods during which specific products may be safely used in the future. [For detailed recommendations pertaining to the preparation, handling, and storage of single-dose and multiple-dose containers of sterile drugs, *see ASHP Technical Assistance Bulletin, Single Unit and Unit Dose Packages of Drugs,* issued 1984, available on the Internet at http://www.ashp.org/bestpractices.]

## Chemical Hazards and Hazard Communication

### What hazardous chemicals may be found in a hospital pharmacy department?

Hazardous substances that are typically found in hospital pharmacy departments include cytotoxic medications, carcinogens, corrosives, phenol, formaldehyde, other toxic chemicals, and known irritants. These substances must be handled in accordance with the requirements of OSHA and other federal and state regulations, and thus hospital pharmacy departments should have detailed policies and procedures in this area. In addition, hospital pharmacy departments must comply with all applicable federal and state regulations governing disposal of hazardous substances, discussed in a later section, **Disposal of Hazardous Waste.**

### What is OSHA's hazard communication standard?

OSHA regulations, known as the hazard communication standard, require employers to notify employees if there are hazardous chemicals present in the workplace and train employees to work with these chemicals. [29 C.F.R. 1910.1200] Although the standard does not apply to drugs, it does apply to other hazardous chemicals to which employees in hospital pharmacy departments may be exposed under normal working conditions. A good source for an initial determination as to what chemicals might give rise to hazard communication concerns for a hospital pharmacy department is the toxic and hazardous substances listing that appears in OSHA regulations. [29 C.F.R. 1910, subpart Z]

In addition to the federal standard, some states have enacted similar laws. Pharmacy leaders should carefully consult state statutes to determine whether additional requirements must be met.

### What must hospitals do to comply with OSHA's hazard communication standard?

The standard requires covered employers to undertake a hazard evaluation in which they identify and list all hazardous chemicals used, released, or stored in the workplace. [29 C.F.R. 1910.1200(d)] To accomplish this, employers must implement a comprehensive hazard communication program that includes such requirements as container labeling and other forms of warning, filling out and maintaining material safety data sheets (MSDSs), and employee education and training. (For further information on Joint Commission hazard communication requirements, refer to discussion of the standards in **Management of the Environment of Care** in Part 3 of this Manual.)

### What specific labeling requirements does the hazard communication standard impose on hospitals?

A hospital's hazard communication program must address labeling of containers of hazardous chemicals. The hospital that purchases hazardous chemicals may rely on the labels provided by its suppliers until the chemicals are transferred into another container. At that time, it becomes the responsibility of the hospital to label the container, unless it is subject to a portable container exemption. Under that exemption, labels are not required for temporary/secondary containers (e.g., mop buckets and other containers that remain in the employer's custody) or for storage cabinets. The information required on a label is the identity of the material, by common trade name or chemical name, and any other warnings. The hazard warning, in general, is a brief statement of the hazardous effects of the chemical. Although there are no specific requirements for label size and color, labels must be in English, legible, and prominently displayed.

### What does the hazard communication standard require in relation to MSDS forms?

Hospitals are required to maintain MSDSs for each hazardous chemical that they use, process, or store. [29 C.F.R. 1910.1200(g)] The MSDS is a document that describes the physical and chemical properties of products, their physical and health hazards, as well as their safe handling and use. The MSDSs must be made available upon request to any employee, employee's designated representative, or the Department of Labor.

The hospital that receives MSDSs from distributors should review them for accuracy and completeness and make sure that the latest MSDS for each hazardous substance is on file. A comparison of new and old MSDSs is useful because it may identify that there is a new hazard associated with an existing chemical or that a new ingredient is included in a currently used product.

Copies of an MSDS for each chemical must be readily accessible at all work times to employees who work in areas where the chemicals are used. The employer is also responsible for ensuring that all employees who use chemicals are familiar with the information on the MSDSs and know where they are kept in the event of an accident or if safety information is needed. (For further information regarding the Joint Commission's MSDS requirements on pharmacies, refer to discussion of the standards in **Management of the Environment of Care** in Part 3 of this Manual.)

---

### Can employers provide the required employee access to MSDSs through electronic means?

OSHA has published a compliance directive stating that employers can meet the access requirements by relaying MSDSs to employees through computers, microfiche machines, the Internet, CD-ROM, and fax machines. However, if employers are using electronic means for this purpose, they must ensure that reliable devices are always readily accessible in the workplace and that employees have adequate training in the use of such devices (i.e., software or Internet training). Moreover, employers must take steps to establish and maintain adequate backup systems so that access is not impaired under circumstances of system failures, power outages, or on-line access delays; as one additional safeguard, employers still must provide employees with access to hard copies of MSDSs upon request, or in the event of medical emergencies, when hard copies must be provided immediately to medical professionals. [OSHA, *Inspection Procedures for the Hazard Communication Standard,* OSHA Instr. CPL 2–2.38D (1998), available on the Internet at http://www.osha.gov]

---

### What are the requirements regarding a written hazard communication program?

The hospital's hazard communication program must include provisions for the maintenance of MSDSs and the labeling of containers of hazardous chemicals, as well as for the dissemination of information and employee training on how to work safely with hazardous materials. The standard also requires that, whenever a hazard changes or a new hazard is introduced in the workplace, the employer must provide additional training. Pharmacy departments should ensure that staff members receive appropriate orientation and training with regard to hazardous materials.

### Are there other regulatory requirements on hospitals with respect to hazard communication?

Hospitals are also subject to the Superfund Amendments and Reauthorization Act of 1986 (SARA) [42 U.S.C. 9601 *et seq.*], a federal law enforced by the EPA. The law contains additional reporting and notification provisions pertinent to hazardous substances. For example, covered employers must comply with right-to-know reporting requirements, such as providing the public with access to information about hazardous chemicals at the work site. More specifically, the employer must submit the MSDS prepared for employees to the local emergency planning committee, state emergency response commissions, and local fire departments. [42 U.S.C. 11023] Regulations also require hospitals to plan for emergencies if they expect to use their employees to handle emergencies involving hazardous substances, and to ensure that employees are trained by an emergency response plan that is approved by the Joint Commission and meets criteria set out in the regulations. [29 C.F.R. 1910.120. *See also* U.S. Department of Health and Human Services, *Hospital and Community Emergency Response—What You Need To Know*, OSHA 3152, issued Dec. 12, 1997, available on the Internet at http://www.osha.gov] (For further information regarding Joint Commission emergency preparedness requirements, refer to discussion of the standards in **Management of the Environment of Care** in Part 3 of this Manual. For a sample pharmacy disaster/emergency plan, see Part 4 of this Manual under **Management of the Environment of Care.**)

In addition, many states have right-to-know laws, which vary but generally require that employers communicate with and train employees regarding the handling and use of toxic or hazardous substances. Typically, such laws also require employers to provide copies of MSDSs to employees upon request. Some state laws also contain hazardous-substance listings different from those of either OSHA or the EPA and may require independent reporting and notification procedures. Thus, in some states, hospitals must comply with OSHA's hazard communication standard, SARA, and applicable state right-to-know laws.

### What are the health risks associated with hazardous drugs?

Many important drugs, such as anti-cancer agents (otherwise known as "cytotoxic" drugs) and anesthetic gases, can cause serious unintended side effects, not only in patients but also in health care workers who may be exposed to these hazardous drugs during their preparation or administration. Health risks potentially caused by exposure to hazardous drugs include cancer and adverse reproductive outcomes (i.e., genetic damage, birth defects, fertility problems, and organ damage). Although there is still significant uncertainty as to actual exposures to hazardous drugs as well as the causal link to adverse health effects, scientific literature increasingly indicates that exposure to such drugs is an emerging occupational safety and health problem that should be given national attention. [*See ASHP Technical Assistance Bulletin, Handling Cytotoxic and Hazardous Drugs*, ASHP, issued 1990, available on the Internet at http://www.ashp.org/bestpractices]

---

**Are there OSHA regulations pertaining to the use of hazardous drugs in health care settings?**

OSHA's Technical Manual describes several aspects of handling hazardous drugs that might involve occupational exposure to hospital pharmacists, including preparation of the drugs without the use of appropriate engineering controls and protective apparel, and handling or working in proximity to potentially contaminated materials used during drug preparation (e.g., gloves, gowns, biosafety cabinets, laminar airflow hoods, sinks).

In addition, OSHA recommends that, where hazardous drugs are used, employers should develop a written hazardous drug safety and health plan that indicates what measures the employer is taking to ensure employee protection in this area. The plan should include the following components:

- standard operating procedures relevant to safety and health considerations to be followed when health care workers are exposed to hazardous drugs
- criteria that the employer uses to determine and implement control measures to reduce employee exposure to hazardous drugs, including engineering controls, the use of personal protective equipment, and hygiene practices
- a requirement that ventilation systems and other protective equipment function properly, and specific measures to ensure proper and adequate performance of such equipment
- provision for information and training, and for ready access to the plan by all employees
- the circumstances under which the use of specific hazardous drugs (e.g., FDA investigational drugs) require prior approval from the employer before implementation
- provision for medical examinations of potentially exposed personnel
- designation of personnel responsible for implementation of the hazardous drug plan, including the assignment of officers or the establishment of a hazardous drug committee
- provision for annual reevaluation and necessary updating of the plan

OSHA also recommends that, where appropriate, employers consider including the following provisions in the hazardous drug plan: establishment of a designated hazardous drug handling area, use of containment devices such as biological safety cabinets, procedures for safe removal of contaminated waste, and decontamination procedures. [OSHA Technical Manual, Section VI, Chapter 2, Controlling Occupational Exposure to Hazardous Drugs, available on the Internet at http://www.osha.gov; *see also ASHP Technical Assistance Bulletin, Hospital Drug*

*Distribution and Control,* ASHP, issued 1980, available on the Internet at http://www.ashp.org/bestpractices] (For a more detailed discussion of regulatory requirements pertaining to disposal of toxic chemicals, see Disposal of Hazardous Waste.)

---

**Do state laws address the preparation and handling of hazardous drugs by hospital pharmacy departments?**

In some states, hospital pharmacy departments must comply with state regulations containing specific requirements pertaining to the safe handling of cytotoxic drugs. In Vermont, for example, institutional pharmacies must take specified measures to ensure the protection of personnel involved with the preparation and handling of cytotoxic drugs. Such measures include

- compounding of drugs in a biosafety cabinet that meets specified criteria and is designated exclusively for hazardous drugs
- provision of protective apparel, in accordance with federal and state standards, by personnel who compound hazardous drugs
- personnel training to ensure appropriate safety and containment techniques for compounding hazardous drugs
- development of written policies and procedures regarding proper disposal of hazardous drugs in accordance with applicable federal, state, and local requirements
- establishment of written policies and procedures for handling spills of hazardous drugs or agents used in preparing these drugs [Code Of Vermont Reg. 04-030-0230 § 4.411, *See also, e.g.,* Wis. Admin. Code ch. Phar. 15, § 15.08]

---

**Are there any guidelines for establishing policies and procedures regarding the safe handling of hazardous drugs?**

The ASHP technical bulletin on the handling of cytotoxic drugs contains detailed recommendations for policies, procedures, and safety materials for controlling, preparing, administering, containing, and disposing of hazardous drugs. [*See ASHP Technical Assistance Bulletin, Handling Cytotoxic and Hazardous Drugs,* ASHP, issued 1990, available on the Internet at http://www.ashp.org/bestpractices] The bulletin outlines recommended policies and procedures for achieving four central objectives:

1. protecting and securing packages of hazardous drugs
2. informing and educating all involved personnel about hazardous drugs and training them in the safe handling procedures relevant to their responsibilities
3. preventing hazardous drugs from escaping their containers when they are handled (e.g., dissolved or otherwise prepared, transferred, administered, or discarded)

4. eliminating the possibility of inadvertent ingestion or inhalation, or direct skin or eye contact with hazardous drugs

Emphasizing the complexity of issues arising from occupational exposure to hazardous drugs, the bulletin also states that the advice of medical experts, occupational physicians, pharmacists, industrial hygienists, legal counsel, and risk managers should be obtained when organizational policies and safety plans in this area are being developed. (For a sample policy, see Part 4 of this Manual under **Management of the Environment of Care.**)

### What is latex sensitivity?

Sensitivity to latex products, or latex allergy, develops in some individuals exposed to natural rubber latex—a plant substance that is used extensively to manufacture latex gloves. Allergic reactions to latex range from skin disease to asthma and anaphylaxis that can result in chronic illness and other disabilities; there is no treatment for these problems other than complete avoidance of latex.

OSHA's sister agency, NIOSH, has issued guidance regarding prevention of latex-related health problems in the workplace. [NIOSH Alert, *Preventing Allergic Reactions to Natural Rubber Latex in the Workplace*, DHHS Pub. No. 97–135 (June 1997), available on the Internet at http://www.cdc.gov/niosh/latexalt.html] NIOSH recommends that hospitals implement policies and procedures to require, or at least encourage, appropriate engineering and work practice controls to reduce the risk of allergic reactions to latex. Such controls include the use of nonlatex gloves for activities that are not likely to involve contact with infectious materials, good housekeeping practice to remove latex-containing dust in latex-contaminated areas, and training materials/education programs about latex allergy.

## Disposal of Hazardous Waste

### What types of regulated waste are potentially generated by a hospital pharmacy department?

A variety of substances and medical equipment managed by hospital pharmacy departments may be linked to occupational and environmental health hazards. When disposed, these materials fall within a range of wastes subject to varying degrees of regulation depending on federal and state definitions of the various wastes. Understanding the various categories of waste potentially generated by a hospital pharmacy department is necessary to determine what regulations govern its disposal. In general, hospital pharmacy departments should be concerned about three types of waste subject to federal and state regulation, discussed below:

1. hazardous waste
2. infectious waste
3. radioactive waste

---

**What precautions should be taken in handling and preparing hazardous drugs?**

In handling and preparing hazardous drugs, it is important to follow precautions to prevent exposure to the drug. The hazards in the pharmacy area should be assessed and appropriate precautions put into place. These precautions include personal protective equipment (PPE) such as eye, hand, or face protection as well as gloves and gowns for all hazardous drugs. Biological safety cabinets (BSC) should be used when preparing hazardous medications. Vertical-flow BSC with vents to the outside are recommended. The BSC should also include covered needle containers for adequate needle disposal and covered waste disposal to dispose of excess fluids. Areas where hazardous drugs are prepared should have restricted access. Activities within the area should also be restricted such as no smoking, drinking, or applying cosmetics. (*OSHA Technical Manual,* Chapter II)

Safe handling of hazardous drugs can also reduce exposure. Safe handling involves preparation of hazardous drugs by pharmacists only with appropriate PPE. Special precautions should be taken when transferring hazardous drugs between containers, when reconstituting or manipulating drugs, when withdrawing needles from drug vials, and when expelling air from a drug-filled syringe that should be done in a BSC. OSHA also recommends that drug administration sets be primed in the BSC prior to addition of the drug and that hazardous drugs should be specifically labeled as requiring Special Handling/Disposal Precautions. (*OSHA Technical Manual,* Chapter V)

---

**What federal laws govern a hospital pharmacy department's disposal of hazardous chemicals?**

All health care facilities are subject to the Resource Conservation and Recovery Act (RCRA), which regulates generators of hazardous waste, transporters of hazardous waste, and owners and operators of hazardous waste treatment facilities. The statute and its implementing regulations, which are administered and enforced by the EPA, impose a "cradle-to-grave" framework for handling and disposal of hazardous wastes. Material is considered "hazardous waste" if it appears on any one of four lists of hazardous wastes contained in the RCRA regulations [40 C.F.R. 261.3] or has characteristics that qualify it as hazardous waste under certain tests. The requirements for handling and disposing of hazardous waste vary depending on the quantity of waste generated by an entity and on the nature of the waste. Also, many states have received EPA approval for state programs that are more stringent than the federal RCRA.

In general, EPA regulations have not classified medical waste as "hazardous"; there are, however, certain medical wastes, such as discarded thermometers containing mercury—a substance with toxic characteristics—that fall within the purview of RCRA. Another example is antineoplastic agents used in chemotherapy and materials contaminated by such drugs. Some chemotherapy drugs currently available at medical facilities appear on the EPA's listing of "hazardous" substances within RCRA regulations, which thereby subjects these drugs to RCRA disposal and recordkeeping requirements not applicable to other biomedical waste.

Accordingly, hospitals must consult the EPA and state solid and hazardous waste agencies, as well as local air and water quality control boards, regarding the classification and appropriate disposal of materials (e.g., drugs or other substances) that are defined as hazardous or toxic chemicals. With respect to hazardous drugs, the EPA categorizes several antineoplastic agents, including cyclophosphamide and daunorubicin, as toxic wastes, while many states have stricter waste standards that classify as "hazardous carcinogens" certain cytotoxic drugs (e.g., azathioprine) and hormonal preparations (e.g., diethylstilbestrol and conjugated estrogens).

---

**What are some typical requirements that hospital pharmacy departments must meet to comply with federal regulations governing the disposal of hazardous chemicals?**

Hospitals must have written policies and procedures governing the proper collection and disposal of hazardous chemical waste. These policies and procedures should establish a system to ensure that hazardous waste materials are identified, contained, and segregated from all other trash. Such a system must include placing hazardous waste, including hazardous drugs, in thick plastic bags or leakproof containers bearing a caution label (e.g., "HAZARDOUS CHEMICAL WASTE"). Hazardous waste receptacles should be specially marked to indicate their use for only hazardous waste and should be kept in all areas where hazardous drugs or materials are commonly used in the workplace. Any waste receptacle used for discarding glass fragments, sharps, and syringes that may be contaminated by hazardous chemicals must be puncture resistant.

With respect to hazardous drug waste, hospitals are allowed to reduce disposal costs by dividing waste materials into trace and bulk-contaminated waste, unless state or local regulations contain restrictions to the contrary. If a hospital pharmacy department opts for separating these two types of wastes, the bulk-contaminated waste must be segregated into more secure receptacles for containment and disposal as toxic waste, whereas less rigorous requirements apply to the disposal of trace wastes. The EPA has defined bulk-contaminated materials as solutions or containers with contents weighing more than three percent of the capacity of the container. For example, under this definition unused final doses of hazardous drugs in intravenous containers would usually be considered bulk-contaminated waste, while empty intravenous containers would fall under the category of trace waste.

Federal, state, and local regulations in this area also contain very specific requirements regarding the temporary storage of hazardous waste materials prior to its offsite disposal, as well as the transportation of such waste to an EPA-permitted, state-licensed hazardous waste incinerator or dump site.

---

**What federal laws govern a hospital pharmacy department's disposal of infectious waste?**

Under RCRA, the EPA has authority to regulate infectious waste, which is generally considered to be any waste capable of producing an infectious disease. In its guidelines, the EPA recommends that every medical facility establish an infectious waste plan to ensure that waste material in this category is handled properly from generation to disposal. The guidelines describe in detail the components of an infectious waste plan, and the EPA's recommendations for policies and procedures addressing identification, handling, storage, and disposal of infectious waste, contingency planning, and staff training. [U.S. Environmental Protection Agency, Office of Solid Waste and Emergency Response, *EPA Guide for Infectious Waste Management,* EPA-530-SW-86–014 (1986)]

Federal regulatory requirements in this area are also contained in OSHA's bloodborne pathogens standard, which mandates that all equipment contaminated or partially contaminated by contact with human blood or other potentially infectious body fluids be appropriately labeled. [29 C.F.R. 1910.1030(g)] Hospitals are also required either to affix labels with a red "biohazard" symbol on all containers of infectious waste, including transport, storage, and waste containers that hold infectious waste materials, or to place such materials in red bags or containers. Waste contained in these specially marked containers must be disposed of separately from routine trash, in accordance with the hospital's policies on disposal and/or incineration of hazardous or potentially infectious waste. [For further guidance in the related area of sharps disposal, *see* U.S. Department of Health and Human Services, *Selecting, Evaluating, and Using Sharps Disposal Containers*, NIOSH Pub. No. 97–111, issued 1998, available on the Internet at http://www.cdc.gov/niosh/sharps1.html]

---

**Do state laws address disposal of infectious waste?**

Many states have enacted laws regulating the collection, storage, transportation, and disposal of infectious waste by medical facilities, and a majority of these laws incorporate EPA recommendations in this area. [*See, e.g.,* MINN. STAT. 116.76.12] In Ohio, for example, the law specifies that all unused, discarded hypodermic sharps, syringes, and scalpels must be placed in rigid, tightly closed, puncture-resistant containers on the premises before they are transported off the premises. Containers containing such wastes must be labeled "sharps" and, if the wastes have not been treated to render them noninfectious, must be conspicuously labeled with the international biohazard symbol. [Ohio Rev. Code Ann. 3734.021]

---

**How do federal and state laws governing the disposal of radioactive waste implicate hospital pharmacy departments?**

Hospital pharmacy departments may have management responsibility over storing, controlling, and distributing radioactive medications or radiographic contrast media. Because proper handling and disposal of radioactive waste is an essential part of a medical facility's radioactive materials license, hospital pharmacy departments must have policies and procedures in this area to ensure compliance with all applicable federal and state regulations.

Both individuals and facilities that operate equipment containing radioactive sources or otherwise handle radioactive materials must obtain a license to do so. On the federal level, the Nuclear Regulatory Commission (NRC) requires a license for the handling of radioactive materials. Most states, however, are controlled by an agreement with the NRC to regulate radioactive materials through a state agency authorized by the NRC to implement its own state plan. State plans must be as restrictive as NRC licensing requirements and are typically more restrictive.

---

**How should a hospital pharmacy department manage the safe handling of radioactive waste?**

Radioactive waste is not handled nor disposed of like any other wastes because it cannot be altered by chemical, physical, or biological treatment; only time can reduce the toxicity of radioactive waste, and therefore it must be dealt with separately from other categories of waste. The complexities of radioactive waste disposal underlie the NRC's decision to require hospitals that are licensed to use radioactive materials to employ or contract with individuals who have specialized training enabling them to assume complete control over policies and procedures regarding collection, management, and disposal of radioactive waste. Accordingly, hospital pharmacy departments should rely on experienced staff or outside experts in developing and implementing effective procedures in this area.

In addition, hospital pharmacy departments should have policies and procedures in place to ensure that any waste contaminated by radioisotopes, whether or not mixed with other wastes, is handled as radioactive material until it is no longer radioactive and can be delabeled. To increase flexibility in the disposal options for radioactive waste, many radioactive waste management programs include procedures for segregating materials contaminated by short half-life isotopes from those contaminated by long half-life isotopes. Short half-life isotopes decay quickly and, once decayed and delabeled, can be categorized under a different waste class (e.g., solid or chemical waste) subject to less stringent disposal requirements.

**What are some federal and state regulatory requirements regarding offsite disposal of radioactive waste?**

Radioactive wastes are classified for management and treatment purposes as high, intermediate, and low level. Hospital pharmacy departments primarily deal with low-level radioisotopes, which may include liquids, vials, bottles, test tubes, and other items contaminated by contact with these radioisotopes. Federal law specifies that licensed material can be disposed of only

- by transfer to an authorized recipient who must dispose of the materials in accordance with several approved handling methods [10 C.F.R. 20.2001]
- by decay in storage [10 C.F.R. 20.2001]
- by release in effluents (within regulation limits) [10 C.F.R. 20.2001]
- under a plan not in the regulations but approved by the NRC [10 C.F.R. 20.2002]
- by release into sanitary sewage if several conditions are met [10 C.F.R. 20.2003]
- by incineration if certain conditions are met [10 C.F.R. 20.2004]

The states often adopt the federal regulations governing low-level radioactive waste by reference; facilities in state-plan states obviously will need to refer to specific requirements within the applicable state law. [*See, e.g.,* CAL. CODE REGS. tit. 17, 30470] State laws, however, may or may not add exceptions or additions to the federal law. Texas law, for example, specifies that the relevant department and commission must ensure that the management of radioactive waste is compatible with applicable federal commission standards. [TEX. HEALTH & SAFETY CODE 401.151] It also indicates, however, that the state commission directly regulates the disposal of radioactive waste and that the person making the disposal must comply with commission rules. [TEX. HEALTH & SAFETY CODE 401.201]

**What activities can an authorized nuclear pharmacist engage in?**

An authorized nuclear pharmacist (ANP) is a pharmacist who has additional radiation training and is authorized to prepare radioactive drugs. This involves preparing the drugs and measuring the amount of radioactivity of the radioactive drug. The ANP must comply with all applicable state and federal laws including: Environmental Protection Agency (EPA) hazardous waste disposal requirements; Nuclear Regulatory Commission (NRC) requirements regarding medical use of radioisotopes in imaging, treatment, and cancer therapy and rules governing medical use of byproduct material (MPS) delineating radiation dose and monitoring requirements; as well as Occupational Safety and Health Administration (OSHA) safety requirements. [67 Fed Reg. 20250 (Apr. 24, 2002); corrected at 67 Fed. Reg. 62872 (Oct. 9, 2002); and 10 C.F.R. 32.72]

## Employee Safety

### What are the workplace safety requirements under OSHA's general duty clause?

OSHA has specific standards and regulations for safety that must be complied with as well as a general duty clause that requires the workplace to be kept free of serious recognized hazards. Hazards to be avoided include anything that could result in death or serious bodily injury to an employee. OSHA will use the general duty clause to cite a safety violation that does not fall within a specific standard. Therefore, the pharmacy department should take precautions to keep the workplace safe even when there is not a specific OSHA standard. When there is a question about workplace safety, OSHA can be contacted for consultation.

OSHA standards give employees the right to file a complaint with OSHA if an employee feels that the workplace is not safe. Employers cannot discriminate against employees who file an OSHA complaint. Many organizations prefer to encourage employees to share safety concerns with management so that improvements can be made to enhance workplace safety on an ongoing basis. Safety recommendations can be part of an ongoing safety program.

### What is OSHA's approach to ergonomics?

OSHA intends to reduce ergonomic injury or musculoskeletal disorders (MSD) that occur in the workplace through the following activities: (1) development of industry or task-specific guidelines; (2) enforcement of ergonomics through the general duty clause; (3) outreach and assistance such as advice and training for employers on ways to implement ergonomic guidelines; and (4) encouraging research to expand knowledge about cause and treatment of MSD. OSHA has indicated that it will not focus enforcement efforts on those who have made good faith efforts to comply with voluntary guidelines.

OSHA issued its first draft guidelines within the health care industry focusing on nursing homes. The draft guidelines for nursing homes focus on developing appropriate management practices such as training, policies and procedures, and reporting. It also focuses on worksite analysis through reviewing workplace practices and activities to determine risk areas for MSD and then establishing control methods to reduce the likelihood of ergonomic injury. [*See* OSHA ergonomic information available at http://www.osha.gov.ergonomics and *Draft Guidelines for Nursing Homes* (Aug. 29, 2002).]

### What factors place employees at risk of violence at work?

Workplace violence is the third-leading cause of fatal occupational injury in the United States. Eighteen percent of violent crimes occur while the victim is at work. The National Institute of Occupational Safety and Health (NIOSH) has identified factors that place an employee at risk for violence. These are:

- public contact;
- money exchange;
- delivery of passengers, goods, or services;
- having a mobile workplace such as a cab;
- working with unstable or volatile persons such as in health care;
- working alone or in small numbers;
- working late at night or during early morning hours;
- working in high-crime areas;
- guarding valuable property or possessions; and
- working in community-based settings.

In health care settings, additional risk factors include the following.

- prevalence of handguns or weapons among patients and their families
- acute and chronic mentally ill patients who are released early without follow-up care
- availability of drugs or money in the hospital or pharmacy
- public access to an area or lengthy waiting times for care or assistance
- low staffing patterns during periods of increased activity
- isolated work area with clients during treatment
- solo work in remote areas on locations with high-crime ratings
- lack of staff training about how to handle and lessen hostile behavior or assaults
- poorly lit parking areas [*See* OSHA Summary Sheet (2002) and *Guidelines for Preventing Workplace Violence in Health Care and Social Service Workers*, OSHA Pub. 3148 (1998).]

---

**What can the pharmacy department do to prevent violence?**

The pharmacy department can prevent violence in a number of ways. OSHA has established guidelines to prevent violence for health care workers that are advisory in nature. Any OSHA enforcement would take place under the general duty clause that requires a safe workplace. It is wise for the pharmacy department to take inventory of the specific risks and hazards in the department and take steps to enhance employee safety. The OSHA guidelines recommend the following aspects of prevention.

*Program Management*—Effective program management begins by establishing a written program with policies and procedures that outline processes to maintain workplace safety, minimize violence, and follow-up when an incident does occur.

*Worksite Analysis*—Worksite analysis occurs when the department reviews specific incidents and trends; security systems; and high-risk factors, locations, or jobs.

*Hazard Prevention and Control*—This involves analysis of engineering controls such as the use of security features, alarms, metal detectors, videos, curved mirrors, enclosed client service areas, patient waiting areas, two exits from rooms, furniture arrangement to prevent entrapment, locking unused doors, bright lighting, and maintenance of locks. This also involves analysis of post-incident response such as victim counseling, treatment, or EAP services. From an administrative standpoint, managers can ensure adequate staff coverage, restrict public access to certain areas, prevent employees from working alone, provide security escorts to and from parking areas, and establish "buddy systems" to prevent threatening situations.

*Training and Education*—All employees should be informed of violence risk factors and be encouraged to watch for warning signs or aggressive behavior that may lead to an assault. Employees should be trained on ways to deal with hostile people. A response action plan should be put in place with each employee knowing his or her part in the response. [*Guidelines for Preventing Workplace Violence for Health Care and Social Service Workers*, OSHA Pub. 3148 (1998).]

---

**What are OSHA recordkeeping and reporting requirements?**

In January 2002 OSHA issued a final rule on recordkeeping and reporting. The rule requires records to be kept of all occupational incidences of death, injury, or illness. A record should be made anytime the injury or illness results in death, days away from work, transfer to another job, medical treatment beyond first aid, loss of consciousness, or diagnosis of a significant injury or illness. OSHA has three forms to use to record information. These forms are available on the Internet at http://www.osha.gov. The forms are:

- *Form 300 Log of Work-Related Injuries and Illnesses*—This is a record of injuries and illnesses as they occur.
- *Form 300A Summary of Work-Related Injuries*—This is an annual summary of injuries and illnesses for the year.
- *Form 301 Injury and Illness Incident Report*—This is a record of medical treatment received for injuries and illnesses on the job.

When there are privacy concerns, an employee record should be kept separate from the standard forms. OSHA considers the following to raise privacy concerns.

(1) injuries or illness of an intimate body part or reproductive system
(2) injury or illness from sexual assault
(3) mental illness
(4) HIV, hepatitis, or tuberculosis
(5) blood contamination by a needle or sharp
(6) when the employee requests the records be kept private. [29 C.F.R. 1904.0-1904.46 and *Recordkeeping Policies and Procedures Manual* CPL 2-0.131 (Jan. 1, 2002).]

## STATE REGULATION OF PHARMACY ACTIVITIES

As pharmacy directors and pharmacists know, nearly every aspect of pharmacy practice is regulated by state law. Because state pharmacy practice acts, hospital licensure laws, and pharmacy regulations are often more detailed or more strict than federal law, compliance with state laws will frequently provide protection from federal violations. This section discusses some of the important aspects of hospital pharmaceutical services that are regulated by state law: prescription and medication order screening, formulary and substitution policies, dispensing practices, patient counseling, and pharmaceutical care legislation. (Joint Commission standards relating to hospital medication distribution are primarily discussed in **Care of Patients: Medication** in Part 3 of this Manual.)

### Prescription and Medication Order Screening

#### What are a hospital pharmacist's duties with regard to screening prescriptions and drug orders?

Prospective Drug Utilization Review (DUR) is a key function of the hospital pharmacy. If the pharmacist's review of the prescription or patient record reveals any potential problem, the information should be relayed to the attending practitioner. ASHP advises hospital pharmacists to review patient profiles for specific potential problems, such as patient allergies, unintended dosage changes, drug duplications, and overlapping therapies before dispensing a drug. [*ASHP Technical Assistance Bulletin, Hospital Drug Distribution and Control,* ASHP, issued 1980, is available on the Internet at http://www.ashp.org/bestpractices] (For a discussion of Joint Commission requirements, see the discussion of standards concerning **Patient Assessment** and **Care of Patients: Medication** in Part 3 of this Manual. For related materials, see Part 4 of this Manual under **Assessment of Patients** and **Care of Patients.**)

#### Do state laws address prescription screening requirements?

Pharmacists should consult their state hospital licensing laws and regulations for a specific list of items to be reviewed before dispensing a drug pursuant to a medication order. In Texas, for example, institutional pharmacists must evaluate medication orders and patient medication records for

- known allergies
- rational therapy—contraindications
- reasonable dose and route of administration
- reasonable directions for use
- duplication of therapy

- drug-drug interactions
- drug-food interactions
- drug-disease interactions
- ADRs
- proper utilization, including overutilization or underutilization, and
- clinical laboratory or clinical monitoring methods to monitor and evaluate drug effectiveness, side effects, toxicity, or adverse effects, and appropriateness to continued use of the drug in its current regimen [22 TEX. ADMIN. CODE 291.74]

---

**What role do computers play in screening?**

Most pharmacies rely on computer software to screen patient profiles and drug orders or prescriptions for potential problems. Although computer screening offers many benefits, such as speed and accuracy, pharmacists should carefully evaluate whether their software performs the checks required by state law. Pharmacists should also assess the currency of the software and the depth of the database. Simply mechanizing the screening process will not satisfy legal requirements. In addition, most clinical pharmacy software programs carry a disclaimer that the information provided is not a substitute for professional judgment.

---

**Should pharmacists screen drug orders and prescriptions for prescriptive authority?**

In addition to screening drug orders and prescriptions with regard to the appropriateness of the drug therapy itself, pharmacy staff must verify that the order or prescription is valid—that is, that it contains all required information and was issued by a health care provider with prescriptive authority. The first consideration is whether the individual health care provider has prescribing privileges in the facility. Second, the classes of health care providers who may prescribe varies from state to state, including nurse practitioners, physician assistants, and pharmacists. The scope of authority to prescribe also varies depending on the circumstances, excluding controlled substances, or requiring a protocol, for example. Institutional pharmacy staff must be intimately familiar with the limitations in their state and must not dispense any medications prescribed outside the scope of a health care provider's authority. (For related materials, see Part 4 of this Manual, under **Care of Patients.**)

---

**What if the pharmacist or a pharmacy staff member has a moral objection to filling a prescription?**

The question has arisen whether a pharmacist may refuse to fill a prescription to which the pharmacist has a moral objection, such as prescriptions for drugs intended for assisted suicide or "morning after" pregnancy termination. State law should be consulted, as legislation in many states specifies that no health care provider may be required to participate in such procedures, if the provider has a moral or religious objection. South Dakota is the first state to enact a statute-shielding pharmacists specifically. According to the statute, a pharmacist may not be required to dispense medication if there is reason to believe the medication would be used to cause an abortion, destroy an unborn child (as defined in the state code), or cause death by assisted suicide, euthanasia, or mercy killing. A pharmacist who refuses to dispense under these conditions may not be sued or subjected to disciplinary action. [S.D. CODIFIED LAWS 36–11–70]

Other states take a more general approach. For example, Kansas law gives the pharmacists the discretion to refuse to fill a prescription if in the pharmacist's professional judgment it should not be filled. [*See* KANSAS STAT. ANN. 65-1637] Indiana gives the pharmacist the right to refuse to fill a prescription from another state when it would be contrary to the law, not in the best interest of the patient, when it would aid addiction, or be contrary to the patient's health. [INDIANA CODE ANN. 25-26-13-16] One court found that the right to refuse is not a mandatory duty or obligation, but gives the pharmacists the freedom to decide whether to fill the prescription or not. [*Hooks SuyperX Inc. v. McLaughlin*, 642 N.E.2d 514 (Ind. 1994).] Other states have general "right to conscience" legislation that allows a health care provider to refuse an action such as abortion or assisted suicide when the provider has a religious or moral objection and protects the provider from liability for such action. [For example, 745 ILL. COMP. STAT. ANN. 70/3( c).]

ASHP recognizes the patient's right to choose or refuse medical treatment and notes that the patient's right to choose assisted suicide is a matter of individual conscience. At the same time, ASHP recognizes the pharmacist's right to object to therapies for religious, moral, or ethical reasons. It encourages establishment of systems that provide for the patient's right to therapy, while allowing conscience objection by the pharmacist. ASHP also notes that the use of drugs in capital punishment is a matter of individual conscience by the pharmacist who should not be subject to discrimination or retaliation for refusal to participate. [ASHP Ethics (2002)] (For further discussion, refer to the **Management of Human Resources** standards in Part 3 of this Manual.)

## Formularies and Substitution

### Do state regulations address hospital formulary development?

State hospital licensure regulations typically require a pharmacy and therapeutics committee to design the formulary and/or may require the hospital pharmacy director to participate in hospital formulary development. Regulations may be more specific, requiring that the formulary be reviewed and updated annually or on an as-needed basis. Formulary development and implementation must comply with state regulations, so pharmacy directors should carefully consult the requirements in their jurisdictions. (For related materials, see Part 4 of this Manual under **Care of Patients.**)

### How do ASHP guidelines address the hospital formulary?

ASHP guidelines require that a hospital's pharmacy and therapeutics committee (or equivalent committee) select the items to be included in the formulary. ASHP recommends that

- the pharmacist be responsible for selecting the generic equivalents that may be dispensed pursuant to a physician's order for a particular drug product
- the prescriber have the option of specifying the brand or supplier of a drug at the time of prescribing, based on pharmacologic or therapeutic considerations for a particular patient
- the pharmacy and therapeutics committee be responsible for determining drug products that will be considered therapeutic equivalents, as well as clearly delineating the conditions and procedures for therapeutic substitution
- medical and nursing staffs be educated about the formulary system
- policies provide for appraisal and use of nonformulary drugs
- the pharmacist be responsible for the quality, quantity, and source of supply of all drugs and other preparations used in the diagnosis and treatment of patients [*ASHP Statements, The Formulary System,* ASHP, issued 1983, is available on the Internet at http://www.ashp.org/bestpractices]

### How do health plan formularies impact prescribing and dispensing for inpatients?

Health plans have taken a variety of approaches with regard to implementing formularies. A plan may cover only formulary drugs (known as a "closed" formulary), present the formulary as a recommendation (an "open" formulary), require preauthorization for nonformulary drugs (the "partially closed," "restricted," or "selective" formulary), or offer financial incentives for prescribers and patients to use listed drugs (the "incentive" formulary). As a general matter, hospital pharmacies, particularly outpatient pharmacies, should consider the reimbursement implications of dispensing hospital formulary drugs that don't appear on health plan formularies. For inpatients, pharmacists are concerned primarily with the institution's formulary. However, health plan formularies are a concern when a patient is admitted on medication from a plan formulary that does not appear on the hospital formulary. Hospital policies and procedures should describe the circumstances under which the patient should be automatically switched to a hospital formulary drug, when the patient's physician must write a new drug order, and when the hospital formulary should obtain and dispense the plan formulary drug.

### How do state laws treat MCO and insurer formularies?

Many states regulate the formulary development and revision process for MCOs and insurers as well. For example, the state of Virginia has enacted a law that prohibits imposing financial penalties on patients who are prescribed medically necessary nonformulary prescription drugs. Under the law, insurers and HMOs offering outpatient prescription drug coverage as part of group accident and sickness plans may implement a prescription drug formulary, as long as the formulary is developed and updated annually by a committee with a majority of membership composed of actively practicing licensed pharmacists, physicians, and other licensed health care providers. If the insurer or HMO adopts a closed formulary, it must make the complete current formulary available to providers and pharmacists. There must also be a "process to allow an enrollee to obtain, without additional cost-sharing beyond that provided for formulary prescription drugs in the enrollee's covered benefits, a specific, medically necessary nonformulary prescription drug." Medical necessity is determined by the insurer or HMO when reasonable investigation and consultation with the prescribing physician leads to the determination that a formulary drug is an inappropriate therapy. Requests for coverage of nonformulary drugs must be made within one business day. [VA. CODE ANN. § 38.2–3407.9:01]

California has adopted extensive legislation regarding formulary and nonformulary prescription drug coverage. State law requires health care services plans that provide prescription drug benefits to maintain an "expeditious" process for prescribers to obtain authorization to prescribe a medically necessary nonformulary prescription drug. A written description of the process must be supplied to providers, members (in evidence of coverage documentation), and the state. If the plan denies coverage, it must notify the enrollee and must state the reasons for the disapproval, indicate that the enrollee can file a grievance, and note any alternative drug or treatment offered by the plan. California has also adopted a "continuity of care provision" that prohibits health plans from limiting or excluding coverage for a drug that was previously covered and is being appropriately prescribed for an enrollee. [CAL. HEALTH & SAFETY CODE 1367.22, 1367.24]

Regarding formulary drugs, California requires every plan that covers prescription drug benefits to disclose, in the evidence of coverage provided to enrollees, whether the plan uses a formulary. The notice must explain what a formulary is, how the plan determines which prescription drugs are included or excluded, and how often the plan reviews the contents of the formulary. The plan must also verify, upon request, whether a particular prescription drug is on the formulary. A phone number for making such requests must be included in the evidence of coverage. Plans must also retain a variety of records related to formulary development and implementation for inspection by the state upon request. For example, plans must retain records that describe the reasoning behind formulary decisions and documentation of arrangements with prescribers, pharmacists, and PBMs aimed at encouraging formulary compliance. [CAL. HEALTH & SAFETY CODE § 1363.01, 1367.24]

After an investigation into health plan formulary deletions, the California Department of Corporations has ordered five health plans to return certain prescription drugs to their formularies. In addition, the department found that these and other plans were "authorized" to delete certain other drugs from their formularies, provided that enrollees who were previously prescribed the medications could continue receiving them after the formulary change, although the state law requiring this type of pharmaceutical care continuity was not yet effective. In its initial investigation letter, the department expressed concern that by preemptively deleting drugs from their formularies before the continuity of care legislation took effect, the health plans were in violation of the public policy embodied in the statutes. The department also argued that the deletions constituted a material modification of health plan operations that should have been submitted to the agency for preapproval in accordance with state law. The challenged deletions included such high-cost drugs as Prozac, Zoloft, and Prilosec. The Department of Corporations sent the order letters to the following health plans:

- Aetna U.S. Healthcare of California
- Health Net
- Kaiser Foundation Health Plan
- Key Health Plan
- Molina Medical Centers

[For copies of the correspondence between the California Department of Corporations Health Plan Division and the health plans, contact Julie Stewart, Assistant Commissioner of Public Affairs, at 916–323–7120. The correspondence was issued between December 1998 and June 1999.]

---

**What is the difference between therapeutic substitution and generic substitution?**

Therapeutic substitution, also known as therapeutic interchange, takes place when a pharmacist dispenses a drug that is the therapeutic equivalent of the drug prescribed. A drug is a therapeutic equivalent if it has a different active ingredient than the prescribed drug but is expected to produce the same therapeutic effect and toxicity. The hospital formulary itself might list therapeutic equivalents, or the pharmacist might consult a source such as the FDA's *Approved Drug Products with Therapeutic Equivalence Evaluations* (known as the Orange Book), to assess whether a drug is a therapeutic equivalent. Typically, hospital protocol established by the pharmacy and therapeutics committee will allow therapeutic substitution of particular drugs without advance prescriber notification. For therapeutic substitutions that are not part of an established protocol, a pharmacist will contact the prescribing physician before substituting a formulary drug.

A generic medication is a chemically equivalent version of a brand name drug. Substitution of generic medications for prescribed brand name drugs is a widely used method of health care cost containment. At one time, pharmacists were prohibited from substituting one brand of drug for another, unless the pharmacist obtained the express consent of the prescriber. Now, every state has enacted legislation permitting the pharmacist to dispense less expensive generic equivalents, or even requiring substitution. In the hospital setting, generic substitution typically does not require prescriber notification.

### How do state laws and regulations affect generic substitution?

Pharmacists should consult their state pharmacy practice laws and regulations to determine

- whether generic substitution is mandatory or merely permitted
- whether the patient must be notified of or consent to substitution
- whether the prescriber must be notified before or consent to substitution
- how the prescriber can prevent substitution (usually by checking a box on the prescription form or designating "brand necessary")
- whether the drug container label must indicate that a generic has been dispensed (Pharmacists should also note that failing to accurately label a generic as such may constitute misbranding under the FDCA.)
- whether the pharmacist must inform the prescriber when the substitution results in financial benefit to the pharmacist
- whether cost savings must be passed on to the patient
- whether the generic substitution laws and regulations exempt hospital or institutional pharmacies

### What are the legal considerations surrounding therapeutic substitution?

Unlike generic substitution, which is governed in detail by state law and regulation, therapeutic substitution poses several questions. Although therapeutic substitution has a long history in hospital pharmacy practice, few state laws address pharmacists' authority to make therapeutic substitution or the procedures for doing so. It is clear that a pharmacist may make a therapeutic substitution with authorization of the prescriber prior to dispensing the drug. There is also little doubt that a pharmacist must not independently make a therapeutic substitution without prescriber knowledge or authorization. The difficulty arises when hospital procedures require pharmacists to make therapeutic substitutions and inform prescribers after the fact, on the understanding that prescribers understand and agree to follow hospital policies and procedures. Pharmacists participating in these substitution programs should consult their state boards of pharmacy to ensure compliance with state law.

### How should substitutions be documented?

Typically, generic substitution is performed without additional specific documentation. Therapeutic substitution, however, should be documented. For therapeutic substitutions, it is important to document the pharmacist's intervention, the physician's response, and the drug that was ultimately dispensed. Documentation options include

- documenting the substitution on the drug order
- documenting the substitution in the patient's medication administration record
- using a "change order" form, to be signed by a pharmacist or the prescriber
- requiring the physician to write a new prescription

(For related materials, see Part 4 of this Manual under **Care of Patients.**)

## Dispensing

### Who may dispense drugs?

Pharmacy personnel other than registered pharmacists may include technicians, assistants, interns, and clerks. States' rules vary in terms of what specific activities nonpharmacists may perform in hospitals. In most states, only pharmacists and practitioners permitted to prescribe medications may dispense, except in limited circumstances. However, pharmacy interns and technicians may be permitted to perform a variety of activities that are part of the dispensing process, including preparing a prescription label, retrieving medication from stock, putting the medication into a container, and placing the label on the container. State regulations vary and often require the direct supervision of a pharmacist. Hospital pharmacy policies and procedures must clearly delineate which types of employees may perform which tasks, as well as the level of pharmacist oversight required. (Joint Commission dispensing requirements are discussed in connection with the **Care of Patients: Medication** standards in Part 3 of this Manual.)

### How are drugs obtained when the pharmacy is closed?

State regulations delineate the procedures for hospital drug distribution when a pharmacist is not on duty. Hospital policies and procedures must comply with the state regulations and must be carefully adhered to by staff in hospitals lacking 24-hour pharmacy services. In Delaware, for example, night cabinets may be used to provide drugs to physicians and other authorized staff when the pharmacist is not on duty, if proper security, policies, and documentation are in place. When medications cannot be immediately obtained from any other source (such as from floor stock), authorized persons may enter the pharmacy, as long as the registered nurse or physician who enters is accompanied by a second nurse, a physician, or approved security personnel; the removal of drugs is documented; and the pharmacy reviews and records the removal when it reopens. [Del. Code Regs. 10–522–01] (For a discussion of Joint Commission requirements in this area, refer to the discussion of the **Care of Patients: Medication** standards in Part 3 of this Manual.)

### Have any courts addressed dispensing authority?

A New York case provides an example of how hospital procedures may run afoul of state dispensing limitations. A hospital and its pharmacist were found guilty of misconduct for permitting nurses to dispense and mix drugs and for delegating the responsibility of measuring, weighing, compounding, and mixing ingredients in preparation of various solutions. After the state censured, reprimanded, and fined the hospital, the pharmacist, and the nurses for professional misconduct, they appealed to the court. The hospital argued that "dispensing" was undefined and that the practice in question had been in place at the hospital for more than 25 years, constituting accepted nursing practice. The court disagreed and upheld the sanctions, finding that the applicable law prohibited nurses from preparing solutions for patients to whom they would not personally administer the solution, as the activity was "dispensing," reserved for pharmacists. [*In re Sheffield*, 571 N.Y.S.2d 350 (App. Div. 1991) appeal denied 588 N.E.2d 98 (1992).]

## Automated Dispensing

### Do any states regulate the use of automated dispensing systems?

Any pharmacy that uses automated dispensing and/or storage systems must closely consult state regulation, as state pharmacy practice or hospital licensing rules may define requirements for the use of these systems. Automated dispensing may not be permitted in all states or practice settings. In Texas, for example, the state attorney general has issued an opinion stating that automated dispensing machines may not be used to dispense prescription drugs at a nursing home, because dispensing prescription drugs is a function reserved to licensed pharmacies. The nursing home in question was not licensed as a pharmacy, and the automated dispensing machine would not be under a pharmacist's continuous on-site supervision. [Tex. Attorney Gen. Opinion No. JC-0186, Feb. 24, 2000, TEXAS OCC. CODE ANN. 562.109 allows automated dispensing under the continuous supervision of a pharmacist]

Where automated dispensing is permitted, detailed requirements may apply. In Illinois, for example, only individuals appropriately licensed to administer medications under state law, or individuals working under the direct supervision of a licensed individual, may have access to the machine for removal of prescription medications for patient use. Further, medication orders must be reviewed by a pharmacist in accordance with policies, procedures, and good pharmacy practice. Containers of medications stored in the system must be packaged as a unit of use for a single patient.

Required documentation in that state includes policies and procedures for system operation, safety, security, accuracy, patient confidentiality, access, controlled substances, data retention, downtime procedures, emergency or first dose procedures, inspection and maintenance, quality assurance, inventory, staff education, and malfunction. All events involving access to the contents of the system must be recorded electronically.

The Illinois regulation also sets standards for

- labeling
- documenting on-site administration
- returning unused medications to the system
- accounting for wasted medications
- error reporting
- responsibilities of the pharmacist in charge. [68 ILL. ADMIN. CODE 1330.98]

---

**What does the Joint Commission say about automated dispensing?**

An automated dispensing device is a tool that is part of a sound medication control system. Therefore, all medication use standards apply to medications obtained through an automated dispensing device to the same extent as medications dispensed through traditional unit-dose drug distribution systems or floor stock. Some hospitals have been penalized on survey when nurses accessed the automated dispensing device before the pharmacist reviewed the prescription orders. Standard TX 3.5.2 requires all medication orders to be reviewed by a pharmacist before administration of the drug except: (1) when the physician controls the ordering, dispensing, and administration of the drug such as in the emergency department, operating room, or endoscopy suite; and (2) in emergency situations when time does not permit a review such as STAT orders or doses where the clinical status of the patient would be compromised by the delay.

The Joint Commission recommends that the best way to comply with the standard is to develop a policy and procedure specifying when nurses can access medications from an automated machine without a pharmacist review. It is recommended that when the nurse bypasses pharmacist review, a second nurse verify the order and medication prior to administration. It is the patient situation that determines that there is an emergency, not the medication itself nor the location. Some pharmacies find it useful to separate the dispensing of the medication from the review of medication orders in order to expedite pharmacy review of orders. When a hospital pharmacy is not open all the time, pharmacy review may be obtained from an independent outside pharmacy. Similarly, night medication administration also should not routinely occur without prior pharmacy review. The Joint Commission recommends the use of a night cabinet with only nursing supervisor access to the cabinet in conjunction with a double-check process to ensure the correct medication. In most cases, drugs used in the Emergency Department are used in emergency situations and will not require a pharmacist review of the order; however, standard labor and delivery orders should be reviewed by the pharmacist because no two patients are the same. It is therefore important to assess for prior allergies and medication responses before determining if the standard protocol is appropriate for the patient. [*See Surveying*

*Medication Use Related to Automated Dispensing Machines* The Joint Commission (Nov.18, 2002).]

## Patient Counseling

### What is the source of the pharmacist's duty to counsel patients on their drug therapies?

In 1990, the Omnibus Budget Reconciliation Act (OBRA) changed the practice of pharmacy by requiring pharmacists to conduct prospective and retrospective drug use review for Medicaid patients and to counsel those patients on use of their medications. Although OBRA does not apply to hospitals (provided the institution uses a formulary system and does not bill Medicaid more than the institution's purchasing cost for the drug) or HMOs, it has brought patient counseling to the forefront. Other authorities, such as state laws and regulations, Joint Commission standards, and ASHP guidelines, impose patient-oriented responsibilities on hospital pharmacists, extending the duty beyond Medicaid patients to all patients. Liability is also a concern, as patient counseling may have become so widespread that it now constitutes the minimum standard of patient care such that failure to counsel may be negligent. (For more on patient counseling, see the **Education** standards in Part 3 of this Manual. For related materials, see Part 4 of this Manual under **Education.**)

### Do state laws address patient counseling in the hospital setting?

State laws generally exempt inpatients from patient counseling requirements but require patient counseling on prescriptions dispensed to hospital outpatients. For outpatient counseling, there is variation from state to state regarding who must make the offer to counsel (e.g., a pharmacist, technician, or other individual), whether the offer must be verbal or in writing, whether and how the offer or counseling session should be documented, and what must be discussed. Pharmacists must consult their state regulations to ensure compliance with counseling requirements.

### Does ASHP have patient counseling recommendations?

ASHP guidelines recommend that pharmacists collaborate with other members of a patient's health care team to identify the information that should be provided to the patient. The organization has developed a list of items that should be discussed with patients for each drug administered. Pharmacists are cautioned that this list is more comprehensive than what most state laws require.

- name of the drug
- intended use and expected action
- expected onset of action and what to do if the action does not occur

- route, dosage form, dosage, and administration schedule
- directions for preparation and administration
- precautions to be observed during use and administration, and risks in relation to benefits
- common and severe side effects, how to avoid them, and what to do if they occur
- techniques for self-monitoring of drug therapy
- proper storage and disposal
- potential drug-drug, drug-food, or drug-disease interactions or other therapeutic contraindications
- issues related to radiologic and laboratory procedures
- prescription refill information
- instructions for 24-hour access to a pharmacist
- action to be taken if a dose is missed
- any other information particular to that patient or drug [*ASHP Guidelines, Pharmacist-Conducted Patient Education and Counseling,* ASHP, issued 1996, is available on the Internet at http://www.ashp.org/bestpractices]

---

### Pharmaceutical Care Legislation

**Do any state laws and regulations authorize pharmacists to engage in pharmaceutical care management?**

Thirty-eight states have passed legislation allowing pharmacists to provide patient care or collaborate with other providers in managing drug therapy. In Mississippi, for example, the practice of pharmacy includes ordering laboratory work in accordance with written guidelines or protocols and providing pharmacotherapeutic consultations. [Miss. Code Ann. 73–21–73] Both West Virginia and Oklahoma allow pharmacists to provide pharmaceutical care services. [W. Va. Code 30–5–1b and 59 Okla. Stat. 353.1] Several states have passed collaborative practice acts. In South Carolina and Ohio, for example, pharmacists can manage drug utilization and therapy with health care practitioners. [Ohio Rev. Code Ann. 4729.01 and S.C. Stat. 40–43–86 (D)] Generally, a pharmacist providing pharmaceutical care services, such as administering laboratory tests and modifying drug therapy accordingly, must work under a written agreement with the patient's treating physician. To determine the parameters of permissible activities, pharmacists should check the status of the law in their states. (For information on billing for pharmaceutical care activities, see Reimbursement, under **Payment and Pricing Issues.**)

---

## PATIENT RECORD DOCUMENTATION AND CONFIDENTIALITY

Patient records and the information they contain play a crucial role in the delivery of health care services in a hospital and, more specifically, in the provision of pharmaceutical services to hospital patients. The pharmacy department not only creates data to be entered in a patient's record but also must rely heavily on the information the record contains. The procurement, provision, and distribution of all drugs used within the hospital by the pharmacy department is a part of a continuum of medical services that are documented in a patient record, which makes it imperative that pharmacy department personnel apply proper documentation techniques and understand the legal rules governing confidentiality. (Joint Commission patient confidentiality requirements are discussed in connection with the **Patient Rights and Organizational Ethics** standards in Part 3 of this Manual.)

---

### What legal rules governing patient record documentation apply to patient-related information gathered by the pharmacy department?

A hospital patient's clinical record is a continuously maintained history of the treatment provided in the hospital. Pharmaceutical care is an important component of the care provided to a hospital patient and has a direct impact on outcomes, and accordingly, activities by the pharmacy department to ensure safe and effective drug administration need to be documented in the patient's medical record. Because this information is part of the patient's chart, it is governed by state and federal law regarding format, authority to enter data, access, and confidentiality.

---

### What legal requirements apply to the type of information that a pharmacy department enters in a patient record?

State and federal law and regulations provide general guidance as well as some specific requirements on what a hospital patient's record should contain. In Florida, for example, the hospital licensing statute sets forth minimum record requirements, while in many jurisdictions, content requirements are issued by regulatory agencies. [FLA. STAT. § 395.1055(1)(b)] Under federal law, all patient records must contain medication records, as appropriate, as well as documentation of unfavorable reactions to drugs. [42 C.F.R. 482.24(c)] Whether or not specific statutory or regulatory guidelines apply, a hospital should adopt a formal, written policy regarding the content of medical records that lists the types of data that need to be included and/or references applicable to statutory or accreditation standards. This policy governs medical record content throughout the facility, including the entries made by pharmacy department personnel.

Although legal requirements vary from state to state, the general rule is that the information recorded by a pharmacy department in a patient's chart should be complete and accurate, and provide a current account of the treatment that was delivered. All clinical actions and recommendations by pharmacists to ensure the safe and effective use of medications and that have a potential effect on patient outcomes should be recorded in the patient's chart. The type of information that may need to be documented to meet this standard includes

- summary of patient's medication history on admission
- notes of oral and written consultations with other health care professionals regarding the patient's drug selection and management
- verbal orders from a physician received directly by a pharmacist
- adjustments to patient's drug dosage, dose frequency and form, and route of administration
- potential drug-related problems requiring supervision
- drug therapy monitoring findings, such as therapeutic appropriateness of drug regimen, therapeutic duplication, notes on patient's compliance with prescribed drug regimen, actual and potential drug interactions, clinical and pharmokinetic laboratory data pertinent to the patient's drug regimen, actual and potential drug toxicity and adverse effects, physical signs and clinical symptoms relevant to patient's drug therapy
- drug-related patient education and counseling [*ASHP Guidelines, Obtaining Authorization for Documenting Pharmaceutical Care in Patient Medical Records,* ASHP, issued 1989, is available on the Internet at http://www.ashp.org/bestpractices]

---

**What standards govern the accuracy and timeliness of medication orders in a patient's record?**

In a hospital setting, physicians or other authorized health care professionals will order medications to be administered to a patient by entering the order in the patient's chart. Hospital licensing regulations in most states require all physician orders to be written in the patient's records and authenticated and frequently provide time periods, ranging from 24 hours to one week, for the transcription and authentication of verbal orders in the record. [*See, e.g.,* S.C. Code Ann. Regs. R.61–16, 601.6] Like other orders relating to patient care, therefore, medication orders should be entered in writing in the patient record. If the order is given verbally, it should be put in writing immediately and countersigned by the prescriber within the time period set by statute and/or hospital policy. Because institutional policies should also be predicated on the concept that only personnel who are qualified to understand verbal orders should receive and transcribe them, policies relating to verbal medication orders should require that only the pharmacist or a registered nurse be authorized to receive such orders.

Because medication orders are not prescriptions, they do not need to comply with all the requirements of a prescription record. These orders are medical record entries, however, and as such must comply with state law and regulations regarding legibility, timeliness, and completeness. State law as well as the licensing regulations for specific facilities frequently contain the requirement that entries in patient records be legible and complete. Federal conditions of participation in Medicare also require that all entries to hospital records be legible and complete. [42 C.F.R. 482.24(c)] To meet these standards, medication orders should be written clearly and include patient identification and location, name of the medication, dosage, frequency of administration, route of administration, signature of the physician or prescriber, and the time and date the order was written. The pharmacist receiving the order is responsible for ensuring that these standards are met and for verifying that all the information is complete and legible before dispensing the medication. Any questions relating to the medication order must be resolved with the prescriber, and a written notation of these discussions should be inserted in the patient's medical record.

---

**Are there legal standards that govern signatures of medication orders in a patient record?**

State professional licensing and certification statutes determine the scope of practice for various health care professionals, and in particular will specify which practitioners have the authority to prescribe medication. (For a more detailed discussion of the authority to prescribe and scope of practice, see **Prescription and Medication Order Screening.**) Medical record entries are typically authored and signed by the clinical provider who delivers the service to the patient, and hospital policy will generally require that these providers function within the scope of their practice and professional competence. Accordingly, medication orders in a patient's record should be signed by the prescribing practitioner.

In computerized medical record systems, each prescriber should have a unique identifier, and this number should be included in all medication orders. Any computerized system of delivering a medication order to a pharmacy should allow the pharmacist to verify drug orders entered into the system by anyone other than an authorized prescriber.

State law or regulations frequently require that written prescriptions be signed by a practitioner who is authorized to prescribe drugs. A Wisconsin appeals court recently ruled that prescription orders e-mailed from a physician to a pharmacist do not violate a state law that requires a physician's signature on written prescriptions, finding that e-mailed prescriptions are more closely analogous to phoned prescriptions, for which state law waives the signature requirement. [*Walgreen Co. v. Wisconsin Pharmacy Examining Board*, 577 N.W.2d 387 (Wis. Ct. App. 1998)]

---

**What should a patient record contain with respect to the administration of medication?**

All administered, refused, or omitted medication doses should be recorded in the patient record in accordance with the hospital's policy governing medication administration. These entries should be made immediately after the medication is administered, which generally means after the patient has taken the dose. Medication administration entries to the record should include the name of the drug, route of administration, date and time the drug was administered, and the initials of the person administering the drug. The pharmacy department should receive copies of all medication error reports or other medication-related incidents.

### Who in the pharmacy department has the authority to make entries in a patient record?

State law typically does not impose restrictions on the type of professional who may write entries in a patient medical record; who may do so is generally a matter of policy within the hospital. Medical record entries are typically authored by the clinical provider who delivers the service to the patient, and as a rule, any person providing care to a patient should be permitted to document that care, regardless of the person's position within the facility. [*See* 42 C.F.R. 482.24(c), requiring that entries to medical records be authenticated and dated by the person (identified by name and discipline) who is responsible for ordering or evaluating the service furnished] Within the hospital, therefore, specific organizational and medical staff committees—such as the medical records committee, the pharmacy and therapeutics committee, and a quality assurance committee—will need to approve authority for pharmacists and pharmacy department personnel to make medical record entries. (For related material, see Part 4 of this Manual under **Management of Human Resources.**)

### What rules of confidentiality govern the patient-related data gathered by a pharmacy department?

A patient record, including information relating to medications administered and prescribed, is a confidential document. Access to a patient record is generally limited to the patient or an authorized representative, the attending physician, and other health care facility staff members possessing legitimate patient care interests. The basic rules of confidentiality and access to medical records are established in most states by statute and regulation. A few states simply specify that a medical record is confidential and impose a general obligation on the facility with custody of the record to develop an appropriate policy for record confidentiality without further statutory or regulatory guidance. [*See, e.g.,* S.D. ADMIN. R. 44:04:09:04] Enactments in other states similarly embody the principle of confidentiality and the patient's right of access. In Connecticut, for example, a Patient's Bill of Rights provides that patients are entitled to confidential treatment of their medical records. [CONN. GEN. STAT. 19a-550(b)(9)] Numerous other statutes, including those of Maryland and Michigan, provide that medical records are confidential and may be disclosed only with the patient's consent or as provided by statute. [MICH. COMP. LAWS 333.6111 & 333.6112 and MD. CODE ANN. HEALTH-GEN. 4–302(a)(2)]

Under federal law, a hospital must have a procedure for ensuring the confidentiality of its patient records [42 C.F.R. 482.24(b)], and patients have the right to the confidentiality of their clinical records. [42 C.F.R. 482.13(d)]

Accordingly, a pharmacy department and its staff must respect and protect patient confidentiality by safeguarding access to both print and electronic sources of patient information. Access to patient information should be granted only to authorized health personnel within the hospital as required for the care of patients. Information that a pharmacy collects is particularly sensitive because other details regarding the nature of a patient's illness and course of treatment can be deduced from the type of medication prescribed. In pharmacy practice, requests for patient information come from a variety of sources, and pharmacists have the obligation to safeguard confidentiality by preventing unauthorized access to this information in accordance with state law and regulations. (For related material, see Part 4 of this Manual under **Management of Human Resources.**)

---

### What confidentiality of patient information issues arise with respect to computerized medical recordkeeping?

The computerization of medical record data, including medication orders and information relating to drug administration, raises a number of confidentiality concerns. Although a computer-based patient record system can improve efficiency and the quality of care rendered by a provider, it may also increase a provider's exposure to liability for improper disclosure of personal health information through computer sabotage committed by persons gaining unauthorized access to a computerized record system.

Legal confidentiality obligations do not vary with the medium on which patient records are stored. Because of the potential for large-scale breaches of data security in a computerized patient record system, however, a provider must implement special safeguards to protect confidentiality against both internal and external users of the system. Appropriate computer security can generally be achieved through a combination of technical measures, system management, and administrative procedures. Some of the technical safeguards relevant to computerized patient record systems are

- personal identification and user verification, which verify a user's identity, frequently through a user password or code or a combination of identifiers
- access control software and audit trails, which limit a user's access to authorized data and resources and locate suspicious patterns of access
- computer architecture, which enhances security by monitoring the computer's activities and thereby preventing users from gaining access to unauthorized data
- encryption, which encodes data so as to permit interpretation only with an appropriate key

---

### What is the Health Insurance Portability and Accountability Act (HIPAA)?

HIPAA is a federal law that addresses two separate issues: health insurance reform and federal standards for transfer of patient information in the health care industry. These standards are referred to as the Administrative Simplification provisions, and are intended to improve the efficiency of the health care system by making technology more uniform. The standards are explained further in the question and answer that follows.

## What does HIPAA compliance entail?

HIPAA compliance is an ongoing process that entails carefully following regulatory developments, analyzing what steps toward compliance are necessary, and then implementing appropriate policies and procedures to ensure compliance. This planning will likely take place outside of the pharmacy department, at the hospital or health care organization level.

Congress vested authority for developing standards for electronic health industry transactions in CMS, a division of HHS, if none was legislated by August 1999. No legislation was passed by that deadline, and CMS has now finalized a number of proposed rules. CMS's first final regulation addresses what are known as the transaction elements of the HIPAA Administrative Simplification provisions, adopting standards for content and format of eight electronic transactions in the health care industry. All health care providers will be able to use the electronic format to bill for their services, and all health plans will be required to accept these standard electronic claims, referral authorizations, and other transactions. [65 Fed. Reg. 50312–50372, amending 45 C.F.R. Parts 160 and 162 (Aug. 17, 2000).]

The second final rule, commonly referred to as the Privacy Rule, addresses requirements for the privacy of individually identifiable health care information. [65 Fed. Reg. 82461–82829, amending 45 C.F.R. Part 160 (Dec. 28, 2000).] Health information is defined in the regulations as any information, whether oral or recorded, that is created or received by a health care provider, health plan, public health authority, employer, life insurer, school or university, or health care clearinghouse, if that information relates to an individual's past, present, or future physical or mental health or condition, the provision of health care to an individual, or future payment for that health care.

The final privacy regulations protect all patient health information or records that have been maintained or disclosed by a hospital or other provider in any form, whether communicated electronically, on paper, or orally. Under the rule, patient health information may not be used or disclosed unless the disclosure is either authorized by the patient or is specifically authorized under HIPAA. Providers must obtain an individual's consent for uses and disclosures of protected health information for treatment of the patient, payment purposes, and health care operations.

There are other significant aspects of the final privacy rule that may apply to hospital pharmacy departments. Disclosures of protected health information within a hospital must be limited to the minimum amount of information necessary to accomplish the purpose for which the information is disclosed. In addition, pharmacy departments must establish privacy-conscious business practices, including training staff about privacy issues and making sure that the appropriate safeguards are in place to protect patient health information from misuse, and sanctioning employees for violating privacy policies.

More recently, the final privacy rule has been modified to clarify the following: that marketing use of data requires the individual's written consent, it expands notice of privacy requirements requiring notice of privacy protections to patients, makes consent for regular health care optional, allows disclosure of information under FDA rules and requirements, allows disclosure for incidental

use such as patient sign-in sheets or health care provi
clarifies that parents have access to medical records of th
provides for a single form for research consent. [67 Fed. Reg
fying 45 C.F.R. 160-164 (Oct. 15, 2002)] CMS has also made
plans available. A model compliance plan had to be filed by O
for an organization to obtain an extension for compliance. [67 Fe
(Apr. 15, 2002)]

Although full compliance with the final privacy regulations is not
until 2003, hospitals should already have begun putting the appropriate pr
policies and procedures into place. Additional proposed federal rules to imp
ment HIPAA are in development, on the subjects of national health plan identifiers, claims attachments, and enforcement. HIPAA and its regulations will ultimately impact all aspects of the management of patient health information, including the safety, security, and integrity of that information.

### What measures should a pharmacy department implement to safeguard the confidentiality of patient information?

Protecting confidential patient information in a pharmacy setting against unauthorized internal and external access involves a variety of different issues that are too numerous and complex to be analyzed in depth in this chapter. Specific measures to protect the confidentiality of records depend on the setting in which pharmacy services are delivered and the format in which the record is maintained. Briefly, however, a pharmacy department should develop specific policies and procedures to ensure confidential handling of patient information. These policies should comply with HIPAA and other federal and state laws regarding confidential patient information and address such issues as

- the physical security of all records containing patient-related data, including patient profile records and physician drug order records
- restrictions on pharmacy department personnel access to these records
- respect for hospital policy regarding subpoenas of pharmacy department records, or any request to access patient-related data by third parties, including employers, third-party payers, and drug marketing companies
- procedures and written documentation for the authorized release of information from the record
- establishment of a private patient/pharmacist counseling area if outpatient dispensing is provided

For related material, see Part 4 of this Manual under **Management of Human Resources.**

## MEDICAL ERROR

Medical error occurs when the wrong medication, wrong dose, or wrong patient occur during medication administration. The Institute of Medicine (IOM) identified medical error as prevalent in its 1999 report titled "To Err is Human."

te of Medicine (1999)] The Joint Commission has also r is one of the top reasons for sentinel events in Joint dication errors can be caused by a number of factors ting, similar sounding or looking drug names, drug abtation of labeling or packaging, miscalculations, lack of ıcorrect administration.

---

**es of medical error?**

dical error that the pharmacist may encounter include the rors; omission errors; wrong time errors; unauthorized drug errors; wrong dose-form errors; wrong dose-preparation trative technique errors; deteriorated drug errors; moni- ıce errors; and other errors. (*See* ASHP Guidelines *Preventing Medical Errors in Hospitals* available on the Internet at http://www.ashp.org/bestpractices.)

---

**What does ASHP recommend pharmacists do to prevent medical error?**

Medication errors comprise 20% of all medical errors. American Society of Health-System Pharmacists (ASHP) recommends that pharmacists take the following actions to prevent medical error.

- Engage in drug therapy monitoring.
- Stay up to date with current with drug therapy practices.
- Be available to prescribers and nurses to give advice.
- Be familiar with organizational ordering systems.
- Question confusing orders.
- Prepare drugs in an orderly and clean work area with each order prepared individually.
- Review the original medication order for appropriate drug, label, packaging, quantity, dose, and instructions.
- Prepare drugs in a form that is ready for administration.
- Use auxiliary labels such as "shake well," "external use only," or "not for injection."
- Deliver medications to patient care areas in a timely manner.
- Observe actual medication use in patient care areas.
- Review medications returned to the department.
- Provide counseling when dispensing to ambulatory patients.
- Review medications ordered on preprinted medication orders.
- Keep pharmacy records to identify patients where medical error occurred. (*See* ASHP Guidelines *Preventing Medical Errors in Hospitals* available on the Internet at http://www.ashp.org/bestpractices.)

ASHP has also established guidelines to prevent medical error with antineoplastic agents. It recommends orientation on medical error reduction, standard drug procurement and storage, standard medication preparation and dispensing, standard medication labeling, and credentialing pharmacists to prepare antineoplastic medication use orders. The pharmacist can play an important role in educating others about risks of medical error; verifying medication doses, routes, and schedules, becoming involved in multidisciplined review of drug use, standardizing prescriptive vocabulary, educating consumers and drug manufacturers about medical error risks. [*See* ASHP Guidelines *Preventing Medication Errors with Antineoplastic Agents* available on the Internet at http://www.ashp.org/bestpractices.]

---

**What action should a pharmacist take when a medication error has occurred?**

When a medication error occurs, the pharmacist can classify the error according to the level of harm caused to the patient. The pharmacist should also be involved in immediate corrective therapy for the patient, make sure the error is documented, gather facts and information in regard to the way the error occurred, review reports for reasons for causation, and report the error to appropriate authorities such as FDA Adverse Drug Reaction (ADR) report or state required reporting. (*See* ASHP Guidelines *Preventing Medical Errors in Hospitals* available on the Internet at http://www.ashp.org/bestpractices.)

---

**What role can the pharmacist assume in the health care system to detect and correct medical error?**

The pharmacist can assume a leadership role in the health care system detection and correction of medical error. ASHP recommends that the pharmacist be involved in the following activities.

- Individual pharmacists can assume professional responsibility to ensure patient safety.
- Encourage statutory liability protection.
- Stay actively involved in decisions to prevent medical error such as handling of look-alike, sound-alike drugs, packaging characteristics that contribute to medical error, and stay informed of documented medical errors.
- Establish pharmacy risk management processes to assess medical use systems for error, implement medical error prevention and review medical errors, and develop a corrective action plan.
- Report medical error by establishing a confidential environment for reporting, analyzing reports, and recommending error prevention strategies.
- Encourage research on ways to reduce medical error. (*See* ASHP Policy Positions *Medication Misadventures* available on the Internet at http://www.ashp.org/bestpractices.)

**What Joint Commission standards impact medical error?**

The Joint Commission has proposed revisions to the Medication Use Standards to take effect January 1, 2004. These standards revisions focus on reducing process variation, error, and misuse through uniform medication processes and practices based on sound medical evidence. These standards require the following.

- Health care professional access to patient and medication information that is important in regard to medication prescribing, dispensing, administration, or monitoring. Each organization will set a minimum amount of information to be available such as age, weight, diagnosis, comorbidities, pregnancy and lactation, medication allergies and sensitivities, and current medications including over-the-counter remedies.
- Continual evaluation of medication use processes with steps to improve processes.
- An inventory of medications to ensure ready availability when ordered. This includes a recall system to retrieve and dispose of discontinued or recalled medications.
- Appropriate and safe storage of medications including securing of prescription medications.
- Policies and procedures on ordering and transcribing to ensure that orders are clear, complete, legible, and without ambiguity. This would include specifying the elements and acceptability for standing orders, medication protocols, titrating orders, taper orders, as needed orders, dose scales, range orders, compounded drugs, use of medication-related devices, use of investigational medication, and discharge orders.
- Use of pharmacy services to review all prescription or medication orders prior to dispensing. Safe preparation of medications including appropriate labeling.
- Medications are safely administered and dispensed and verified before the medication is administered. Proper administration includes correct identification of the patient, verification of the medication based on the order and label, verification that the medication is stable, verification that there is no contraindication for the medication because of allergies, medication incompatibility, patient condition, lab results, prior drug reactions, age considerations, or family discussions.
- Prompt response to adverse drug reactions.
- Special procedures and processes are set forth for medications with a high potential for serious adverse drug effects.
- Investigational drugs are safely stored and dispenses.

[Comprehensive Accreditation Manual for Hospitals, Proposed Revisions to Medication Use Standards, Joint Commission, effective Jan. 1, 2004.]

### What potentially dangerous abbreviations can lead to medication errors?

A major cause of medication error is the use of abbreviations and dose expressions. For example, when using "U" for units, the U may be interpreted as a zero. Similarly the use of a zero after a decimal point such as 2.0 may be misinterpreted as 20 or failing to put a zero before a decimal point such as .2 may be interpreted as 2. When an infant was prescribed .5 mg IV morphine for post-operative pain, the order was transcribed as 5 mg morphine that an experienced nurse gave. Four hours after the second dose, the infant died. Other confusing abbreviations include: "D/C" which could stand for discharge or discontinue; "DPT" which could be demoralk phenergan, thorazine or diptheria, pertussis, tetanus vaccine; "MgSO4" or "MS04" which could be magnesium sulfate or morphine sulphate; "Qhs" which could be read every evening or every hour, or "Sub q" which could be read as subcutaneous or every so often.

The Joint Commission has recommended the following risk reductions strategies: (1) develop a list of unacceptable abbreviations that is shared with all prescribers; (2) develop a policy requiring medical staff to refer to the list; and (3) establish a policy that if an unacceptable abbreviation is used, the prescription order is verified with the prescriber before being filled. [*Medication errors related to potentially dangerous abbreviations,* Joint Commission Sentinel Event Alert, Issue 23 (Sept. 2001); *Please don't sleep through this wake up call,* ISMP Medication Safety Alert, (May 2, 2001); *Eliminating dangerous abbreviations and dose expressions in the print and electronic world,* ISMP Medication Safety Alert, (Feb. 20, 2002) with a table of dangerous abbreviations linked to the article available on the Internet at http://www.ismp.org]

### How can error be reduced for look-alike, sound-alike drugs?

The following can reduce error for look-alike, sound-alike drugs.

- Do not store problem medications by name, but in an alternative location.
- Ensure both generic and brand name of drug on orders to avoid duplication.
- Be sure the purpose of the medication is on the prescription.
- Provide written information about drugs to patients. [*Look-alike, sound-alike drug names,* Joint Commission Sentinel Event Alert, Issue 19 (May 2001)]

## SAFETY

### What is the role of the pharmacy department in emergency preparedness?

In response to the events of September 11, 2001, ASHP has issued a statement on the role of health-system pharmacists in emergency preparedness. Generally,

ASHP indicates that pharmacists play a key role in pharmaceutical distribution and control as well as drug therapy management in the event of attack with chemical, biological, or nuclear agents. Pharmacists can provide expertise to facilitate selection of pharmaceuticals for emergency situations; ensure proper packaging, storage, handling, labeling, and dispensing of supplies; deploy emergency supplies, develop guidelines for diagnosis and treatment of victims; and counsel people receiving medications. Pharmacists can also advise public health officials on pharmaceutical information and collaborate with prescribers in drug therapy management.

ASHP recommends that all hospital pharmacists do the following.

- Stay up to date with potential agents of terror including diagnostic and treatment options.
- Share information on pharmaceuticals used to respond to terror attacks.
- Prevent panic and irrational responses to terror.
- Discourage personal stockpiles of drugs used to treat chemical, biological, or nuclear attacks.
- Assist with emergency supply distribution and help manage individual victims.
- Develop and maintain first aid skills.

[ASHP Statement *Role of the Health-System Pharmacist in Emergency Preparedness* available on the Internet at http://www.ashp.org/bestpractices]

**PART 2**

# Joint Commission Survey Questions and Answers

Part 2 Contents

## INTRODUCTION

This section presents first-person accounts of the Joint Commission accreditation process from the point of view of the pharmacy department. The following interviews describe the Joint Commission survey experience as a whole, as well as how recently surveyed hospitals demonstrate their performance improvement activities. The following pages detail the concerns of Joint Commission survey teams—including what the surveyors did and didn't ask during their visits—and the innovative methods used in some hospitals to share their performance improvement successes with the surveyors. In addition, several hospitals shared their views on the new Joint Commission survey process that will go into effect in 2004.

## SURVEY FOCUS

**Question:** What did the Joint Commission survey team focus on when they visited your pharmacy department?

**Answers:**

**Don Buckley**
Director of Pharmacy
South Haven Community Hospital
South Haven, MI
Joint Commission Site Visit: December 2002

For the surveys that I've participated in, both this month and several others over the years, patient safety is the buzzword. They want to know what your institution is doing about medication errors.

I have a large binder with all the documentation that addresses what the pharmacy is doing to prevent medication errors. The surveyor reviewed that documentation and programs I had started regarding patient safety and medication safety before we met. He was evidently impressed.

We are not open 24 hours a day, so he was concerned about the quantity of drugs that the nursing supervisors had in the night pharmacy. He wants us to reduce that number so that only emergent drugs are available when the pharmacy is closed. He was looking for the minimum amount needed overnight—the thrust from the Joint Commission surveyor is that the pharmacist needs to review orders before any medications are given, and of course you can't do that when you're not there. I look at the orders as soon as I arrive the next morning, so they are reviewed within 8 or 10 hours, and he was satisfied with that.

He looked at floor stock and had no problem with the way we handle it. He also looked at crash carts; I had just installed a new system with interchangeable trays, and he liked that. The survey of the hospital's nine physician practices or clinics went very well too with regard to drugs.

The trend I get from talking to my colleagues around the state, plus my experience from several past surveys, is that they're not looking at the pharmacy per se, but at pharmacy interactions with other departments. They know we're trying to do a good job, and they're looking at compliance with medications at the other end. For example, our surveyor had a concern with the nursing department's documentation of wastage of controlled substances.

We're a small rural hospital, only 25 beds, and because of that they didn't do any after-hours visits, but I've heard that they are doing that in other facilities. My "watchword" through all the Joint Commission surveys I've been through is to make sure you're doing what you say you're doing. If you can't meet a requirement of your policy, then change the policy to reflect what you can do.

**Nancy Czarnecky, RPh**
Clinical Staff Pharmacist
PHC—Lake Havasu, Inc.
Lake Havasu City, AZ
Joint Commission Site Visit: October 2002

We actually did not have a long visit in the pharmacy because of the size of the hospital, but I toured the floors with the surveyors. They were very focused on medication processes and patient safety. They wanted to make sure that for all patient procedures and medications, we had processes in place to ensure that we had the right patient, and we charged and credited the patient correctly.

They spent a great deal of time checking the documentation in the chart. In our automated dispensing system medication has to be dispensed against a specific patient name. They were interested in seeing that process and how we know we have the right patient. The nurses are the primary ones who work with the dispensing machines on the floors, so they wanted to see that whole process from start to finish, mainly as a security issue. For example, how does the nurse get an order for a patient medication, who has access to the medication room, and how does a nurse get the medication out of the dispensing machine? Also, how do we handle narcotic wastage?

There was a big concern about after-hours entry into the pharmacy and the security of the pharmacy. They asked who has access and, as a related concern, how do we deal with floor nurses needing medications for patients after hours, and what kind of system we have in place for that. They wanted to know what we're doing in terms of patient safety, cost, and accessibility.

The surveyors were interested in viewing a current patient profile and what kind of information we had access to (i.e., whether we could access things like lab results, and how integrated our system is with other systems in the hospital).

We also spent some time talking about drug samples. They asked what the drug representatives bring, and we assured them that the representatives do not bring actual drug samples—just a lot of pens, paper, and donuts.

On the floors they checked to see that our medication protocol information and our policies were current. It's interesting how after you've been anywhere for a long time, you tend to overlook things like posters that have been hanging up for years. We had a consultant group come in before the survey to do some mock reviews with us, and that was really good because doing that makes you take a fresh look at things. They would ask questions such as, "What's this doing here? What's the purpose of this? What happens when patients bring their own medications into the hospital?" etc.

It was very educational to see the connections among all the departments, and it's motivational to know that the surveyors are coming. Similar to company coming to your house, you tend to get projects done that have been around awhile.

**Jorge Este-McDonald, MD**
Director, Pharmacy Department
River Oaks, Inc.
New Orleans, LA
Joint Commission Site Visit: October 2002

Our pharmacy is small, so we don't deal with all the same issues that larger hospitals do. We started in the conference room, and then did the physical visit.

In the conference room, we talked a lot about partial patients, the night cart, and about how the dietitians interfaced with nursing staff and the pharmacy. The surveyor wanted to talk about what type of reports we generate for the nurses and dietitians. If the patients are on particular drugs, the cafeteria has to be aware of what the patients can have. He wanted to know who receives the report from the pharmacy. It goes to the nurse units, who refer it to the dietitians to monitor how food is given out.

The night cart was a big issue with them. They were interested in the whole process of the night cart—it's basically a pharmacy without a pharmacist, because there is no one there to control the drugs coming out of that room.

The only thing they asked a great deal about was our partial-patient program and how that was managed. We don't dispense drugs, but I have to review the charts of outpatients. Those particular medications are provided by outside physicians, so it seemed kind of odd for us to be involved. We may discontinue that program because we can't do any kind of interventions with those patients.

For the physical visit the surveyor was able to take a very brief look around since we're small. He checked to see if the shelves were clean and basically gave the department a once-over to see what the place is like. He put more emphasis on process than on the pharmacy's operation.

He looked at how the pharmacy is set up and how it is organized. He didn't focus much on controlled drugs. He did not ask for any records of any sort—no permits, or any type of patient records, etc. He did not observe me triaging any patients or putting information into the computer. He focussed a lot more on asking basic questions on operations, but he did not actually go in-depth on any one particular thing. I think a lot of his questions had been answered during his meeting in the conference room. He was focussed more on operations than on whether the controlled drugs were correct, or even if we were compliant with Board of Pharmacy rules. He did focus more on the nurse medication rooms.

**Floyd Handley, RPh, MPA**
Director of Pharmacy
Ogden Regional Medical Center
Ogden, UT
Joint Commission Site Visit: November 2002

They didn't spend very long within the department, only about 15 or 20 minutes. They focussed on our communication with other departments to coordinate patient care. Their questions in every nursing station were geared toward finding out what clinical things we were doing and how we were monitoring patients.

On the nursing stations, they also looked at floor stock control and controlled substance control. We had our magnesium sulfate prefilled 5g emergency syringes in a locked cupboard, but the surveyors also wanted them to be individually wrapped and sealed to stop someone from opening them. The surveyors did not look at controlled substances, but they did observe control procedures at one of the nursing stations, i.e., documentation procedures for sign out and waste.

They checked out samples in the areas outside the pharmacy where samples are kept. They also looked for unlabelled pre-drawn syringes by anesthesiology in such areas as Endo and OR.

Training was discussed in another session with human resources, so our training program was reviewed there. The surveyors had no comments, so evidently that passed.

**Mark Kester, RPh**
Pharmacy Manager
North Adams Regional Hospital
North Adams, MA
Joint Commission Site Visit: September 2002

We're a small hospital of about 50 beds, so the surveyor's visit to the pharmacy was pretty basic. They didn't spend a lot of time in the pharmacy, maybe 15 minutes or half an hour. We had two reviewers, a nurse and an administrator.

They asked to see one of the pharmacists entering an order into the computer, and they wanted to know how we orient a new technician employee and what things we look for in a new hire. They also asked for a copy of the orientation checklist that the new hire has to complete. I believe that tied into the human resources review.

Their major focus was on documentation completeness. I noticed that one of the reviewers was here late one night, and I think he spent a lot of time going over documents. They did focus on narcotic records and requested to see all the records for January. The surveyors picked out one unit and looked at the whole file. They looked at each drug administration for that unit, and they found some items such as missing or illegible initials. For example, there were unclear entries on some of the narcotic forms. The surveyor's point was that if he couldn't read it, then it wasn't complete. That was a Type I for us.

**Ken Lundgren, PharmD**
Pharmacy Services Manager
Atascadero State Hospital
Atascadero, CA
Joint Commission Site Visit: November 2002

The Joint Commission initiated their survey at our facility by reviewing all of our pharmacy policies and procedures. A primary area of focus for the Joint

Commission was how our controlled drug policy addressed issues of accountability involving schedule II, III, IV, and V drugs throughout our facility. A specific area of interest within the controlled drug policy involved our processes related to the accountability of special dosage forms such as the Fentanyl patches. Fortunately, we had anticipated a special set of problems associated with the uniqueness of the Fentanyl patches related to the ordering, dispensing, administering, and wasting of the product. These issues were addressed in a separate policy concerning specialized controlled dosage forms.

The surveyors did not spend a lot of time physically in the pharmacy itself. Instead, they concentrated their efforts on patient units determining how well the hospital's nursing service and other disciplines understood and adhered to the pharmacy's policies and procedures. Also, while on the units, the surveyors were ascertaining the level of involvement and participation of the pharmacists at the patient level. For example, was the pharmacist a part of the unit interdisciplinary team that reviews the patient treatment plan monthly? Are the pharmacists present on the patient units on a regular basis? Do the pharmacists interact with the other disciplines? As the pharmacist's activities involve more direct patient care, they become more of an asset to the hospital and ultimately improve patient outcomes.

**Jill Michaud, PharmD, BCPS**
Director of Pharmacy
Community Health Care—Wausau Hospital
Wausau, WI
Joint Commission Site Visit: August 2002

The surveyor specifically asked how we handle range doses; we haven't really solved range doses, but that is something we've been working on with our pharmacy and therapeutics committee, starting with high-risk types of drugs.

Our pharmacy system uses automated dispensing cabinets, so the surveyor was interested to hear that we have the profile system in place. We did get some questions about anesthesia narcotic handling, and we have an exchange box system where the anesthesiologist returns the waste to us in that box.

The surveyor asked about physician involvement in pharmacy decision making, which in our case is through the pharmacy and therapeutics committee. He was basically looking for physician input on formulary decisions and services offered.

In the patient care units, the survey team was interested in the pharmacy's involvement with the patient, looking for signs of interdisciplinary care.

As part of the patient care interviews, they asked about medication errors versus adverse drug reactions and how those were reported, but that was discussed in terms of our process improvement plans.

The visit in the pharmacy was very brief. The surveyor who came into our department did not look at any documentation, although we had our 10 binders ready! The most common questions were along patient safety lines and how physicians are involved in the pharmacy, whether it's process improvements or medication errors. The surveyor wanted to know that the physicians were involved and participated in the process.

**Robert Nordin, RPh**
Pharmacy Director
Regions Hospital
Saint Paul, MN
Joint Commission Site Visit: October 2002

Their main areas of focus were narcotic control/wastage documentation, medication security, and patient safety.

Regarding narcotics wastage, we did an audit of seven months of records (5,000 cards) looking for two signatures on the documentation. The surveyor specifically picked out five clinical departments: the emergency room, intensive care unit, labor and delivery, the med-surg unit, and another nursing unit. He went through the whole cycle of drug usage in order, from the chart to dispensing and proper wastage. He wanted to know that we documented the cycle of medication orders through usage. That was the major effort, to see what kind of cycle we had for control of narcotics and proper documentation of wastage.

The surveyor asked about our efforts to enhance patient safety. We participate in the "Safest in America" effort, which is a collaboration of all hospitals in a geographic area. Our efforts have concentrated on safe handwriting, standardization of acronyms, and looking at several high-risk drugs. We also did a self-survey on patient education. We showed him everything we had been working on. He also wanted to know the number of medical errors we had and how we treat them, as well as how we communicate, such as for shortages of drugs.

The surveyors looked at drug security everywhere, making sure no medications were left unattended, whether it's in the operating suite or any of the clinical units. They went through nursing floor inspections and looked for locked drug cabinets. This is not just for narcotics, but regular medications as well. All cabinet doors had to have locks. We had installed almost 40 different keyless entry locks, so everything was secure. The surveyors liked that. They also checked our crash cart security. Who has control over the crash carts? Who has access? Who controls the security seals? One interesting suggestion they made is that we put a different kind of lock on a cart after it has been partially used. In other words, while the staff is waiting for a new cart to come up to replace the used one, they should put a different color lock on the partially used one immediately.

The surveyors were very interested in our interdisciplinary work. They would go into the nursing units and ask the clinical pharmacist, "What's your role in here? If there is a drug-food interaction, how do you deal with this? How do you handle this patient with experimental drugs?" Overall there were many interdisciplinary questions. They wanted to know that the staff was doing what was actually in the policies.

The surveyors also went through our computer screens to see documentation of medications. They were interested in our sample drugs policy and how that was documented.

Some of the inspection was not much different than previous years, like refrigeration temperature documentation. They covered the basics, but their main areas of concern were medication security, narcotics wastage, and patient safety.

**Judy Sikes, PhD**
Director of Accreditation and Medical Staff Services
Parkview Medical Center
Pueblo, CO
Joint Commission Site Visit: October 2002

The surveyor was very thorough, and security was a major focus. We have a dumbwaiter system that we use, and shortly before the survey we had purchased six internal lock boxes—one for each unit. We secured them all inside the dumbwaiter, and the surveyor really liked that extra security measure.

She had the staff run a PYXIS report on narcotics wastage. We did get a citation on medication security because the report showed a chart in which a nurse had wasted a narcotic and didn't get a second signature.

Our pharmacy department has an obligation to check all medication rooms every month, and she wanted to see those logs. She was looking not only at the on-site medication rooms, but also at any facility that's part of the hospital system, because that's part of the main pharmacy's responsibility.

The surveyor would visit a particular unit and find a chart that had a patient with an allergy, for instance, to codeine. She'd take that name and have the pharmacy get the profile on that patient to make sure that the chart had the allergy and/or weight on it. She wanted to know that the chart on the floor matched the chart in the pharmacy.

She spent a lot of time asking about the medication error process, both what we have done and what we are currently doing in that area. We looked at all the sentinel event alerts, and the high-alert medications, such as potassium chloride (KCl). For instance, we removed KCl from all areas of the hospital because the bottle looked just like the one for sodium chloride (NaCl), and since that posed a potential risk of choosing the wrong bottle, they shouldn't be stored together.

She also asked about competencies, what kind of inservices we give, and the standard questions for any department in the hospital.

**Pharmacist**
Winston Salem, NC
Joint Commission Site Visit: November 2002

The team's main focus was on age-specific competencies. They were looking for specific documentation of the hands-on experience of the technicians. The surveyors especially wanted us to have demonstrated competence specific to medications with pediatric patients regarding measuring pediatric dosages, and to other issues directly related to medication use.

The other major focus was medication safety. They were concerned that all medications were secure in all areas, and that even in the operating room setting, medications were under double lock. They went through and checked locks; they also opened drawers looking for accessible medications that should be secure. They were concerned with the PYXIS machine, and that any discrepancies in the system were reconciled right away. They actually wanted the nurse to have the ability to reconcile a discrepancy right away, but we felt that eliminated the pharmacy's ability to come back and track down any problems. If the nurses took care of it right away, we would not be so likely to come back to it. They wanted any discrepancy to be resolved as soon as possible after it occurred, but absolutely within 24 hours. We're not a 24-hour pharmacy, so we disagreed with that recommendation.

**Bob Wishner, RPh, MBA**
Pharmacy Director
Alexian Brothers Behavioral Hospital
Hoffman Estates, IL
Joint Commission Site Visit: September 2002

The surveyor seemed to focus on two things. One was getting information about the drugs we dispensed and how they related to particular patients. In other words, how do we know the drugs dispensed are appropriate for a particular patient? How do we get a patient's diagnosis? He checked our computer for the diagnosis information and patient demographics pertaining to health care issues.

Another thing the surveyor focussed on, since we're not a 24-hour pharmacy, is how a nurse supervisor can obtain a specific drug when the pharmacy is closed, since access is denied when a pharmacist is not present. He inspected the night locker and its associated sign-out log, and he was interested in how it was arranged in terms of obtaining drugs and how we dealt with the safety issues surrounding drug procurement at night. He seemed to be interested in how a nurse supervisor would obtain a specific drug. In addition, we were asked to show our unit inspection logs as well as the logs for controlled drugs that were dispensed to the units.

I know they went through documents pertaining to other issues during a different part of the survey.

## PERFORMANCE IMPROVEMENT

**Question:** How did you demonstrate performance improvement to the Joint Commission?

**Answers:**

**Don Buckley**
Director of Pharmacy
South Haven Community Hospital
South Haven, MI
Joint Commission Site Visit: December 2002

The medication error performance improvement project was presented by a risk manager; I wasn't there for that but had submitted my material. I pay a lot of attention to the sentinel alerts, so I addressed 19 issues, and where I saw opportunities for improvement I set up procedures. For example, if the standard dose of a particular medication is two tablets, then I put two tablets in a clearly labeled bag. The Joint Commission wants to see voluntary reporting of medication errors. They are also looking for a nonpunitive medication safety program, and it's difficult to come up with that. We're still working on that as a task force.

I also read and post ISMP practices, which is a biweekly bulletin, and I included those as a reference. The surveyor liked that and I highly recommend that pharmacies use them. Whenever there is a caution, we would start a PI project addressing that. If you respond in any way to an issue that comes up, that really helps the surveyors know that you're willing to jump into action.

My advice is don't wait until the last minute. If a pharmacy can visibly show that it's addressing issues through policies and procedures—or, in my case, through memoranda and a binder—that's good and they'll leave you alone. Just showing the effort is important. You don't have to be perfect, but you have to be working.

**Jorge Este-McDonald, MD**
Director, Pharmacy Department
River Oaks, Inc.
New Orleans, LA
Joint Commission Site Visit: October 2002

They asked about performance improvement, but not specifically for the pharmacy department. A presentation was made by various nurses and representatives from Comprehensive Pharmacy Services (CPS), which is contracted by River Oaks to provide pharmacy services. A lot of the presentation consisted of slides done by the nurses. One of the CPS representatives came over and made some comments, but it was not a pharmacy-specific presentation.

We are able to do things that larger hospitals cannot do quickly because of our size. It's much easier to implement policies and procedures. So we are ahead with the quality improvement part because for us, it does not require a lot of staff training. The communication is a lot better: I can just walk over to the other buildings to talk to the staff. The surveyor was impressed that we're far along with the performance improvement. They don't require that you're finished, but they're more impressed if you're further along. That good first impression really set the tone for the visit.

**Floyd Handley, RPh, MPA**
Director of Pharmacy
Ogden Regional Medical Center
Ogden, UT
Joint Commission Site Visit: November 2002

I had a policy book assembled with policies across department lines; that was pre-prepared and given to them in the beginning of the survey. They did ask a few brief questions to verify that I did have a performance improvement policy, but they did not ask to see any other policies. In addition, my employee file had all kinds of training documentation they saw before the pharmacy department visit, so they didn't ask for training documentation during the pharmacy visit. During nursing station reviews, questions were asked about pharmacy involvement in patient care and improving processes. Generally, questions could be grouped into three areas: communication (with nursing/physicians); clinical activities (renal dosing review/ABX review); and DUE activities (Vancomycin review). Pharmacy involvement with patient safety programs (i.e., competency validation/improvement, medication safety programs) was reviewed and discussed, as was improving the medication process and error identification/discussion. The quality management department gave an opening presentation describing the Medication Safety Committee efforts and successes.

**Mark Kester, RPh**
Pharmacy Manager
North Adams Regional Hospital
North Adams, MA
Joint Commission Site Visit: September 2002

Performance improvement was covered in our group discussion on patient safety, the interview with all the different disciplines present. It went very well. They asked about our adverse drug reporting. They had reviewed the documentation and had some questions about how our procedure operated. Our major performance improvement project, which is hospitalwide and pharmacy specific, is that we're in the midst of installing a new pharmacy computer dispensing system (Baxter-AUTROS Point of Care). That involves new software for the pharmacy plus dispensing cabinets on nursing units and bar code scanning for all medications. That's our short-term and long-term goal for improving patient care and medication safety. Discussion of that project answered PI questions across the board. We had a demo of the system that we showed them with an example of a medication box and of the hand-held scanners. The project encompasses all departments, but affects mainly pharmacy and nursing.

**Ken Lundgren, PharmD**
Pharmacy Services Manager
Atascadero State Hospital
Atascadero, CA
Joint Commission Site Visit: November 2002

The pharmacy has been working on a major project for the last two years to develop a system that will improve the detection and reporting of medication errors, which we call Medication Systems Failures. Through the efforts of an initial pharmacy pilot project, we developed a hospitalwide medication systems failures process in collaboration with hospital administration, nursing, and the hospital's Joint Commission standards compliance department. We were able to isolate and analyze each process involving the complex medication system into individual components of that process. Tally sheets and weekly reports that were developed as part of the program helped us to identify areas of process improvement in our hospital medication delivery system. Prior to the implementation of the medication systems failures program, the hospital staff was unwilling to report medication process failures because they felt doing so was punitive. One of the pharmacy's main goals in implementing this program was to instill a medication error "blame free" culture in the hospital, concentrate our efforts on improving the processes that were involved in the medication delivery system, and not to point fingers at individuals. Training of hospital staff and interdisciplinary communication has contributed greatly to the success of the program.

We had a tremendous amount of data from the program and were ready to overwhelm the surveyors with it, but they basically reviewed the policy with no follow-up questions.

**Jill Michaud, PharmD, BCPS**
Director of Pharmacy
Community Health Care—Wausau Hospital
Wausau, WI
Joint Commission Site Visit: August 2002

Our major process improvement was implementation of the profile system and automated dispensing cabinet. That's one of the things we told nursing to talk about if they were asked about performance improvement projects they had been involved with. We had a storyboard that was on display in a meeting room the surveyors used.

**Robert Nordin, RPh**
Pharmacy Director
Regions Hospital
Saint Paul, MN
Joint Commission Site Visit: October 2002

We showed them some projects such as improved turnaround time for outpatient drug prescriptions and our adverse drug reporting. They didn't ask us the rate, but wanted to make sure we had a process in place. We were also asked who is in charge of the process—this was in general conversation. They asked for documentation from Quality Assurance and we just added to that in our walk-through. In Quality Assurance, the surveyors looked through committee minutes and went through HR charts to make sure all our pharmacists had age-related competencies.

**Judy Sikes, PhD**
Director of Accreditation and Medical Staff Services
Parkview Medical Center
Pueblo, CO
Joint Commission Site Visit: October 2002

She asked what performance improvement activities we had done in the past year. We shared with her our improvement process on look-alike/sound-alike drugs. We explained that in the computer system we flag sound-alike drugs, so if someone asks for one that has a sound-alike name, a question will come up on the computer reminding the pharmacist to make sure they're requesting the right one. For look-alike drugs, we first try to separate them physically, such as by moving them to different shelves. If that's not possible, we relabel the bottles with different colors.

We had done an FMEA (Failure Mode and Effects Analysis) on our MAR (Medication Administration Record) to make it better and safer. The FMEA was provided in the document review session, so in the department she just asked a few follow-up questions on that.

**Pharmacist**
Winston Salem, NC
Joint Commission Site Visit: November 2002

We had a process improvement presentation that the surveyors actually decided to present to the Joint Commission as a standard. It was about assessment of the medication allergies of patients at the pre-anesthesia visit. We gave the surveyors a PowerPoint presentation of our project. (We had a storyboard also, but we did the presentation on PowerPoint.) When patients come in, we ask them what their allergies are, what type of allergies they are, and what the severity is. We ask them to rank the severity of their allergies as mild, moderate, or severe, or by using story faces like the ones used for pain assessment, which is very helpful for patients who can't express the severity very well. We also ask if they're allergic to latex and what their home pharmacy is, and we get a pharmacy phone number in case it's needed later. With this information in hand, we can actually treat the patient much quicker. We don't have to ask them allergy-related questions after surgery when they're not very coherent, but can get the information we need from their completed allergy documentation form. The nurses know whether they can give a certain medication without contacting the physician for allergy clarification or a change in order, or if other procedures have to be followed for a particular patient based on criteria associated with the type and severity of reaction.

**Bob Wishner, RPh, MBA**
Pharmacy Director
Alexian Brothers Behavioral Hospital
Hoffman Estates, IL
Joint Commission Site Visit: September 2002

We addressed performance improvement issues as part of hospital interviews. The surveyors went over our ADRs (adverse drug reactions) and DUEs (drug utilization evaluations). In addition, they looked at the Pharmacy and Therapeutics (P&T) Committee minutes.

We have a hospitalwide program for performance improvement, and they went through that as well. The pharmacy presents monthly performance improvement reports at the P&T Committee meetings, and we report quarterly to the Organizational Improvement Committee. All of those records were available for inspection. They were able to see how changes we made resulted in improvements in the areas we were concentrating on.

## THE NEW SURVEY PROCESS

**Question:** Are you aware of the new Joint Commission survey process (going into effect in 2004)? If so, how do you anticipate adjusting your processes?

**Answers:**

**Floyd Handley, RPh, MPA**
Director of Pharmacy
Ogden Regional Medical Center
Ogden, UT
Joint Commission Site Visit: November 2002

I know that they're out there, but we haven't had a chance to look at them yet. We have been discussing the five goals for 2003 in our patient safety committee.

**Ken Lundgren, PharmD**
Pharmacy Services Manager
Atascadero State Hospital
Atascadero, CA
Joint Commission Site Visit: November 2002

I have read some issues related to how we will be processing the Joint Commission sentinel event alerts, but beyond that I do not know the specifics involved with their next survey. However, the pharmacy is striving to implement processes and programs that will promote pharmacist involvement in the enhancement and outcome of patient care activities. Adjustments to these programs will be made as the intent of the new recommendations is incorporated into our processes.

**Jill Michaud, PharmD, BCPS**
Director of Pharmacy
Community Health Care—Wausau Hospital
Wausau, WI
Joint Commission Site Visit: August 2002

I've heard there's going to be a new process, but I've heard that many times. It sounds as though with the new process, you do a lot of the work ahead of time and it's not as intense or has a different focus when the surveyors are on site—more of a self-assessment. I haven't given a lot of thought to adjusting our processes, because we have a philosophy of continual regulatory readiness. It's just a matter of responding to the questions beforehand instead of after the fact.

**Robert Nordin, RPh**
Pharmacy Director
Regions Hospital
Saint Paul, MN
Joint Commission Site Visit: October 2002

We're really into continuous improvement. We do so much work all the time, and we're always doing new things. Overall, I've been through five or six surveys, and some things really haven't changed. I think we could pass another one right now.

**Judy Sikes, PhD**
Director of Accreditation and Medical Staff Services
Parkview Medical Center
Pueblo, CO
Joint Commission Site Visit: October 2002

I was reviewing some of the drafts for the 2004 standards, and I think the new process will help somewhat to limit the variation among the surveyors. I hope that the Joint Commission continues to work on surveyor variation. I have to give them credit, because I do know they're trying. I have done consultant work with a lot of hospitals, and the biggest complaint I hear is about surveyor variation.

**Bob Wishner, RPh, MBA**
Pharmacy Director
Alexian Brothers Behavioral Hospital
Hoffman Estates, IL
Joint Commission Site Visit: August 2002

I'm becoming aware of changes now; what the new process will evolve into is now being looked at. We want to be compliant in areas such as medication management standards and initiatives for patient safety. This includes new orders written at times when the pharmacy is not in operation.

# PART 3

# Hospital Accreditation Standards Analysis

## Part 3 Contents

## INTRODUCTION

Part 3 of the *Pharmacy Department Compliance Manual* analyzes the standards in the *Comprehensive Accreditation Manual for Hospitals: The Official Handbook* (CAMH), published by the Joint Commission on Accreditation of Healthcare Organizations (Joint Commission) and updated quarterly. Part 3 was prepared on the basis of the standards updated through the November 2002 supplement to the CAMH.

The information in Part 3 is presented in a chart format for easy reference. The chart format contains five columns: Standard, Comments, Evidence, Staff Questions, and Reference.

- The **Standard** column designates those particular Joint Commission standards that uniquely apply to the pharmacy department.
- The **Comments** column provides a brief explanation of each standard and special considerations for the pharmacy department.
- The **Evidence** column outlines specific types of evidence that may be used to show pharmacy department compliance with the standard. The types of evidence suggested include both written documentation review and physical inspection.
- The **Staff Questions** column lists detailed questions to use in preparing staff for the Joint Commission survey.
- The **Reference** column indexes sample forms, policies and procedures, and other items in Part 4 that can be used to demonstrate compliance with the standard.

# PATIENT RIGHTS AND ORGANIZATIONAL ETHICS

| Standard | Comments | Evidence | Staff Questions | Reference |
|---|---|---|---|---|
| RI.1 through RI.1.2.1 | These standards require that the organization address ethical issues in patient care, that patients' right to treatment or service be protected, and that patients be involved in all aspects of care, including the informed consent process (and, beginning in 2001, pain management).<br><br>Pharmacy leaders should ensure that pertinent pharmacy-related issues are addressed in the organization's ethics policies.<br><br>Further, pharmacy leaders should ensure that ethical practices are employed in the selection and procurement of pharmaceuticals for the organization.<br><br>Appropriate conflict of interest and disclosure documents should be utilized.<br><br>Many of the issues in RI.1.2 are covered in more detail in subsequent standards. | • Patient, family, and staff interviews<br>• Open and closed medical records<br>• Patient rights policies and procedures<br>• Organizational policies and procedures regarding conflict of interest, ethics, disclosure, etc.<br>• Informed consent policy<br>• Ethics, confidentiality staff orientation and continuing education materials, training records<br>• Consent forms designed and written in terms, language the patient can understand<br>• Executed consent forms<br>• Drug selection and procurement policies—special focus on how drugs and vendors are selected, who is involved in the process, ethics employed by the Pharmacy and Therapeutics or Formulary committee<br>• Pharmacy involvement with the Ethics committee or functioning of ethics resolution process, as necessary<br>• Pharmacy involvement with the Patient and Family Education committee<br>• Minutes of Ethics committee<br>• Educational materials distributed or accessible to patients, families regarding patient rights, responsibilities, advance directives, accessing the ethics | • Describe how pharmacy associates learn about patient rights.<br>• Who is responsible for ensuring that patients make informed decisions about their treatment options? How is patient understanding and consent documented?<br>• Provide examples of consent forms for investigational drug studies.<br>• What mechanisms are in place for obtaining investigational drug study informed consent from non–English-speaking patients?<br>• How does the pharmacy service ensure that the appropriate informed consent is obtained prior to the dispensing of an investigational drug?<br>• How does the pharmacy service ensure ethical selection of medication vendors and specific products?<br>• How are potential conflicts of interest with medication selection and procurement identified and handled?<br>• What are the ethical issues the pharmacy service has targeted for improvement? | 4–1 to 4–3<br>4–14 to 4–17<br>4–36 |

*continues*

**Patient Rights and Organizational Ethics**

| Standard | Comments | Evidence | Staff Questions | Reference |
|---|---|---|---|---|
| RI.1 through RI.1.2.1 *continued* | | resolution process, investigational drugs, etc. | | |
| RI.1.2.1.1 through RI.1.2.1.5 | These standards address implementation of organizationwide policies and procedures for addressing the rights of patients asked to participate in an investigational study/ clinical trial.<br><br>The pharmacy leaders must ensure that patients receive and understand the appropriate information regarding the risks and benefits of investigational drug protocols prior to receiving an investigational drug. | • Staff, patient, and family interviews<br>• Policy on investigational drugs<br>• Open and closed medical records<br>• Executed consent forms<br>• Investigational drug policy staff orientation and continuing education materials, training records<br>• Educational materials distributed to patients on investigational drugs | • How is staff oriented regarding the organization's informed consent policies and procedures?<br>• Who obtains consent for patients participating in investigational drug protocols and research projects? Where is informed consent documented?<br>• What information is given to patients participating in investigational drug studies or clinical trials?<br>• What happens when patients refuse to participate in a research project/ clinical trial? How does this affect their access to services? | 4–6 |
| RI.1.2.2 | This standard concerns informing patients and, when appropriate, their families, about the outcomes of care that the patient or family must be knowledgeable about in order to make decisions about the patient's care, including unanticipated outcomes. This would include advising the patient if he or she has been harmed by the care provided (i.e., if medical errors were made). | • Patient, family, staff interviews<br>• Policies and procedures on communication of outcomes to patients<br>• Open and closed medical records<br>• Staff orientation and continuing education<br>• Patient satisfaction surveys/results | • What is the pharmacy service policy regarding communications with patients regarding adverse outcomes?<br>• What information is given to patients or their families regarding outcomes or procedures when those outcomes differ significantly from the expected outcomes? | 4–73<br>4–74 |

*continues*

**Patient Rights and Organizational Ethics**

| Standard | Comments | Evidence | Staff Questions | Reference |
|---|---|---|---|---|
| RI.1.2.3 | This standard addresses family (or surrogate decision maker [i.e., health proxy]) participation in patient care decisions.<br><br>Pharmacy leaders should ensure that pharmacy associates understand the patient's right or need for family or surrogate decision maker participation in care decisions, including the organization's policies and procedures for living wills, health care proxies, advance directives, etc. | • Staff, patients, and family interviews<br>• Open and closed records<br>• Organizational policies related to the following:<br>– Guardianship<br>– Family/surrogate decision maker's involvement in care decisions<br>– Living wills and health care proxies<br>– Access to legal counsel regarding care decisions<br>– Patient and family education<br>• Pharmacy associate orientation and continuing education materials, training records relating to guardianship, living will, health care proxy, advance directive, etc. | • How is staff oriented and educated regarding the organization's policies and procedures relating to family or surrogate decision making, living wills, health care proxies, advance directives?<br>• When applicable, does the family or surrogate engage in the patient's drug therapy treatment decisions?<br>• What is the policy when the patient does not have the mental or physical capacity to make care decisions?<br>• Who is responsible for determining whether or not a patient has advance directives, a health care proxy, and/or a living will? | |
| RI.1.2.4 | This standard concerns ethical dilemmas that may arise during the admission, treatment, or discharge of a patient.<br><br>Pharmacy leaders should, through the provision of pharmaceutical care, ensure that patients are involved in decisions regarding their medication treatment options. | • Patient, family, and staff interviews<br>• Open and closed records—specific documentation of patient's participation in medication therapy decisions<br>• Patient rights policies and procedures, specifically resolving conflicts in care decisions/ethical dilemmas<br>• Patient and family education policies, materials flow sheets (e.g., brochure on access to ethics resolution process)<br>• Results of patient satisfaction surveys | • Please describe how conflicts in care (e.g., end of life decisions) are resolved.<br>• How do pharmacists facilitate a patient's participation in the medication therapy decision process?<br>• What is the organization's process for informing patients, families, and staff about the ethics resolution process? | 4–8 to 4–9<br>4–63 to 4–64<br>4–69 to 4–70 |

*continues*

**Patient Rights and Organizational Ethics**

| Standard | Comments | Evidence | Staff Questions | Reference |
|---|---|---|---|---|
| RI.1.2.5 through RI.1.2.9 | These standards address the issues of advance directives, appropriate pain assessment and management, withholding resuscitative services, forgoing or withdrawing life-sustaining treatment, care at end of life, and the patient's right to appropriate assessment and management of pain.<br><br>Pharmacy leaders should ensure that communication mechanisms between the clinical staff and the pharmacy services include pertinent information regarding advance directives.<br><br>Policies and procedures should address the care of patients to provide for communication to patients about effective pain relief. | • Patient and staff interviews<br>• Open and closed medical records<br>• Documentation of staff orientation and records and content outlines of continuing education materials, documentation regarding advance directives, pain management<br>• Policies and procedures addressing:<br>– Advance directives<br>– Forgoing or withdrawing life-sustaining treatment<br>– Do not resuscitate (DNR) orders<br>– Effective pain management<br>– Care at the end of life<br>– Alternative therapies (e.g., herbal medications, holistic treatments, etc.)<br>• Treatment algorithms, clinical pathways include appropriate pain management strategies and document the patient's wishes<br>• Patient and family educational material available concerning patient rights (e.g., advance directives, care at end of life, spiritual support)<br>• Policy regarding patient family education on pain management using medications and other pain management techniques | • Describe how the pharmacist and the rest of the patient care team are informed of pertinent information relating to a patient's advance directive status.<br>• What advance directive educational materials are distributed to patients, family, and staff?<br>• Describe the organization's procedure for assisting patients who do not have an advance directive but wish to create one.<br>• What orientation and training is provided to staff regarding end of life ethical and legal issues?<br>• Describe how attempts to treat pain and meet comfort, spiritual needs are documented.<br>• How do pharmacy staff members ensure effective management of pain for patients?<br>• How do pharmacists facilitate the patient's participation in their pain management and needs for alternate therapies?<br>• Describe how pharmacists educate patients and families regarding their roles in managing pain, as well as potential limitations and side effects of pain treatments.<br>• Are there any educational programs for pharmacy staff regarding pain assessment and treatment? | 4–1 to 4–5<br>4–9<br>4–70 |

*continues*

**Patient Rights and Organizational Ethics**

| Standard | Comments | Evidence | Staff Questions | Reference |
|---|---|---|---|---|
| RI.1.3 through RI.1.3.6.1.1 | These standards address patient needs and privacy. The organization is responsible for establishing and maintaining methods of ensuring that patients' rights to communication and information are addressed and preserved.<br><br>Pharmacy leaders should ensure systems are in place to ensure that patient rights, resolution of complaints, and communication regarding medication therapy and pharmacy services are addressed. | • Staff, patient, and family interviews<br>• Open and closed medical records<br>• Policies and procedures addressing:<br>– Patient confidentiality<br>– Safety and security<br>– Patient complaint resolution<br>– Patient rights<br>– Patient/family medication education<br>– Handling/securing medications brought into the organization by patients and/or family<br>• Staff orientation and continuing education documentation regarding confidentiality, safety/security, complaint resolution, patient education<br>• Medication education materials translated into appropriate languages<br>• Patient satisfaction data, surveys, results (e.g., complaint tracking)<br>• Examples of pharmacy-related patient complaint resolution<br>• Performance improvement (PI) studies concerning privacy, confidentiality, security, complaints, pastoral care, and/or communication<br>• Patient and family education materials distributed on patient rights, pastoral care, access to advocates, Ethics committee, etc.<br>• Site inspections/ observations of phar- | • Describe the mechanisms the pharmacy service employs to ensure privacy for patients while waiting for pharmacy services or counseling.<br>• How does the pharmacy service keep patient information confidential?<br>• What is your mechanism to resolve patient and family complaints?<br>• Are all pharmacy areas where patients are cared for secure?<br>• What procedures are employed to handle or secure medications brought into the organization by the patient or the patient's family?<br>• How do you communicate with patients who are deaf or speak another language?<br>• What are your patient population's primary and secondary languages? | 4–7<br>4–44<br>4–69 to 4–71<br>4–114<br>4–115 |

*continues*

**Patient Rights and Organizational Ethics**

| Standard | Comments | Evidence | Staff Questions | Reference |
|---|---|---|---|---|
| RI.1.3 through RI.1.3.6.1.1 *continued* | | macy areas to ensure appropriate handling of confidential information, patient privacy, and security | | |
| RI.2 | This standard calls for an organizational policy and procedure for procuring, donating organs and other tissues developed with staff participation.<br><br>Pharmacy leaders should ensure that all pharmacy associates know the organizational policies and how to direct patient or family questions. | • Organ and tissue procurement and donation policy<br>• Staff interviews<br>• Staff orientation and continuing education documentation regarding organ and tissue procurement and donation<br>• Discuss the organization's mechanism to address procurement and donation of organs.<br>• What type of education did you receive about organ/tissue procurement and donations? | | |
| RI.3 through RI.3.1 | These standards relate to the protection of patient rights during research, investigation, and clinical trials.<br><br>All consent forms contain the required information to ensure participants' rights to privacy, confidentiality, and safety.<br><br>(See standards RI.1.2.1.1 through RI.1.2.1.5 as well.)<br><br>Pharmacy leaders should ensure participation in the organization's Investigational Review Board (IRB), with specific focus on the appropriate content of the informed | • Staff, patient, and family interviews<br>• Patient education materials regarding clinical trials or research<br>• Open and closed medical records<br>• Pharmacy membership on IRB<br>• Sample informed consent forms in the medical record | • What body reviews investigational drugs protocols?<br>• If investigational drugs are dispensed within the organization, how are pharmacy associates educated on the drugs?<br>• How is the pharmacy service represented on the organization's IRBs? | 4–6 |

*continues*

**Patient Rights and Organizational Ethics**

| Standard | Comments | Evidence | Staff Questions | Reference |
|---|---|---|---|---|
| RI.3 through RI.3.1 *continued* | consent form and its use within the organization. | | | |
| RI.4 through RI.4.2 | Pharmacy department policies, procedures, and performance must be in compliance with the organization's ethical code, and staff members must be well informed about the content and practical application of the code.<br><br>Pharmacy leaders should ensure adherence to the organization's code of ethical behavior in all pharmacy practices (e.g., patient care, drug selection and procurement). | • Patient and staff interviews<br>• Open and closed medical records<br>• Policies and procedures supporting ethical business and patient care practices (e.g., code of ethics, governing body and Medical Staff Bylaws, conflict of interest policies, etc.)<br>• Organization's mission, vision, value statements, code of ethics<br>• Drug selection and procurement policies—special focus on how drugs and vendors are selected, who is involved in the process, ethics employed by the Pharmacy and Therapeutics or Formulary committee<br>• Staff orientation and continuing education documentation relating to organizational ethics and conflict of interest policies | • Does your organization have a written code of ethics? Describe how you were informed about it. What is the purpose of the code of ethics?<br>• What ethical issues pertain to the provision of pharmaceutical care to patients?<br>• How does the pharmacy service select and purchase pharmaceuticals used within the organization?<br>• How does the pharmacy service bill patients for pharmaceuticals and related services? | 4–15 |
| RI.4.3 | Pharmacy leaders should ensure that the organization has self-medication policies or policies allowing for the administration of medications to patients by family members. | • Staff, patient, and family interviews<br>• Open and closed medical records<br>• Policies and procedures addressing self-medication and/or administration of medications by family members<br>• Staff orientation and continuing education documentation regard- | • What is the process to allow patients to self-medicate or to allow family members to administer medications?<br>• How are pharmacy associates and other clinical staff educated on organizational policies regarding self-medication? | 4–44<br>4–69 |

*continues*

**Patient Rights and Organizational Ethics**

| Standard | Comments | Evidence | Staff Questions | Reference |
|---|---|---|---|---|
| RI.4.3 *continued* | | ing self-medication administration<br>• Medication education materials translated into appropriate languages<br>• Patient satisfaction data, surveys, results | | |

# PATIENT ASSESSMENT

| Standard | Comments | Evidence | Staff Questions | Reference |
|---|---|---|---|---|
| PE.1 and PE.1.1 | Pharmacy department policies and procedures in these areas should be consistent with organizationwide standards. Standards concern performing a thorough initial assessment of patient care needs.<br><br>Pharmacy leaders should ensure that systems are in place to allow for appropriate pharmacy assessment of drug therapy, drug allergies, drug history, and patient's drug therapy desires upon admission and throughout the course of treatment. | • Open and closed records indicating pharmacist participation in the patient medication therapy assessment upon admission and for further assessments (when indicated)<br>• Policies and procedures regarding interdisciplinary assessment of medication therapy<br>• Medication assessment documentation<br>• Clinical pathways, algorithms include pharmacist's participation in the medication assessment process<br>• Pharmacy associate orientation, continuing education materials re: assessment procedures and expectations<br>• Translation services available for assessing patients | • In review of a medical record, answer the following:<br>– When was the patient's medication therapy first assessed?<br>– What assessment data were collected by each discipline?<br>– Was there an opportunity to involve family members in gathering medication assessment information?<br>– How will follow-up assessments be conducted?<br>– Where is medication allergy status documented? How is this information updated?<br>• How were you oriented to the medication assessment procedures?<br>• How was the patient included in his or her medication therapy plan? | 4–8<br>4–10<br>4–69 to 4–70 |
| PE.1.2 | This standard requires assessment of nutritional status.<br><br>Pharmacy leaders should ensure that systems are in place to include the appropriate assessment for enteral and parenteral nutrition by a member of the interdisciplinary team. | • Staff interviews<br>• Policy regarding the responsibilities of the interdisciplinary team members for assessing enteral and/or parenteral nutrition needs<br>• Documentation of assessment function in open and closed medical records | • Describe how patients are assessed to be at nutritional risk and in need of enteral and/or parenteral nutrition. | |
| PE.1.4 | Requires assessment of pain for all patients, not only patients at the end of life.<br><br>Pharmacy leaders should ensure pharmacist participation in all | • Documentation of assessment in open and closed medical records<br>• Staff interviews<br>• Organizational and department-specific policies regarding pain assessment | • What role do pharmacists play in pain assessment protocols (for children, adults, cognitively impaired patients, elderly patients)?<br>• How were you trained in pain management? | 4–1 to 4–5,<br>4–8 to 4–9<br>4–69 to 4–70<br>4–83 to 4–86 |

*continues*

**Patient Assessment**

| Standard | Comments | Evidence | Staff Questions | Reference |
|---|---|---|---|---|
| PE.1.4 *continued* | aspects of pain assessment, including data collection and evaluation, patient education and counseling, intervention documentation, and measurement of medication outcomes.<br><br>Appropriate pain medication and assessment documentation should be utilized.<br><br>Pharmacists should demonstrate competency in pain assessment and related processes. | • Clinical pathways or clinical practice guidelines<br>• Documentation of staff orientation and educational materials re: pain management<br>• Patient and family education materials<br>• Patient and family interviews<br>• Observation of assessment interviews<br>• Pharmacy participation in PI initiatives relating to pain assessment<br>• Pain assessment tools and aggregate data | • How are pain assessment findings recorded?<br>• How is a patient's response to pain medication measured? What happens next? | |
| PE.1.5 and PE.1.5.1 | These standards relate to performing testing to determine patient's health care or treatment needs and providing the appropriate clinical interpretation, when necessary.<br><br>Pharmacy leaders should ensure that laboratory testing for antimicrobial susceptibility, serum or urine drug concentration reporting, and laboratory data to guide drug dosing and monitoring therapy are adequately reported and available to be used in the patient's initial and continual assessment and treatment plans. | • Organizational and department-specific policies regarding microbiology, toxicology, and chemistry testing and reporting procedures or protocols relating to medications<br>• Clinical pathways include testing/reporting requirements relating to drug therapy<br>• Laboratory and radiology reports<br>• Open and closed medical records<br>• Pharmacy involvement in the planning and monitoring of drug-related laboratory testing needs of patients (e.g., pharmacy involvement with antimicrobial susceptibility review process, development and monitoring of select "panic values" for serum drug concentrations, pharmacokinetic | • Describe the involvement of the pharmacy in determining the appropriate laboratory monitoring to assist in patient assessment and treatment.<br>• How does the pharmacy service participate in the development of the organization's antibiogram? How is this information disseminated throughout the organization?<br>• What happens when a toxic serum drug concentration is reported by the laboratory? | 4–8 to 4–9<br>4–122 |

*continues*

**Patient Assessment**

| Standard | Comments | Evidence | Staff Questions | Reference |
|---|---|---|---|---|
| PE.1.5 and PE.1.5.1 *continued* | | assessments and monitoring service, etc.) | | |
| PE.1.7 through PE.1.7.1 | These standards concern assessments that should be conducted and documented following guidelines and time frames established by the organization.<br><br>Pharmacy leaders should ensure that medication assessment, patient medication education needs, and assessment of admission medication orders and new medication orders meet organizationally agreed upon time frames. | • Staff and patient interviews<br>• Policies and procedures regarding interdisciplinary assessment of medication therapy time frames<br>• Clinical pathways with established medication assessment time frames<br>• Open and closed medical record documentation<br>• PI data regarding medication order turnaround times, medication assessment procedures, patient medication education needs, etc. | • How is the pharmacy service involved with the planning and service agreements regarding time frames for medication order assessment and turnaround time?<br>• How do you ensure that initial and follow-up medication assessments are completed within the standards set by the organization? | |
| PE.1.8 | This standard outlines requirements for preoperative assessment and documentation. Pharmacy leaders should ensure that systems are in place in all anesthesia areas or areas where conscious sedation may be performed to document a comprehensive medication history, including an in-depth drug allergy history, or to retrieve this information from a previous admission/encounter. | • Staff interviews<br>• Closed and open medical records<br>• PI monitoring regarding medication history and allergy documentation | • What staff are responsible for documenting medication and allergy histories? Where is this information documented? Who has access to this information?<br>• What PI data are collected in monitoring the appropriate documentation of medication and allergy history in preoperative assessment? | 4–10<br>4–11 |
| PE.1.9 | This standard concerns the identification of victims of abuse using established criteria set by the organization. | • Staff and patient interviews<br>• Open and closed medical records<br>• Staff records indicating attendance at manda- | • What orientation and training did you receive to assist you in identifying victims of abuse? | |

*continues*

**Patient Assessment**

| Standard | Comments | Evidence | Staff Questions | Reference |
|---|---|---|---|---|
| PE.1.9 *continued* | Pharmacy leaders should ensure that all pharmacy associates are familiar with the criteria used to identify abuse victims and how this information should be communicated to the appropriate individuals within the organization. | tory orientation, continuing education sessions regarding identifying and handling victims of abuse<br>• Pertinent interdisciplinary PI initiatives relating to identification and handling of abuse victims | • If you suspect a patient is being abused, what process do you follow? | |
| PE.2 through PE.2.4 | These standards concern reassessment of patients to meet their continuing care needs.<br><br>Pharmacy leaders should ensure that appropriate systems are in place for the reassessment of each patient's medication therapy (doses/duration of therapy, etc.) and medication needs with each change in medication orders, including transfer of patients from one setting to another. | • Policies and procedures regarding interdisciplinary assessment of medication therapy, procedures that include reassessment practices upon changes in medication therapy and transfer from one setting to another<br>• Clinical pathways with established medication assessment time frames<br>• Open and closed records | • When are a patient's medication therapy needs reassessed? How frequently?<br>• What is included in medication therapy reassessment? How are patients and their families included in this medication reassessment process? | 4–8 to 4–10 |
| PE.3 and PE.3.1 | These standards concern the integration of assessments to assign priorities to care needs and make care decisions.<br><br>Pharmacy leaders should see these standards as an opportunity to advance pharmaceutical care initiatives. Particular focus should be on the pharmacist's direct interaction with the patient to identify and document the patient's medication therapy desires in an effort to | • Open and closed records<br>• Policies and procedures regarding pharmacist responsibility/participation with the interdisciplinary assessment of medication therapy<br>• Medication assessment documentation<br>• Clinical pathways, algorithms that include pharmacist's participation in the medication assessment process<br>• Interdisciplinary progress notes, pharmaceutical care plans, forms, flowsheets, critical pathways | • Describe how the pharmacy service participates in the collaborative process of prioritizing specific patient care needs.<br>• How is the pharmacist's interaction with the patient to develop a pharmaceutical care plan documented? Who has access to this assessment and plan? | 4–8 to 4–10 |

*continues*

**Patient Assessment**

| Standard | Comments | Evidence | Staff Questions | Reference |
|---|---|---|---|---|
| PE.3 and PE.3.1 *continued* | avoid potential drug-related problems and ensure desired therapy outcomes. These interactions should be adequately documented in the medical record and utilized by other members of the interdisciplinary team in making care decisions. | • Scope of care identifying pharmacy associates' responsibilities<br>• Criteria for requests for specific pharmacy consultations | | |
| PE.4 and PE.4.1 | The scope of assessment performed by each discipline must be defined in writing.<br><br>Pharmacy leaders should ensure that medication-related assessment activities and pharmacist's contribution to that process are included in organizational policies and procedures, and that systems are in place to facilitate this contribution. | • Policies and procedures regarding interdisciplinary assessment of medication therapy and pharmacist responsibility/participation with the interdisciplinary process<br>• Departmental pharmaceutical care plan or policies/procedures<br>• Medication assessment documentation<br>• Clinical pathways, algorithms that include pharmacist's participation in the medication assessment process<br>• Closed and open medical records | • Describe how the scope of medication assessment and pharmaceutical care for patients in need of drug therapy was developed. | 4–8 to 4–10<br>4–71 |
| PE.5 | This standard measures an organization's compliance with individualizing the assessment processes for specific patient populations:<br>• infant<br>• child<br>• adolescent<br><br>Pharmacy leaders should ensure that additional assessment data for this patient population are included in the overall assess- | • Staff interviews<br>• Open and closed records<br>• Policies and procedures regarding medication assessment policies and procedures specific to type, age of patient, and condition<br>• Staff orientation, position description questionnaires, performance evaluations, and continuing education materials regarding age-specific competencies | • Describe the medication assessment process for infant, child, and adolescent patients.<br>• Where do you document medication allergy history and immunization status for these patients?<br>• How were you oriented/ trained to care for this patient population?<br>• What medication-related resources are available to you to provide appropriate medication assess- | 4–99 to 4–109 |

*continues*

**Patient Assessment**

| Standard | Comments | Evidence | Staff Questions | Reference |
|---|---|---|---|---|
| PE.5 *continued* | ment process. This includes, but is not limited to, medication allergy status, immunization status/history, appropriate doses/routes of medication administration, etc. Pharmacist competency for this unique patient population should be addressed. | • Specific pediatric medication-related assessment algorithms, clinical pathways<br>• Available clinical drug information resources specific to the infant, pediatric, and adolescent patient populations | ment and care to this patient population? | |

## CARE OF PATIENTS: PLANNING AND PROVIDING CARE

| Standard | Comments | Evidence | Staff Questions | Reference |
|---|---|---|---|---|
| TX.1 through TX.1.2 | Standards TX.1 through TX.1.1 refer to individualized patient care plans to meet the needs of patients served.<br><br>Standard TX.1.1 refers to care plans that focus on patients' urgent care needs. Those needs deferred and not defined as part of the care plan need to be documented within the medical record.<br><br>Standard TX.1.2 requires that clinical staff involved in a patient's care work together as a team to plan care.<br><br>Pharmacy leaders should ensure that pharmacists are integrally involved in care planning, with specific attention paid to age- and disease-specific medication competencies and pharmacists' documented contribution to medication-related care planning and monitoring of the plan.<br><br>The appropriate level of pharmacy services to meet defined patient demands is essential (e.g., pediatric services, chemotherapy preparation facilities, etc.). | • Pharmacy policies and procedures regarding:<br>– Medication assessment/reassessment<br>– Age-specific competencies/procedures<br>– Admission procedures<br>– Provision of urgent or stat medications<br>• Open and closed medical records<br>• Use of standards of care, decision algorithms, clinical pathways, protocols, care guidelines, etc.<br>• Guidelines for assessment and care of patients with specific conditions, disorders, injuries, and types of patients that include medication-related issues. Examples might include: dose adjustment in geriatric and pediatric patients; patients with impaired renal/hepatic function, specific infectious disease processes and therapies; etc.<br>• Pharmacy services scope of services or service agreements with care units<br>• Position description questionnaires, performance evaluations that include specific competencies<br>• Attendance, educational materials from continuing education programs on medication assessment, provision of pharmaceutical care<br>• Evidence of adherence to appropriate American Society of Health- | • Where in the medical record is the plan of care?<br>• Describe how the pharmacy service collaborates with other providers in planning care, documenting care/treatment, and monitoring the effectiveness of that care.<br>• Have appropriate resources been allocated to the pharmacy to meet its patient care goals?<br>• What is your mechanism for ensuring competent pharmacist coverage for various patient care settings?<br>• What is your procedure for documenting when assessed medication-related problems are not addressed?<br>• What medication-related practice standards, protocols, and guidelines do you use? How did the pharmacy service contribute to these guidelines?<br>• How were pharmacy associates educated about these guidelines?<br>• How do you evaluate and monitor that pertinent pharmacy services meet the intent of ASHP guidelines and standards for the provision of comprehensive pharmacy services? | 4–8 to 4–10<br>4–39<br>4–67 to 4–68<br>4–83<br>4–99 to<br>4–106<br>4–109 |

*continues*

**Care of Patients: Planning and Providing Care**

| Standard | Comments | Evidence | Staff Questions | Reference |
|---|---|---|---|---|
| TX.1 through TX.1.2 *continued* | | System Pharmacists (ASHP) guidelines and standards relating to the provision of comprehensive pharmacy services within organized health care settings | | |
| TX.1.3 | This standard concerns evaluation of goals set in care plans.<br><br>Pharmacy leaders should ensure that the pharmacy service contributes to the development of pathways and guidelines so that pertinent medication-related issues are included. A mechanism for pharmacist monitoring of care plans to ensure that medication-related issues are addressed is essential. | • Clinical pathways, guidelines, protocols<br>• Policies and procedures for medication assessment/reassessment, care planning<br>• Requirements for pharmacy consultations, service agreements<br>• Open and closed medical records demonstrating medication assessment, reassessment, and medication outcomes<br><br>*See also*<br><br>• Patient Assessment section<br>• TX.1–TX.1.2 above | • Describe how pharmacists participate in the planning and revision of medication-related care plans based on reassessment and outcome monitoring to prevent medication-related problems.<br>• Describe how pharmacists are consulted for specific medication-related problems. | 4–66 |

# CARE OF PATIENTS: ANESTHESIA

| Standard | Comments | Evidence | Staff Questions | Reference |
|---|---|---|---|---|
| TX.2 through TX.2.1 | These standards are related to presedation and preanesthesia assessments, and the necessity for qualified individuals to perform moderate or deep sedation and anesthesia.<br><br>The standards apply to patients who receive drugs causing general, spinal, or other major regional anesthesia or moderate or deep sedation that may cause a loss of protective reflexes. Minimal/moderate/deep sedation and anesthesia are defined in the *Comprehensive Accreditation Manual for Hospitals*.<br><br>Because sedation puts patients at significant risk for the loss of protective reflexes, the organization should develop protocols and guidelines for the use of sedation and anesthesia throughout the organization.<br><br>Pharmacy leaders should ensure that organizational policies regarding conscious sedation include the medications, dosages, and routes of administration approved for use in conscious sedation. Although some of these medications may be considered anesthetics and sedatives, special attention should be paid to the appropriateness of use in specific patient care settings as well. | • Staff interviews<br>• Specific policies and procedures for anesthesia and conscious sedation, with a focus on the types of medications, dosages, and routes of administration approved for each indication and special patient types (e.g., pediatric)<br>• Anesthesiology, Pharmacy, and Pharmacy and Therapeutics committee or Formulary committee approval of the types of medications, dosages, and routes of administration approved for conscious sedation<br>• Evidence of pharmacy service participation in the development and continuous review of conscious sedation policies, protocols, guidelines<br>• Attendance records for orientation, training, continuing education regarding the organization's conscious sedation policy, with particular focus on medications<br>• Inclusion of risks associated with the use of conscious sedation drugs in discussions with the patient or family prior to consent to the procedure<br>• Policies regarding the availability of emergency medications in areas where procedures requiring conscious sedation are performed | • How was the pharmacy service involved with the design of organizational policy regarding conscious sedation?<br>• How were the medications used for conscious sedation according to the organizational policy approved by the medical staff?<br>• How are staff oriented to the conscious sedation policy and associated approved medications?<br>• Are emergency medications available in areas where procedures requiring conscious sedation are performed? | 4–11<br>4–56 |

*continues*

**Care of Patients: Anesthesia**

| Standard | Comments | Evidence | Staff Questions | Reference |
|---|---|---|---|---|
| TX.2.2 | This standard concerns making the patient and family aware of sedation and anesthesia alternatives and risks. Pharmacy leaders should ensure that the medications used by anesthesiology are included in the discussion of sedation and anesthesia options and risks. Adequate pharmacist and drug information resources to support this standard should be available. | • Clinical staff interviews<br>• Presedation and preanesthesia assessment policy and procedure that include specific medications, their expected effects and side effects, and the risks of each<br>• Open and closed record review<br>• Informed consent policy and forms<br>• Pharmacy and Therapeutics committee or Formulary committee documents/minutes addressing sedation and anesthesia medications approved for use within the organization<br><br>*To patients:*<br><br>• How were the effects and side effects of the medications used by the anesthesiologist described to you prior to your surgery/procedure? | *To staff:*<br><br>• Who decides the type of sedation or anesthesia medication for each patient?<br>• Who is responsible for outlining risks and options to patients and families?<br>• Where is the discussion of potential risks of these medications documented?<br>• Who approves the medications available to be used in sedation and anesthesia?<br>• How is the competency of individuals who administer sedation and anesthesia medications measured? | |

# CARE OF PATIENTS: MEDICATION

This section is extremely important to pharmacy leaders, as it outlines the current standards for medication use throughout the entire organization. These standards address medication selection, procurement, and storage; prescribing or ordering; preparation and dispensing; administration; and monitoring effects on the patient. Special attention should be paid to areas where medications are stored, prepared, dispensed, administered, and monitored beyond the pharmacy areas and acute care facility (e.g., off-site clinics, mobile treatment vehicles, etc.).

*Note:* As a result of an internal review of its standards for all of its accreditation programs, the Joint Commission has proposed revisions to the existing medication use standards. The purpose of the revisions is to reduce the number of standards and clarify the remaining standards, reduce the paperwork associated with compliance with the standards, and align the standards requirements with surveyor assessment and scoring protocols. The revised standards are not new; the proposed modifications represent deletions, consolidations, or clarifications of existing standards. The revised standards are expected to be approved in February 2003, and implementation of the modified standards is scheduled for January 2004.

At the conclusion of the following chart outlining the medication use standards as they are currently written, there is a separate chart that outlines the proposed medication management standards. The outline of the proposed standards is italicized to avoid confusion.

| Standard | Comments | Evidence | Staff Questions | Reference |
|---|---|---|---|---|
| TX.3 through TX.3.2 | These standards are related to the use, selection, prescription, ordering, and procuring of medications.<br><br>Pharmacy leaders should focus on standardizing processes for medication use across the organization. Standardized policies, procedures, and practices for all patient care areas are required. A medication formulary addressing the needs of the patients cared for is a valuable tool in ensuring compliance with this standard. The formulary process should be collaborative and representative of all disciplines and types of patients serviced. Safety, effectiveness, and economics should be stressed. A process for the timely acquisition of medications not usually available in the organization should be a | • Clinical staff interviews<br>• Formulary document<br>• Policies and procedures regarding medication usage that adhere to local and federal law, regulations, and professional standards of practice, including:<br>– Ordering or prescribing<br>– Preparation and dispensing<br>– Administration<br>– Monitoring<br>– Procurement<br>– Formulary management<br>– Storage of medications<br>– Security of medications inside and outside of pharmacy areas<br>– Procurement of drugs when pharmacy areas are closed<br>– Patient medication education<br>– Dispensing of medications to patient at discharge from | • Pharmacy and Therapeutics or Formulary committees and subcommittees (e.g., Antibiotic Surveillance, Medication Usage Evaluation, etc.) policies and procedures, and minutes<br>• Evidence of physician knowledge and participation in the formulary process<br><br>*Note:* Most of the questions in the medication use section are addressed in the formal medication use and nutrition interview that is usually conducted by the physician, nurse, and administrator surveyor. The organization should ensure that the appropriate pharmacy leadership and staff are in attendance as well as medical, nursing, and administrative staff involved in the formulary management process and other medication use processes throughout the organization. Questions from the medication use | 4–12 to 4–24<br>4–41 to 4–42<br>4–48<br>4–52<br>4–72 to 4–73<br>4–82 |

*continues*

**Care of Patients: Medication**

| Standard | Comments | Evidence | Staff Questions | Reference |
|---|---|---|---|---|
| TX.3 through TX.3.2 *continued* | component of the formulary process.<br><br>*Note:* The examples of evidence of compliance to current medication use standards significantly overlap from standard to standard. This may be reflected in the repetitiveness of the elements listed in each section. In addition, different surveyors may review the same evidence of compliance wherever medications are prescribed, stored, dispensed, or administered throughout the organization. | emergency department<br>– Sample drugs<br>– Adverse drug reaction (ADR) reporting mechanism<br>– Medication error reporting mechanism<br>• Open and closed records showing compliance with organizational policies and legal and regulatory requirements, controlled substance records, documentation of monitoring for compliance<br>• Medical, nursing, pharmacy, respiratory staff personnel records indicating staff responsibilities for medication usage, education activities (job descriptions, orientation, performance evaluations, continuing education records)<br>• Pharmacy and organizationwide PI activities concerning medication usage (e.g., ADRs, medication errors, medication usage evaluations)<br><br>*Note*: These PI initiatives should be interdisciplinary and address prescribing, dispensing, administering, and monitoring functions. | interview may also be asked throughout the survey by any surveyor to any associate throughout the organization involved with medication ordering, prescribing, preparing, dispensing, administering, and monitoring for effect.<br><br>• Describe the role of the Pharmacy and Therapeutics or Formulary committee.<br>• How is the medical staff involved in the selection of drugs for the formulary?<br>• How are drugs added to the formulary?<br>• What role does nursing play in the formulary process?<br>• What happens if a patient needs a drug that is not on the formulary?<br>• How is the organization's clinical staff made aware of drugs that are added to/deleted from the formulary?<br>• How do you report an ADR?<br>• How do you report a medication error?<br>• What PI initiatives regarding medication use are you involved with?<br>• What orientation and continuing education have you received regarding the use of medications?<br><br>In addition, all licensed personnel authorized to handle controlled substances should know the law and regulations regarding appropriate documenta- | |

*continues*

**Care of Patients: Medication**

| Standard | Comments | Evidence | Staff Questions | Reference |
|---|---|---|---|---|
| TX.3 through TX.3.2 *continued* | | | tion for perpetual inventory, administration, waste, and procurement of controlled substances. | |
| TX.3.3 | This standard requires policies and procedures that support the safe prescription and ordering of medications. The standard also requires procedures for using pain management techniques, such as patient-controlled analgesia and spinal/epidural or intravenously administered (IV) medication.<br><br>Pharmacy leaders should ensure organizational, legal, and regulatory adherence to the following medication use functions: | • Prescription, distribution, administration, proper storage, and control of all medications with special focus on controlled substances, investigational drugs, medication samples, radioactive medications, blood derivatives, and radiographic contrast.<br>• Discontinuance or holding of medication orders<br>• "As needed" (PRN) medication orders<br>• Discharge medications<br>• Clinical staff interviews<br>• Organizational and pharmacy service policies and procedures regarding:<br>– Medication review and dispensing<br>– Labeling of medications<br>– Floor stock medication control processes to minimize the risk of ADRs or medication errors (e.g., unit dose system, pharmacy-based IV additive program, etc.)<br>– Patient medication profiles<br>– Expired medication surveillance<br>– Investigational drug processes<br>– Control, handling, and documentation of | • Describe how medication preparation and dispensing processes are controlled. Is there a unit dose system in use?<br>• Is there a pharmacy-based IV additive program in use? If not, how is the appropriate and safe preparation of IV medication ensured?<br>• How are pharmacists involved in reviewing medication orders and drug therapy regimens?<br>• Who is responsible for maintaining patient medication profiles? Who has access to this information?<br>• What systems are in place to ensure that expired medications are not used for patients?<br>• Are sample medications used within the organization?<br>• What is the policy and procedure for the use of sample medications (e.g., security, labeling, and dispensing method; documentation requirements; recall mechanism)?<br>• Describe the organization's medication stop order policy.<br>• Who is authorized to prescribe investigational drugs?<br>• Where are investigational drugs stored? Who has access to them? | 4–16<br>4–18 to 4–20,<br>4–23<br>4–41 to 4–42<br>4–45 to 4–46 |

*continues*

**Care of Patients: Medication**

| Standard | Comments | Evidence | Staff Questions | Reference |
|---|---|---|---|---|
| TX.3.3 *continued* | | radioactive medications<br>–Control, handling, and documentation of blood products<br>–Control, handling, and documentation of radiographic contrast media<br>–Sample medication policies<br>–PRN medications<br>–Medication stop order policies<br>–Discharge medication dispensing<br>• Open and closed records focusing on appropriate documentation of prescribing, dispensing, administering, and monitoring for effect<br>• Controlled substance records and documentation<br>• PI initiatives involving medication usage<br>*Tour of medication areas:*<br>• Controlled substance documentation<br>• Patient medication dispensing and administration documentation/profiles<br>• Medication labeling (including medications given to patients at discharge, sample medications, investigational medications, multidose medications)<br>• Repackaging and IV/total parenteral nutrition production areas and records<br>• Security of medication storage areas<br>• Expired medications | • Are there any special policies or procedures for wasting a controlled substance? Who has access to controlled substances?<br>• Have any significant controlled substance losses been reported to the Drug Enforcement Administration (DEA) within the last year?<br>• Who is responsible for handling radioactive medications? What special orientation or continuing education did you receive regarding radiographic contrast drugs?<br>• Who is responsible for handling blood derivatives? What special orientation or continuing education did you receive regarding blood derivative drugs?<br>• How do pain management techniques relate to medication administration? | |

*continues*

**Care of Patients: Medication**

| Standard | Comments | Evidence | Staff Questions | Reference |
|---|---|---|---|---|
| TX.3.4 | This standard relates to the preparation and dispensing of medications in accordance with law, regulations, licensure, and professional standards of practice.<br><br>Pharmacy leaders should ensure that the organization complies with legal and professional standards of pharmacy practice. Where applicable, standards and guidelines established by the ASHP, the American Pharmaceutical Association, Occupational Safety & Health Administration (OSHA), and other professional organizations should be utilized.<br><br>Special attention should be paid to local and federal laws and regulations and professional standards of practice governing:<br>• Medication labeling<br>• Medication storage<br>• Control of single dose and multidose vials and packages<br>• Required medication production records and documentation<br>• Controlled substances<br>• Required licensures<br>• Functions and authority of licensed practitioners (pharmacists, physicians, nurses, etc.)<br>• Utilization of pharmacy support personnel | • Clinical staff interviews<br>• Policies and procedures:<br>– Applicable local/federal laws governing licensed personnel and the use of medications (e.g., controlled substances, medication production and labeling, limitations of support personnel functions, etc.)<br>• Packaging and production records<br>• Applicable standards and guidelines from professional organizations incorporated into departmental and/or organizational policies and procedures regarding:<br>– Medication procurement and storage<br>– Procedures for aseptic technique and the preparation of parenteral products<br>– The use, storage, and labeling of single dose and multidose parenteral, ophthalmic, and topical products<br>• Medication refrigerator temperature logs in all medication storage areas, including patient care areas (previous 12 months of records required). *Note:* The appropriate temperature range should be defined.<br>• Appropriate laminar flow hood and clean room cleaning records | • What information is required by law on inpatient and outpatient prescription labels?<br>• Can any practitioner prescribe controlled substances? How do you know who is authorized to prescribe controlled substances?<br>• Are there any restrictions regarding the use of support personnel in the pharmacy?<br>• What is the organizational policy regarding the storage of medication? In what refrigerators are medications stored? How are those refrigerators labeled?<br>• Where are medication refrigerator temperature logs maintained?<br>• What is the appropriate temperature range for the medication refrigerator? What do you do if the temperature is outside of this range?<br>• How often are laminar flow hoods and other equipment used in the preparation of pharmaceuticals certified?<br>• How is the competency of the staff preparing parenteral products ensured?<br>• Who keeps clean room cleaning records?<br>• Are single-unit-of-use vials, eyedrops, and topical preparations used whenever possible?<br>• What is the policy for the use, labeling, and storage of multidose parenteral, ophthalmic, and topical products? | 4–16<br>4–22 to 4–23<br>4–36<br>4–38<br>4–39 to 4–40<br>4–91<br>4–116 to 4–118 |

*continues*

**Care of Patients: Medication**

| Standard | Comments | Evidence | Staff Questions | Reference |
|---|---|---|---|---|
| TX.3.4 *continued* | | • Required certification documents for equipment used in the preparation of medications (i.e., balances, laminar flow hoods, automated parenteral mixing devices, etc.)<br>• Multidose parenteral, ophthalmic, and topical product storage locations and labeling<br>• Multidisciplinary orientation and continuing education materials and attendance records regarding legal and regulatory requirements for controlled substances and medication use, and multidose product use, storage, and labeling.<br><br>*See TX.3 through TX.3.3 above* | | |
| TX.3.5 through TX.3.5.2 | These standards concern the control of preparation and dispensing of drugs, medication dose system, and pharmacy review of orders.<br><br>Pharmacy leaders should ensure that policies and procedures are in place to ensure control of all medications used within the organization.<br><br>Policies and procedures should include the following:<br><br>• Prospective pharmacist's review of each medication prescription or order prior to dispensing; some exceptions may | • Clinical staff interviews<br>• Pharmacy and organizational policies and procedures regarding:<br>– Prescription writing and ordering<br>– Authorized or credentialed prescribers<br>– Unit dose distribution system<br>– Dispensing and distribution of medications by the pharmacy and other patient care areas<br>– Medication prescribing restrictions (e.g., antibiotics, chemotherapy agents, etc.)<br>– Patient medication assessment<br>– ADR surveillance | • Who is authorized/credentialed to prescribe medications throughout the organization? How do you know?<br>• Can certain drugs be prescribed only by specific physicians?<br>• How are these prescribing restrictions and list of authorized prescribers disseminated to the clinical staff?<br>• How does the unit dose drug distribution system work?<br>• Who has access to information contained on the medication profiles?<br>• Who is responsible for reviewing the appropriateness of prescribed medications? | 4–8 to 4–10<br>4–13<br>4–17 to 4–20<br>4–24 to 4–36<br>4–38<br>4–48<br>4–50 to 4–52<br>4–52 to 4–54<br>4–77<br>4–93<br>4–198 |

*continues*

**Care of Patients: Medication**

| Standard | Comments | Evidence | Staff Questions | Reference |
|---|---|---|---|---|
| TX.3.5 through TX.3.5.2 *continued* | include medications used in certain treatment areas (e.g., cardiac catheterization lab, OR) or during medical emergencies<br>• A process for contacting the prescriber for medication order clarification<br>• Standardized medication labeling throughout the organization<br>• Dispensing of medications in individual doses to minimize potential errors<br>• Utilization of point of use distribution or automated dispensing technologies, if applicable | –Medication error surveillance<br>–Communication with various health care practitioners<br>–Medication order profiling (manual vs. computerized)<br>–Medication profiles<br>–Pharmacy-based IV additive services<br>–Parenteral nutrition and chemotherapy prescribing, profiling, production, and dispensing<br>–Controlled substances procedures and documentation<br>–Point of use distribution technologies<br>–Automated dispensing technologies<br>• Open and closed medical records for pharmacist intervention documentation<br>• Patient medication profiles<br>• Medication labels<br>• Stocking and dispensing records, fill lists, checklists<br>• Orientation and continuing education records for pharmacy associates, nurses, physicians, and other prescribers regarding the preparation and dispensing of medications<br>• Prescriber's signature verification logs, narcotics registration numbers<br>• Tours of pharmacy and other areas where medications are prepared and dispensed | • How do pharmacists document drug therapy interventions?<br>• How many drug therapy interventions are documented annually?<br>• Who has access to medications stored in the point of use distribution cabinets? How is the stock of medications in these units maintained? How often are they checked?<br>• What checks and balances are in place to prevent potential distribution or dispensing errors with chemotherapy products? With point of use distribution cabinets or automated dispensing machines?<br>• How do you report a suspected ADR or medication error?<br>• How were you oriented to the medication use policies and procedures within the organization? | |

*continues*

**Care of Patients: Medication**

| Standard | Comments | Evidence | Staff Questions | Reference |
|---|---|---|---|---|
| TX.3.5.3 | This standard concerns using patient information to prepare and dispense medications safely.<br><br>Pharmacy leaders should ensure that the pharmacists and appropriate clinical staff throughout the organization have access to the patient's medication profile to ensure the safe prescribing, dispensing, and administering of medications.<br><br>Minimum requirements for the content of medication profiles should be defined. | • Clinical staff interviews<br>• Pharmacy and organizational policies and procedures regarding:<br>– Unit dose distribution system<br>– Minimum requirements for the content of the medication profile, including, but not limited to: patient demographics, diagnosis and disease state information, medication/food allergies, height/weight/body surface area, current medications and medication history, medication dosages, routes of administration, frequencies and duration of therapy, dispensing history, patient care and medication order comments and clarification, and pharmacist intervention documentation<br>– Dispensing and distribution of medications by the pharmacy and other patient care areas<br>– Patient medication assessment<br>– ADR surveillance<br>– Medication error surveillance<br>– Medication order profiling (manual vs. computerized)<br>– Medication profiles<br>– Parenteral nutrition and chemotherapy prescribing, profiling, production, and dispensing | • What important information is included in the patient medication profile?<br>• Who has access to the patient medication profile?<br>• Describe the medication order profiling process.<br>• Besides the patient medication profile, where is pertinent patient care information necessary for safe and accurate medication preparation and dispensing obtained?<br>• How is a patient's medication and/or food allergy history obtained and documented?<br>• Who is able to update information on the patient's medication profile (manual vs. computerized)? | 4–8 to 4–10<br><br>4–14<br>4–36<br>4–38<br>4–48 to 4–54 |

*continues*

**Care of Patients: Medication**

| Standard | Comments | Evidence | Staff Questions | Reference |
|---|---|---|---|---|
| TX.3.5.3 *continued* | | • Patient medication profiles<br>• Orientation and continuing education records for pharmacy associates, nurses, physicians, and other prescribers regarding the use of the medication profile and pertinent patient information in medication preparation and dispensing | | |
| TX.3.5.4 | This standard relates to the availability of pharmacy services.<br><br>Pharmacy leaders should ensure that the appropriate policies and procedures are in place if pharmacy services are not available 24 hours a day, seven days a week. This should include a retrospective review by a pharmacist of the activities during hours when the pharmacy is closed or unavailable. | • Clinical staff interviews<br>• Organizational and pharmacy policies and procedures regarding:<br>– Pharmacy services when the pharmacy is closed<br>– Use, regulation, and replenishment of night cabinets, point of use distribution systems<br>– Authorized non-pharmacists in the pharmacy after hours<br>– Retrospective pharmacist review of all after-hour medication access<br>– Quantities and doses of available medications<br>– Emergency access to a pharmacist for preparation and dispensing of unavailable medications<br>• Records regarding after-hours access to the pharmacy, dispensing, and inventory<br>• Night cabinet and point of use system pharmacy inspection documents | • How are medications obtained, prepared, and dispensed when the on-site pharmacy service is closed or unavailable?<br>• Who has access to night cabinets, after-hours carts, or point of use distribution cabinets?<br>• How are night cabinets, after-hours carts, or point of use distribution cabinets replenished?<br>• Who has access to the pharmacy after hours?<br>• Is there an "on-call" pharmacist schedule for emergencies?<br>• How are staff members oriented to the organizational policies and procedures regarding accessing medications when the pharmacy is closed or unavailable? | |

*continues*

**Care of Patients: Medication**

| Standard | Comments | Evidence | Staff Questions | Reference |
|---|---|---|---|---|
| TX.3.5.4 *continued* | | • Orientation and continuing education records of personnel required to access medications after hours | | |
| TX.3.5.5 | This standard relates to emergency medication system issues.<br><br>Pharmacy leaders should ensure adherence to organizational policy regarding emergency medications.<br><br>*Note*: The security of medications on patient care areas is a shared pharmacy/nursing responsibility. All nursing staff members should routinely check secured emergency medication locations.<br><br>Sealed, pharmacy-controlled emergency kits or boxes are not required to meet the intent of this standard; however, this may be the most appropriate means to ensure organizational compliance with this far-reaching standard. | • Clinical staff interviews<br>• Organizational, nursing, and pharmacy policies and procedures regarding:<br>– Availability and control of emergency medications to include the organizational process for availability, security, multidisciplinary monitoring responsibilities, and control of emergency boxes and locks, if applicable<br>– Routine organizational review of emergency medication inventory, policies, authorized patient care areas (e.g., through Pharmacy and Therapeutics or Formulary committee, Cardiopulmonary Arrest committee, Risk Management committee, etc.)<br>– Logs, checklists, etc., supporting organizational policy regarding monitoring of emergency medication availability, control, expiration dating, and security (previous 12 months of records required)<br>• Orientation and continuing education records for staff regarding the organiza- | • How does the organization ensure that emergency medications are always available, controlled, and secured?<br>• Who is responsible for inspecting emergency medication supplies? How often?<br>• How do staff know what is the appropriate inventory, location, and security of emergency medications?<br>• How is the availability, control, and security of emergency medications routinely reviewed?<br>• Who is responsible for the availability, control, and security of emergency medications?<br>• How long are records regarding emergency medication availability, control, and security kept and where? | 4–14<br>4–18<br>4–90 |

*continues*

**Care of Patients: Medication**

| Standard | Comments | Evidence | Staff Questions | Reference |
|---|---|---|---|---|
| TX.3.5.6 *continued* | | tional policies and procedures for the availability, control, and securing of emergency medications<br><br>*Note:* Pharmacy areas and patient care areas throughout the entire organization where emergency medications are stored will be a focus for surveyors. Special attention will be paid to adherence with organizational, nursing, and pharmacy policies and procedures. | | |
| TX.3.5.6 | This standard relates to medication recall systems.<br><br>Pharmacy leaders should ensure that comprehensive medication recall policies and procedures are followed wherever medications are used or stored throughout the organization. | • Clinical staff interviews<br>• Organizational and pharmacy service policies and procedures regarding a comprehensive medication recall system. This system should include:<br>– Identification of all potential areas where the recalled medication was used or stored<br>– Process for retrieval, quarantine, recordkeeping, and return of recalled medications<br>– Organizationwide notification process<br>• Complete records of all medication recalls with verification of on-hand inventory checks for identified manufacture lot numbers<br>• Orientation and continuing education records for staff regarding their responsibilities for the organization's medication recall system | • What is the organizational and pharmacy service policy and procedure for recalled medications?<br>• How is the organization informed of medication recalls?<br>• How does the pharmacy service notify areas where medications are used or stored of a medication recall?<br>• How are recalled medications disposed of?<br>• Where are records of recalled medications kept?<br>• How were you oriented to the organization's medication recall policy? | 4–43 |

*continues*

**Care of Patients: Medication**

| Standard | Comments | Evidence | Staff Questions | Reference |
|---|---|---|---|---|
| TX.3.6 | This standard concerns measuring the effectiveness of policies relating to verifying orders and identifying patients prior to drug administration.<br><br>Pharmacy leaders should ensure that medication profiling, dispensing, and administration policies and procedures include prescription or order verification by competent pharmacy, medical, or nursing personnel prior to administration. A process for identifying a patient prior to medication administration is vital. | • Additional policies and procedures regarding:<br>– Medication administration; these should outline the various checks and balances in medication prescribing, profiling, dispensing, and administering and the responsibilities of the physicians, pharmacists, and nurses involved in the process<br>– Available resources (pharmacists, references, databases) for clarification of perceived problems with medication prescriptions or orders<br>– Escalation process for conflicts with or errors in medication prescribing, dispensing, and administering<br>• Orientation and continuing education for staff regarding medication administration policies and procedures<br><br>*Note:* During the tour of patient care areas, the surveyors may observe medication administration for adherence to organizational policies and procedures.<br><br>*See TX.3.5 through TX.3.5.2* | • Describe the process of verifying prescription orders before medication administration to a patient.<br>• How are patients identified and verified prior to medication administration?<br>• How are the various responsibilities for medication prescription, dispensing, and administration delineated?<br>• What do you do if an incorrect medication is administered to a patient?<br>• What resources are available when clarification of perceived problems with medication prescriptions or orders is required?<br>• How were you oriented to the organization's medication administration policy and procedure? | 4–44<br>4–45<br>4–49<br>4–52 |
| TX.3.7 | This standard concerns the organization's alternative medication administration systems. | • Clinical staff, patient, and family interviews<br>• Organizational and pharmacy policies and procedures regarding: | • What are the organizational policies and procedures regarding medications brought into the organization by a | 4–44 |

*continues*

**Care of Patients: Medication**

| Standard | Comments | Evidence | Staff Questions | Reference |
|---|---|---|---|---|
| TX.3.7 *continued* | Pharmacy leaders should ensure that policies and procedures are in place to prevent the use of medications brought in by patients or families without verification by a pharmacist.<br><br>Additionally, the organization should, under appropriate procedures, allow for the self-administration of medications. | –Medication administration<br>–The use of medications brought into the organization by patients, family, or friends; this should include identification, verification, and labeling of these medications by pharmacy and nursing staff prior to administration or self-administration<br>–Administration of medications by patients or family members<br>• Orientation and continuing education records regarding medications brought into the organization by patients or family members and self or family medication administration policies and procedures | patient or family member?<br>• Are patients permitted to administer medications to themselves?<br>• Are family members permitted to administer medications to patients?<br>• How were you oriented to the organization's policies and procedures regarding medications brought into the organization and self or family medication administration? | |
| TX.3.8 | This standard relates to the safe control of investigational drugs.<br><br>Pharmacy leaders should ensure that appropriate policies and procedures are in place so that the organization conducts investigational medication studies safely, and that investigational medications not used during the study are safely destroyed or returned to the study sponsor. | • Clinical staff interviews<br>• Organizational and pharmacy policies and procedures regarding:<br>–Investigational drug services<br>–Informed consent<br>–Medication administration, including investigational medication prescription, dispensing, and administration responsibilities of the various disciplines involved with investigational medications<br>• Investigational drug inventory documents, reports of study | • Where are investigational medications stored?<br>• Who is authorized to prescribe, dispense, and administer investigational medications?<br>• What becomes of unused investigational medications?<br>• How were you oriented to the organization's investigational medication prescription, dispensing, and administration policies and procedures?<br><br>*See RI.1.2.1 through RI.1.2.1.5, RI.3, and RI.3.1* | 4–45 to 4–47 |

*continues*

**Care of Patients: Medication**

| Standard | Comments | Evidence | Staff Questions | Reference |
|---|---|---|---|---|
| TX.3.8 *continued* | | monitors or regulatory agencies (e.g., National Institutes of Health, etc.)<br>• Specific investigational medication protocols and waste/return guidelines<br>• Orientation and continuing education records for staff involved with investigational medications<br><br>*Note:* During the tour of the pharmacy and medication storage areas, the surveyor may well review the security of all medications, and may focus on the storage and security of investigational medications.<br><br>*See RI.1.2.1 through RI.1.2.1.5, RI.3, and RI.3.1* | | |
| TX.3.9 | This standard relates to monitoring medication effects.<br><br>Pharmacy leaders should ensure that organizational and pharmacy service programs, policies, and procedures are in place to ensure that medication monitoring is collaborative and includes the patient and/or family. Medication outcome monitoring programs should be designed to improve the patient's medication therapy. A comprehensive program should ensure that: | • Clinical staff interviews<br>• Organizational and pharmacy service policies and procedures regarding:<br>– Medication assessment<br>– Unit dose distribution system<br>– Medication profiling (manual vs. computerized)<br>– Pharmacist intervention documentation<br>– ADR surveillance<br>– Medication error surveillance<br>– Medication usage evaluation program<br>– Medication prescribing, dispensing, administering, and monitoring | • Who is responsible for the continual monitoring of medication effects on patients?<br>• How are the effects of medications monitored by nurses, pharmacists, and physicians?<br>• How does the organization document monitoring for medication effectiveness?<br>• How does the organization determine which medications should be reviewed under the medication usage evaluation program? How does it work? Where/how does the medical center communicate aggregate medication usage evaluation information? | 4–1 to 4–11<br>4–36 to 4–38<br>4–40<br>4–48 to 4–54<br>4–66 to 4–68<br>4–71 to 4–78 |

*continues*

**Care of Patients: Medication**

| Standard | Comments | Evidence | Staff Questions | Reference |
|---|---|---|---|---|
| TX.3.9 *continued* | • Practitioners monitor therapeutic responses to medications.<br>• Practitioners review the appropriateness of the choice and dosage of medication(s), and prevent therapeutic duplication or contraindications.<br>• Interactions with prescribers to avoid potential medication-related adverse events are routinely documented by pharmacists, nurses, and other clinicians. | – Medication order conflict resolution and escalation process for conflicts with or errors in medication prescribing, dispensing, and administering<br>– Medication profile<br>– Pain assessment<br>– Parenteral nutrition and chemotherapy prescription, profiling, production, and dispensing<br>• Pharmacist intervention documentation<br>• Drug-related information resources, databases, on-line subscription services for minimum/maximum doses, drug interaction checking, duplication checking, compatibility checking, etc.<br>• ADR and medication error surveillance data (previous 12 months of data required)<br>• Pharmacy and Therapeutics or Formulary committee minutes or other committee minutes (Quality, Risk Management, etc.) where ADR, medication error, and medication use PI are reported and tracked<br>• PI initiatives and data regarding medication use and monitoring<br>• Open and closed medical record review for daily documentation regarding nursing (as well as multidisciplinary) monitoring and | • How do you report a suspected drug interaction? Medication error?<br>• What performance improvement initiatives have you been involved with regarding medication use and the prevention of negative medication outcomes?<br>• What is the organization's definition of an ADR? A medication error?<br>• What PI initiatives have been implemented within the last 12 months to improve the reporting of suspected ADRs and medication errors?<br>• How do you report a serious ADR to the Food and Drug Administration (FDA) and manufacturer?<br>• What information resources are available to assist with the monitoring for medication effectiveness and the prevention of negative medication outcomes?<br>• How are medication overdoses identified and prevented?<br>• How is the effectiveness of medications used to treat patients in pain monitored and documented?<br>• How is the effectiveness of parenteral nutrition monitored and documented?<br>• How are the effects of chemotherapy agents monitored and documented?<br>• How were you oriented to the organization's policies, procedures, and programs regarding | |

*continues*

**Care of Patients: Medication**

| Standard | Comments | Evidence | Staff Questions | Reference |
|---|---|---|---|---|
| TX.3.9 *continued* | | reporting of medication effects<br>• Orientation and continuing education records of staff involved with medication prescribing, dispensing, administering, and monitoring for medication effects<br><br>*See TX.3 through TX.3.2, TX.3.5 through TX.3.5.3, TX.3.6, PI.3 through PI.3.1.3, and PI.4 through PI.4.6.* | medication use and monitoring for medication effects?<br><br>*See TX.3 through TX.3.2, TX.3.5 through TX.3.5.3, TX.3.6, PI.3 through PI.3.1.3, and PI.4 through PI.4.6.* | |

The following chart outlines the proposed modifications to the medication management standards that are expected to be approved in early 2003 and implemented in January 2004. The proposed standards focus special attention on an organization-wide systems approach to safe medication use. They address risk points in medication use systems and cover processes and procedures that contribute to safe medication practices, augmented with an error reporting, performance improvement process.

| Standard | Comments | Evidence | Staff Questions | Reference |
|---|---|---|---|---|
| TX.3 and TX.3.1 | The proposed standards concern the organization and systematization of medication use processes throughout the hospital organization, and the organization's adherence to laws, regulations, and professional practice standards concerning medication use practices.<br><br>Pharmacy leaders should focus on standardizing processes for medication use across the organization. Standardized policies, procedures, and practices for all patient care areas are required. A medication formulary addressing patient needs | • Clinical staff interviews<br>• Formulary document<br>• Policies and procedures regarding medication management that adhere to local and federal law, regulations, and professional standards of practice, including:<br>– Ordering or prescribing<br>– Preparation and dispensing<br>– Administration<br>– Monitoring<br>– Procurement, including when pharmacy areas are closed<br>– Formulary management<br>– Security of medications inside and outside of pharmacy area | • How is the medical staff involved in selecting drugs for the formulary?<br>• How are drugs added to the formulary?<br>• What role does nursing play in the formulary process?<br>• What happens if a patient needs a drug that is not on the formulary?<br>• How is the clinical staff made aware of drugs that are added to or deleted from the formulary?<br>• How do you report an ADR or a medication error?<br>• What PI initiatives regarding medication management are you involved with?<br>• What orientation and continuing education have you received | |

*continues*

**Care of Patients: Medication**

| Standard | Comments | Evidence | Staff Questions | Reference |
|---|---|---|---|---|
| TX.3 and TX.3.1 *continued* | is a valuable tool in ensuring compliance with this standard.<br><br>Pharmacy leaders should adhere to applicable laws and regulations, professional licensure, and accepted professional practice standards governing safe medication use and the safe operation of pharmacy services. | – Storage<br>– Dispensing of medications to patient at discharge from emergency department<br>– Patient medication education<br>– Sample drugs<br>– Mechanisms for reporting adverse drug reactions, medication errors<br>• Open and closed records showing compliance with organizational policies and legal and regulatory requirements, controlled substance records, documentation of monitoring for compliance<br>• Pharmacy, medical, nursing, respiratory staff personnel records indicating staff responsibilities for medication management, education activities<br>• Pharmacy and hospitalwide PI activities concerning medication (e.g., ADRs, medication errors, medication usage evaluations)<br>• Pharmacy and Therapeutics of Formulary committees and subcommittees (e.g., Antibiotic Surveillance, Medication Usage Evaluation, etc.) policies and procedures, and minutes<br><br>Note: Most of the questions in this section are addressed in the formal medication use | regarding the management of medications? | |

*continues*

**Care of Patients: Medication**

| Standard | Comments | Evidence | Staff Questions | Reference |
|---|---|---|---|---|
| TX.3 and TX.3.1 *continued* | | and nutrition interview that is usually conducted by the physician, nurse, and administrator surveyor. The hospital should ensure that the appropriate pharmacy leadership and staff attend, as well as medical, nursing, and administrative staff involved in the formulary management process and other medication management processes throughout the organization. Any surveyor may also ask questions from thc medication use interview to any associate throughout the organization involved with medication management processes, including ordering, prescribing, preparing, dispensing, administering, and monitoring for effect. | | |
| TX 3.2 | The proposed standard requires that health professionals involved in the medication use process have access to and use patient and medication information that is important in prescribing, dispensing, administering, and monitoring medications.<br><br>(Formerly addressed in TX.3.5.3)<br><br>Pharmacy leaders should ensure that pharmacists and appropriate clinical staff have readily available information relevant to | Minimum requirements for the content of medication profiles should be defined.<br><br>• Clinical staff interviews<br>• Organizational and pharmacy service policies and procedures regarding minimum requirements for medication-related patient information that is made available to the pharmacist and other clinical staff, including, but not limited to: patient diagnosis and disease state information, medication/food | • How does the pharmacy service assure that medication-related patient information is accessible?<br>• Who is responsible for maintaining patient medication profiles? Who has access to this information?<br>• What important information is contained in each patient's medication profile?<br>• How is a patient's medication and/or food allergy history obtained and documented?<br>• Who is able to update information on the patient's medication | |

*continues*

**Care of Patients: Medication**

| Standard | Comments | Evidence | Staff Questions | Reference |
|---|---|---|---|---|
| TX 3.2 *continued* | each patient's medication regimen in order to facilitate continuity of care and create an accurate drug profile and to ensure the safe dispensing and administering of medications. | allergies, height/weight/body surface area, comorbidities, pregnancy and lactation status, current medications and medication history (including prescription, over-the-counter, herbal medications and home remedies), medication dosages, routes of administration, frequencies and duration of therapy, dispensing history, patient care and medication order comments and clarification, and pharmacist intervention documentation<br>• Open and closed records showing compliance with organizational policies regarding patient medication profiles<br>• Patient medication profiles<br>• Orientation and continuing education records for pharmacy associates, nurses, and prescribers regarding the use of the medication profile and pertinent patient information in medication preparation and dispensing | profile (manual vs. computerized)?<br>• Describe the medication order profiling process and give an example of how a patient medication profile is used in dispensing a medication. | |
| TX 3.3 | This proposed standard relates to the organization's ongoing evaluation and improvement of its medication use processes.<br><br>Pharmacy leaders should participate in | • Clinical staff interviews<br>• Organizational and pharmacy policies and procedures regarding:<br>–Evaluation of emerging technologies and medication systems<br>–Evaluation of techniques shown to | • How are pharmacists involved in reviewing and evaluating new medication systems and procedures?<br>• What is the organization's policy for evaluating medication | |

*continues*

**Care of Patients: Medication**

| Standard | Comments | Evidence | Staff Questions | Reference |
|---|---|---|---|---|
| TX.3.3 *continued* | the organization's review and evaluation of new technologies, systems, and procedures that have been demonstrated to improve the safety and accuracy of the medication use process as it relates to selection, procurement, storage, preparation, and dispensing of medications and monitoring of their effects on patients, and if feasible, ensure that those systems and procedures are implemented. | improve the safety and accuracy of medication systems in other organizations (e.g., best practices) | systems in other organizations? | |
| TX.3.4 and TX.3.4.1 | The proposed standards require that the organization identify and select appropriate medications available for prescribing or ordering within the organization, and have a process for procuring medications not usually available.<br><br>(These standards incorporate the issues addressed by former TX.3 through TX.3.2.)<br><br>Pharmacy leaders should participate in the organization's development and maintenance of an inventory of medications to ensure that medications prescribed or ordered are readily available, and should ensure that a formulary of medications that are always available for immediate use is maintained. The | • Clinical staff interviews<br>• Formulary document<br>• Documentation of criteria used in selection of medications for inclusion in formulary, demonstrating that need, effectiveness, risks, and cost impact have been taken into consideration<br>• Documentation of reviews of recently approved medications<br>• Organizational and pharmacy policies and procedures regarding procurement, formulary management, storage of medications, security of medications inside and outside of pharmacy areas, procurement of drugs when pharmacy areas are closed, dispensing of medications to patient at discharge from emergency department, and sample drugs | • Describe the role of Pharmacy and Therapeutics or Formulary committee.<br>• How is the medical staff involved in the selection of drugs for the formulary?<br>• How are drugs added to the formulary?<br>• What role does nursing play in the formulary process?<br>• What happens if a patient needs a drug that is not on the formulary?<br>• How is the organization's clinical staff made aware of drugs that are added to/deleted from the formulary?<br>• How does the organization handle drug shortages and outages? | |

*continues*

**Care of Patients: Medication**

| Standard | Comments | Evidence | Staff Questions | Reference |
|---|---|---|---|---|
| TX.3.4 and TX.3.4.1 *continued* | formulary process should be collaborative and represent all disciplines and types of patients serviced. Safety and patient need should be stressed as well as economics. The formulary process should include a process for the timely acquisition of medications not usually available in the organization. | • Pharmacy and Therapeutics or Formulary committees and subcommittees (e.g., Antibiotic Surveillance, Medication Usage Evaluation, etc.) policies and procedures, and minutes<br>• Evidence of physician knowledge and participation in the formulary process<br>• Evidence of pharmacy staff education regarding responsibilities for medication usage (e.g., ADRs, medication errors, medication usage evaluations, protocols for handling drug shortages, approved substitution protocols, etc.) | | |
| TX.3.5 | The proposed standard relates to the storage of medications under proper conditions of sanitation, temperature, light, moisture, ventilation, segregation, and safety, consistent with applicable laws and regulations and accepted standards of practice.<br><br>(This standard incorporates portions of former TX.3.3 and TX.3.4 as they related to medication storage.)<br><br>Pharmacy leaders should ensure organizational, legal, and regulatory adherence to proper storage and securing of all medications, with special focus | • Clinical staff interviews<br>• Organizational and pharmacy service policies and procedures regarding:<br>– Labeling of medications<br>– Expired medication surveillance<br>– Investigational drug processes<br>– Control, handling, and documentation of blood products<br>– Control, handling, and documentation of radioactive medications<br>– Control, handling, and documentation of radiographic contrast media<br>– Sample medication policies | • What systems are in place to ensure that expired medications are not used for patients?<br>• Are sample medications used within the organization?<br>• What is the policy and procedure for the use of sample medications (e.g., security, labeling, and dispensing method, documentation requirements, recall mechanism)?<br>• Where are investigational drugs stored? Who has access to them?<br>• Are there any special policies or procedures for wasting a controlled substance? Who has access to controlled substances? | |

*continues*

**Care of Patients: Medication**

| Standard | Comments | Evidence | Staff Questions | Reference |
|---|---|---|---|---|
| TX.3.5 *continued* | on controlled substances, investigational drugs, medication samples, radioactive medications, blood derivatives, and radiographic contrast. | • Controlled substance records and documentation<br>• Open and closed records focusing on appropriate documentation of storage and securing of medications<br>• Applicable standards and guidelines from professional organizations incorporated into departmental and/or organizational policies and procedures regarding medication storage<br>• Medication refrigerator temperature logs in all medication storage areas, including patient care areas (previous 12 months of records required), defining the appropriate temperature range<br>• Multidose parenteral, ophthalmic, and topical product storage locations and labeling<br>• Multidisciplinary orientation and continuing education materials and attendance records regarding legal and regulatory requirements for controlled substances and medication use and storage, and multidose product use, storage, and labeling<br><br>Tour of medication areas:<br><br>• Medication labeling (including medications given to patients at discharge, investigational medications, sample medications, multidose medications) | • Have any significant controlled substance losses been reported to the Drug Enforcement Administration (DEA) within the last year?<br>• Are there special storage requirements for medications with a high potential for serious medication errors, such as sound-alike and look-alike drugs?<br>• How often are storage areas inspected to ensure that expired, discontinued, or contaminated medications are removed? | |

*continues*

**Care of Patients: Medication**

| Standard | Comments | Evidence | Staff Questions | Reference |
|---|---|---|---|---|
| TX.3.5 *continued* | | • Security of medication storage areas<br>• Expired medications<br>• Controlled substance documentation<br>• Segregation of medications to minimize storage-associated errors (e.g., dangerous non-drug chemicals separated from medications) | | |
| TX.3.5.1 | The proposed standard requires that emergency medications and supplies be consistently available, controlled, and secure in the pharmacy and patient care areas.<br><br>(This standard was formerly designated as TX.3.5.5.)<br><br>Pharmacy leaders should adhere to organizational policies that ensure that emergency medications and supplies are available for use in all patient care areas when needed, but are properly secured and are either locked or under constant surveillance by licensed health care professionals.<br><br>Note: The security of medications in patient care areas is a shared pharmacy/nursing responsibility. All nursing staff members should routinely check secured emergency medication locations.<br><br>Sealed, pharmacy-controlled emergency | • Clinical staff interviews<br>• Organizational, pharmacy, and nursing policies and procedures regarding:<br>– Availability and control of emergency medications to include the process for availability, security, multidisciplinary monitoring responsibilities, and control of emergency boxes and locks, if applicable<br>– Routine organizational review of emergency medication inventory, policies, authorized patient care areas (e.g., through Pharmacy and Therapeutics or Formulary committee, Risk Management committee, etc.)<br>– Logs, checklists, etc., supporting organizational policy regarding monitoring of emergency medication availability, control, expiration dating, and security (previous 12 months of records required | • How does the organization ensure that emergency medications are always available, controlled, and secured?<br>• Who is responsible for inspecting emergency medication supplies? How often?<br>• How do staff know what is the appropriate inventory, location, and security of emergency medications?<br>• How are the availability, control, and security of emergency medications routinely reviewed?<br>• Who is responsible for the availability, control, and security of emergency medications?<br>• How long are records regarding emergency medication availability, control, and security kept and where? | |

*continues*

**Care of Patients: Medication**

| Standard | Comments | Evidence | Staff Questions | Reference |
|---|---|---|---|---|
| TX.3.5.1 *continued* | kits or boxes are not required to meet the intent of this standard; however, this may be the most appropriate means to ensure organizational compliance with this far-reaching standard. | • Orientation and continuing education records for staff regarding the organizational policies and procedures for the availability, control, and securing of emergency medications<br><br>Note: Pharmacy areas and patient care areas throughout the organization where emergency medications are stored will be a focus for surveyors. Special attention will be paid to adherence with organizational, pharmacy, and nursing policies and procedures. | | |
| TX. 3.5.2 | The proposed standard relates to a medication recall system that provides for retrieval and safe disposition of recalled and discontinued medications.<br><br>(This standard was formerly designated as TX.3.5.6).<br><br>Pharmacy leaders should ensure that comprehensive medication recall policies and procedures are followed wherever medications are used or stored throughout the organization. | • Clinical staff interviews<br>• Organizational and pharmacy service policies and procedures regarding a comprehensive medication recall, which should include:<br>– Identifying any medication subject to discontinuation for safety reasons or a recall, and all potential areas where the medication was used or stored<br>– Process for retrieving and disposing of recalled medication, quarantine, replacement with a safe substitute, and returning recalled medications, as directed on the recall notice<br>– Informing physicians, staff, and others, as appropriate, of the | • What is the organizational and pharmacy service policy and procedure for recalled or discontinued medications?<br>• How is the organization informed of medications recalls?<br>• How does the pharmacy service notify areas where medications are used or stored of a medication recall?<br>• How are recalled medications disposed of?<br>• Where are records of recalled medications kept?<br>• How were you oriented to the organization's medication recall policy? | |

*continues*

**Care of Patients: Medication**

| Standard | Comments | Evidence | Staff Questions | Reference |
|---|---|---|---|---|
| TX.3.5.2 *continued* | | recall or discontinuance and of patients who may have received any medication that was recalled or discontinued for safety reasons<br>• Complete records of all medication recalls with verification of on-hand inventory checks for identified manufacturer lot numbers<br>• Orientation and continuing records for staff regarding their responsibilities for the organization's medication recall system | | |
| TX.3.6 and TX.3.7 | The proposed standard concerns the development and implementation of policies for safe medication prescribing or ordering and transcribing.<br><br>(This standard consolidates the standards contained in former TX.3.5 through TX.3.5.1.)<br><br>Pharmacy leaders should ensure that policies and procedures are in place to ensure control of all medications used within the organization. Policies and procedures should include:<br>• Standardized medication labeling throughout the organization<br>• Dispensing of medications in individual doses to minimize potential errors | • Clinical staff interviews<br>• Pharmacy and organizational policies and procedures regarding:<br>– A process for ensuring that all medication orders are clear, accurate, complete, legible, and unambiguous, including defining<br>1. The required elements of a complete medical order<br>2. Abbreviations, symbols, acronyms, and codes that are unacceptable because of possible misinterpretation<br>3. When generic or trade drug names are acceptable as part of a medication order<br>4. When indication for use is required on a medication order | • Who is authorized/ credentialed to prescribe medications throughout the organization? How do you know?<br>• Can certain drugs be prescribed only by specific physicians?<br>• How are these prescribing restrictions and list of authorized prescribers disseminated to the clinical staff?<br>• Who has access to information contained on the medication profiles?<br>• How do pharmacists document drug therapy interventions?<br>• How many drug therapy interventions are documented annually?<br>• Who has access to medications stored in the point of use distribution cabinets? How is the stock of medications in these units maintained? How often are they checked? | |

*continues*

**Care of Patients: Medication**

| Standard | Comments | Evidence | Staff Questions | Reference |
|---|---|---|---|---|
| TX.3.6 and TX.3.7 *continued* | • Utilization of point of use distribution or automated dispensing technologies, if applicable | 5. Special procedures for ordering drugs with look-alike or sound-alike names<br>6. Actions to be taken when medication orders are unclear, incomplete or illegible<br>–Minimizing the use of verbal medication orders and defining a process for validating the accuracy of verbal medication orders<br>–A process for using, reviewing, and updating preprinted order sheets<br>–Defining situations in which all or some of a patient's medication orders can be permanently or temporarily canceled, and mechanisms for reinstating them<br>–Specifying the unacceptability of blanket orders<br>–"As needed" (PRN) vs. scheduled prescriptions<br>–Standardizing times of dose administration, concentration of IV medications, and dose scales<br>–Appropriate use of patient-controlled analgesia (PCA), spinal/epidural or IV medication administration, and other pain management techniques<br>–Specifying the appropriate use, required elements, and approval process for | • What checks and balances are in place to prevent potential distribution or dispensing errors with chemotherapy products? With point of use distribution cabinets or automated dispensing machines?<br>• How do you report a suspected ADR or medication error?<br>• How does the unit dose drug distribution system work?<br>• How were you oriented to the medication use policies and procedures within the organization? | |

*continues*

**Care of Patients: Medication**

| Standard | Comments | Evidence | Staff Questions | Reference |
|---|---|---|---|---|
| TX.3.6 and TX.3.7 *continued* | | 1. Standing orders<br>2. Medication protocols<br>3. Titrating orders<br>4. Taper orders<br>5. PRN orders<br>6. Dose scales<br>7. Range orders<br>8. Orders for compounded drugs<br>9. Orders for medication-related devices<br>10. Orders for investigational medications, home remedies, and herbal products<br>11. Discharge orders<br>• Policies and procedures regarding:<br>–Authorized or credentialed prescribers<br>–Patient medication assessment<br>–ADR surveillance<br>–Medication error surveillance<br>–Parenteral nutrition and chemotherapy prescribing, profiling, production, and dispensing<br>–Controlled substances procedures and documentation<br>• Open and closed medical records for pharmacist intervention documentation<br>• Patient medication profiles<br>• Medication labels<br>• Stocking and dispensing records, fill lists, checklists<br>• Orientation and continuing education records for pharmacy | | |

*continues*

**Care of Patients: Medication**

| Standard | Comments | Evidence | Staff Questions | Reference |
|---|---|---|---|---|
| TX.3.6 and TX.3.7 *continued* | | associates, nurses, physicians, and other prescribers regarding the preparation and dispensing of medications<br>• Prescriber's signature verification logs, narcotics registration numbers<br>• Tours of pharmacy and other areas where medications are prepared and dispensed | | |
| TX.3.7 and TX.3.7.1 | These standards relate to pharmacist review of prescriptions or medication orders and consideration of pharmaceutical issues in selecting the appropriate method for administering the medication.<br><br>These standards were formerly designated as TX.3.5.2.<br><br>A pharmacist should review each prescription or medication order against the medication profile and other relevant patient information before the drug is dispensed in order to identify:<br>• Appropriateness of the drug, dose, frequency, and route of administration<br>• Therapeutic duplication in the patient's medication regimen<br>• Any medication allergies<br>• Real or potential significant interactions of the drug with | • Clinical and administrative staff interviews<br>• Tour of the pharmacy and other areas where medications are prepared and dispensed<br>• Pharmacy and organizational policies and procedures addressing:<br>– Prospective pharmacist review of each medication prescription or order prior to dispensing<br>– Process for contacting the prescriber for medication order clarification<br>– Dispensing and distribution of medications by the pharmacy and other patient care areas<br>– Medication error surveillance<br>– Medication order profiling (manual vs. computerized)<br>– Medication profiles<br>– Criteria for selecting appropriate method of administration (e.g., the use of an infusion control device) based on the | • Who has access to information contained on the medication profiles?<br>• Who is responsible for reviewing the appropriateness of prescribed medications?<br>• How do pharmacists document drug therapy interventions?<br>• What happens when a question arises about a medication order or prescription?<br>• How do you report a suspected medication error?<br>• How were you oriented to the medication management policies and procedures within the organization? | |

*continues*

**Care of Patients: Medication**

| Standard | Comments | Evidence | Staff Questions | Reference |
|---|---|---|---|---|
| TX.3.7 and TX.3.7.1 *continued* | other drugs, food, lab, or disease<br>• Contraindications to use<br>• Any organizational criteria for use or for selecting the method of administration<br>Exceptions to this procedure include:<br>• During medical emergencies and STAT orders<br>• Medications used in certain treatment areas where a licensed independent practitioner controls the prescribing and administration of the medication, e.g., cardiac catheterization, endoscopy, surgery, radiology, emergency department, or during cardiorespiratory arrest resuscitation<br>• Medication orders that have been entered by a physician into a computerized physician order entry (CPOE) system that has an active physician alert mechanism and an approved set of checks and balances; however, when a CPOE system is in use, a pharmacist must review medication orders retrospectively as soon as possible<br>For organizations that do not provide 24-hour/day pharmacy services, nurses may administer | medication and dose to be administered<br>• Orientation and continuing education records for pharmacy associates regarding review of medication orders against medication profiles. | | |

*continues*

**Care of Patients: Medication**

| Standard | Comments | Evidence | Staff Questions | Reference |
|---|---|---|---|---|
| TX.3.7 and TX.3.7.1 *continued* | any medication without prior pharmacist's review when a pharmacist is not on the premises; in such cases, however, the organization must develop an alternative system for medication order review that must include:<br>• Retrospective review of the orders by a pharmacist as soon as the pharmacy reopens<br>• A qualified health care professional review of the order prior to administration of the medication for appropriateness against an information database<br>• Ongoing monitoring of this process for the incidence of medication errors | | | |
| TX.3.8 | This standard concerns the safe preparation of medications under proper conditions.<br><br>The standard addresses issues that were addressed by former TX.3.4 and TX.3.5.<br><br>Pharmacy leaders should ensure that policies and procedures are in place to ensure that medications are safely and accurately prepared. When applicable, standards and guidelines established by the ASHP, the American Pharmaceutical Association, OSHA, and other professional | • Clinical staff interviews<br>• Pharmacy and organizational policies and procedures regarding:<br>– Preparing medications and products using appropriate pharmaceutical and aseptic techniques<br>– Preparing medication according to approved directions<br>– Using the metric measurement system<br>– Visually inspecting ingredients and final products for inappropriate particulate matter or signs of deterioration or of microbial contamination | • How often are laminar flow hoods and other equipment used in the preparation of pharmaceuticals certified?<br>• How is the competency of the staff preparing parenteral products ensured?<br>• Who keeps clean room cleaning records?<br>• Are there any restrictions regarding the use of support personnel in the pharmacy? | |

*continues*

**Care of Patients: Medication**

| Standard | Comments | Evidence | Staff Questions | Reference |
|---|---|---|---|---|
| TX.3.8 *continued* | organizations should be utilized. | – Using accepted quality control systems<br>– Using packaging processes that ensure the safety of personnel and prevent error<br>– Preparing and packaging medications (including labeling and expiration dating) according to United States Pharmacopoeia (USP) standards and all applicable laws and regulations<br>– Preparing sterile medications under proper conditions in accordance with laws and regulations and accepted standards of practice<br>• Required certification documents for equipment used in preparation of medications (i.e., balances, laminar flow hoods, automated parenteral mixing devices, etc.)<br>• Appropriate laminar flow hood and clean room cleaning records<br>• Packaging and production records<br>• Applicable standards and guidelines from professional organizations incorporated into organizational and/or pharmacy policies and procedures regarding medication preparation, procedures for aseptic technique, and the preparation of parenteral products<br><br>Tour of medication preparation areas: | | |

*continues*

**Care of Patients: Medication**

| Standard | Comments | Evidence | Staff Questions | Reference |
|---|---|---|---|---|
| TX.3.8 *continued* | | • Clean, uncluttered, functionally separate areas for sterile product preparation<br>• Laminar airflow hood or other class 100 environment for preparing sterile products<br>• Safety equipment (e.g., biological safety cabinets) to protect personnel preparing cytotoxic or hazardous medications)<br>• Clean, disinfected work surfaces that are free of materials, paper, and equipment unnecessary for preparing a given medication or TPN therapy solution | | |
| TX.3.9 | The proposed standard relates to appropriate labeling of medications.<br><br>Pharmacy leaders should ensure that policies and procedures are in place to ensure that all medications are properly labeled, and if medications are prepared or dispensed by departments other than the pharmacy, that the labeling requirements and information on the label are equivalent throughout the organization. Special attention should be paid to local and federal laws and regulations and professional standards of practice governing medication labeling. | • Clinical staff interviews<br>• Pharmacy and organizational policies and procedures implementing a standardized method for labeling all medications dispensed to or prepared for use by patients, including:<br>– Drug name<br>– Strength<br>– Amount (if not apparent by the container, e.g., gradations on a syringe)<br>– Expiration date<br>– If dispensed for administration by another individual, any applicable cautionary statements (e.g., requires refrigeration, for IM use only, etc.)<br>– Scheduled date, time, and rate of adminis- | • What information is required by law on inpatient and outpatient prescription labels?<br>• What is the policy and procedure for labeling sample medications? Multidose medications? Medications dispensed to patients at discharge?<br>• How were you oriented to the medication labeling procedures within the organization? | |

*continues*

**Care of Patients: Medication**

| Standard | Comments | Evidence | Staff Questions | Reference |
|---|---|---|---|---|
| TX.3.9 *continued* | | tration (compounded IV admixtures and TPN solutions)<br>– Infusion products (including plain IVs) have label on the container, not the overwrap<br>• Medication labels (including medications given to patients at discharge, sample medications, investigational medications, multidose medications)<br>• Multidisciplinary orientation and continuing education materials and attendance records regarding legal, regulatory, and organizational requirements for medication labeling | | |
| TX.3.10 | The proposed standard concerns the organization's implementation of a safe and effective patient medication dose distribution system.<br><br>This standard was formerly designated TX.3.5.1.<br><br>Pharmacy leaders are responsible for controlling and distributing all medications used in the organization. When departments other than the pharmacy distribute medications, the pharmacy must design, monitor, and assure that the medication distribution system and controls used meet applicable laws and regula- | • Clinical staff interviews<br>• Organizationwide and pharmacy policies and procedures ensuring that medications are dispensed in the most ready-to-administer form possible<br>• Policies and procedures regarding unit dose distribution system<br>• Policies and procedures regarding dispensing and distribution of medications by the pharmacy and other patient care areas | • How does the unit dose drug distribution system work?<br>• How were you oriented to the unit dose distribution system within the organization? | |

*continues*

**Care of Patients: Medication**

| Standard | Comments | Evidence | Staff Questions | Reference |
|---|---|---|---|---|
| TX.3.10 *continued* | tions, accepted standards of practice, and organizational policies and procedures. | | | |
| TX.3.11 | The proposed standard concerns the organization's process to ensure that medications are dispensed accurately to the patient for whom they are prescribed.<br><br>Pharmacy leaders are responsible for implementing procedures to ensure that medications are prepared, dispensed, and distributed to the patient in a timely manner, using a system that ensures accuracy and safety and documents all dispensing activities. | • Clinical staff interviews<br>• Policies and procedures regarding:<br>– Control of the preparation, dispensing, and distribution of medications<br>– Dispensing medications to patients at discharge<br>Procurement, storage, control, and distribution of medications obtained from outside sources<br>– Procurement, storage, control, distribution, administration, and documentation of radioactive medications<br>– Procurement, storage, control, distribution, administration, monitoring, and documentation of blood derivatives, radiographic contrast media and other diagnostic drugs, and IV solutions<br>– Floor stock medication control processes to minimize the risk of ADRs or medication errors<br>– Expired medication surveillance<br>– Controlled substance records and documentation<br>– Investigational drug processes<br>– Sample medication policies<br>– PRN medications | • Describe how medication preparation and dispensing processes are controlled.<br>• Is there a pharmacy-based IV additive program in use? If not, how is the appropriate and safe preparation of IV medication ensured?<br>• What systems are in place to ensure that expired medications are not used for patients?<br>• What is the policy and procedure for the use of sample medications (e.g., security, labeling and dispensing methods; documentation requirements)?<br>• Describe the organization's medication stop order policy.<br>• Where are investigational drugs stored? Who has access to them?<br>• Are there any special policies or procedures for wasting a controlled substance? Who has access to controlled substances?<br>• Who is responsible for handling radioactive medications? What special orientation or continuing education did you receive regarding radiographic contrast drugs?<br>• Who is responsible for handling blood derivatives? What special orientation or continuing | |

*continues*

**Care of Patients: Medication**

| Standard | Comments | Evidence | Staff Questions | Reference |
|---|---|---|---|---|
| TX.3.11 *continued* | | – Medication stop order policies<br>– PI initiatives involving medication usage<br>• Open and closed records focusing on appropriate documentation of preparation, dispensing, and distribution of medications<br>• Applicable standards and guidelines from professional organizations incorporated into departmental and/or organizational policies and procedures regarding medication procurement and storage, control, distribution, administration, and monitoring<br>Tour of medication areas:<br>Patient medication dispensing and administration documentation/ profiles<br>• Controlled substance documentation<br>• Medication labeling<br>• Repackaging and IV/ total parenteral nutrition production areas and records<br>• Security of medication storage areas<br>• Expired medications | education did you receive regarding blood derivative drugs? | |
| TX.3.12 | The proposed standard concerns the organization's provision of pharmacy services when the on-site pharmacy is closed or unavailable.<br><br>This standard is similar to former TX.3.5.4. | • Clinical staff interviews<br>• Organizational and pharmacy policies and procedures regarding:<br>– Pharmacy services when the pharmacy is closed<br>– Use, regulation, and replenishment of night cabinets, point | • How are medications obtained, prepared, and dispensed when the on-site pharmacy service is closed or unavailable?<br>• Who has access to night cabinets, after-hours carts, or point of use distribution cabinets? | |

*continues*

**Care of Patients: Medication**

| Standard | Comments | Evidence | Staff Questions | Reference |
|---|---|---|---|---|
| TX.3.12 *continued* | Pharmacy leaders should ensure that the appropriate policies for the safe provision of pharmacy services are in place at times when the pharmacy is closed. These policies should include a retrospective review by a pharmacist of the activities during hours when the pharmacy is closed or unavailable.<br><br>Organizational and pharmacy policies should limit the conditions under which non-pharmacist health care professionals are used to obtain medications when the pharmacy is closed, as follows:<br>• The medication supply is limited to an approved set of medications that may be stored in a night cabinet, automated medication device, or a limited section of the pharmacy<br>• Limited personnel are involved and are trained on the process and the medications available<br>• A qualified pharmacist is available either on-call or at another location to answer staff questions or provide unavailable medications<br>• There is an ongoing monitoring of the process, of which medications are accessed and why, and of the incidence | of use distribution systems<br>– Authorized non-pharmacists in the pharmacy after hours<br>– Quantities and doses of available medications<br>– Emergency access to a qualified pharmacist for answers to drug information questions and preparation and dispensing of unavailable medications<br>– Retrospective pharmacist review of all after-hours medication access<br>• Records regarding after-hours access to the pharmacy, dispensing, and inventory<br>• Night cabinet and point of use system pharmacy inspection documents<br>• Orientation and continuing education records of personnel required to access medication after hours | • How are night cabinets, after-hours carts, or point of use distribution cabinets replenished?<br>• Who has access to the pharmacy after hours?<br>• Is there an "on-call" pharmacist schedule for times when the pharmacy is closed or unavailable?<br>• How is staff oriented to the organization's policies and procedures for accessing medications when the pharmacy is closed or unavailable? | |

*continues*

**Care of Patients: Medication**

| Standard | Comments | Evidence | Staff Questions | Reference |
|---|---|---|---|---|
| TX.3.12 *continued* | of medication errors as compared to when the pharmacy is open | | | |
| TX.3.13 | The proposed standard concerns the safe and accurate administration of medications after prescriptions or orders have been verified and the patient identified.<br><br>The standard was formerly addressed in TX.3.6.<br><br>Pharmacy leaders should ensure that medication profiling, dispensing, and administration policies and procedures include prescription or order verification by competent pharmacy, medical, or nursing personnel before a medication is administered. A process for identifying a patient prior to medication administration is vital. | • Clinical staff interviews<br>• Additional policies and procedures for medication administration regarding:<br>– Identifying staff members who are qualified to administer medications with and without supervision<br>– Limiting administration of medication to qualified staff who are knowledgeable about the patient, the medication, and the method of administration (including any medication administration device)<br>– The process for the administration of any first dose of any new medication<br>– Special precautions and requirements for high-risk or high-alert drugs<br>– Checks and balances in medication prescribing, profiling, dispensing, and administering, and the responsibilities of the pharmacists, physicians, and nurses involved in the process<br>– Available resources (pharmacists, references, databases) for clarification of perceived problems with medications | • Describe the process of verifying prescription orders before medication is administered to a patient.<br>• How are patients identified and verified prior to medication administration?<br>• How are the various responsibilities for medication prescription, dispensing, and administration delineated?<br>• Describe the procedure for administering the first dose of a new medication to a patient.<br>• What do you do if an incorrect medication is administered to a patient?<br>• What resources are available when you need clarification of a problem with a medication order or prescription?<br>• How were you oriented to the organization's medication administration policy and procedure? | |

*continues*

**Care of Patients: Medication**

| Standard | Comments | Evidence | Staff Questions | Reference |
|---|---|---|---|---|
| TX.3.13 *continued* | | – Escalation process for conflicts with or errors in medication prescribing, dispensing, and administering<br>• Orientation and continuing education for staff regarding medication administration policies and procedures<br><br>Note: During the tour of patient care areas, surveyors may observe medication administration for adherence to organizational policies and procedures. | | |
| TX.3.13.1 | The proposed standard relates to the organization's response to adverse drug events.<br><br>Pharmacy leaders should be involved in the organization's development of a process for those who administer medications to respond appropriately to adverse drug events, adverse drug reactions, toxic drug reactions, and anaphylaxis. | • Clinical staff interviews<br>• Organizational and pharmacy service policies and procedures regarding:<br>– Maintaining a list of common signs and symptoms of adverse drug events and toxicity for various classes of medication<br>– The appropriate action to be taken when an adverse drug event occurs<br>– The availability of appropriate medications, supplies, and equipment to respond to adverse drug events<br>– Protocols for administering medications or treatments to respond to adverse drug events<br>– Notification of the patient's physician, the prescriber (if different), the pharmacist, and others | • Describe your organization's policy regarding the appropriate action to take when an adverse drug event, ADR, toxic drug reaction, or anaphylaxis occurs.<br>• Who do you notify in the event of an adverse drug event?<br>• How do you report a suspected drug interaction? Medication error?<br>• What is the organization's definition of an adverse drug event?<br>• How do you report a serious adverse drug reaction to the Food and Drug Administration (FDA) and manufacturer? | |

*continues*

**Care of Patients: Medication**

| Standard | Comments | Evidence | Staff Questions | Reference |
|---|---|---|---|---|
| TX.3.13.1 *continued* | | involved in the patient's care<br>– Any related patient instruction<br>– Reporting the occurrence both internally and externally (e.g., to FDA, USP)<br>• Adverse drug event reports (previous 12 months of data)<br>• Pharmacy and Therapeutics or Formulary committee minutes or other committee minutes (Quality, Risk Management, etc.) where adverse drug events, medication errors are reported and tracked<br>• Orientation and continuing education records of staff involved with medication dispensing, administering, and monitoring for medication effects | | |
| TX.3.14 | The proposed standard concerns the organization's process for managing medications brought in by the patient and for the safe self-administration of medications.<br><br>The content of this standard was formerly designated as TX.3.7.<br><br>Pharmacy leaders should participate in the organization's development of written criteria to determine when medications brought in by patients or families can safely be | • Clinical staff, patient, and family interviews<br>• Organizational and pharmacy policies and procedures regarding:<br>– Medication administration<br>– The use of medications brought into the hospital by patients, family, or friends; this should include written criteria that must be met before such medications may be used, and identification, verification, and labeling of such medications by pharmacy and nursing staff prior to | • What are the hospital's policies and procedures regarding medications that a patient or family member brings into the hospital?<br>• Are patients permitted to administer medications to themselves? If so, under what circumstances?<br>• Are family members permitted to administer medications to patients? If so, under what circumstances?<br>• How were you oriented to the organization's policies and procedures regarding medications brought into the organi- | |

*continues*

**Care of Patients: Medication**

| Standard | Comments | Evidence | Staff Questions | Reference |
|---|---|---|---|---|
| TX.3.14 *continued* | used. When the criteria have been met and the prescriber has ordered self-administration, the pharmacy participates in procedures that ensure safe and accurate self-administration, including appropriate training and supervision of the patient, appropriate storage of medications for self-administration, and documentation of administration. | administration or self-administration<br>– Administration of medications by patients or family members<br>• Orientation and continuing education records regarding medications brought into the hospital by patients or family members and self or family medication administration policies and procedures | zation and self or family medication administration? | |
| TX.3.15 | This proposed standard relates to monitoring medication effects.<br><br>This standard was formerly designated as TX.3.9.<br><br>Pharmacy leaders should ensure that organizational and pharmacy service programs, policies, and procedures are in place to ensure that medication monitoring is collaborative and includes the patient and/or family. Medication outcome monitoring programs should be designed to improve the patient's medication therapy. A comprehensive program should ensure that:<br>• Each patient is monitored on an ongoing basis for medication effectiveness and actual or potential medication-related problems, which may include: | • Clinical staff interviews<br>• Organizational and pharmacy service policies and procedures regarding:<br>– Medication assessment<br>– Unit dose distribution system<br>– Medication profiling (manual vs. computerized)<br>– Pharmacist intervention documentation<br>– ADR surveillance<br>– Medication error surveillance<br>– Medication usage evaluation program<br>– Medication prescribing, dispensing, administering, and monitoring<br>– Medication order conflict resolution and escalation process for conflicts with or errors in prescribing, dispensing, and administering medication<br>– Medication profile<br>– Pain assessment | • Who is responsible for the continual monitoring of medication effects on patients?<br>• How are the effects of medications monitored by nurses, pharmacists, and physicians?<br>• How does the organization document monitoring for medication effectiveness?<br>• How does the organization determine which medications should be reviewed under the medication usage evaluation program? How does it work? Where/how does the organization communicate aggregate medical usage evaluation information?<br>• How do you report a suspected drug interaction or medication error?<br>• What PI initiatives have you been involved with regarding medication use and preventing negative medication outcomes?<br>• How does the organization define an ADR? A medication error? | |

*continues*

**Care of Patients: Medication**

| Standard | Comments | Evidence | Staff Questions | Reference |
|---|---|---|---|---|
| TX.3.15<br>*continued* | –Needing drug therapy but not receiving it<br>–Taking or receiving the wrong drug<br>–Taking or receiving too little or too much of the correct drug<br>–Experiencing an adverse drug reaction or drug interaction<br>–Not taking or receiving the prescribed drug<br>–Taking or receiving a drug for which there is no valid indication<br>–Abuse or misuse of a drug (such as a chemical restraint)<br>–Therapeutic duplication of a drug or contraindications<br>• Interactions with prescribers to avoid potential medication-related adverse events routinely documented by pharmacists, nurses, and other clinicians | –Parenteral nutrition and chemotherapy prescription, profiling, production, and dispensing<br>• Documentation of pharmacist intervention<br>• Drug-related information resources, databases, online subscription services for minimum/maximum doses, drug interaction checking, duplication checking, compatibility checking, etc.<br>• ADR and medication error surveillance data (previous 12 months of data required)<br>• Pharmacy and Therapeutics or Formulary committee minutes or other committee minutes where ADR, medication error, and medication use PI are reported and tracked<br>• PI initiatives and data regarding medication use and monitoring<br>• Open and closed medical record review for daily documentation regarding nursing and multidisciplinary monitoring and reporting of medication effects<br>• Orientation and continuing education records of staff involved with medication prescribing, dispensing, administering, and monitoring for medication effects | • What PI initiatives have been implemented within the last 12 months to improve the reporting of suspected ADRs and medication errors?<br>• How do you report a serious ADR to the FDA and manufacturer?<br>• What information resources are available to assist with monitoring for medication effectiveness and preventing negative medication outcomes?<br>• How are medication overdoses identified and prevented?<br>• How is the effectiveness of medications used to treat patients in pain monitored and documented?<br>• How is the effectiveness of parenteral nutrition monitored and documented?<br>• How are the effects of chemotherapy agents monitored and documented?<br>• How were you oriented to the hospital's policies, procedures, and programs regarding medication use and monitoring for medication effects? | |

*continues*

**Care of Patients: Medication**

| Standard | Comments | Evidence | Staff Questions | Reference |
|---|---|---|---|---|
| TX.3.16 through TX.3.19 | These proposed standards address the procedures and processes the organization uses for the safe control of special medications, i.e., those with a high potential for serious adverse drug events; investigational medications; sample medications; and controlled substances.<br><br>Pharmacy leaders should participate in the development and use of special procedures and processes for special medications, including:<br>• Extra safety steps and quality control steps for procuring, storing, prescribing or ordering, transcribing, preparing, dispensing, administering, and monitoring high-risk medications (i.e., those that resulted in a sentinel event at the organization or as nationally reported, and those identified in the literature with a high potential for significant adverse drug events)<br>• Processes to ensure that investigational or clinical medication studies are conducted safely, specifically addressing:<br>– Procuring investigational medications<br>– Obtaining information about the medication's use, | • Clinical staff interviews<br>• Organizational and pharmacy policies and procedures regarding medications with a high potential for serious adverse drug events, investigational medications<br>• Investigational drug inventory documents, reports of study monitors or regulatory agencies (e.g., National Institutes of Health, etc.)<br>• Specific investigational medication protocols and waste/return guidelines<br>• Organizational and pharmacy policies and procedures regarding storage, control, dispensing, and disposal of sample medications<br>• Open and closed records showing compliance with organizational policies and legal and regulatory requirements<br>• Controlled substance records and documentation<br>• Orientation and continuing education records for staff involved with investigational medications, high-risk medications, sample medications, and/or controlled substances | • How are you made aware of medications that have resulted in sentinel events, either at the organizations or nationally?<br>• What safety checks and quality control steps do you take regarding high-risk medications?<br>• Where are high-risk medications stored?<br>• Where are investigational medications stored? Sample medications?<br>• Who is authorized to prescribe, dispense, and administer investigational medications?<br>• What becomes of unused investigational medications?<br>• What is the policy and procedure for the use of sample medications (e.g., security, labeling, and dispensing method; documentation requirements; recall mechanism)?<br>• Can any practitioner prescribe controlled substances? How do you know who is authorized to prescribed controlled substances?<br>• Are there any restrictions regarding the use of support personnel in the pharmacy?<br>• Are there any special policies or procedures for wasting a controlled substance? Who has access to controlled substances?<br>• Have any significant controlled substance losses been reported to the Drug Enforcement | |

*continues*

**Care of Patients: Medication**

| Standard | Comments | Evidence | Staff Questions | Reference |
|---|---|---|---|---|
| TX.3.16 through TX.3.19 *continued* | action, and side effects that is made available to all involved health care professionals<br>–Specific inventory control procedures<br>–Safe dispensing and distribution of medications<br>–Appropriate labeling of investigational medicines<br>–Documentation requirements<br>–Security<br>–Making pertinent parts of the investigational protocol available to all involved health care professionals, including the pharmacist<br>–Readily identifying all medication recipients<br>–Providing a continuum of care for patients who are admitted and already involved in an investigational medication protocol<br>–Destruction of investigational medications that are not used during the study<br>• A process for the storage, control, dispensing, and disposal of sample medications, to include:<br>–Appropriate selection of sample medications that will be stored within the organization, including any | | Administration (DEA) within the last year?<br>• How were you oriented to the organization's policies and procedures regarding investigational medications/high-risk medications/sample medications/controlled substances? | |

*continues*

**Care of Patients: Medication**

| Standard | Comments | Evidence | Staff Questions | Reference |
|---|---|---|---|---|
| TX.3.16 through TX.3.19 *continued* | acceptable non-formulary sample medications<br>– Proper storage, control, and accountability of sample medications<br>– Proper labeling and dispensing of sample medications, including documentation of dispensing<br>– An effective recall mechanism for sample medications<br>– Monitoring the effects of sample medications in patients<br>• Processes for controlling, dispensing, administering, disposing of, and reconciliation of controlled substances that are consistent with state and federal laws and regulations, to include:<br>– Receiving, delivering, distributing, controlling, and accounting for all controlled substances, designed to detect and prevent diversion<br>– Adequately documenting and accurately reconciling Schedule II controlled substances<br>– Appropriate disposal of all controlled substances | | | |

## CARE OF PATIENTS: NUTRITION CARE

| Standard | Comments | Evidence | Staff Questions | Reference |
|---|---|---|---|---|
| TX.4 through TX.4.1 | These standards concern nutrition care planning and the development of interdisciplinary nutrition therapy plans.<br><br>Pharmacy leaders should ensure the review, assessment, and monitoring of medications that affect nutritional status. Pharmacy leaders should also ensure that an assessment of the need for parenteral nutrition or the continued need for parenteral nutrition should be included in the nutritional assessment and reassessment. Competent pharmacists to provide this specialized service are essential. | • Staff and patient interviews<br>• Open and closed records<br>• Pharmacy service policies and procedures regarding medication assessment and reassessment, food-drug interaction checking, parenteral nutrition assessment and treatment, consultative pharmacy services<br>• Attendance and educational materials documenting pharmacist competency in parenteral nutrition assessment and monitoring | • How are pharmacists involved in the assessment and reassessment of patients requiring or receiving parenteral nutrition?<br>• How are food-drug interactions monitored?<br>• How are pharmacy and nutrition staff educated as to the appropriate assessment and reassessment of food-drug interactions and the need for parenteral nutrition?<br>• Has the organization identified the most clinically important food-drug interactions? How is a drug with a potential for a food-drug interaction identified?<br>• What laboratory indicators are used by the pharmacy service to adequately monitor the effect of food-drug interactions or parenteral nutrition? | 4–22 to 25<br>4–69 to 4–71 |
| TX.4.2 | This standard concerns the timely prescription and ordering of food and nutrition products.<br><br>Pharmacy leaders should work collaboratively with the nutrition service and other appropriate clinical departments to ensure that only authorized prescribers are ordering and reordering parenteral nutrition. | • Staff interviews<br>• Policies and procedures regarding the identification of authorized prescribers of parenteral nutrition (e.g., individual prescribers, services, parenteral nutrition team)<br>• Attendance and educational materials of orientation and continuing education regarding authorized prescribers of parenteral nutrition | • How do you know who is authorized to prescribe parenteral nutrition? | 4–21 |

*continues*

**Care of Patients: Nutrition Care**

| Standard | Comments | Evidence | Staff Questions | Reference |
|---|---|---|---|---|
| TX.4.3 and TX.4.4 | These standards relate to the safe administering and monitoring of food and nutrition products.<br><br>Pharmacy leaders should ensure that appropriately trained pharmacist resources are allocated to prepare and monitor the safe, accurate, and timely administration of parenteral nutrition products. | • Policies and procedures regarding the safe and accurate preparation and monitoring of parenteral nutrition, and fluid and electrolytes<br>• Evidence that appropriate ASHP guidelines and standards for safe and accurate preparation and monitoring of parenteral nutrition are utilized<br>• Orientation, training, and continuing education attendance and educational materials regarding parenteral nutrition preparation and monitoring<br>• Appropriate quality assurance documentation regarding safe and accurate parenteral nutrition preparation (e.g., protocols, guidelines, sterility/microbiology testing, expiration checking, inspection and calibration of automated mixing devices, laminar flow hood certification, and quality checks)<br>• Nursing policies and procedures regarding the safe administration and monitoring of parenteral nutrition products<br>• PI initiatives regarding safe and accurate parenteral nutrition preparation and monitoring<br>• Documentation of Hazard Analysis Critical Control Point (HACCP) process with regard to | • What resources are available to pharmacists to ensure the accurate and safe preparation and monitoring of parenteral nutrition and fluid and electrolytes?<br>• What orientation, education, or training do pharmacists receive to ensure safe and accurate parenteral nutrition preparation and monitoring?<br>• How are parenteral nutrition products tested for accuracy and sterility?<br>• How are nurses oriented or trained to appropriately administer and monitor parenteral nutrition therapy?<br>• Describe, if applicable, how automated mixing devices are used in the safe and accurate preparation of parenteral nutrition. How were pharmacy associates oriented and trained to utilize this technology?<br>• Who is responsible for the accuracy and safety checks on any automated equipment?<br>• What mechanism is in place for intervention once a potential fluid or electrolyte problem associated with parenteral nutrition is identified? | 4–22 to 4–25<br>4–83 to 4–86<br>4–110<br>4–116 to 4–117 |

*continues*

**Care of Patients: Nutrition Care**

| Standard | Comments | Evidence | Staff Questions | Reference |
|---|---|---|---|---|
| TX.4.3 and TX.4.4 *continued* | | food and enteral tube-feeding safety | | |
| TX.4.5 | This standard concerns nutrition care monitoring for the patient.<br><br>Pharmacy leaders should ensure that appropriately trained pharmacists are allocated to monitor the outcome of patients receiving parenteral nutrition. This may be accomplished through formal pharmacy participation on a nutrition or parenteral nutrition team or committee or by individual pharmacist contributions. A focus on monitoring each patient's therapy for pertinent food-drug interactions in collaboration with the nutrition service is important. | *See TX.4.2 through TX.4.4 above* | *See TX.4.2 through TX.4.4 above* | 4–22 to 4–25 |

## CARE OF PATIENTS: OPERATIVE AND OTHER PROCEDURES

| Standard | Comments | Evidence | Staff Questions | Reference |
|---|---|---|---|---|
| TX.5.2 through TX.5.2.2 | These standards relate to ensuring that patients receive all information necessary to give an informed consent.<br><br>Pharmacy leaders should ensure that the relative risks of all medications and blood components are included in the informed consent document. | • Staff and patient interviews<br>• Policies and procedures regarding informed consent that include potential use of medications and blood products<br>• Medical staff approval of blood products to be used within the organization (e.g., through Pharmacy and Therapeutics or Formulary committee)<br>• Open and closed records<br>• Consent forms<br>• Reasons for failure to obtain consent documented in medical record | • How was the pharmacy service involved with the design of informed consent policies and forms?<br>• Where is the discussion of relative risks of medications and blood components documented? | 4–45 to 4–46<br>4–53 |
| TX.5.4 | This standard concerns postprocedure monitoring of patients, including physiological and mental status, pathological conditions, IV fluids and drugs administered, impairments and functional status, pain intensity and quality and response to treatment, and unusual events or complications and their management. Monitoring of pain is a component of this standard.<br><br>Pharmacy leaders should ensure that medications (including blood products) administered and the patient's response to medications during the postprocedure period are included in the clinical monitoring and assessment. | • Staff interviews<br>• Policies and procedures regarding assessment, patient transfer from one postprocedure setting to another, medication and blood product administration documentation<br>• Open and closed records<br>• Inclusion of patient care checklists, tools, scoring sheets, etc., as part of the medical record, including medications administered and the response to these medications<br>• PI studies, medical record review data, and any corrective action plans regarding documentation of medications used and their response | • How was the pharmacy service involved with the design of postprocedure assessment and documentation policies, guidelines, checklists, etc.?<br>• Where is medication and blood product administration documented? Where is the patient's response to these medications and/or blood products documented? Is this a part of the medical record? | 4–1 to 4–3 |

## CARE OF PATIENTS: REHABILITATION CARE

| Standard | Comments | Evidence | Staff Questions | Reference |
|---|---|---|---|---|
| TX.6 through TX.6.5 | These standards relate to the development of a rehabilitation plan.<br><br>The providing of rehabilitation services is guided by an interdisciplinary rehabilitation plan developed by qualified professionals in conjunction with the patient and his or her family social network, and based on a functional assessment of the patient's needs.<br><br>Pharmacy leaders should ensure that pharmacist consultation is available to assist in the design and monitoring of the interdisciplinary rehabilitation plan as it relates to medications that may impact the outcome of the plan, particularly with respect to pain management. | • Pharmacy and rehabilitation medicine policies and procedures regarding medication assessment, reassessment, planning, etc.<br>• Open and closed records<br>• Staff education materials regarding pharmacy consultation/contribution to the rehabilitation care plan | • How do pharmacists contribute to the patient's rehabilitation care plan?<br>• How can pharmacists be consulted to identify or prevent specific medication-related problems? | 4–1 to 4–3<br>4–9<br>4–69 to 4–70 |

## CARE OF PATIENTS: SPECIAL INTERVENTIONS

| Standard | Comments | Evidence | Staff Questions | Reference |
|---|---|---|---|---|
| TX.7.1 through TX.7.5.5 | These revised standards address the use of restraints and seclusion. Joint Commission standards specifically exclude chemical restraints, or "the use of any psychoactive medication that is not a usual or customary part of a medical diagnostic or treatment procedure, and that is used to restrict a patient's freedom of movement," from the definition of a restraint as contemplated by these standards. However, pharmacy leaders are cautioned that the Center for Medicare and Medicaid Studies' (CMS, formerly the Health Care Financing Administration) definition of restraints includes the use of chemical restraints, thus triggering the requirements found in Medicare Conditions of Participation for hospitals that receive Medicare funds. For those hospitals, a physician or other licensed independent practitioner must evaluate the patient within one hour of the initiation of restraints.<br><br>For updates, check the Joint Commission's Web site at http://www.jcaho.org.<br><br>In any event, although most of the standards in this chapter do not apply to pharmacy | • Staff, patient, and family interviews<br>• Policies, procedures, and protocols regarding restraint and seclusion<br>• Participation in PI activities to reduce restraint and seclusion use<br>• Open and closed medical records, with particular emphasis on timed orders, qualification of the practitioner entering the order, clinical justifications, attempts at less restrictive alternatives, and patient monitoring<br>• Staff records, including orientation and continuing education on restraint and seclusion, with a focus on prevention and alternative strategies | • Were any pharmacy associates involved in designing your organization's restraint and seclusion policy?<br>• Describe how staff are aware of their roles and responsibilities in assessing the need for restraints and seclusion and selecting alternatives.<br>• Describe what a pharmacist may evaluate upon assessment of a patient being evaluated for the need for restraints or seclusion. Where is this information found?<br>• Describe orientation, education, or training focused on strategies to reduce the use of restraints and/or seclusion.<br>• When may chemical restraints be used?<br>• Who may order chemical restraints?<br>• How do you ensure that only qualified staff order chemical restraints?<br>• How do you document use of chemical restraints? | |

*continues*

**Care of Patients: Special Interventions**

| Standard | Comments | Evidence | Staff Questions | Reference |
|---|---|---|---|---|
| TX.7.1 through TX.7.5.5 *continued* | services, pharmacy leaders should ensure that drug therapies causing behavior that may trigger the need for restraints or seclusion are considered in the assessment and, if necessary, removed from the patient's therapeutic regimen as an alternative to restraints or seclusion. Conversely, drug therapy may be a viable alternative to physical restraint or seclusion. Assessment should include pharmacy participation to focus on these two issues.<br><br>Pharmacy leaders should ensure that appropriate policies and procedures for the use of chemical restraints are developed and that pharmacists are competent to participate in the monitoring for effectiveness of utilized medications. | | | |

## EDUCATION

| Standard | Comments | Evidence | Staff Questions | Reference |
|---|---|---|---|---|
| PF.1 through PF.1.1 | These standards measure whether the education the hospital provides is planned and supports the coordination of patient education activities in all settings to assist in meeting the hospital's mission. Education must be relevant to the patient's unique set of circumstances and characteristics. In addition, the patient should receive information related specifically to his or her treatment and services. | • Inclusion of pharmacy services in patient education plan<br>• Interdisciplinary patient and family education assessment and flowsheets<br>• Patient education materials<br>• Interdisciplinary discharge and medication summary/instructions<br>• Open and closed medical records<br>• Patient, staff, and family interviews<br>• Direct observation of patient education occurring<br>• Patient and family education plan, policy, procedure, and PI activities<br>• Evidence of education material for patients and families (e.g., brochures, handouts, videos, closed circuit television education channel, education display rack, bulletin boards, poster projects )<br>• Committee minutes, budgets, staff development plans | *To staff:*<br>• Do you have a Patient and Family Education committee that coordinates activities across health settings?<br>• Does your hospital promote and support a learning environment for staff, patients, and families?<br>• What type of patient and family education activities do you provide to improve outcomes, promote self-care?<br>• What information is assessed upon admission concerning patient education needs?<br>• Show me your assessment of the patient's education needs and corresponding flowsheet.<br>• What education have you received about teaching techniques? Have you had a competency in educating your patients and families?<br>• How do you assess and address cultural or language barriers to learning?<br>• How do you assess a patient's ability to learn?<br>• How are your patients educated on medication? Food and drug interactions? Medical equipment? How to obtain further treatment?<br>*To patient:*<br>• What education have you received or do you expect to receive regarding your care? | 4–1 to 4–3<br>4–69 to 4–71 |

*continues*

**Education**

| Standard | Comments | Evidence | Staff Questions | Reference |
|---|---|---|---|---|
| PF.1 through PF.1.1 *continued* | | | • Was your family included in the education process?<br>• Were you referred to any community education resources?<br>• Were you informed where to seek additional treatment, if needed?<br>• What were you told about your medications?<br>• Was your pain addressed? | |
| PF.2 | Patient education should be collaborative if care involves multiple disciplines. This standard assesses whether the hospital uses an interdisciplinary approach to the provision of patient care.<br><br>*Note:* Medication education and counseling should be an interdisciplinary process. Nurses, physicians, respiratory therapists, etc., in addition to pharmacists, may provide these services; however, it is the expectation that the pharmacy service is responsible for the medication education and tools provided to patients. Interdisciplinary involvement should be reflected in the organizational policy and procedures. | • Policies, procedures, and plans related to patient education demonstrating collaborative efforts by caregivers, including pharmacists<br>• Open and closed records demonstrating interdisciplinary participation in patient education<br>• Clinical pathways incorporating patient and family education<br>• Patient interview | • What role do pharmacists and pharmacy staff play in developing and implementing patient and family education?<br>• Do you have an interdisciplinary Patient and Family Education committee or other group supporting this function?<br>• Can you describe a case that would depict how you would demonstrate compliance with providing collaborative, interdisciplinary education? | |
| PF.3 | Assessing patient and family education needs is critical to ensure a favorable outcome for | • Patient interview | • What information is assessed upon admission concerning patient | 4–69 to 4–71 |

*continues*

**Education**

| Standard | Comments | Evidence | Staff Questions | Reference |
|---|---|---|---|---|
| PF.3 *continued* | the patient. Pharmacy staff should consider cultural, religious, emotional, and language barriers; readiness to learn (motivation level); physical and cognitive limitations; financial impact of medication decisions; and the learning method (e.g., demonstration, verbal, video) preferred by the patient and family. | | medication education needs?<br>• How do you get the patient and/or family involved in care or services involving medications before they are discharged?<br>• How do you know that the patient and/or family understands the medication education efforts?<br>• Where is this information documented?<br>• What grade level do you use for instructional material?<br>• What actions do you take if you know there are barriers preventing understanding? How do you make accommodations for limitations identified? Can you describe a challenging case that was successfully managed?<br>• How do you incorporate education factors in the care planning process (i.e., creating individual education plans, prioritizing education needs, etc.)?<br>• Do you have an interdisciplinary patient and family education form?<br>• Show me how your assessment process addresses barriers to learning.<br>• Show me a record that demonstrates you have assessed for barriers to learning.<br>• How do you determine a patient's preference for learning?<br>• Can you describe a challenging case where you had to overcome a | |

*continues*

**Education**

| Standard | Comments | Evidence | Staff Questions | Reference |
|---|---|---|---|---|
| PF.3 *continued* | | | patient or family barrier to learning? | |
| PF.3.1 through PF.3.5 | These standards are related to education provided to the patient and/or family (special focus on safety and effectiveness) regarding the following topics: | • PF.3.1: medication usage (e.g., medication handouts)<br>• PF.3.2: nutrition counseling, oral health, and drug-food interactions (e.g., evidence of literature/brochures regarding diet)<br>• PF.3.3: medical equipment (e.g., crutches)<br>• PF.3.4: pain management as a part of the treatment plan<br>• PF.3.5: habilitation or rehabilitative techniques (e.g., special adaptations provided to patients to ensure maximal independence) | *To pharmacy associates:*<br>• What type of patient and family medication education activities do you provide?<br>• Where is medication education provided by pharmacists documented? Show examples of documented assessment of patient's medication education needs, as well as evidence that you educated patients on the safe and effective use of medications prescribed.<br>• Indicate evidence of instructions provided regarding medical equipment, special diet needs, and/or any rehabilitative techniques offered to the patient and/or family (if applicable) in reviewing a chart.<br>*To patient:*<br>• What medication education or counseling have you received or do you expect to receive regarding your medication therapy?<br>• Who educated or counseled you regarding your medications? | 4–69 to 4–71 |
| PF.3.4 | This standard requires that patients be educated about pain and about methods of pain management as a part of treatment. | • Documentation that patient was educated regarding:<br>– Pain management options offered during treatment<br>– Methods for management of | *To pharmacy associates:*<br>• Describe your policies on educating patients and their families about the management of pain.<br>• What type of patient and family pain management | 4–1 to 4–3 |

*continues*

**Education**

| Standard | Comments | Evidence | Staff Questions | Reference |
|---|---|---|---|---|
| PF.3.4 *continued* | | postprocedure pain<br>– Follow-up for management of pain at home<br>– When to contact a physician or health care provider when pain symptoms worsen | education activities do you provide?<br>• Where is pain management education provided by pharmacists documented? Show examples of documented assessment of patient's pain management education needs, as well as evidence that you educated patients on pain management.<br>*To patient:*<br>• What medication education or counseling have you received or do you expect to receive regarding pain management options?<br>• Who educated or counseled you regarding pain management? | |
| PF.3.6 | Patients and families are educated about what other resources are available and how to obtain further care, services, and treatment as necessary to meet patients' identified needs. | • Evidence of referrals to community groups, consultation notes<br>• Patient and family education materials<br>• Clinical staff, patient, and family interviews | • What community resources do you promote prior to discharge and include in your discharge instructions? | |
| PF.3.7 | Patients and families are educated on their responsibilities and role in the treatment process, and specifically, their role in helping to facilitate the safe delivery of care.<br>Patient responsibilities include:<br>• Following instructions, rules, and regulations (e.g., providing as much | • Handout/brochure of patient rights and responsibilities regarding the medication therapy plan<br>• Open and closed medical records for education about patient/family responsibilities<br>• Posting of patient rights and responsibilities in waiting areas<br>• Patient and staff interviews | • Do you have any booklet or handout to orient your patient and family to the pharmacy department?<br>• Describe your procedure for educating patients and their families on their responsibilities for care appropriate to the patient's assessed needs, e.g., safe use of medications, medical equipment, pain management. | 4–8 to 4–10 |

*continues*

**Education**

| Standard | Comments | Evidence | Staff Questions | Reference |
|---|---|---|---|---|
| PF.3.7 *continued* | complete information as possible to allow a complete history to be gathered, reporting changes to condition, providing feedback on expectations, reporting perceived risks in their care, asking questions when they do not understand what they have been told or what they are expected to do, following instructions, treatment plan or medication therapy plan, accepting outcomes if not following treatment plan or medication therapy plan, following regulations regarding noise control, visitation, smoking, security/property, etc.)<br>• Acting with consideration and respect for pharmacy staff and property<br>• Meeting financial commitments | | | |
| PF.3.8 | This standard relates to the patient's being able to care for self (e.g., hygiene, grooming). | • Open and closed records<br>• Observation of patients<br>• Clinical staff interviews<br>• Policies and procedures related to education, self-care | • If a need is indicated by visual inspection of the patient, what follow-up education is provided to ensure that the patient receives proper hygiene and grooming resources?<br>• Can you demonstrate that hygiene and grooming are assessed upon admission?<br>• Where in your education materials do you have evidence that you instructed a patient and/or family on hygiene and grooming? | |

*continues*

**Education**

| Standard | Comments | Evidence | Staff Questions | Reference |
|---|---|---|---|---|
| PF.3.9 | Discharge instruction is given to the patient and family, as well as other caregivers. | • Discharge planning policy and procedure<br>• Open and closed records<br>• Discharge medication summary/instructions incorporating education issues (e.g., lifestyle changes), current pharmacist contact, etc. | • What type of medication information or instructions are provided to patient and family, the patient's primary health care provider, and community pharmacist upon discharge?<br>• Who provides the information? | 4–69 to 4–71<br>4–79 |

## CONTINUUM OF CARE

| Standard | Comments | Evidence | Staff Questions | Reference |
|---|---|---|---|---|
| CC.1 | This standard addresses the organization's process to provide patients access to appropriate level of care based on their assessed needs.<br><br>Pharmacy leaders should ensure that pharmaceutical care is accessible to patients and appropriate to the setting. This should include appropriate medications, personnel resources, and up-to-date pharmacy technology and information systems. | • Policies and procedures regarding:<br>1. Formulary management<br>2. Provision of distributive pharmacy functions<br>3. Provision of clinical pharmacy functions<br>– Assessment<br>– Medication education and counseling<br>– Drug therapy outcome monitoring<br>• Pharmacy and Therapeutics or Formulary committee minutes<br>• Medication use evaluation documentation<br>• Leadership interviews<br>• Observation of patient entry to organization, flow through system<br>• Handouts for community resources | • How do you know patients receive the pharmacy-related care needed in the appropriate setting?<br>• What is the scope of pharmacy services you provide?<br>• Do you have sufficient staff, equipment, and medication information resources to provide pharmacy services to meet the needs of your patient population?<br>• How do you access the services of other departments within the organization?<br>• How do you obtain a nonformulary medication that is needed for a patient?<br>• How is the medication use evaluation process used to monitor drug therapy outcomes and improve care? | 4–8 to 4–10<br>4–15<br>4–48<br>4–52 to 4–53 |
| CC.3 and CC.3.1 | These standards require hospitals to provide continuity over time among the patient services provided to ensure a smooth and safe transition during the care process.<br><br>Pharmacy leaders should ensure seamless pharmacy services from inpatient to outpatient settings, with particular focus on the availability and transfer of pertinent medication and related information across the organization to facilitate care. | • Staff, leadership, patient interviews<br>• Open and closed records<br>• Departmental policies and procedures regarding:<br>– Assessment<br>– Care planning<br>– Medication education<br>– Discharge planning<br>• Communication of a patient's medication-related information to other departments and services (e.g., home care, social services, primary care physician, case managers, community pharmacists, etc.)<br>• Availability of information management (e.g., | • How does the pharmacy service ensure effective communication of a patient's medication-related information to care providers in various settings? | 4–8 to 4–10<br>4–69 to 4–71 |

*continues*

**Continuum of Care**

| Standard | Comments | Evidence | Staff Questions | Reference |
|---|---|---|---|---|
| CC.3 and CC.3.1 *continued* | | computer, software) for facilitating continuous care | | |
| CC. 4.1 | This standard requires that the established follow-up process provides for continuing care to meet patients' needs. Follow-up planning should identify the patient's symptom management needs (e.g., for pain, nausea, or dyspnea) and ensure that the patient and family be informed in a timely manner of the need for planning for discharge and for continuing care, if necessary.<br><br>*Note:* Pain assessment and management standards became effective January 1, 2001.<br><br>Pharmacy leaders should ensure that patients' medication education needs are identified prior to discharge so as not to delay the transition to the outpatient setting. This would include pertinent medication education and counseling, referral to medication-related support groups and/or home health agencies, etc. | • Patient, leadership, staff interviews<br>• Lists of pharmacy-related community resources and medication-related support groups given to patients and families<br>• Open and closed records documenting the patient's medication-related continuing care needs following discharge<br>• Policy and procedures regarding:<br>– Followup/discharge planning<br>– Medication education and counseling<br>• Medication education materials | • What is the pharmacist's role in the follow-up/discharge planning process as it relates to medication?<br>• What medication-related information does the patient and/or family receive prior to or upon discharge?<br>• How do you ensure that the patient receives necessary follow-up pharmacy services or counseling?<br>• What do you do if a patient cannot read medication instructions or educational materials? | 4–41 to 4–42<br>4–69 to 4–71<br>4–103 to 4–106 |
| CC.4.1 | This standard concerns the need to inform the patient in a timely manner about the need to plan for discharge or transfer to another level of care. | • Medical records<br>• Hospital and departmental policies and procedures<br>• Interviews with staff, patients | • When pharmacy staff anticipate some level of continuing care, including medications, after a patient's discharge, what is the procedure for | |

*continues*

**Continuum of Care**

| Standard | Comments | Evidence | Staff Questions | Reference |
|---|---|---|---|---|
| CC.4.1 *continued* | | | keeping the patient and family informed of the care process?<br>• Describe the information that is provided to the patient and family regarding continuing care. | |
| CC.5 | This standard requires that appropriate information related to the services provided is exchanged at key points in the continuum of care (admission, transfer, referral for consultation or treatment, discharge, and when services are discontinued).<br><br>Pharmacy leaders should ensure that appropriate patient medication-related information is available across the organization and that medication history summaries are available upon discharge. | • Open and closed records (e.g., review of discharge medication summaries)<br>• Clinical pathways demonstrating flow of pertinent medication-related information from admission to discharge, and beyond<br>• Use of information systems to assist with the flow of patient medication information among providers and various health care settings | • Describe the flow of clinical medication information when patients are admitted, transferred, and discharged, and when services are discontinued.<br>• What type of information management support does the pharmacy service have for the exchange of patient medication information?<br>• How is the confidentiality of the medication-related patient information ensured as it is made available at various settings across the organization? | 4–7 |

## IMPROVING ORGANIZATION PERFORMANCE

| Standard | Comments | Evidence | Staff Questions | Reference |
|---|---|---|---|---|
| PI.1 through PI.1.1 | These standards require pharmacy leaders and staff to participate in organizationwide performance improvement (PI) initiatives.<br><br>Emphasis is on the pharmacy staff's collaboration in PI activities organization-wide rather than isolated within the department. | • Staff interviews<br>• PI orientation, continuing education, other materials distributed to pharmacy staff<br>• Staff involvement with PI planning<br>• Interdisciplinary PI projects, planning documents reflecting pharmacy participation<br>– Meeting minutes<br>– Attendance sheets<br>– Reports<br>– Storyboards/ storybooks<br>• Demonstration of pharmacy and/or medication use initiatives as part of the organization's strategic planning process | • Describe how the pharmacy service collaborates with other departments and disciplines to improve patient care.<br>• What is your organization's PI model?<br>• How did you learn about your PI plan?<br>• Have you been part of a PI team?<br>• Give an example of a medication use process you have improved.<br>• How did you measure the results? | 4–53<br>4–80 to 4–82<br>4–98 |
| PI.2 | This standard is used to evaluate the design of new and modified processes. The Joint Commission's intent describes the criteria for "good process design." The design may be for a new pharmacy service in response to a new product line, a change in an existing service, or opening of a new facility.<br><br>Examples of criteria to consider for designing new processes include:<br>• Relationship to mission, vision, and values of the organization<br>• Customer needs<br>• Successful practices<br>• Literature ("best practice") guidelines | • Staff interviews<br>• PI planning documents<br>• Flowcharts, process maps, etc., before and after implementation of the process<br>• Evidence that the new process is consistent with the mission and vision of the pharmacy and the organization | • How do you identify issues for the pharmacy's PI plan?<br>• What is the staff's role in this process?<br>• What improvements have been made in the pharmacy during the last year?<br>• How did you measure continuous or sustained improvement?<br>• Describe three PI tools and what they are used for. | 4–80 to 4–82<br>4–98 |

*continues*

**Improving Organization Performance**

| Standard | Comments | Evidence | Staff Questions | Reference |
|---|---|---|---|---|
| PI.2 *continued* | • Consistency with sound business practices<br>• PI activity results<br>• Information about potential risks to patients and sentinel events within the organization and at other facilities<br>• Analysis and/or pilot testing of whether the proposed design is an improvement | | | |
| PI.3 through PI.3.1.3 | These standards describe the organization's responsibility systematically to collect data to monitor performance and identify areas and methods for improvement initiatives. The pharmacy staff should be prepared to show compliance with organizationwide and department-specific data collection activities, as well as evidence that the data have been used to improve pharmacy processes.<br><br>PI focus is on high-risk, high-volume, problem-prone processes and functions, as well as sentinel events. Data collection must also include areas targeted for further study and PI efforts. Those processes that have greatest impact on processes and outcomes should be measured. | • Staff interviews, PI team interviews<br>• Plans and strategies for data collection<br>• Data collection tools used (e.g., surveys, flow sheets, graphs, charts)<br>• Orientation and continuing education materials regarding data collection and measurement<br>• Measurement and improvement reports, minutes<br>• Participation in a reference database (i.e., benchmarking pharmacy service measurements against those of comparable organizations)<br>• PI plans, reports based on data collected<br>• Graphs interpreting medication use and pharmacy service PI processes, data collected, other trend analysis<br>• Documentation illustrating the periodic evaluation of common pharmacy activities (e.g., calendars depicting pharmacy PI | • What aspects of pharmacy services are you measuring as part of improvement activities?<br>• Who is responsible for collecting pharmacy and medication use PI data? Where are the data reported and how will they be used to improve the medication use system?<br>• Do you use external comparative data (e.g., Press Gainey, Gallup, comparisons with other organizations)?<br>• Are pharmacy-related data included in the aggregated organization data?<br>• Describe a medication use process for which data have been collected and analyzed including the strategy for data collection and analysis (e.g., sampling process, timing of sampling).<br>• How do you measure the quality of medication use and pharmacy services provided to patients undergoing invasive and noninvasive procedures | 4–1 to 4–3<br>4–52 to 4–53<br>4–77 to 4–78 |

*continues*

**Improving Organization Performance**

| Standard | Comments | Evidence | Staff Questions | Reference |
|---|---|---|---|---|
| PI.3 through PI.3.1.3 *continued* | | initiatives, medication usage evaluations, medication error surveillance, ADR surveillance, occurrence reports, sentinel events, standard quality control measures, appropriate documentation)<br>• Use of data collection tools to measure performance as related to the following important processes:<br>–Operative, other invasive, and noninvasive procedures (outcomes and complications of conscious sedation should be assessed)<br>–Medication use<br>–The use of blood and blood products<br>–Appropriateness/ effectiveness of pain management<br>–Patient satisfaction<br>–PI opportunities identified by pharmacy associates<br>–Perceptions of risks to patients as identified by pharmacy associates, and suggestions for improving patient safety<br>–Quality control (i.e., pharmaceutical equipment used to prepare medications)<br>• Pharmacy staff willingness to report medical/ health care errors<br>• Use of data collection tools to measure staffing effectiveness | that place the patient at risk?<br>• What sampling methods are used for medication use PI initiatives?<br>• Describe the data collected on the following processes and how the data are used throughout the organization to improve performance.<br>–Appropriateness of medication and blood product use<br>–Medication errors/ sentinel events<br>–ADRs<br>–Medication errors<br>• How is this information used at the time of medical staff reappointment? | |

*continues*

**Improving Organization Performance**

| Standard | Comments | Evidence | Staff Questions | Reference |
|---|---|---|---|---|
| PI.4 through PI.4.4 | These standards focus on the organization's assessment and analysis of collected data. The organization must use the data to identify changes that will not only improve performance and patient safety, but also reduce the risk of sentinel events. Pharmacy service leaders in collaboration with staff need to be prepared to discuss the analysis and use of data collected, especially where undesirable trends have been identified.<br><br>Statistical analysis tools are helpful in comparing the organization's performance with historical trends, as well as against that of other organizations, and in assessing variations. | • Staff and PI team member interviews<br>• Orientation and continuing education material on statistical analysis, assessment techniques<br>• Reports and minutes evaluating data using tools such as control charts, histograms, run charts, etc.<br>• Documents reflecting poor performance, major discrepancies, undesirable patterns, and unacceptable variability (usually defined as data indicating greater than two standard deviations from the mean)<br>• Root cause analysis<br>• Material from external sources such as recent scientific, clinical, and management literature, including relevant Joint Commission *Sentinel Event Alerts*<br>• Evidence of appropriate analysis and follow-up action concerning opportunities for improvement once unacceptable variability is identified.<br>• Intensive assessment of adverse reactions to medications and blood products to identify opportunities to prevent future occurrences<br>• Intense analysis of staffing effectiveness issues | • How are managers trained in statistical analysis?<br>• Can you describe tools you use to analyze data collected?<br>• What statistical methods do you use to analyze medication use PI data?<br>• When opportunities for improvement in medication use were identified, what corrective actions were implemented (give examples)?<br>• Does the organization participate in a reference database (e.g., adverse drug or medication error benchmarking studies)?<br>• What internal resources are available to assist in statistical analysis?<br>• How do you review and respond to information and recommendations the Joint Commission provides about sentinel events?<br>• What do you do if there is a sentinel event? | 4–52 to 4–53<br>4–77 |
| PI.5 | This standard measures whether PI is sustained over time. | • Staff, PI team interviews | • Are the medication use improvement efforts consistent with the | |

*continues*

**Improving Organization Performance**

| Standard | Comments | Evidence | Staff Questions | Reference |
|---|---|---|---|---|
| PI.5<br>*continued* | Pharmacy leaders and staff need to demonstrate their ongoing collaborative efforts to continuously improve performance within the pharmacy service as well as overall medication use throughout the organization. | • Records of PI activities, reports<br>• Staff files showing PI orientation and continuing education<br>• Inclusion of the following in all organizational and departmental PI strategies:<br>– Planning<br>– Testing<br>– Assessment/redesign<br>– Implementation<br>• Evidence of the Joint Commission's 10-step process or a modified Find, Organize, Clarify, Uncover, Start-Plan, Do Check, Act (FOCUS-PDCA) | priorities established by the organization?<br>• Is PI around medication use an ongoing activity in your organization?<br>• Are PI initiatives evident in the planning and implementation of pharmacy services throughout the organization?<br>• Do you receive feedback about departmental PI activities?<br>• How do medication use and other pharmacy PI initiatives incorporate the concepts of planning, testing, assessing, and implementing?<br>• Show an example of how the planning, testing, assessing, and implementing concepts are incorporated into medication use and pharmacy PI initiatives. | |

# LEADERSHIP

| Standard | Comments | Evidence | Staff Questions | Reference |
|---|---|---|---|---|
| LD.1 through LD.1.1.2 | These standards discuss leaders' role in organizationwide, systematic planning.<br><br>Pharmacy leaders must show participation in the organizational planning as well as the development of a mission/vision for pharmacy services that is in synchrony with the organization's strategic, operational, and programmatic mission vision. | • Leadership interviews<br>• Meeting minutes demonstrating pharmacy leaders' participation in organizationwide planning activities<br>• Documents indicating that the planning of pharmacy services and medication use initiatives are addressed at the organizational level (such as at budget meetings, space planning, new program development)<br>• Department policies and procedures supporting organizationwide policy<br>• Departmental mission/vision statement clearly encompassing the organizationwide plans | *To pharmacy leaders:*<br><br>• Describe your participation in strategic and operational planning.<br>• What is the process for requesting additional resources, such as space or staff, new medications, new technology/automation?<br>• Describe how the needs of the pharmacy service throughout the organization are coordinated with organizationwide plans. | 4–79 to 4–82 |
| LD.1.2 | Pharmacy leaders must educate pharmacy staff regarding the organization's mission.<br><br>Further, the mission for pharmacy services and how it corresponds to the organizationwide mission must be communicated to the pharmacy staff. | • Organization mission posted within the department<br>• Mission, vision, and values for pharmacy services posted within the department<br>• Minutes of meetings discussing organization and departmental mission and vision<br>• Orientation materials on mission for new staff and staff orientation documentation<br>• Examples of activities supporting the organizationwide and pharmacy service mission and strategic plans | *To staff:*<br><br>• What is the organization's mission?<br>• What is the organization's vision?<br>• What is the mission and vision for pharmacy services throughout the organization?<br>• Describe how leaders communicate the organization's mission and plans (i.e., PI)<br>• How does the mission and vision for pharmacy services contribute to the organization's mission and strategic plan? | 4–80 to 4–81 |

*continues*

**Leadership**

| Standard | Comments | Evidence | Staff Questions | Reference |
|---|---|---|---|---|
| LD.1.3 through LD.1.3.3.1 | These standards measure organization service planning to meet the needs of patients and the community served by the organization.<br><br>Pharmacy leaders must participate in this process. | • Use of data collected concerning patients' needs (e.g., patient satisfaction surveys, community focus group sessions)<br>• Evidence that patient and community data are used in planning for pharmacy services provided to the organization<br>• Planning documents involving pharmacy services demonstrating process or service design based on patient needs, consideration of the mission, human resources (HR), and material resources | • Does the organization have a written plan for the provision of patient care?<br>• How do you know that the services provided by the pharmacy are suitable for the organization?<br>• How are community needs determined and considered in your planning process?<br>• What have you done to make improvements based on patient satisfaction? | |
| LD.1.3.4 | This standard evaluates the timeliness of organizational services, their availability, and whether the services meet patient needs.<br><br>Pharmacy services should address the timeliness of all types of medication-related services provided to inpatients and outpatients.<br><br>*Note:* Ambulatory patient and inpatient service needs should be incorporated. | • Pharmacy scope of services, timeliness of services provided<br>• Patient, family, nursing, physician satisfaction surveys<br>• Clinical pathways including medication use and related pharmacy services<br>• Open and closed chart review indicating that pharmacy services are provided within organizational standards<br>• Tools used to measure medication turnaround time, and readiness and availability to provide patient medication counseling | • Describe how you ensure that patients' pharmaceutical care needs are appropriately being met.<br>• How do you measure improvements in pharmacy services?<br>• Do you measure any of the following:<br>– Medication delivery at times of limited staffing (e.g., evenings and nights)<br>– Response of pharmacists to patient medication counseling requests<br>– Pharmacy staffing to patient care demand | |
| LD.1.6 | This standard measures uniformity of care across services.<br><br>The organization and the pharmacy service | • Pharmacy enforcement of organizationwide policies and procedures relating to medication use across the organization. | • How do leaders and staff ensure one standard of pharmacy care across the organization?<br>• Provide documents that outline the standards of | 4–9 |

*continues*

**Leadership**

| Standard | Comments | Evidence | Staff Questions | Reference |
|---|---|---|---|---|
| LD.1.6 *continued* | need to demonstrate that, no matter where the patient enters the system, he or she will be provided the same level of pharmaceutical care. | *Note:* As much as possible, one standard of pharmaceutical care and pharmacy service should be provided to inpatients and outpatients, regardless of the practice setting. Exceptions should be clearly explained and justified in organizational and departmental policies and procedures.<br>• Pharmacy implementation and support for organizationwide programs<br>• Pharmacy's consistent enforcement of medication use within critical pathways and treatment protocols<br>• Adherence to medical staff bylaws, credentialing, privileging requirements as they relate to medication use<br>• Pharmacy participation in organizationwide PI projects, committees (e.g., patient and family education, patient assessment, care delivery planning)<br>• Staffing plans that relate to demands of patient care and address specific staff qualifications/competencies (e.g., availability of resources for special patient populations) | pharmaceutical care and services provided to meet patient demand.<br>• Are pharmacists with special patient-specific competencies (e.g., pediatrics, oncology) available to meet the patient care demand?<br>• Do all pharmacists providing care and services throughout the organization meet a minimal standard for pharmacists? Who determines that standard and how is it evaluated and documented? | |
| LD.1.7 through LD.1.7.1 | These standards pertain to the scope of departmental services. | • Department policies and procedures outlining scope of services provided | • Is the scope of pharmacy services written? Who approved it?<br>• Is the scope of pharmacy services consistent with | 4–8 to 4–10<br>4–69<br>4–79 |

*continues*

**Leadership**

| Standard | Comments | Evidence | Staff Questions | Reference |
|---|---|---|---|---|
| LD.1.7 through LD.1.7.1 *continued* | The Joint Commission's intent for these standards establishes a list of considerations that must be addressed in departmental policy and procedure development. | • Departmental goals and objectives<br>• Staff interviews<br>• Minutes of meetings at which pharmacy service planning is discussed | the organization's mission statement?<br>• Is pharmacy staffing adequate to serve your patient population?<br>• Describe your staffing plan. | |
| LD.1.8 | Surveyors will assess the participation of pharmacy leaders and staff in decision making.<br><br>An emphasis will be placed on how the pharmacy leadership collaborates with other organizational leaders. | • Documentation of pharmacist involvement with interdisciplinary care throughout the organization, including the role of the pharmacy and medication use in care plans, critical pathways, etc.<br>• Documentation reflecting pharmacy participation in development of organizationwide programs, plans, and policies<br>• Staff and leadership interviews<br>• Pharmacy and medication use PI projects | • Describe how the pharmacy participates in organizationwide planning.<br>• Does the pharmacy have representatives participating in organizationwide committees or projects (e.g., strategic planning, PI, patient and family education, patient assessment, protocol and clinical pathways)?<br>• How does information regarding pharmacy's participation and representation in organizationwide initiative get communicated to staff? | |
| LD.1.9 and LD.1.9.1 | These standards assess leaders' efforts in developing and educating staff.<br><br>*See also HR.3.1* | • Pharmacy staffing plan<br>• Pharmacy service budgets<br>• Continuing education activities, plans, and budgets<br>• Staff orientation/ training/education records<br>• Annual performance evaluations including a focus on professional development and education | *To pharmacy leaders:*<br><br>• How has pharmacy staff competence been improved?<br>• Describe the internal and external continuing education opportunities provided to pharmacists and support staff.<br>• Have any employees left because they were unhappy?<br>• How do you know your staff meet the needs of your patients?<br>• How would you describe pharmacist morale?<br>• Are you doing anything to reduce turnover? | |

*continues*

**Leadership**

| Standard | Comments | Evidence | Staff Questions | Reference |
|---|---|---|---|---|
| LD.1.9 and LD.1.9.1 *continued* | | | *To staff:*<br>• What continuing education have you received in the past year?<br>• Do you have opportunities for training and education?<br>• Does your annual performance evaluation provide an opportunity for you to identify opportunities for professional growth? | |
| LD.1.10 through LD.1.10.3 | These standards discuss the selection of clinical practice guidelines for improving processes. This is a hospitalwide standard with which pharmacy leaders may be asked to show participation. | • Leadership and staff interviews<br>• Minutes of meetings documenting pharmacy participation in discussions of clinical practice guideline evaluation and use<br>• Examples of guideline use or modification for PI, including results<br>• Staff training materials | • What is an example of a clinical practice guideline implemented with the participation of the pharmacy?<br>• Why was it adopted?<br>• How was it selected?<br>• How has it affected patient care?<br>• When was it last reviewed? Who participated in the review?<br>• How are staff trained regarding this guideline?<br>• What do you do if you receive a medication order that deviates from an adopted guideline? | 4–37 |
| LD.2.1 through LD.2.10 | These standards are used to evaluate the performance of department leaders.<br><br>The standards outline specific activities in which the pharmacy leadership should be prepared to demonstrate consistent performance. | • Leadership and staff interviews<br>• Observation of department director interacting with staff<br>• Scope of services that includes the integration of pharmacy services with other departments<br>• Pharmacy policies and procedures that reflect and support the integrated scope of services<br>• PI plans, documentation, and reports | *To any staff member:*<br>• Is this pharmacy adequately staffed?<br>• Are the space, equipment, and supplies in the pharmacy adequate for you to care for patients?<br>• Are you involved in any PI projects?<br>• What is the organization's mission and vision?<br>• What is the mission and vision for pharmacy services? | 4–79<br>4–99 to 4–110 |

*continues*

**Leadership**

| Standard | Comments | Evidence | Staff Questions | Reference |
|---|---|---|---|---|
| LD.2.1 through LD.2.10 *continued* | | • Meeting minutes from medical staff, governing body, Interdisciplinary Care, and Performance Improvement committees<br>• Documented staffing plan that meets the patient care demand<br>• Job descriptions and competencies for pharmaceutical care providers<br>• Annual performance evaluations<br>• Staff orientation materials and attendance records<br>• Policies on staff development, training, and competency<br>• Staff continuing education records<br>• Pharmacy staffing budget<br>• Organization's budget for medications and related supplies<br>• Quality control records in accordance with departmental, organizational, and regulatory standards and requirements.<br><br>*Note:* Records from the previous 12 months are required. | • How does the mission and vision for pharmacy services correspond to the organizational plans?<br>• What improvements in the medication use system have been implemented in the last year?<br><br>*To the pharmacy leadership:*<br>• How do you build PI into the ongoing activities and functions within the pharmacy?<br>• How do you create an environment to help the pharmacy associates meet the established goals for pharmaceutical services?<br>• Describe the orientation program for new staff.<br>• How does the pharmacy coordinate services with other departments?<br>• How do you know the pharmacists and support staff are competent?<br>• Who trains the professional and nonprofessional pharmacy staff?<br><br>*To the Medical Director regarding pharmacy services:*<br>• Can you demonstrate that there are an adequate number of pharmacists and pharmacy services to meet patient care demands?<br>• How many pharmacists and pharmacy support staff are in the organization at any time?<br>• Is there a pharmacy on-call schedule?<br>• Are all pharmacy services available 24 hours a day?<br>• What credentials do pharmacy staff members have? | |

*continues*

**Leadership**

| Standard | Comments | Evidence | Staff Questions | Reference |
|---|---|---|---|---|
| LD.2.1 through LD.2.10 *continued* | | | • Who defines the qualifications?<br>• How is the clinical competency of pharmacy staff documented? | |
| LD.2.11 through LD.2.11.3 | Standards address the qualifications of pharmacy leaders (licenses, credentials, education, and training). | • Pharmacy leaders' position description questionnaires<br>• Pharmacy leaders' personnel files, credentials, licenses, etc.<br>• Pharmacy leaders' recent performance evaluation<br>• Medical staff bylaws, rules, and regulations (if applicable) | *To pharmacy leaders:*<br>• What are your qualifications?<br>• Where are they defined?<br>• How is your performance evaluated? | |
| LD.3 through LD.3.4 | These standards assess coordination of patient care and of improvements to patient safety between pharmacy leaders and other organizational departments, leaders, and individuals. | • Scope of pharmacy services describing the integration and the coordination with other services and departments throughout the organization<br>• Leadership and staff interviews<br>• Meeting minutes<br>• Medication availability and medication use policies and procedures that clearly indicate development in collaboration with various disciplines and departments (e.g., Pharmacy and Therapeutics, and Formulary committee)<br>• Internal and external communications, satisfaction surveys, customer expectations, etc.<br>• Patient care guidelines and clinical pathways developed in coordination with pharmacy services and other | • How are practitioners within the organization made aware of medications available to care for patients?<br>• How do practitioners request new drugs for use within the organization?<br>• How do practitioners know of the variety of pharmacy services and expertise available to patients within the organization?<br>• Describe the process for interdisciplinary development of medication use policies. | 4–96 |

*continues*

**Leadership**

| Standard | Comments | Evidence | Staff Questions | Reference |
|---|---|---|---|---|
| LD.3 through LD.3.4 *continued* | | departments and disciplines<br>• Evidence of participation in interdepartmental PI projects<br>• Documentation of measurement/analysis of variations in performance of high-risk processes that affect patient safety | | |
| LD.4 through LD.4.5 | These standards require organization leaders to participate in all aspects of organizational PI and safety improvement activities, including those dealing with adequacy and allocation of resources.<br><br>Pharmacy leadership should be prepared to demonstrate pharmacy's contribution. | • Leadership and staff interviews<br>• Orientation and ongoing staff education related to performance improvement and patient safety improvement<br>• Performance and patient safety improvement initiatives and assessment tools<br>• Organizationwide PI and patient safety improvement activities include pharmacy representation<br>• Documentation of education related to PI and patient safety improvement attended by pharmacy leaders<br>• Use of PI and patient safety improvement tools in medication use and pharmacy service initiatives<br>• Integration of PI and patient safety improvement into all aspects of pharmacy services<br>• Evidence that data and other information necessary to improve pharmacy service performance are identified, gathered, and assessed | • What pharmacy resources are committed to PI? To patient safety improvement?<br>• What medication use issues or pharmacy service issues have you improved over the past year?<br>• Who is responsible for PI? For patient safety improvement?<br>• How do pharmacy associates learn about the outcomes of medication use and pharmacy service PI and patient safety improvement projects?<br>• Are the PI and patient safety improvement priorities consistent with pharmacy mission and vision? With the mission and vision of the organization?<br>• How do you evaluate the effectiveness of your contribution to improving medication use and pharmacy service performance throughout the organization? | 4–43<br>4–53<br>4–78 |

*continues*

**Leadership**

| Standard | Comments | Evidence | Staff Questions | Reference |
|---|---|---|---|---|
| LD.4 through LD.4.5 *continued* | | • Communication of interdisciplinary medication use and pharmacy service PI and patient safety improvement projects, storyboards/storybooks<br>• Allocation of adequate human and other resources to PI and patient safety improvement activities<br>• Pharmacy leadership incorporation of self-evaluations in PI and patient safety improvement planning and implementation | | |
| LD.5 through LD.5.3 | These standards require organization leaders to implement and give high priority to an organizationwide patient safety program, including processes for identifying and managing sentinel events and for reducing medical errors. The intent is to proactively identify potential patient safety risks and prevent adverse occurrences. Pharmacy leaders should be prepared to demonstrate pharmacy department contribution. | • Interviews with leaders, staff<br>• Orientation, continuing staff education re: patient safety improvement program<br>• Patient safety program initiatives, priority planning, lists, assessment tools<br>• Organizationwide patient safety improvement activities that include pharmacy department representation<br>• Department and organizational evaluations of patient safety programs<br>• Allocation of human and other resources to patient safety improvement activities<br>• Documentation of mechanisms, procedures for immediate response to medical/ health care errors and other occurrences, e.g., root cause analysis of a sentinel event | • What do you do when you discover that a medical/health care error has been made by the pharmacy department?<br>• What is a sentinel event?<br>• Is a "near miss" considered to be a sentinel event?<br>• How would you report a sentinel event? | 4–73<br>4–75<br>4–95 to 4–96 |

## MANAGEMENT OF THE ENVIRONMENT OF CARE

| Standard | Comments | Evidence | Staff Questions | Reference |
|---|---|---|---|---|
| EC.1.1, EC.1.1.1, EC.1.5.1, EC.2.1, EC.2.8, EC.2.10.1 | These standards relate to the safety management plan for the protection of patients and workers and how well it is implemented in the pharmacy department. The surveyor will walk through the patient care areas, including the pharmacy department if applicable, to assess ongoing risk monitoring and compliance at the department level. The surveyor will assess whether the environment is consistent with the organization's mission and whether the organization abides by the rules of regulatory and accrediting agencies.<br><br>Hazardous surveillance surveys should be performed in the pharmacy semiannually to reduce safety risks. | • Leadership and staff interviews<br>• Organization and pharmacy-specific safety policies and procedures accessible to staff<br>• Documentation supporting implementation of safety plan<br>• Pharmacy participation in Safety committee as indicated by meeting minutes, agendas, attendance lists<br>• Feedback and action plans concerning pharmacy safety surveillance rounds<br>• PI projects, measurement of performance standards, action plans in response to safety trends<br>• Safety orientation and continuing education materials, education schedules, staff attendance records<br>• Mechanism for training, informing pharmacy associates of environment of care plans, policies, and procedures<br>• Preventive maintenance logs, service logs<br>• Reporting of trends in occupational illness, personnel injuries<br>• Building plans if renovation of pharmacy is underway<br><br>*Site inspection:*<br><br>• Tours of pharmacy area showing area free of hazards, such as exposed electrical wiring, hallway obstructions | • Describe your safety orientation.<br>• How often do you receive safety updates?<br>• Is there a Safety committee?<br>• How does the pharmacy service participate in the Safety committee (if applicable)?<br>• How do you ensure that pharmacy areas are safe to take care of patients?<br>• Describe the frequency of any surveillance rounds in the pharmacy area. What data are collected?<br>• How do you contribute to eliminating and minimizing safety risks?<br>• What is the procedure for reporting an incident or threat involving a patient or visitor?<br>• How do you prevent patient falls?<br>• What is the policy on allowing equipment (e.g., stretchers, portable radiographic equipment, etc.) in hallways?<br>• Describe any safety risks you encounter during your job. How do you protect yourself?<br>• What activities have been implemented to increase worker safety?<br>• What incident trends have been noted in the pharmacy area? | 4–83<br>4–84<br>4–97<br>4–116 to 4–119 |

*continues*

**Management of the Environment of Care**

| Standard | Comments | Evidence | Staff Questions | Reference |
|---|---|---|---|---|
| EC.1.1, EC.1.1.1, EC.1.5.1, EC.2.1, EC.2.8, EC.2.10.1 *continued* | | • Key near locked doors<br>• Exit signs visible and operational<br>• Negatively vented rooms for airborne substance isolation | | |
| EC.1.1.2 | This standard concerns enforcement of the organization's non-smoking policy in the pharmacy, including in visitor areas. | • Orientation and continuing education material on efforts to communicate and enforce the nonsmoking policy<br>• Nonsmoking policy and procedure<br>• Patient and family education materials on smoking cessation programs and activities<br>• No smoking signs posted, as appropriate | • Where can I smoke in the organization?<br>• Describe how patients, families, visitors, and staff learn about the nonsmoking policy.<br>• What do you do if a patient asks to smoke?<br>• If you observe someone smoking in the building, what is the procedure to follow?<br>• Has the organization been involved in any PI projects to promote smoking cessation? | |
| EC.1.2, EC.2.2, EC.2.8 | These standards relate to monitoring and compliance with the organizationwide security plan assessed by the surveyor during the pharmacy walk-through. | • Implementation of organizationwide and pharmacy-specific security plan and related policies and procedures<br>• Pharmacy associates should have knowledge of the following applicable policies and procedures:<br>–Security and key/lock/alarm control of pharmacy areas and medication areas outside of the pharmacy<br>–Security and key/lock/alarm control of mobile or automated medication storage and distribution devices in the pharmacy and in medication areas outside of the pharmacy | • What type of security do you have in the pharmacy areas? in the hospital or organization?<br>• Do you think there is enough coverage?<br>• Did you receive a security orientation? Do you receive continuing education on security?<br>• What is the telephone number of security?<br>• Who do you call if a patient or visitor threatens violence?<br>• Describe what you do if a patient has a weapon.<br>• Who is responsible for the metal detector, and how was that person trained?<br>• How do you identify a staff member in the pharmacy? In the organization? | 4–94 |

*continues*

**Management of the Environment of Care**

| Standard | Comments | Evidence | Staff Questions | Reference |
|---|---|---|---|---|
| EC.1.2,<br>EC.2.2,<br>EC.2.8<br>*continued* | | – Security during transport of medications throughout the organization<br>– Security incidents, including those related to civil disturbances, handling VIPs and the media, and staffing during disasters<br>– Identification/ID badge/visitor control<br>– Authorization processes for access to computerized systems and associated pharmacy technologies<br>– Management of patient property<br>– Kidnapping<br>– Workplace violence<br>– Patients with weapons<br>– Metal detector use, if applicable<br>– Care of prisoner guidelines<br>– Vehicular access to emergency department<br>– Access to sensitive areas secured<br>– Method for reporting security incidents<br>– Method for reporting missing patient or family property<br>• Security orientation, continuing education materials, education schedules, staff files<br>• PI projects, measurement of performance standards, action plans in response to security trends<br>*Site inspection:*<br>• Staff wearing ID badges<br>• Panic buttons for staff | • What do you do when you see someone without an ID badge?<br>• How do you report a security incident?<br>• What are your most common security incidents?<br>• Can you describe a security improvement in the pharmacy?<br>• Give me an example of a process for reducing security risks.<br>• How responsive is security when you call?<br>• Describe the procedure you use when a patient's belongings are missing. | |

*continues*

**Management of the Environment of Care**

| Standard | Comments | Evidence | Staff Questions | Reference |
|---|---|---|---|---|
| EC.1.2,<br>EC.2.2,<br>EC.2.8<br>*continued* | | • Physical design of pharmacy and medication areas outside of the pharmacy that includes locked doors to prevent public access to appropriate areas<br>• Appropriate securing of pharmacy areas<br>• Telephone numbers for security and police posted and/or readily available | | |
| EC.1.3,<br>EC.2.3,<br>EC.2.8 | These standards measure the department's ongoing monitoring of risk and compliance with the organization's hazardous waste plan.<br><br>Because the pharmacy has a high volume of certain hazardous materials, pharmacy associates should pay particular attention to policies related to organizational, departmental, and regulatory requirements.<br><br>Pharmacy leaders should ensure appropriate staff knowledge and monitoring and inspection activities, emergency and incident reporting, and the inspection, preventive maintenance, and testing of equipment. | • Staff and leadership interviews<br>• Material safety data sheets (MSDSs) accessible to staff<br>• Hazardous materials and waste plan, policies, communication<br>• Specific policies regarding the appropriate disposal of chemotherapy waste and sharps<br>• Orientation, continuing education, staff files indicating hazardous materials and waste training<br>• Compliance with reporting procedures for hazardous material spills<br>• PI projects, measurement of performance standards, action plans in response to hazardous material trends (e.g., pharmacy associate knowledge of what to do in the event of a hazardous material or chemotherapy spill)<br><br>*Site inspection:*<br><br>• Inspection showing proper use and disposal | • What orientation and continuing education did you receive concerning hazardous materials?<br>• What personal protective devices are available to you when you work with hazardous materials?<br>• Where do you store hazardous materials?<br>• What are some examples of hazardous materials used in the pharmacy?<br>• What does MSDS stand for?<br>• Where are MSDSs located?<br>• What information is contained in an MSDS?<br>• What procedure is followed when chemotherapy or hazardous material is spilled?<br>• How is a chemotherapy or hazardous material or waste spill reported?<br>• What procedure is followed if someone comes in contact with a hazardous material?<br>• What procedure do you follow if you encounter an unknown chemical?<br>• How do you dispose of contaminated sharps or gauze contaminated with body fluids? | 4–94<br>4–95 |

*continues*

**Management of the Environment of Care**

| Standard | Comments | Evidence | Staff Questions | Reference |
|---|---|---|---|---|
| EC.1.3,<br>EC.2.3,<br>EC.2.8<br>*continued* | | of chemotherapy and hazardous materials<br>• Appropriate space and ventilation, if required, for the safe handling and storage of hazardous materials and waste<br>• Labeling of hazardous materials, including chemotherapy and radioactive waste, in accordance with federal, state, and local regulation, in a manner adequate to protect patient, visitor, and staff safety<br>• Appropriate hazardous waste containers to minimize potential harm to patients, staff, and visitors<br>• Hazardous waste containers located appropriately throughout the pharmacy (off the floor)<br>• Flammable liquids stored in fire-resistant cabinets or room<br>• Toxic, corrosive materials segregated and appropriately stored and labeled<br>• Poison control number accessible to staff in all pharmacy areas | • Where do you keep information regarding poisons?<br>• Where is the telephone number of the local poison control center? | |
| EC.1.4,<br>EC.2.4,<br>EC.2.8,<br>EC.2.9,<br>EC.2.9.1,<br>EC.2.10.4.1 | These standards measure the compliance with and implementation of all phases of the organizationwide emergency management plan, to include mitigation, preparedness, response, and recovery. The standards include cooperative planning with other health care organizations that | • Organization's emergency management plan<br>• Pharmacy service emergency management plan, policy, role of staff<br>• Staff and leadership interviews<br>• Pharmacy participation in Safety and/or Emergency (Disaster) Management commit- | • Describe your orientation and continuing education on emergency preparedness.<br>• How does the pharmacy service manage demands in emergency situations (e.g., assigning staff, making space accommodations, ensuring availability of medications and supplies)? | 4–94<br>4–95<br>4–97<br>4–98<br>4–110 |

*continues*

**Management of the Environment of Care**

| Standard | Comments | Evidence | Staff Questions | Reference |
|---|---|---|---|---|
| EC.1.4,<br>EC.2.4,<br>EC.2.8,<br>EC.2.9,<br>EC.2.9.1,<br>EC.2.10.4.1<br>*continued* | provide services to a contiguous geographic area to facilitate information and resource sharing (to be scored effective January 1, 2003).<br><br>Pharmacy leaders should ensure the appropriate involvement of pharmacy services and associates in meeting the organizational plan. The Joint Commission requires that the organization participate in two drills annually, a minimum of four months apart and no more than eight months apart. The pharmacy service should participate in the drills. The drills may be executed in response to an actual emergency or may be planned drills. | tee, minutes of meetings<br>• Orientation and continuing education records demonstrating training of pharmacy associates<br>• PI projects, measurement of performance standards, action plans in response to emergency management (e.g., indicator might be the use of disaster critiques to prepare for future disasters)<br>• Dispensing and administration records for medications used in emergencies and drills<br>• Updated pharmacy service disaster call list/ on-call list<br>• Assessment and inventory of emergency medications<br>• Policy for communication to the pharmacy during an emergency or disaster<br>– Policy for communication with pharmacies in other local health organizations to facilitate sharing of information and resources in an emergency response<br>• Policy, if any, for granting emergency privileges within the pharmacy during an emergency or disaster<br>• Backup communication plan<br>• List of duties to be performed in an emergency<br>*Site inspection:*<br>• Emergency supplies accessible, stocked; | • When was the last emergency preparedness drill? What was the role of the pharmacy service and your particular role in the last emergency preparedness drill?<br>• Describe the community's involvement in the last drill.<br>• What was the feedback after the last emergency preparedness drill? What did you learn from the last drill?<br>• How often do you have drills?<br>• How is communication to the pharmacy conducted during a emergency or disaster drill?<br>• Describe any backup communication systems and alternatives to utilities.<br>• How would you manage patients in need of radioactive or chemical isolation and decontamination?<br>• Describe your evacuation routes. Describe your role in an evacuation.<br>• Who authorizes an evacuation?<br>• What equipment is available for transporting patients in emergencies?<br>• Where are the medical records to go during an evacuation?<br>• What is your procedure for notifying authorities when emergency measures are initiated?<br>• What is the alternative care site if evacuation is necessary? | |

*continues*

**Management of the Environment of Care**

| Standard | Comments | Evidence | Staff Questions | Reference |
|---|---|---|---|---|
| EC.1.4, EC.2.4, EC.2.8, EC.2.9, EC.2.9.1, EC.2.10.4.1 *continued* | | supplies (including electrical) in working condition<br>• Posting education/ procedures for managing emergencies, if available (e.g., Utility Systems Failure Guide, bomb threat procedures, etc.)<br>• Emergency preparedness drill records indicating pharmacy involvement/participation<br>• Evacuation routes posted | | |
| EC.1.5, EC.2.5, EC.2.8, EC.2.9.2, EC.2.10.2 | The life safety plan, or fire prevention plan, is organizationwide. Surveyors will look for monitoring and compliance in the pharmacy to determine whether the care area is fire safe. These standards measure compliance with and implementation of the organization's life safety plan.<br><br>Pharmacy leaders should be prepared to demonstrate a fire-safe environment within all pharmacy areas and nonpharmacy areas where medications are stored.<br><br>Pharmacy leaders should ensure appropriate staff knowledge, skills, and participation, as well as monitoring and inspection activities, emergency and incident reporting, and the inspection, preventive maintenance, and testing of equipment. | • Staff and leadership interviews<br>• Organizationwide and departmental life safety plan and department's role in contributing to, supporting, and implementing plan<br>• Implementation of fire response plan<br>• Orientation and continuing education materials, attendance records<br>• PI projects, measurement of performance standards, corrective action plans in response to life safety issues (e.g., staff knowledge of topic)<br>• Compliance with life safety codes and reporting of fire protection deficiencies, failures, and user errors<br><br>*Note:* Tabletop or poster fire drills do not satisfy the intent of this standard. | • Pharmacy associates may be asked to describe:<br>– Orientation and continuing education on life safety/fire safety<br>– The type of life safety training/fire safety training pharmacy associates receive<br>– Required and actual frequency of fire drills<br>– Whether drills are performed at least 50 percent of the time on all shifts<br>– Whether drills are conducted without notice<br>– How staff performance during drills is evaluated and whether feedback is provided to the staff<br>– What to do if there is a fire<br>– The location of the closest fire exit<br>– The location of the closest fire alarm and how to operate it | |

*continues*

**Management of the Environment of Care**

| Standard | Comments | Evidence | Staff Questions | Reference |
|---|---|---|---|---|
| EC.1.5,<br>EC.2.5,<br>EC.2.8,<br>EC.2.9.2,<br>EC.2.10.2<br>*continued* | | *Site inspection:*<br>• Roles and responsibilities of disaster plan<br>• Reporting of fire<br>• Inspection showing department compliance (e.g., hallways and designated fire exits unobstructed, electrical systems intact, fire alarm systems functional)<br>• Portable fire extinguishers properly identified, mounted, inspected<br>• Up-to-date inspection tags on all life safety equipment<br>• Building compartmentalization—smoke and fire partitions<br>• Interim life safety measures in effect during relevant construction projects (e.g., access to normal exit, entrance blocked, etc.) | – The location of the closest fire extinguisher and how to operate it<br>– Procedures to follow to contain smoke and fire<br>– Who is responsible for turning off oxygen valves in the event of a fire and for closing doors and windows<br>– How the pharmacy areas are evacuated during a fire<br>– What life safety measures take effect if a construction project blocks access to the pharmacy exits or entrances<br>– How the fire alarms are tested<br>– How to report life safety/fire safety concerns or violations<br>– Who the organization's safety officer(s) are | |
| EC.1.6,<br>EC.2.6,<br>EC.2.8,<br>EC.2.10.3 | These standards measure compliance with the organization's medical equipment management plan.<br><br>The pharmacy must demonstrate monitoring of risk and compliance with the medical equipment management plan. Any specific pharmacy policies and procedures must be consistent with the organizationwide plan. Pharmacy leaders should ensure that pharmacy equipment, especially equipment used in preparing, com- | • Staff and leadership interviews<br>• Organizationwide medical equipment plan and policies<br>• Pharmacy service's role in supporting and implementing the organizational plan<br>• Policies, procedures, and staff competencies related to pharmacy equipment used in the preparation, compounding, dispensing, and administration of medications<br>• Orientation, continuing education materials, and attendance records | • Pharmacy associates may be asked to describe:<br>– Orientation and continuing education on pharmacy equipment<br>– Who is competent and authorized to utilize pharmacy equipment and how this is determined<br>– How a piece of equipment is operated, including what to do if it malfunctions<br>– Who trains staff on using the pharmacy equipment and what the training process is when new equipment is introduced | |

*continues*

**Management of the Environment of Care**

| Standard | Comments | Evidence | Staff Questions | Reference |
|---|---|---|---|---|
| EC.1.6,<br>EC.2.6,<br>EC.2.8,<br>EC.2.10.3<br>*continued* | pounding, dispensing, and administering medications, meets the intent of the organization's equipment management plan, including appropriate maintenance strategies.<br><br>This should include packaging/repackaging/compounding equipment for oral, topical, and parenteral products, laminar flow hoods, automated medication storage and distribution devices, medication storage cabinets and refrigerators, medication, and administration pumps. | • Inventory of pharmacy equipment used in the preparation, compounding, dispensing, and administration of medications; this may be required during the Environment of Care Document Review (may show pharmacy inventory of equipment if surveyor inquires)<br>• Records indicating that equipment is properly maintained consistent with strategies to minimize risks identified in the equipment management plan, and that equipment carries inspection tags, and service logs are completed<br>• Organizational and pharmacy policies and procedures for reporting defective equipment and supplies to vendors, the FDA, etc.<br>• Documentation of actions taken regarding equipment recalls, medical device defects, medication recalls<br>• Specific pharmacy equipment competencies and pharmacy associate competency assessments<br>• Documentation of acting on equipment recalls and medical device sentinel events<br>• PI projects, measurement of performance standards, corrective action plans in response to medical equipment management (e.g., pharmacy | – How staff competency to use equipment is assessed<br>– What procedure is followed and who is informed if a given piece of equipment malfunctions<br>– How often a given piece of equipment is serviced or inspected and how this is known<br>– What the procedure is for checking the infusion administration pumps and defibrillators, and who is responsible<br>– What the policy and procedures are for reporting defective equipment or devices within the organization and to regulatory agencies<br>– What the policy is on safety testing of equipment prior to initial use<br>– What the policy is on safety testing for contracted equipment<br>– Who does the performance testing of sterilizers<br>– How and from whom training was received<br>– Whether equipment is loaned to other organizations, and what the process is | |

*continues*

**Management of the Environment of Care**

| Standard | Comments | Evidence | Staff Questions | Reference |
|---|---|---|---|---|
| EC.1.6, EC.2.6, EC.2.8, EC.2.10.3 *continued* | | staff knowledge of response to equipment failure, preventive maintenance, etc.) | | |
| EC.1.7, EC.1.7.1, EC.2.7, EC.2.8, EC.2.10.4, EC.2.10.4.1 | The utility systems plan is an organizationwide plan that promotes a highly functioning, adequately monitored, operational utility system by reducing the risks associated with utility failure. | • Staff and leadership interviews<br>• Organizationwide medical utility management plan and policies; pharmacy's role in implementing plan<br>• Orientation, continuing education materials, attendance records for instructional programs on utilities, medical gas management<br>• Utility inventory usually displayed in pharmacy document review<br>• PI projects, measurement of performance standards, action plans in response to utilities (e.g., staff knowledge of actions to take, emergency procedures to follow, in a utility system failure)<br>• Documentation in meeting minutes of any utility management issues within the pharmacy<br>• Inspection records of preventive maintenance, testing of utilities prior to initial use and at scheduled intervals based upon manufacturers' recommendations and organizational experience (most likely reviewed during review of Environment of Care | • What orientation and continuing education have you received on utility management?<br>• What do you do if the power goes out?<br>• How would you turn off the medical gas, if necessary?<br>• What would you do if you learned the water was unsafe for drinking?<br>• How do you report a utility problem, failure, or user error?<br>• Who examines, maintains, and tests critical operating components in the pharmacy? What is the inspection schedule for these critical components?<br>• Identify alternative sources of utilities.<br>• Describe clinical interventions that care providers may need to perform if there is a complete power outage. | |

*continues*

**Management of the Environment of Care**

| Standard | Comments | Evidence | Staff Questions | Reference |
|---|---|---|---|---|
| EC.1.7,<br>EC.1.7.1,<br>EC.2.7,<br>EC.2.8,<br>EC.2.10.4,<br>EC.2.10.4.1<br>*continued* | | documents or building tour)<br>*Site inspection:*<br>• Location of emergency shut-off controls for pharmacy utilities<br>• Labeling of control panels within pharmacy (performed during Environment of Care building tour)<br>• Appropriate emergency telephone numbers posted | | |
| EC.3<br>through<br>EC.3.4 | The survey will assess pharmacy compliance with organizationwide policy on environmental considerations related to patient services, dignity, and privacy. | • Policy for patient confidentiality and privacy<br>• Pharmacy budget for expansion projects, if applicable<br>• Door locking policies and procedures (for observation units, bathrooms, forensic patients, etc.)<br>• Documentation of risk assessment related to planned construction or renovation that might compromise patient care in the pharmacy<br>*Site inspection:*<br>• Appropriate space for services, cleanliness, etc.<br>• Adequate auditory and visual privacy for patients<br>• Patients not placed on stretchers in hallways<br>• Patient privacy not violated on overhead paging system<br>• Appropriate patient clothing, considering clinical condition | • Is there a telephone available for patients, as needed?<br>• Is there enough space in the pharmacy area to provide services? Manage a code?<br>• How are you sensitive to patients' needs for privacy, respect, and dignity in the waiting area and treatment rooms? | 4–106<br>4–112 |

*continues*

**Management of the Environment of Care**

| Standard | Comments | Evidence | Staff Questions | Reference |
|---|---|---|---|---|
| EC.3 through EC.3.4 *continued* | | • Place provided for private telephone conversations<br>• Doors closed where appropriate<br>• Emergency access to locked rooms, such as bathrooms<br>• Adequate lighting for patient care activities<br>• Acceptable ventilation<br>• Safe, clean and attractive environment<br>• Clearly marked exterior circulation<br>• Paths to the pharmacy | | |
| EC.4 through EC.4.4 | These standards address the organizational compliance regarding the social environment, ensuring that it meets the needs of the populations served.<br><br>Pharmacy leaders should ensure that the acute and ambulatory pharmacy areas where patients are cared for are appropriate in size, design, and appearance to foster patient safety, privacy, and dignity. | • Organizational and departmental policies for patient confidentiality and privacy<br>• Staff and patient interviews<br>• Privacy, respect, and dignity orientation; continuing education materials; and attendance records<br>• Pharmacy budget for expansion projects, if applicable<br>• Pharmacy environment of care data, environmental safety issues, and recommendations for improvement are integrated into the hospitalwide patient safety program (*effective January 1, 2002*)<br><br>*Site inspection:*<br>• Appropriate space for pharmacy care services, cleanliness, etc.<br>• Adequate auditory and visual privacy for patients<br>• Appropriate areas available for patient | • Is there enough space in the ambulatory pharmacy areas to provide private, dignified pharmacy services to patients?<br>• How did you receive orientation or continuing education regarding patient privacy, respect, and dignity?<br>• How are you sensitive to patients' needs for privacy, respect, and dignity in the pharmacy areas, patient care areas, as well as in any waiting areas? What safeguards are in place to ensure patient privacy, respect, and dignity? | |

continues

**Management of the Environment of Care**

| Standard | Comments | Evidence | Staff Questions | Reference |
|---|---|---|---|---|
| EC.4 through EC.4.4 *continued* | | medication education and counseling<br>• Patient information not posted or available in public areas—patient name not associated with any clinical information<br>• Patient privacy not violated on overhead paging system | | |
| EC.4 through EC.4.3 | These standards focus on whether the organization, including the pharmacy, seeks to improve environmental conditions. | • Environment of care data are collected on identified deficiencies and opportunities for improvement (e.g., use of surveillance data, risk assessments)<br>• Evidence of meeting minutes, reports, analysis of environment of care findings by multidisciplinary PI teams, plans for improvement to resolve any identified issues<br>• Outcomes and improvement reports, including annual reports of scope, objectives, and effectiveness for each of the environment of care plans. Reports demonstrate that recommendations for the environment of care have been communicated at least annually to hospital leaders for consideration. | • What data have you collected to measure the effectiveness of the environment of care plans in your area?<br>• What strategies have you implemented to improve the environment of care in your unit?<br>• How do you monitor the effectiveness of any new environment of care recommendations implemented?<br>• Describe how you resolve environment of care issues identified in your system? Service area? What other disciplines have you worked with to improve the environment of care? | |

## MANAGEMENT OF HUMAN RESOURCES

| Standard | Comments | Evidence | Staff Questions | Reference |
|---|---|---|---|---|
| HR.1, HR.2, and HR.2.1 | Pharmacy leaders should set standards for pharmacy practitioners that meet the needs and mission of the organization and the patients for whom it cares.<br><br>Pharmacy leaders should verify that there are sufficient pharmacy associates with the education, training, licensure, and knowledge consistent with legal requirements and organization requirements, and should use data on service and HR screening indicators in relation to patient outcomes to identify staffing needs and assess staffing effectiveness.<br><br>Further, all pharmacy associates' files should contain appropriate documents. | • Staff and leadership interviews<br>• HR policies and procedures<br>• Pharmacy associate personnel files that include:<br>– Licensure, if applicable<br>– Certification, if applicable<br>– Position description questionnaires/clinical privileges<br>– Orientation (organizationwide and departmental)<br>– Proof of continuing education credits<br>– Competency assessments (equipment, age-specific competencies, clinical knowledge base, etc.)<br>– Performance evaluations<br>• Job descriptions that reflect state law requirements for licensing and scope of practice<br>• Pharmacy staffing plan—including the numbers of each type of position needed to provide services on each shift each day<br>• Pharmacy organizational chart<br>• Data on clinical/service screening indicators such as family or patient complaints, patient falls, adverse drug events, injuries to patients, postoperative infections, urinary tract infection, upper GI bleeding, and shock/cardiac arrest | • Pharmacy leaders should be able to describe:<br>– Process for defining staff qualifications and responsibilities<br>– Mechanism for evaluating staff<br>– Method for matching staffing needs against the experience of staff<br>– Process for monitoring staffing and adjusting based on patient need<br>– Process for assigning staff to specific patient care areas (e.g., pediatrics, oncology, geriatrics)<br>– Method for ensuring that job descriptions meet essential job requirements<br><br>*To pharmacy associates:*<br>• What knowledge and abilities do you need to work in this organization?<br>• What special training or continuing education have you received in the last year to help you perform your job better?<br>• How are you trained to perform specific tasks or operate specific technology?<br>• How is your performance evaluated? Are there an adequate number of pharmacy associates on all shifts? | 4–99 to 4–111 |

*continues*

**Management of Human Resources**

| Standard | Comments | Evidence | Staff Questions | Reference |
|---|---|---|---|---|
| HR.1, HR.2, and HR.2.1 *continued* | | • Data on human resource screening indicators such as overtime, staff turnover and vacancy rates, staff satisfaction, understaffing as compared with the hospital's staffing plan, and sick time<br><br>*Note:* Personnel files representing the various positions within the pharmacy (e.g., pharmacist, pharmacy technician, pharmacy leaders/managers) will be reviewed in the HR interview | | |
| HR.3 and HR.3.1 | These standards relate to ongoing evaluation of staff competencies and improvement of competencies through self-improvement and learning.<br><br>Pharmacy leaders are responsible for planning continuing staff education initiatives that include a means of measuring how well pharmacy associates continually improve performance. Continuing education plans should be consistent with legal and regulatory requirements for licensure, certification, and/or registration. | • Staff and leadership interviews<br>• Pharmacy policies and procedures for continuing education standards consistent with legal and regulatory requirements for licensure, certification, and/or registration<br>• Current licenses, certifications, and/or registrations for applicable pharmacy associates<br>• Position description questionnaires and a performance evaluation process that links specific pharmacy competencies from the position description questionnaires with competency measures<br>• Orientation and annual competency evaluation related to the following areas (as applicable):<br>– Age-specific patient care | *To pharmacy leaders:*<br>• How do you ensure that staff have the pharmacy skills needed for their jobs?<br>• Describe how you identify staff learning needs.<br>• How do you monitor staff education requirements?<br>• What training have you planned for your department within the past year?<br>• How do you address the educational and staff development needs of the evening and night shift associates?<br>• Do staff pursue higher advanced degrees and training?<br>• How many internal educational programs have been made available to staff in the past year?<br>• How many external educational opportunities | 4–99 to 4–111 |

*continues*

**Management of Human Resources**

| Standard | Comments | Evidence | Staff Questions | Reference |
|---|---|---|---|---|
| HR.3 and HR.3.1 *continued* | | –Pharmacy equipment use<br>• Records of attendance for continuing education programs, self-assessments, outside seminars, etc.<br>• Evidence of pharmacy associate participation in professional organizations<br>• Rewards program/ career ladders for staff development initiatives<br>• Documentation for education budgets<br>• Employee satisfaction surveys relating to continuing education and staff development | have you offered staff in the past year?<br>• Is your staff development/education budget adequate to meet the educational needs of the pharmacy associates?<br>*To staff:*<br>• What type of educational programs are available? How often?<br>• Do they carry continuing education credits?<br>• If yes, how many continuing education programs did you attend in the last year?<br>• Are adequate resources available for continuing education (e.g., audiovisual aids, seminars, and conferences)?<br>• What was the last continuing education session you attended?<br>• How has it helped you to improve patient care?<br>• How were you oriented and continually educated to treat different age groups (e.g., infants, children, adolescents, geriatric patients)?<br>• How were you oriented and continually educated on the use of equipment and technologies used to compound and dispense medications to patients?<br>• How do you provide feedback to pharmacy leaders on your continuing education needs and concerns? | |
| HR.4 | This standard outlines the organizational and department orientation programs. | • Staff and leadership interviews<br>• Position description questionnaires, performance evaluation, | • Describe how a new member of the pharmacy service would receive the following: | 4–99 to 4–111 |

*continues*

**Management of Human Resources**

| Standard | Comments | Evidence | Staff Questions | Reference |
|---|---|---|---|---|
| | Pharmacy leaders are responsible for ensuring that orientation processes assess associates' abilities to fulfill specific responsibilities and familiarize associates with their jobs and the work environment, including job-related aspects of patient safety, before beginning their jobs. | competency, orientation, policies and procedures, etc.<br>• New employee orientation for the organization and pharmacy service:<br>–Attendance records<br>–Training materials<br>–Assessment tools and tests | –An orientation to the organization and pharmacy services—which would include specific equipment, policies and procedures, patient safety<br>–An evaluation determining that he or she is ready to perform the responsibilities of the job<br>• If volunteers, temporary employees, or agency employees work in the pharmacy, how were they oriented to the organization and the pharmacy service? | |
| HR.4.2 | This standard concerns staff participation in continuous education and training programs to improve competence and support an interdisciplinary approach to patient care.<br><br>The pharmacy leaders should ensure that pharmacy associates participate in the continuous education and inservice programs required by the organization.<br><br>*See also HR.3* | • Staff and leadership interviews<br>• Organizational and department-specific inservice and continuous education policies and procedures<br>• Training and staff development program schedules<br>• Documentation of interdepartmental and department-specific training concerning job-related aspects of patient safety, reporting of medical/health care errors<br>• Staff files indicating position description questionnaires, orientation certifications, performance evaluations, competencies, continuing education<br>• PI studies related to staff education and training<br>• Training tools | • Can you describe the organizational and departmental educational curriculum?<br>• Are training and continuing education programs designed for specific job classifications, patient populations, pharmacy technologies, and equipment?<br>• Describe any training you have participated in regarding patient safety and reporting of medical errors.<br>• Give examples of educational programs and/or educational tools available to meet continuing education and training needs. | |

*continues*

**Management of Human Resources**

| Standard | Comments | Evidence | Staff Questions | Reference |
|---|---|---|---|---|
| HR.4.3 | The pharmacy department participates by submitting and responding to data collected from pharmacy associates' training and continuing education initiatives. | • Staff and leadership interviews<br>• Records indicating that applicable data were submitted on pharmacy associate performance and competence to the organization's governing body<br>• Action plans addressing ways to improve staff competence | *To pharmacy leaders:*<br>• Describe trends in your pharmacy associates' competency and performance.<br>• Provide aggregate data that track and trend pharmacy associate competency and performance.<br>• How do you identify training needs?<br>• If applicable, what changes have been made in pharmacy associate education and training based on data trends identified? | 4–109 |
| HR.5 | This standard concerns the assessment of competencies related to specific patient age groups for staff with regular clinical contact with patients.<br><br>It is the responsibility of pharmacy leaders to ensure that this standard is consistently met. | • Staff and leadership interviews<br>• Organization and department-specific policies and procedures<br>• Pharmacy associate files and records including:<br>– Position description questionnaire<br>– Orientation curriculum and documentation<br>– Performance evaluations<br>– Competency certification for specific age groups (as applicable), pharmacy equipment and technologies, etc.<br>– Continuing education, training documentation<br>• Tools for measuring age-specific and equipment/technology competencies for specific pharmacy tasks<br>• PI studies involving performance evaluation and associated competency issues | • How are pharmacy associates evaluated for job performance competency?<br>• When applicable, do evaluations measure competencies and abilities to care for specific age groups? | 4–99 to 4–111 |

*continues*

**Management of Human Resources**

| Standard | Comments | Evidence | Staff Questions | Reference |
|---|---|---|---|---|
| HR.6 through HR.6.2 | Pharmacy leaders should be prepared to discuss the organizational and departmental policy in cases when a pharmacy associate requests not to perform a specific patient care task, with specific attention to ensuring that the patient care needs are met.<br><br>It is incumbent upon the pharmacy leadership to discuss with potential employees specific tasks that may conflict with their cultural values or religious beliefs and subsequently influence their desire for employment.<br><br>Pharmacy leaders should attempt to accommodate an associate's request to be excused from a specific task; however, in an emergency situation, when accommodations cannot be made, the associate may need to perform assigned duties so that the patient receives the care he or she needs. | • Staff and leadership interviews<br>• Organizational and departmental policy and procedure regarding the associate's right to request not to participate in any aspect of care because of cultural or religious beliefs<br>• Meeting minutes, Ethics committee meeting minutes | *To pharmacy leaders and managers:*<br><br>• Describe the organizational and departmental policy for accommodating the religious and ethical concerns of staff members.<br>• How would you ensure that patients receive needed treatment when an associate requests not to participate in a particular aspect of care?<br>• Describe how these policies are discussed with potential employees.<br>• How many times in the last year has a pharmacy associate requested to be excused from participating in providing care based on cultural values or religious beliefs? How did you accommodate this request without compromising patient care? | 4–112 |

## MANAGEMENT OF INFORMATION

| Standard | Comments | Evidence | Staff Questions | Reference |
|---|---|---|---|---|
| IM.1 through IM.1.1.2 | This standard addresses the hospital that has an information management (IM) plan created by assessing the organization's information management needs. Representatives from the pharmacy department must demonstrate they have participated and that their IM needs have been assessed so that these needs are incorporated within the IM planning process.<br><br>Surveyors may focus on:<br>• How pharmacy services are involved in the planning and design of IM processes<br>• How pharmacy leaders make their IM needs known to senior leadership<br>• How pharmacy resources are allocated to meet the scope and complexity of services provided<br>• How pharmacy associates participate in selecting, integrating, and using IM technology | • Staff and leadership interviews<br>• Pharmacy participation in IM planning, strategic plans, needs assessment surveys, requests to administration, etc.<br>• Meeting minutes indicating IM planning<br>• Evidence of IM planning for pharmacy services<br>• Medication use and pharmacy service PI projects that include outcomes improving patient information processes (e.g., plans for or observation of new computer system, charting, scheduling system, etc.)<br>• Information system generated utilization and work flow reports | *To pharmacy leaders:*<br><br>• Describe how you participate in IM planning.<br>• How has the organization assessed the pharmacy service's IM needs?<br>• Give an example of how the pharmacy service had an IM need met.<br>• Show IM reports and documents that pharmacy associates routinely use to provide service and care to patients and other organizational services and disciplines.<br>• How were you oriented to IM systems within the organization?<br>• How were you educated to translate to utilize available data in patient care decisions? | 4–8 to 4–10 |
| IM.2 through IM.2.3 | The pharmacy department should ensure that IM practices comply with organizational policies and procedures while allowing access to data and information in a timely fashion. To protect confidentiality and prevent loss, destruction, or tampering, pharmacy policies | • Staff, leadership, and patient interviews<br>• IM policies relating to access to information, confidentiality, release of information, preservation of the medical record, and destruction of records/copies<br>• Pharmacy policies relating to access to information, confiden- | • Describe how pharmacy associates preserve the confidentiality and security of data/information.<br>• What pharmacy associates have access to patient records? to the computerized information system?<br>• What backup procedures are in place to prevent | 4–7<br>4–114<br>4–115 |

*continues*

**Management of Information**

| Standard | Comments | Evidence | Staff Questions | Reference |
|---|---|---|---|---|
| IM.2 through IM.2.3 *continued* | and procedures should limit access to patient information based on need. Systems must be implemented to protect the integrity of the data (e.g., medical record, computer system, stored records, etc.).<br><br>Also, adequate backup procedures should be in place to prevent permanent loss or damage to medication information. | tiality, and the release of information—specific attention should be paid to the control of access to computerized pharmacy information systems and automated technologies, backup procedures<br>• IM plans and policies for protecting the integrity of data (e.g., operation of backup systems, contingency plans, down-time procedures, data retrieval, measures for protection against emergencies, security systems that include passwords, codes)<br>• Upon inspection, ensure that:<br>– Clinical information identifying patients is secure<br>– Active and inactive patient information is secure<br>– Confidential, sensitive patient information is not discussed in areas where it may be overheard by individuals other than the patient<br>– Computer terminals automatically log off when not in use<br>– Paper pharmacy records and records to be archived are secured and accessible only by authorized individuals<br>• Protective measures implemented to prevent distribution of sensitive information to public (e.g., proce- | permanent loss or damage to medication information?<br>• What information is accessible to pharmacy associates on the computerized information system? Do all pharmacy associates have the same levels of access?<br>• What do you do to ensure that confidential, sensitive patient information is not discussed publicly?<br>• What do you do if a family member asks to look at a patient's record?<br>• What is your policy on releasing clinical information or copies of the record? Do you get a consent for the release of information?<br>• How do you manage inquiries regarding patients?<br>• How are you trained on confidentiality and security of information issues? What special procedures do you have to protect patient information (e.g., staff sign confidentiality statements on hire or when using computer system)?<br>• What measures does the pharmacy take to protect information from being revealed to individuals not having permission? What processes protect the data or information from security breaches, harm, or alteration? | |

*continues*

**Management of Information**

| Standard | Comments | Evidence | Staff Questions | Reference |
|---|---|---|---|---|
| IM.2 through IM.2.3 *continued* | | dural schedules, not having patient sign-in log where patient information could be viewed by others)<br>• Measures to protect records from damage (e.g., sprinklers, fireproof cabinets) | | |
| IM.3 | These standards relate to the use of standard data terminology, definitions and abbreviations, as well as uniform data collection methodologies.<br><br>Where applicable, the pharmacy service should collaborate with the appropriate services and disciplines to ensure that the definitions and terms relating to medication use (e.g., medication administration frequencies, abbreviations, definitions for ADRs and medication errors) are consistently defined and standardized throughout the organization. | • Staff and leadership interviews<br>• Open and closed review of medical records as well as pharmacy records<br>• Minutes, feedback from medical record reviews distributed throughout the organization<br>• Medication use and pharmacy service PI studies, ADR and medication error surveillance data<br>• Definitions for ADRs and medication errors approved by the medical staff<br>• Medication administration frequencies and abbreviations tables approved by the medical staff<br>• Formulary document/ information | • How does the pharmacy service participate in standardizing medication-related definitions, abbreviations, and terminology used in data collection and review?<br>• How are the definitions for ADRs and medication errors used throughout the organization established and distributed? Do these definitions meet industry standards (e.g., those of World Health Organization, FDA, ASHP)? | 4–43<br>4–78 |
| IM.4 | This standard concerns educating staff on IM and addresses the education resources available to analyze data and transform it into information.<br><br>Pharmacy leaders should ensure that appropriate individuals understand security, confidentiality, data | • Education curriculum on IM that includes:<br>– Confidentiality, security, access to information<br>– Use of computers, software, databases<br>– Documentation in medical records<br>– Access to literature, library services<br>– Data collection techniques, | • What resources does the organization have to support IM education?<br>• What type of IM training has pharmacy staff received? From the organization? From the pharmacy? What elements does the education include? From the pharmacy viewpoint, has there been any specialized education? Have you | |

*continues*

**Management of Information**

| Standard | Comments | Evidence | Staff Questions | Reference |
|---|---|---|---|---|
| IM.4 *continued* | measurement instruments, tools, and methods to interpret and use data in decision making and process improvement. | ensuring of accuracy of collecting data<br>– Use of data, exchange of information, interpretation of data<br>– Tools available<br>– PI techniques for using data to support decisions, statistical and nonstatistical analysis methods<br>• Position description questionnaires indicating required IM skills<br>• Personnel files indicating IM training provided, based on the individual's job requirements and information needs<br>• Performance evaluation indicating adequate understanding and application of IM principles, data analysis methods, statistical tools<br>*Site inspection:*<br>• Staff interactions, use of data, computer system<br>• Pharmacy and medication resources (e.g., literature, books, journals, computer software, audiovisual tools) available to the staff | added any IM systems or support specific to your area?<br>• How are pharmacy associates selected to be trained in IM?<br>• How do you assess staff knowledge of IM?<br>• Who evaluates that these pharmacy associates understand and utilize IM principles? Statistical tools?<br>• What pharmacy indicators are collected to improve systems and processes? How do you ensure consistency when gathering the data? Have you trended your data? Do you use statistical techniques to interpret the data? | |
| IM.5 through IM.5.1 | This standard requires that appropriate, complete, and correct information, both written and verbal, be transmitted and disseminated among caregivers and other users in a standardized | • Staff interviews<br>• Policies and procedures for standardized medication administration frequencies and abbreviations approved by the medical staff<br>• PI data regarding the timeliness of specific | • Describe mechanisms used to ensure that information necessary for the medication use process is collected, received, and used in a timely and accurate manner. | |

*continues*

**Management of Information**

| Standard | Comments | Evidence | Staff Questions | Reference |
|---|---|---|---|---|
| IM.5 through IM.5.1 *continued* | fashion to facilitate interpretation.<br><br>Pharmacy leaders should ensure that accurate patient-specific medication information is available to other disciplines as appropriate.<br><br>Further, appropriate standardization to minimize the misinterpretation of medication information should be employed. | communication systems around the medication use process<br>• Policies, procedures, and indicators, organizationwide or specific to the pharmacy, including:<br>– Mechanism for ensuring that systems are compatible for accurate transmission and assimilation of data for analysis and reporting<br>– Medication record entry accuracy<br>• PI data, chart reviews, practices that ensure accuracy of data and information (e.g., use of standard abbreviations, codes, definitions, turnaround time, chart completion rates)<br>• Standardization of the record | • Can you give examples of how the organization standardizes medication use data and information (e.g., approved abbreviations and standardized administration frequencies)?<br>• How long does it take to receive medication orders from patient care areas?<br>• How long does it take to process and distribute or deliver medications to the patient care areas?<br>• How do medication orders get communicated to the pharmacy?<br>• Give an example of how the pharmacy service identified and improved the process of medication order turnaround. | |
| IM.6 | This standard concerns the use of the IM process to integrate and interpret data and information from different sources to support decision making.<br><br>Pharmacy leaders should ensure that the applicable laws and regulations regarding the retention of medication- and pharmacy-related information are followed, and that records are easily retrievable and accessible, if necessary. | • IM system structure that collects, organizes, analyzes, and assists with interpreting data<br>• IM plans, policies, and procedures on data management<br>• Interviews with pharmacy staff who collect, analyze, and use data<br>• Agreement with reference or external databases<br>• Applicable pharmacy policies and procedures outlining the retention policies for medication and pharmacy-related records as required by law, regulatory agen- | • If you have clinical systems, are they linked to your financial and billing system?<br>• How are department systems linked (e.g., pharmacy with laboratory)?<br>• Do you trend reports on volumes, staffing patterns, billing records?<br>• What are the legal and regulatory requirements for medication and pharmacy-related record retention?<br>• How are medication and pharmacy-related records retained, and who has access to retrieve any necessary information? | |

*continues*

**Management of Information**

| Standard | Comments | Evidence | Staff Questions | Reference |
|---|---|---|---|---|
| IM.6 *continued* | | cies, and clinical practice<br>• Reports demonstrating the integration of data from various sources, clinical with non-clinical information<br>• Examples of data being used for individual care, management, research, chart documentation, education<br>• Medication data and information transfer and storage policies and procedures that ensure confidentiality and ease of acccessibility | | |
| IM.7 through IM.7.2 | These standards require that a medical record be maintained for every patient treated or assessed, with entries made only by authorized individuals, and outline the patient-specific data that should be in the medical record in order to facilitate patient care. The medical record must contain information sufficient to identify the patient; describe and support the diagnosis; document tests and results relevant to managing the patient's condition; document the plan of care, progress of case, prognosis, and results; and promote continuity of care. This process displays how the organization captures, analyzes, transforms, transmits, and reports patient data and | • Staff interviews<br>• Open and closed medical records<br>• Pharmacy policies and procedures relating to required information on patient medication profiles<br>• Review of pharmacy patient medication profiles<br>• Compliance with medical staff bylaws, rules, regulations regarding pharmacy associates' privileges to enter medication use information in the patient medical record<br>• Quarterly medical record review results, use of performance data, outcomes (involving those elements listed in the intent of the standard)<br>• Evidence of involvement with PI initiatives relating to the adequate documentation of medication use infor- | • When reviewing a medical record, the surveyor may ask pharmacy associates the following:<br>– Where is the patient's identification data (i.e., name, age, account or medical record number, Social Security number)?<br>– Why did this patient come to the medical center? What was the diagnosis and treatment plan?<br>– What medication education did the patient receive?<br>– Who can document medication-related information in the patient record?<br>– Where is it noted that medications are given to the patient?<br>– Were any referrals made to internal or external care providers to ensure that the patient's continuing care needs | |

*continues*

**Management of Information**

| Standard | Comments | Evidence | Staff Questions | Reference |
|---|---|---|---|---|
| IM.7 through IM.7.2 *continued* | information. Medical records must be retained based on applicable state law and regulations. Patient care, research, PI, legal requirements, and educational endeavors may contribute to the length of time a record is retained. Patient-specific data and information may be used for clinical care; for financial, PI, and risk management issues; for support of research projects; and for decision making.<br><br>Pharmacy leaders should ensure that information required to adequately care for the patient is included in the medication section of each patient record. Information required by legal and regulatory agencies should also be included. Further, systems to ensure that only authorized pharmacy associates make entries into patient records should be in place. | mation in the patient record | are met? Where would that be documented?<br>• When reviewing a patient medication profile, the surveyor may ask pharmacy associates the following:<br>– What information is required on the patient medication profile?<br>– Who has the authority to document information on the patient's medication profile?<br>– Who has access to the patient's medication profile?<br>– How long are your records maintained? | |
| IM.7.3 through IM.7.3.5 | These standards concern documentation in the medical record of pre-, intra-, and postoperative (and/or other) procedures and the use of anesthesia or sedation.<br><br>Pharmacy leaders should ensure that the appropriate anesthesia documentation for the | • Staff interviews<br>• Open and closed document review<br>• Anesthesia records<br>• Policies and procedures regarding the medication administration documentation in the OR and recovery room, with particular attention to the appropriate documentation of controlled substances | • How are medications (including intravenous fluids) ordered in the OR and the recovery room?<br>• Where are medication orders and medication administration documented in the patient's operating and recovery room records? Who is responsible for documenting this information? | 4–78 |

*continues*

**Management of Information**

| Standard | Comments | Evidence | Staff Questions | Reference |
|---|---|---|---|---|
| IM.7.3 through IM.7.3.5 *continued* | administration of medications during the perioperative period is completed. This extends to unusual medication-related events or postoperative complications and their management. | as required by law<br>• Medication-related occurrence reports generated in the OR and recovery room<br>• Controlled substance inventory and administration documents | • How do medication-related occurrence reports get generated, and where is the information forwarded?<br>• How is the patient and/or family informed of a medication-related occurrence?<br>• How are controlled substances ordered and obtained from the pharmacy service?<br>• Where is the administration of controlled substances documented in the patient's OR or recovery room record?<br>• Who has access to controlled substances in the OR and the recovery room? | |
| IM.7.4 and IM.7.4.1 | These standards require that summary lists be developed for ambulatory care patients by the patient's third visit.<br><br>This standard is more applicable to outpatient settings such as family health centers and clinics. Pharmacy leaders should ensure that standards for ambulatory patient care records include pertinent drug allergy and medication information. | • Records of patients receiving ambulatory care services containing summary lists that include drug allergies and medications | • Do you have a policy on information required in ambulatory care patient records?<br>• Are drug allergies and medication profiles a part of the ambulatory care patient record?<br>• Who is responsible for ensuring that medication-related information is included in the ambulatory care patient record? | 4–10 |
| IM.7.7 | This standard addresses verbal medication orders.<br><br>Verbal orders for medications are common in many health care settings. It is | • Staff and leadership interviews<br>• Organizational verbal order policy and procedure—this should include a specific section regarding verbal orders for medications | • Describe the organization's verbal medication order policy and procedure.<br>• Describe the pharmacy service's verbal medication order policy and procedure. | 4–13 |

*continues*

**Management of Information**

| Standard | Comments | Evidence | Staff Questions | Reference |
|---|---|---|---|---|
| IM.7.7 *continued* | important that pharmacy leaders ensure compliance with organizational, legal, and regulatory requirements relating to verbal medication orders. | (reflecting legal and regulatory requirements) and the medical staff bylaws, rules, and regulations regarding verbal orders<br>• Pharmacy service verbal medication order policy and procedure<br>• Open and closed medical records, medication administration records, and patient medication profiles demonstrating that verbal medication orders are properly transcribed and processed, implemented, and countersigned<br>• PI indicator data used to monitor the effectiveness of the organization's policies relating to verbal medication orders | • How do you know that a verbal medication order has been acted on and completed?<br>• Who is authorized to give a verbal medication order?<br>• Who may transcribe a verbal medication order?<br>• Do verbal medication orders require follow-up countersignatures or approval? If so, what is the acceptable time frame for countersignature or approval?<br>• Are PI indicators in place to monitor the effectiveness of the organization's policies relating to verbal medication orders? | |
| IM.7.8 | This standard relates to medical record authentication.<br><br>This standard should be implemented on an organizationwide basis; however, pharmacy leaders should ensure that these standards are applied to all medication-related documentation in the patient record. | • Organizational policy and procedure regarding the dating, author identification, and, when necessary, authentication of entries in the medical record<br>• Pharmacy service policy and procedure regarding the dating, author identification, and, when necessary, authentication of medication orders<br>• Manual and/or computerized information system processes and documents showing dating, author identification, and authentication in effect | • Describe the organization's policy on identifying the author of a medication order and, when necessary, authenticating the medication order.<br>• How do you know that a prescriber is authorized to write for medications?<br>• Are there any medications that are restricted to specific services or types of prescribers? If so, what are these medications? How are prescribers authorized to write for restricted medications identified and, when necessary, authenticated?<br>• What do you do if you cannot identify or | 4–36<br>4–38 |

*continues*

**Management of Information**

| Standard | Comments | Evidence | Staff Questions | Reference |
|---|---|---|---|---|
| IM.7.8 *continued* | | • Open and closed records demonstrating compliance with policy and procedure<br>• PI data regarding authentification of data on medication orders<br>• Medical staff bylaws, rules, regulations, policies<br>• Manual and/or computerized lists of physician staff authorized to prescribe medications—including restricted medications (i.e., select antibiotics, chemotherapy agents, etc.)—that are easily accessible to clinical staff | authenticate the author of a medication order? | |
| IM.7.9 | This standard refers not only to pharmacy access to patient records but also to pharmacy contribution to the record in a manner that makes information accessible to staff providing follow-up care.<br><br>Pharmacy leaders should ensure that patient medication profiles are available to supplement the medication-related information in the patient medical record. | • Pharmacy policies and procedures relating to the availability of online or manual patient medication profiles<br>• Staff, leadership interviews<br>• Observation of staff accessing computerized or manual records | • Describe how pharmacy-related patient information can be obtained.<br>• Who is authorized to access patient medication profile information either online or manually?<br>• Show how to access a patient's medication profile.<br>• What if the pharmacy records for a specific patient exist in more than one location? How quickly can you assemble the pharmacy records from different settings (e.g., hard copy or screen display) or databases?<br>• How long are patient medication profile records kept in the pharmacy (computerized or manual) after a patient has been discharged or transferred? | |

*continues*

**Management of Information**

| Standard | Comments | Evidence | Staff Questions | Reference |
|---|---|---|---|---|
| IM.8 | This standard refers to the collection and analysis of clinical and administrative aggregate data. Scoring is based on a detailed list of data collection elements.<br><br>Pharmacy leaders should focus on the aggregate data regarding pharmacy transactions required by law, investigational drugs inventory and dispensing, medication error and ADR surveillance, defect reporting for medications or equipment used in the compounding or delivery of medication to pharmaceutical vendors and the FDA, and the documentation of radionuclides and radiopharmaceuticals obtained, administered, and disposed of within the organization. | • Policies and procedures relating to the maintenance of medication- and pharmacy-related documents in accordance with legal and regulatory agencies<br>• Policies and procedures relating to the maintenance of investigational drug inventories and dispensing records<br>• IM staff interviews<br>• Medication error and ADR surveillance policies and procedures and aggregate data<br>• Maintenance and quality assurance records for equipment used in the compounding or delivery of medication to patients<br>• Pharmacy policies and procedures for medication, product, or equipment defect reporting or recalls with associated tracking of reports submitted to vendors and/or the FDA<br>• Pharmacy and/or nuclear medicine policies and procedures for the procurement, administration, and disposal of radionuclides and radiopharmaceuticals used within the organization | • How are medication-and pharmacy- related documents maintained and stored in accordance with legal and regulatory agencies?<br>• How are investigational drug inventories maintained and recorded?<br>• How do medication error and ADR data get compiled and reported within the organization?<br>• What quality assurance records are available for equipment used in the compounding or delivery of medication to patients?<br>• How do you report a defective medication, product, or piece of equipment to the vendor and/or the FDA? How are these events tracked?<br>• How are medication recalls handled within the organization? Where are records of medication recalls and associated actions kept?<br>• Describe the process for procurement, administration, and disposal of radionuclides and radiopharmaceuticals used within the organization. | 4–78 |
| IM.9 through IM.9.1 | These standards concern the knowledge-based ("literature") IM needs of the organization. The standards also address where knowledge-based information is provided on site. A hospital need | • Staff and leadership interviews<br>• Availability of current knowledge-based medication literature and information systems (manual and online, internal and | • Describe resources available to meet your knowledge-based ("literature") medication information needs.<br>• How do you access knowledge-based medication information? | |

*continues*

**Management of Information**

| Standard | Comments | Evidence | Staff Questions | Reference |
|---|---|---|---|---|
| IM.9 through IM.9.1 *continued* | not have an on-site library but must demonstrate that information may be obtained in a timely manner by sharing services with another resource.<br><br>Pharmacy leaders should focus on the availability of authoritative, current systems, resources, and services to facilitate knowledge-based medication information. Pharmacy leaders should periodically assess the medication-related information needs of the clinical staff. | external) in pharmacy locations, patient care areas, and/or accessible library locations<br>• Survey of medication information needs of clinical staff<br>• Evidence of improvement and enhancement of the availability of knowledge-based medication information throughout the organization | • How do you provide input to the organization and/or the pharmacy service on the knowledge-based medication information needs you require to care for patients?<br>• Demonstrate how you access a piece of knowledge-based medication information.<br>• How have you used knowledge-based information to support management decisions and PI? | |
| IM.10.1 through IM.10.3 | Standards describe how comparative external reference databases are used to improve services provided by the organization.<br><br>Specific pharmacy-related benchmarking studies should be used to measure the performance of the pharmacy services provided against that in other similar organizations. | • Staff and leadership interviews<br>• Pharmacy participation in various comparative databases and surveys<br>• Proposals and recommendations for pharmacy systems–related improvement based on benchmarking comparisons<br>• Use of organizational patient satisfaction information (e.g., Press Gainey, Gallop) incorporated into pharmacy PI initiatives | • Describe the aggregate pharmacy data used to support patient care and operational decision making.<br>• What external databases are used by the organization for comparative data? What data do the pharmacy contribute?<br>• How have you used comparative benchmarking data to improve pharmacy services or pharmaceutical care provided to patients? | |

## SURVEILLANCE, PREVENTION, AND CONTROL OF INFECTION

| Standard | Comments | Evidence | Staff Questions | Reference |
|---|---|---|---|---|
| IC.1 | This standard refers to the organization's infection control (IC) program and selection of surveillance program based on specific criteria. The aim of the IC program is to reduce risks of infections among patients, staff, contracted workers, volunteers, students, and visitors.<br><br>Pharmacy leaders are responsible for contributing to the organizationwide IC and surveillance program by ensuring that pharmacy- and medication-related issues are included in the organization's program. | • Staff interviews<br>• Organizational and departmental IC plan, policies, and procedures<br>• IC committee minutes demonstrating pharmacy membership and/or contributions to the committee and function<br>• Pharmacy and Therapeutics/Formulary committee minutes related to IC<br>• Pharmacy meetings relating to IC issues<br>• Staff orientation and education that includes IC plan and ways to minimize risk of endemic and epidemic nosocomial infections in patients and health care workers<br>• Educational materials<br>• Specific policies and procedures for postneedlestick prophylaxis<br>• Specific medication- or pharmacy-related IC indicators tracked by the pharmacy service (e.g., needlesticks, return of used needles and syringes from patient care areas, appropriate disposal of needles and syringes, antibiotic resistance patterns) | • What is the organization's process for prevention, surveillance, and control of infection (i.e., standard precautions)?<br>• How does the pharmacy service contribute to the organization's IC program and surveillance?<br>• Describe the organization's IC training program.<br>• Where are the IC policies and procedures kept within pharmacy areas?<br>• What do you do if you are accidentally stuck with a needle?<br>• What PI initiatives has the pharmacy performed or participated in during the past year related to IC? | 4–116<br>4–120<br>4–123<br>4–127 |
| IC.1.1 | This standard refers to organizationwide management of IC by a qualified individual. | • IC plan, policies, and procedures<br>• Meeting minutes, plans reflecting qualifications of those overseeing IC/environmental health program | • Do you know who oversees IC and employee health?<br>• How do you find out about the activities of the IC committee? | |

*continues*

**Surveillance, Prevention, and Control of Infection**

| Standard | Comments | Evidence | Staff Questions | Reference |
|---|---|---|---|---|
| IC.2 | This standard addresses organizational data collection and surveillance regarding IC and employee health issues.<br><br>Pharmacy leaders should ensure participation in and contribution to organizationwide data collection and surveillance related to employee health issues. | • Staff observation and interviews<br>• Implementation of organizationwide and departmental IC policies and procedures<br>• Records of IC surveillance rounds, reports, and corrective action plans<br>• Pharmacy IC data collection that complies with organization requirements<br>• Records of employees' annual health assessments and nosocomial infections | • Describe your process for collecting data on pharmacy associates' health issues.<br>• What is a nosocomial infection?<br>• How do you monitor compliance with pharmacy IC procedures?<br>• What pharmacy- or medication-related IC issues have you identified in the last year? | |
| IC.3 | This standard concerns the organization's duty to report to public health agencies.<br><br>Pharmacy leaders should ensure that antibiotic resistance patterns are tracked and trended and made available to clinicians and appropriate organizational leaders. | • Policies and procedures on tracking, trending, and reporting antibiotic resistance patterns within the organization, and to public health agencies when appropriate<br>• Policies on reporting employee illness of epidemiological significance to public health agencies | • Describe the procedure for tracking, trending, and reporting antibiotic resistance patterns within the organization.<br>• How are employee health issues tracked, trended, and reported?<br>• Who do you contact within the organization regarding IC surveillance issues?<br>• Who is responsible for informing public health agencies of IC hazards? | 4–121 |
| IC.4 and IC.5 | These standards relate to reducing the risk of nosocomial infection throughout the organization.<br><br>Pharmacy leaders should be prepared to discuss the pharmacy service's contributions toward ensuring adherence to IC policies and procedures to limit risk of infection and decrease the incidence of antibiotic resistance. | • Staff observation and interviews<br>• IC orientation and continuing education material, attendance records for IC training<br>• Policies and procedures for the appropriate use, dating, and storage of drugs, specifically multidose and single dose vials of parenteral drugs, expired medications, and open oral medication containers | • Have you had any outbreaks of nosocomial infections identified within the past year related to medication or pharmacy issues? If yes, how have you responded to control the outbreak?<br>• How do you reduce the incidence of nosocomial infections?<br>• Describe IC orientation and continuing education programs for pharmacy associates. | 4–118 to 4–119<br>4–122<br>4–124<br>4–126 to 4–127 |

*continues*

**Surveillance, Prevention, and Control of Infection**

| Standard | Comments | Evidence | Staff Questions | Reference |
|---|---|---|---|---|
| IC.4 and IC.5 *continued* | | • Medication- or pharmacy-related PI projects to assist in the surveillance and control of identified outbreaks of nosocomial infections (e.g., antibiotics used for prophylaxis in surgery, appropriate antibiotic selection and utilization throughout the organization)<br><br>*Site inspection:*<br><br>• Proper disposal of waste that may transmit infection—needle boxes not overflowing and off the floor<br>• Appropriate clean room procedures and aseptic technique during the preparation of intravenous products for patients<br>• Staff demonstration of proper handwashing techniques<br>• Appropriate dating and storage of multidose and single dose parenteral vials and open oral medication containers<br>• Medication refrigerators:<br>– Clean<br>– Free of outdated containers<br>– No nondrug items present<br>– Thermometer and appropriate temperature ranges, logs | • If a pharmacy associate becomes ill on the job, what is the procedure to take care of the associate?<br>• Describe the process of antibiotic use in the operating room to prevent surgery-related infections.<br>• How are postoperative nosocomial infections tracked and trended? How is this information used to prevent further nosocomial infections and outbreaks?<br>• Name a few ways the pharmacy service ensures that the intravenous products made in the pharmacy are free of contaminants that may harm patients.<br>• What is the single most important way of preventing the spread of infection?<br>• Show me where you wash your hands.<br>• Why do you have an annual PPD (tuberculin) test?<br>• What is the procedure to follow in the event of an accidental sharp exposure or needlestick?<br>• Who is responsible for ensuring that areas where medications are stored and medication refrigerators are in compliance with organizational and departmental policies and procedures?<br>• What do you do when you discover expired medications? | |

*continues*

**Surveillance, Prevention, and Control of Infection**

| Standard | Comments | Evidence | Staff Questions | Reference |
|---|---|---|---|---|
| IC.6 through IC.6.2 | These standards concern organizationwide efforts to reduce the risk of infection transmission between patients and staff. Emphasis is placed on the use of management systems and automated IC data collection, analysis, and improvement efforts.<br><br>Pharmacy leaders should ensure that the pharmacy service contributes to the overall organizational IC processes to decrease transmission risk.<br><br>*See IC.4 and IC.5* | • Staff knowledge of objectives of IC program<br>• Employee health records regarding surveillance and immunization status of all employees<br>• Pharmacy service process for participating in IC program<br>– Knowledge of data collection efforts<br>– Data from specific PI initiatives to reduce the potential for antibiotic resistance and the contamination of intravenous products prepared by the pharmacy service<br>• Resources dedicated to IC surveillance initiatives<br><br>*See IC.4 and IC.5* | • What resources support IC practices within the pharmacy service? Are there adequate management staff and data systems resources dedicated to IC surveillance and practices within the pharmacy service?<br>• Describe one activity performed by pharmacy associates to reduce infections between patients and staff.<br>• How are pharmacy associates made aware of pharmacy-related IC surveillance data and trends?<br>• How do you provide feedback to pharmacy leaders to improve the IC-related processes within the pharmacy?<br><br>*See IC.4 and IC.5* | |

# PART 4

# Reference Materials for Pharmacy Department Compliance

The following forms serve as examples. Hospitals should consult with counsel or other appropriate advisors before adapting the forms in this part to suit particular purposes.

## Part 4 Contents

# 4–1
# Pain Management Chart Review Form

**ONLY REVIEW CHARTS ON PATIENTS WHO RECEIVE PAIN MEDICATIONS AT LEAST ONCE (INCLUDES ANY MEDICATION TO RELIEVE PAIN)**

**Name of Reviewer/Date:** ______________________________

| **DATA (attach copy of face sheet if information is accurate):** | |
|---|---|
| Unit/Campus: | ______________________ |
| Medical Record Number: | ______________________ |
| Date of Admission: | ______________________ |
| Primary/Secondary Diagnoses: | ______________________ |
| Patient Age/Sex: | ______________________ |
| Attending Physician: | ______________________ |

| **QUESTIONS** | **YES** | **NO** | **N/A** |
|---|---|---|---|
| Was the pain scale completed on the RN assessment? If YES, indicate intensity (0–10). | 1 2 3 4 5<br>6 7 8 9 10 | | |
| Was pain assessed prior to administration of medication (see progress notes)? | | | |
| Was pain assessed after medication administered (see progress notes)? | | | |
| Was any *patient and/or family* education documented in the record regarding the administration of pain medication/side effects, etc.?<br>If YES, indicate location of documentation. | __ Progress notes<br>__ Pt./family education sheet<br>__ Medication Kardex<br>__ Other | | |

* How many times was pain assessed (#)? ______________________

How many times did the patient receive pain medication (#)? ______________________

How many times was pain reassessed after receiving medication (#)? ______________________

Pain scale used to reassess? ______________________
YES NO

**List on back of this review sheet the following:**

___ Medications being administered to patient (may attach copy of list already within chart)

___ Comments/Opportunities for improvement

*Any entry in the progress note indicating the patient's pain was assessed by the physician or nurse. An assessment is not performed if the patient is in pain and pain medications are given without any documentation of an assessment. An assessment is when the patient is interviewed to determine the type of pain, intensity, location/scope as communicated by the patient verbally or non-verbally.

Source: Adapted from Kennedy Health System, Voorhees, New Jersey.

# 4–2
# Guide to Pain Management

Introduction: All patients have the right to have their pain assessed, treated, and reassessed. Assess pain using the pain scale. If the patient is unable to communicate, assess pain based on behavioral cues. The following are guidelines for the appropriate use of medications for the management of pain.

## Opioid Agonist Drugs

| Drug | Dose equianalgesic to 10 mg IM morphine | | Dosing Schedule | Duration of Action | Comments |
|---|---|---|---|---|---|
| | IM/IV[1] | Oral[1] | | | |
| ***Opioid Agonist Drugs Customarily Used To Treat Moderate Pain (Step 2)*** | | | | | |
| Codeine | 130 mg | 200 mg | q 4h | 2–4 | Usually combined with a non-opioid. |
| Oxycodone* | 15 mg | 30 mg | q 4–6h | 2–4 | Used for moderate pain when formulated in combination with a non-opioid. |
| Hydrocodone *(Vicoden)* | — | 5–10 mg | q 4–6h | 3–4 | Usually combined with a non-opioid. |
| ***Opioid Agonist Drugs Customarily Used To Treat Severe Pain (Step 3)*** | | | | | |
| Morphine | 10 mg | 30 mg (repeated dose) | IR: q 4h<br>SR: q 8–12h | 3–4 | Morphine-6-glucuronide in renal failure may predispose to additional toxicity. Available in IR and SR formulations. |
| Oxycodone | 15 mg | 30 mg | IR: q 6h<br>SR: q 12h | 2–4 | Formulated as single agent it can be used for severe pain. Available in IR and SR formulations. |
| Hydromorphone *(Dilaudid)* | 1.5 mg | 7.5 mg | q 3–6h | 2–4 | Alternative to morphine. |
| Methadone | 10 mg | 20 mg | q 6–8h | 4–8 | Plasma accumulation may lead to delayed toxicity. Dosing should be initiated on a p.r.n. basis. In opioid tolerant patients, start with 10–25% of the equianalgesic dose. |
| Fentanyl, Transdermal System *(Duragesic)* | — | — | q 72h | 48–72 | Patches available to deliver 25, 50, 75, and 100 mcg/h. Opioid naïve patients should be started at 25 mcg/h. |

*When combined with a non-opioid.
[1]Duration of analgesia is dose dependent; the higher the dose, the longer the duration.

Note: When switching from one opioid to the equianalgesic dose of another, initiate the new regimen at 50% to 75% of the equianalgesic dose.

**Management of Opioid Induced Constipation.** All patients on opioid therapy should be on an individualized bowel regimen unless clinically contraindicated.

Prevention - Docusate 100 mg bid plus Senna 1–2 tabs bid.

Bisacodyl 10 mg PO/PR at bedtime if no bowel movement in last 24 hours. Patients who do not have a bowel movement in any three-day period should be evaluated for impaction.

*continues*

4–2 continued

## Non-Opioid Analgesics

Indications for non-opioid analgesics:

- Mild pain. Start with a non-opioid. Acetaminophen or an NSAID (Non-Steroidal Anti-Inflammatory Agent) alone often provides adequate relief.
- Moderate to severe pain. Pain of any severity may be at least partially relieved by a non-opioid, but an NSAID alone usually does not relieve severe pain.
- Pain that requires an opioid. Consider adding a non-opioid for the opioid dose-sparing effect.

### Non-Steroidal Anti-Inflammatory Agents

| Drug | Recommended Starting Dose (mg/dose) | | Dosing Schedule | Max. Rec. Dose (mg/day) | Comments |
|---|---|---|---|---|---|
| | Oral | IV/IM | | | |
| Acetaminophen | 325–650 mg | — | q 4–6h | 4000 mg | Overdoses produce hepatic toxicity. No anti-inflammatory activity. No GI, platelet toxicity. |
| Aspirin | 325–650 mg | — | q 4–6h | 4000 mg | GI and platelet toxicity. Newer NSAIDs better tolerated. |
| Celecoxib *(Celebrex)* | 100–200 mg | — | QD–q 12h | 400 mg | Contraindicated in patients allergic to sulfonamides, ASA. Can cause GI toxicity. Use lower doses in patients <50 kg. |
| Ibuprofen | 200–800 mg | — | q 4–8h | 3200 mg | Contraindicated in patients allergic to ASA. Causes GI and platelet toxicity. Use with caution in decreasing renal, hepatic function. |
| Ketorolac *(Toradol)* | 10 mg | 15–30 mg | q 6h | 40 mg PO or 120 mg IV/IM | Recommended for use for 5 days. Use with caution in patients with renal insufficiency. Adjust dose for patients > 65. Causes GI toxicity. Contraindicated in patients allergic to ASA. Causes GI and platelet toxicity. |
| Naproxen | 250–500 mg | — | q 8–12h | 1250 mg | Caution in elderly patients. Decrease dose 50% for hepatic insufficiency. Monitor LFTs, BUN, $Cl_{er}$. Causes GI and platelet toxicity. Contraindicated in patients allergic to ASA. |
| Rofecoxib *(Vioxx)* | 12.5 mg | — | QD | 25 mg | **Contraindicated in patients allergic to ASA. No platelet toxicity.** Use with caution in decreasing renal, hepatic function. |

### Gastroprotective therapies for the prevention of ulcers in patients taking NSAIDs:

- Administer with food
- Misoprostol 100–200 mcg q.i.d.
- Sucralfate 1 g q.i.d.
- Antacids
- Famotidine 20 mg PO bid
- Lansoproazole 15 mg qd

*continues*

4-2 continued

## Adjuvant Analgesics Used for Chronic Pain

| Drug | Usual Starting Dose (mg/day) | Usual Effective Dose Range (mg/day) | Dosing Schedule | Comments |
|---|---|---|---|---|
| ***Anticonvulsants—Useful for Lancinating Neuropathic Pain*** | | | | |
| Carbamazepine *(Tegretol)* | 200 mg | 600–1200 mg | q 6–8h | Increase dose every 3–5 days. May cause Leukopenia or Thrombocytopenia. |
| Clonazepam *(Klonopin)* | 0.5 mg | 0.5–3 mg | q 8h | |
| Valproate Na+ *(Depakote)* | 500 mg | 1500–3000 mg | q 8h | Monitor LFTs. Titrate dose weekly by 5–10 mg/kg/day. |
| Phenytoin *(Dilantin)* | 300 mg | 300 mg | qhs | |
| Gabapentin *(Neurontin)* | 100–300 mg | 300–3600 mg | q 8h | Adjust doses for renal impairment. |
| ***Tricyclic Antidepressants—Useful for Neuropathic Pain*** | | | | |
| Amitriptyline *(Elavil)* | 10–25 mg | 50–150 mg | qhs | Increase doses q 3–5 days to a max of 300 mg/day. |
| Desipramine *(Norpramin)* | 10–25 mg | 50–150 mg | qhs | Increase as needed q 3–5 days to a max of 300 mg/day. Divide doses > 150 mg. |
| Doxepin *(Sinequan)* | 10–25 mg | 50–150 mg | qhs | Increase as needed q 3–5 days to a max of 300 mg/day. Divide doses > 150 mg. Decrease dose for hepatic impairment. |
| Imipramine *(Tofranil)* | 10–25 mg | 50–150 mg | qhs | Increase as needed q 3–5 days to a max of 300 mg/day. |
| Nortriptyline *(Pamelor)* | 10–25 mg | 50–150 mg | qhs | Increase as needed q 3–5 days to a max of 300 mg/day. |
| ***Miscellaneous Agents*** | | | | |
| Baclofen *(Lioresal)* | 15 mg | 30–80 mg | q 8h | Useful for lancinating and neuropathic pain. Titrate dose q 3 days to a max of 80 mg/day. Adjust doses for renal impairment. |
| Clonidine Oral *(Catapres)* | 0.1 mg | — | q 12h | Useful for neuropathic pain. Increase dose by 0.1 mg/day q 3–5 days to a max of 2.4 mg/day. Adjust doses for renal impairment. Available in a patch containing 0.1, 0.2, or 0.3 mg per 24 hr. Apply patch q 7 days. |
| Clonidine Epidural *(Duracion)* | 30 mcg/h | titrate | — | Adjust dose prn. Minimal experience with doses > 40 mcg/h. |
| Mexiletine *(Mexitil)* | 150 mg | 900–1200 mg | q 8h | Useful for neuropathic pain. Monitor plasma levels to decrease risk of toxicity. Use with caution in CV disease. |
| Lidocaine CIVI* | 2.5 mg/kg/h | — | CIVI* | Useful for neuropathic pain. Adjust for hepatic impairment. |
| Dexamethasone | 16–96 mg | — | q 6–q 8h | Useful for pain associated with brain metastasis and spinal cord compression. |

*Continuous intravenous infusion

The cause of pain must always be properly assessed. These guidelines are for the management of pain only. Patients may require a different dose or a different treatment approach. Patients who are already taking opioids will require higher doses to control new or worsening pain.

Consult with Palliative Care Service, Substance Abuse Consultation, Service or Pain Service as clinically indicated.

Courtesy of Montefiore Medical Center, Bronx, New York.

## 4–3
## Pain Control Plan

Pain control plan for ______________________________

At home, I will take the following medicines for pain control:

| Medicine | How To Take | How Many | How Often | Comments |
|---|---|---|---|---|
| ________ | ________ | ________ | ________ | ______________________ |
| ________ | ________ | ________ | ________ | ______________________ |
| ________ | ________ | ________ | ________ | ______________________ |

Medicines that you may take to help treat side effects:

| Side Effect | Medicine | How To Take | How Many | How Often | Comments |
|---|---|---|---|---|---|
| ________ | ________ | ________ | ________ | ________ | ______________________ |
| ________ | ________ | ________ | ________ | ________ | ______________________ |

Constipation is a very common problem when taking opioid medications. When this happens, do the following:

___ Increase fluid intake (8 to 10 glasses of fluid per day).

___ Exercise regularly.

___ Increase fiber in the diet (bran, fresh fruits, vegetables).

___ Use a mild laxative, such as milk of magnesia, if no bowel movement in 3 days.

___ Take ________________________ every day at ____________ (time) with a full glass of water.

___ Use a glycerin suppository every morning. (This may help make a bowel movement less painful.)

Nondrug pain control methods:

______________________________

______________________________

______________________________

Additional instructions:

______________________________

______________________________

______________________________

Important phone numbers:

Your doctor ______________________________

Your nurse ______________________________

Your pharmacy ______________________________

Emergencies ______________________________

Call your doctor or nurse immediately if your pain increases or if you have new pain. Also call your doctor early for a refill of pain medicines. Do not let your medicines get below 3 or 4 days' supply.

Source: Managing Cancer Pain, Consumer Version, Clinical Practice Guideline No. 9, Agency for Health Care Policy and Research, Public Health Service, U.S. Department of Health and Human Services, March 1994.

## 4–4
## Observation of a Patient

### STANDARD

All patients have the right to appropriate assessment and management of pain. Pain is assessed initially and on an on-going basis.

### PURPOSE

The pain management flowsheet is used to facilitate a regular assessment, treatment, and reassessment of pain. Multiple sites of pain can be recorded as needed.

The patient is involved in the management of pain. They are educated on the use of the pain scale and are involved in setting a comfort/function goal.

### PROCEDURE

1. The flowsheet is initiated by the nurse when the patient experiences pain.
2. Record the date, time location of pain, quality (use key), pain rating (use appropriate pain scale). Use signs of pain (use key) if patient unable to give a self-report of pain.
3. Record the medication name, dose and route and/or other non-pharmological pain relief treatments.
4. Record the patient's response by entering date, time, pain rating (signs of pain if unable), sedation rating (use key), and side effects (use key).
5. Initial/signature in space provided.
6. Indicate that the patient was educated on the use of the pain scale in space provided.
7. Record the patient's comfort/function goal.
8. The flowsheet may be kept with the patient's MAR to facilitate documentation. The form will be placed in the narrative notes section of the patient's medical record.

*continues*

**4–4** continued

| **Patient Assessment/Treatment** | | | | | | | | | | |
|---|---|---|---|---|---|---|---|---|---|---|
| Date | | | | | | | | | | |
| Time | | | | | | | | | | |
| Location | | | | | | | | | | |
| Quality | | | | | | | | | | |
| Pain Rating | | | | | | | | | | |
| If Unable, Signs of Pain | | | | | | | | | | |
| Med/Dose/Route | | | | | | | | | | |
| Other Treatment | | | | | | | | | | |
| Initials | | | | | | | | | | |
| **Patient Response IV/IM 30 Min. PO 60 Min.** | | | | | | | | | | |
| Date | | | | | | | | | | |
| Time | | | | | | | | | | |
| Pain Rating | | | | | | | | | | |
| If Unable, Signs of Pain | | | | | | | | | | |
| Sedation Rating | | | | | | | | | | |
| Side Effects | | | | | | | | | | |
| Initiate | | | | | | | | | | |

Patient Educated On Pain Scale: ☐

Patient's Comfort/Function Goal: ______________________

**Sedation Rating:**
1 = Wide Awake
2 = Drowsy
3 = Dozing
4 = Sleeping, (easy to arouse)
5 = Somnolent, (difficult to arouse)

0 No Hurt | 2 Hurts a little | 4 Hurts a little more | 6 Hurts even more | 8 Hurts a whole lot | 10 Hurts the worst

0 1 2 3 4 5 6 7 8 9 10

| **Int.** | **Signature** |
|---|---|
| ______ | ______________________ |
| ______ | ______________________ |
| ______ | ______________________ |
| ______ | ______________________ |
| ______ | ______________________ |

**Side Effects:**
1. Nausea
2. Constipation
3. Rash/Itching/Hives
4. Urinary Retention
5. Resp. Rate $\geq$ 10/min.
6. None

**Signs of Pain:**
1. Frown
2. Grimace
3. Restlessness
4. Guarding
5. Generalized Tension
6. Groaning/Moaning
7. Crying
8. None

**Quality:**
1. Sharp
2. Dull
3. Aching
4. Throbbing
5. Burning
6. Radiating
7. Stabbing
8. Cramping
9. Pressure

**PAIN MANAGEMENT FLOWSHEET**

Courtesy of Women's Health Services, Henry County Memorial Hospital, New Castle, Indiana.

## 4–5
## Baby Pain Scale

The FLACC Pain Assessment Scale, a behavioral scale for scoring pain will be used for neonates. In addition to changes in vital signs, the presence of pain behaviors may indicate the level of pain or discomfort present.

| Category | 0 | 1 | 2 |
|---|---|---|---|
| **Face** | No particular expression or smile | Occasional grimace or frown, withdrawn, disinterested. | Frequent to constant quivering chin, clenched jaw |
| **Legs** | Normal position or relaxed | Uneasy, restless, tense | Kicking or legs drawn up |
| **Activity** | Lying quietly, normal position, moves easily | Squirming, shifting back and forth, tense | Arched, rigid or jerking |
| **Cry** | No cry, awake or asleep | Moans or whimpers, occasionally | Crying steadily, screams or sobs, frequent complaints |
| **Consolability** | Content, relaxed | Reassured by occasional touch, hugging, or being talked to, distractible | Difficult to console or comfort |

Each one of the five categories is scored from 0-2, which results in a total score between 0 and 10.

**Scoring range:**
0 = no pain
5 = moderate pain
10 = worst pain

This score should be recorded in your nurse's notes with each set of vital signs and after procedures like circumcision, blood draws, etc.

Courtesy of Lee Memorial Health System, Fort Myers, Florida.

# 4-6
# Protection of Human Subjects Assurance Identification/IRB Certification/ Declaration of Exemption (Common Rule)

*Policy:* Research activities involving human subjects may not be conducted or supported by the Departments and Agencies adopting the Common Rule (56FR28003, June 18, 1991) unless the activities are exempt from or approved in accordance with the Common Rule. See section 101(b) of the Common Rule for exemptions. Institutions submitting applications or proposals for support must submit certification of appropriate Institutional Review Board (IRB) review and approval to the Department or Agency in accordance with the Common Rule.

Institutions must have an assurance of compliance that applies to the research to be conducted and should submit certification of IRB review and approval with each application or proposal unless otherwise advised by the Department or Agency.

| 1. Request Type<br>[ ] ORIGINAL<br>[ ] CONTINUATION<br>[ ] EXEMPTION | 2. Type of Mechanism<br>[ ] GRANT [ ] CONTRACT [ ] FELLOWSHIP<br>[ ] COOPERATIVE AGREEMENT<br>[ ] OTHER: ________________ | 3. Name of Federal Department or Agency and, if known, Application or Proposal Identification No. |
|---|---|---|
| 4. Title of Application or Activity | | 5. Name of Principal Investigator, Program Director, Fellow, or Other |

6. Assurance Status of this Project *(Respond to one of the following)*

[ ] This Assurance, on file with Department of Health and Human Services, covers this activity:
Assurance Identification No. ________________, the expiration date ___________ IRB Registration No. ______________

[ ] This Assurance, on file with *(agency/dept.)* ________________________________, covers this activity. Assurance No. ______________, the expiration date ____________ IRB Registration/Identification No. ______________ *(if applicable)*

[ ] No assurance has been filed for this institution. This institution declares that it will provide an Assurance and Certification of IRB review and approval upon request.

[ ] Exemption Status: Human subjects are involved, but this activity qualifies for exemption under Section 101(b), paragraph ____.

7. Certification of IRB Review (Respond to one of the following IF you have an Assurance on file)

[ ] This activity has been reviewed and approved by the IRB in accordance with the Common Rule and any other governing regulations.

by: [ ] Full IRB Review on (date of IRB meeting) __________ or [ ] Expedited Review on (date) ________

[ ] If less than one year approval, provide expiration date __________

[ ] This activity contains multiple projects, some of which have not been reviewed. The IRB has granted approval on condition that all projects covered by the Common Rule will be reviewed and approved before they are initiated and that appropriate further certification will be submitted.

8. Comments

| 9. The official signing below certifies that the information provided above is correct and that, as required, future reviews will be performed until study closure and certification will be provided. | 10. Name and Address of Institution |
|---|---|
| 11. Phone No. *(with area code)*<br>12. Fax No. *(with area code)*<br>13. Email: | |
| 14. Name of Official | 15. Title |
| 16. Signature | 17. Date |

Authorized for local Reproduction

Sponsored by HHS

Public reporting burden for this collection of information is estimated to average less than an hour per response. An agency may not conduct or sponsor, and a person is not required to respond to, a collection of information unless it displays a currently valid OMB control number. Send comments regarding this burden estimate or any other aspect of this collection of information, including suggestions for reducing this burden to: OS Reports Clearance Officer, Room 503 200 Independence Avenue, SW., Washington, DC 20201. *Do not return the completed form to this address.*

## 4-7
## HIPAA Privacy Rules: HHS's Final Version

**Background**

In 1996, Congress recognized the need for national patient privacy standards and, as part of the Health Insurance Portability and Accountability Act of 1996 (HIPAA), set a three-year deadline for it to enact such protections. HIPAA also required that if Congress did not meet this deadline HHS was to adopt health information privacy protections via regulation based upon certain specific parameters included in HIPAA. Congress did *not* enact health privacy legislation by the deadline.

HHS proposed federal privacy standards in 1999 and, after reviewing and considering more than 52,000 public comments on them, published final standards in December 2000, but had to make changes to address the serious unintended consequences of the rule that would have interfered with patients' access to quality care.

For example, patients would have been required to visit a pharmacy in person to sign paperwork before a pharmacist could review protected health information in order to fill their prescriptions. Similar barriers would have arisen when a patient was referred to a specialist and in other situations. In effect, the prior regulation, while well-intentioned, would have forced sick or injured patients to run all around town getting signatures before they could get care or medicine.

In March 2001, Secretary Thompson requested additional public input and received more than 11,000 comments, which helped to shape the improvements proposed in March 2002. Today's final improvements reflect public comments received on that proposal. The privacy rule is part of a set of standards required under HIPAA's "administrative simplification" provisions.

The final version, which was published in the August 14th *Federal Register*, includes some key revisions to address public concerns. The rule is available at http://www.hhs.gov/ocr/hipaa/.

Under the privacy rule:

- Patients must give specific authorization before entities covered by this regulation could use or disclose protected information in most nonroutine circumstances—such as releasing information to an employer or for use in marketing activities. Doctors, health plans, and other covered entities would be required to follow the rule's standards for the use and disclosure of personal health information.
- Covered entities generally will need to provide patients with written notice of their privacy practices and patients' privacy rights. The notice will contain information that could be useful to patients choosing a health plan, doctor, or other provider. Patients would generally be asked to sign or otherwise acknowledge receipt of the privacy notice from direct treatment providers.
- Pharmacies, health plans, and other covered entities must first obtain an individual's specific authorization before sending him or her marketing materials. At the same time, the rule permits doctors and other covered entities to communicate freely with patients about treatment options and other health-related information, including disease-management programs.
- Specifically, improvements to the final rule strengthen the marketing language to make clear that covered entities cannot use business associate agreements to circumvent the rule's marketing prohibition. The improvement explicitly prohibits pharmacies or other covered entities from selling personal medical information to a business that wants to market its products or services under a business associate agreement.
- Patients generally will be able to access their personal medical records and request changes to correct any errors. In addition, patients generally could request an accounting of nonroutine uses and disclosures of their health information.

*continues*

4–7 continued

HHS' privacy regulation is designed to enhance the protections afforded by many existing state laws. Stronger state laws and other federal laws continue to apply, so the federal regulation provides a national base of privacy protections. The standards for covered entities apply whether its patients are privately insured, uninsured, or covered under public programs such as Medicare or Medicaid.

Most covered entities have until April 14, 2003 to comply with the patient privacy rule; under the law, certain small health plans have until April 14, 2004 to comply.

HHS' Office for Civil Rights (OCR) conducts outreach and education targeted to health plans, health care providers, consumers, and others affected by the privacy regulation. These efforts include developing appropriate technical assistance materials, which includes fact sheets, handbooks, and other materials, as well as responding to frequently asked questions. HHS also will hold national educational conferences in the fall of 2002 to address issues related to key parts of the privacy regulation. Technical assistance materials will be posted on OCR's privacy rule Web site at http://www.hhs.gov/ocr/hipaa/.

Organizations governed by the new rules, or "covered entities," include health plans, health care clearinghouses, and health care providers who transmit any health information in electronic form in connection with standard transactions (e.g., claims submission and eligibility inquiries) identified under HIPAA. The Privacy Standards apply to "protected health information"—namely, individually identifiable information transmitted or stored in any form (i.e., paper, oral, or electronic) that concerns the individual's past, present, or future physical or mental health or that relates to the provision of health care to or payment of health care for the individual.

Covered providers who have a direct treatment relationship with an individual must obtain his or her written consent in order to use or disclose information for treatment, payment, or health care operations (e.g., training, credentialing, and business management activities). Use and disclosure of protected health information is permitted *without* the individual's consent, authorization, or agreement for specified public policy purposes (e.g., public health activities, law enforcement purposes, research, and serious threats to health or safety). For any other use or disclosure of such information, a covered entity must obtain the individual's written authorization (a more extensive document than a consent). Except with respect to disclosures to a provider for treatment purposes, covered entities must "reasonably ensure" that all uses and disclosures of information are limited to the minimum amount of information required to accomplish the intended purpose of the use or disclosure.

Covered entities will generally be permitted to disclose protected health information to "business associates," provided that they obtain contractual assurances from the business associate that it will safeguard the information. A business association is created when the right to use or disclose information belongs to the covered entity and another party requires the information either: (1) to perform a function for, or on behalf of the covered entity (e.g., billing or practice management services); or (2) to provide certain specified services (e.g., legal and accounting) to the covered entity. A business associate contract is not required where a disclosure is made for treatment purposes from one provider to another.

Courtesy of Julia J. Dodd., R.Ph., J.D., Cowles & Thompson, P.C., Dallas, Texas.

# 4–8
# Pharmacy Department Patient Assessment Policy
## DEPARTMENT OF PHARMACY

**Subject:** Patient Assessment
**Manual Code:**
**Date Issued:**
**Date Revised:**
**Approved by:** Director of Pharmacy ______________________________
**Reviewed by/Date:** ________ ________ ________ ________

## PURPOSE

The primary mission of the Department of Pharmacy is to advance rational, patient-oriented drug therapy and promote the application of pharmaceutical care concepts to contemporary pharmacy practice.

Pharmaceutical care is defined as the responsible provision of drug therapy for the purpose of achieving definite outcomes that improve a patient's quality of life. These outcomes are

- cure of a disease
- elimination or reduction of patient symptomatology
- arresting or slowing of a disease process
- preventing a disease or symptomatology

The purpose of patient assessment activities by the Department of Pharmacy is to ensure that patients are receiving the most appropriate, safe, and effective drug therapy for their clinical condition on admission as well as throughout their hospital course.

## SCOPE

The Department of Pharmacy cares for all patients admitted to the Medical Center. All inpatients and medication orders are assessed by the Department of Pharmacy as outlined in this policy.

## RESPONSIBILITIES

1. **Initial Basic Pharmacy Assessment**

   1.1 All patients and their admission medication orders are assessed by a Pharmacist upon admission to the Medical Center. All Pharmacists within the department perform Basic Pharmacy Assessment of patients and medications. The Initial Pharmacy Assessment is conducted within 8–12 hours of the admission and is initiated when the admission medication orders are received by the Pharmacy Department. This process begins with physicians making diagnostic and therapeutic treatment decisions resulting in admission orders.

   1.2 Initial Pharmacy Assessment includes but is not limited to:

   - Evaluation of medication order appropriateness in relation to the patient's active disease states and diagnoses.

*continues*

**4–8** continued

- Determination of appropriateness of medication dosages, routes of administration, frequency, and duration of therapy in relation to the patient's clinical status, age, drug absorption/elimination capacity (e.g., oral versus IV administration, GI absorption, renal/hepatic elimination), and desired therapeutic drug outcomes.
- Identification of any drug–drug, food–drug, and/or drug–disease interactions that could represent potential harm to the patient, that would indicate duplication of therapy, or would interfere with achieving the desired therapeutic drug outcome.

1.3 Clinical medication issues identified during the Initial Basic Pharmacy Assessment that require resolution are clarified and resolved by the Pharmacist in collaboration with the physician and/or nurse as soon as possible upon discovery.

Resolved medication order issues are documented by the Pharmacist in the patient's medical record with the use of the Drug Change Order/Clarification Form. Many medication issues are resolved by the physician discontinuing the medication order in question and writing a new order based upon discussion with the Pharmacist. Pharmacists also document these interventions to improve the quality of medication use through the Pharmacy Department's Intervention Documentation process.

2. **Continuous Pharmacy Basic Reassessment**

2.1 Patients and their medication orders are reassessed throughout their hospital course by a Pharmacist each time medication orders are renewed or changed or when new medications are ordered.

Continuous Pharmacy Basic Reassessment is triggered by changes in treatment plans made by the physician and initiated when new medication orders are presented to the Pharmacy Department.

2.2 The Continuous Pharmacy Basic Reassessment process includes the same activities outlined in sections 1.2 and 1.3 above.

3. **Pharmaceutical Care Assessment**

3.1 The Department of Pharmacy provides a more intensive assessment of patients and medication therapy for specifically defined patient populations within the medical center. This is termed a Pharmaceutical Care Assessment. Pharmaceutical Care Assessments in these targeted areas are completed within 24–48 hours after the patient is admitted to the clinical setting.

3.2 Pharmaceutical Care Assessment is patient-specific. It is prospective, because the primary responsibility of the Pharmacist conducting the Pharmaceutical Care Assessment is to prevent drug-related problems.

Pharmaceutical Care Assessment requires that the Pharmacist engage in a systematic comprehensive process whereby a patient's actual and potential drug-related problems are identified. To accomplish this, the Pharmacist must know what drug-related problems exist and identify what needs to be done to resolve them.

A drug-related problem is an undesirable event—a patient experience—that involves or is suspected to involve drug therapy, and that actually, or potentially, interferes with a desired patient outcome. There are two primary components of a drug-related problem:

- The patient experiences an undesirable event or incurs a risk. It can take the form of a medical complaint, symptom, diagnosis, disease, impairment, disability, or syndrome and can result from psychologic, physiologic, social, or even economic condition.
- Some relationship must exist (or be suspected to exist) between the undesirable event and drug therapy.

Almost always, a drug-related problem can be assigned to one of eight general categories or scenarios, as follows:

- A patient needing pharmacotherapy but not receiving it (a drug indication)

*continues*

**4–8** continued

- A patient taking or receiving the wrong drug
- A patient taking or receiving too little of the correct drug
- A patient taking or receiving too much of the correct drug
- A patient experiencing an adverse drug reaction
- A patient experiencing a drug–drug, drug–food, drug–disease interaction
- A patient not taking or receiving the drug prescribed
- A patient taking or receiving a drug for which there is no valid medical indication

3.3 The primary resources needed for the Pharmacist to establish the relationship necessary to conduct Pharmaceutical Care Assessments are:

- Access to the patient and all medical record and diagnostic information
- A clear, articulate understanding of the components of the Pharmaceutical Care Assessment process and the knowledge base to integrate the clinical patient information with existing pharmacotherapy skills
- A sound ability to articulate pathophysiologic, diagnostic, pharmacologic, pharmacokinetic, and pharmacodynamic principles as they relate to drug therapy treatment decisions
- An ability to communicate with the patient, physician, nurse, or other health care professional
- Dedication and commitment to provide pharmaceutical care reassessment and related functions from the beginning of the patient care process to its end

Pharmaceutical Care Assessments are performed by Clinical Pharmacy Managers and other specifically trained and skilled Pharmacists who perform a variety of clinical and administrative pharmacy functions.

3.4 Clinical Pharmacy Managers and appropriately trained and skilled Pharmacists provide Pharmaceutical Care Assessments for specifically defined patient populations within the medical center. These populations are targeted because the Pharmacy Department in collaboration with the Medical Staff has determined these patients to be at a high risk for developing a drug-related problem either because of their disease state, therapeutic drug regimen, or age-related complications.

These patient types include, but are not limited to, geriatric patients, infectious disease patients, family medicine patients, neurology patients, critical care patients, adult medicine patients, AIDS patients, renal dialysis patients, neonatal intensive care patients, pediatric patients, and patients on investigational drug protocols.

3.5 Any of the Clinical Pharmacy Managers and Pharmacists can be requested to perform a Pharmaceutical Care Assessment consult. These consults can be called by any physician or nurse caring for the patient and will be completed within 24–48 hours of the consult being called.

3.6 Documentation of Pharmaceutical Care Assessments is recorded in the patient's medical record allowing access by all health care professionals within the medical center.

3.7 Clinical medication issues identified during the Pharmaceutical Care Assessment that require resolution are clarified and resolved by the Clinical Pharmacy Manager and Pharmacists in collaboration with the physician and/or nurse as soon as possible upon discovery as outlined in section 1.3 above.

Source: Adapted from Montefiore Medical Center, Bronx, New York.

# 4–9
# Pharmaceutical Care Plan

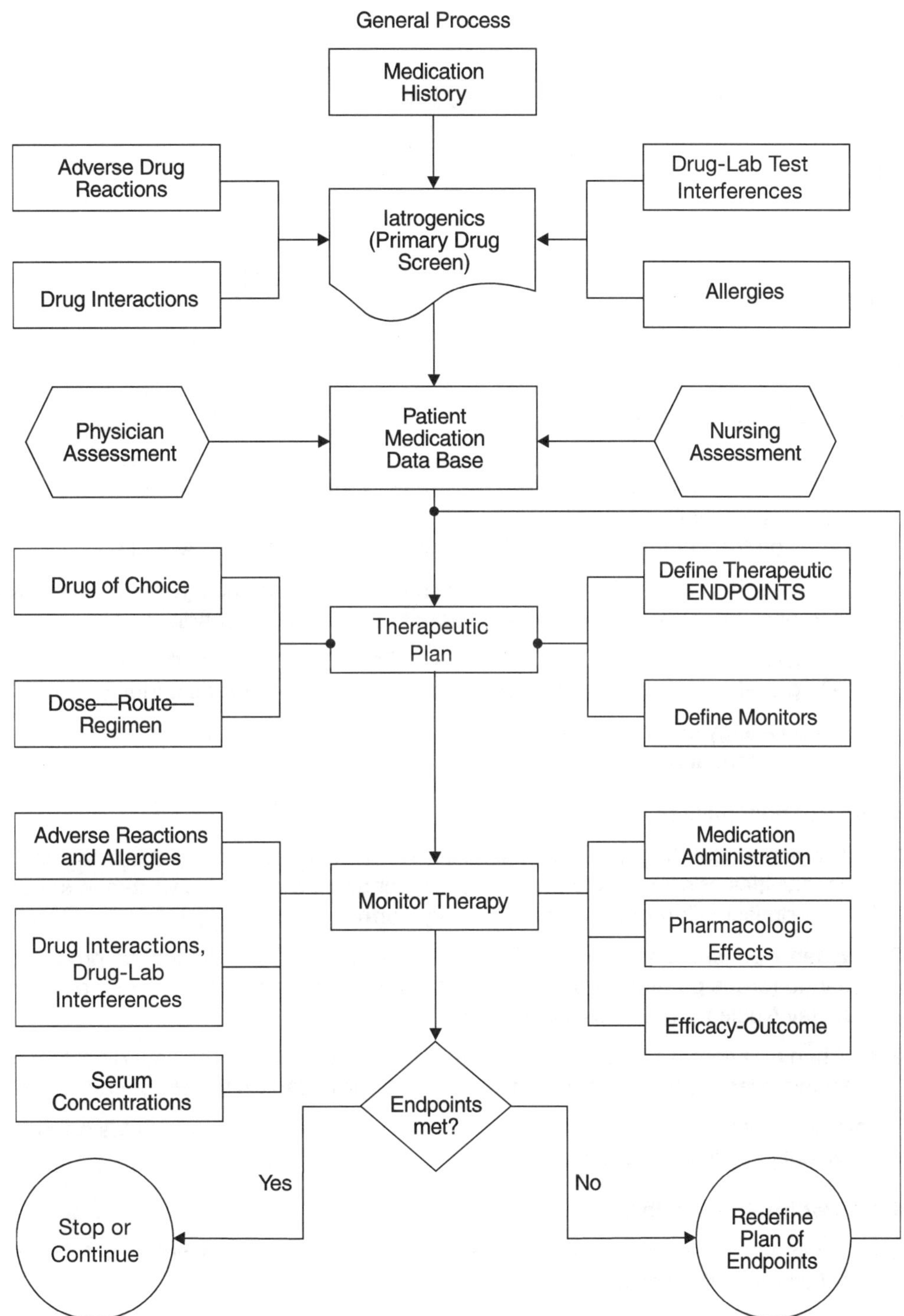


Courtesy of Johns Hopkins Bayview Medical Center, Baltimore, Maryland.

# 4–10
# Drug Sensitivities and Allergy Reporting
## DEPARTMENT OF PHARMACY

**Subject:** Drug Sensitivities and Allergy Reporting
**Manual Code:**
**Date Issued:**
**Date Revised:**
**Approved by:** Director of Pharmacy ____________________
**Reviewed by/Date:** ________ ________ ________ ________

**1. INPATIENTS**

1.1 **Physician's Responsibilities**

1.1.1 When preparing the patient's admission notes, the admitting house officer must include complete information concerning the patient's known drug sensitivities and allergies. This information shall be listed individually by allergy or drug sensitivity in the patient's admission notes on the Patient Progress Observation Record as such: "Allergies–PCN," etc.

Likewise, the same information above shall be noted on the left-hand side of the first page of the Doctor's Order Sheet along with the admitting diagnosis, condition, etc.

If the patient does not have any known drug sensitivities or allergies, this information shall be noted as such: "Allergies–None Known" in the spaces provided (e.g., Doctor's Order Sheet).

**Note:** Medication allergy information should be entered into the appropriate fields on the patient profile of the Clinical Information System.

1.2 **Nursing Responsibilities**

1.2.1 The nurse admitting the patient shall inquire as to whether the patient has any known drug sensitivities or allergy. Any drug sensitivity or allergies must be written in the space provided on the Admission Interview–Nursing History Form.

1.2.2 When a patient is sent to another area of the hospital for a diagnostic procedure, the nurse caring for the patient will write known drug allergies or sensitivities in the space provided on the X-Ray Nuclear Medicine Checklist Form.

1.2.3 When a patient is to be sent to the Operating Room, the nurse caring for the patient must record known allergies and sensitivities in the space provided on the Preoperative Checklist Form.

**Note:** Medication allergy information should be entered into the appropriate fields on the patient profile of the Clinical Information System.

1.3 **Unit Secretary Responsibilities**

1.3.1 When either a physician or nurse notes a drug sensitivity or allergy, the following "Alerts" will be activated by the unit secretary:

1.3.1.1 Drug allergies will be written on the top portion of each Doctor's Order Sheet, the medication administration sheet, the Kardex, and the cover of the chart binder.

*continues*

**4–10** continued

1.3.1.2 An allergy sticker will be placed on the patient's door card, identification bracelet, Kardex, Hollister Sign, and spine of the binder.

1.3.1.3 A Drug Sensitivity and/or Allergy label (NR7774) will be affixed to the Discharge Summary Sheet (AD 3751).

1.4 **Pharmacist's Responsibility**

Medication allergy information should be entered into the appropriate fields on the patient profile of the Clinical Information System.

1.5 **Medical Records Department Responsibility**

If an adverse drug reaction is noted upon review of the patient's medical record, the medical record coder shall check whether a Drug Sensitivity and/or Allergy label is affixed to the Discharge Summary Sheet. Finding none, he/she shall forward the chart to the Director for Clinical and Educational Pharmacy Services for review and allergy update.

**2. AMBULATORY PATIENTS**

2.1 **Physician's Responsibilities**

The physician caring for the patient shall list all known drug sensitivities and allergies in the intake history in the Patient Progress Observation Record. If there are no known allergies, this should be recorded as such: "Allergies–None Known."

2.2 **Nursing Responsibilities**

Whenever a drug allergy or sensitivity is noted, the nurse shall affix a Drug Sensitivity and/or Allergy label on the fact sheet and the chart cover.

2.3 **One-Day Stays**

The physician and/or nurse in the admission assessment will document any drug sensitivities or allergies and the associated adverse reaction(s) in the space provided on the Short Stay Admission and Ambulatory Surgery Form.

Source: Adapted from Montefiore Medical Center, Bronx, New York.

# 4-11
# Conscious Sedation Guidelines—Drugs Used for Sedation

**Note:** *The following is excerpted from Conscious Sedation Guidelines Policy, Johns Hopkins Bayview Medical Center, Baltimore, Maryland.*

**Recommended Intravenous Dosages of Drugs Commonly Used for Sedation**

**Adult Dosages**

| | Dose/Rate of administration | Maximum total dose | Onset (min) | Peak (min) | Duration (hr) |
|---|---|---|---|---|---|
| Fentanyl | 25–50 mcg/2–3 min | 3.5 mcg/kg | 1–2 | 15 | 1–2 |
| Meperidine | 10–20 mg/2–3 min | 1.5 mg/kg | 1–2 | 15 | 2–4 |
| Morphine | 1–3 mg/2–3 min | 0.15 mg/kg | 1–2 | 15 | 2–4 |
| Nalbuphine | 1–2 mg/2–3 min | 0.15 mg/kg | 2–3 | 5–15 | 4–6 |
| Diazepam | 1–2 mg/2–3 min | 0.15 mg/kg | 1–5 | 10 | 1–2 |
| Midazolam | 0.5–1 mg/2–3 min | 0.15 mg/kg | 2–5 | 15 | 2–6 |
| Lorazepam | 1–2 mg/2–3 min | 6 mg/h4 | 2–5 | 60–120 | 12–24 |

**Pediatric dosages**—onsets, peaks, and durations approximate those for adults

| | Dose/Rate of administration | Maximum total dose |
|---|---|---|
| Fentanyl* | 0.5–1 mcg/2–3 min | 3.5 mcg/kg |
| Meperidine | 0.5–1 mg/kg/2–3 min | 1.5 mg/kg |
| Morphine | 0.05–0.1 mg/kg/3 min | 0.15 mg/kg |
| Diazepam | 0.05–0.1 mg/kg/3 min | 0.15 mg/kg |
| Midazolam | 0.05–0.1 mg/2–3 min | 0.20 mg/kg |
| Ketamine** | 0.25–0.5 mg/kg iv | 0.5 mg/kg |
| | 2–3 mg/kg im | 3 mg/kg |

*See Appendix I for dosing guidelines for transbuccal fentanyl (Oralet®) and nasal, oral, and rectal midazolam.

**Give with atropine 0.03 mg/kg iv or im or glycopyrrolate 0.015 mg/kg iv or im to reduce oral secretions; ketamine is contraindicated in patients < 3 months of age.

There is wide variability in patient responses to sedative drugs. The drugs should be titrated slowly and the patient's response evaluated prior to giving additional doses of the same drug or another agent. Patients may require more or less than the recommended doses, depending on special needs or problems.

Dosages should usually be decreased in elderly or debilitated patients.

If the maximum dose is exceeded in order to obtain adequate conscious sedation, the physician must document the reason.

*continues*

**4–11** continued

No opioid or benzodiazepine may be used by continuous infusion.

In the future, additional drugs for intravenous conscious sedation may be approved by the Pharmacy and Therapeutics Committee.

## ADVERSE OUTCOMES/MANAGEMENT

Notify physician for

- oxygen saturation decrease of 3 points
- heart rate change of 20
- blood pressure change of 20 mm Hg

If ventilatory depression occurs

- Stimulate the patient.
- Call for assistance if no response.
- Perform a jaw thrust to relieve airway obstruction by the tongue.
- Assist or control ventilation with an Ambu bag/mask and 100% oxygen.
- Give naloxone if an opioid was given and/or flumazenil if a benzodiazepine was given.**
- The duration of action of naloxone and flumazenil is shorter than that of the opioids and benzodiazepines, thus the patient must be closely monitored for the recurrence of ventilatory depression.
- Call the arrest team (for those units serviced by the arrest team) if response to these maneuvers is inadequate.

**Recommended doses of naloxone and flumazenil (intravenous)

- Naloxone—Adult: 0.04 mg increments up to 0.1–0.2 mg/2–3 min to desired degree of reversal

Pediatric: 0.005 mg–0.01 mg/2–3 min to desired degree of reversal

- Flumazenil—Adult: Initial dose: 0.2 mg over 30 seconds. Repeat doses of 0.2–0.5 mg over 30 seconds given every minute to desired degree of reversal, not to exceed 3 mg/hr.

Pediatric: Flumazenil pediatric dosing is not well established, give initial dose 0.1 mg regardless of size. If ineffective, double dose in 1 minute.

### References

Guidelines for Monitoring and Management of Pediatric Patients during and after Sedation for Diagnostic and Therapeutic Procedures. *Pediatrics* 89:1112, 1992.

*Standards for Basic Intraoperative Monitoring,* American Society of Anesthesiologists, adopted October 6, 1986; amended October 18, 1989; effective January 1, 1990.

*Sedation for Diagnostic, Operative or Invasive Procedures. Interdisciplinary Clinical Practice Manual.* Policy Number PAT009. Johns Hopkins Hospital, p. 1–20, Dec. 1995.

Sedation for the pediatric patient. A review. *Pediatric Clinics of North America.* 41(1):31–58, Feb. 1994.

Practice Guidelines for Sedation and Analgesia by Non-Anesthesiologists. *Anesthesiology* 1996; 84:459–471.

*continues*

**4–11** continued

## Appendix I

The following drugs, although not administered intravenously, may produce hypoventilation. Therefore, pulse oximetry must be used and the readings documented as per this policy. Postprocedure monitoring standards must also be followed.

### Transmucosal Fentanyl Citrate (Oralet®)

Dosing:

- Pediatrics: 10–15 mcg/kg, not to exceed 400 mcg
- Adults: 5 mcg/kg, not to exceed 400 mcg
- Geriatrics: 2.5–5 mcg/kg

Hypoventilation may occur approximately 30 minutes after administration. Dose-dependent facial flushing, pruritus, and nausea and vomiting may occur. If an adequate response is achieved, or if excessive sedation develops before the lozenge is completely consumed, the remaining portion should be removed from the patient's mouth immediately.

### Midazolam

The intravenous form is administered nasally, orally, or rectally. The intravenous form tastes bitter and is often administered with liquid acetaminophen or cola.

- Nasal: 0.2–0.3 mg/kg, onset < 5–10 min
- Oral: 0.5–0.75 mg/kg, onset 20 min
- Rectal: 0.3–1 mg/kg, onset 10 min

*continues*

**4–11** continued

# Appendix II
# Drug Profiles

## Opioids

Clinical effects: analgesia, sedation

Side effect profile: All opioids have the same profile—nausea/vomiting, sedation, dose-related respiratory depression, pruritus, and hypotension. Morphine causes histamine release that may result in localized erythema or bronchospasm.

Special concerns

1. All opioids are potentiated by benzodiazepines, tricyclic antidepressants, alpha-2 agonists (clonidine), antihistamines, and acute alcohol ingestion.
2. Avoid concomitant use of opioid agonist-antagonists (e.g., Stadol, Nubain).
3. All opioids should be administered conservatively to elderly, opioid-naive patients, and patients with renal and/or hepatic insufficiency.
4. Meperidine should **NOT** be given to patients taking MAO inhibitors (coma or sudden death may result). Meperidine is vagolytic and may cause tachycardia.
5. Fentanyl, if given in large dosages rapidly, may cause apnea and chest wall rigidity, which may impair the ability to mask ventilate the patient.

## Benzodiazepines

Clinical effects: sedation, anxiolysis, amnesia

Side effect profile: dose-related respiratory depression, hypotension, confusion, dry mouth, visual disturbances

Special concerns

1. Respiratory depressant effects are potentiated by concomitant opioid administration.
2. Reduce dosages in patients with renal and/or hepatic insufficiency.
3. Stop administration if agitation and hyperactivity occur.
4. Diazepam is contraindicated in patients with untreated glaucoma. Diazepam has active metabolites that may be active 72 hours or more after administration.

## Ketamine

Clinical effects: analgesia, amnesia, sedation

Side effect profile: nystagmus, increased oral secretions, tachycardia, hypertension, hallucinations, dysphoria

Special concerns

1. An antisialogogue (atropine or glycopyrrolate) is usually given with ketamine to reduce oral secretions.
2. In adults, a small dose of benzodiazepine may be given prior to ketamine to reduce the incidence of hallucinations and dysphoria.

*continues*

**4–11** continued

**Reversal Agents**

Clinical effects: reverse side effects (mainly respiratory depression) caused by opioids and/or benzodiazepines

Side effect profile: Reversal agents may cause arrhythmias, seizures, hypertension, and angina due to catecholamine release.

Special concerns

1. Administration is not recommended for routine use for the purpose of hastening recovery.
2. Titrate slowly to desired effect; avoid overcorrection that would precipitate profound catecholamine release.
3. Seizure activity may be induced when flumazenil is given to patients with a history of seizures or tricyclic antidepressant poisoning.
4. Withdrawal symptoms may occur in patients with chronic opioid or benzodiazepine exposure when the antagonist is administered.

*continues*

**4–11** continued

## Appendix III
## Single Medication Administered Orally (PO), Rectally (PR), or Intramuscularly (IM) under Which the Sedation Protocol Does Not Apply

Whenever these or similar drugs are used by themselves as single doses and are given PO, PR, or IM, the sedation protocol does not apply.

Examples of single dose sedating drugs for adults:

| **Drug** | **Dose (mg)** | **Route** |
|---|---|---|
| Lorazepam | 1–2 | PO |
| Diphenhydramine | 25–50 | PO |
| Chloral hydrate | 500–1,000 | PO |
| Meperidine | 25–100 | IM |
| Morphine | 5–10 | IM |
| Phenobarbital | 15–60 | PO |
| Diazepam | 5–10 | PO |

____________________________ Vice President of Patient Care Services

____________________________ Chairman, Medical Board

Source: Adapted from Johns Hopkins Bayview Medical Center, Baltimore, Maryland.

# 4–12
# Medication Use Process: 16 Box Model with Subprocesses

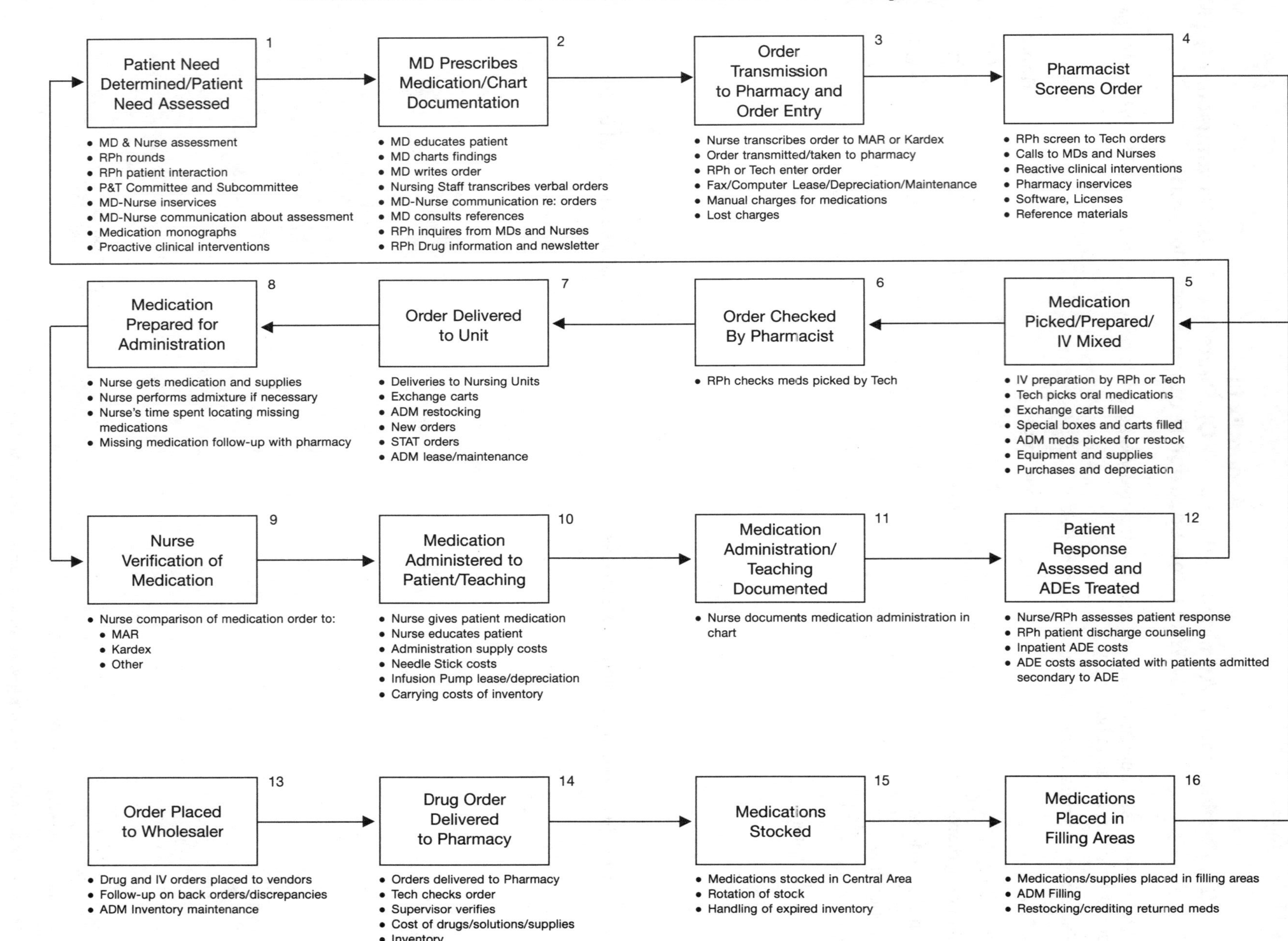


Courtesy of McKesson-HBOC.

# 4–13
# Prescribing Medications

**Manual:** Medication

**Issued by:** Pharmacy and Drug Information Service

**Revised:**

**Effective:**

**Department:** Pharmacy and Drug Information Service

**Authorization:**

**Prepared by:**

**Subject:** Prescribing Medications

## PURPOSE

To define who may prescribe medications and the requirements of a medication order.

## POLICY

A. Only physicians and dentists licensed to practice in the State of ___________ and appointed to the medical staff by the Board of Trustees of __________ Medical Center shall be allowed to issue orders for medications for diagnosis or treatment of ___________ patients.

B. All physicians and dentists on staff at _____________ must apply to the Drug Enforcement Agency for their DEA registration numbers. This number must be on file in the Pharmacy and Drug Information Service.

C. Medical Associates and Medical Assistants who meet the requirements outlined in Medical Staff Bylaws may issue orders for medications within the scope of their licensure/certification.

D. Resident physicians-in-training who have a graduate license and a license without restriction are permitted to write orders for all medications at the sole discretion and responsibility of the designated physician member of the Medical Staff responsible for the patient's care. These residents may prescribe controlled substances for outpatients only with a valid DEA certification.

   Resident physicians-in-training who have only a graduate license are permitted to write orders for medications pursuant to the following conditions:

   - the resident must be currently registered by the State Board of Medicine (i.e., have a graduate license) to participate in a training program;
   - the resident may write only noncontrolled (nonscheduled) prescriptions for inpatients or outpatients treated at or in affiliation with _____________ Medical Center;
   - the medical staff appointee responsible for the care of the patient is responsible for the orders and progress notes written by the resident on that patient's chart.

E. All drugs and medications ordered shall be those listed in the latest edition of the ____________ Formulary. Other drugs may be exceptions, if used in full accordance with all regulations of the Food and Drug Administration and as authorized by the Medical Center's Pharmacy and Therapeutics Committee. (NOTE: See Page ___ of _____ Medical Center Formulary.)

F. Ordered medications and iv solutions that are conditional on approval of another licensed medical practitioner (e.g., give Lasix 40 mg po x 1 if ok with Dr. X) will *not* be honored. Medication orders contingent on patient assessment are acceptable.

*continues*

**4–13** continued

G. All *medication* orders must contain

- drug name
- specific dose and dosage form (when appropriate—e.g., liquid, SR, etc.)
- range dosing (e.g., 50–60 mg) is disallowed
- route of administration
- frequency of administration

NOTE: prn orders must include maximum frequency (e.g., “PRN pain” is not acceptable; Q X hrs PRN pain is acceptable).

H. *Parenteral continuous infusion orders* must include

- base solution and volume
- medication(s) and dosage(s) to be added per volume
- rate of administration in volume/time (e.g., ml/hour, mg/min)
- in lieu of rates, an order to titrate to a defined endpoint is acceptable (titrate to maintain BP > 60).

I. All *changes* to IV solutions must include those items outlined in H above.

J. *Medications ordered to be held* will be automatically discontinued and will need to be rewritten unless

- Hold is conditional for a specific time frame (hold for 24 hours) or patient assessment (hold is BP > 160).

Source: Adapted from Hamot Medical Center, Erie, Pennsylvania.

# 4–14
# Intravenous Potassium Policy

**Subject:** Intravenous Potassium Administration Guidelines

**Manual Code:**

**Date Issued:**

**Date Revised:**

**Approved by:** ______________________________

**Reviewed by/Date Reviewed:** ________ ________ ________ ________

The intravenous administration of potassium salts (chloride, acetate, phosphate) may be indicated if a patient is unable to take potassium orally or if the patient's clinical symptoms warrant rapid drug administration. In general, oral administration is safer than intravenous administration. The risk of intravenous potassium therapy depends upon the rate and the concentration of the infusion. All concentrated potassium must be adequately diluted before administration. *Infusion of undiluted potassium salts could be fatal.*

## I. General Guidelines

A. Vials of concentrated potassium (chloride, acetate, phosphate) are not considered floor stock in any medical center location.

B. All intravenous infusions containing potassium should be administered with a volumetric OR syringe pump.

C. Premixed potassium chloride solutions are available as floor stock in adult medical/surgery patient care areas and should be utilized whenever possible to decrease the risk of medication errors.

D. If burning or pain occurs at the site of infusion, further dilution may be necessary. Check the IV site for infiltration or phlebitis.

E. The following guidelines do NOT apply to total parenteral nutrition solutions, which often contain higher potassium concentrations.

F. Oral potassium supplementation should not be given following the last soluset without a potassium level being drawn.

## II. Pediatric Guidelines

A. All orders for IV potassium chloride will be clearly written as mEq/L. All orders for IV potassium acetate will be clearly written as mEq/L. All orders for IV potassium phosphate will be clearly written as mEq/L or mM/L.

B. Intravenous potassium orders over a concentration of 80 mEq/L (potassium phosphate [$KPO_4$]: 55 mM/L) require written or verbal approval by the Pediatrics Critical Care attending physician. The attending physician must speak directly to the responsible nurse administering the medication. All orders must be countersigned within 24 hours.

C. Potassium solutions administered *peripherally* should not exceed a concentration of 60 mEq/L ($KPO_4$: 41 mM/L), except in emergent situations and with the approval of the Pediatric Critical Care attending, not to exceed a concentration of 80 mEq/L ($KPO_4$: 55 mM/L) over 1 hour.

D. Intravenous potassium administration should not exceed 0.5 mEq/kg/h ($KPO_4$: 0.34 mM/kg/h) without attending physician approval. The physician will write in the "comments" section of the order sheet the IV potassium rate (mEq(mM)/kg/h).

*continues*

**4–14** continued

E. Bolus administration of IV potassium at 0.5 mEq/kg/h over 1 hour (to an adult maximum of 20 mEq) must be administered by syringe pump for infants of less than 10 kg body weight. Intravenous potassium 0.5 mEq/kg should be diluted to a maximum concentration of 1 mEq/3 mL and should be infused over 1 hour.

Example: A 1.5-mEq potassium chloride order in a 3-kg infant (0.5 mEq/kg) should be diluted in 5 mL $D_5W$ and run at 5 mL/h over 1 hour.

Microbore tubing should be used to connect the bolus infusion from the syringe pump to the patient's central venous line. Syringe pumps may also be used for patients weighing more than 10 kg.

F. Concentrated IV potassium must be diluted prior to administration. Intravenous potassium will be diluted in either 500-ml or 1,000-ml *bags* (not solusets). The finished product will be labeled and appropriately initiated by the associate preparing the solution. Potassium-containing infusions for pediatric patients will be compounded by the Pediatric Pharmacy Satellite.

Please refer to Table 1 for specific administration guidelines.

**III. Neonatal Intensive Care Unit Guidelines***

A. All orders for IV potassium chloride will be clearly written as mEq/L. All orders for IV potassium acetate will be clearly written as mEq/L. All orders for IV potassium phosphate will be clearly written as mEq/L or mM/L.

B. All intravenous potassium infusions must be administered through a syringe pump. Continuous EKG monitoring is mandatory for both peripheral and central infusions.

C. Acute treatment of symptomatic hypokalemia with potassium chloride should begin at 0.5 to 1.0 mEq/kg/h, over 1 hour. Potassium chloride administration should not exceed this rate without attending physician approval.

D. The maximum concentration for potassium chloride peripheral infusions is 40 mEq/L and 80 mEq/L for central venous infusions. The rate of any maintenance infusion should depend on the clinical needs of the patient.

Please refer to Table 1 for a summary of administration guidelines.

**IV. Adult Guidelines**

A. All orders for IV potassium chloride will be clearly written as mEq/L. All orders for IV potassium acetate will be clearly written as mEq/L. All orders for IV potassium phosphate will be clearly written as mEq/L or mM/L.

B. Orders for potassium chloride infusions other than the commercially available solutions or for any other IV potassium salts (acetate, phosphate) will require dispensing on a patient-specific order only. The pharmacist will dispense only enough potassium to administer a 24–48 hour infusion. Individual vials will be labeled with the appropriate patient demographic information and necessary warning labels (i.e., CONCENTRATED POTASSIUM: DILUTE PRIOR TO USE!).

C. The maximum concentration for potassium-containing maintenance infusions is generally 40 mEq/L ($KPO_4$: 27 mM/L). The rate of any maintenance infusion should depend on the clinical needs of the patient.

D. For patients with serum potassium concentrations of less than 3 mEq/L, potassium chloride boluses should be infused at a maximum rate of 10 to 20 mEq/h.

E. Concentrations of IV potassium greater than 40 mEq/100 mL ($KPO_4$: 27 mM/100 mL) must be administered centrally. Potassium chloride 20 mEq/100 mL boluses should be administered either through a large peripheral or central vein.

F. Potassium concentrations should be monitored at least daily or at the completion of the bolus infusions. The infusion site should be inspected daily for signs of vein irritation or phlebitis.

Please refer to Table 1 for specific administration guidelines.

---

* Information abstracted from *Neofax*, 1998.

*continues*

**4–14** continued

## Table 1
## Guidelines for Intravenous Potassium Administration

| | *Type of Infusion* | *Maximum Rate* | *Site of Infusion* | *Maximum Concentration* | *Monitoring* |
|---|---|---|---|---|---|
| **Neonatal ICU** | | | | | |
| | Maintenance (KCL only) | 0.5–1 mEq/kg/d | Peripheral | 40 mEq/L | Serum $K^+$ at least daily; routine inspection of infusion site; continuous ECG monitoring |
| | | 0.5–1 mEq/kg/d | Central | 80 mEq/L | (See above) |
| | Acute (bolus) (KCL only) | 0.5–1 mEq/kg/h over 1 hour | Peripheral or central | (See above) | (See above) |
| **Pediatrics**[a] | | | | | |
| | Maintenance | 0.5 mEq/kg/h[b] ($KPO_4$: 0.34 mM/kg/h)[d] | Peripherally | 60 mEq/L[c] ($KPO_4$: 41 mM/L) | Serum $K^+$ at least daily; routine inspection of infusion site |
| | Acute (bolus) (KCL and K acetate only) | 0.5 mEq/kg/h[b] | Peripherally | 60 mEq/L[c] | Serum $K^+$ after KCL infused; routine inspection of infusion site |
| | | 0.5 mEq/kg/h[b] ($KPO_4$: 0.34 mM/kg/h) | Centrally | Variable—per patient status[c] | Serum $K^+$ after KCL infused; continuous ECG monitoring. Potassium concentrations above 80 mEq/L ($KPO_4$: 55 mM/L) require approval of the Pediatric Critical Care attending |
| **Adults** | | | | | |
| | Maintenance (continuous infusion) | Variable | Peripheral or central | 40 mEq/L ($KPO_4$: 27 mM/L)[d] | Serum $K^+$ at least daily; routine inspection of infusion site |
| | Acute (bolus) (KCL and K acetate only) | 10 mEq/h for serum $K^+$ $\geq$ 3 mEq/L | Peripheral | 20 mEq/100 mL | Serum $K^+$ at end of three 10-mEq solusets; routine inspection of infusion site |
| | | 10–20 mEq/h for serum $K^+$ < 3 mEq/L if asymptomatic | Peripheral or large vein (ie, antecubital) | 20 mEq/100 mL | Serum $K^+$ 2 hours after a total of 30 mEq infused; continuous EKG monitoring for rates of $\geq$ 20 mEq/h; routine inspection of infusion site |
| | | 20 mEq/h for serum $K^+$ < 3 mEq/L and symptomatic | Central line only | 20 mEq/50 mL | Serum $K^+$ after 20 mEq/h infused; continuous ECG monitoring |

a. IV potassium will be diluted in either 500-ml or 1,000-ml bags (not solusets). Potassium-containing infusions will be compounded by the Pediatric Pharmacy Satellite.

b. IV potassium administration should not exceed 0.5 mEq/kg/h ($KPO_4$: 0.34 mM/kg/h) without Pediatric attending physician approval.

c. Potassium orders over 80 mEq/L (potassium phosphate [$KPO_4$]: 55 mM/L) require written or verbal approval by Pediatric Critical Care attending physician.
Potassium-containing solutions administered *peripherally* should not exceed 60 mEq/L ($KPO_4$: 41 mM/L), except in emergent situations and with the approval of the Pediatric Critical Care attending.

d. $KPO_4$ = Potassium phosphate. $KPO_4$ will be clearly written as mEq/L or mM/L.

Source: Adapted from Montefiore Medical Center, Bronx, New York.

## 4–15
## Formulary Decisions Algorithm

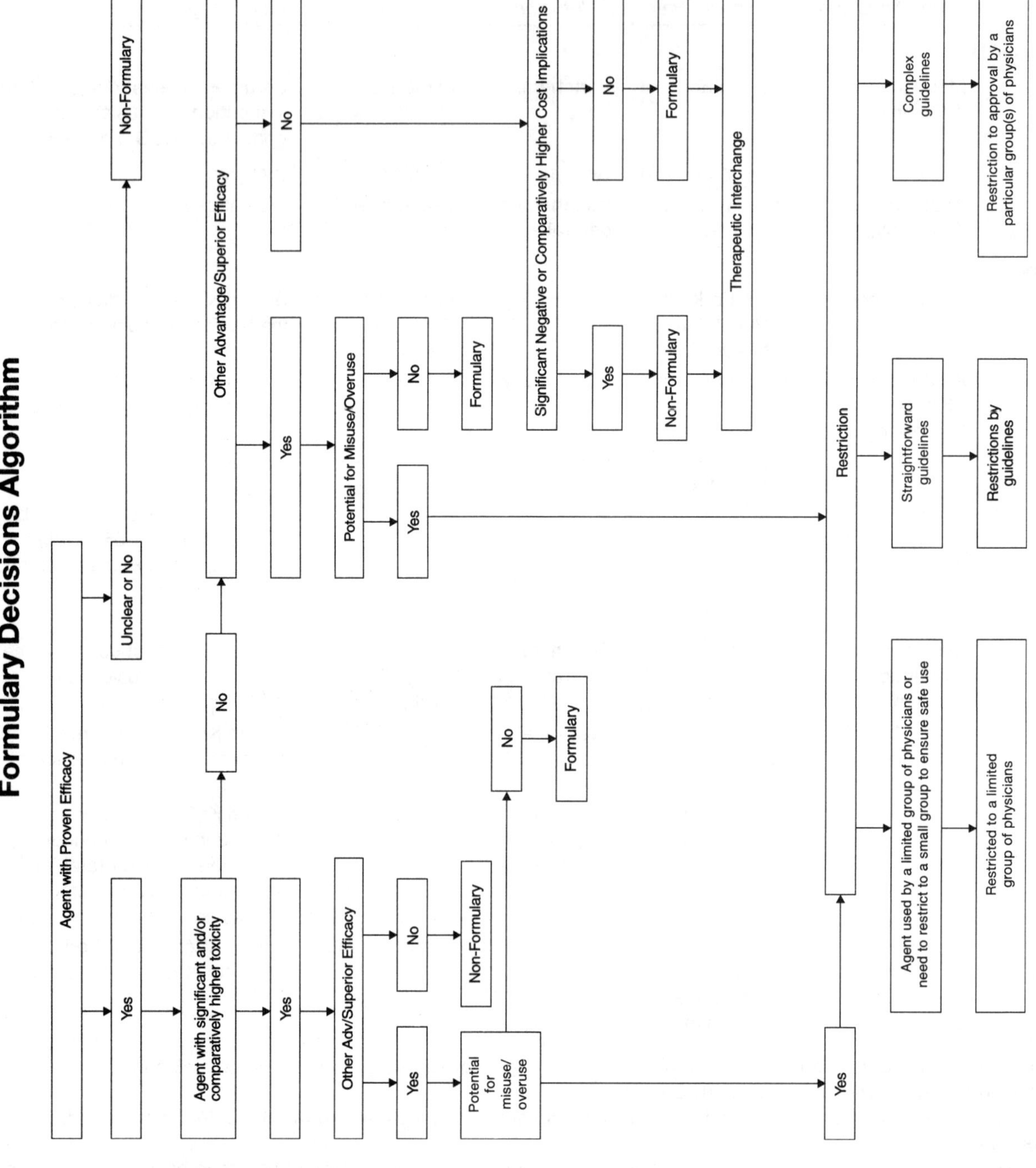


Courtesy of Hamot Medical Center, Erie, Pennsylvania.

## 4–16
## Controlled Substance Distribution and Administration

**Policy:** The Pharmacy will administer the ordering, dispensing, and recordkeeping functions for controlled substances established by state (PHL §§ 3300 *et seq.* and 10 NYCRR Part 80) and federal law (21 U.S.C. §§ 801–970) in cooperation with the medical staff and the nursing staff at Moses-Ludington Hospital and the Heritage Commons Nursing Home.

**Procedure:**

**Pharmacy:**

Ordering: Based on the regulations of the New York State Department of Health (DoH) and the federal Drug Enforcement Administration (DEA), the Pharmacy will order to maintain those Formulary items ordered for MLH and Heritage Commons patients.

Distribution: When needed, a new supply will be delivered to the nursing unit. Pharmacy personnel will obtain the signature of the individual receiving the medication acknowledging the specific quantity.

Records: Pharmacy will maintain the following records for a period of five years from the date of the transaction.
- invoices, C-II separate from CIII-V, separate from noncontrolled substances
- official DEA order form (222) separate from other records
- prescriptions
- distribution receipts
- dispensing/administration records
- cumulative running inventory of all controlled substances
- official biennial inventory

**Nursing:**

Receipt: Designated nursing personnel will sign for controlled substances delivered by Pharmacy. A contemporaneous entry will be made on the appropriate Controlled Substance Record Sheet with signature, date, quantity, and new total.

Storage: Unit-based substocks of controlled substances will be maintained in securely double-locked, substantially constructed cabinets.

Administration: After administration of medication, in addition to making the required notation on the MAR, the nurse will deduct the quantity administered on the Controlled Substance Record Sheet indicating the patient's name, the time of administration, the nurse's signature, and the name of the physician.

Partial Doses: After administering the prescribed dose, the remainder shall be "wasted" by pouring into the sink and flushing with a copious amount of water. This shall be witnessed by another nurse or pharmacist, with a notation made and signed on the reverse of the Controlled Substance Record Sheet.

Inventory: At each change of shift the nurse leaving shall make an inventory of each controlled substance with the nurse beginning the new shift with each making his or her signature certifying the physical quantity.

Discrepancies: Should be investigated by the discovering parties. If the record cannot be reconciled readily, the charge nurse should be notified and a narra-

*continues*

**4–16** continued

tive about the discrepancy should be made on the reverse of the Controlled Substance Record Sheet. The charge nurse should give notice to the supervisor and pharmacist as appropriate.

**Medical Staff:** Write medication orders according to DoH guidelines and review at least every seven days for hospital patients and every 30 days for nursing home patients.

Approved:

______________________________
Medical Staff President

______________________________
Director of Nursing

______________________________
CEO

Courtesy of Inter-Lakes Health, Pharmacy Department, Ticonderoga, New York.

# 4–17
# Compounded IVs

## POLICY

Any IV (including TPN solutions) compounded at facilities other than this medical center will not be administered to patients at this facility.

## PROCEDURE

Compounding intravenous medication is defined as the manual manipulation of a drug into another volume of drug or IV solution acquired from a pharmaceutical manufacturer for a specific patient. Manipulation includes (but is not limited to) removing and adding drug to vials, syringes, ampoules, bottles, and bags.

Compounding is subject to strict industrywide rules and hospital-specific policies and procedures designed to ensure patient safety. These rules and policies include (but are not limited to) guidelines concerning IV preparation technique, compatibility, maximum safe concentrations, and stability.

Safety cannot be guaranteed for any IV medication not compounded at this facility. Therefore, the administration of any compounded IV medication (including TPN solutions) not prepared at this facility is NOT permissible.

**Signed by** ______________________________

**Effective** ______________________________

Source: Courtesy of Judy Sikes, PhD, CPHQ, Director of Accreditation/Medical Staff Services, Parkview Medical Center, Pueblo, Colorado.

# 4–18
# Labeling of Medication

**Effective Date:**

**Revision Date:**

## PURPOSE

To ensure that all medication labeling meets federal and state regulations; to promote safety in administering the right drug, in the right quantity, to the right patient.

## POLICY STATEMENT

### A. Outpatient Prescriptions

All outpatient prescriptions shall have a hospital pharmacy label affixed to the container and contain the following information:

- pharmacy name, address, telephone number
- prescription number
- patient name
- date of dispensing
- directions for use
- prescriber's name
- drug, dose, and quantity dispensed
- pharmacist's initials
- any auxiliary labeling/precautions

### B. Inpatient Medication Orders

All new orders will have a new medication order label affixed to the zip-lock bag containing the following information:

- hospital name
- patient's name, ID #, and nursing unit/room number
- medication name, dose, quantity
- date dispensed
- pharmacist's initials
- any precautionary statements/auxiliary labels

### C. Parenteral Solutions

Labels for parenteral solutions will contain the following information:

- hospital name
- patient's name, ID #, and nursing unit/room number

*continues*

**4–18** continued

- medication name (trade & generic) and quantity for each additive
- base solution's name and volume
- date, time, and rate of administration
- expiration information (if applicable)
- pharmacist's initials
- any precautionary statements/auxiliary labels

### D. Containers Smaller Than Prescription Labels

Pursuant to ORC 4729-5-16, at least the prescription number and patient name must be placed on a strip label and affixed to all prescription containers that are too small to bear a complete prescription label. Examples of affected drugs are ophthalmic drugs, nitroglycerin, otics, etc. The small container is then placed into an outer container bearing the complete prescription label.

### E. Prepackaged Drugs

Drugs extemporaneously prepackaged by the hospital pharmacy shall contain at least the following information:

- trade name
- generic name
- strength
- lot number/expiration date

A prepackaging log shall be maintained that indicates all information required by law regarding prepackaging (e.g., above information plus original manufacturers' lot/expiration and date/initials of checking pharmacist).

RECOMMENDER: ______________________________ ____________________

______________________________ ____________________

### References

Drug Laws of the State

Source: Adapted from Department of Pharmacy Services, St. Joseph Health Center, Warren, Ohio.

# 4–19
# Quarterly Medication Sample Inventory Check

**Date:** ____________ **Unit:** ____________ **Responsible Person:** ____________

**Procedure:** Please list medication, quantities, expiration date, and lot numbers for all medication samples stocked in your unit on this form and return it to the Pharmacy, attention ____________ .

| Medication (Drug, Strength, & Package Size) | Quantity of Packages | Expiration Date | Lot # | Medication (Drug, Strength, & Package Size) | Quantity of Packages | Expiration Date | Lot # |
|---|---|---|---|---|---|---|---|
| | | | | | | | |
| | | | | | | | |
| | | | | | | | |
| | | | | | | | |
| | | | | | | | |
| | | | | | | | |
| | | | | | | | |
| | | | | | | | |
| | | | | | | | |
| | | | | | | | |
| | | | | | | | |
| | | | | | | | |
| | | | | | | | |

Source: Adapted from Hamot Medical Center, Erie, Pennsylvania.

## 4–20
## Sample Medication Distribution Log

| Date | Patient Name | Phone Number | M.R.# | Drug/Strength | Qty. | Lot # |
|---|---|---|---|---|---|---|
| | | | | | | |
| | | | | | | |
| | | | | | | |
| | | | | | | |
| | | | | | | |
| | | | | | | |
| | | | | | | |
| | | | | | | |
| | | | | | | |
| | | | | | | |
| | | | | | | |
| | | | | | | |
| | | | | | | |
| | | | | | | |
| | | | | | | |
| | | | | | | |
| | | | | | | |

Source: Adapted from Hamot Medical Center, Erie, Pennsylvania.

# 4–21
# Ordering Parenteral Nutrition

## POLICY

Initial orders and formulation changes for parenteral nutrition utilize the standard preprinted physician's order. Pharmacists will screen TPN formulations for compatibility and completeness.

## PROCEDURE

1. Initial Orders
   A. The initial physician's order for Parenteral nutrition will be written on the facility's standard preprinted physician's order.
2. Pharmacists will perform an initial evaluation of the formulation order, making sure there are no compatibility problems, including (not a complete list) the following.
   A. TPN formulas containing calcium and phosphate MUST also include amino acids.
   B. The amount of calcium and phosphate in the TPN must be checked to make sure no precipitation will occur (calcium/phosphate solubility curve).
   C. No TPN formula may include electrolytes containing a bicarbonate anion.
   D. Compare the additives ordered with lab values to make sure they are appropriate.
3. Subsequent Formulation Changes
   A. Formulation changes may be written on blank physician's orders.
   B. After making the necessary drug profile changes, pharmacy will do the following.
      1. Generate an extra computer label.
      2. Affix the label to a blank copy of the standard preprinted parenteral nutrition physician's order.
      3. Make sure the order is placed in the physician's order section of the patient's chart.
   C. Unless specified, formulation changes will be made with the next bag of parenteral nutrition.

**Signed by** ______________________________

**Effective** ______________________________

Courtesy of Judy Sikes, PhD, CPHQ, Director of Accreditation/Medical Staff Services, Parkview Medical Center, Pueblo, Colorado.

# 4–22
# Preparation of Parenteral Nutrition

**POLICY:**

Bags of parenteral nutrition will be compounded in such a manner that solutions are free from contamination and particulate matter.

**PROCEDURE:**

1. Pharmacy personnel must pass an initial IV technique evaluation before compounding TPN bags.
2. Pharmacy personnel compounding TPN solutions must have IV technique-compounding skills reevaluated at least once a year.
3. Total parenteral nutrition (TPN) bags are compounded using a pump that delivers preset volumes of dextrose, amino acids, fats, and water.
4. The order of mixing electrolyte additives is extremely important.
    a. Use the TPN compounder to add diluents first.
    b. The phosphate-containing ingredient must be added next, followed by shaking.
    c. Add all other components EXCEPT the calcium-containing ingredient next, followed by shaking.
5. Add the calcium-containing ingredient last.
6. A pharmacist will check the TPN bag twice before it leaves the pharmacy.
    a. The first check includes the following:
        1. The macronutrient bags attached to the pump are correct.
        2. The pump display indicated the correct volume of macronutrient was pumped into the bag.
        3. The weight of the TPN bag is correct.
        4. The additives are inspected for identity and volume BEFORE they are added to the TPN bag.
        5. The sequence of addition to the TPN bag is correct.
    b. The second check includes looking for leaks and "cores."

**Signed by** ______________________________

**Effective** ______________________________

Courtesy of Judy Sikes, PhD, CPHQ, Director of Accreditation/Medical Staff Services, Parkview Medical Center, Pueblo, Colorado.

# 4–23
# Changing or Adjusting PN Additives to a Current Solution

## POLICY:

The medical center pharmacy staff, using aseptic technique in a laminar flow hood, will prepare all parenteral nutrition (PN) solutions. **PN additives shall not be added to a bag unless by aseptic technique in the laminar flow hood.**

Adding to a PN bag after it has been hung increases the likelihood of contamination, inappropriate concentration of additive(s), which may adversely affect the electrolyte/metabolic status, and finally may increase the likelihood of admixture incompatibility.

## PROCEDURE

If a bag has been prepared, and the physician/NST has written orders for changes before the bag has been spiked and hung, the bag may be returned to the pharmacy for PN additive changes where possible.

If a bag has been spiked and hung, additive changes may not be made under any circumstance.

**Signed by** ______________________________

**Effective** ______________________________

Courtesy of Judy Sikes, PhD, CPHQ, Director of Accreditation/Medical Staff Services, Parkview Medical Center, Pueblo, Colorado.

# 4–24
# Parenteral Nutritional Support Distribution

**POLICY**

Parenteral Nutrition will be delivered to the nursing area in a timely manner and be hung within the specified time constraints.

**PROCEDURE**

1. The initial bag of parenteral nutrition (PN) will be sent at 1700, unless specified otherwise by the physician. Bags are compounded with sufficient volume to last 24 hours.
2. Subsequent bags will also be sent at 1700. A pharmacist will screen the most recent lab values in advance of making the bag to make sure there are no pending formula changes. Bags are compounded with sufficient volume to last 24 hours.
   A. A physician may request a "Bridge Bag" if lab values are abnormal. These bags contain enough volume to last until 1700 and reflect the change in formula content.
3. PN bags must be infused by midnight of the expiration day indicated on the PN bag.
   A. PN bags may be kept at room temperature or under refrigeration.
4. An in-line filter will be sent along with each PN bag daily.

**Signed by** ______________________________

**Effective** ______________________________

Courtesy of Judy Sikes, PhD, CPHQ, Director of Accreditation/Medical Staff Services, Parkview Medical Center, Pueblo, Colorado.

## 4–25
## Monitoring of Parenteral Nutrition Lab Values

**POLICY:**

Lab value monitoring will be performed in order to minimize complications and maximize the benefit from parenteral nutrition (PN).

**PROCEDURE**

1. Pharmacists will monitor lab values on all patients receiving parenteral nutrition.
   A. Initial assessment of lab values will be performed before the first PN bag is compounded.
   B. Daily assessment will be done in order to anticipate or recommend changes in the PN formula.
      1. Pharmacists will communicate with the physician or nutritional support team as appropriate if an abnormal lab value is in need of assessment.
         a. The pharmacist will check with the patient's nurse first to see if the problem has already been communicated to the physician and/or the nutritional support team.
         b. If the pharmacist is unsure of a course of action based on abnormal lab values, consultations will be made with appropriate support staff (pharmacy clinical coordinator, nutritional support clinical staff, physician, etc.).
2. Lab values are to be reassessed with each new request for a PN bag in order to anticipate pending formulation changes and minimize waste.
3. Lab values monitored by the pharmacist will include the following: sodium, potassium, chloride, carbon dioxide, glucose, BUN, creatinine, calcium, albumin, phosphate, triglyceride, and magnesium.
4. The pharmacist will check the patient medication profile on a daily basis for treatment with Coumadin: If a patient is found to be anticoagulated with Coumadin and the PN formula contains Vitamin K, the physician and/or the nutritional support team will be notified as appropriate.

**Signed by** ______________________________

**Effective** ______________________________

Courtesy of Judy Sikes, PhD, CPHQ, Director of Accreditation/Medical Staff Services, Parkview Medical Center, Pueblo, Colorado.

# 4–26
# Drug Distribution

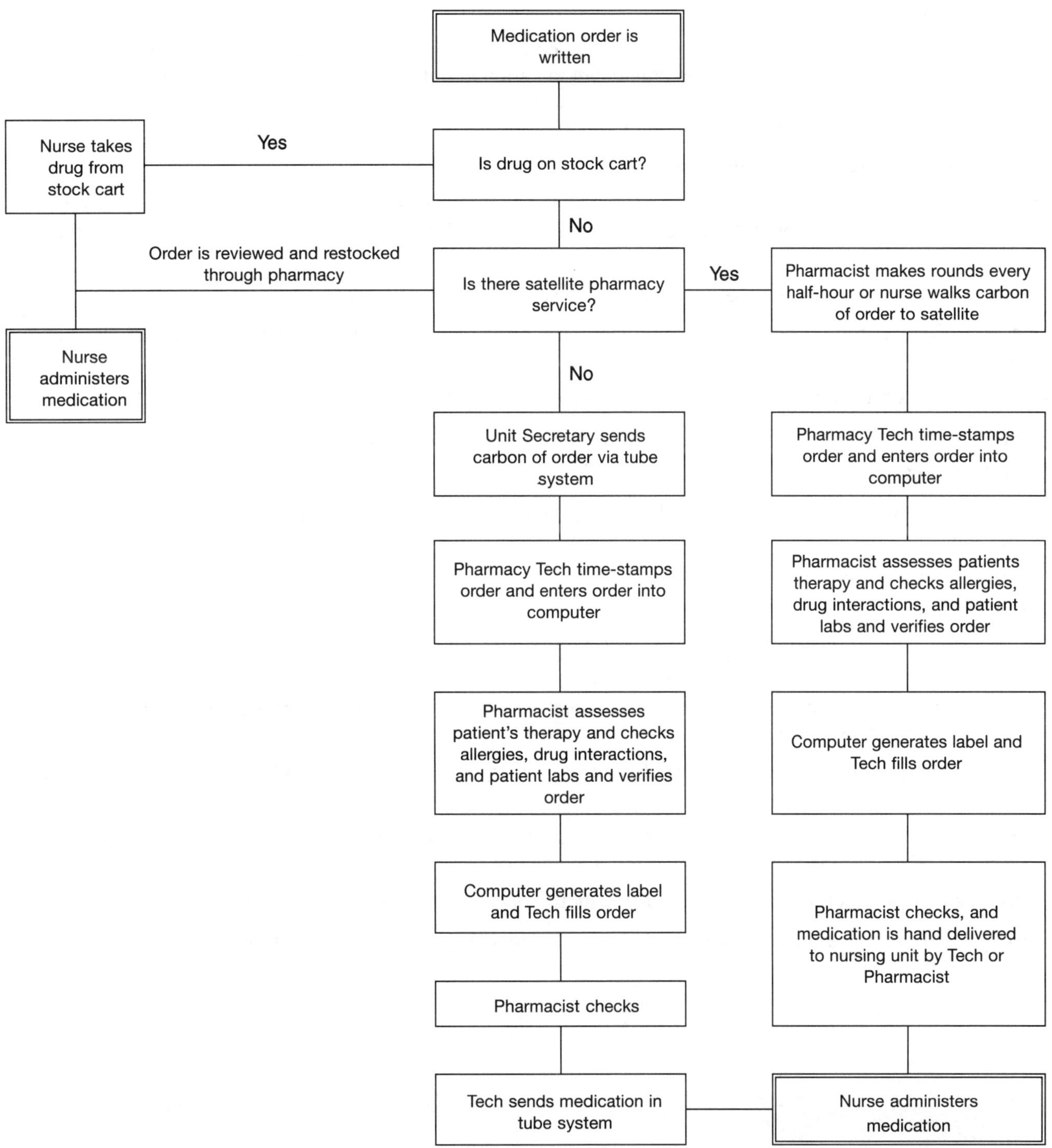


Source: Adapted from Hamot Medical Center, Erie, Pennsylvania.

# 4–27
# Job Description: Medication Safety Practitioner

**Position Title:** Nurse Specialist—Medication Administration

**Job Summary:**

The Nurse Specialist will act as a clinician to assess, coordinate and provide patient care related to specialty; as an educator to conduct opportunities for staff development and patient education; as a consultant to serve as a resource to staff, patients and other health care providers; and as a researcher to participate and conduct studies, review literature and disseminate information to others.

**Essential Values-Based Competencies:**

Demonstrates value based competencies in line with the four core values that are the foundation of all activities performed by employees in order to achieve the Mission of the Hospital (see attached list of behavioral definitions):

Dignity: Demonstrates competence in communication and interpersonal relations.

Excellence: Demonstrates competence in continuous improvement, continuous learning, accountability and teamwork.

Service: Demonstrates competence in customer/patient focus and adaptability.

Justice: Demonstrates competence in community orientation and stewardship

**Essential Functions:**

1. Coordinates processes to improve/evaluate medication administration through pharmacy, nursing, and the medical staff.
2. Serves as liaison between nursing, pharmacy, and the medical staff to ensure safe/standardized medication practices.
3. Collaborates in the development of policy and procedures through identification and/or revision with nursing, pharmacy, and the medical staff.
4. Designs and implements educational presentations, which facilitates the attainment and maintenance of safe medication practice standards within the organization.
5. Promptly investigates medication errors based on severity index/potential severity in order to improve staff performance and patient care.
6. Serves as a resource person by consulting with nursing/pharmacy concerning professional and education problems related to medication and/or medication safety.
7. Analyzes nursing techniques and other medication processes and recommends modifications.
8. Coordinates with pharmacy/nursing/medical staff the trial of new products, facilitating education and training.

Courtesy of Covenant Health Systems, Lubbock, Texas

# 4–28
# ISMP's Table of Dangerous Medical Abbreviations

| **SPECIAL ISSUE—Do not use these dangerous abbreviations or dose designations** | | | |
|---|---|---|---|
| **Abbreviation/ Dose Expression** | **Intended Meaning** | **Misinterpretation** | **Correction** |
| Apothecary symbols | dram<br>minim | Misunderstood or misread (symbol for dram misread for "3" and minim misread as "mL"). | Use the metric system. |
| AU | aurio uterque (each ear) | Mistaken for OU (oculo uterque—each eye). | Don't use this abbreviation. |
| D/C | discharge<br>discontinue | Premature discontinuation of medications when D/C (intended to mean "discharge") has been misinterpreted as "discontinued" when followed by a list of drugs. | Use "discharge" and "discontinue." |
| Drug names | | | Use the complete spelling for drug names. |
| ARA□A | vidarabine | cytarabine (ARA□C) | |
| AZT | zidovudine (RETROVIR) | azathioprine | |
| CPZ | COMPAZINE (prochlorperazine) | chlorpromazine | |
| DPT | DEMEROL-PHENERGAN-THORAZINE | diphtheria-pertussis-tetanus (vaccine) | |
| HCl | hydrochloric acid | potassium chloride (The "H" is misinterpreted as "K.") | |
| HCT | hydrocortisone | hydrochlorothiazide | |
| HCTZ | hydrochlorothiazide | hydrocortisone (seen as HCT250 mg) | |
| MgSO4 | magnesium sulfate | morphine sulfate | |
| MSO4 | morphine sulfate | magnesium sulfate | |
| MTX | methotrexate | mitoxantrone | |
| TAC | triamcinolone | tetracaine, ADRENALIN, cocaine | |

*continues*

4–28 continued

| **SPECIAL ISSUE—Do not use these dangerous abbreviations or dose designations** ***continued*** | | | |
|---|---|---|---|
| **Abbreviation/ Dose Expression** | **Intended Meaning** | **Misinterpretation** | **Correction** |
| ZnSO4 | zinc sulfate | morphine sulfate | |
| Stemmed names | | | |
| "Nitro" drip | nitroglycerin infusion | sodium nitroprusside infusion | |
| "Norflox" | norfloxacin | NORFLEX (orphenadrine) | |
| mg | microgram | Mistaken for "mg" when handwritten. | Use "mcg." |
| o.d. or OD | once daily | Misinterpreted as "right eye" (OD—oculus dexter) and administration of oral medications in the eye. | Use "daily." |
| TIW or tiw | three times a week | Mistaken as "three times a day." | Don't use this abbreviation. |
| per os | orally | The "os" can be mistaken for "left eye." | Use "PO," "by mouth," or "orally." |
| q.d. or QD | every day | Mistaken as q.i.d., especially if the period after the "q" or the tail of the "q" is misunderstood as an "i." | Use "daily" or "every day." |
| qn | nightly or at bedtime | Misinterpreted as "qh" (every hour). | Use "nightly." |
| qhs | nightly at bedtime | Misread as every hour. | Use "nightly." |
| q6PM, etc. | every evening at 6 PM | Misread as every six hours. | Use 6 PM "nightly." |
| q.o.d. or QOD | every other day | Misinterpreted as "q.d." (daily) or "q.i.d. (four times daily) if the "o" is poorly written. | Use "every other day." |
| sub q | subcutaneous | The "q" has been mistaken for "every" (e.g., one heparin dose ordered "sub q 2 hours before surgery" misunderstood as every 2 hours before surgery). | Use "subcut." or write "subcutaneous." |

*continues*

**4–28** continued

**SPECIAL ISSUE—Do not use these dangerous abbreviations or dose designations *continued***

| Abbreviation/ Dose Expression | Intended Meaning | Misinterpretation | Correction |
|---|---|---|---|
| SC | subcutaneous | Mistaken for SL (sublingual). | Use “subcut.” or write “subcutaneous.” |
| U or u | unit | Read as a zero (0) or a four (4), causing a 10-fold over-dose or greater (4U seen as “40” or 4u seen as 44”). | “Unit” has no acceptable abbreviation. Use “unit.” |
| IU | international unit | Misread as IV (intravenous). | Use “units.” |
| cc | cubic centimeters | Misread as “U” (units). | Use “mL.” |
| x3d | for three days | Mistaken for “three doses.” | Use “for three days.” |
| BT | bedtime | Mistaken as “BID” (twice daily). | Use “hs.” |
| ss | sliding scale (insulin) or ½ (apothecary) | Mistaken for “55.” | Spell out “sliding scale.” Use “one-half” or use “½.” |
| > and < | greater than and less than | Mistakenly used opposite of intended. | Use “greater than” or “less than.” |
| / (slash mark) | separates two doses or indicates “per” | Misunderstood as the number 1 (“25 unit/10 units” read as “110” units. | Do not use a slash mark to separate doses. Use “per.” |
| Name letters and dose numbers run together (e.g., Inderal40 mg) | Inderal 40 mg | Misread as Inderal 140 mg. | Always use space between drug name, dose and unit of measure. |
| Zero after decimal point (1.0) | 1 mg | Misread as 10 mg if the decimal point is not seen. | Do not use terminal zeros for doses expressed in whole numbers. |
| No zero before decimal dose (.5 mg) | 0.5 mg | Misread as 5 mg. | Always use zero before a decimal when the dose is less than a whole unit. |

Source: Reprinted with permission from: *ISMP Medication Safety Alert!* May 2, 2001. 

# 4–29
# Failure Mode, Effect and Criticality Form

**High Risk Process:** ______________________

**Severity**

☐ 3— An event occurred that resulted in the need for treatment and/or intervention and caused temporary patient harm

☐ 4— An event occurred that resulted in initial or prolonged hospitalization, and caused temporary patient harm.

☐ 5— An event occurred that resulted in permanent patient harm or near death event, such as anaphylaxis

☐ 6—An event occurred that resulted in patient death.

**Selected Through:**

☐ Joint Commission Sentinel Event Alert on ________ (attach alert)

☐ Patient Safety Tracking Tool (PSTT)-Event: ____________

☐ Multiple PSTTs—# of events ________ within ________ months

☐ Other (specify): ______________________

Review conducted by: ______________ Date: ________ Participants: ______________

**Complexity** (Steps in process from initial activity to identification of error)

| | Would failure at this step adversely affect patient? | If yes, rank possibility:<br>1 = remote<br>5 = already documented elsewhere<br>10 = documented and almost certain to occur | If yes, rank severity of overall failure:<br>1 = no harm to patient<br>5 = may affect patient adversely<br>10 = injury or death will occur | If yes, likelihood of detection BEFORE accident takes place:<br>1 = will always be detected<br>5 = might be detected<br>10 = detection not possible | Criticality Index: (mean of possibility, severity, detection—divide by 3):<br>1 = no action needed<br>5 = action must be considered<br>10 = action a must |
|---|---|---|---|---|---|
| 1. | | | | | |
| 2. | | | | | |
| 3. | | | | | |
| 4. | | | | | |
| 5. | | | | | |
| 6. | | | | | |
| 7. | | | | | |
| 8. | | | | | |
| 9. | | | | | |
| 10. | | | | | |

Is Root Cause Analysis (RCA) indicated (anything above 5 in Severity or in Criticality Index)? If yes, attach RCA Summary and complete information on reverse side of this form.

*continues*

**4–29** continued

## ERROR REDUCTION ACTION(s)

**Remove Alternatives**

- ☐ Eliminate dangerous items/procedures
- ☐ Limit use or access
- ☐ Certification or privileging
- ☐ Avoid potential confirmation bias (look-alike containers, names, abbreviations)
- ☐ Minimize consequence of error
- ☐ Other (specify): ____________

**Improve Detection**

- ☐ Orientation, education, additional training
- ☐ Protocols and procedures
- ☐ Hazard warnings and signs
- ☐ Technology
- ☐ Improved inspection process
- ☐ Other (specify): ____________

**Prevent Completion of Action**

- ☐ Fail safe (automatic shut-off, locking device, etc.)
- ☐ Forcing function (non-compatible connectors, etc.)
- ☐ Technology (automatic med dispensing system, etc.)
- ☐ Other (specify): ____________

**Minimize Consequence of Error**

- ☐ Reduce supply (volume, concentration, number, etc.)
- ☐ Modify defaults
- ☐ Other (specify): ____________

## FOLLOW-UP FOR EFFECTIVENESS OF ERROR REDUCTION ACTION(s)

Date of First Review: ______________________ Reviewer: ______________________ (individual or committee)

- ☐ Action(s) resolved problem
- ☐ Action(s) reduced problem. Needs modification as follows: ____________ ____________ ____________ Date action will commence: ____________
- ☐ Action did not resolve problem. New action to be implemented: ____________ ____________ ____________ Date action will commence: ____________
- ☐ If not completely resolved, review on: ____________ (date)

Date of Second Review: ______________________ Reviewer: ______________________ (individual or committee)

- ☐ Action(s) resolved problem
- ☐ Action(s) reduced problem. Needs modification as follows: ____________ ____________ ____________ Date action will commence: ____________
- ☐ Action did not resolve problem. New action to be implemented: ____________ ____________ ____________ Date action will commence: ____________
- ☐ If not completely resolved, review on: ____________ (date)

Source: Reprinted with permission from Marie Conti, ARM, CPHRM.

# 4–30
# Medication Safety: Computerized Physician Order Entry (CPOE)

Computerized Physician Order Entry (CPOE) is a practice that has been advocated for reducing medication errors. Such a system is used in conjunction with a pharmacy software program designed to detect potential contraindications, dosing errors or inappropriate routes of administration. The ultimate goal is the reduction of adverse drug events (ADEs) related to preventable causes.

**Application of Criteria to CPOE**

1. **There is sufficient evidence for effectiveness**

   There is evidence to support that CPOE systems reduce medication errors. The AHRQ assessed CPOE with clinical decision support systems (CDSS) as a safety practice with "medium" strength of evidence regarding its impact and effectiveness and placed it on its list of practices for which further research would be highly beneficial. The AHRQ found no published study that documented a significant reduction in serious adverse drug events (ADEs) through the use of CPOE, acknowledging the statistical challenges of the relatively infrequent occurrence of ADEs. The most frequently cited study of CPOE is from the Brigham and Women's Hospital. In their study, CPOE reported a 55% decrease in serious medication errors, but the decline in preventable ADEs was only 17% and not statistically significant.

2. **There is sufficient evidence for greater effectiveness of the practice than alternatives**

   While CPOE with decision support should decrease medication error rates, other interventions have also demonstrated good outcomes (see below). Clinical information systems with pharmacy modules are able to proactively detect many errors, including therapy duplication, dosing errors, allergies, drug-drug interactions, and contraindicated route of administration. Examples of non-CPOE, system-driven initiatives that have demonstrated decreased adverse drug events include:

   Albany Medical Center published a description of their 14-year process to reduce medication errors. This institution is a 631-bed tertiary care center with 26,000 admissions a year. By 1999, their Prescribing Error Program was detecting 2,500 prescribing errors per year. These results were achieved without CPOE, using a refined system that included a central drug distribution process with a pharmacy computer software system and a McKesson Automated Health RxRobot.

   Good Samaritan Regional Medical Center (GSRMC) in Phoenix, AZ reported the outcomes from their intervention to reduce ADEs using a computer alert system. The system incorporated integrated patient-specific data including pharmacy orders, patient allergies, demographics, radiology orders and laboratory results. GSRMC reported the ADE alert system detected opportunities to reduce preventable ADE injuries at a rate of 64/1000 patient admissions.

3. **There is freedom from known implementation issues**

   The limited outcomes data related to CPOE likely reflect the infancy of this promising practice and the challenges of implementing this intervention in a resource-constrained environment. The estimated development and implementation cost of CPOE at the Brigham and Women's Hospital was $1.9 million, with $500,000 maintenance costs per year. The AHRQ assessed that the cost of purchasing and implementing large, commercial systems varied substantially, but could be on the order of tens of millions of dollars.

4. **There is evidence of successful transfer from research to non-research settings**

   CPOE has been implemented in relatively few hospitals in a non-research, non-beta-test site capacity. Implementation experience and outcomes from these hospitals have not been published in peer-reviewed journals. The AHRQ located published evidence of the effectiveness of CPOE with CDSS for only two hospitals, both of which were teaching hospitals. A separate evaluation of medication error-reducing technologies conducted in 2001 also located few sites with sufficient experience to report outcomes.

**Summary:** It is clear that CPOE with computerized decision support holds much promise as an initiative that will improve patient safety, but the evidence is insufficient at this time to establish CPOE as a standard of care. CPOE should be considered as one of many practices that a hospital could consider for reducing its ADEs.

Source: *"The Challenge of Assessing Patient Safety in American Hospitals."* © 2002 American Hospital Association and Protocare Sciences.

# 4–31
# Medication Safety—Clinical Pharmacists

One practice to decrease adverse drug events (ADEs) is the use of clinical pharmacists as part of patient care teams (i.e., clinical pharmacists make "rounds" with the patient care team and are available for consultation regarding patients).

**Application of Criteria to Clinical Pharmacists**

1. **There is sufficient evidence for effectiveness**

   There are numerous reports documenting the effectiveness of pharmacists in detecting and preventing ADEs, but few published reports specifically evaluating the use of clinical pharmacists consultation services/participation in rounds. One of the most frequently cited reports is that of Leape et al, who reported that pharmacist participation in physician rounds in the ICU decreased medication ordering errors significantly (66%). The AHRQ rated clinical pharmacist consultation services as a patient safety practice with medium strength of evidence regarding impact and effectiveness.

2. **There is sufficient evidence for greater effectiveness of the practice than alternatives**

   There is no evidence that clinical pharmacist consultation services are superior to other practices in reducing ADEs.

3. **There is freedom from known implementation issues**

   AHRQ rated the cost of implementing clinical pharmacist consultation services as high. This is most likely due to the increase in costs due to salaries and benefits. However, studies examining resource utilization and cost savings in the inpatient setting indicate overall cost savings due to clinical pharmacist activities. Currently, there is a pharmacist shortage in some areas of the United States.

4. **There is evidence of successful transfer from research to non-research settings**

   Clinical pharmacist consultation services have been used across hospital types (academic, community, public).

**Summary:** There is evidence that clinical pharmacist consultation decreases preventable ADEs. While the use of clinical pharmacists as part of patient care teams is relatively widely implemented, the activities of the clinical pharmacists vary from hospital to hospital (e.g., consultation for pharmacokinetic services, attendance at rounds), which may yield different outcomes of this practice. Clinical pharmacist participation on patient care teams should be considered one of many practices that a hospital can implement to reduce ADEs.

Source: *"The Challenge of Assessing Patient Safety in American Hospitals."* 

# 4–32
# Medication Safety—Unit Dose Medication Distribution Systems

A practice that is intended to reduce Adverse Drug Events (ADEs) is the use of Unit Dose (UD) distribution systems. A UD distribution system is the dispensing of medications in a package that is ready to administer to the patient. Each package is labeled with the drug name, strength, and expiration date. There are a variety of ways in which the UD medication reaches the patient in a hospital. The UD medication may be placed in patient-specific medication cassettes, stocked in automated dispensing devices, or provided to nursing stations as "ward stock" medications.

**Application of Criteria to Unit Dose Distribution Systems**

1. **There is sufficient evidence for effectiveness**

   The published literature regarding the effectiveness of unit dose distribution systems is of relatively poor quality. Unit dose systems are effective in reducing medication errors compared to floor stock systems with bulk containers of medications. Based upon its evaluation of published literature, AHRQ rated unit dose distribution systems as a safety practice with lower impact and/or strength of evidence.

2. **There is sufficient evidence for greater effectiveness of the practice than alternatives**

   Older published studies demonstrated that UD distribution systems are superior to bulk bottle ward stock systems. However, given that unit dose distribution systems are a Joint Commission standard, there are few alternatives to these systems. The evidence is insufficient to determine the superior method for distribution of the unit dose medications (e.g., dispensed in patient cassettes, dispensed in automated dispensing devices, etc.)

3. **There is freedom from known implementation issues**

   Unit dose distribution systems are widely accepted and implemented in hospitals throughout the United States. As such, the cost of implementation and complexities associated with implementation is low.

4. **There is evidence of successful transfer from research to non-research settings**

   Unit dose distribution systems are widely used. In a 1994 survey conducted by the American Society of Health-system Pharmacists (ASHP), 92% of hospitals practiced unit dose dispensing.

**Summary:** The use of unit dose medication distribution systems illustrates a commonly used practice that has evolved into a standard over the past two decades, but which would not meet today's evidence requirements for a practice that should be elevated to a standard. There are numerous studies that demonstrate decreased dispensing-related medication errors with unit dose systems and decreased costs/drug wastage compared to nursing floor-stock systems. However, the methodology described within those published studies does not meet today's requirements of rigor in health care studies, as performed by the AHRQ evaluation. The relatively modest AHRQ rating regarding the effectiveness of Unit Dose Distribution systems in decreasing ADEs is largely due to the lack of well-designed studies that measured and reported outcomes. The use of unit dose systems is widespread through America's hospitals, has additional benefits for hospitals (help reduce wastage and increase nursing productivity), and currently has few alternatives, so it is unlikely that more rigorous studies will be performed in the near future. Other specific practices related to unit dose distribution systems, such as the newer technology of automated devices, complicate the measurement of the effectiveness of unit dose distribution systems as a "stand alone" practice. Thus, unit dose distribution systems represent an example of a practice that does not have reasonable alternatives against which a comparison can be made for greater effectiveness, but does not appear to introduce any additional "harm" into the medication distribution system and has additional benefits that are not directly related to an objective of reduced ADEs.

Source: *"The Challenge of Assessing Patient Safety in American Hospitals."* 

# 4–33
# Recommendations To Reduce Medication Errors Associated with Verbal Medication Orders and Prescriptions

## Preamble

Confusion over the similarity of drug names accounts for approximately 25% of all reports to the USP Medication Errors Reporting (MER) Program. To reduce confusion pertaining to verbal orders and to further support the Council's mission to minimize medication errors, the following recommendations have been developed.

In these recommendations, verbal orders are prescriptions or medication orders that are communicated as oral, spoken communications between senders and receivers face to face, by telephone, or by other auditory device.

## Recommendations

1. Verbal communication of prescription or medication orders should be limited to urgent situations where immediate written or electronic communication is not feasible.
2. Health care organizations should establish policies and procedures that:
   - Describe limitations or prohibitions on use of verbal orders
   - Provide a mechanism to ensure validity/authenticity of the prescriber
   - List the elements required for inclusion in a complete verbal order
   - Describe situations in which verbal orders may be used
   - List and define the individuals who may send and receive verbal orders
   - Provide guidelines for clear and effective communication of verbal orders.
3. Leaders of health care organizations should promote a culture in which it is acceptable, and strongly encouraged, for staff to question prescribers when there are any questions or disagreements about verbal orders. Questions about verbal orders should be resolved prior to the preparation, or dispensing, or administration of the medication.
4. Verbal orders for antineoplastic agents should **NOT** be permitted under any circumstances. These medications are not administered in emergency or urgent situations, and they have a narrow margin of safety.
5. Elements that should be included in a verbal order include:
   - Name of patient
   - Age and weight of patient, when appropriate
   - Drug name
   - Dosage form (e.g., tablets, capsules, inhalants)
   - Exact strength or concentration
   - Dose, frequency, and route
   - Quantity and/or duration
   - Purpose or indication (unless disclosure is considered inappropriate by the prescriber)
   - Specific instructions for use
   - Name of prescriber, and telephone number when appropriate
   - Name of individual transmitting the order, if different from the prescriber.

*continues*

**4–33** continued

6. The content of verbal orders should be clearly communicated:
   - The name of the drug should be confirmed by any of the following:
     - Spelling
     - Providing both the brand and generic names of the medication
     - Providing the indication for use
   - In order to avoid confusion with spoken numbers, a dose such as 50 mg should be dictated as "fifty milligrams . . . five zero milligrams" to distinguish from "fifteen milligrams...one five milligrams."
   - Instructions for use should be provided without abbreviations. For example, "1tab tid" should be communicated as "Take/give one tablet three times daily."
7. The entire verbal order should be repeated back to the prescriber, or the individual transmitting the order, using the principles outlined in these recommendations.
8. All verbal orders should be reduced immediately to writing and signed by the individual receiving the order.
9. Verbal orders should be documented in the patient's medical record, reviewed, and countersigned by the prescriber as soon as possible.
10. Health care organizations include community pharmacies, physicians' offices, hospitals, nursing homes, home care agencies, etc.

Adopted February 20, 2001

# 4–34
# Quality Control of Automated Dispensing System Robot Rx

## POLICY

I. **Maintenance**—Preventative maintenance of the robot's hardware will be provided by McKesson Automated, Inc. on a routine basis (at least every six weeks) based on part replacement trends and the Pharmacy's requirements. Software releases will also be installed when available.

II. **Repackaging**—All repackaging performed on site will be verified by a licensed Pharmacist. All doses in a batch will be checked for accuracy including drug name, strength, lot number, and expiration date. The batch sheet will then be initialed by the Pharmacist and maintained in a log book for five years. Any errors will be indicated on the sheet and the packager will be notified. Medications that have been checked will be placed into off-line inventory in the main Pharmacy.

III. **Dispensing**—Medications dispensed by the robot will be checked on a scheduled basis for accuracy. On a daily basis, 5% of all medication bins will be checked by a Pharmacist for accurate filling. The tolerable error rate is less than 0.01% and any error is significant enough to require thorough check of dispensing system. This check will be performed by a Pharmacist in the morning on carts filled by the night shift and documented on the daily cart check sheet.

IV. **Expired Medications**—The robot will reject any medication that is expired and periodically (every 30 days) rotate stock based on expiration date. Any errors of dispensing expired medications will result in immediate contacting of McKesson and resolution of the problem prior to continuing with automated dispensing.

V. **Manual Picks**—Any medication not dispensed by the robot will be checked by a licensed Pharmacist. Cart checking will be initialed on the daily cart check sheet and first doses will be initialed on the dispensing label by the Pharmacist prior to dispensing.

VI. **Returns**—Medications returned from patient care areas will be reviewed by a Technician for integrity and then returned to the robot if appropriate. Any opened packaging will result in repackaging of the medication. Damaged medication or opened unit dose packaging will result in destruction of the medication.

Source: Courtesy of Strong Health, Rochester, New York.

# 4–35
# Robot Rx Dispensing Procedures

## POLICY

I. **The robot is utilized for cart filling and initial dose (new order) dispensing when appropriate using the following procedure:**

1. New Order is entered (or cart fill lists are generated).
2. Bar-coded patient name label is affixed to bin and placed on conveyor for robot filling.
3. Manual picks (items not in the robot) are then selected by the technician.

II. **Packaging Procedures:**

1. Packaging technician is responsible for set up and operation of packaging machine. Machine is set up for each individual medication, including verification of lot number and expiration date.
2. Upon completion of packaging, each item is checked for accuracy by a Pharmacist and recorded in the packaging logs.

III. **Down Time Procedures**

In the event that the robot is inoperable, a manual dispensing process will be implemented. All medications will be selected based on orders that are assessed and entered in the Pharmacy Computer system. All orders picked by a technician will be verified by a licensed Pharmacist prior to dispensing and the label will be initialed.

Courtesy of Strong Health, Rochester, New York.

# 4–36
# Medication Ordering Privileges, Authorization
## DEPARTMENT OF PHARMACY

**Subject:** Medication Ordering Privileges, Authorization

**Manual Code:**

**Date Issued:**

**Date Revised:**

**Approved by:** Director of Pharmacy ______________________________

**Reviewed by/Date:** ________ ________ ________ ________

Medications are administered only on the order of an authorized member of the Medical Staff, house staff, or other legally authorized practitioner who has been granted clinical privileges to order medications.

The granting of clinical privileges to members of the medical staff shall include authorization to prescribe any unrestricted medication. Selected medications may be restricted by policy or the recommendation of the Pharmacy and Therapeutics Committee. Restricted medications may be prescribed only by selected members of the medical staff on the basis of education, training, or experience and must be renewed annually.

The Medical Staff Office is responsible for confirming medical staff attending credentials and individuals with privileges to write medication orders for patients. The House staff office is responsible for confirming house staff credentials and individuals with privileges to write medication orders for patients.

The Pharmacy Department receives a signature card for each privileged physician. Signature on these cards indicates compliance with the medical center's Formulary process and DEA number. This card is maintained in the Pharmacy and authorizes the Pharmacy Department to dispense therapeutically equivalent generic medications and therapeutic alternates per Pharmacy and Therapeutics Committee and medical center policy. The cards also act to inform pharmacists that the physician is privileged to order medications at the Medical Center.

Signature cards are kept on file in the Pharmacy Department.

Additionally, physicians credentialed and authorized to prescribe are maintained within the Clinical Information System. This serves as an alternate reference of physicians authorized to prescribe medications at the Medical Center.

Source: Adapted from Montefiore Medical Center, Bronx, New York.

## 4–37
## New or Unusual Drug Privileges

A. Drugs Not Requiring Delineation of Privileges

Most of the drugs in the pharmacy will be put to use in the hospital by the pharmacist and will not require special privileges. However, in time, the Pharmacy and Therapeutics Committee shall review all drugs. A pharmacist shall be a member of the committee.

B. Unusual or Special Drugs Requiring Delineation of Privileges

1. Unusual drugs like chymopapain need special precaution and shall require delineation of privileges. The pharmacist or Pharmacy and Therapeutics Committee or physician intending to use an unusual or special drug shall identify the drug.
2. Physicians shall request privileges before using unusual or special drugs. An application form shall be completed, presenting written documentation of training and experience.
3. The Pharmacy and Therapeutics Committee shall investigate the drug under consideration and forward its recommendations to the Credentials Committee. This committee shall forward its recommendations to the Executive Committee, which in turn shall submit its recommendations to the Hospital Board of Trustees.

C. Drugs Not in Stock

Drugs not in stock, expensive, and hard to find but not requiring special privileges such as Zovirax (Acyclovir), may be obtained from another hospital or pharmacy if a substitute drug is not in stock.

D. Experimental Drugs

Experimental drugs shall be investigated by the Pharmacy and Therapeutics Committee, which after its investigation shall forward its recommendations to the Credentials Committee; this committee shall forward its recommendations to the Executive Committee, which in turn shall submit its recommendations to the Hospital Board of Trustees.

### NEW OR UNUSUAL PROCEDURES

New or unusual procedures such as use of chymopapain in the chemonucleolysis of the nucleus pulposus and/or other procedures requiring training and experience shall have delineation of privileges. The physician requesting these privileges shall complete an application form listing written documentation of training and experience in performing the procedure.

Source: Adapted from Saint Barnabas Health Care System, Livingston, New Jersey.

# 4–38
# Restricted Drugs Policy, Antibiotic Restriction
## DEPARTMENT OF PHARMACY

**Subject:** Restricted Drugs Policy, Antibiotic Restriction

**Manual Code:**

**Date Issued:**

**Date Revised:**

**Approved by:** Director of Pharmacy ______________________________

**Reviewed by/Date:** ________ ________ ________ ________

The Pharmacy and Therapeutics Committee, in approving the addition of certain antibiotics to the Formulary, may restrict their use because of toxicity, and in an attempt to prevent, or at least delay the development of resistant bacterial strains. The monitoring of the usage of these antibiotics is the responsibility of the Antibiotic Surveillance Subcommittee, the Division of Infectious Diseases, and the Pharmacy Department.

1. A physician wishing to prescribe any of the antibiotics listed in Form 4–27 shall contact a member of the Division of Infectious Diseases (I.D). The I.D. consultant and prescribing physician will discuss the patient to determine appropriate drug use and dose. If the situation warrants the use of the restricted antibiotic, the I.D. consultant will call the Pharmacy and provide the following information:

   - Name of patient
   - Location within the institution
   - Drug name, dosage, route, frequency of administration, duration of therapy
   - Name of approving I.D. physician

   In those instances when the prescribing physician is unable to reach a member of the Division of Infectious Diseases within one hour, the order should be rewritten and the Pharmacy informed of the situation. The Pharmacist will attempt to contact the Infectious Diseases consultant within the next half hour. If unsuccessful, the Pharmacy shall notify the Division of Infectious Diseases of this situation at the beginning of the next working day.

2. Upon receipt of an *order* for a restricted antibiotic, the Pharmacist profiles the order (both approved and unapproved) into the Clinical Information System and sends the appropriate number of doses of medication to the patient unit. The Pharmacist enters a "U" into the report flag field indicating I.D. approval is pending.

   2.1 Upon receipt of *approval* for a restricted antibiotic from I.D., the Pharmacist obtains the patient's medication profile and specifies the approval in the Patient Notes. The "U" in the report flag field should be changed to an "A" for approved.

      2.1.1 The approval given by the Division of Infectious Diseases will be valid for the number of days specified.

      2.1.2 Approval for use beyond the specified date will necessitate additional I.D. approval.

      2.1.3 The prescribing physician, once initial approval is granted, will then write the order and have the order sent to the Pharmacy.

      2.1.4 The Pharmacist should indicate the appropriate stop date and time in the Pharmacy patient profile.

*continues*

**4–38** continued

2.2 If the restricted antibiotic has *not* been approved by I.D., the Pharmacist notes in the *Patient Notes* section that the drug that has been profiled has not yet been approved.

2.2.1 When the antibiotic is approved by I.D., the Pharmacist should purge the note that the approval is pending and enter the appropriate note as indicated above and proceed as described above.

3. The following adjustments in restricted antibiotic therapy will be regarded as a new order and will require additional approval from the Division of Infectious Diseases as described in Section 1:

3.1 Increased dose of the drug

3.2 Increased frequency of administration

3.3 Changing from the oral to the parenteral route of administration

4. At the beginning of each shift, the Clinical Pharmacy Manager or designee shall review the Restricted Drug Report indicating which antibiotics have not been approved or authorized for dispensing by I.D.

4.1 It is the responsibility of the Pharmacist on duty to ensure that each restricted antibiotic is approved by I.D. in a timely fashion.

4.2 The Director for Clinical and Educational Pharmacy Services will ensure that restricted antibiotics are approved by the responsible department through scheduled Pharmacy Performance Improvement Initiatives.

The List of Restricted Antibiotics is updated annually (Form 4–36) and distributed to all associates throughout the medical center.

Source: Adapted from Montefiore Medical Center, Bronx, New York.

# 4–39
# Chemotherapy Dispensing Pin

## POLICY

In order to ensure the safety of pharmacy personnel and sterility of the compounded product, a chemo dispensing pin will always be used for preparing and transferring any chemotherapy solution or diluent from rubber stoppered vials in the chemo hood (EXCEPTION = TAXOL).

## PROCEDURE

When used properly, this device facilitates the safe withdrawal and/or addition of chemotherapeutic IV medications and diluents. The vent in the pin eliminates the need to pull air out after adding diluent, or push air in the vial when withdrawing the medication that could result in the solution being sprayed when the needle is withdrawn due to pressure buildup.

To use, place the drug to be reconstituted, the diluent, and two chemo dispensing pins in the hood. Gown up and wear gloves as usual. All normal precautions are to be taken when using the pin as when not. Swab the diluent vial and the vial containing the antineoplastic agent with alcohol. Remove one dispensing pin from the outer wrap, and plug it into the diluent vial in a "sideways" plane. Plug the second pin into the vial of antineoplastic agent in the same manner. Remove the cap from both chemo dispensing pins. Affix the appropriately sized syringe (minus the needle) to the diluent vial by screwing the syringe into the pin in a "sideways" plane. As you remove the needed amount of diluent, MAKE SURE THE SYRINGE/PIN/VIAL ARE STRAIGHT UP AND DOWN WITH THE VIAL ON TOP. THIS WILL PREVENT THE PAPER VENT FROM BEING SOAKED. Unscrew the syringe from the diluent vial (in a sideways plane) and screw it into the antineoplastic vial (sideways plane). You now have a closed system. WITH THE SYRINGE/PIN/VIAL STRAIGHT UP AND DOWN, AND THE VIAL ON THE BOTTOM push the diluent into the powder. WITH THE SYRINGE STILL ATTACHED TO THE VIAL shake the reconstituted powder. After the powder is dissolved, withdraw the needed amount of solution into the attached syringe. You may now unscrew the syringe (in a sideways plane). Attach a needle to the syringe and inject the solution into the final bag/bottle.

Discard the chemo dispensing pins in the chemo waste container.

**Signed by** ______________________________

**Effective** ______________________________

Courtesy of Judy Sikes, PhD, CPHQ, Director of Accreditation/Medical Staff Services, Parkview Medical Center, Pueblo, Colorado.

# 4-40
# Chemotherapy Orders

| | | Manual Code: |
|---|---|---|
| **Subject:** | Chemotherapy Orders | |
| **Effective:** | | **Supersedes:** |
| **Distribution:** | All Manual Holders | |

## PURPOSE

Policy to provide a safe and efficient method of ordering chemotherapy agents for the treatment of cancer throughout the medical center.

## PROCEDURE

I. Physicians, Fellows, Physician Assistants, and Nurse Practitioners
   A. All chemotherapy orders for the treatment of cancer should be entered on the Doctor's Chemotherapy Order Sheet.
   B. Only those physicians, fellows, physician assistants, and nurse practitioners associated with the Oncology Service, and authorized to prescribe chemotherapeutic agents for the treatment of cancer, will order these drugs.
   C. Chemotherapy orders written by fellows, physician assistants, and nurse practitioners must be countersigned by an attending physician prior to preparation in pharmacy.
   D. If a specific protocol is being followed, it should be so noted in the designated space at the top of the order form. In addition, a note to this effect should be written in the progress sheet.

      A copy of investigational protocols must be placed in a notebook at each nursing unit where chemotherapy is administered, and given to the Department of Pharmacy Services.
   E. All orders will be legibly written and include the following, each in the area designated on the order form. Patient's weight (at time of admission), height, and body surface area, protocol or regimen (if applicable), as well as the diagnosis and chemotherapy cycle number must be indicated each time an order is written.
   F. Associated nonchemotherapy agents, i.e., hydration, antiemetic, etc., must be ordered on the same order form in the designated section. The order must be complete, including name, dose, and route of administration. Specify what type of fluid is to be given along with chemo (main IV line). Check compatibility of additives to main line with chemotherapy before sending orders.
   G. Chemotherapy agents must be ordered in the designated section. Orders shall include each of the following components:
      1. Dosage of each drug must be written both as per/m$^2$ (or per/kg) as well as the total dose to be given, based on the patient's surface area or body weight.
      2. Route of administration; if parenteral, specify rate of infusion. (Infusion should be specified in hours.) Specify route of administration. When protocol specifies rate of infusion over time, e.g., write, "Over 24 hours," *not* 21 ml/hr)
      3. Diluent, final volume, and rate of administration must also be specified.
      4. Frequency or duration of therapy as well as the date(s) clearly delineated that each drug and dose is to be administered, i.e., 2/4, 2/5, 2/6. Do not use "D" to abbreviate day or dose (e.g., for 4 days or 4 doses). Write the entire word.
         - In the case of continuous infusions, write the start date of each dose.

*continues*

**4–40** continued

- H. All orders are to be dated (month, day, and year), timed, and legibly signed by the practitioner. The practitioner's page number is to be listed following the name.
- I. Verbal orders for chemotherapy will not be accepted.
- J. When changes or modifications to nonchemotherapy orders are required, they may be made on a regular "Direct Doctor's Order Form."
- K. All changes or modifications to chemotherapy orders must be made on a new Chemotherapy Order Form.
- L. In order to minimize the risk of error when ordering medications, trailing zeros should never be used (e.g., 10.0 mg can easily be read as 100 mg). The word "unit" should be written fully, not abbreviated. A zero should precede numbers less than a whole unit (e.g., 0.5 mg, so as not to be interpreted as 5 mg).
- M. Abbreviations or number prefixes (such as 5FU) should be avoided because they can be confused with dosage instructions, misconstrued, or misread.

II. Pharmacists

- A. Pharmacists competent and experienced in oncology care and chemotherapy will be assigned to the preparation of antineoplastic agents.
- B. The service or physician will provide the Pharmacy Department with a copy of the investigational protocol for review and reconstitution. Chemotherapy orders will be checked against the protocol.
- C. Pharmacists shall honor chemotherapy prescriptions only when written on the appropriate order form, and in compliance with this policy. The pharmacy will be sent the "NCR" (or fax) copy of the order.
- D. Chemotherapy orders written by fellows, physician assistants, and nurse practitioners must be countersigned by an attending physician prior to preparation in pharmacy.
- E. Dispensation of investigational drugs must be accurately documented in a timely manner on the Investigational Drug Inventory form. Entries must be complete, including date (M-D-Y), patient's initials, and CALGB, POG, GOG I.D. number (when appropriate), dose, quantity dispensed, transferred or received, the balance, manufacturer and lot #, and pharmacist's initials. Transfers must be clearly indicated, i.e., "To ACT" (Ambulatory Chemotherapy & Transfusion Unit).
- F. All orders must be signed and dated by the pharmacist who prepared the chemotherapy. Whenever possible, two pharmacists will check each other's work comparing both the chemotherapy order and the reconstituted medication to the protocol or accepted dosing ranges. The second pharmacist should also sign and date the order.
- G. The pharmacist will verify with the physician/fellow, physician assistant, or nurse practitioner any order he/she deems questionable. For example, if an order does not comply with a protocol or when entered into the computer the dose is either above or below the dosage range, the pharmacist is to discuss the order with the responsible physician. If there is still a question, the order is to be discussed with the Director of Pharmacy Services and the Chief of Hematology/Oncology (either Adult or Pediatric as appropriate). Orders will not be dispensed until all issues are resolved. If the order is received for preparation at night, and it is impossible or impractical to get in touch with the physician, the night pharmacist will defer the problem to the morning until it can be resolved. In no case will any medication be dispensed until all questionable orders are clarified and resolved.

III. Nurses

Refer to Nursing Policy and Procedure.

IV. Errors

All errors will be evaluated by the Medication Variance Subcommittee of the Pharmacy and Therapeutics Committee and appropriate action will be taken to avoid a recurrence of the error.

**Approvals:**

Source: Adapted from Pharmacy Services, Long Island Jewish Medical Center, New Hyde Park, New York.

## 4–41
## Outpatient Ambulatory Care and Dismissal Prescriptions

### POLICY

The pharmacy does not fill dismissal prescriptions or outpatient ambulatory care prescriptions for use outside of the Medical Center. In emergency situations (i.e., all retail pharmacies are closed or patient is indigent), exceptions will be made only if deemed necessary to provide quality patient care. The pharmacy will fill prescriptions for radiology outpatients regarding a preparation for a radiology procedure.

### PROCEDURE

1. All outpatient ambulatory care prescriptions filled will be in compliance with all state and federal laws and recognized standards of practice in all respects (i.e., labeling, recordkeeping, counseling, etc.).
2. Ambulatory care patient prescription labels will bear the following information.
   - Name, address, and phone number of the pharmacy
   - Date filled
   - Pharmacy's identifying serial number
   - Full name of the patient
   - Name of the drug, strength, and amount dispensed
   - Directions for use
   - Name of the prescriber
   - Initials of the dispensing pharmacist
   - Pertinent cautionary labels including those required by the DEA
3. The face of the outpatient prescription will bear the following information.
   - Brand, lot number, and expiration date of the drug dispensed (in order to effect drug recalls on outpatient prescriptions)
   - Name of the patient
   - Address of the patient when required by law
   - Initials of the dispensing pharmacist and date filled
   - Full signature of dispensing pharmacist on Rxs for CII controlled substances
   - Red "C" on Rxs for controlled substances CIII–CV
   - Pharmacy's identifying serial number
4. The storage, documentation, and distribution of all medications for ambulatory care dispensing will be in accordance with all applicable state and federal laws. Nothing in this policy shall be deemed to take the place of, supersede, or release the pharmacy from the responsibility of being in accordance with those laws.

**Signed by** ______________________________

**Effective** ______________________________

Courtesy of Judy Sikes, PhD, CPHQ, Director of Accreditation/Medical Staff Services, Parkview Medical Center, Pueblo, Colorado.

# 4–42
# Relabeling of Patient Medications at Discharge

## POLICY

Bulk medications (i.e., topical preparations, inhalers, insulin, etc.) that have been dispensed to patients may be sent home with the patient if so ordered by the physician. Any medication sent home will be properly labeled in adherence with guidelines set forth in Pharmacy policy 025-15 Outpatient Ambulatory Care and Dismissal Prescriptions.

## PROCEDURE

1. The physician must indicate to nursing personnel via a written or verbal order that bulk medications that have been dispensed to the patient are to be sent home.
2. Nursing personnel must bring medications to be sent home to the pharmacy along with the order authorizing such.
3. Pharmacy will write out a prescription for the drug assigning a new Rx number in the usual manner. The medication will be labeled as outlined in Pharmacy policy 025-15. The face of the prescription will contain information as detailed in Pharmacy policy 025-15. The Rx and information will be recorded in the outpatient Rx log book.
4. Refilling of any inpatient prescriptions upon dismissal is not permissible and no subsequent refills from PMC are allowed.
5. The relabeled prescription is given to the patient by nursing with appropriate discharge medication education as outlined in Pharmacy policy 115-10.

**Signed by** ______________________________

**Effective** ______________________________

Courtesy of Judy Sikes, PhD, CPHQ, Director of Accreditation/Medical Staff Services, Parkview Medical Center, Pueblo, Colorado.

# 4–43
# Drug Product Defect Reporting
## DEPARTMENT OF PHARMACY

**Subject:** Drug Product Defect Reporting

**Manual Code:**

**Date Issued:**

**Date Revised:**

**Approved by:** Director of Pharmacy ____________________

**Reviewed by/Date:** ________ ________ ________ ________

It is the policy of the Pharmacy Department that any product problems observed or suspected must be reported to the United States Pharmacopeia (USP) Drug Product Reporting Program. This program is designed to immediately inform participating product manufacturers and the FDA of potential health hazards and defective products based on submitted reports. From collaboration with this USP program, it is hoped that improvement in the quality of commercially available prescription and OTC drug products will be achieved. Examples of reportable product problems are poor product quality, therapeutic ineffectiveness, packaging and labeling problems, and possible product tampering. Reports shall be submitted in writing, using the USP report form.

The following procedures shall be used to implement the reporting program:

1. Any staff who notices a drug defect (packaging, labeling, color precipitate, odor, etc.) or who is notified of a drug defect by another member of the hospital staff, or, as is sometimes the case, a patient, shall immediately contact his or her immediate supervisor.
2. In addition to contacting his or her supervisor, a pharmacy practitioner shall collect a sample of the drug having the defect for evaluation.
3. The nature of the defect and the probable cause, such as change in potency, degradation, poor storage conditions, or contamination, will be evaluated. A determination shall then be made if any immediate action is necessary; that is, whether any stock on hand should be immediately quarantined and an in-hospital recall initiated until the matter is resolved.
4. If action is deemed necessary, the Director of Pharmacy or designee shall fill out and submit the FDA's Drug Product Problem Reporting Form.
5. The Director of Pharmacy shall inform Risk Management, if necessary.

Source: Adapted from Montefiore Medical Center, Bronx, New York.

# 4–44
# Medications: Patient's Own

**REFERENCE:**

**SUPERSEDES:**

**ORIGINATED:**

**PAGE:**

**APPROVAL:** ______________________________
Chief Executive Officer

**Policies/Procedures:**

________________ Medical Center

**Subject:** Medications: Patient's Own

By: **MEDICATION USE FUNCTION TEAM**

______________________________
Senior Vice-President

**Revised:** New

**Authority:** Comprehensive Accreditation Manual for Hospital Medication Use Standards California Code of Regulations Title XXII

## PURPOSE

To safely administer patient's own medications when so ordered in compliance with regulatory requirements.

## POLICY

A. Patients are discouraged from using their own medications while hospitalized. Medications brought to the hospital by a patient or a patient's family and not ordered or authorized by pharmacy for use in the hospital shall be sent home with the family or placed in a "valuables envelope" by nursing personnel and picked up by Security personnel.

B. In patient care areas where a child may be present, containers for oral medications must have a safety cap. In Children's Hospital, acceptable bedside medications include vitamins (except A and D), multivitamins, antacids, topical medications, and food supplements.

C. Medications brought to the hospital by the patient and ordered for use in the hospital must comply with the following requirements before they may be administered to the patient or self-administered:

1. Complete prescriber's order must be written identifying drug name, strength, and directions for use.
2. Medication container must be clearly and properly labeled.
    a. Prescription drugs must meet prescription label requirements including: patient name, prescriber name, drug name, strength, quantity, directions for use, and expiration date if needed.
    b. Over-the-counter drugs must have complete manufacturer label and will also be labeled with patient name and room number.
3. Medication(s) must be examined and positively identified by a pharmacist or physician. Document in TDS if physician positively identifies a medication. A sticker will be placed on the bottle indicating a pharmacist approval. Must not be a Home TPN or IV solution prepared by outside firms.

*continues*

**4–44** continued

D. The Pharmacist is responsible to communicate with the patient's physician if any of the above three conditions cannot be met and will issue ordered medications from the hospital drug supply.

E. Patient's own medications must be kept in a medication cart or a locked drawer in their original containers.

F. Self-administration of any medication by a patient must be specifically ordered by a physician, whether the medication is brought into the hospital by the patient or is obtained from hospital supply. Patients who administer medications to themselves should have the mental capacity to understand the drug use and be capable of administering the drug appropriately; e.g., proper dose and frequency. The ordering prescriber shall make this evaluation.

G. A pharmacist or RN may remove any medication from the patient's bedside if abuse or misuse of the medication is suspected.

H. Patient's own medications that are left behind will be placed in a valuables envelope and picked up by the Security personnel. Medication not claimed by the patient will be returned to Pharmacy for appropriate disposal.

Source: Adapted from Long Beach Memorial Medical Center, Long Beach, California.

## 4–45
## Investigational Drugs: Approval, Consent, Dispensing, and Disposal

**REFERENCE:**

**SUPERSEDES:**

**ORIGINATED:**

**PAGE:**

**APPROVAL:** ______________________________
Chief Executive Officer

**Policies/Procedures:**

________________ Medical Center

**Subject:** Investigational Drugs: Approval, Consent, Dispensing, and Disposal

By: **MEDICATION USE FUNCTION TEAM**

______________________________
Senior Vice-President

**Revised:**

**Authority:** Investigational Review Board; Research Council

### PURPOSE

To administer medications in a safe and effective manner.

### DEFINITION OF TERMS

An investigational drug is defined as any new drug approved for investigational use in patients pursuant to Federal and State Law.

FDA: Food and Drug Administration

NCI: National Cancer Institute

### POLICY

All investigational drugs must be approved prior to their use. The Research Council is responsible for the approval and review of investigational drugs used in research.

### SCOPE AND RESPONSIBILITY

A. Scope:

This policy applies to all patients.

B. Responsibility:

Compliance with this policy is the responsibility of Pharmacy Services, Medical Staff, and Nursing Staff.

*continues*

**4–45** continued

## PROCEDURE

A. The Approval Process

1. Approval is given by the Research Council for research protocols and by the Chairman of the Research Council and Director of Pharmacy Services or their designees for one-time use in emergency situations, or continuation of investigational drugs started outside the hospital (see section E.2 of this policy).
2. Emergency drug request: The attending physician must make a request for use to the Chairman of the Research Council or the Director of Pharmacy Services or their designees. A notice of approval will be sent to the physician and the pharmacy.

B. Informed Consent

The prescriber is responsible for obtaining from the patient a signed informed consent and a signed patient bill of rights and placing them on the patient's chart prior to initiation of therapy. A surgical consent form is not acceptable.

C. Information Regarding Investigational Drugs

1. The following information is required at the nursing substation or patient's medical record and in the pharmacy prior to use of investigational drugs:
   a. Dosage form, route of administration, strength
   b. Actions, uses
   c. Side effects, adverse effects
   d. Interactions and symptoms of toxicity

D. Source of Investigational Drugs

All investigational drugs used at Memorial Medical Center must be approved as investigational drugs by the FDA or NCI and be supplied by a source authorized to distribute the drug in the United States.

E. Orders for Investigational Drugs

1. A written order for the investigational drug must be in the patient's medical record. All orders must be from an approved investigator. A house officer whose name is not listed on the research application cannot write orders for investigational drugs; e.g., changing dosage. The order must include the following information:
   a. Drug name
   b. Strength
   c. Dose and dosing frequency
   d. Route of administration
   e. If appropriate, duration of therapy
2. If a patient is admitted to the hospital on an investigational drug that was started at another site, the admitting physician or designee must contact the approved investigator to confirm that the investigational drug should be continued and the correct dosage regimen. This must be documented in the patient's chart. Verification of informed consent and information on the drug must be available in the patient care area to allow continued therapy.

*continues*

**4–45** continued

3. Storage and Dispensing of Investigational Drugs

   a. Investigational drugs must be stored in the Pharmacy and dispensed by pharmacy personnel (see Title 22, Joint Commission Requirements and 301.4 Stockroom, Pharmacy).

   b. The pharmacist is responsible for proper labeling, storage, and distribution of the investigational drug. A dispensing record will be kept in the pharmacy.

4. Disposal of Investigational Drugs

   In the event that a patient does not use an investigational drug, it will be returned to pharmacy by the nurse. The unused drug will be recorded and returned to the manufacturer or destroyed according to the manufacturer's guidelines.

Source: Adapted from Long Beach Memorial Medical Center, Long Beach, California.

## 4–46
## Waiver of Storage for Investigational Drugs
### DEPARTMENT OF PHARMACY
### Investigational Drug Services

It is hospital policy that all investigational drugs be stored by the Department of Pharmacy. However, in instances where this is not practical, Principal Investigators may obtain approval from the Department of Pharmacy to store their own investigational drug supplies. To obtain approval, please complete and sign this waiver and return it to the Department of Pharmacy at your earliest convenience.

To assist you in the proper storage of investigational drugs, it is essential that you adhere to the following guidelines:

1. Store your investigational drugs in a locked, secure area.
   (For information on storing controlled substances, please refer to the guidelines listed in the Controlled Substances Act Handbook. This may be obtained from the Department of Pharmacy.)
2. Store your investigational drugs appropriately (i.e., room temp., refrigeration).
   **Please check one:** __ Room Temp. __ Refrigeration __ Freezer
3. Label all your investigational drugs appropriately prior to dispensation.
4. Maintain accurate inventory logs that reflect the receipt and dispensation of any investigational drugs.
5. Return any unused investigational drugs upon study completion.

By signing this form, Principal Investigators agree to follow the above guidelines. If you have any questions regarding this matter, please contact the Department of Pharmacy at _______________ .

**Protocol Name:**

IND# ____________________ Protocol# ______________________

Drug Name, Strength, Dosage Form: ______________________________ Sponsor: ________________

Anticipated Quantity of Medication: ____________________ Designated Storage Area: ________________

________________________ M.D. Dept:______ Location:__________ Contact: ___________
Principal Investigator Name (Print)

________________________ M.D. Date: ______ / ______ / ______
Principal Investigator Name (Signature)

Source: Adapted from Montefiore Medical Center, Bronx, New York.

# 4–47
# (Medications) Investigational Drugs

## Policy

Investigational medication (a therapeutic agent undergoing clinical investigation that has not been approved for general use by the FDA) and those in clinical trials (a drug that has been approved by the FDA that is being used in a manner different than that for which it is approved) will be safely controlled, administered, and destroyed.

## Procedure

1. The Institutional Review Board (IRB) must approve the use of all investigational drugs.
2. Investigational drugs shall be used only under the direct supervision of the principal investigator (a member of the medical staff).
3. When a patient who is enrolled in an investigational protocol from another institution is admitted to the facility, notification by the admitting physician will be given to the principal investigator at that institution. It will be the responsibility of the admitting physician to notify the Chair of the IRB. The admitting physician will document in the patient's chart that the drug is investigational and that the IRB chair has been notified.
4. The original consent form is to be placed in the patient's chart.
5. The pharmacy shall be responsible for the storage, control, and dispensing of these drugs. Transfer of the drug to the pharmacy shall be arranged if received directly by the principal investigator.
6. The pharmacy will be responsible for having available information about the drug. Pharmacy will place in the patient chart a copy of the investigative protocol, reviewing basic pharmacologic information to include, but not limited to: indication; route, dose; adverse effects; and the need to return unused drug to the pharmacy. Nursing will not administer the investigational drug to the patient until familiar with the information provided in the chart. A pharmacist will be available as a resource person.
7. Disposal of any unused drug will be handled in the manner prescribed by the investigational protocol.

**Signed by** ______________________

**Effective** ______________________

Courtesy of Judy Sikes, PhD, CPHQ, Director of Accreditation/Medical Staff Services, Parkview Medical Center, Pueblo, Colorado.

# 4–48
# Adverse Drug Reactions

National experience is that approximately 10% to 15% of hospital admissions result in significant adverse drug reactions. This means that your hospital would be expected to report, on a monthly basis, adverse drug reactions equivalent to 10% to 15% of its average monthly discharge rate. Not too many hospitals achieve this figure. As surveyors, our experience has been that most often one or both of two factors appear to be responsible for this underreporting. Either the description of an adverse drug reaction is too extreme, or the reporting mechanism is faulty.

## DESCRIPTIONS OF AN ADVERSE DRUG REACTION

Quite often, the definition elaborated by the medical staff stipulates the reporting as an adverse drug reaction of the occurrence of any unsuspected or undesirable event that results in the discontinuance or modification of the dose of a drug, requires or prolongs hospitalization, results in disability, requires treatment with a prescription drug, or results in anaphylactic shock or death. Operationally, this requires the reporting individual to determine that a *significant* adverse drug reaction has already occurred before reporting it as a *suspected* one and, of course, drastically limits the number of events reported for evaluation. The best method of operating is to require the individual to report any suspected adverse drug reaction and allow the Pharmacy and Therapeutics Committee (or other medical staff group) to evaluate the circumstances in order to determine whether it was indeed a significant adverse reaction. (They are the ones who should be making this determination anyway.)

I suggest that the medical staff start with the broadest definition possible and then, if too many charts fall out, keep narrowing the definition until a comfortable number is reached and is one that results in the recording of a more appropriate number of adverse drug reactions. The broadest definition is also the simplest: merely the occurrence, after the administration of the drug, of any unexpected or undesirable sign or symptom that had not been present before the drug was administered. If this results in too many charts falling out for evaluation, then start narrowing the definition in a stepwise manner.

First, exclude any *known, predictable, commonly occurring* side effects. If more exclusion is needed, then known, predictable side effects should be eliminated. Finally, known side effects can be eliminated if needed. This, of course, would bring the definition to the beginning point at which a significant adverse drug reaction would be defined, mainly discontinuing the drug or modifying the dose. Key here is the concept that *suspected* adverse drug reactions should be reported. The medical staff and not the reporting individual should determine whether a significant reaction occurred.

The above methodology provides a hierarchical series of events that allow an adjustable setpoint for defining a suspected adverse drug reaction. The hierarchy is:

1. Occurrence of undesirable sign/symptom not present prior to administration
2. Occurrence of #1, not due to known commonly occurring predictable side effect
3. Occurrence of #1, not due to known commonly occurring side effect
4. Occurrence of #1, not due to known side effect
5. Occurrence of #1, requiring discontinuation of the drug or modification of the dose
6. Occurrence of #1, requiring treatment with a prescription drug
7. Occurrence of #1, resulting in anaphylactic shock
7. Occurrence of #1, requiring hospitalization or increase in level of acuity of care
   **(Numbered the same due to debatable level in hierarchy)**

*continues*

**4–48** continued

8. Occurrence of #1, resulting in disability
9. Occurrence of #1, resulting in death

## REPORTING OF SUSPECTED ADVERSE DRUG REACTIONS

More often than not, the underreporting hospitals tell us that any individual discovering an adverse drug reaction is responsible for reporting it. Again, speaking operationally, this means that *no one* is responsible for reporting it, since no one person is designated as accountable for the action. Clearly, some single individual should be made accountable for reporting the reactions, and since the nurses are the only individuals observing the patient on a 24-hour basis, they should be the ones designated for reporting.

Suggested steps to take to establish an effective reporting mechanism are as follows:

1. By hospital policy, designate the nurse attending the patient as the person responsible for reporting adverse drug reactions.
2. Inservice the nurses in the initial definition established for reporting of a *suspected* adverse drug reaction. Make certain they understand they are being required to report suspected reactions and are not asked to judge whether a significant reaction has occurred. Keep them apprised of any changes in the definition.
3. Provide them with a rubber stamp to record the report in the Progress Notes (see below).

The P & T Committee will take over from here.

## RUBBER STAMP REPORT FORM

The rubber stamp as a reporting form fulfills a number of requirements. First of all, it saves an extra form in the chart. This also means no one has to worry about neglected reporting due to inability to locate the report form, since the stamps are almost always kept in a holder at the charting desk, providing instant access. Further, the rubber stamp will stand out like a sore thumb in the Progress Note and serve as a very rapid means of written communication to all members of the treatment team, as well as those involved in screening charts for drug reactions. Last, it puts the report right in the middle of the action describing the event (the Progress Notes) and provides a more cohesive description for the treatment team as well as the P&T Committee. Any time communication among team members is increased, the probability of improving patient care is also increased.

A suggested format for the stamp is as follows:

### SUSPECTED ADVERSE DRUG REACTION ALERT

Drug ______________________ Finding(s) ______________________

Dose ______________________ Date ______________________

Route ______________________ Time ______________________

Action/Interventions ____________________________________________

Signature ____________________________ R.N.

Source: Adapted from Saint Barnabas Health Care System, Livingston, New Jersey.

## 4–49
## Adverse Drug Reaction (ADR) Assessment Form

**DEFINITION**

An Adverse Drug Reaction (ADR) is any unintended, undesirable, or unexpected response to a drug. It includes any reaction that results in the discontinuation of a drug, necessitates additional drug therapy, or causes a hospital admission, prolongation of hospital stay, permanent injury, or death.

**Patient:** ______________________ **Hosp #:** __________ **Age:** ________ **Sex:** ____________

**Diagnosis:** ____________________ **Room #:** __________ **ADM:** __/__/__ **Disch:** __/__/__

**Date of Reaction:** __/__/__ **Number of Doses Admin:** ____________

**Known Drug Allergies:** ______________________________________________

**Current Medications:** ______________________________________________

**Medication Suspected** (generic and trade name, route, dose, frequency, lot #):

______________________________________________________________

**Reaction Description:** ______________________________________________

______________________________________________________________

**Relevant Lab Data** (drug serum concentration, electrolytes, etc.): ____________________

______________________________________________________________

**TREATMENT:** ______________________________________________

**ADDITIONAL COMMENTS:** ______________________________________

**PATIENT OUTCOME**

____ Slight morbidity—may/may not require change in drug therapy

____ Moderate morbidity—drug therapy must be discontinued

____ Severe morbidity—potential for life-threatening or irreversible reaction

____ Death

**CLASSIFICATION**

____ Definite—reaction appears after rechallenge

____ Probable—reaction disappears after drug DC'd, but without rechallenge

____ Possible—reaction fits known response pattern, but may also be caused by other elements of the patient's disease

____ Unrelated—reaction is unrelated to drug therapy (does not meet ADR definition)

____ Unclear

Source: Adapted from Mercy Health Partners, Wilkes-Barre, Pennsylvania.

# 4–50
# MedWatch—Medical Products Reporting Form

MEDWATCH

THE FDA MEDICAL PRODUCTS REPORTING PROGRAM

For **VOLUNTARY** reporting by health professionals of adverse events and product problems

Page ___ of ___

**FDA Use Only**

**Triage unit sequence #**

## A. Patient Information

1. **Patient Identifier** In confidence
2. **Age at time of event:** or ______ **Date of birth:**
3. **Sex** __ female __ male
4. **Weight** ___ lbs or ___ kgs

## B. Adverse event or product problem

1. __ **Adverse event** and/or __ **Product problem** (e.g., defects/malfunctions)
2. **Outcomes attributed to adverse event** (check all that apply)
   - __ death ______________ (mo/day/yr)
   - __ life-threatening
   - __ hospitalization—initial or prolonged
   - __ disability
   - __ congenital anomaly
   - __ required intervention to prevent permanent impairment/damage
   - __ other: ______________
3. **Date of event** (mo/day/yr)
4. **Date of this report** (mo/day/yr)
5. **Describe event or problem**
6. **Relevant tests/laboratory data,** including dates
7. **Other relevant history, including preexisting medical conditions** (e.g., allergies, race, pregnancy, smoking and alcohol use, hepatic/renal dysfunction, etc.)

**Mail to:** MEDWATCH
**5600 Fishers Lane**
**Rockville, MD 20852-9787**

*or* FAX to:
**1-800-FDA-0178**

## C. Suspect medication(s)

1. **Name (give labeled strength & mfr/labeler, if known)**
   #1 ______________
   #2
2. **Dose, frequency & Route used**
   #1 ______________
   #2
3. **Therapy dates** (if unknown, give duration from/to (or best estimate)
   #1 ______________
   #2
4. **Diagnosis for use** (indication)
   #1 ______________
   #2
5. **Event abated after use stopped or dose reduced**
   #1 __ yes __ no __ doesn't apply
   #2 __ yes __ no __ doesn't apply
6. **Lot #** (if known)
   #1 ______________
   #2
7. **Exp. date** (if known)
   #1 ______________
   #2
8. **Event reappeared after reintroduction**
   #1 __ yes __ no __ doesn't apply
   #2 __ yes __ no __ doesn't apply
9. **NDC #** (for product problems only
10. **Concomitant medical products** and therapy dates (exclude treatment of event)

## D. Suspect medical device

1. **Brand name**
2. **Type of device**
3. **Manufacturer name and address**
4. **Operator of device**
   - __ health professional
   - __ lay user/patient
   - __ other: ________
5. **Expiration date** (mo/day/yr)
6. **model #** ______________
   **catalog #** ______________
   **serial #** ______________
   **lot #** ______________
   **other #** ______________
7. **If implanted, give date** (mo/day/yr)
8. **If explanted, give date** (mo/day/yr)
9. **Device available for evaluation?** (Do not send to FDA)
   __ yes __ no __ returned to manufacturer on ______________ (mo/day/yr)
10. **Concomitant medical products and therapy dates** (exclude treatment of event)

## E. Reporter (see confidentiality section on back)

1. **Name, address & phone #**
2. **Health professional?** __ yes __ no
3. **Occupation**
4. **Also reported to:**
   - __ manufacturer
   - __ user facility
   - __ distributor
5. **If you do NOT want your identity disclosed to the manufacturer, place an "X" in this box.** ___

**FDA Form 3500 (6/93) Submission of a report does not constitute an admission that medical personnel or the product caused or contributed to the event.**

Source: Department of Health and Human Services, Public Health Service, Food and Drug Administration, Rockville, Maryland.

# 4–51
# Vaccine Adverse Event Reporting System Form

**VACCINE ADVERSE EVENT REPORTING SYSTEM**
24 Hour Toll Free Information 1-800-822-7967
P.O. Box 1100, Rockville, MD 20849-1100
**PATIENT IDENTITY KEPT CONFIDENTIAL**

***For CDC/FDA Use Only***
VAERS Number ____________
Date Received ____________

| Patient Name: | Vaccine administered by (Name): | Form completed by (Name): |
|---|---|---|
| Last First M.I.<br>Address<br><br>City State Zip<br>Telephone no. (___) ____________ | Responsible Physician ____________<br>Facility Name/Address<br><br>City State Zip<br>Telephone no. (___) ____________ | Relation to Patient __ Vaccine Provider __ Patient/Parent __ Manufacturer __ Other<br>Address *(if different from patient or provider)*<br><br>City State Zip<br>Telephone no. (___) ____________ |

| 1. State | 2. County where administered | 3. Date of birth<br>__/__/__<br>mm dd yy | 4. Patient age | 5. Sex<br>__ M __ F | 6. Date form completed<br>__/__/__<br>mm dd yy |
|---|---|---|---|---|---|

7. Describe adverse event(s) (symptoms, signs, time course) and treatment, if any

8. Check all appropriate:
__ Patient died (date __/__/__ ) mm dd yy
__ Life threatening illness
__ Required emergency room/doctor visit
__ Required hospitalization (____ days)
__ Resulted in prolongation of hospitalization
__ Resulted in permanent disability
__ None of the above

9. Patient recovered __ YES __ NO __ UNKNOWN

12. Relevant diagnostic tests/laboratory data

10. Date of vaccination __/__/__ mm dd yy
Time ____________ AM PM

11. Averse event onset __/__/__ mm dd yy
Time ____________ AM PM

13. Enter all vaccines given on date listed in no. 10

| | Vaccine (type) | Manufacturer | Lot number | Route/Site | No. Previous Doses |
|---|---|---|---|---|---|
| a. | | | | | |
| b. | | | | | |
| c. | | | | | |
| d. | | | | | |

14. Any other vaccinations within 4 weeks prior to the date listed in no. 10

| | Vaccine (type) | Manufacturer | Lot number | Route/Site | No. previous doses | Date given |
|---|---|---|---|---|---|---|
| a. | | | | | | |
| b. | | | | | | |

15. Vaccinated at:
__ Private doctor's office/hospital __ Military clinic/hospital
__ Public health clinic/hospital __ Other/unknown

16. Vaccine purchased with:
__ Private funds __ Military funds
__ Public funds __ Other/unknown

17. Other medications

18. Illness at time of vaccination (specify)

19. Pre-existing physician-diagnosed allergies, birth defects, medical conditions (specify)

20. Have you reported this adverse event previously? __ No __ To doctor __ To health department __ To manufacturer

***Only for children 5 and under***

22. *Birth weight* ____ lb. ____ oz.

23. *No. of brothers and sisters*

21. Adverse event following prior vaccination (check all applicable, specify)

| | Adverse Event | Onset Age | Type Vaccine | Dose no. in series |
|---|---|---|---|---|
| __ in patient | | | | |
| __ in brother or sister | | | | |

***Only for reports submitted by manufacturer/immunization project***

24. *Mfr./imm. proj. report no.*

25. *Date received by mfr./imm. proj.*

26. *15 day report?* __ Yes __ No

27. *Report type* __ Initial __ Follow-Up

Health care providers and manufacturers are required by law (42 USC 300aa-25) to report reactions to vaccines listed in the Table of Reportable Events Following Immunization. Reports for reactions to other vaccines are voluntary except when required as a condition of immunization grant awards.

*continues*

**4–51** continued

**DIRECTIONS FOR COMPLETING FORM**

**(Additional pages may be attached if more space is needed)**

**GENERAL**

Use a separate form for each patient. Complete the form to the best of your abilities. Items 3, 4, 7, 8, 10, 11, and 13 are considered essential and should be completed whenever possible. Parents/Guardians may need to consult the facility where the vaccine was administered for some of the information (such as manufacturer, lot number, or laboratory data).

Refer to the Reportable Events Table (RET) for events mandated for reporting by law. Reporting for other serious events felt to be related but not on the RET is encouraged.

Health care providers other than the vaccine administrator (VA) treating a patient for a suspected adverse event should notify the VA and provide the information about the adverse event to allow the VA to complete the form to meet the VA's legal responsibility.

These data will be used to increase understanding of adverse events following vaccination and will become part of CDC Privacy Act System 09-20-0136, "Epidemiologic Studies and Surveillance of Disease Problems." Information identifying the person who received the vaccine or that person's legal representative will not be made available to the public, but may be available to the vaccinee or legal representative.

Postage will be paid by addressee. Forms may be photocopied (must be front and back on same sheet).

**SPECIFIC INSTRUCTIONS**

Form Completed By: To be used by parents/guardians, vaccine manufacturers/distributors, vaccine administrators, and/or the person completing the form on behalf of the patient or the health professional who administered the vaccine.

| | |
|---|---|
| Item 7: | Describe the suspected adverse event. Such things as temperature, local and general signs and symptoms, time course, duration of symptoms diagnosis, treatment, and recovery should be noted. |
| Item 9: | Check "YES" if the patient's health condition is the same as it was prior to the vaccine, "NO" if the patient has not returned to the pre-vaccination state or health, or "UNKNOWN" if the patient's condition is not known. |
| Items 10 and 11: | Give dates and times as specifically as you can remember. If you do not know the exact time, please indicate "AM" or "PM" when possible if this information is known. If more than one adverse event, give the onset date and time for the most serious event. |
| Item 12: | Include "negative" or "normal" results of any relevant tests performed as well as abnormal findings. |
| Item 13: | List ONLY those vaccines given on the day listed in Item 10. |
| Item 14: | List any other vaccines that the patient received within 4 weeks prior to the date listed in Item 10. |
| Item 16: | This section refers to how the person who gave the vaccine purchased it, not to the patient's insurance. |
| Item 17: | List any prescription or non-prescription medications the patient was taking when the vaccine(s) was given. |
| Item 18: | List any short term illnesses the patient had on the date the vaccine(s) was given (i.e., cold, flu, ear infection). |
| Item 19: | List any pre-existing physician-diagnosed allergies, birth defects, medical conditions (including developmental and/or neurologic disorders) for the patient. |
| Item 21: | List any suspected adverse events the patient, or the patient's brothers or sisters, may have had to previous vaccinations. If more than one brother or sister, or if the patient has reacted to more than one prior vaccine, use additional pages to explain completely. For the onset age of a patient, provide the age in months if less than two years old. |
| Item 26: | This space is for manufacturers' use only. |

Source: Department of Health and Human Services, Public Health Service, Food and Drug Administration, Rockville, Maryland.

## 4–52
## Prescribing and Dispensing Errors Data Collection Form

Date: ______________ Patient Unit: ______________ Pharmacist: ______________

| **Medication Error Initiative** | | Directions: Please indicate implicated medication and *briefly* describe error. Access to the patient's medical record (MR) may be necessary. PLEASE remember to note the total number of medications the patient is receiving. Thanks!! | | | | | |
|---|---|---|---|---|---|---|---|
| | | MR#: | | MR#: | | MR#: | |
| Total number of medications | | | | | | | |
| | | Prescribe | Dispense | Prescribe | Dispense | Prescribe | Dispense |
| Prescribing errors | Dispensing errors | | | | | | |
| Incorrect indication/contraindication for the med. / incorrect medication in cassette | | | | | | | |
| Incorrect dose based on weight, renal/hepatic function prescribed or dispensed | | | | | | | |
| Incorrect number of doses dispensed (DISPENSING ERROR ONLY) | | | | | | | |
| Delay in drug delivery (DISPENSING ERROR ONLY) | | | | | | | |
| Expired medication dispensed (DISPENSING ERROR ONLY) | | | | | | | |
| Medications prescribed / dispensed with incorrect or missing<br>Route of administration<br>Frequency<br>Strength<br>Duration<br>Dosage form<br>Miscellaneous ( ________________ ) | | | | | | | |
| Inappropriate abbreviation or poorly written order (PRESCRIBING ERROR ONLY) | | | | | | | |
| Therapeutic duplication for prescribed or dispensed drug | | | | | | | |
| No rational indication for prescribed or dispensed drug | | | | | | | |
| Drug allergy to prescribed drug not noted in medical record /Drug allergy to dispensed drug OR no allergy noted in medical record | | | | | | | |
| Significant drug interaction to prescribed/ dispensed drug not noted in medical record | | | | | | | |
| Prescribed restricted medications are not approved/Restricted medication is dispensed | | | | | | | |
| When necessary, prescribed/dispensed medications are not appropriately monitored or are NOT monitored | | | | | | | |
| Miscellaneous | | | | | | | |

Exceptions to above: ______________________________

______________________________

Source: Adapted from Montefiore Medical Center, Bronx, New York.

# 4–53
# Medications/Parenterals/Blood Components Quality Review Sheet

Occurrence Date: __________ Time: ________ Reported Date: ______________ Time: ________________

Employee Name: ______________________________ Title: ______________ Unit: ______________________

Patient Name: _________________________________ MR#: ______________ Acct#: ____________________

Medication/Product Name: ______________________ Strength: __________ Dose Form: ________________

Description of Incident: ___________________________________________________________________

____________________________________________________________________________________

____________________________________________________________________________________

**Check All That Apply**

**A. OCCURRENCE TYPE**

**Nursing Service** . . . . . . . . . . . . . . . . . . . . . . **Pts**

**Documentation:**

___ Failure to record administered dose on Medication Administration Record (MAR) IV Kardex or Narcotic Administration Record (NAR) for Patient Controlled Analgesia (PCA) pump . . . . . . . . . . . . . . . . . . . 1
___ Failure to report any discrepancy on the NAR update label to a pharmacist . . . . . . . . . . 2
___ Failure to report any MAR discrepancy on the MAR Variance Report . . . . . . . . . . . . . . 2
___ Failure to transcribe an order correctly on the MAR . . . . . . . . . . . . . . . . . . . . . . . . . . . 2
___ Failure to transcribe an order on the MAR . . . . 2

**Administration:**

___ Wrong patient . . . . . . . . . . . . . . . . . . . . . . . . . 4
___ Wrong medication/product . . . . . . . . . . . . . . . . 3
___ Wrong dose . . . . . . . . . . . . . . . . . . . . . . . . . . 2
___ Wrong route . . . . . . . . . . . . . . . . . . . . . . . . . . 1
___ Wrong time . . . . . . . . . . . . . . . . . . . . . . . . . . 1
___ Omitted dose . . . . . . . . . . . . . . . . . . . . . . . . . 1
___ Unordered medication . . . . . . . . . . . . . . . . . . 4
___ Incorrect IV rate . . . . . . . . . . . . . . . . . . . . . . . 2
___ Wrong IV solution . . . . . . . . . . . . . . . . . . . . . . 3
___ Discontinued med given . . . . . . . . . . . . . . . . . 2
___ Expired/deteriorated/contaminated medication given . . . . . . . . . . . . . . . . . . . . . . 2
___ Allergy to medication . . . . . . . . . . . . . . . . . . . 4
___ Pyxis discrepancy . . . . . . . . . . . . . . . . . . . . . . 1
___ Other _________________ . . . . . . . . . . . . . ___

**Pharmacy Service** . . . . . . . . . . . . . . . . . . . . **Pts**

**Order Entry:**

___ Wrong patient . . . . . . . . . . . . . . . . . . . . . . . . . 4
___ Wrong medication . . . . . . . . . . . . . . . . . . . . . 4
___ Wrong dose . . . . . . . . . . . . . . . . . . . . . . . . . . 2
___ Wrong frequency . . . . . . . . . . . . . . . . . . . . . . 1
___ Wrong time . . . . . . . . . . . . . . . . . . . . . . . . . . 1
___ Missed order . . . . . . . . . . . . . . . . . . . . . . . . . 2
___ Wrong route . . . . . . . . . . . . . . . . . . . . . . . . . 1
___ Wrong dose form . . . . . . . . . . . . . . . . . . . . . . 1
___ Wrong order form . . . . . . . . . . . . . . . . . . . . . 1
___ Incorrect message . . . . . . . . . . . . . . . . . . . . . 1
___ Failure to discontinue med . . . . . . . . . . . . . . . 1
___ Failure to suspend/unsuspend med . . . . . . . . . 1
___ Causing a medication to be dispensed without an order . . . . . . . . . . . . . . . . . . . . . . . 4
___ Failure to resolve a drug allergy issue . . . . . . . 4
___ Failure to resolve a duplicate therapy issue . . . 2
___ Failure to resolve a clinically significant drug interaction/contraindication issue . . . . . . . . . . 4
___ Other _______________________ . . . . . . . ___

**Compounding/Dispensing:**

___ Wrong patient . . . . . . . . . . . . . . . . . . . . . . . . . 2
___ Wrong medication . . . . . . . . . . . . . . . . . . . . . 2
___ Wrong dose . . . . . . . . . . . . . . . . . . . . . . . . . . 1
___ Wrong dose form . . . . . . . . . . . . . . . . . . . . . . 1
___ Date . . . . . . . . . . . . . . . . . . . . . . . . . . . . . . . 1
___ Incorrect label . . . . . . . . . . . . . . . . . . . . . . . . 2
___ Outdated/deteriorated/contaminated medication . . . . . . . . . . . . . . . . . . . . . . . . . . 2
___ Incorrect compounding of formulation . . . . . . . 3
___ Other _______________ . . . . . . . . . . . . . . . . ___

**A. SUBTOTAL** _____________

*continues*

4–53 continued

**B. ROUTE SEVERITY** ........................ **Pts**
___ IV/epidural/IT ........................ 4
___ IM/SC ........................ 3
___ PO/NG ........................ 2
___ Other (PR, top) ........................ 1

**B. SUBTOTAL** ____________

**C. NUMBER OF DOSES**
(1 pt for each dose) ____________

**C. SUBTOTAL** ____________

**D. OUTCOME SEVERITY CODE** (Check one) — **FACTOR**
___ Corrective action prior to error occurring .......... 0.5 (No Incident Report Required)
___ Error—no harm to patient .......... 1 (Incident Report Required)
___ Error—increased monitoring—no harm to patient ... 2 (Incident Report Required)
___ Error—increased monitoring—increased morbidity, increased level of care, increased LOS .......... 3 (Incident Report Required)
___ Error—death .......... 4 (Incident Report Required)

**D. SEVERITY FACTOR** ____________

**E. ERROR POINTS**
Occurrence Type (A) + Route Severity (B) + Doses (C) × Severity Factor (D) = Error Points

**TOTAL POINTS** ____________

**F. CONTRIBUTING CAUSES** (Check all that apply)

**Prescriber Related:**
___ Incorrectly prescribed medication
___ Illegibly written order
___ Ambiguously written order
M.D. number: ____________

**Individual:**
___ Miscalculation
___ Typographical error
___ Policy/procedure not followed
___ Failure to communicate
___ Needed assistance note requested
___ Failure to ID patient
___ Error in judgment
___ Insufficient attention to detail
___ Other: ____________

**Equipment:**
___ Poor fax quality
___ Defective/malfunctioning equipment
___ Other: ____________

**Organizational:**
___ No/ineffective policy/procedure
___ Staff assignment issue
___ Education/training issue
___ Other system related:
____________
____________
____________
____________

**G. CORRECTIVE ACTION** (Check all that apply)

**Individual:**
___ Counseling
___ Restriction of duties
___ Inservice/education
___ Progressive discipline
___ Other: ____________

**Departmental:**
___ Establish policy/procedure
___ Inservice/training
___ Revise policy/procedure
___ Reviewed at staff meeting
___ Equipment repair or replacement
___ Other: ____________

**Organizational:**
___ Refer to Pharmacy and Therapeutics
___ Refer to administration
___ Other: ____________

**COMMENTS:** ____________
____________
____________

**Date Reviewed:**

**Employee Signature:** ____________

**Supervisor Signature:** ____________

## 4–54
## Pharmacist's Intervention Form

Stamp patient information in this space

Record #: ______________________________

Date: ____________ Inpatient room: ____________ or ___ Outpatient

Patient name: ______________________________ M.R. #: ______________________________

**Fill out date and patient information (Or use addressograph at upper right)**

Att. M.D.: ______________________________ H.O./M.D.: ______________________________

Drug order(s): ______________________________

______________________________

Report time spent: ____________ (min) R.Ph.: ______________________________

Problem Description:

Intervention Action Taken:

Outcome:

Check all that apply:
Intervention was: __ Resolved __ Unresolved
Intervention: __ Prevented potential problem __ Patient received potentially problematic doses

__ Further follow-up necessary __ Administrative: __ Unusual occurrence __ Incident report
__ Drug information
__ Pharmacist on next shift

CONFIDENTIAL: This material is prepared pursuant to Utah Code Annotated. Title 26-25-1, et seq., and 58-12-43 (7, 8, and 9), for the purpose of evaluating health care rendered by hospitals or physicians and is NOT PART of the medical record.

*continues*

**4–54** continued

Complete each section, circle all that apply:

__ Proactive __ Reactive
*Reactive = in response to a med order

**Type of Intervention**

Adverse Reaction (ADR)
Allergy/Contraindication (Alt/CI)
Consultation (Consult)
Dosage Individualization (Dosage)
Drug Dose __ High __ Low
Drug-Drug Interactions (Dr-Dr)
Drug-Food Interactions (Dr-Food)
Duplicate Treatment (Duplic)
Duration of Treatment (Durat)
Incomplete Order (Inc Ord)
Indication for Drug (Indic)
Interval (Interv)
Investigational Drug (INV)
Lab Monitoring (Lab)
Non-Formulary (NF)
Nutritional Assessment (Nutr)
Omission of Drug (Omiss)
Pharmacokinetics (Pkin)
Route (Route)
Drug Administration (DA)
Transcription
Other: ________________

**Drug Categories**

| | | | |
|---|---|---|---|
| 04.00 | Antihistamines | 40.00 | Electrolytic, Caloric and Water Balance |
| 08.00 | Anti-infective Agents (Except penicillins, cephalosporins, and aminoglycosides) | 44.00 | Enzymes |
| 08.1202 | Aminoglycosides | 48.00 | Antittussive, Expectorants and Mucolytic Agents |
| 08.1206 | Penicillins/Cephalosporins | 52.00 | EENT Preps |
| 10.00 | Antineoplastic Agents | 56.00 | Gastrointestinal Agents |
| 12.00 | Autonomic Drugs | 60.00 | Gold Compounds |
| 16.00 | Blood Derivatives | 64.00 | Heavy Metal Antagonists |
| 20.00 | Blood Formulation/ Coagulation | 68.00 | Hormones and Synthetic Substitutes |
| 24.00 | Cardiovascular Drugs | | Local Anesthetics |
| 28.00 | CNS Agents (not otherwise classified) | 72.00 | Oxytocics |
| 28.04 | General Anesthetics | 76.00 | Serums Toxoids |
| 28.08 | Analgesics (NSAIDs, exc Narcs) | 80.00 | Vaccines |
| 28.0808 | Narcotics | | Misc. Topical Agents |
| 28.12 | Anticonvulsants | 84.00 | Skin and Muscle |
| 28.16 | Psychotherapeutic Agents | 86.00 | Relaxants (incl. Theophylline) |
| 28.24 | Anxiolytics, Sedatives, Hypnotics | 92.00 | Unclassified Agents |
| 36.00 | Diagnostic Agents | 98.00 | TPN |
| | | Other: | ________________ ________________ |

**Clinical Service Categories**

Transplant __ Kidney __ Heart __ Other __
General Medicine (MED)
(Include all Medicine Divisions)
Hematology/Oncology (HEM)
Emergency Room (ER)
General Surgery (GSR)
Orthosurgery (OSR)
Neurosurgery (NSR)
Burn Unit
Plastic Surgery (PSR)
Cardiothoracic Surgery (TSR)
Neurology (NRO)
Obstetrics/Gynecology (OBG)
Otolaryngology (ENT)
Urology (URO)
Pediatrics (PED)
Neonatology (PNE)
Psychiatry (PSY)
Rehabilitation (REH)
Ophthalmology (EYE)
Anesthesiology/Pain Service (ANE)
Other: ______________________________
______________________________

Source: Rawley M. Guerrero, Linda S. Tyler, and Nancy A. Nickman, "Documenting the Provision of Pharmaceutical Care," *Topics in Hospital Pharmacy Management*, Vol. 11:4, Aspen Publishers, Inc., © 1992.

## 4–55
# Application for Registration Under Controlled Substances Act of 1970

**APPROVED OMB NO. 1117-0014**
**FORM DEA-224 (11-00)**
***Previous editions are obsolete***

**READ INSTRUCTIONS BEFORE COMPLETING**
**USE BLACK INK**

No registration will be issued unless a completed application form has been received (21 CFR 1301.13).

NAME: APPLICANT OR BUSINESS (LAST)

(First, MI)

TAX IDENTIFYING NUMBER and/or SOCIAL SECURITY NUMBER

**The Debt Collection Improvement Act of 1996 (PL 104-134) requires that you furnish your Taxpayer Identifying Number and/or Social Security Number to DEA. This number is required for debt collection procedures should your fee become uncollectable.**

PROPOSED BUSINESS ADDRESS *(When using a P.O. Box you must also provide a street address)*

CITY STATE ZIP CODE

APPLICANT'S BUSINESS PHONE NUMBER APPLICANT'S FAX NUMBER

**FOR DEA USE ONLY**

## REGISTRATION CLASSIFICATION

**1. BUSINESS ACTIVITY: (Fill-in Circle)**
A. ○ RETAIL PHARMACY B. ○ HOSPITAL/CLINIC C. ○ PRACTITIONER - (Specify professional degree, e.g., DDS, DO, DVM, MD, etc.)
D. ○ TEACHING INSTITUTION (Instructional purposes only) M. ○ MID-LEVEL PRACTITIONER (MLP) (Specify professional degree, e.g. PA, NP, OD, NH, AMB, AS, etc.)

**2. INDICATE HERE IF YOU REQUIRE ORDER FORM BOOKS.** ○

**3. DRUG SCHEDULES:** (Fill-in all circles that apply)
○ SCHEDULE II NARCOTIC ○ SCHEDULE II NON NARCOTIC ○ SCHEDULE III NARCOTIC ○ SCHEDULE III NON NARCOTIC ○ SCHEDULE IV ○ SCHEDULE V

**4. ALL APPLICANTS MUST ANSWER THE FOLLOWING:**

(a) Are you currently authorized to prescribe, distribute, dispense, conduct research, or otherwise handle the controlled substances in the schedules for which you are applying under the laws of the **state** or jurisdiction in which you are operating or propose to operate?

○ Yes - State License No. ○ PENDING ○ N/A

○ Yes - State Controlled Substance No. ○ PENDING ○ N/A

(b) Has the applicant ever been convicted of a crime in connection with controlled substances under state or federal law? ○ YES ○ NO

(c) Has the applicant ever surrendered or had a federal controlled substance registration revoked, suspended, restricted or denied? ○ YES ○ NO

(d) Has the applicant ever surrendered or had a state professional license or controlled substance registration revoked, suspended, denied, restricted, or placed on probation? Is any such action pending? ○ YES ○ NO

(e) If the applicant is a corporation (other than a corporation whose stock is owned and traded by the public), association, partnership, or pharmacy, has any officer, partner, stockholder or proprietor been convicted of a crime in connection with controlled substances under state or federal law, or ever surrendered or had a federal controlled substance registration revoked, suspended, restricted or denied, or ever had a state professional license or controlled substance registration revoked, suspended, denied, restricted, or place on probation? ○ YES ○ NO ○ N/A

**ATTENTION** ▶ **FEE IS $210. FOR 3 YRS**

**ATTACH CHECK HERE**

Continued on Reverse ▶

*continues*

4–55 continued

**4. CONTINUED**

**(f) MLP** only: Applicant is authorized to engage in the following controlled substance activites by the **state** in which applicant practices. (Fill-in all circles that apply.)

| | Prescribe | Administer | Dispense | Procure* |
|---|---|---|---|---|
| SCHEDULE II NARCOTIC | O | O | O | O |
| SCHEDULE II NON NARCOTIC | O | O | O | O |
| SCHEDULE III NARCOTIC | O | O | O | O |
| SCHEDULE III NON NARCOTIC | O | O | O | O |
| SCHEDULE IV | O | O | O | O |
| SCHEDULE V | O | O | O | O |

*Procure means to individually obtain controlled substances by purchase or receipt of samples from a manufacturer or distributor. It does not include receipt of controlled substances from, or pursuant to an order from a collaborating or supervising physician.

**5. EXPLANATION FOR ANSWERING "YES" TO ITEM(S) 4(b), (c), (d), OR (e).** Applicants who have answered "YES" to item(s) 4(b), (c), (d), or (e) are required to submit a statement explaining such response(s). The space provided below should be used for this purpose. If additional space is needed, use a separate sheet and return with application.

**6. PAYMENT METHOD (Fill-in only one circle)**

O VISA  O MASTER CARD  O CHECK  O U.S. MONEY ORDER

**FEES ARE NOT REFUNDABLE**

CREDIT CARD NUMBER

**EXPIRATION DATE**

SIGNATURE OF CARD HOLDER

**7. CERTIFICATION FOR FEE EXEMPTION (Fill-in Circle)**

O **FILL-IN CIRCLE IF APPLICANT NAMED HEREON IS A FEDERAL, STATE, OR LOCAL GOVERNMENT OPERATED HOSPITAL, INSTITUTION, OR OFFICIAL. The undersigned hereby certifies that the applicant named hereon is a federal, state or local government operated hospital, institution, or official, and is exempt from payment of the application fee.**

| SIGNATURE OF CERTIFYING OFFICIAL **(Other than applicant)** | DATE |
|---|---|
| PRINT OR TYPE NAME OF CERTIFYING OFFICIAL | PRINT OR TYPE TITLE OF CERTIFYING OFFICIAL |

**8. APPLICANT SIGNATURE (*must be an original signature in ink*) ► Remove form from package before signing**

SIGNATURE  DATE

**I hereby certify that the foregoing information furnished on this application is true and correct.**

Print or Type Name

Print or Type Title (e.g., President, Dean, Procurement Officer, etc...)

**MAKE A COPY FOR YOUR RECORDS.**

**RETURN COMPLETED APPLICATION WITH FEE IN ATTACHED ENVELOPE**

*MAKE CHECK OR MONEY ORDER PAYABLE TO*

***DRUG ENFORCEMENT ADMINISTRATION***

UNITED STATES DEPARTMENT OF JUSTICE
DRUG ENFORCEMENT ADMINISTRATION
CENTRAL STATION
P.O. BOX 28083
WASHINGTON, D.C. 20038-8083

For information, call 1 (800) 882-9539
See "Privacy Act" Information on last page of application.

# 4–56
# Anesthesiology Controlled Substance Distribution and Accountability

## POLICY

The purpose of this policy is to describe the procedure for handling and distribution of controlled substances for the Anesthesia Department. An individual issue system shall be instituted for controlled substances administered by Anesthesia in the Operating Suites or other areas in the hospital where an anesthesiologist or a certified registered nurse anesthetist (CRNA) administer controlled substances. Each anesthesiologist and CRNA shall be issued and responsible for the control and documentation of controlled substances.

## DEFINITION

**Class II** Substances are narcotics as defined by the federal government

**Class III, IV, V** Items are drugs defined by the federal government

In this policy, the term "controlled substance" will be for narcotics or controlled substances.

The terms "schedule" and "class" are used interchangeably.

Inventory report is list of all control items in the pharmacy.

Log file report is list of all drug transactions in a specific period of time.

Doses shall be documented onto the controlled substances sheets using metric units, for example micrograms (mcg), milligrams (mg), or milliliters (ml).

Proper documentation of usage includes the administration date, patients name, drug administered, dose administered, wastage (cosigned) if applicable, and the anesthesiologist or CRNA signature.

CDS order form is form used to order control items.

CDS substance destruction is list of all items destroyed and witnessed.

## PROCEDURE

### Distribution of Controlled Substances

1. All controlled substances received from vendors in the hospital shall be entered and accounted for in the NARCO program, a computerized inventory system. A pharmacist shall have his/her own password to access the computer. Only a registered pharmacist shall issue controlled substances.
2. When an item is issued or received in the Pharmacy, the transaction shall be recorded on the NARCO system and a physical inventory shall be performed to verify the accuracy of the inventory transaction.
3. All anesthesiologists and CRNAs' must be properly credentialed by the normal medical staff credentialing process and have an identification badge prior to dispensing controlled substances. No controlled substance shall be dispensed without proper identification, a signature card, and DEA number on file with the Department of Pharmacy.
4. The anesthesiologist and CRNA receiving controlled substances shall be legally responsible to secure and properly document the usage of controlled substances, thereby leaving a paper trail, of the received controlled substances.

*continues*

4–56 continued

5. The anesthesiologist and CRNA requiring an initial supply of controlled substances shall report to the pharmacy dispensing window, present a hospital ID badge and request on a standard initial supply of controlled substances.
6. The anesthesiologist and CRNA shall open the numbered controlled substance box in the presence of pharmacy personnel and each party will verify the count. The anesthesiologist and CRNA shall then "sign out" the contents of the box on the Anesthesia Controlled Substance Disposition Record.

**SECURITY**

7. The Anesthesiologist and CRNA shall store the keyed controlled substance box in a keyed cart or other device permanently fixed to the wall or floor in the keyed Anesthesia workroom while not in use. All locks are to be locked at all times except when in use and under the direct supervision of the Anesthesiologist or CRNA. The controlled substances boxes and keys may not be shared. There shall be only one key per controlled substance box with a master key located in the Department of Pharmacy safe or vault. Each individual receiving a key shall sign for the receipt of a controlled substance key, i.e., controlled substance box, cart, and room. Keys may not be reproduced.
8. If a key is lost or misplaced the locks will be changed and the cost incurred by the appropriate party.
9. The anesthesiologist and CRNA shall ensure the controlled substances are secure at all times and maintain an accurate perpetual inventory.

**DOCUMENTATION**

10. When controlled substances are administered, they shall be noted on the anesthesia OR record and Patient Record of Controlled Substance log sheet. All wastage shall be documented on the Patient Record of Controlled Substance log sheet. A licensed health professional witnessing wastage shall document by cosigning the controlled substance log sheet adjacent to the documented wastage.
11. At the end of the shift the anesthesiologist and CRNA shall verify the count for their supply and that wastage/usage is properly documented. Appropriately labeled syringes containing unused drug shall be wasted with a witness to cosign. All controlled substances shall be exchanged and reconciled at least twice a week.
12. When additional controlled substances are required, the anesthesiologist and/or CRNA shall return Request Additional Controlled Substances (CS) on their Patient Record of Controlled Substance and drop it off at the pharmacy at the end of the shift. The pharmacy will prepare as previously described and deliver to the Anesthesia Suite between 10:00 AM and 10:30 AM the next working day. The CS will be checked, signed and added onto the Patient Record of Controlled Substance by representatives of pharmacy and anesthesia.
13. A count by the anesthesiologist or CRNA with pharmacy personnel shall occur comparing the inventory recorded on the to the sign-out log to the physical inventory twice a week, typically Wednesday and Friday. Pharmacy personnel shall visit the Anesthesia Suite during the agreed upon times . Once this is verified to be accurate the new supply shall be issued as described in #6. If a discrepancy is identified—the discrepancy shall be rectified prior to providing any additional controlled substances to the Anesthesiologist or CRNA. This shall also be noted on the incident report.
14. Discrepancies shall be resolved as discovered. Unresolved discrepancies shall be reported to the Director of Pharmacy, Chief of Anesthesia, and the appropriate regulatory agencies (U.S. Drug Enforcement Agency, State Board of the appropriate discipline, and others as required by law).

*continues*

**4–56** continued

15. A random review shall occur of control substance sign out records compared to documentation in the patient anesthesia record shall occur weekly. Pharmacy shall randomly verify contents of returned syringes.
16. The NARCO program shall consider each anesthesiologist and CRNA, with privileges at a certain campus, as a separate unit receiving controlled substances and tracked as such.
17. All anesthesia controlled substance records shall be kept in a separate file according to the date and year.

Courtesy of Kennedy Health Systems, Voorhees, NJ

## 4–57
## Sample Letter 1

08/29/02

Dear Dr ____________________,

A review of your anesthesia controlled substance box, with an anesthesia representative present in your absence, on 8/28/01 revealed a discrepancy in the count of ________and/or_________ unlabeled filled syringe(s).

To avoid regulatory and licensure issues, it is imperative the recordkeeping and drug count for all controlled substances be timely and accurate.

To decrease the risk of serious medication errors, it is imperative all syringes be properly labeled. If the syringe was not prepared in a sterile environment and properly labeled, it must be destroyed at the end of the shift. All controlled substance wastage must be witnessed and documented by a second party.

Please ensure these matters are immediately corrected. We appreciate your cooperation in the future to ensure compliance with all regulatory and standards of care.

Sincerely,

PharmD, BCPS, FASCP

Cc

Courtesy of Kennedy Health System, Voorhees, New Jersey.

## 4–58
## Sample Letter 2

8/28/02

Dear ____________________,

A review of anesthesia controlled substances records revealed you did not properly return the Anesthesia Controlled Substance box to the Pharmacy on ________. The anesthesia controlled substance box issued to locum tenens, must be returned each day at the end of their shift. This will help ensure compliance with regulatory and licensure issues.

It is imperative the recordkeeping and drug count for all controlled substances are timely, accurate, and compliant with the hospital policies and procedures.

Please ensure this matter is immediately corrected. We appreciate your cooperation in the future to ensure compliance with all regulatory and standards of care.

Sincerely,

PharmD, BCPS, FASCP

Cc

Courtesy of Kennedy Health System, Voorhees, New Jersey.

# 4–59
# Operational Policy for Controlled Substances

## PURPOSE

To conform practice and procedure regarding controlled substances to the needs of patients and the demands of the state and federal laws, rules and regulations. Procedures will include but are not limited to the following activities: ordering and receiving, distribution, destruction, and recordkeeping.

## POLICY

Employees that are authorized to handle controlled substances shall do so only as specified by the relevant law and hospital policy.

## PROCEDURES

### Ordering and Receiving

Based on the regulations of the state DoH and the federal DEA, the Pharmacy will place wholesale orders to maintain those Formulary items ordered for patients.

### Distribution

When needed, a new supply will be delivered by Pharmacy personnel to the nursing unit Pyxis. Pharmacy personnel will log the medication into the Pyxis unit acknowledging the specific quantity and verifying the correct inventory.

### Records

Pharmacy will maintain the following records for a period of five (5) years from the date of the transaction:

- invoices, C-II separate from CIII-V, separate from non-controlled substances
- official DEA order form (222) separate from other records
- prescriptions
- distribution receipts
- dispensing/administration records
- cumulative running inventory of all controlled substances
- official biennial inventory

### Inventory

Pharmacy will make a complete inventory of all controlled substances in the department during the annual complete department inventory in satisfaction of the federal Controlled Substances Act and the State Public Health Law. Additional inventories of infrequently used items will be conducted periodically.

*continues*

**4–59** continued

**REFERENCES**

1. NY Public Health Law §§ 3300–3396 and 10 NYCRR Subchapter K.
2. Federal Controlled Substances Act § 21 U.S.C. *et seq.* and 21 C.F.R., *et seq.*
3. Pharmacy Law Digest, Facts and Comparisons, 35th Edition, Chapter 3.

APPROVED BY:________________________, Director of Pharmacy

________________________, VP for Clinical Services

EFFECTIVE DATE: September 17, 2001

SUPERSEDES: None

Courtesy of Seton Health System, Troy, New York.

# 4-60
# Order Form for Recombinant Activated Protein C
## *drotrecogin alfa (activated) (Xigris™)*

For a patient to qualify for use of drotrecogin alfa (activated), the patient must meet:

1. the Infection Criterion,
2. the modified Systemic Inflammatory Response Syndrome (SIRS) Criteria,
3. the Dysfunctional Organs or Systems Criteria, and
4. have no contraindications to this therapy.

Consultation with Infectious Disease Personnel is required prior to submission of this form to the Department of Pharmacy Services.

***1. The patient must have a known or suspected infection.***

| Infection criterion | Definition and comments (if applicable) |
|---|---|
| ☐ Infection | As evidenced by one or more of the following:<br>• positive cultures;<br>• white blood cells in a normally sterile body fluid;<br>• perforated viscus;<br>• radiographic evidence of pneumonia in association with the production of purulent sputum; or<br>• a syndrome associated with a high risk of infection. |

***2. The patient must meet at least three of the following four modified SIRS criteria.*** These events must be believed to be related to the onset of sepsis and not attributable to an underlying disease process or the effects of concomitant therapy.

| Modified SIRS criteria | Definition and comments (if applicable) |
|---|---|
| ☐ Hyperthermia/ hypothermia | Core temperature ≥ 38°C (100.4°F) or ≤ 36°C (96.8°F). |
| ☐ Leukocytosis/ leukopenia | White blood cell count ≥ 12,000 cells/mm³, white blood cell count ≤ 4,000 cells/mm³, or a differential count showing > 10% immature neutrophils (bands). |
| ☐ Tachycardia | Heart rate ≥ 90 beats/minute, except in patients with a medical condition known to increase the heart rate or those receiving treatment (e.g., beta blockers) that would prevent tachycardia. |
| ☐ Tachypnea | Respiratory rate ≥ 20 breaths/minutes, $PaCO_2$ ≤ 32 mm Hg, or need for mechanical ventilation to treat an acute respiratory process. |

*continues*

**4–60** continued

3. ***The patient must meet at least two of the following dysfunctional organs or systems criteria <u>within 24 hours of administration including laboratory evidence of DIC</u>.*** These must be newly developed in the context of the changes in vital signs listed in SIRS criteria and not explained by the underlying disease process or concomitant therapy.

| Dysfunctional organs or systems criteria | Definition and comments (if applicable) |
|---|---|
| ☐ DIC | The **patient must have laboratory evidence** of a DIC, at least two of the following:<br><br>Platelet < 100K or 50% decrease in past 3 days<br>PT or APTT >1.2× ULN<br>D-Dimer > ULN<br>Fibrinogen ≤ ULN<br>Protein C, Protein S or Antithrombin < LLN |
| ☐ Cardiovascular | Arterial systolic blood pressure ≤ 90 mm Hg or mean arterial pressure ≤ 70 mm Hg for ≥ 1 hour despite adequate fluid resuscitation (IV bolus of ≥ 500 ml crystalloid, 20g albumin or 200 ml other colloids over 30 minutes), adequate intravascular volume (PCWP ≥ 12 mm Hg or CVP ≥ 8 mm Hg), <u>or</u> use of vasopressors (dopamine at ≥ 5 mcg/kg/min, epinephrine, norepinephrine or phenylephrine) to in an attempt to maintain systolic blood pressure ≥ 90 mm Hg or mean arterial pressure ≥ 70 mm Hg. |
| ☐ Hematologic | Platelet count < 80,000 cells/$mm^3$, <u>or</u> a 50% decrease over the 3 days preceding administration. |
| ☐ Metabolic acidosis (unexplained) | pH ≤ 7.30, <u>or</u> base deficit ≥ 5.0 mmol/L in association with a plasma lactate level > 1.5 times the upper limit of normal. |
| ☐ Renal | Urine output < 0.5 ml/kg/hr for ≥ 1 hour despite adequate fluid resuscitation as described above. |
| ☐ Respiratory | $PaO_2/FiO_2 \leq 250$ in the presence of other dysfunctional organs or systems, <u>or</u> $PaO_2/FiO_2 \leq 200$ if the lung is the only dysfunctional organ. |

4. ***Patients will be excluded from the use of drotrecogin alfa (activated) if they meet any of the contraindications for therapy listed below.***

| Contraindication | Definition and comments (if applicable) |
|---|---|
| ☐ Age < 18 years | |
| ☐ Pregnancy or breast feeding | |
| ☐ Weight > 135 kg | |
| ☐ APACHE II score < 25 | Acute Physiologic and Chronic Health Evaluation II Score: **calculated by the Medical or Surgical critical care service.** |

*continues*

4–60 continued

***4. Patients will be excluded from the use of drotrecogin alfa (activated) if they meet any of the contraindications for therapy listed below.*** *continued*

| Contraindication | Definition and comments (if applicable) |
|---|---|
| ☐ Prior administration | Patients that have received drotrecogin alfa (activated) in the past. |
| ☐ Thrombocytopenia | Inability to maintain a platelet count > 30,000 cells/mm³. |
| ☐ Increased risk of bleeding | • Surgery requiring general or spinal anesthesia (within 12 hours); or potential need for such surgery during the infusion;<br>• evidence of active bleeding postoperatively;<br>• history of severe head trauma requiring hospitalization, intracranial surgery or stroke within 3 months;<br>• any history of intracerebral arteriovenous malformation, cerebral aneurysm or mass lesions of the central nervous system;<br>• history of congenital bleeding diatheses;<br>• gastrointestinal bleeding within 6 weeks unless corrective surgery or therapeutic endoscopy has been performed; and<br>• trauma. |
| ☐ Patients receiving medications that can cause bleeding | • Antiplatelet agents within 3 days including aspirin at > 650 mg/day;<br>• warfarin within 7 days and if the INR is > 3.0;<br>• unfractionated heparin ≥ 15,000 units/day (within 8 hours) to treat an active thrombotic event;<br>• low molecular-weight heparin at a higher dose than recommended for prophylactic use as specified in the package insert within 12 hours;<br>• use of direct thrombin inhibitors within 7 days;<br>• glycoprotein IIb/IIIa inhibitor within 7 days;<br>• systemic thrombolytic therapy within 3 days;<br>• antithrombin III infusion of > 10,000 units within 12 hours or nonactivated protein C infusion within 24 hours.<br>*All these medications must be withheld during the 96-hour infusion of drotrecogin alfa (activated).* |
| ☐ Known hypercoaguable conditions | • Activated protein C resistance;<br>• hereditary deficiency of protein C, protein S or antithrombin III;<br>• anticardiolipin antibody, antiphospholipid antibody, lupus anticoagulant, or homocysteinemia;<br>• deep venous thrombosis documented within 3 months; or<br>• highly suspected deep vein thrombosis or pulmonary embolism. |
| ☐ Acquired Immune Deficiency Syndrome | Human immunodeficiency virus infection in association with a last known CD4 count of ≤ 50 cells/mm³. |
| ☐ Chronic renal failure | Requiring hemodialysis or peritoneal dialysis. *Acute renal failure is not an exclusion criterion*. |
| ☐ Liver failure | Known or suspected portosystemic hypertension, chronic jaundice, cirrhosis, or chronic ascites |

*continues*

4–60 continued

***4. Patients will be excluded from the use of drotrecogin alfa (activated) if they meet any of the contraindications for therapy listed below.*** *continued*

| Contraindication | Definition and comments (if applicable) |
|---|---|
| ☐ Acute pancreatitis | Acute pancreatitis with no established source of infection. |
| ☐ Transplant patients | Patients with bone marrow, liver, lung, pancreas, or small bowel transplantation. |
| ☐ Poor prognosis | Patient not expected to survive 28 days because of an uncorrectable medical condition or moribund state in which death is perceived to be imminent. |
| ☐ Code status | Patient's surrogate decision maker or physician not in favor of aggressive treatment to last at least the 96-hour period required to complete the infusion; or an advanced directive to withhold life-sustaining treatment irrespective of potential acute reversibility of the condition (e.g., sepsis). |

**Administration issues:**

1. Only patients with APACHE II scores > 25 completing the 96-hour infusion of drotrecogin alfa (activated) are known to benefit.
2. Drotrecogin alfa (activated) is stable for 12 hours. Bags will be prepared in concentrations of 10 mg drotreccogin alfa in 100 ml normal saline or 20 mg drotrecogin alfa in 100 ml normal saline, depending on patient weight
3. Coordination of replacement of drug infusions with the patient's current infusion volume is critical.
4. Replacement solutions should be prepared ≤ 1 hour prior to actual need. Nurses must call the pharmacy for a new bag at least 1 hour prior to the actual need.
5. Patient will receive 96 hours of actual infusion.
6. **Infusion interruption recommandations:**
   - Stop the infusion 2 hours before percutaneous or surgical procedures.
   - Restart the infusion 1 hour after a percutaneous bedside procedure if there is no evidence of active bleeding.
   - Restart the infusion 12 hours after surgery in the absence of bleeding complications.
7. Drotrecogin alfa (activated) requires a dedicated line. Maintenance fluids with ≤ 40 mEq K+ may run in the same line.
8. **Any unused/unspiked drotrecogin alfa (activated) solution should be returned to the central pharmacy immediately.**

**For a patient to qualify for use of drotrecogin alfa (activated), the patient must meet the Infection Criterion, modified Systemic Inflammatory Response Syndrome (SIRS) Criteria, Dysfunctional Organs or Systems Criteria, and have no contraindications to therapy. Approval of the infectious disease consult team is required prior to submission of this form to the Department of Pharmacy Services.**

Weight: __________kg Allergies: ______________________________

*continues*

4–60 continued

| Date | Time | Drug | Administration rate |
|---|---|---|---|
| | | Drotrecogin alfa (activated) 24 mcg/kg/hour continuous intravenous infusion × 96 hours | mcg/hour |

*Infusion bags will be rounded down to the nearest 5 mg

| Ordering Physician Signature | Physician Printed Name and pager # | Transcription | |
|---|---|---|---|
| | | Initials | Time |
| | | | |

| Approving Infectious Disease Attending Physician Signature | Physician Printed Name and pager # | Date | Time |
|---|---|---|---|
| | | | |
| | | | |

| Approving Administrative (CMO or DOP only) Signature | Administrative printed name and pager # | Date | Time |
|---|---|---|---|
| | | | |

Courtesy of Kennedy Health System, Voorhees, New Jersey.

## 4–61
## Inpatient Epoetin Alpha Order

This form is required to be completed by the physician prior to submission to the Department of Pharmacy Services. Consultation with the renal or hematology may be considered.

For a patient to qualify for inpatient use of epoetin alpha, the patient must meet: (all categories must be checked)

☐ The anemia criteria, the approved indication, and the approved dose and duration (See below)

☐ Have no uncontrolled hypertension

☐ Have no allergy to any component of epoetin or allergy to mammalian cell-derived products, AND

☐ Have no allergy to Albumin

### *1. The patient must have an anemia responsive to epoetin alfa and not be iron deficient.*

| Anemia and Iron Stores | Definition and comments |
|---|---|
| ☐ Indicators of Anemia | Hemoglobin less than 10 g or hematocrit less than 30% |
| **AND** | |
| ☐ Indicators of adequate iron stores | Transferrin saturation over 20% and Ferritin over 100 ng/ml |

### *2. The patient must have an approved indication.*

| Approved Indication | Definition and comments |
|---|---|
| ☐ | Anemia with chronic renal failure on dialysis with HCT < 30% |
| ☐ | Chronic renal failure not on dialysis with symptomatic anemia and HCT< 30%; |
| ☐ | Anemia in patients with non-myeloid malignancies where anemia (Hb at or below 10 g/dL) is due to chemotherapy |
| ☐ | Anemia with zidovudine-treated HIV-Infected Patient with HCT < 30%, endogenous epo level < 500 mUnits/ml and zidovudine dose < 4,200 mg per day |

*continues*

4–61 continued

**3. *The patient starting dose follows from the indication.***

| Indication | Starting Dose |
|---|---|
| ☐ Anemia with chronic renal failure on dialysis (Evidence does not support maintaining Hct over 36% compared to a Hct 30 to 36%) | 50 U/kg SC 3 times per week |
| ☐ Anemia with chronic renal failure not on dialysis with HCT< 30%* (Evidence does not support maintaining Hct over 36% compared to a Hct 30 to 36%) | 50 to 100 U/kg SC 3 times per week |
| ☐ Anemia in patients with non-myeloid malignancies where anemia (Hb at or below 10 g/dL) is due to chemotherapy* | 150 U/kg SC 3 times per week |
| ☐ Anemia with zidovudine-treated HIV-infected patient for 8 weeks, then titrated dose to maintain response * | 100 U/kg/week SC 3 times per week |

*Increases in hematocrits are not typically seen for 4 to 6 weeks after beginning epoetin alfa *(Epogen, Procrit).*

Erythropoetin ____________U/kg S.C. Monday, Wednesday, and Friday at 10 AM or________________

Patient Weight ____________kg (Pharmacists will prepare dose to limit waste)

Erythropoetin ____________U S.C. Monday, Wednesday, and Friday at 10 AM or ________________.
**(ESRD Patients on established dose)**

| Ordering Physician Signature | Physician Printed Name and pager # | Transcription | |
|---|---|---|---|
| | | Initials | Time |
| | | | |

Courtesy of Kennedy Health System, Voorhees, New Jersey.

## 4–62
## Policy and Procedure on After Hours Access to Medication

### DISTRIBUTION

Medical Staff, Nursing, and Pharmacy Services

### PURPOSE

To provide access to urgently needed medication when the Pharmacy Department is closed. When delay in therapy would compromise patient care, the Nursing Supervisor may obtain required doses.

### PROCEDURES

1. The Patient Care Coordinator (PCC) shall determine, in conjunction with the patient's nurse, if the ordered medication is required to satisfy an urgent need that, in its absence, would clinically compromise the patient's condition. If so the medication can be obtained from the Night Cabinet Pyxis located outside the Pharmacy.
2. Prior to administration of the newly ordered medication the order shall be reviewed against a database of patient and drug specific information including:
    - diagnosis,
    - known patient allergies and sensitivities,
    - contraindications,
    - the medication profile for drug-drug, drug-disease, and drug-food interactions,
    - dose modifying co-morbidities,
    - brand and generic names,
    - the medication obtained is independently verified by two nurses and double-checked against the original order.

    Note: The Lexicomp® drug information database is available on the Night Cabinet Pyxis and a Meditech® terminal is located in proximity for patient specific information. An on-call pharmacist is available for consultation.
3. The PCC shall not enter the pharmacy except in consultation with the on-call pharmacist when the ordered medication is not otherwise available. Keys are maintained in the Night Cabinet to track access to the Pharmacy.
4. A pharmacist shall review all after hour orders as soon as possible the following morning.

Courtesy of Seton Health System, Troy, New York.

# 4–63
# Operational Procedures: Drug Recalls

## DISTRIBUTION

Pharmacy Services

## PURPOSE

The Pharmacy Department shall facilitate immediate removal of recalled medication from all patient care areas (i.e., Nursing units, primary care sites, ancillary departments, and long-term care sites).

## PROCEDURES

In the event of a drug recall, pharmacy personnel shall:

1. Determine whether any quantity of the lots of the involved medication have been purchased by the hospital. If a recalled medication may be present, the Pharmacy personnel shall do the following:
   a. Remove recalled items from Pharmacy stock and sequester;
   b. Initiate "Recall" mode in the Pyxis dispensing units to prevent further dispensing and remove from each unit as soon as possible;
   c. Notify appropriate personnel at each the primary care sites, request removal from active stock, and return to the Pharmacy.
2. Document findings in Drug Recalls book.
3. Return recalled medication and products as directed in the Recall notification.
4. Report information about recalls to the Safety Committee periodically.

APPROVED BY:____________________________, Director of Pharmacy

____________________________, VP for Clinical Services

EFFECTIVE DATE:

SUPERCEDES:

Courtesy of Seton Health System, Troy, New York.

## 4–64
## Policy and Procedure on the Use of Fentanyl (Duragesic®) Topical Patches

**PURPOSE:** Standard practice for administration, management, and destruction of this Schedule II controlled medication.

**PROCEDURES:**

1. With each new patch the administering nurse shall write the date, time, and his or her initials on the patch in indelible ink or magic marker. The administered patch shall be inspected for this documentation on a daily basis and compared to the MAR.
2. The patch shall be inspected for cuts, needle marks, and a dried out appearance. If these or any other unusual circumstances are discovered the charge nurse and Pharmacy shall be notified immediately, a notation shall be made on the Controlled Substance Administration Record, and an incident report shall be filed.
3. Immediately after the routine removal the patch shall be destroyed by folding the patch in half by attaching the adhesive edges, and placing in a "sharps" container in the presence of a witness. This destruction shall be documented and countersigned on the Controlled Substance Administration Record.

Formulated: ______________________________
Pharmacist

Approved: ______________________________
Medical Staff President

______________________________
Director of Clinical Services

______________________________
Director of Nursing, Nursing Home

______________________________
CEO

## 4–65
## Notice of Inspection of Controlled Substances

U.S. DEPARTMENT OF JUSTICE
DRUG ENFORCEMENT ADMINISTRATION

| **NOTICE OF INSPECTION OF CONTROLLED PREMISES** | **DEA USE ONLY** |
|---|---|
| | FILE NUMBER |

| | | |
|---|---|---|
| NAME OF INDIVIDUAL | TITLE | |
| NAME OF CONTROLLED PREMISES | | DEA REGISTRATION NO. |
| NUMBER AND STREET | | DATE |
| CITY AND STATE ZIP CODE | | TIME *(Initial Inspection)* |

*STATEMENT OF RIGHTS*

1. You have a constitutional right not to have an administrative inspection made without an administrative inspection warrant.
2. You have the right to refuse to consent to this inspection.
3. Anything of an incriminating nature which may be found may be seized and used against you in a criminal prosecution.
4. You shall be presented with a copy of this Notice of Inspection.
5. You may withdraw your consent at any time during the course of the inspection.

*ACKOWLEDGEMENT AND CONSENT*

I, ______________________________ have been advised of the above Statement of Rights by DEA
*(Name)*

__________________________________________________________, who has
*(Title and Name)*

identified himself/herself to me with his/her credentials and presented me with this Notice of Inspection containing a copy of sections 302(f) and 510(a), (b) and (c) of the controlled Substances Act (21 U.S.C. 822(f) and 21 U.S.C. 880(a), (b) and (c)), printed hereon, authorizing an inspection of the above-described controlled premises. I hereby acknowledge receipt of this Notice of Inspection. In addition, I hereby certify that I am the ____________________ for the premises described in this Notice of Inspection, that I have read the
*(President) (Manager) (Owner)*

foregoing and understand its contents; that I have authority to act in this matter and have signed this Notice of Inspection pursuant to my authority.

I understand what my rights are concerning inspection. No threats or promises have been made to me and no pressure of any kind has been used against me. I voluntarily give consent for inspection of these controlled premises.

*continues*

**4–65** continued

______________________________
*(Signature)*

______________________________
*(Date)*

**WITNESSES:**

| | |
|---|---|
| ____________________ | ________ |
| *(signed)* | *(date)* |
| ____________________ | ________ |
| *(signed)* | *(date)* |

**DEA Form**
**(June 1962)** - 82

Source: U.S. Department of Justice, Drug Enforcement Administration, Washington, D.C.

## 4–66
## Adult Vaccine Order and Protocol

**Order:**

Administer the **pneumococcal vaccine, 0.5ml IM**, to all employees and patients who are eligible per protocol between September 1, 2002 and December 31, 2003.

Administer the **influenza vaccine, 0.5ml IM**, to all employees and patients who are eligible per protocol between October 1, 2002 and March 31, 2003.

Administer the **tetanus and diphtheria toxoid, 0.5ml IM**, to all employees and patients who are eligible per protocol between September 1, 2002 and December 31, 2003.

Administer the **hepatitis B series**, to all employees and patients who are eligible per protocol between September 1, 2002 and December 31, 2003.

For anaphylactic reactions associated with any of the above administer epinephrine 1:1000, 0.3ml by subcutaneous injection.

**Protocol:**

In connection with each patient the administering registered professional nurse ("RN") shall ensure that each potential recipient is assessed for contraindications. In addition, the RN shall ensure each recipient's record of immunization shall include the manufacturer and lot number, or the refusal of immunization by the patient. Emergency anaphylaxis treatment agents, related syringes, needles, and supplies shall be available. Also the RN shall:

- Inform each patient about potential side effects and adverse reactions, orally and in writing, prior to administration;
- Provide written instructions to the recipient concerning the appropriate course of action in the event of an adverse reaction;
- Obtain written consent from the patient or legally responsible party prior to administration;
- Provide a signed certificate of immunization noting the recipient's name, date, address of administration, administering nurse, immunization agent, manufacturer, and lot number;
- Communicate the fact of administration to the recipient's primary care provider if there is one;
- Report all adverse reactions to the Vaccine Adverse Reporting System (VAERS) on the designated form; and
- Ensure that a record is kept of all potential recipients, noting those who refused to be immunized.

This order is effective from October 1, 2002 through September 30, 2003.

________________________________________ ____________________

Physician or Certified Nurse Practitioner signature | License number

________________________________________ ____________________

Printed name | Date

Courtesy of Inter-Lakes Health, Pharmacy Department, Ticonderoga, New York.

## 4–67
## Thrombolytic Order Form for Acute Myocardial Infarction

Allergies: ______________________________________________

1. Prior to Retavase (Retaplase) administration obtain patient weight (________ kg)
   a) 12 lead EKG
   b) Draw CBC, Basic Metabolic Panel (BMP), PT, aPTT, Lipid Panel
   c) Cardiac Iso-enzymes (check to activate order)
      ☐ Per protocol
   d) Other: ______________________________
2. Begin $O_2$ by nasal cannula at _________ L/min
3. Attempt to establish at least 2 IV access sites (multiple port catheters may be used)
4. Record Vital Signs q15 minutes until the completion of the Retavase administration.
5. ☐ Aspirin 325 mg po now ____ Time given
   ☐ Aspirin not ordered because: ____________________
   ☐ Nitroglycerin 1/150 5L × 3 Q 5 minutes
6. ☐ Retavase 10 units IV bolus (Administer over 2 minutes) ____ Time given
   Retavase 10 units IV bolus 30 minutes after initial bolus. (Administer over 2 minutes) ____ Time given
7. **Post Retavase administration**
   a) 12 lead EKG at the completion of the Retavase administration

8a. Heparin 60 unit/kg **Bolus** (Max 4000 units) ______________ units ____ Time given

**THEN**

8b. ☐ Heparin 25,000 units in 250 ml D5W (100 units/ml)
Heparin 12 units/kg/hr (Max 1000 units/hr) ______________ units
Obtain aPTT 8 hours after starting heparin.

9. ☐ IV Nitroglycerin 50 mg/250 ml D5W. Start at ______________ mcg/min
   Titrate to decreased chest pain. Hold for SBP <____________
10. ☐ IV Metoprolol 5 mg Q5° × _____, then 25 mg PO × 1 ____ Time given
    ☐ Beta blocker not ordered because: ______________________________

**I have read all of the above orders and have checked, filled in, or deleted as I desire.**

Date: __________ Time: __________ Physician Signature: ____________________

Date: __________ Time: __________ Unit Secretary Signature: ____________________

Date: __________ Time: __________ RN Signature: ____________________

***(Authorization is given to dispense and administer another brand of a generic equivalent product, identical in dosage form and content or active therapeutic ingredient(s) unless marked "no substitution.")***

Form # (11/02)

Courtesy of Kennedy Health System, Voorhees, New Jersey.

# 4–68
# Pulmonary Embolism or Venous Thrombosis Heparin/Anticoagulation Order Form

**(Lower doses are used for Acute Myocardial Ischemia receiving Thrombolytic or GPIIb/IIIa antagonist agents)**

**EFFECTIVE START DATE—____________**

Allergies: ____________________________________________

____________________________________________

**Diagnosis for Order:** ____________________________

1. Weigh Patient = _______ kg (calculate using actual body weight, round weight down)
   *(If greater than 100kg, base initial dosing on 100kg maximum)*
2. Laboratory STAT: PTT, CBC
   CBC with platelet count every (3) days
   <u>STAT</u> PTT six (6) hours after heparin bolus *(PTT must be drawn peripherally)*
3. BOLUS HEPARIN, 80 units/kg = _______ units IV × 1
4. IV HEPARIN INFUSION, 18 units/kg/hr = ______ units/hr *(select one of the following):*
   _______ 25,000 units Heparin in 250 ml D5W, 100 units/ml
   _______ 25,000 units Heparin in 250 ml 0.45% NSS, 100 units/ml
5. ADJUST Heparin infusion based on sliding scale when PTT results available: *(modify scale if appropriate)*

| | |
|---|---|
| PTT < 38 seconds | Rebolus with 80 units/kg = _________ units<br>**Increase** drip rate by 4 units/kg/hr = _________ units/hr |
| PTT 38–49 seconds | Rebolus with 40 units/kg = _________ units<br>**Increase** drip rate by 2 units/kg/hr = _________ units/hr |
| PTT 50–59 seconds | No Change |
| PTT 60–72 seconds | **Reduce** drip rate by 2 units/kg/hr = _________ units/hr |
| PTT > 72 seconds | Hold heparin for one (1) hour then,<br>**Reduce** drip rate by 3 units/kg/hr = _________ units/hr |

*(Round off dose to nearest ml/hr (i.e. nearest 100 units/kg))*

6. **PTT six (6) hours after any dosage change until PTT is therapeutic. When one (1) PTT is therapeutic order PTT every morning. <u>Call physician with any signs of bleeding.</u>**
7. If PTT is > 72 seconds twice consecutively, hold heparin for 2 hours then decrease drip rate by another 3 units/kg/hr and notify physician.
   If PTT is > 72 seconds for third time consecutively call physician. Consider Hematology consult.
8. Warfarin therapy: **(Cross out #8 if not being ordered)**
   Warfarin order _______ mg today, then ordered daily based on INR/PT.
   **LAB:** PT in morning

Physician ______________________ Date/Time ______________ Beeper # ____________

**WHITE - CHART** **CANARY - PHARMACY**

1150.34 (04/02)

Courtesy of Kennedy Health System, Voorhees, New Jersey.

## 4–69
## Pharmacy Patient Education Record

Patient's name ______________________________ Medical record # ____________________

Date of admission ________________________ Location ____________________________

Patient was referred to pharmacy by: ______ Self ______ RN ______ MD ______ Others

Diagnosis: ______________________________________________________________

| | *Drug* | *Dose* | *Frequency* | | *Drug* | *Dose* | *Frequency* |
|---|---|---|---|---|---|---|---|
| 1. | | | | 6. | | | |
| 2. | | | | 7. | | | |
| 3. | | | | 8. | | | |
| 4. | | | | 9. | | | |
| 5. | | | | 10. | | | |

Content of Discussion: ________________________________________________________

______________________________________________________________________________

______________________________________________________________________________

Written educational material given? ______ Yes ______ No

Type of written educational material given: ______ USPDI ______ Others (please specify)

______________________________________________________________________________

Was the pharmacist's business card given to the patient? ______ Yes ______ No

Assessment of the patient's understanding: ______________________________________

______________________________________________________________________________

______________________________________________________________________________

Signature of pharmacist ___________________________________ Date _______________

Source: Adapted from Montefiore Medical Center, Bronx, New York.

# 4–70
# Interdisciplinary Patient/Family Health Education Record

A.
Who will be taught: _____ Patient _____ Family/SO ____________________
Name/Relationship

ADDRESSOGRAPH

| POTENTIAL BARRIER TO LEARNING | PT. | Family | | PT. | Family | PREFERENCE FOR LEARNING | PT. | Family |
|---|---|---|---|---|---|---|---|---|
| 1. Unable To Be Taught and No Family Available | | | 6. Unable To Read/ Write | | | 1. One to One | | |
| 2. Religious/Cultural | | | 7. English Is Not Primary Language | | | 2. Group | | |
| 3. Physical/Auditory/ Visual | | | 8. Interpreter Needed | | | 3. Video | | |
| 4. Mental/Emotional | | | 9. Cognitive | | | 4. Written Material | | |
| 5. Motivational/Financial | | | | | | 5. Other | | |

Signature/RN ______________________________ Date ______________

B.

| | READINESS | | | TOPIC | | | | | | | | | | | | | | | | MEDIA | | | LEARNED OUTCOME | | |
|---|---|---|---|---|---|---|---|---|---|---|---|---|---|---|---|---|---|---|---|---|---|---|---|---|---|
| DATE/INITIALS | NO EDUCAT. NEEDS | UNCOOPERATIVE | RECEPTIVE | DISEASE/COMPLIC | PRE-OP POST-OP | TEACHING | FOLLOW-UP CARE | COMM RESOURCES | DISCHARGE PLAN | HYGIENE | SELF-CARE | NUTRITION | REHAB/ACTIVITY | MEDICATIONS | PROCEDURES/TESTS | EQUIPMENT | FINANCIAL/OTHER | ADVANCE DIRECTIVES | COMMENTS | VIDEO | LITERATURE | INDIV INSTR | NEEDS REVIEW | RETURN DEMONSTR | UNDERSTANDS |
| | | | | | | | | | | | | | | | | | | | | | | | | | |
| | | | | | | | | | | | | | | | | | | | | | | | | | |
| | | | | | | | | | | | | | | | | | | | | | | | | | |
| | | | | | | | | | | | | | | | | | | | | | | | | | |
| | | | | | | | | | | | | | | | | | | | | | | | | | |
| | | | | | | | | | | | | | | | | | | | | | | | | | |
| | | | | | | | | | | | | | | | | | | | | | | | | | |
| | | | | | | | | | | | | | | | | | | | | | | | | | |
| | | | | | | | | | | | | | | | | | | | | | | | | | |
| | | | | | | | | | | | | | | | | | | | | | | | | | |
| | | | | | | | | | | | | | | | | | | | | | | | | | |
| | | | | | | | | | | | | | | | | | | | | | | | | | |

| C. INIT. | SIGNATURE | TITLE | INIT. | SIGNATURE | TITLE |
|---|---|---|---|---|---|
| | | | | | |
| | | | | | |
| | | | | | |
| | | | | | |
| | | | | | |

*continues*

**4–70** continued

D.

| DATE | COMMENTS | INITIALS |
|---|---|---|
| | | |
| | | |
| | | |
| | | |
| | | |
| | | |
| | | |
| | | |
| | | |
| | | |
| | | |
| | | |
| | | |
| | | |
| | | |
| | | |
| | | |
| | | |
| | | |
| | | |
| | | |
| | | |
| | | |
| | | |
| | | |
| | | |
| | | |
| | | |
| | | |
| | | |
| | | |

Source: Adapted from Montefiore Medical Center, Bronx, New York.

# 4–71
# Drug-Nutrient Interactions Policy

| | | |
|---|---|---|
| | Policy No.: | |
| **PATIENT CARE PRACTICES** | Original Date: | |
| | Previous Date: | |
| **DRUG-NUTRIENT INTERACTIONS** | Revised Date: | |

## POLICY

1. Prior to discharge, patients will receive general instructions about avoiding drug-nutrient interactions and more specific education about the potential interactions between certain foods and selected medications that may have clinically significant adverse outcomes.
2. Medications for more detailed education will be selected by the Departments of Pharmacy and Clinical Nutrition on the basis of scientific evidence of significant adverse events due to the interactions of medications and nutrients.

## PURPOSE

1. To educate the patient and other caregivers about the potential interactions between certain medications and foods they will be taking to promote the safe use of medications.

## RESPONSIBILITIES

1. Nursing will screen for selected drugs upon admission and notify Clinical Nutrition via established policy.
2. Nursing is responsible for the education of patients receiving disulfiram from the Chemical Dependency Unit or metronidazole from A2W.
3. Nursing is responsible for the education of patients receiving calcium channel blockers.
4. Clinical Nutrition is responsible for the drug-nutrient education for patients being discharged on the following medications.
   a. Isoniazid
   b. Monoamine oxidase inhibitors (MAOI)
   c. Warfarin
   d. Cyclosporin
5. The Pharmacy will prepare the monographs in coordination with the Patient Education Committee and other appropriate groups. Pharmacists may provide medication use counseling that includes drug-nutrient interaction information as necessary.

## PROCEDURES

1. Verbal and written information will be provided to the patient or the caregiver of a patient being discharged on the designated medication by a nurse, clinical dietitian, or pharmacist.
2. The Pharmacy will provide a list of patients on the targeted medications to the Clinical Nutrition Department on a daily basis.

*continues*

**4–71** continued

3. Nursing will identify patients receiving either disulfiram (A2C) or metronidazole (A2W) through a review of the Medication Administration Record, Pyxis profile, or physician-ordered discharge medications. Nursing will screen for admission medications that are at risk for drug-nutrient interactions and refer patients to the Clinical Nutrition Department, utilizing the *Identified Risk Referral Form.*
4. Patients being discharged on warfarin may be referred to the Anticoagulation Clinic for follow-up by the appropriate caregivers.
5. Clinical Nutrition will educate the patient and/or the patient's caregivers receiving the identified medications from the list of patients identified by Pharmacy.
6. Drug information master sheets will be maintained by the Pharmacy and distributed to the patient care areas and Clinical Nutrition (see Attachments A and B for examples).
7. Documentation will be completed by all disciplines on the Patient Education Assessment and Documentation Form. Dietitians will also document drug-nutrient education with the patient/caregiver in the progress notes of the medical record using the standard nutrition education form. This form documents the written and verbal learning responses obtained.

*REVIEWED BY:*

______________________________ Director, Pharmacy and Management Services

______________________________ Director, Clinical Nutrition

| ______________________________ | ______________________________ |
|---|---|
| Vice-President of Patient Care | Chair, Medical Board |

*continues*

4–71 continued

## ATTACHMENT A
## CALCIUM CHANNEL BLOCKERS

**DRUG:** Calcium Channel Blockers

- Nifedipine—Adalat or Procardia
- Nimodipine—Nimotop
- Amlodipine—Norvasc
- Felodipine—Plendil
- Verapamil—Calan or Isoptin

**USES:** Calcium channel blockers are used to treat angina (chest pain) or to manage hypertension (high blood pressure) or stroke (nimodipine only).

**HOW TO TAKE THIS MEDICATION:** The tablet, capsule, or caplet form (which is a capsule-shaped tablet) should be taken with food.

**Do not take any of these medicines with GRAPEFRUIT JUICE. The action and side effects of these drugs is greatly enhanced by grapefruit juice.**

Do not stop taking this medication suddenly without your doctor's permission. Your dose may need to be gradually decreased.

**SIDE EFFECTS:** This drug may cause dizziness and lightheadedness, especially during the first few days. When you sit or lie down for a while and get up, get up slowly to allow your body to adjust and minimize dizziness.

You may also experience nausea, blurred vision, weakness, lowered blood pressure, muscle cramps, headache, flushing, or constipation. Inform your doctor if these effects persist or worsen.

Notify your doctor if you develop breathing difficulties, rash, chest pain, swelling of the hands or feet, or an irregular heartbeat.

**PRECAUTIONS:** Tell your doctor if you have heart, liver, or kidney disease or any allergies, particularly any allergies to drugs.

Limit alcohol while taking this medication.

During pregnancy, this drug should be used only when clearly needed. Discuss the risks and benefits with your doctor. This drug is excreted into breast milk. Although there are no known problems with taking this drug while breast-feeding, because of the possibility of adverse effects on the infant the manufacturer of this drug recommends that this drug be discontinued or that nursing be stopped. Consult your doctor before breast-feeding.

**DRUG INTERACTIONS:** Tell your doctor of all nonprescription or prescription drugs you take, especially beta blockers, digoxin, disopyramide, high blood pressure medication, calcium, quinidine, carbamazepine, rifampin, theophylline, lithium, cyclosporine, dantrolene, phenobarbital, or muscle relaxants.

Avoid any drugs than increase your heart rate—decongestants, for example. These drugs are commonly found in over-the-counter cough and cold products.

**NOTES:** Occasionally the outer shell of some kinds of tablets passes through the digestive system unchanged. If it appears in your stool, there is no reason for concern, as this is harmless.

**MISSED DOSE:** If you miss a dose, take as soon as remembered. Do not take if it is almost time for the next dose; instead, skip the missed dose and resume your usual dosing schedule. Do not "double-up" the dose to catch up.

**STORAGE:** Store at room temperature away from sunlight and moisture.

**LIMIT ALCOHOLIC BEVERAGES; MAY ENHANCE DIZZINESS.**

*continues*

**4–71** continued

## ATTACHMENT B
## AVOIDING FOOD AND DRUG INTERACTIONS

Food can interact with drug ingredients to reduce or alter absorption so that the medications don't work as intended.

When taking a prescription or over-the-counter (OTC) medication:

- Read directions, warnings, and precautions. OTC products print information on the package; prescription drugs generally have fact sheets.
- Don't stir medications into food. Acid or minerals in some foods can alter drug ingredients. Breaking apart pills can also destroy the time-released mechanism that some drugs have to allow slow, uniform absorption.
- Don't mix medicine into hot beverages. Heat can destroy or alter drug ingredients.
- Avoid alcohol. It can increase or reduce a drug's effects.
- Don't take a vitamin and mineral supplement with your medication. Nutrients can bind with drug ingredients, reducing their absorption or speeding their elimination.
- Take medications with water on an empty stomach. Drugs generally are absorbed fastest when taken with a full glass of water an hour before or two hours after a meal. Do not take drugs with milk, fruit juices, or soda unless directed by a pharmacist.
- Generally, do not take antacids with your medications; they may decrease the effectiveness of your medication. Your doctor or pharmacist may suggest that you take your medication with meals if the drug can cause stomach irritation or upset.
- If you have any questions, you should ask your doctor, pharmacist, or other health care provider to help you understand what is best for you.

Source: Adapted from Johns Hopkins Bayview Medical Center, Baltimore, Maryland.

# 4–72
# Adverse Drug Reaction Definition and Reporting

## POLICY

An adverse drug reaction (ADR) is defined as "A significant response to a drug which causes an undesirable, unintended or unexpected effect that requires discontinuing a drug, modifying a dose, prolonging hospitalization, providing supportive treatment to the patients, treatment with a prescription drug or results in disability or death."

Adverse drug reactions (ADRs) are to be reported to the physician by the nurse at the time the reaction occurs. The ADR Hotline and/or the Risk Manager must be notified as applicable. A summary of ADRs will be reported to the Pharmacy and Therapeutics committee by the pharmacy.

## EXAMPLES OF ADRs:

1. ADR that results in additional illness, complications, or death (i.e., anaphylaxis reaction, arrhythmia with treatment, higher level of care or intubation)
2. ADR requiring intervention to prevent further significant impairment or damage (i.e., hives, rash, nausea/vomiting, or wheezing)
3. ADR that resolves without the need for a reversal drug or treatment (i.e., drug discontinued)

## EXAMPLES THAT ARE NOT CONSIDERED ADRs:

1. Therapy for the prevention or treatment of constipation in patients receiving narcotics
2. Topical steroids used for minor rashes without withdrawing medication

## PROCEDURE

After conferring with the physician, the nurse is to document the event in the medical record including documentation of any interventions and reaction outcomes.

If the ADR results in critical complications or death, the Risk Manager should be notified within 24 hours.

**Signed by** ______________________________

**Effective** ______________________________

Courtesy of Judy Sikes, PhD, CPHQ, Director of Accreditation/Medical Staff Services, Parkview Medical Center, Pueblo, Colorado.

## 4–73
## Nonpunitive Error Reporting

**PURPOSE:** This facility is committed to a learning environment that encourages reporting of errors and hazardous conditions. The organization recognizes that if we are to succeed in creating a safe environment for our patients, we must create an environment in which it is safe for caregivers to report and learn from errors. The organization will promote openness and require that mistakes be reported, while ensuring that reported mistakes and "near misses" will be handled without a threat of punitive action. This facility strives to create this safe environment by:

- Supporting the organization's mission, vision, and values
- Directing error prevention efforts at the root cause of a particular system or process, not at an individual
- Ensuring no reprisals occur for reporting of errors and injuries—both actual occurrences and potential conditions known as "near misses"
- Developing a culture in which communication flows freely, regardless of authority or position

**POLICY:** This facility encourages reporting of all types of errors, injuries, and "near misses" (potential for error or injury) as a means to assess and improve processes and provide a safe environment for patients and health care workers. Staff is required to participate in the detection and reporting of errors, injuries, and near misses; to assist in the identification of the system-based causes of errors; and the implementation of system enhancements to reduce the likelihood of errors.

In most instances, the "General Event Report" shall be used to report errors. There may also be situations for which immediate reporting is more prudent, such as by telephone or verbal communication.

The focus of the program is performance improvement, not punishment. It is assumed that staff members are doing their best and that errors are not the result of incompetence or misconduct. This policy does not remove the medical center's obligations to take appropriate educational or performance actions to protect patients. Staff is not subject to disciplinary action when making or reporting errors/injuries/near misses **except** in the following circumstances:

- Staff repeatedly fail to participate in the detection and reporting of errors/injuries/near misses and the system-based prevention remedies
- There is reason to believe criminal activity or criminal intent may be involved in the making or reporting of an error/injury
- Staff engages in intentional wrongful acts that compromise patient safety
- False information is provided in the reporting, documenting, or follow-up of an error/injury

If an employee believes that he or she is being punished for making or reporting an error/injury/near miss, he or she may seek assistance from his or her department or unit manager, Risk Management, or Human Resources.

Courtesy of St. Alexius Medical Center, Bismarck, North Dakota.

# 4–74
# Disclosure of Unanticipated Outcomes

**POSITION:** An integral part of the diagnostic or treatment process is to provide the patient with continuous information so that informed decisions may be made regarding future treatment. This information may be an expected outcome or unexpected outcome and may be considered a positive or negative outcome. Regardless, this facility is committed to providing our patients and their families with information, disclosing unanticipated outcomes that result in significant differences from that which was planned or anticipated.

**PURPOSE:** When an unanticipated outcome occurs, causing injury or a negative result, the patient and/or family is entitled to receive a truthful and compassionate explanation. The following policy has been developed to provide medical center employees and medical staff members with guidelines for disclosing unanticipated outcomes with an emphasis on negative or adverse events.

**PROCEDURE:**

**RESPONSE TO EVENTS:**

The staff involved in the event shall:

1. Take immediate action to stabilize the patient.
2. Report the event immediately to the attending physician and department/unit manager or the nursing department's Management Representative.
3. Notify Administration and Risk Management (usually done by the department/unit manager).
4. Complete necessary documentation and reporting requirements, such as a "General Event" form.

**DISCLOSURE TO PATIENT:**

1. Disclosure of the event shall take place as soon as practical.
2. A team approach to disclosure of the event shall be undertaken. In most instances, the disclosure communication and discussion with the patient and family will be conducted by the attending physician in collaboration with at least one representative from the medical center.
3. Communication guidelines include:
    a. Truthful and compassionate explanation about the event, including time, place, circumstances, and facts that are known at the time.
    b. Apology that an adverse outcome has occurred.
    c. Definite consequences, as well as potential or anticipated consequences, to the extent known.
    d. Actions taken to treat the consequences of the event.
    e. Proximate cause of the event, if known. Speculation should be avoided. Focus on what is known at the time of discussion.
    f. Assurance that a full analysis is underway.
    g. Names of individuals who are available for future questions and ongoing communications.
    h. Internal and external resources for support and counseling.

*continues*

**4–74** continued

4. For discussion anticipated to be complex or difficult, patients and/or family should be given the option of having another person with them as a support during the discussion.
5. Assignment of individual blame or staff identity should not be included in the discussion with the patient or family.
6. The purpose of disclosure to the patient and/or family is not to accept or negate liability but to explain the event, consequences, and future treatment plan.
7. Medical center staff shall document, on a "General Event Form," what was communicated to the patient and any response or other discussion. Documentation guidelines include:
    a. Time, date, and place of the discussion;
    b. Name and relationship of all those present;
    c. Discussion of the unanticipated outcome;
    d. Documentation of an offer to be of assistance and the response to it;
    e. Documentation of any questions posed by the patient or family and the answers that were provided by the caregiver;
    f. Identity of person(s) who should receive future communication or updates; and
    g. Any follow-up discussions should be documented, using the above guidelines.

Documentation shall be forwarded to the Risk Manager.

### NONDISCLOSURE TO A PATIENT OR FAMILY

In specific cases in which a decision is made to withhold some or all information, appropriate documentation shall be made describing the reasons(s) for the decision. The primary rationale for this decision shall be to protect the safety and welfare of the patient as permitted by law.

Developed: ____________________

Last Review/Revision: ____________________

Dept Responsible: ____________________

Resources: ____________________

Final Approval: ____________________

Distribution/Cross Ref: ____________________

Joint Commission Ref: ____________________

Key Word Search: ____________________

Courtesy of St. Alexius Medical Center, Bismarck, North Dakota

# 4–75
# To Err Is Human: Medication Errors

Julia Dodd, R.Ph., J.D.
Heather McClure, J.D., LL.M.

Recently, another headline-grabbing medication error in the *Washington Post* captured the attention of many as a story unfolded about an unseen decimal point that led to the tragic death of a 9-month-old baby girl just one week earlier. The baby's physician had prescribed morphine ".5 mg" IV for the management of post-operative pain. However, a unit secretary did not see the decimal point and transcribed the order by hand onto a medication administration record (MAR) as "5 mg." An experienced nurse followed the directions on the MAR without question and gave the baby 5 mg of IV morphine initially and another 5 mg dose two hours later. About four hours after the second dose, the baby stopped breathing and suffered a cardiac arrest.

## I. How Did We Get Here?

Events like this, coupled with numerous published reports regarding adverse drug events (ADEs), have focused the public's attention on patient safety issues like never before. In November of 1999, the IOM (Institute of Medicine) published a report entitled: *To Err is Human: Building a Safer Heath System*, in which much attention was given to patient safety issues, including medication errors.

Then, in January of 2000, the GAO (General Accounting Office) published a report to Congress called *Adverse Drug Events.* In it, the authors stated that analgesics, antibiotics, and cardiovascular and psychotropic drugs are among the classes of drugs consistently associated with medication errors. However, the number of errors was found to be a function of how often the drugs in the class were used.

Additionally, some drugs were found to have a high medication error rate because their pharmacological properties make them difficult to use, even when administered in generally recommended doses. For example, both the anticoagulant Warfarin and the cardiac stimulant Digoxin have narrow therapeutic indexes, meaning that the dosage levels for therapeutic effectiveness are close toxic, and both require careful adjustment of dosage levels in individual patients. Known drug interactions pose additional risks, since some drugs interact in potentially dangerous ways with many other pharmaceuticals. For example, the label for Warfarin indicates clinically significant interactions with approximately a hundred other drugs.

Drugs with similar names can also lead to medication errors. Physicians may confuse names when prescribing drugs and pharmacists may do the same when dispensing them. Recently, concern has been raised about possible confusion between Celebrex, Celexa, and Cerbyx, names that look and sound alike, but represent very different drugs—a pain medication used to treat arthritis, an antidepressant, and an anti-seizure drug, respectively. (GAO report, Jan. 2000)

Joint Commission (Joint Commission for Accreditation of Healthcare Organizations) weighed in on the issue and has issued new recommendations on sound-alike/look-alike drug names. Additionally, the National Coordinating Council for Medication Errors Reporting and Prevention (NCC-MERP) is a resource for reporting of "Sentinel" events regarding medication errors. They have published a series of recommendations including: reducing errors associated with verbal orders; promoting and standardizing bar coding on medication packaging; correcting error-prone prescription writing, dispensing, and administration of drugs; and standards for manufacturers regarding labeling.

*continues*

4–75 continued

## II. What is the Problem?

A steady stream of reported errors due to misinterpreting of dose expressions and abbreviations has led the Institute for Safe Medication Practices to repeatedly recommend abandoning their use for almost three decades. Others have joined ISMP in advocating this important error reduction step. For example, in 1996, the first recommendations issued from the NCC-MERP were aimed at establishing safe prescribing practices through avoidance of a short list of dangerous abbreviations and dose expressions (including naked decimal points).

It is equally important to avoid these dangerous abbreviations and dose expressions in other communications such as computer-generated labels, MARs, labels for drug storage bins/shelves, preprinted orders and protocols, and pharmacy and prescriber computer order entry screens. For example, it could be argued that computerized prescriber order entry (CPOE) could have prevented the tragic death of the infant described earlier through clear communication of the prescribed dose. However, many computer systems display drug doses using naked decimal points or trailing zeros, and use dangerous abbreviations such as QD and U. Thus, misinterpretation of an order is still a very real possibility with CPOE when these dangerous forms of communication are used. Groups have also urged the pharmaceutical industry and FDA to avoid the use of dangerous abbreviations and dose expressions on medication labeling, packaging, and advertisements.

Medication errors occur at any point in the medication administration process—during ordering, transcription (the process of manually transferring the physician order onto medication sheets), dispensing, and administering medications. However, as shown in Table 1, the majority of errors occur during the ordering and administration stages:

---

**Table 1***
**Percent of Medication Errors Occurring Within The Four Stages of the Medication Process**

Physician ordering: 39%–49%
Nursing administration: 26%–38%
Transcription: 11%–12%
Pharmacy dispensing: 11%–14%

*Sources: (1) D.W. Bates et al., *Incidence of Adverse Drug Events and Potential Adverse Drug Events*, 274(1) JAMA 29–34 (1995). (2) L.L. Leape et al., *Systems Analysis of Adverse Drug Events*, 274(1) JAMA 35–43 (1995).

---

*continues*

4–75 continued

Table 2 shows the percent for selected types of errors that were commonly associated with ADEs:

**Table 2**
**Studies of Medication Errors as Causes of Adverse Drug Events: Percent of ADEs for Each Cause**

**Study:** D.W. Bates et al., *Relationship Between Medication Errors and Adverse Drug Events*, 10(4) J. GEN. INTERN. MED. 199–205 (1995).

**Dose error:** 31.0%
**Known allergy:** 4.0%
**Wrong drug/patient:** 4.0%
**Route error:** 10.0%
**Frequency:** 17.0%

**Study:** L.L. Leape et al., *Systems Analysis of Adverse Drug Events*, 274(1) JAMA 35–43 (1995).

**Dose error:** 28.0%
**Known allergy:** 8.0%
**Wrong drug/patient:** 9.0%
**Route error:** 2.0%
**Frequency:** 6.0%

**Study:** T.S. Lesar et al., *Factors Related To Errors In Medication Prescribing*, 277(4) JAMA 312–17 (1997).

**Dose error:** 58.3%
**Known allergy:** 12.9%
**Wrong drug/patient:** 5.4%
**Route error:** 3.3%

**Study:** E.J. Thomas et al., *Costs of Medical Injuries in Utah and Colorado*, 36(3) INQUIRY 255–64 (1999).

**Dose error:** 7.9%
**Known allergy:** 5.7%
**Wrong drug/patient:** 20.9%
**Frequency:** 4.6%

Other specific errors not shown in Table 2 that have also been associated with ADEs** include:

Missed dose (7%).
Wrong technique (6%).
Illegible order (6%).
Duplicate therapy (5%).
Drug-drug interaction (3%–5%).
Equipment failure (1%).
Inadequate monitoring (1%).
Preparation error (1%)

***Source: Reducing and Preventing Adverse Drug Events to Decrease Hospital Costs*. Research in Action, Issue 1. AHRQ Publication Number 01-0020, March 2001. Agency for Healthcare Research and Quality, Rockville, MD.

*continues*

4–75 continued

A table of dangerous abbreviations and dose expressions most often associated with misinterpretation and patient harm (as reported to the USP-ISMP Medication Errors Reporting Program) appears on the following two pages (May 2, 2001 issue of the Institute for Safety Medication Practices' "Hazard Alert").

**III. What Should We Do?**

A recent issue of Joint Commission's *Sentinel Event Alert* focuses specifically on medication errors resulting from confusing look-alike or sound-alike drug names and recommendations for minimizing risk and preventing potential errors.

With tens of thousands of brand name and generic drugs currently on the market, the potential for error due to confusing drug names is significant. "Health care professionals often report confusion between similar brand and generic names," says Diane Cousins, R.Ph., Vice President, Practitioner and Product Experience Department, U.S. Pharmacopeia. "Contributing to the confusion are complications such as illegible handwriting, incomplete knowledge of drug names, newly available products, similar packaging or labeling, and incorrectly selecting a drug from a computerized list," says Cousins. In fact, similar drug names, either written or spoken, account for approximately 15% of all reports to the USP Medication Errors Reporting program.

New names that are similar to existing names continue to be approved and medication errors continue to occur despite review before introduction to the market by a number of U.S. and international organizations, including pharmaceutical manufacturers, the U.S. Pharmacopeia, the International Nonproprietary Names Committee of the World Health Organization, the Food and Drug Administration, the U.S. Adopted Names Council, and the U.S. Patent and Trademark Office. "This ever-increasing number of confusing name sets represents such a broad range of products and therapeutic drug classes that every health care practitioner is vulnerable to making this type of error," says Cousins. "While similarly named products may not be perceived to pose a public health threat, USP has received reports of patient harm and fatalities that have occurred as a result of this problem."

In March 2001, the USP released "Use Caution, Avoid Confusion," an updated list highlighting hundreds of confusing drug name sets and identifying more than 750 unique drug names that have been reported to the Medication Errors Reporting program. A poster and a laminated, quick-reference card are available for health care professionals free of charge from the USP by contacting USP's Practitioner and Product Experience department at (800) 487-7776, or the list may be accessed from USP's Web site at www.usp.org/reporting/review/rev_076.htm.

While the FDA recently instituted an intensive risk analysis system for the review and evaluation of proposed proprietary drug names, and in fact rejects approximately one-third of all proposed names because of their potential for confusion, it is important for health care professionals to integrate systems and establish practices to reduce the possibility of ordering, dispensing, or administering, the incorrect drug.

"To prevent errors, we must never rely solely on one's memory of problem name pairs," says Michael Cohen, M.S., FASHP, president, Institute for Safe Medication Practices. "I strongly recommend that organizations routinely monitor information from the error reporting programs and then apply it. For example, through careful formulary selection of alternative medications without nomenclature problems or through the use of interactive reminders in computer systems or auxiliary reminder labels on product containers." Other suggestions for minimizing the risk of errors include:

- Do not store problem medications alphabetically by name. Store such identified medications out of order, or in an alternate location.
- Provide or ask for both the generic and brand names of drugs for medication orders in order to provide patients and staff with information to avoid unintentional duplication.
- Write the purpose of the medication on the prescription. This inexpensive and efficient method to minimize errors helps the pharmacist in screening the medication order for proper dose, duration, and appropriateness,

*continues*

4–75 continued

and it may also enable the pharmacist to intervene when multiple prescribers unknowingly order duplicative therapy for the same patient. It also minimizes the risk of confusion due to look-alike names of medications as well as the risk of misinterpretation due to poorly handwritten orders.

- Develop a policy for taking verbal or telephone orders. For example, when taking verbal drug orders, clearly repeat the name of the drug, the dosage ordered, and request or provide correct spelling. This is particularly important for sound-alike drugs. The NCC–MERP recently released comprehensive recommendations to reduce medication errors associated with verbal prescription orders.
- Provide the generic and brand name on all medication labels. Joint Commission standards in all programs (e.g., TX.3.5.1 in Comprehensive Accreditation Manual for Hospitals) require that all dispensed medications are appropriately and safely labeled using a standardized method in the most ready-to-administer form possible to minimize opportunities for error. This includes having both the generic name and, when different from the generic name, the brand name of the drug on the medication order. Surveyors will evaluate if the drug name on the medication order, medication label, and nursing MAR are the same. Providing both names on the label ensures consistency between the documents and helps to prevent misinterpretation of orders.
- Provide patients with written information about their drugs including the brand and generic names. Inquire if the prescribed drug is a routine medication and withhold medications that the patient questions or does not recognize.

Joint Commission standards for hospitals, ambulatory, and behavioral health organizations (e.g., TX.3.1 in Comprehensive Accreditation Manual for Hospitals) require that organizations maintain a list of medications that are always available within the organization (i.e., a formulary). Organizations must develop and follow criteria for selecting drugs that are stocked within an institution (i.e., added to the formulary), and one of the required criteria in the intent of the standard that must be considered is the potential for medication errors. Sound-alike names and similar labeling of generic products should be considered in determining the formulary selection of products. When look-alike and sound-alike drugs are allowed on the formulary, or are ordered on a nonformulary basis, they should be identified as being medications at "high risk" for potential error and extra steps should be taken to ensure safety in ordering, dispensing, and administering such products.

Additionally, avoid using dangerous abbreviations or dose designations:

*continues*

**4–75** continued

***Avoid these dangerous abbreviations or dose designations***

| Abbreviation/ Dose Expression | Intended Meaning | Misinterpretation | Correction |
|---|---|---|---|
| Apothecary symbols | dram<br>minim | Misunderstood or misread (symbol for dram misread for "3" and minim misread as "mL"). | Use the metric system. |
| AU | aurio uterque (each ear) | Mistaken for OU (oculo uterque—each eye). | Don't use this abbreviation. |
| D/C | discharge<br>discontinue | Premature discontinuation of medications when D/C (intended to mean "discharge") has been misinterpreted as "discontinued" when followed by a list of drugs. | Use "discharge" and "discontinue." |
| Drug names | | | Use the complete spelling for drug names. |
| ARA-A | vidarabine | cytarabine (**ARA-C**) | |
| AZT | zidovudine **(RETROVIR)** | azathioprine | |
| CPZ | **COMPAZINE** (prochlorperazine) | chlorpromazine | |
| DPT | DEMEROL-PHENERGAN-THORAZINE | diphtheria-pertussis-tetanus (vaccine) | |
| HCl | hydrochloric acid | potassium chloride (The "H" is misinterpreted as "K.") | |
| HCT | hydrocortisone | hydrochlorothiazide | |
| HCTZ | hydrochlorothiazide | hydrocortisone (seen as HCT250 mg) | |
| MgSO4 | magnesium sulfate | morphine sulfate | |
| MSO4 | morphine sulfate | magnesium sulfate | |
| MTX | methotrexate | mitoxantrone | |
| TAC | triamcinolone | tetracaine, **ADRENALIN**, cocaine | |
| ZnSO4 | zinc sulfate | morphine sulfate | |
| Stemmed names | | | |
| "Nitro" drip | nitroglycerin infusion | sodium nitroprusside infusion | |
| "Norflox" | norfloxacin | **NORFLEX** (orphenadrine) | |
| µg | microgram | Mistaken for "mg" when handwritten. | Use "mcg." |
| o.d. or OD | once daily | Misinterpreted as "right eye" (OD—oculus dexter) and administration of oral medications in the eye. | Use "daily." |
| TIW or tiw | three times a week | Mistaken as "three times a day" | Don't use this abbreviation. |

*continues*

4–75 continued

***Avoid these dangerous abbreviations or dose designations (cont'd)***

| Abbreviation/ Dose Expression | Intended Meaning | Misinterpretation | Correction |
|---|---|---|---|
| per os | orally | The "os" can be mistaken for "left eye." | Use "PO," "by mouth," or "orally." |
| q.d. or QD | every day | Mistaken as q.i.d., especially if the period after the "q" or the tail of the "q" is misunderstood as an "i." | Use "daily" or "every day." |
| qn | nightly or at bedtime | Misinterpreted as "qh" (every hour). | Use "nightly." |
| qhs | nightly at bedtime | Misread as every hour. | Use "nightly." |
| q6PM, etc. | every evening at 6 PM | Misread as every six hours. | Use 6 PM "nightly." |
| q.o.d. or QOD | every other day | Misinterpreted as "q.d." (daily) or "q.i.d. (four times daily) if the "o" is poorly written. | Use "every other day." |
| sub q | subcutaneous | The "q" has been mistaken for "every" (e.g., one heparin dose ordered "sub q 2 hours before surgery" misunderstood as every 2 hours before surgery). | Use "subcut," or write "subcutaneous." |
| SC | subcutaneous | Mistaken for SL (sublingual). | Use "subcut." or write "subcutaneous." |
| U or u | unit | Read as a zero (0) or a four (4), causing a 10-fold overdose or greater (4U seen as "40" or 4u seen as 44"). | "Unit" has no acceptable abbreviation. Use "unit." |
| IU | international unit | Misread as IV (intravenous). | Use "units." |
| cc | cubic centimeters | Misread as "U" (units). | Use "mL." |
| x3d | for three days | Mistaken for "three doses." | Use "for three days." |
| BT | bedtime | Mistaken as "BID" (twice daily). | Use "hs." |
| ss | sliding scale (insulin) or ½ (apothecary) | Mistaken for "55." | Spell out "sliding scale." Use "one-half" or use "½." |
| > and < | greater than and less than | Mistakenly used opposite of intended. | Use "greater than" or "less than." |
| / (slash mark) | separates two doses or indicates "per" | Misunderstood as the number 1 ("25 units/10 units" read as "110" units. | Do not use a slash mark to separate doses. Use "per." |

*continues*

4–75 continued

***Avoid these dangerous abbreviations or dose designations (cont'd)***

| Abbreviation/ Dose Expression | Intended Meaning | Misinterpretation | Correction |
|---|---|---|---|
| Name letters and dose numbers run together (e.g., Inderal40 mg) | Inderal 40 mg | Misread as Inderal 140 mg. | Always use space between drug name, dose and unit of measure. |
| Zero after decimal point (1.0) | 1 mg | Misread as 10 mg if the decimal point is not seen. | Do not use terminal zeros for doses expressed in whole numbers. |
| No zero before decimal dose (.5 mg) | 0.5 mg | Misread as 5 mg. | Always use zero before a decimal when the dose is less than a whole unit. |

**IV. Case Studies**

1. RAPAMUNE

Several reports of medication errors have been related to labeling of the immunosuppressant, RAPAMUNE (sirolimus) unit dose liquid packets. The label identifies the strength of the liquid as 1 mg/mL but it is available in 1 mL, 2 mL, and 5 mL packets (a photo appears below). The information is listed in very small print that is not easy to read. One hospital alone has had at least two instances in which patients received the wrong dose of medication because of this packaging. They have since put auxiliary labels on the products. In another hospital, a 5 mg dose of Rapamune was ordered. However, the pharmacy was asked to dispense 1 mg packets to allow titration. The patient's mother was instructed by the nurse to give five (1 mg) packets to start, but the pharmacy dispensed 5 mg packets without realizing it. The patient was given 25 mg × 2 doses! In yet another case, a patient was to receive 4 mg Rapamune oral solution. Four packets labeled as 1 mg/mL were sent by the pharmacy. However, pharmacy did not recognize that these were each 2 mL (2 mg) packets. The nurse administered 8 mg, double the dose ordered. According to the product's manufacturer, Wyeth Laboratories, efforts are now underway to improve the labeling. In the meantime, pharmacy-applied auxiliary labeling, as undertaken at the hospital above, is probably the best way to prevent errors. (January 24, 2001 issue of Institute for Safe Medication Practices, "Hazard Alert")

*continues*

**4–75** continued

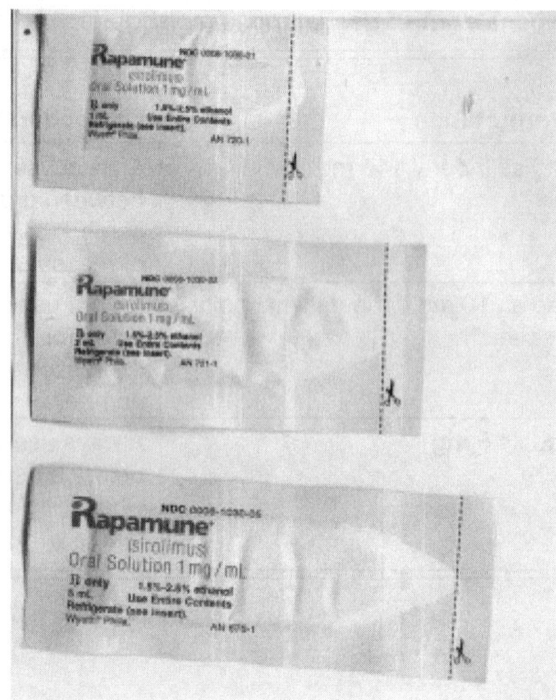


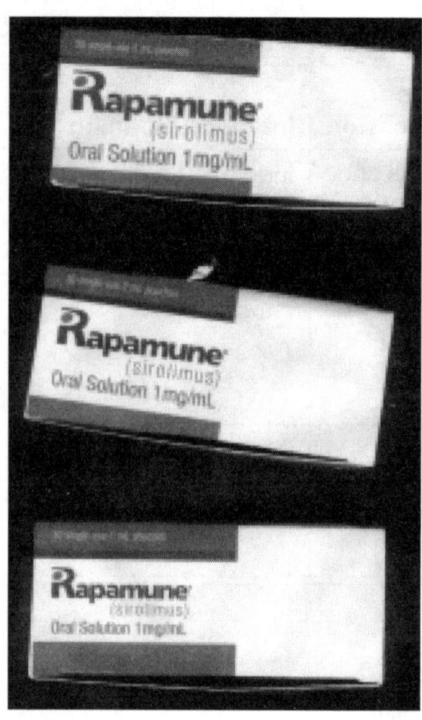


Pictures of Rapamune packaging, ISMP

2. CHLORPROPAMIDE/CHLORPROMAZINE

A pharmacist recently reported two incidents involving mix-ups between UDL's unit dose packages of the oral hypoglycemic, chlorpropamide 100 mg, and the antipsychotic, chlorpromazine 100 mg. The printed labels are so similar that one must look very closely to notice the difference (see below for a photo). Because the storage bins for both drugs were near each other, a pharmacy technician pulled the wrong drug and a pharmacist missed the error during a routine check. Chlorpropamide was then placed into an automated drug distribution module instead of chlorpromazine. Nurses did not notice the error and, unfortunately, two patients received the drug for 4–5 doses each. In this case, neither patient suffered serious harm, but in other cases (ISMP Medication Safety Alert! May 19, 1999) patients have suffered permanent CNS impairment or have died because of hypoglycemia from the chlorpropamide. In order to conform to the requirements for unit dose blister package labeling, UDL feels there is limited potential for change. However, we have asked them to consider using a combination of large and small letters (e.g., chlorproMAZINE and chlorproPAMIDE). This method has successfully eliminated similar problems with other products (M.R. Cohen, ed. Medication Errors (American Pharmaceutical Association, Washington, D.C.

*continues*

**4–75** continued

1999). Pharmacists have been urged to consider repackaging the 100 mg tablets or eliminating unit dose packages of chlorpromazine 100 mg and using 2 × 50 mg instead.

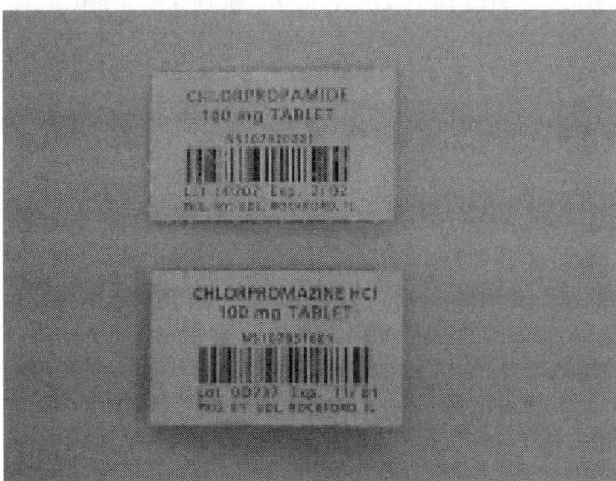


Picture of UDL unit dose packaging of chlorpropamide and chlorpromazine, ISMP

3. SUCCINYLCHOLINE/QUELICIN

Anesthesia professionals have been hit hard by the nationwide shortage of anesthetics and muscle relaxants. Avoiding the pitfalls of using less desirable alternatives has not been easy. We recently wrote about a few serious errors that occurred when sufentanil was used as a replacement for fentanyl. Recently, a potentially serious situation occurred due to the shortage of succinylcholine. A technician ordered a supply of 10 mL vials of QUELICIN (succinylcholine) directly from the manufacturer, Abbott Laboratories. The pharmacy expected to receive the usual concentration of 20 mg/mL, but instead received 10 mL vials of 100 mg/mL, a strength used less frequently in hospitals. Side by side, the 10 mL vials are slightly different in size, but the labels look very similar (see photo below). If the more concentrated strength had been dispensed to anesthesia unnoticed, serious patient harm could have resulted. The hospital is unsure if the technician simply ordered the drug by volume only (10 mL vials) or if the manufacturer just sent the only strength available. If nonpharmacists are ordering products, be sure they know and specify the drug's strength and vial size. Equally important, be sure to verify the medications when the shipment arrives before placing them into stock. (March 7, 2001 issue of ISMP's "Hazard Alert")

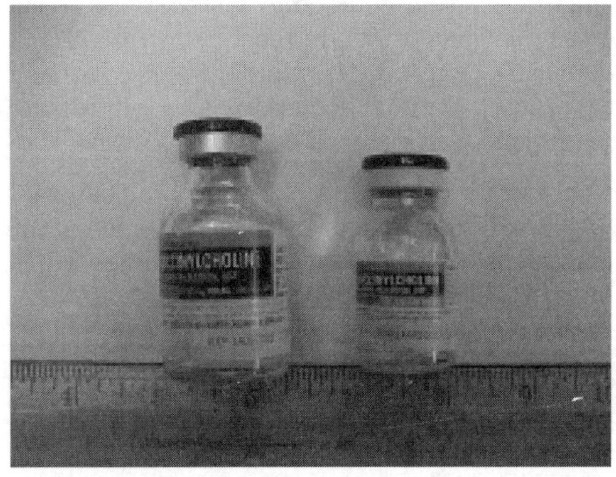

Succinylcholine pictures, ISMP

*continues*

4–75 continued

4. HEPARIN PRODUCTS

Low molecular weight heparin products offer effective prophylaxis and treatment against deep vein thrombosis and are useful in preventing ischemic complications in unstable angina and non-Q-wave myocardial infarction. Since these products have been on the market, we have seen clear evidence—three voluntarily reported deaths in the past year—that safeguards may not be in place to prevent concomitant use of low molecular weight heparin and unfractionated heparin. The first reported death involved a 62-year-old patient with unstable angina who died after receiving an initial dose of FRAGMIN (dalteparin) in the emergency department, and then IV heparin along with a thrombolytic when he exhibited signs of an acute myocardial infarction. In another case, a 42-year-old patient with an upper extremity thrombosis died from intracranial hemorrhage after a physician accidentally prescribed LOVENOX (enoxaparin) and initiated a heparin protocol.

The most recent case led to the death of a hospitalized 86-year-old woman with a history of atrial fibrillation, hypertension, lethargy, and constipation. A consulting cardiologist prescribed enoxaparin 60 mg every 12 hours subcutaneously. On the following day, Warfarin was added to the drug regimen. Later in the week, a gastroenterologist recommended a colonoscopy to rule out colorectal cancer. Warfarin was discontinued and a heparin infusion was ordered (5,000 unit bolus and 1,000 units/hour). However, enoxaparin administration continued every 12 hours and the heparin order was never faxed to the pharmacy. To administer the bolus and begin the infusion, the nurse borrowed a vial of heparin and a premixed solution that the pharmacy had dispensed for another patient. Several hours later, the patient's aPTT was supratherapeutic at greater than 90 seconds. The heparin infusion was decreased to 900 units/hour. By morning, the patient's aPTT was still elevated, her hemoglobin and hematocrit had dropped, and there was evidence of internal bleeding. Heparin and enoxaparin were discontinued immediately, but the patient died despite aggressive treatment.

Thorough review of the patient's total drug regimen is key to safe use of all forms of heparin. It's imperative for prescribers, pharmacists, and nurses to consider current and recent drug therapy before ordering, dispensing, and administering any of these products. However, that's not an easy task. Many times, low molecular weight heparin is prescribed and administered in the emergency department (ED). Consequently, those orders are rarely communicated to the pharmacy or screened for safety. In addition, communication of drug therapy administered in the ED may not be standardized and may not appear on the patient's drug therapy profile after admission, especially if it was a one-time dose. Protocols, guidelines, and standard order forms should prominently remind practitioners to assess all drug therapy (including in the ED) and avoid concomitant use when indicated (e.g., a heparin infusion should not be started if low molecular weight heparin has just been administered, etc.).

For inpatients, a summary of current and discontinued medications (including one-time doses) generated from the pharmacy computer system may be helpful if placed on the patient's chart daily for easy reference. One hospital pharmacist reported that alert stickers stating, "Patient on low molecular weight heparin," are affixed to the front of the chart to help communicate this information. A system must be in place to communicate all orders for heparin products to the pharmacy (including those prescribed in the ED, if patients are admitted) so that screening can occur for unsafe duplication of products and contraindications. Be sure that computer alerts for duplicate therapy have not been suppressed. Restrict access to heparin products (except flushing solutions) when feasible and dispense these drugs from the pharmacy as needed.

Educate nurses about the risks inherent in borrowing high alert medications from other patients' supplies. If some of these medications must be stored in patient care areas (e.g., emergency department, etc.), display alerts on automated dispensing cabinet screens or affix them to other storage areas. Ensure that heparin products stored in automated dispensing cabinets outside the ED cannot be removed via "override" before the pharmacy has screened the order.

Build a safety net by requiring an independent check by two individuals before administering heparin products. As part of the check system, consider including an independent review of the patient's entire drug therapy profile and recent laboratory results. (February 21, 2001 issue of ISMP's "Hazard Alert")

*continues*

4–75 continued

5. NIMBEX (cisatracurium besylate) injection CONTAINERS

This neuromuscular blocking agent is available in a 20 mg/10 mL (2 mg/mL) multiple dose vial as well as a 200 mg/20 mL (10 mg/mL) single dose vial meant for preparing infusions. The vials are distributed in individual cartons that are exactly the same size. Both use teal print for the drug name and black print for the strength. In the past three weeks, we received two error reports as well as one report about the potential for confusion. In one case, a patient experienced prolonged recovery after it was discovered that the 200 mg/20 mL concentration was used for a bolus injection. Abbott Laboratories told us that label enhancements are now underway. In the meantime, if Nimbex is available, communicate with all who may use this drug, including OR staff, pharmacists, and pharmacy technicians. In addition, draw attention to the product strengths by circling the concentration on the carton labels. (August 8, 2001 issue of ISMP's "Hazard Alert")

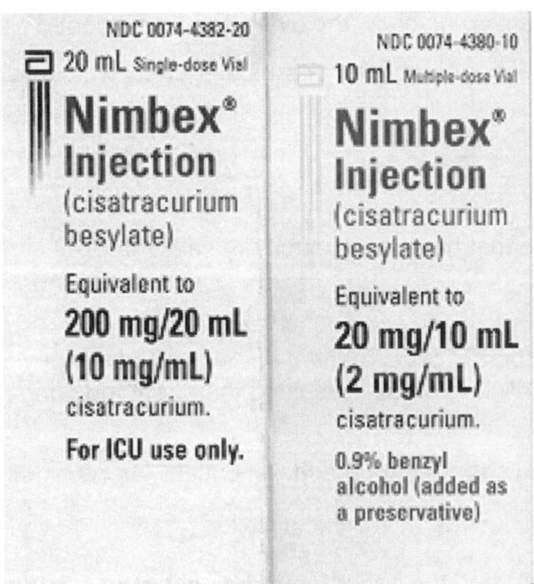


Nimbex injection containers, ISMP

**V. Conclusion**

Together, we can work to reduce medication errors and increase patient safety. Although with all the new medications coming out, it may seem like an overwhelming task, if you know where to look, you can find help. Use the resources available to you. Your facility should have a set of materials to keep you updated on new medications, and should have written policies regarding the use of abbreviations, etc.

At present, the Institute for Safe Medication Practices, the USP, and the FDA collect and track medication errors and make information available to health care providers and the public. Information and alerts about confusing drug names and current initiatives to have confusing names changed may be obtained from the organizations' Web sites: www.ismp.org, www.usp.org, www.fda.gov, www.nccmerp.org, or www.jcaho.org.

To err may be human, but in the context of medication errors, serious, consistent, and vigilant care must be taken to avoid mistakes. With increased awareness, and adjustments in the system, great progress can be made, and tragedy avoided.

Courtesy of Julia J. Dodd, R.Ph., J.D., Cowles & Thompson, P.C., Dallas, Texas.

# 4–76
# NCC-MERP Taxonomy of Medication Errors

## PATIENT OUTCOME

NCC-MERP recommends that medication error information be collected and reported as soon as possible, while the information is still fresh. It is recognized that the eventual patient outcome may change from the time when the medication error initially occurs. For example, the patient may initially require hospitalization due to the error, but eventually die as a result of the error after several weeks of treatment and support in the hospital. If the patient outcome or other variables should change, the medication error information can be updated or corrected at a later time.

In selecting the patient outcome category, select the highest level severity that applies during the course of the event. For example, if a patient suffers a severe anaphylactic reaction (Category H) and requires treatment (Category F) but eventually recovers completely, the event should be coded as Category H (33.4).

Select only one of the medication error categories or subcategories, whichever best fits the error that is being reported.

31 <u>NO ERROR</u>

31.1 Category A
Circumstances or events that have the capacity to cause error

32 <u>ERROR, NO HARM</u>

[Note: Harm is defined as temporary or permanent impairment of the physical, emotional, or psychological function or structure of the body and/or pain resulting therefrom requiring intervention.]

32.1 Category B
An error occurred but the error did not reach the patient (An "error of omission" <u>does</u> reach the patient.)

32.2 Category C
An error occurred that reached the patient, but did not cause patient harm
32.2.1 Medication reaches the patient and is administered
32.2.2 Medication reaches the patient but not administered

32.3 Category D
An error occurred that reached the patient and required monitoring to confirm that it resulted in no harm to the patient and/or required intervention to preclude harm

33 <u>ERROR, HARM</u>

33.1 Category E
An error occurred that may have contributed to or resulted in temporary harm to the patient and required intervention

33.2 Category F
An error occurred that may have contributed to or resulted in temporary harm to the patient and required initial or prolonged hospitalization

33.3 Category G
An error occurred that may have contributed to or resulted in permanent patient harm

*continues*

**4–76** continued

33.4 Category H
An error occurred that required intervention necessary to sustain life

34 <u>ERROR, DEATH</u>

34.1 Category I
An error occurred that may have contributed to or resulted in the patient's death.

Source: 

# 4–77
# Medication Error Tracking Form

TODAY'S DATE ____________________

DATE OF EVENT ______________ TIME OF EVENT ______________

WHERE DID IT OCCUR: ______________________________
(be specific, i.e., operating room, recovery, 2 South, etc.)

(addressograph)

MEDICATION (drug, dose, form) ______________________________

MEDICATION CLASS (i.e., narcotic, sedative, etc.) ______________________________

TYPE OF PERSONNEL INVOLVED (circle all that apply) MED STAFF, AHP, RN, LPN, R.PH, AGENCY, STUDENT, CLERICAL

*Medication Error Definition* *A medication error is any error made in the process of prescribing, transcribing, dispensing or administering a drug whether or not any adverse consequences occurred.*

**Place a check mark next to statement(s) that best describe the event. If other, please provide details:**

| | | |
|---|---|---|
| 1. Integrity Compromised: | ☐ | Expired, improper storage, or contamination issues. |
| 2. Not Labeled: | ☐ | The information on the label is missing (i.e., Med added to bag, not written on label). |
| 3. Omitted: | ☐ | Dose is not received by the patient due to a dispensing error. |
| | ☐ | Dose is not received by the patient due to an administration error. |
| 4. Prescribing Error: | ☐ | A prescribing error may include wrong patient, rate, route, and/or form orders, illegibility, allergy/drug interaction, dose, drug. (attach copies of documentation if appropriate) |
| 5. Wrong Dosage Dispensed: | ☐ | The correct drug is dispensed, but in a strength other than ordered. |
| 6. Transcription Error: | ☐ | Order transcribed incorrectly from orders by nursing, clerical and/or pharmacy staff (includes verbal orders). |
| Wrong Dose: | ☐ | An amount of Med greater or less than the amount ordered is administered. |
| 8. Wrong Med: | ☐ | A Med other than that ordered is dispensed. |
| | ☐ | A Med other than that ordered is administered. |
| 9. Wrong Patient: | ☐ | Med is dispensed to the wrong patient. |
| | ☐ | Med is administered to the wrong patient. |
| 10. Wrong Rate: | ☐ | The administration of IV or enteral products is administered at wrong rate. |
| 11. Wrong Route/Site Administration: | ☐ | The correct form of the drug is administered, but not in the correct site (i.e., IM vs IV or drug ordered IM and tablets dispensed). |
| 12. Wrong Time: | ☐ | Patient does not receive Med within the Med Administration Guidelines |

13. Other:

**Please circle the risk level that best describes this case:**

A. Circumstance or events that have the capacity to cause potential harm or error. Examples: illegible order, alike/same patient names, similar sounding/spelled drug names, etc. (please attach the example).

B. Incident/error occurred before reaching the patient. Example: pharmacy dispensed the wrong drug, but nursing discovered error before administration of drug to patient.

C. Incident/error occurred, but did not cause patient harm.

*D. Incident/error occurred that resulted in the need for increased patient monitoring (i.e., vital signs, observations, testing, etc.) but did not cause the patient harm.

*E. Incident/error that resulted in the need for treatment or intervention (i.e., warm compress, sutures, medication administration, etc.) that caused temporary patient harm.

*F. Incident/error occurred that resulted in admission of or prolonged hospitalization of patient and caused temporary harm to patient.

*G. Incident/error occurred that resulted in permanent patient harm.

*H. Incident/error occurred that resulted in near-death event (i.e., anaphylaxis, cardiac arrest, hemorrhage) of patient.

*I. Incident/error occurred that resulted in patient death.

For Risk Manager Use Only:
☐ Ordering ☐ Preparation, dispensing & delivery
☐ Transcription and verification ☐ Admin & monitoring

*(please continue on back)*

**AFTER COMPLETING, PLEASE FORWARD TO RISK MANAGEMENT IMMEDIATELY**
**NOT A PART OF THE MEDICAL RECORD—FOR QUALITY ASSURANCE PURPOSES ONLY**

*continues*

**4–77** continued

Were any diagnostic or treatment measures taken following the discovery of the event? ____ YES ____ NO

If so, please describe measures taken ____________________

Describe event ____________________

1. Is staff member involved in event aware of occurrence? ______ Yes ______ No
2. What follow-up has been done? ____________________
3. Does the event involve another department? ______ Yes ______ No
   If so, which department(s) ____________________
4. Documentation: ______ N/A
   A. Physician notification documented in chart? ______ Yes ______ No
   B. Charting includes description of event? ______ Yes ______ No
   C. Charting includes corrective actions taken? ______ Yes ______ No
5. Describe your suggestions to prevent a future event. ____________________

Name (OPTIONAL) ____________________

*Department Director Response (For Risk Levels D–I) ____________________

Risk Management Notes ____________________

**AFTER COMPLETING, PLEASE FORWARD TO RISK MANAGEMENT IMMEDIATELY**
**NOT A PART OF THE MEDICAL RECORD—FOR QUALITY ASSURANCE PURPOSES ONLY**

Courtesy of Judy Sikes, PhD, CPHQ, Director of Accreditation/Medical Staff Services, Parkview Medical Center, Pueblo, Colorado.

# 4–78
# Medical Error Reporting

## PURPOSE

To provide a standardized mechanism for identifying, reporting, and monitoring medication errors and adverse drug events (ADEs) and to provide a consistent mechanism for improving the medication use process.

## SCOPE

This policy applies to medication therapy for all patients cared for in hospital departments and outpatient services regardless of where the medication was originally prescribed.

## POLICY

The hospital encourages reporting of medical errors, to include medication errors, as well as potential medication errors as a means to assess and improve the medication use process and provide a safe environment for patient care. The purpose of the reporting errors is to learn about their causes and enhance the medication system to make it difficult for practitioners to err. Practitioners involved in medication use are required to participate in the detection and reporting of errors, the identification of the system-based causes of errors, and the facilitation of system enhancements to reduce the likelihood of errors. Thus, the focus of the program is quality improvement, not punishment. The hospital assumes that practitioners are doing their very best and that errors are rarely the result of incompetence or misconduct. Therefore, employees are not subject to disciplinary action when making or reporting errors except in the following circumstances:

- The employee consistently fails to participate in the detection, reporting, and the system-based remedies to prevent errors;
- There is reason to believe criminal activity or criminal intent may be involved in the making or reporting of an error;
- False information is provided in relation to the report or investigation.

The reporting program is coordinated through the Medical Error Reduction Team, as part of the hospital's performance improvement and peer review function, with participation by Nursing and Pharmacy departments and the medical staff.

The Team reviews monthly error reports and makes recommendations to trend data or initiate intensive analysis or root cause analysis with the appropriate personnel.

Pharmacists report Adverse Drug Reactions (ADRs) to the FDA if they are serious, associated with a new drug, or not mentioned in the drug's labeling.

Medication errors are reported by physicians, nurses, pharmacists, patients, medical records/QA personnel, or any member of hospital staff. To report an error, a Medication Error Tracking Form is completed, a call is made to the Risk Manager or an incident report is submitted to the Risk Manager.

Staff members identifying a medication error will immediately report the event to the Risk Manager who will evaluate the event and, as a result, may invoke the Sentinel Event Policy and Procedure. A root cause analysis is conducted in such cases as outlined in the Procedure for Conducting a "Root Cause Analysis."

*continues*

4–78 continued

**DEFINITIONS**

**MEDICAL ERROR:** An unintended act (either of omission or commission) or one that does not achieve its intended outcome in all stages in the process of care that caused or might have caused a temporary or permanent injury or death to a patient. There are two kinds of failures: either the correct action does not proceed as intended (error of execution) or the original intended action is not correct (error of planning).

**MEDICAL ERROR REDUCTION TEAM:** A multidisciplinary team with oversight of the Medical Error System of Focus of Parkview Medical Center reviews errors, trends, and significant medical errors. These include medication errors, equipment errors, safety concerns and fall prevention and sentinel event prevention (such as suicide of a patient; infant abduction or discharge to the wrong family; rape; hemolytic transfusion reaction involving administration of blood or blood products having major blood group incompatibilities, or surgery on the wrong patient or wrong body part). The Team makes recommendations for system-based changes to improve the medication use process and other hospital system processes.

**MEDICATION ERROR:** A medication error is any error made in the process of prescribing, transcribing, dispensing, or administering a drug whether or not any adverse consequences occurred.

**SEVERITY LEVELS OF MEDICATION ERRORS:** The severity of a medication error is graded A through I and is reviewed, evaluated, and final assignment made by Risk Management.

**DESCRIPTION OF ERROR**

| | |
|---|---|
| Integrity Compromised: | Expired, improper storage, or contamination issues |
| Not Labeled: | The information on the label is missing (i.e., Med added to bag, not written on label). |
| Omitted: | Dose is not received by the patient due to a dispensing error. |
| | Dose is not received by the patient due to an administration error. |
| Prescribing Error: | A prescribing error may include wrong patient, rate, route, and/or form orders, illegibility, allergy/drug interaction, dose, drug. |
| Wrong Dosage Dispensed: | The correct drug is dispensed, but in a strength other than ordered. |
| Transcription Error: | Order transcribed incorrectly from orders by nursing, clerical, and/or pharmacy staff (includes verbal orders). |
| Wrong Dose: | An amount of Med greater or less than the amount ordered is administered. |
| Wrong Med: | Med other than that ordered is dispensed. |
| | Med other than that ordered is administered. |
| Wrong Patient: | Med is dispensed to the wrong patient. |
| | Med is administered to the wrong patient. |
| Wrong Rate: | The administration of IV or enteral products is administered at wrong rate. |
| Wrong Route/Site Admin: | The correct form of the drug is administered, but not in the correct site (i.e., IM vs. IV or drug ordered IM and tablets dispensed). |
| Wrong Time: | Patient does not receive Med within the Med Administration Guidelines. |
| Other: | |

*continues*

**4–78** continued

**MEDICATION ERROR TRACKING FORM:** Form completed by any member of PMC staff to document a possible medication error and sent to Risk Manager within 24 hours. It is treated by Risk Management as an incident report and has the same legal protections.

**PROCEDURES AND RESPONSIBILITIES**

**IDENTIFYING A MEDICATION ERROR**

1. Staff who suspect a medication error notify prescriber immediately if the event is significant or may alter the patient's plan of care.
2. Staff assesses the patient.
3. Staff collaborate with clinical and supervisory resource personnel if unsure how to proceed.
4. Staff implement adjustments in patient's treatment as ordered.
5. Staff documents the factual description of the error, notification of physician, and subsequent monitoring in the progress record.

**REPORTING A MEDICATION ERROR**

1. Staff completes the Medication Error Tracking form located on the unit or in Meditech or notifies the hospital Risk Manager within 24 hours of the error identification.
2. Error forms are mailed, confidentially, to the Risk Manager or entered into the Meditech system.

**SECURITY OF INFORMATION**

1. No copies are made of the Medication Error Tracking forms.
2. Clinical interventions are migrated into a secure data base.
3. Forms and data are secured in the Risk Management and/or IS and accessed by key or password.

**REVIEWING ERRORS**

1. Supervisor/manager completes timely evaluation of the circumstances surrounding high-risk event.
2. Error reviewers assess all reports, to verify and collect additional data, and assign severity level.
3. In the case of significant error or medication-related sentinel events, reviewers confirm notification of department director or manager, as well as compliance with sentinel event policy.
4. Error reports are reviewed and categorized by: location, severity, product information, and therapeutic classification, type, causes, and contributing factors.
5. Adverse Drug Reactions (ADRs) are further evaluated to determine:

   –Appropriateness of medication for patient's condition

   –Predisposing contraindications to medication

   –Appropriate documentation of allergies

   –Appropriate management and monitoring of ADR

*continues*

**4–78** continued

## TRENDING/REPORTING/IMPROVING THE MEDICATION USE PROCESS

1. The Risk Management Department performs the data entry, trending, and report distribution.
2. Risk Management and Administration prepares a monthly analysis of errors.
3. The Medical Error Reduction Team forwards monthly trending reports to Directors, Administration, Medical Staff, and Board, as appropriate.
4. Directors are responsible for analyzing their department data and responding with performance improvement activities, as appropriate.
5. The Medical Error Reduction Team reviews the monthly report, significant events, results of root cause analysis, and completion of consequent recommendations and makes recommendations for improvements to the medication use process.

## EXCEPTIONS

1. Adverse reactions that occur following the administration of investigational drugs are reported according to the specific protocol for that drug by contacting the principal investigator.
2. A probationary employee may be terminated if basic competencies related to the medication use process are not demonstrated.

**Signed by** ______________________________

**Effective** ______________________________

Courtesy of Judy Sikes, PhD, CPHQ, Director of Accreditation/Medical Staff Services, Parkview Medical Center, Pueblo, Colorado.

# 4–79
# Pharmacy Scope of Services

Policy Number:
Date Originated:
Date Revised:
Page: 1 of 3

**Pharmacy Services Policy Subject: Scope of Service**

## I. MISSION

A. We are dedicated to improving the therapeutic outcomes of all patients through safe, rational, and cost-effective pharmaceutical care, education, and research.

## II. VISION

A. We will continue to be the site for our region's highest quality pharmacy services where

1. patients receive quality pharmaceutical care and education,
2. physicians and nurses receive accurate and responsive pharmacy services, and
3. pharmacy employees are motivated to work as a team and to excel.

## III. SERVICES

A. **Pharmacy services focus on four basic areas:** medication distribution/dispensing, patient-centered services, medication use/outcome assessment, and educational services.

B. **Medication Distribution/Dispensing:** unit dose system, prescription service IV admixture service, Pyxis medstations, extemporaneous packaging, compounded products, automated narcotic control, drug formulary, computerized medication profile, cost containment, and drug purchasing.

C. **Patient-Centered Services:** medication order review, drug information, pharmacist-managed drug therapies, CPR team member, medication response assessment, prescribing error prevention, pharmacokinetic analysis, drug serum level evaluations, and drug-related research.

D. **Medication Use/Outcome Assessment:** drug use evaluations, target drug programs, CQI, drug therapy audits, adverse drug reaction reporting, prescribing error analysis, drug formulary management, and medication error analysis.

E. **Educational Services:** drug information, pharmacokinetics, pharmacoeconomics, residency program, USC/UCSF teaching, drug formulary, cost containment, DIS Newsletter, New Drug Evaluations, physician and nursing education, pharmacy staff inservices, patient/family education, and professional publications.

## IV. CUSTOMERS

A. The scope of care provided by Pharmacy Services is designed to meet the needs of its various customers; e.g., patients, nurses, physicians, Carelines, Risk Management, etc. All types and ages of patients are served including pediatric, adult, and geriatric.

## V. PROVISION OF SERVICES

A. Inpatient Pharmacy Services provides patient-centered and medication distribution services to all patient care areas of the medical center 24 hours a day including nights, weekends, and holidays utilizing a unit dose drug distribution system and preparation of intravenous admixtures and parenteral nutrition.

*continues*

**4–79** continued

Policy Number:

Date Originated:

Date Revised:

Page: 2 of 3

B. Experienced pharmacists with a support team of pharmacy technicians have decentralized and centralized assignments to best meet the needs and complexity of individual patients in a timely manner.

C. Patient care pharmacy offices are located on the ______ floor, ______________ .

D. Drug distribution services for these areas are provided from the Central Pharmacy located on the ground floor. The Central Pharmacy is complemented by a dedicated pneumatic tube system, a pharmacy computer system with an interface to the hospital information system, e.g., SAM, a dumbwaiter lift, and a Pyxis drug delivery system. Patient-centered and drug distribution services are provided from satellite pharmacies located on the ____________ floor (serving critical care patients on __________ floor), __________ Hospital and ____________ with support from the Central Pharmacy.

E. Retail Pharmacy Services are provided from four locations to best meet the needs of the patients we serve.

   1. The Outpatient Pharmacy serves hospital employees, patients being discharged from the hospital, emergency room patients, selected inpatients (for bedside and relabeled prescriptions), and others. Hours of operation: 7 days a week from 0800 to 2400. The pharmacy provides after hours, emergency services to patients of the other retail pharmacies.

   2. HomeCare Pharmacy provides services to patients of Family Medicine, Occupational Medicine, California Children's Service recipients and other patients to whom they have contracts. Services include pharmaceuticals, ostomy supplies, wound healing supplies, and other medical supplies. Hours of operation: Monday through Friday from 0830 to 1730.

   3. PharmaCare Pharmacy provides prescription service mainly to patients seen by physicians in the Medical Group building. Hours of operation: Monday through Friday from 0830 to 1730, and provides delivery service to the same areas as HomeCare Pharmacy.

   4. The Children's Clinic Pharmacy serves patients of the Children's Clinic. Hours of operation: Monday through Friday from 0930 to 1800.

**VI. PATIENT ASSESSMENT**

A. Pharmacists evaluate the appropriateness of all prescribed drug and parenteral nutrition orders. Concerns about the appropriateness of care are reviewed with the prescriber and/or the patient's nurse within eight hours of request. Pharmacists evaluate all drug orders prior to dispensing medications for known patient drug allergies.

B. When appropriate, pharmacists make notations in the patient's medical record regarding actions taken. Pharmacist interventions (resulting in concurrence by the prescriber and a change in order) for significant prescribing errors, including potential allergy conflicts, are documented outside the patient's medical record for tabulation and review by the quality improvement committees and the medical directors.

C. Review new orders, including

   1. all medication orders and the patient's medication profile,

   2. pharmacists identify patients for further assessment and monitoring based upon criteria that include those with a high degree or changing acuity,

   3. those receiving high-risk medications, atypical drug dosages, or combinations of medications,

*continues*

4–79 continued

Policy Number:
Date Originated:
Date Revised:
Page: 3 of 3

4. those with compromised renal function or other critical systems,
5. those at risk of adverse drug reactions or drug interactions.

D. Pharmacists contact the physician to recommend changes in therapy as needed to improve patient outcomes.

E. Pharmacists are actively involved in assessing the appropriateness and clinical necessity of a variety of treatment modalities, e.g., heparin per pharmacy, which are evaluated and managed in accordance with medical staff-approved guidelines. All such pharmacist-managed care is performed under the supervision of the patient's physician. When ordered "per pharmacy," pharmacists routinely assess the patient within two hours or less depending upon the patient's acuity for initiation (or change) of drug therapy as indicated by the prescriber. Pharmacists regularly reassess the patient's progress at least daily toward achieving the defined goals of the "per pharmacy" therapy and routinely document their decisions and assessment in the patient's medical record. Patient assessments by the pharmacist are based upon patient interviews or immediate observation of the patient, interviews with the patient's nurse, and by review of clinical data in the patient's medical record.

**VII. REQUIREMENTS FOR STAFF**

A. Pharmacists typically have a PharmD degree with completion of a hospital pharmacy residency.

B. Pharmacy technicians performing skilled functions typically have attended a pharmacy technician training program or have comparable experience. Pharmacy technicians must be licensed by the state.

C. Staff have fulfilled certification, life safety, infection control, and other requirements as needed.

**VIII. STAFFING**

A. Pharmacy staffing is provided 7 days a week, 24 hours a day including night shift, weekends, and holidays. Pharmacy staffing is based upon a team concept. Each team has a pharmacist supervisor who is responsible for scheduling team members. Pharmacists and technicians are assigned to primary teams in which they have expertise. Each work area has a pharmacist in charge.

B. Pharmacy technicians and interns work under the direct supervision of the pharmacist in charge. A pharmacist is typically immediately available in a decentralized assignment. If not, a pharmacist within the medical center is designated as the responsible pharmacist and is available at any time by telephone or page.

C. A pharmacy manager is on call at all times to respond to staffing, drug procurement, or other patient care or procedural concerns.

Source: Adapted from Long Beach Memorial Medical Center, Long Beach, California.

# 4–80
# Pharmacy Vision Statement

It is the vision of the Pharmacy to exercise leadership in all matters relating to the use of drugs at this medical center, thereby ensuring patient safety and the most appropriate drug therapy.

Our vision is that the principles of the practice of pharmacy will enable us to fulfill our mission.

**Definition of the Practice of Pharmacy:**

The practice of pharmacy is the responsibility for provision of appropriate drug therapy to achieve positive outcomes that improve a patient's quality of life. The ethical imperative of pharmacy practice is the patient as the focus of any endeavor. The practice of pharmacy engages the whole patient and does not view the person as only individual medical conditions.

Our work life will be governed by this facility's core VALUES of:

- Continuous Improvement
- Teamwork
- Knowledge
- Respect for Individuals
- Leadership At All Levels
- Customer Focus
- Integrity and Honesty

**Signed by** ______________________________

**Effective** ______________________________

Courtesy of Judy Sikes, PhD, CPHQ, Director of Accreditation/Medical Staff Services, Parkview Medical Center, Pueblo, Colorado.

## 4–81
## Pharmacy Mission Statement

The Pharmacy Department mission is to provide the most efficacious, safe, and cost-effective drug therapy to patients while working in collaboration with the medical staff and all health care providers.

The Pharmacy Department will strive to:

- Provide high value to the medical center (Value = Quality/Cost);
- Deliver the right drug, right dose, and right frequency at the right time all the time;
- Provide drug information and continuing education to physicians, nurses, other health care professionals, and patients;
- Meet and exceed customer expectations as they relate to the practice of pharmacy (see definition in Pharmacy Vision statement).

The Pharmacy Department will work to fulfill our mission by encouraging a practice setting for pharmacists that allows for patient-oriented clinical duties and collaboration with physicians, nurses, and other health care providers. Qualified pharmacy technicians will be utilized in all departmental functions as allowed by law. Pharmacist's clinical work and technicians distributive endeavors will be within the scope of the department's competency program and all state and federal laws and regulations.

The Pharmacy Department will track progress through the use of PM/PI indicators. The FOCUS-PDSA process will be employed to reach the goals of our mission.

**Signed by** ______________________________

**Effective** ______________________________

Courtesy of Judy Sikes, PhD, CPHQ, Director of Accreditation/Medical Staff Services, Parkview Medical Center, Pueblo, Colorado.

# 4–82
# Drug Formulary

I. AUTHORITY

The Drug Formulary of this medical center is authorized and sponsored by the Medical Staff of the hospital. It is based upon the recommendations of the Pharmacy and Therapeutics Committee and is implemented by the Pharmacy Department.

II. DESCRIPTION

The formulary system is a method whereby the Medical Staff, working through the Pharmacy and Therapeutics Committee (P&T), evaluates, appraises, and selects from among the numerous available drug classes those that have a demonstrated need and are considered the most safe, efficacious, and cost effective. Sound-alike names are also taken into account in the decision-making process.

These drug selections are published as a reference for staff use. The Drug Formulary is a selected (closed) formulary. Listings are by generic name.

The P&T Committee has identified certain drugs suitable for dispensing under the therapeutic equivalent policy (see Section IV).

The formulary includes non-legend medication.

All drugs, chemicals, and biologicals meet national standards of quality.

III. GENERIC EQUIVALENTS

Where several preparations differing only in the trade name of the manufacturer are available, those of the highest quality, prepared by the most experienced firms, and obtained at the most reasonable cost are to be selected for inclusion.

Drugs purchased on a generic basis will meet official compendia standards. Bioavailability and bioequivalence data are desirable and manufacturers providing such data will be preferred. All generic equivalents selected are listed as being acceptable in the United States Pharmacopoeia's "Orange Book."

IV. THERAPEUTIC EQUIVALENTS

Drug products differing in composition or in their basic drug entity that are considered to have very similar pharmacological and therapeutic activities are therapeutic equivalents. The P&T Committee is responsible for determining those drugs that shall be considered therapeutic equivalents.

The committee may designate certain classes of drugs for inclusion in the therapeutic equivalency dispensing routine. The Committee will review designated drug groups at scheduled meetings. Input will be obtained from the appropriate medical committee(s) (depending on the type of drug) regarding the proposed interchange. Decisions made by the P&T Committee will be considered final.

Dispensing done by pharmacy according to the therapeutic equivalency procedure will be communicated to the appropriate nursing unit and to the prescribing physician via a physician order filled out by the pharmacist.

V. CURRENT CONSENT

Prior consent of physicians, under the formulary system, for the dispensing of generic and/or automatic therapeutic interchanges is not necessary.

*continues*

4–82 continued

To ensure the ability of the physician to exercise his or her right of professional judgment, the current consent statement on this facility's physician order forms reads "Authorization is given to dispense under the formulary system unless checked here."

VI. PUBLICATION

The drug formulary is available on all clinical units in the hospital via the MediTech computer system. It will be made current on a regular and continuing basis. Additions or deletions may be made at any scheduled P&T Committee meeting.

VII. DELETIONS

The Committee may move to delete any drug from the formulary that has been found to be of no value, that has adverse effects on patients, that has not been used for a period of time, that has been superseded by a superior drug, that has been replaced by a therapeutic equivalent, or for any reason the P&T Committee feels is valid.

VIII. ADDITIONS/NON FORMULARY DISPENSING

When a physician prescribes a medication not included on this facility's formulary, a pharmacist will call to suggest the use of an appropriate formulary alternative. If the physician deems it necessary to use the nonformulary agent, a limited supply will be obtained for that specific patient.

If the physician desires that the drug be added to the formulary and routinely stocked, an application for formulary inclusion must be made. Applications will be considered at P&T meetings. For those medications considered complex or that may pose significant risk to the patient, it is necessary for the sponsoring physician to present the proposed drug to the formulary.

**Signed by** ______________________________

**Effective** ______________________________

Courtesy of Judy Sikes, PhD, CPHQ, Director of Accreditation/Medical Staff Services, Parkview Medical Center, Pueblo, Colorado.

# 4–83
# Antineoplastic Drug Order Entry and Preparation

## POLICY

Pharmacy personnel will follow specialized procedures when processing a physician's order for cancer chemotherapy to ensure accurate dispensing.

Pharmacy personnel will use specialized equipment and techniques in preparing and disposing of cancer chemotherapeutic agents to minimize their exposure to these agents.

## PROCEDURE

1. Each patient receiving chemotherapy will have a folder maintained containing all details of previous chemotherapy regimens.
2. Upon receiving a chemotherapy order, the pharmacist will locate the patient's folder or create one if necessary.
3. The pharmacist will carefully evaluate the order for appropriateness of dose and frequency using available references. Any clarifications necessary will be made with the prescriber.
4. The pharmacist will completely fill out a chemotherapy flowsheet.
5. After entering the orders in the computer, the pharmacist will print a copy of the order from Pyxis Connect. A second pharmacist will check the order entry for accuracy.
6. The pharmacist originally entering the order will calculate the amount of drug necessary for the entire course of therapy and write it on the "want book" for reordering.
7. Cancer chemotherapeutic drugs shall be prepared in a Class II biological safety cabinet using strict aseptic technique. (Referred to as a "chemo hood").
8. The chemotherapy agents, diluents, and IV solutions, along with any other material required to prepare the medication, are assembled in the chemo hood. All other material is to be removed from the hood.
9. The technician will ask a pharmacist to check the medications and diluents gathered before any reconstitution is begun.
10. Hands must be thoroughly washed prior to and immediately after preparing the medication. Gowns, facemask, and latex chemo gloves are to be worn and scrupulous sterile technique is to be employed. (In the event of a latex allergy, latex-free gloves will be worn underneath the latex chemo gloves.)
11. The latex chemo gloves are not sterile; therefore washing with Hibiclens after putting on the gloves is necessary.
12. A chemotherapy-dispensing pin will be used when withdrawing a chemotherapy agent from a vial. (See policy 050-16 Chemo Dispensing Pin) In the event that the chemotherapy agent in question cannot be successfully withdrawn from the vial using a dispensing pin, a pin will not be used (i.e., Taxol).
13. When the compounding of the chemotherapy is complete, the technician will ask a pharmacist to check the final product. (This preferably will be a different pharmacist than the one performing the original check of ingredients.)
14. The pharmacist performing the initial check, the preparing technician, and the pharmacist performing the final check will initial the chemotherapy worksheet.

*continues*

**4–83** continued

15. The "check labels" for the chemo are affixed to the back of the copy of the physician's order. Both the chemotherapy worksheet and the copy of the physician's order are placed in the patient folder.
16. Partially used multiple dose vials of chemotherapy agents may be left in the hood for use later the same day for the same patient.
17. All materials, including diluents used in the preparation of the chemotherapy agents, must be disposed of by placing them in the special boxes with "Bio Hazard" markers. When full, the boxes will be placed in the designated area in the pharmacy. They will be picked up by Environmental Services for proper disposal.
18. The biological safety cabinet is to be cleaned immediately after use and all cleaning materials will be disposed of as hazardous waste.
19. All chemotherapy agents will be received, handled, stored, used, and disposed of according to procedures outlined in the MSDS.
20. The procedure for cleaning cytotoxic drug spills is based on the size and location of the spill. Small spills are considered to be less than 5 ml or 5 GM of a cytotoxic drug spilled outside of a biological safety hood.
    - Clean up spills immediately.
      1. SMALL SPILLS
         a. Clean up small amounts of liquids using gauze pads. Then clean the area with 70% isopropyl alcohol or alcohol pads.
         b. Clean up small amounts of solids using wet absorbent gauze pads.
      2. LARGE SPILLS
         a. In the event of a large chemotherapy spill, personnel will retrieve a Cytotoxic Drug Spill Kit Emergency Response Pack from under the chemo hood.
         b. Persons cleaning these spills should wear double chemo gloves, eye protection, and a disposable lint-free, low permeability-fabric gown, with a closed front and long sleeves with elastic or knit cuffs. The cuffs must be tucked under the gloves. (All supplies are included in the kit.)
         c. Contain the spill with absorbent pads or if a powder is involved, use damp cloths or towels.
         d. Gather and place broken glassware and disposable contaminated material into a leak-proof, puncture-resistant container and then place the container into a sealable 4-mil polyethylene or 2-mil polypropylene bag labeled "caution antineoplastic drug." Place bag in "Chemo Waste" container.
         e. Clean the spill area three times using a detergent followed by clean water.
         f. Place contaminated reusable items in the sink. Specially trained personnel wearing double chemo gloves should wash these items with a detergent.
         g. Document the incident according to established medical center policies. An event report shall be completed if a large spill comes in contact with personnel/patient.
      3. When a chemotherapy spill kit will not handle the quantity, staff will do the following:
         a. Use the steps listed above under Large Spills;
         b. Use large absorbent pillow(s) stored in the pharmacy;
         c. Double bag all used supplies, containers, etc., in thick, yellow chemotherapy waste bags in the IV room;

*continues*

**4–83** continued

d. Notify Environmental Services once all contaminated material is contained. (They will bring a container and coordinate with Safety/Security to have material placed in the "Hazardous Waste Area"); and

e. Notify safety office by message if this occurs on the weekend or off-hours.

21. Personnel who are pregnant or are planning on becoming pregnant will not prepare chemotherapy.

**Signed by** ______________________________

**Effective** ______________________________

Courtesy of Judy Sikes, PhD, CPHQ, Director of Accreditation/Medical Staff Services, Parkview Medical Center, Pueblo, Colorado.

# 4–84
# Pharmacy Disaster/Emergency Plan
## DEPARTMENT OF PHARMACY

**Subject:** Disaster/Emergency Plan

**Manual Code:**

**Date Issued:**

**Date Revised:**

**Approved by:** Director of Pharmacy ______________________________

**Reviewed by/Date:** __________ __________ __________ __________

**1. INTRODUCTION**

A. Definitions of Terms

(1) **Internal Disaster**

An internal disaster is one within the hospital, such as fire, explosion, or incident affecting a large internal area.

(2) **External Disaster**

An external disaster is one beyond the immediate boundaries of the hospital resulting in a sudden arrival of a large number of casualties.

(3) **"CODE 7," "CODE 8"**

This term refers to the hospital's communication system for alerting all staff of the decision to immediately invoke the emergency preparation plan described in this policy.

B. The actual number of patients creating an overload and calling for the initiation of the Emergency Preparedness Plan is a variable to be identified at the discretion of the Vice-President of Operations or designee, in consultation with the Medical Director of the Emergency Department and the Director of Nursing or designees.

C. A restricted access telephone circuit will be established immediately upon the initiation of the "Code 7" signal and will remain open until the emergency situation is declared over.

The responsible manager or pharmacist should remain on the emergency extension in contact with the disaster command center.

**2. TREATMENT AND ALTERNATIVE TREATMENT AREAS**

A. **Emergency Department**—Stage 1

Triage is carried out in the Emergency Department. Patients may be treated in the Emergency Department, transferred to the Operating Room, Critical Care areas, or inpatient units.

B. **Outpatient Department**—Stage 2

If the Emergency Department capacity is exceeded, the Outpatient Department may be opened for treatment of less seriously injured or sick ambulatory patients.

The Outpatient Department will be used only upon the authorization of the Vice-President of Operations or designee.

C. **Cafeteria**—Stage 3

In the event that there are nonambulatory patients who cannot be treated in the Emergency Department and who require treatment and admission, the Cafeteria will be cleared and used as an additional treatment and holding area.

The Cafeteria will be used only upon the authorization of the Vice-President of Operations or designee.

*continues*

**4–84** continued

## 3. EMERGENCY CALL LIST

In the event of Disaster or Fire Emergency Situation, the pharmacist in charge should contact the management personnel per the manager emergency call listing until one individual is reached.

## 4. ALL PHARMACY PERSONNEL

All pharmacists, upon hearing of a nearby disaster via news media, are expected to telephone the Pharmacy to inquire if their assistance is needed. Within the medical center, the sound of seven (7) fire bells and voice page "Code 7" signals an emergency disaster situation requiring immediate response.

A. The Director for Pharmacy Operations or designee is responsible for providing drugs to the disaster treatment areas.

B. The Director for Clinical Pharmacy Services or a designated Clinical Pharmacy Manager shall be stationed in the Emergency Room and other activated treatment areas to provide assistance, answer questions, and communicate with the Inpatient Pharmacy to obtain additional drugs and supplies as needed.

## 5. PROCEDURAL GUIDELINES AND RESPONSIBILITIES FOR THE PHARMACY WEEKDAYS—DAY SHIFT

A. A Pharmacy Manager shall be stationed at the Inpatient Pharmacy making necessary assignments and answering calls to dispatch needed drugs and supplies. This individual will be stationed at the emergency extension phone for the duration of the emergency situation.

B. The manager shall assign one pharmacist to prepare and deliver to the Emergency Department the controlled drug kit containing the drugs below. The controlled drug kit is kept in a large box labeled "Disaster Drugs" in the Inpatient Pharmacy.

- 5 × 10 tubex Meperidine Injection 50 mg
- 2 × 10 tubex Morphine Injection 15 mg
- 2 × 25 Lorazepam tablets 1mg
- 10 Tubex Holders

C. The pharmacist delivering the controlled drugs to the Emergency Department remains stationed there and dispenses these drugs to the requesting physicians and nurses as needed. The pharmacist is responsible for making the necessary entries on all certificates of disposition for Schedule II and III drugs as they are issued. Requisitions for controlled drugs issued to the treatment areas need not be prepared until after the emergency situation has passed.

D. Supportive personnel should be assigned to deliver a filled Disaster Truck #1 to the Emergency Department. This individual shall remain stationed in the Emergency Department to assist in obtaining additional drugs and supplies as needed.

E. The Director for Clinical and Educational Pharmacy Services should report to the Emergency Department to provide clinical pharmacy support.

F. A second and third controlled drug box shall be prepared and delivered to the Outpatient Department by an Outpatient Pharmacist and the Cafeteria by an Inpatient Pharmacist when these treatment areas are activated. A pharmacist shall be stationed in each area to dispense controlled drugs and maintain appropriate records. Supportive personnel will be assigned to deliver the filled Disaster Truck #2 and #3 to the outpatient area and the Cafeteria. These individuals shall remain stationed at these locations to assist in obtaining additional drugs and supplies as needed.

G. The Clinical Pharmacy Manager for Critical Care will be assigned to the Outpatient Department to provide clinical pharmacy support. The Clinical Pharmacy Manager for Medicine/Cardiology will be assigned to the Cafeteria to provide clinical pharmacy support.

*continues*

**4–84** continued

## 6. PROCEDURAL GUIDELINES AND PHARMACY RESPONSIBILITIES—OFF-HOURS

The following procedures shall be initiated and applied to personnel on duty weekdays between 5:00 PM to 8:00 AM and 24 hours on Saturday, Sunday, and holidays.

The Pharmacy Manager, Pharmacy Resident, or Responsible Pharmacist shall proceed as follows:

A. Assign one pharmacist to prepare and deliver the controlled drug box to the Emergency Department.

B. One technician on duty will deliver the filled Disaster Truck #1 Herman Miller Locker to the Emergency Department.

C. Telephone pharmacy managers according to the sequence of the Emergency Call List.

D. Answer calls from the treatment area(s) and dispatch drugs and supplies as needed, until additional pharmacy managers arrive.

## 7. PROCEDURAL GUIDELINES AND RESPONSIBILITIES FOR THE PHARMACY NIGHT SHIFT

A. The responsible pharmacist shall proceed as follows:

1. Assign one technician on duty to deliver a filled Disaster Truck #1 to the Emergency Department and return to the inpatient pharmacy.
2. Telephone pharmacy managers according to the Emergency Call List until one individual is reached.
3. Prepare the controlled drug box, call operator and inform nursing office that pharmacy will be closed until further notice, and close the pharmacy and deliver the controlled drugs to the treatment area. The pharmacist shall remain in the treatment area to dispense the controlled drugs as needed. Technicians remaining in the pharmacy shall continue routine work activity and respond to phone directives by the pharmacist. The technician may not respond to any other phone calls or send drugs to a patient unit while the pharmacy is closed or until a manager arrives.

B. The pharmacy manager receiving the pharmacist's call shall respond as follows:

1. All management personnel are contacted as well as additional pharmacists depending on the extent of the emergency.
2. During the night, the first pharmacist arriving at the hospital shall open the pharmacy and resume normal operation, and answer the calls and dispatch needed drugs and supplies to the treatment area(s) until the manager arrives.
3. Additional pharmacists responding to the alert or who have been called shall work under the directives of the manager.

Source: Adapted from Montefiore Medical Center, Bronx, New York.

# 4–85

# OSHA's Form 300: Log of Work-Related Injuries and Illnesses

**Attention:** This form contains information relating to employee health and must be used in a manner that protects the confidentiality of employees to the extent possible while the information is being used for occupational safety and health purposes.

Year 20__ __

**U.S. Department of Labor**
**Occupational Safety and Health Administration**

Form approved OMB no. 1218-0176

*You must record information about every work-related death and about every work-related injury or illness that involves loss of consciousness, restricted work activity or job transfer, days away from work, or medical treatment beyond first aid. You must also record significant work-related injuries and illnesses that are diagnosed by a physician or licensed health care professional. You must also record work-related injuries and illnesses that meet any of the specific recording criteria listed in 29 CFR Part 1904.8 through 1904.12. Feel free to use two lines for a single case if you need to. You must complete an Injury and Illness Incident Report (OSHA Form 301) or equivalent form for each injury or illness recorded on this form. If you're not sure whether a case is recordable, call your local OSHA office for help.*

Establishment name ______________________

City ______________ State ______________

| Identify the person | | | Describe the case | | | Classify the case | | | | | | | | | | |
|---|---|---|---|---|---|---|---|---|---|---|---|---|---|---|---|---|
| | | | | | | **Using these four categories, check ONLY the most serious result for each case:** | | | | **Enter the number of days the injured or ill worker was:** | | **Check the "injury" column or choose one type of illness:** (M) | | | | |
| | | | | | | Death | Days away from work | Remained at work | | | | | | | | |
| (A) Case no. | (B) Employee's name | (C) Job title (e.g., *Welder*) | (D) Date of injury or onset of illness | (E) Where the event occurred (*e.g., Loading dock north end*) | (F) Describe injury or illness, parts of body affected, and object/substance that directly injured or made person ill (*e.g., Second degree burns on right forearm from acetylene torch*) | (G) | (H) | Job transfer or restriction (I) | Other recordable cases (J) | On job transfer or restriction (K) | Away from work (L) | Injury (1) | Skin disorder (2) | Respiratory condition (3) | Poisoning (4) | All other illnesses (5) |
| ___ | ___ | ___ | ___/___ month/day | ___ | ___ | ☐ | ☐ | ☐ | ☐ | ___ days | ___ days | ☐ | ☐ | ☐ | ☐ | ☐ |
| ___ | ___ | ___ | ___/___ month/day | ___ | ___ | ☐ | ☐ | ☐ | ☐ | ___ days | ___ days | ☐ | ☐ | ☐ | ☐ | ☐ |
| ___ | ___ | ___ | ___/___ month/day | ___ | ___ | ☐ | ☐ | ☐ | ☐ | ___ days | ___ days | ☐ | ☐ | ☐ | ☐ | ☐ |
| ___ | ___ | ___ | ___/___ month/day | ___ | ___ | ☐ | ☐ | ☐ | ☐ | ___ days | ___ days | ☐ | ☐ | ☐ | ☐ | ☐ |
| ___ | ___ | ___ | ___/___ month/day | ___ | ___ | ☐ | ☐ | ☐ | ☐ | ___ days | ___ days | ☐ | ☐ | ☐ | ☐ | ☐ |
| ___ | ___ | ___ | ___/___ month/day | ___ | ___ | ☐ | ☐ | ☐ | ☐ | ___ days | ___ days | ☐ | ☐ | ☐ | ☐ | ☐ |
| ___ | ___ | ___ | ___/___ month/day | ___ | ___ | ☐ | ☐ | ☐ | ☐ | ___ days | ___ days | ☐ | ☐ | ☐ | ☐ | ☐ |
| ___ | ___ | ___ | ___/___ month/day | ___ | ___ | ☐ | ☐ | ☐ | ☐ | ___ days | ___ days | ☐ | ☐ | ☐ | ☐ | ☐ |
| ___ | ___ | ___ | ___/___ month/day | ___ | ___ | ☐ | ☐ | ☐ | ☐ | ___ days | ___ days | ☐ | ☐ | ☐ | ☐ | ☐ |
| ___ | ___ | ___ | ___/___ month/day | ___ | ___ | ☐ | ☐ | ☐ | ☐ | ___ days | ___ days | ☐ | ☐ | ☐ | ☐ | ☐ |
| ___ | ___ | ___ | ___/___ month/day | ___ | ___ | ☐ | ☐ | ☐ | ☐ | ___ days | ___ days | ☐ | ☐ | ☐ | ☐ | ☐ |
| ___ | ___ | ___ | ___/___ month/day | ___ | ___ | ☐ | ☐ | ☐ | ☐ | ___ days | ___ days | ☐ | ☐ | ☐ | ☐ | ☐ |
| ___ | ___ | ___ | ___/___ month/day | ___ | ___ | ☐ | ☐ | ☐ | ☐ | ___ days | ___ days | ☐ | ☐ | ☐ | ☐ | ☐ |
| | | | | | **Page totals ➤** | ___ | ___ | ___ | ___ | ___ | ___ | ___ Injury (1) | ___ Skin disorder (2) | ___ Respiratory condition (3) | ___ Poisoning (4) | ___ All other illnesses (5) |

*Be sure to transfer these totals to the Summary page (Form 300A) before you post it.*

Page ___ of ___

Public reporting burden for this collection of information is estimated to average 14 minutes per response, including time to review the instructions, search and gather the data needed, and complete and review the collection of information. Persons are not required to respond to the collection of information unless it displays a currently valid OMB control number. If you have any comments about these estimates or any other aspects of this data collection, contact: US Department of Labor, OSHA Office of Statistics, Room N-3644, 200 Constitution Avenue, NW, Washington, DC 20210. Do not send the completed forms to this office.

Source: U.S. Department of Labor, Occupational Safety & Health Administration. http://www.osha.gov.

# 4–86
# How to Fill Out the Log

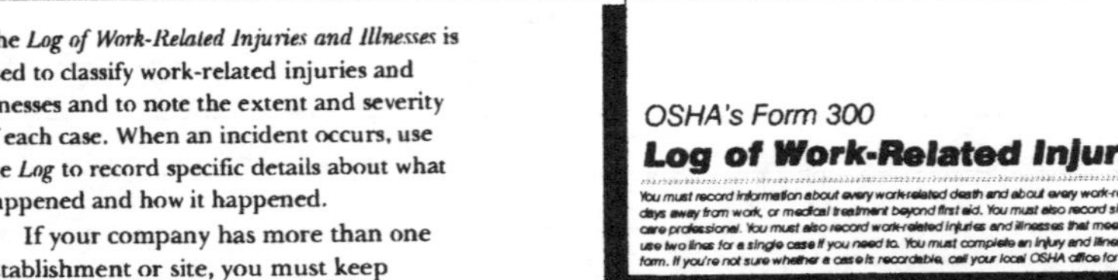


The *Log of Work-Related Injuries and Illnesses* is used to classify work-related injuries and illnesses and to note the extent and severity of each case. When an incident occurs, use the *Log* to record specific details about what happened and how it happened.

If your company has more than one establishment or site, you must keep separate records for each physical location that is expected to remain in operation for one year or longer.

We have given you several copies of the *Log* in this package. If you need more than we provided, you may photocopy and use as many as you need.

The *Summary* — a separate form — shows the work-related injury and illness totals for the year in each category. At the end of the year, count the number of incidents in each category and transfer the totals from the *Log* to the *Summary*. Then post the *Summary* in a visible location so that your employees are aware of injuries and illnesses occurring in their workplace.

**You don't post the Log. You post only the Summary at the end of the year.**

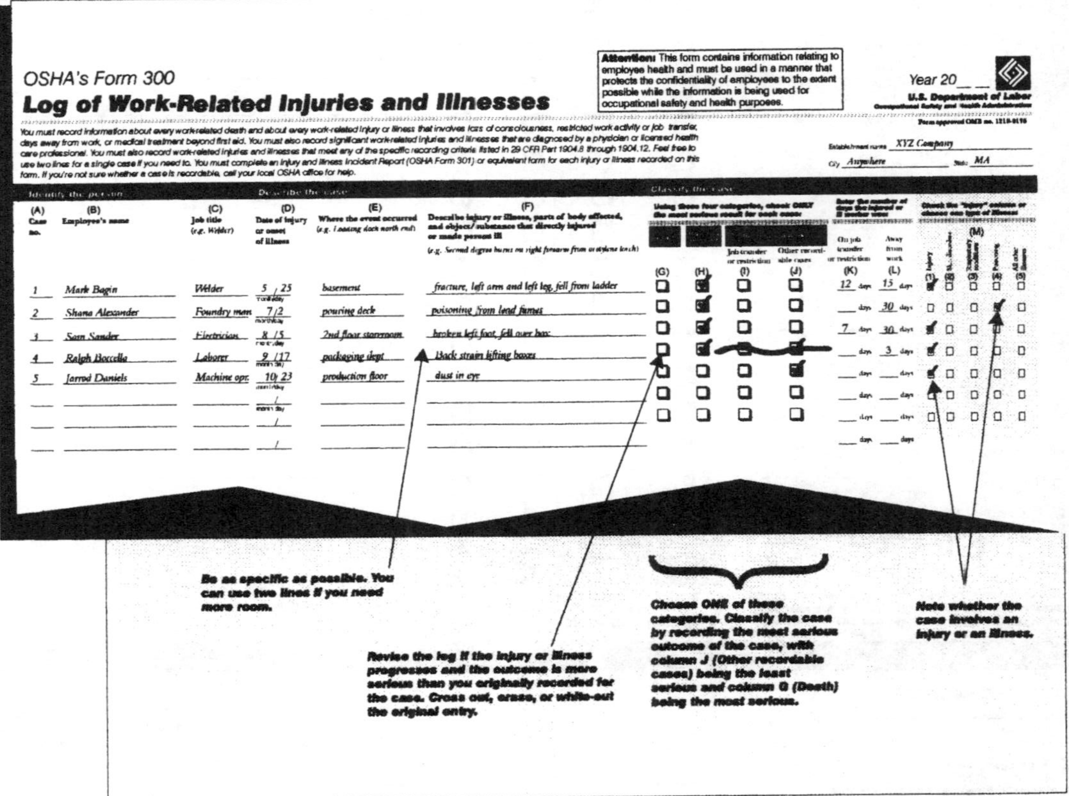


Source: U.S. Department of Labor, Occupational Safety & Health Administration. http://www.osha.gov.

# 4–87
# OSHA's Form 300A: Summary of Work-Related Injuries and Illnesses

Year 20__ __

**U.S. Department of Labor**
**Occupational Safety and Health Administration**

Form approved OMB no. 1218-0176

*All establishments covered by Part 1904 must complete this Summary page, even if no work-related injuries or illnesses occurred during the year. Remember to review the Log to verify that the entries are complete and accurate before completing this summary.*

*Using the Log, count the individual entries you made for each category. Then write the totals below, making sure you've added the entries from every page of the Log. If you had no cases, write "0."*

*Employees, former employees, and their representatives have the right to review the OSHA Form 300 in its entirety. They also have limited access to the OSHA Form 301 or its equivalent. See 29 CFR Part 1904.35, in OSHA's recordkeeping rule, for further details on the access provisions for these forms.*

## Number of Cases

| Total number of deaths | Total number of cases with days away from work | Total number of cases with job transfer or restriction | Total number of other recordable cases |
|---|---|---|---|
| ______ | ______ | ______ | ______ |
| (G) | (H) | (I) | (J) |

## Number of Days

| Total number of days of job transfer or restriction | Total number of days away from work |
|---|---|
| ______ | ______ |
| (K) | (L) |

## Injury and Illness Types

Total number of . . .
(M)

(1) Injuries ______

(2) Skin disorders ______

(3) Respiratory conditions ______

(4) Poisonings ______

(5) All other illnesses ______

**Post this Summary page from February 1 to April 30 of the year following the year covered by the form.**

Public reporting burden for this collection of information is estimated to average 50 minutes per response, including time to review the instructions, search and gather the data needed, and complete and review the collection of information. Persons are not required to respond to the collection of information unless it displays a currently valid OMB control number. If you have any comments about these estimates or any other aspects of this data collection, contact: US Department of Labor, OSHA Office of Statistics, Room N-3644, 200 Constitution Avenue, NW, Washington, DC 20210. Do not send the completed forms to this office.

### Establishment information

Your establishment name ______________________

Street ______________________

City ______________ State ____ ZIP ______

Industry description (*e.g., Manufacture of motor truck trailers*)

______________________

Standard Industrial Classification (SIC), if known (*e.g., SIC 3715*)

___ ___ ___ ___

### Employment information
*(If you don't have these figures, see the Worksheet on the back of this page to estimate.)*

Annual average number of employees ______

Total hours worked by all employees last year ______

### Sign here

**Knowingly falsifying this document may result in a fine.**

I certify that I have examined this document and that to the best of my knowledge the entries are true, accurate, and complete.

______________________
Company executive — Title

( ) - ______________ / /
Phone — Date

Source: U.S. Department of Labor, Occupational Safety & Health Administration. http://www.osha.gov.

# 4–88
# Optional Worksheet To Help You Fill Out the Summary

U.S. Department of Labor
Occupational Safety and Health Administration

*At the end of the year, OSHA requires you to enter the average number of employees and the total hours worked by your employees on the summary. If you don't have these figures, you can use the information on this page to estimate the numbers you will need to enter on the Summary page at the end of the year.*

**How to figure the average number of employees who worked for your establishment during the year:**

❶ **Add** the total number of employees your establishment paid in all pay periods during the year. Include all employees: full-time, part-time, temporary, seasonal, salaried, and hourly.

The number of employees paid in all pay periods = ❶ ________

❷ **Count** the number of pay periods your establishment had during the year. Be sure to include any pay periods when you had no employees.

The number of pay periods during the year = ❷ ________

❸ **Divide** the number of employees by the number of pay periods.

❶ / ❷ ________ = ❸ ________

❹ **Round the answer** to the next highest whole number. Write the rounded number in the blank marked *Annual average number of employees.*

The number rounded = ❹ ________

For example, Acme Construction figured its average employment this way:

| For pay period... | Acme paid this number of employees... |
|---|---|
| 1 | 10 |
| 2 | 0 |
| 3 | 15 |
| 4 | 30 |
| 5 | 40 |
| ▼ | ▼ |
| 24 | 20 |
| 25 | 15 |
| 26 | +10 |
| | 830 |

● Number of employees paid = 830
● Number of pay periods = 26
● 830/26 = 31.92
● 31.92 rounds to 32
32 is the annual average number of employees

**How to figure the total hours worked by all employees:**

Include hours worked by salaried, hourly, part-time and seasonal workers, as well as hours worked by other workers subject to day to day supervision by your establishment (e.g., temporary help services workers).

Do not include vacation, sick leave, holidays, or any other non-work time, even if employees were paid for it. If your establishment keeps records of only the hours paid or if you have employees who are not paid by the hour, please estimate the hours that the employees actually worked.

If this number isn't available, you can use this optional worksheet to estimate it.

**Optional Worksheet**

________ **Find** the number of full-time employees in your establishment for the year.

X ________ **Multiply** by the number of work hours for a full-time employee in a year.

________ This is the number of full-time hours worked.

\+ ________ **Add** the number of any overtime hours as well as the hours worked by other employees (part-time, temporary, seasonal)

________ **Round** the answer to the next highest whole number. Write the rounded number in the blank marked *Total hours worked by all employees last year.*

Source: U.S. Department of Labor, Occupational Safety & Health Administration. http://www.osha.gov.

# 4–89
# OSHA's Form 301: Injury and Illness Incident Report

**Attention:** This form contains information relating to employee health and must be used in a manner that protects the confidentiality of employees to the extent possible while the information is being used for occupational safety and health purposes.

**U.S. Department of Labor**
Occupational Safety and Health Administration

Form approved OMB no. 1218-0176

This *Injury and Illness Incident Report* is one of the first forms you must fill out when a recordable work-related injury or illness has occurred. Together with the *Log of Work-Related Injuries and Illnesses* and the accompanying *Summary*, these forms help the employer and OSHA develop a picture of the extent and severity of work-related incidents.

Within 7 calendar days after you receive information that a recordable work-related injury or illness has occurred, you must fill out this form or an equivalent. Some state workers' compensation, insurance, or other reports may be acceptable substitutes. To be considered an equivalent form, any substitute must contain all the information asked for on this form.

According to Public Law 91-596 and 29 CFR 1904, OSHA's recordkeeping rule, you must keep this form on file for 5 years following the year to which it pertains.

If you need additional copies of this form, you may photocopy and use as many as you need.

Completed by ______

Title ______

Phone (____)____-____ Date ___/___/___

### Information about the employee

1) Full name ______

2) Street ______

City ______ State ______ ZIP ______

3) Date of birth ___/___/___

4) Date hired ___/___/___

5) ☐ Male
☐ Female

### Information about the physician or other health care professional

6) Name of physician or other health care professional ______

7) If treatment was given away from the worksite, where was it given?

Facility ______

Street ______

City ______ State ______ ZIP ______

8) Was employee treated in an emergency room?
☐ Yes
☐ No

9) Was employee hospitalized overnight as an in-patient?
☐ Yes
☐ No

### Information about the case

10) Case number from the *Log* ______ *(Transfer the case number from the Log after you record the case.)*

11) Date of injury or illness ___/___/___

12) Time employee began work ______ AM / PM

13) Time of event ______ AM / PM ☐ Check if time cannot be determined

14) **What was the employee doing just before the incident occurred?** Describe the activity, as well as the tools, equipment, or material the employee was using. Be specific. *Examples:* "climbing a ladder while carrying roofing materials"; "spraying chlorine from hand sprayer"; "daily computer key-entry."

15) **What happened?** Tell us how the injury occurred. *Examples:* "When ladder slipped on wet floor, worker fell 20 feet"; "Worker was sprayed with chlorine when gasket broke during replacement"; "Worker developed soreness in wrist over time."

16) **What was the injury or illness?** Tell us the part of the body that was affected and how it was affected; be more specific than "hurt," "pain," or sore." *Examples:* "strained back"; "chemical burn, hand"; "carpal tunnel syndrome."

17) **What object or substance directly harmed the employee?** *Examples:* "concrete floor"; "chlorine"; "radial arm saw." *If this question does not apply to the incident, leave it blank.*

18) ***If the employee died, when did death occur?*** Date of death ___/___/___

Public reporting burden for this collection of information is estimated to average 22 minutes per response, including time for reviewing instructions, searching existing data sources, gathering and maintaining the data needed, and completing and reviewing the collection of information. Persons are not required to respond to the collection of information unless it displays a current valid OMB control number. If you have any comments about this estimate or any other aspects of this data collection, including suggestions for reducing this burden, contact: US Department of Labor, OSHA Office of Statistics, Room N-3644, 200 Constitution Avenue, NW, Washington, DC 20210. Do not send the completed forms to this office.

Source: U.S. Department of Labor, Occupational Safety & Health Administration. http://www.osha.gov.

# 4–90
# Medication Dispensing in the ED

## POLICY

The dispensing of medication from Emergency Department stock to a patient discharged from the Emergency Department will be in compliance with all state and federal law and recognized standards of practice in all respects.

## PROCEDURES

1. Emergency Department will dispense medication in a childproof amber container to which a PMC prescription label has been attached.
2. The label will bear the patient name, date, Rx number, name/strength/amount of drug, directions to patient, and the name of the Emergency Department physician. A duplicate copy of each label is created. Periodically, the duplicate label records are forwarded to the pharmacy for storage. The pharmacy will stamp a red "C" on all CIII-CV Rxs as required by law.
3. Name, strength, and quantity of drug dispensed will be noted in the patient record.
4. Only enough medication to last the patient until prescriptions can be filled at a retail pharmacy, but not to exceed a 24-hour supply, will be dispensed.
5. Dispensed drugs will be charged to the patient through the Pyxis system in the usual manner.
6. The storage, documentation, and distribution of all medications dispensed to patients discharged from the Emergency Department will be in accordance with all applicable state and federal laws. Nothing in this policy shall be deemed to take the place of, supersede, or release the Emergency Department or Pharmacy from the responsibility of being in accordance with those laws.

**Signed by** ______________________________

**Effective** ______________________________

Courtesy of Judy Sikes, PhD, CPHQ, Director of Accreditation/Medical Staff Services, Parkview Medical Center, Pueblo, Colorado.

# 4–91
# Medication Repackaging

## POLICY

Proper medication repackaging ensures the stability and maintains the quality and integrity of medications. Proper repackaging must include correct and complete labeling and accessory cautionary statements when applicable, as well as the expiration date. It is the responsibility of the pharmacist to ensure the above.

## PROCEDURE

1. All repackaging methods used at this facility will comply with all USP standards for medication repackaging.
2. Competent technicians under the direct supervision of a pharmacist will do repackaging.
3. In order to provide consistency and minimize error all repackaged medications will be labeled in the order as follows:
   a. Generic name of drug;
   b. Brand name of drug (or sub for brand name);
   c. Dosage strength;
   d. The facility's six-digit lot number (the lot number will be the date the medication is repackaged followed by a letter to designate which repackage of the day it is, e.g., the third repackage on October 1, 1996 = 100196C);
   e. The expiration date (see guidelines in #4);
   f. If overfilled, the label will state "OVERFILL"; and
   g. Miscellaneous information as needed for proper use (e.g., Shake Well, Chewable Tablet, Dilute Before Use, etc.).

   SAMPLE LABELS

   DIGOXIN<br>(LANOXIN)<br>0.25 MG TABS<br>LOT: 100696<br>EXP: 4/6/97

   DESIPRAMINE<br>(SUB FOR NORPRAMIN)<br>50 MG TABS<br>LOT: 100696<br>EXP: 12/31/96

   CEFACLOR SUSP<br>(CECLOR)<br>LOT: 100696<br>125MG/5ML<br>EXP: 10/20/96<br>SHAKE WELL/OVERFILL

4. The expiration date required on all repackaged medication labels will conform to the following:
   a. Oral Solids—Not more than six months or 25% of time remaining on manufacturer's dating, whichever comes first;
   b. Oral Liquids—Not more than six months or 25% of time remaining on manufacturer's dating, whichever come first;

*continues*

**4–91** continued

   c. Reconstituted Liquids/Suspensions—as recommended by manufacturer; and
   d. Unpreserved Oral Liquids—not more than two weeks.

5. Determining 25% of the time remaining on the manufacturer's expiration date will be standardized as follows:
   a. Count the remaining months left on the manufacturer's expiration. (Month #1 is the next full month. Ignore any time remaining in the current month.)
   b. The expiration date after repackaging will be that number of weeks from today. (i.e., if the expiration is six months away, the expiration will be six weeks from today.)
6. All repackaged liquids will conform to the following overfill guidelines:
   a. Suspensions—overfill 2 ml;
   b. Solutions—overfill 2 ml;
   c. Elixirs—overfill 2 ml;
   d. Digoxin—NO OVERFILL; and
   e. Controlled Substances—overfill 2 ml.
7. Medications that need to be repackaged will be placed in the repackaging area.
8. A technician will print labels for each product and place the labels and product in a wire basket.
9. The technician will record the repackaging of the drug on the repackaging log. (Alternatively, this may be done after the repackaging is complete.)
10. The following information will be recorded in the repackaging log: drug name and strength; drug NDC #; manufacturer and/or distributor; manufacturers lot number; manufacturers expiration date; lot number; expiration date; and the quantity repackaged. A copy of the label used for repackaging will accompany the entry.
11. A pharmacist will check all labels before medication is packaged. The pharmacist checking at this point is verifying the accuracy of labeling and that the label conforms to all standards as outlined in #6. The pharmacist will signify that the label is correct, including the expiration date, by initialing either on the "log" label or directly on the repackaging log. The pharmacist will draw a line completely through all labels that do not conform.
12. After the label has been verified as being correct, the product may be repackaged.
13. To prevent mislabeling, ONLY ONE container will be open in the repackaging area at any given time. Medication from the open container shall be completely labeled and sealed before any other container will be opened.
14. To prevent touch contamination, the repackaging technician will wear latex-free exam gloves. To prevent cross-contamination with other medications, the technician will reglove if the glove becomes dusty from tablets or if penicillin or sulfa products, chemotherapy agents or disulfiram is packaged.
15. To prevent cross-contamination with other medications, the Euclid machine will not be used to prepackage penicillin products, sulfa products, chemotherapy agents, or disulfiram.
16. After repackaging, the product will be left in the wire tray with the accompanying drug container. A pharmacist will conduct a final check that will:
    - Verify contents of all packages;
    - Include a visual inspection to ensure contaminant-free packages;

*continues*

**4–91** continued

- Verify the accuracy of the entry in the repackaging log; and
- Verify that all "bubbles" contain at least, but not more than, one tablet or capsule.

17. After checking a repackaged item the pharmacist will put the medication in the wire racks in the cart fill area for technicians to put away.
18. NO medications shall leave the repackaging area until a pharmacist has completed the final check and initialed the log book.

**Signed by** ______________________________

**Effective** ______________________________

Courtesy of Judy Sikes, PhD, CPHQ, Director of Accreditation/Medical Staff Services, Parkview Medical Center, Pueblo, Colorado.

# 4–92
# Sample Drugs

**POLICY:**

The distribution of drug samples is discouraged and will be effectively controlled in all areas of the Medical Center. In the event of a drug recall, the location of any affected samples will be easily identified.

**PROCEDURES:**

1. Any area keeping and distributing samples must notify pharmacy of its intent to do so.
2. A list will be maintained in the pharmacy of samples stored in each area along with lot numbers and expiration dates. This list is filed in the "Drug Recall" file and is maintained by the Pharmacy Purchasing Technician or his or her designee.
3. The Pharmacy Purchasing Technician is the contact person in the pharmacy.

**DIABETES CARE CENTER MEDICATION SAMPLES:**

1. The contact person will be one of the diabetes nurse educators.
2. Insulin samples will be kept in a locked refrigerator in the DCC (the only drug samples kept in the DCC are insulin).
3. The DCC contact person will conduct regular monthly inspections checking all samples for expiration dates. Any expired samples will be returned to the Pharmacy for proper disposal.
4. Each month, the DCC contact person will generate a list of all samples in the DCC. This list will include the name of the drug, quantity, lot number, and expiration date. The list will be sent to the Pharmacy Purchasing Technician and placed in the Pharmacy "Drug Recall" file.
5. In the event of a manufacturer recall, the Pharmacy Purchasing Technician will be responsible for making sure the DCC drug sample list is inspected to see if any recalled drugs are in stock. If a drug sample in the DCC corresponds to a drug on the recall list, the Materials Management Tech will inform the DCC. Recalled samples will be returned to the pharmacy for proper disposal.
6. NO CONTROLLED SUBSTANCES are to be kept in the DCC as drug samples.
7. No nonformulary medications will be kept as drug samples.
8. This policy/procedure will be included in the DCC P&P on the Intranet.
9. Patients who receive drug samples are not assessed a charge.
10. Any sample dispensed to the patient will be recorded in a logbook. The log will be kept near the refrigerator. The log will include the name of the drug, number of vials dispensed, lot number, expiration date, name of patient and patient phone number. In the event of a drug recall, any patient receiving the drug in question will be called and arrangements made for the dispensed sample to be returned for disposal.
11. This policy will be listed under Diabetes Care Center policies on the Intranet.

**CONTINENCE CENTER:**

1. A list will be maintained in the Pharmacy of samples stored in the Continence Center. This list will include the drug name, drug strength, lot number, expiration date, and quantity at the time of recording.

*continues*

**4–92** continued

2. The Pharmacy contact person will be the Pharmacy Purchasing Technician.
3. The Continence Center contact person will be one of the Continence Center nurses.
4. During the regular monthly Continence Center inspection, the Continence Center contact person will check all samples for expiration dates. Any expired samples will be returned to the Pharmacy for proper disposal.
5. The sample list will be sent to Pharmacy on a monthly basis and kept in the Drug Recall file. In the event of a manufacturer recall, the Pharmacy Purchasing Tech will be responsible for making sure the Continence Center drug sample list is inspected to see if any recalled drugs are in stock. If a drug sample in the Continence Center corresponds to a drug on the recall list, the Pharmacy Purchasing Tech will inspect the Continence Center drug samples log to see if the lot number in question is in stock. Recalled samples will be returned to the Pharmacy for proper disposal.
6. Patients who receive samples will not be assessed a charge.
7. The Continence Center will maintain a Drug Sample Dispensing Log that will be used to record samples dispensed to patients. The log will include drug name, drug strength, lot number, expiration date, patient name and patient phone number. In the event of a recall, the patient will be contacted and alerted to return the drug to the Continence Center for proper disposal.
8. The Drug Sample Dispensing Log Manual will be kept near the drug cabinet where the samples are stored.
9. No controlled substances are to be kept in the Continence Center as drug samples.
10. No nonformulary medications will be kept as drug samples.

**Signed by** ______________________________

**Effective** ______________________________

Courtesy of Judy Sikes, PhD, CPHQ, Director of Accreditation/Medical Staff Services, Parkview Medical Center, Pueblo, Colorado.

# 4–93
# Medication Review

Organization: ______________________

Please complete the following tasks:

A. Pull the medication logs for the departments listed and for the dates indicated; then pull the medical record of each patient that received the medication and complete the attached form (Controlled Substance Process Monitor). You may need to make additional copies of the form.

| DATE | DEPARTMENT | MEDICATION | COMMENTS |
|---|---|---|---|
| | Labor/Delivery | | |
| | Surgery | | |
| | Emergency Room | | |
| | ICU | | |

B. Count the number of episodes of wasting of controlled substances and the number that were not cosigned (witnessed) appropriately for the month of ______________ for the following departments:

**Cath Lab**

**Radiology Special Procedures**

**C section OR**

C. Calculate the percentage of compliance of emergency cart checks for the organization for the month ______.

*continues*

4–93 continued

## CONTROLLED SUBSTANCE PROCESS MONITOR

Organization ______________________

Department Emergency Room

| Medical Record # Date | PE 1.4 (1) Pain Measured (2) Pain Docum.—character, frequency, location, duration | TX 3.3 (1) Order for med (2) Appropriate (No ranges) | TX 3.5 Doc. of Actual Amount taken from Supply | TX 3.5 Doc. of Actual Amount Given | TX 3.5 (1) Documentation of Wastage (2) 2 Signatures | TX 3.5 Multiple Doses Given from One Vial/amp | TX 3.9 Documentation of Effect of Med. (e.g., pain/nausea relief) |
|---|---|---|---|---|---|---|---|
| | (1) Y N<br>(2) Y N | (1) Y N<br>(2) Y N | Y N | Y N | (1) Y N<br>(2) Y N | Y N<br>NA | Y N |
| | (1) Y N<br>(2) Y N | (1) Y N<br>(2) Y N | Y N | Y N | (1) Y N<br>(2) Y N | Y N<br>NA | Y N |
| | (1) Y N<br>(2) Y N | (1) Y N<br>(2) Y N | Y N | Y N | (1) Y N<br>(2) Y N | Y N<br>NA | Y N |
| | (1) Y N<br>(2) Y N | (1) Y N<br>(2) Y N | Y N | Y N | (1) Y N<br>(2) Y N | Y N<br>NA | Y N |
| | (1) Y N<br>(2) Y N | (1) Y N<br>(2) Y N | Y N | Y N | (1) Y N<br>(2) Y N | Y N<br>NA | Y N |

Department ICU

| Medical Record # Date | PE 1.4 (1) Pain Measured (2) Pain Docum.—character, frequency, location, duration | TX 3.3 (1) Order for med (2) Appropriate (No ranges) | TX 3.5 Doc. of Actual Amount taken from Supply | TX 3.5 Doc. of Actual Amount Given | TX 3.5 (1) Documentation of Wastage (2) 2 Signatures | TX 3.5 Multiple Doses Given from One Vial/amp | TX 3.9 Documentation of Effect of Med. (e.g., pain/nausea relief) |
|---|---|---|---|---|---|---|---|
| | (1) Y N<br>(2) Y N | (1) Y N<br>(2) Y N | Y N | Y N | (1) Y N<br>(2) Y N | Y N | Y N |
| | (1) Y N<br>(2) Y N | (1) Y N<br>(2) Y N | Y N | Y N | (1) Y N<br>(2) Y N | Y N | Y N |
| | (1) Y N<br>(2) Y N | (1) Y N<br>(2) Y N | Y N | Y N | (1) Y N<br>(2) Y N | Y N | Y N |
| | (1) Y N<br>(2) Y N | (1) Y N<br>(2) Y N | Y N | Y N | (1) Y N<br>(2) Y N | Y N | Y N |
| | (1) Y N<br>(2) Y N | (1) Y N<br>(2) Y N | Y N | Y N | (1) Y N<br>(2) Y N | Y N | Y N |

**Make an additional copy and as per instructions under pharmacy doc entitled pharmacy consulting also use this form to do five emergency room records with dates indicated.**

*continues*

4–93 continued

## CONTROLLED SUBSTANCE PROCESS MONITOR

Organization ______________________

Department Operating Room/PACU

| Medical Record # Date | PE 1.4 (1) Pain Measured (2) Pain Docum.—character, frequency, location, duration | TX 3.3 (1) Order for med (2) Appropriate (No ranges) | TX 3.5 Doc. of Actual Amount taken from Supply | TX 3.5 Doc. of Actual Amount Given | TX 3.5 (1) Documentation of Wastage (2) 2 Signatures | TX 3.5 Multiple Doses Given from One Vial/amp | TX 3.9 Documentation of Effect of Med. (e.g., pain/nausea relief) |
|---|---|---|---|---|---|---|---|
| | (1) Y N<br>(2) Y N | (1) Y N<br>(2) Y N | Y N | Y N | (1) Y N<br>(2) Y N | Y N | Y N |
| | (1) Y N<br>(2) Y N | (1) Y N<br>(2) Y N | Y N | Y N | (1) Y N<br>(2) Y N | Y N | Y N |
| | (1) Y N<br>(2) Y N | (1) Y N<br>(2) Y N | Y N | Y N | (1) Y N<br>(2) Y N | Y N | Y N |
| | (1) Y N<br>(2) Y N | (1) Y N<br>(2) Y N | Y N | Y N | (1) Y N<br>(2) Y N | Y N | Y N |
| | (1) Y N<br>(2) Y N | (1) Y N<br>(2) Y N | Y N | Y N | (1) Y N<br>(2) Y N | Y N | Y N |

Department Labor/Delivery

| Medical Record # Date | PE 1.4 (1) Pain Measured (2) Pain Docum.—character, frequency, location, duration | TX 3.3 (1) Order for med (2) Appropriate (No ranges) | TX 3.5 Doc. of Actual Amount taken from Supply | TX 3.5 Doc. of Actual Amount Given | TX 3.5 (1) Documentation of Wastage (2) 2 Signatures | TX 3.5 Multiple Doses Given from One Vial/amp | TX 3.9 Documentation of Effect of Med. (e.g., pain/nausea relief) |
|---|---|---|---|---|---|---|---|
| | (1) Y N<br>(2) Y N | (1) Y N<br>(2) Y N | Y N | Y N | (1) Y N<br>(2) Y N | Y N | Y N |
| | (1) Y N<br>(2) Y N | (1) Y N<br>(2) Y N | Y N | Y N | (1) Y N<br>(2) Y N | Y N | Y N |
| | (1) Y N<br>(2) Y N | (1) Y N<br>(2) Y N | Y N | Y N | (1) Y N<br>(2) Y N | Y N | Y N |
| | (1) Y N<br>(2) Y N | (1) Y N<br>(2) Y N | Y N | Y N | (1) Y N<br>(2) Y N | Y N | Y N |
| | (1) Y N<br>(2) Y N | (1) Y N<br>(2) Y N | Y N | Y N | (1) Y N<br>(2) Y N | Y N | Y N |

**Make an additional copy and as per instructions under pharmacy doc entitled pharmacy consulting also use this form to do five emergency room records with dates indicated.**

Courtesy of Judy Sikes, PhD, CPHQ, Director of Accreditation/Medical Staff Services, Parkview Medical Center, Pueblo, Colorado.

## 4–94
## Emergency Preparedness

### POLICY

THE PHARMACY SHALL HAVE A PLAN TO ADEQUATELY PREPARE FOR ANY EMERGENCY OR DISASTER. THE PLAN WILL BE IN ACCORDANCE WITH THE MEDICAL CENTER'S DISASTER MANUAL AND WILL ASSURE THE PROVISION OF PHARMACY SERVICES ADEQUATE FOR THE NEEDS OF THE FACILITY.

### PROCEDURE

For each emergency code and other emergencies, pharmacy personnel will respond as outlined in the Medical Center's Disaster Manual. Definitions for Codes and other situations and specific pharmacy responses, if applicable, are outlined below:

**CODE ORANGE: A Code Orange is called when a large influx of patients to the Medical Center is expected *or* any situation where additional resources are needed to support patient care.**

A. Management and Direction

   Upon notification of a disaster by overhead page ("CODE ORANGE") or other means, the Director of Pharmacy, Administrative Coordinator, Clinical Coordinator, or Pharmacy Shift Leader (in that order) will assume responsibility for directing and coordinating the activities of the Pharmacy Department. The director may delegate responsibilities, as circumstances require.

B. Notification of Personnel

   Upon notification of a disaster, the director or designee will initiate contacting all staff on the pharmacy roster.

   1. The pharmacy roster is maintained and kept up to date by the Pharmacy Director and/or his or her designee with information supplied by the staff. The pharmacy roster is distributed and posted as changes are required.
   2. Upon initiation of the call list, each employee will be called and each employee's availability will be determined.
   3. All pharmacy personnel will be asked to report to duty or to remain on stand-by to be called if necessary.

C. Duties and Responsibilities

   All employees already on duty must report to the pharmacy. Employees who are asked to come in to work will park in and enter the medical center as outlined in the Disaster Manual, reporting directly to the pharmacy. All employees must have a name badge or driver's license as identification for entrance into the hospital.

   Pharmacy personnel will provide routine service to existing inpatients and will organize to expand and accelerate its normal function to supply all emergency patient care areas with essential drugs consistent with the requirements of the emergency.

   1. Director of Pharmacy or Designee
      a. The Director of Pharmacy will respond to the Ancillary Coordinator as to the availability of departmental personnel, including those employees who are in-house and those who are potentially available.

*continues*

**4–94** continued

b. The director or designee will coordinate activities within the department.

c. The director of pharmacy or his or her designee has the responsibility for pharmacy staffing adequate to handle the emergency and at the same time to ration staff to ensure continuous service during the duration of the situation. In addition, regular service to inpatients must be maintained.

d. The director or designee will ensure adequate supplies during the disaster. Additional supply/equipment needs will be coordinated with the Supply Coordinator.

e. The director will provide staffing schedules in order to account for all staff.

2. Pharmacy Staff

   a. Pharmacy staff must perform their regular duties.

   b. In addition to their regular duties, staff is expected to perform the following duties as directed by the Director or his or her designee.

      i. Deliver drugs to areas as necessary.

      ii. Answer the telephone and handle emergency and routine requests.

      iii. Change shifts, extend shifts into overtime, and change work duties, as needed.

      iv. Perform any activity as requested by the director, his or her designee, or the Command Center Administrator.

3. Pharmacy Responsibilities

   a. Pharmacy will maintain a reasonable reserve of disaster inventory of drugs in anticipation of medical emergencies. Pharmacy will have the capability of securing further supplies of any drug needed from other institutions or suppliers at any time.

   b. The pharmacy will supply auxiliary inpatient and emergency treatment units with drugs as needed.

   c. The pharmacy will maintain records of drugs dispensed.

   d. When appropriate, during operation of the Disaster Plan, deliveries of drugs to patient care areas will be made by non-pharmacist staff members. This includes rounds of the disaster treatment areas.

   e. Professional staff will remain in the department as much as possible.

   f. Knowledge of Pharmacy Department policies is the responsibility of each employee.

**CODE BLACK: A bomb threat**

Pharmacy will strictly follow the hospitalwide procedure in the Disaster Manual.

**CODE GREEN: Abduction or kidnapping.**

Pharmacy will follow the hospitalwide procedure in the Disaster Manual.

Pharmacy personnel will search the areas outside of the pharmacy including the stairwells for any suspicious activity. Security will be notified for any sighting of the abductor or abductee.

**CODE RED: A fire**

Pharmacy will follow the hospitalwide procedure in the Disaster Manual.

*continues*

4–94 continued

**CODE RESPOND: Out of control person**

Pharmacy will follow the hospitalwide procedure in the Disaster Manual.

**COR-ZERO: Respiratory/Cardiac Arrest**

Pharmacy will follow the hospitalwide procedure in the Disaster Manual.

**CODE BLUE: Practice Cor-Zero**

**HAZARDOUS MATERIALS/CHEMICAL SPILL OR RELEASE ON MEDICAL CENTER PROPERTY:**

Pharmacy will follow the hospitalwide procedure in the Disaster Manual.

**HOSTAGE: A PERSON HELD AS SECURITY PENDING THE FULFILLMENT OF CERTAIN TERMS**

Pharmacy will follow the hospitalwide procedure in the Disaster Manual.

**TORNADO THREAT:**

Pharmacy will follow the hospitalwide procedure in the Disaster Manual. Pharmacy personnel will evacuate into the hallway.

**VIOLENCE, THREATS, AND WEAPONS:**

Pharmacy will follow the hospitalwide procedure in the Disaster Manual.

**EVACUATION:**

Pharmacy personnel will evacuate only if notified to do so by Security or human life is in immediate danger. Evacuation routes will be followed as posted in the floor hallways.

**Signed by** ______________________________

**Effective** ______________________________

Courtesy of Judy Sikes, PhD, CPHQ, Director of Accreditation/Medical Staff Services, Parkview Medical Center, Pueblo, Colorado.

## 4–95
## Haz-Mat/Chemical Handling

### POLICY

It is the policy of the Pharmacy Department to maintain a safe and hazardous-free work environment. The Pharmacy Department shall adhere to the policies and procedures spelled out in Risk Management Policy J100.021 (Hazard Communication Program). In addition, the following procedures for the receipt, handling, storage, use, and disposal of hazardous materials/chemicals in the pharmacy will be followed. The proper handling of hazardous materials/chemicals is imperative to ensure the health and well-being of all patients, personnel, visitors, and physicians in the facility.

### PROCEDURE

1. Ordering: No materials shall be ordered without the authorization of the Director of the department or his or her designee. The authorizing person shall evaluate the need for the requested material and shall determine if there is an alternate material/chemical that can be used. Upon determination that the material/chemical is to be ordered, the order is processed by the Materials Management Technician.
2. Receipt: Upon the receipt of the material/chemical, the person receiving it shall ensure that there is an MSDS (Material Safety Data Sheet) on file in the MSDS book located in the department. If there is not, the material/chemical **must not be used** until receipt of an MSDS. Notify the Safety Officer immediately and request an MSDS. Also, there must be a label on the container that clearly states the name of the product, identity of the hazardous chemicals, appropriate hazard warnings, and name and address of the manufacturer, importer, or other responsible party.
3. Handling and Usage: All materials/chemicals must be handled and used in the manner for which they are intended. Follow all directions and precautions on the label and on the MSDS.
4. Storage: Follow the directions for storage on the label and the MSDS. All materials/chemicals must be stored away from any food products and in an area that prevents accidents, misuse, or spills.
5. Disposal: Dispose of container and/or chemical or material as directed on the label or MSDS.
6. Chemotherapeutic Agents: See Pharmacy Policy 050-15 Anti Neoplastic Drugs.

**Signed by** ________________________________

**Effective** ________________________________

Courtesy of Judy Sikes, PhD, CPHQ, Director of Accreditation/Medical Staff Services, Parkview Medical Center, Pueblo, Colorado.

# 4–96
# Pharmacy Safety Policies

**POLICY:**

The Pharmacy maintains a safe environment for all patients, visitors, and employees.

**PROCEDURE:**

1. Current copies of the Hospital Disaster and Safety Manual are kept in the Pharmacy Department. One is kept in the dispensing area, one in the director's office. Each employee must review the information contained in the manual on an annual basis.
2. It is the responsibility of each employee to know the department-specific safety policies and procedures in addition to all information contained in the Hospital Disaster and Safety Manual.
3. All new employees will be trained on the use of all equipment before using. This will be documented on the training and orientation check-off sheet. Existing employees will be trained on the use of any new equipment. This will be documented on a training check-off sheet.
4. All new employees will be familiar with all policies and procedures. This will be documented on the training and orientation check-off sheet. Existing employees will be made aware of new policies and procedures via MOX messaging. Each employee is responsible for familiarizing himself or herself with the content of new policies and procedures they are notified of.
5. A new pharmacy employee is not permitted to work in the IV room until IV training is complete and documented.
6. The Pharmacy area and all storage areas shall be maintained in an orderly condition. Passageways shall be kept clean; tiles and mats shall be clean and undamaged. Floors will be kept dry and clean and free from any projections. Floors and countertops will be as free from waste and clutter as possible.
7. Case goods will be stored off the floor on pallets. Heavy and/or bulky items will be moved on appropriate carts.
8. Pharmacy employees will have access to hospital-supplied weight belts when moving heavy weights.
9. No employee shall handle any combustibles, acids, corrosives, or other chemicals unless he or she is completely familiar with their use.
10. Pharmacy employees will be familiar with the location and use of the MSDS manual.
11. All electrical equipment shall be in good working order and grounded according to standards. All equipment will be inspected and tagged by Biomedical Engineering according to hospital policy.
12. Pharmacy employees will be familiar with the location and proper use of all fire extinguishers in the department.
13. Pharmacy employees will demonstrate knowledge of hospital and departmental safety issues in regularly scheduled competency reviews
14. Smoking is not permitted in the medical center.

**Signed by** ____________________________

**Effective** ____________________________

Courtesy of Judy Sikes, PhD, CPHQ, Director of Accreditation/Medical Staff Services, Parkview Medical Center, Pueblo, Colorado.

# 4–97
# ASHP Statement on the Role of Health-System Pharmacists in Emergency Preparedness

As the United States began to enhance counterterrorism measures in response to the homeland terrorist attacks of September 11, 2001, it became clear that hospital and health-system pharmacists have an essential role to play in those measures. The American Society of Health-System Pharmacists (ASHP) believes that hospital and health-system pharmacists must assertively exercise their responsibilities to counter terrorist acts, and the leaders of emergency planning at the federal, regional, state, and local levels must call on pharmacists to participate in the full range of issues related to pharmaceuticals.

## GENERAL PRINCIPLES

1. On the basis of their education, training, experience, and legal responsibilities, pharmacists should have a key role in the planning and execution of (a) pharmaceutical distribution and control and (b) drug therapy management of patients in the event of a homeland terrorist attack with weapons of mass destruction (WMD), especially chemical, biological, and nuclear agents.
2. The expertise of the pharmacist must be sought in (a) selecting pharmaceuticals and related supplies for national and regional stockpiles and local emergency inventories in counterterrorism programs, (b) ensuring proper packaging, storage, handling, labeling, and dispensing of emergency supplies of pharmaceuticals, (c) ensuring appropriate deployment of emergency supplies of pharmaceuticals in the event of a terrorist attack, (d) developing guidelines for the diagnosis and treatment of victims of WMD, and (e) ensuring appropriate education and counseling of individuals who receive pharmaceuticals from an emergency supply after a terrorist attack.
3. Pharmacists must be in a position to advise public health officials on appropriate messages to convey to the public about the use of essential pharmaceuticals after terrorist attacks, giving consideration to issues such as adverse effects, contraindications, the effectiveness of alternative pharmaceuticals, and the potential development of drug-resistant infectious agents.
4. In the event of a terrorist attack, pharmacists should be called on to collaborate with physicians and other prescribers in the drug therapy management of individual victims.

## ADVICE TO HOSPITAL AND HEALTH-SYSTEM PHARMACY DIRECTORS

Every hospital and health-system pharmacy director (or designee) should

1. Become thoroughly informed of federal, regional, state, local, and institutional plans for emergency preparedness, especially those related to the distribution, control, and use of pharmaceuticals;
2. Ensure that the pharmaceutical components of the institution's emergency plans are coordinated with the overall local preparedness plans involving other institutions, community pharmacies, and wholesalers as well as coordinated with federal, regional, and state plans;
3. Ensure that the appropriate pharmaceuticals and related equipment and supplies are in stock at the institution, consistent with the overall local preparedness plan, which should account for the interim between the occurrence of a terrorist attack and the receipt of federal or state assistance;
4. Ensure that information about the appropriate use of pharmaceuticals in response to a terrorist attack is available to the health professionals in the institution;

*continues*

**4–97** continued

5. Ensure that the institution does not engage in stockpiling of pharmaceuticals without regard to local counterterrorism plans that are designed to meet the needs of the whole community; and
6. Ensure that pharmacy personnel are trained to implement the institution's emergency plans.

## ADVICE TO HOSPITAL AND HEALTH-SYSTEM PHARMACISTS

Every hospital and health-system pharmacist should

1. Become well informed about the threats of chemical, biological, and nuclear terrorism, including potential agents that could be used in an attack and the related diagnostic and treatment issues;
2. Share with professional colleagues and patients evidence-based information on pharmaceuticals used to respond to terrorist attacks;
3. Act assertively to prevent and allay panic and irrational responses after acts of terrorism;
4. Strongly discourage individuals from developing personal stockpiles of pharmaceuticals for use in the event of chemical, biological, or nuclear terrorism;
5. Consider volunteering in advance of any terrorist attack to assist in (a) distributing emergency supplies of pharmaceuticals and (b) managing the drug therapy of individual victims; and
6. Develop and maintain first-aid skills.

## ADVICE TO HOSPITAL AND HEALTH-SYSTEM ADMINISTRATORS

Hospital and health-system administrators should

1. Ask the pharmacy director to participate in preparing the institution's emergency preparedness plan;
2. Consult with the pharmacy director to coordinate the institution's participation in the building of emergency pharmaceutical supplies for use in the community;
3. Refrain from building institutional stockpiles of pharmaceuticals that are not coordinated with the local plan;
4. Encourage local preparedness-planning officials to involve pharmacists in the full range of issues related to pharmaceuticals; and
5. Encourage and enable pharmacy personnel employed by the institution to volunteer for community service in the event of a terrorist attack.

## ADVICE TO EMERGENCY PREPAREDNESS PLANNERS

Emergency preparedness planners at the federal, regional, state, and local levels should

1. Consult with qualified pharmacists in all areas in which the pharmacist's expertise is necessary to make workable plans;
2. Inform pharmacists, through national and state pharmacy organizations, of plans for deployment of emergency pharmaceutical supplies so that appropriate plans can be made at the local level; and
3. Consult with qualified pharmacists on messages that should be conveyed to the public about the appropriate use of pharmaceuticals in the event of chemical, biological, or nuclear terrorism.

*continues*

**4–97** continued

## ADVICE TO STATE SOCIETIES OF HEALTH-SYSTEM PHARMACISTS

State societies of health-system pharmacists should

1. Offer their assistance to state and local disaster-planning officials;
2. Advise their members of information unique to the state regarding pharmacists' participation in emergency preparedness planning and deployment efforts; and
3. Consider establishing a volunteer network of health-system pharmacists for deployment in the event of a terrorist attack.

## COMMITMENTS MADE BY ASHP

In support of the efforts of health-system pharmacists in counterterrorism, ASHP will

1. Maintain an electronic communications network of hospital pharmacy department directors that can be used to transmit urgent information related to counterterrorism;
2. Disseminate promptly to ASHP members important new information related to pharmacist involvement in counterterrorism;
3. Disseminate to ASHP members and others in the health care community timely evidence-based information about pharmaceuticals used when responding to chemical, biological, or nuclear terrorism; and
4. Meet with government officials and others when necessary to clarify promptly important issues that affect the involvement of health-system pharmacists in counterterrorism.

---

Approved by the ASHP Board of Directors on November 27, 2001, and ratified by the ASHP House of Delegates on June 2, 2002.



The ASHP House of Delegates voted on June 2, 2002, to change the title of this document from "ASHP Statement on the Role of Health-System Pharmacists in Counterterrorism" to "ASHP Statement on the Role of Health-System Pharmacists in Emergency Preparedness." Inconsistencies between the title and content will be addressed by ASHP's Council on Professional Affairs. Until then, the bibliographic citation for this document is as follows: American Society of Health-System Pharmacists. ASHP Statement on the Role of Health-System Pharmacists in Counterterrorism. *Am J Health-Syst Pharm.* 2002; 59:282–3.

# 4–98
# Medication System Failures

In June 2000, the Pharmacy Department began to take a comprehensive look at Medication Failures. Recognizing the lack of an effective program, the Pharmacy Department initiated the formation of a hospitalwide multidisciplinary Quality Action Team to analyze the complexities of the medication processes at Atascadero State Hospital. Based on significant research and analysis of the hospitalwide medication delivery system, the Pharmacy Department recommended a program to monitor the medication processes to be called Medication Systems Failures. This nomenclature was chosen to accurately describe the fact that medication ordering, delivery, and administration are interrelated processes and not just individual events. Based upon this preliminary work, the Hospital Quality Action Team produced Nursing Policy #310, which is a hospitalwide Medication System Failure reporting program that encompasses failures that reach the patient, and failures that are successfully intervened.

## POLICY

The Department of Pharmacy has established and participates in a quality assurance program that documents and assesses Medication System Failures as outlined in Nursing Policy #310. This Quality Assurance program will determine cause and an appropriate response as part of a mission to improve the quality of Pharmacy Services and to prevent Medication System Failures.

## GENERAL

It is the responsibility of each person to report *making, observing,* or *recognizing* medication systems failures. A Medication System Failures Report Form, AT 2951 (Attachment A), is completed for each system failure. A Special Incident Report (MH 2506) is completed if the system failure reaches the patient and the severity of patient outcome is equal to or greater than two as indicated on the Medication System Failures Report.

## PURPOSE

A. To protect the health/safety of the patient

B. To prevent recurring Medication System Failures

C. To ensure accountability for medication doses

D. To ensure that each employee's practice in the administration of medication is competent

E. To assist in the gathering of data regarding Medication System Failures for analysis

F. To provide a basis for system improvement/corrective action based on objective data

## DEFINITION

A. A Medication System Failure is any breakdown in the medication usage process resulting in a preventable event that may cause or lead to inappropriate use or patient harm, while the medication is in the control of the health care professional or patient.

B. Such events may be related to professional practice, health care products, procedures, and systems including: prescribing; order communication; product labeling; packaging and nomenclature; compounding; dispensing; distribution; administration; education; monitoring; or use.

*continues*

**4–98** continued

**PROCEDURE**

A. Medication System Failures that **Do Not** reach the patient.

1. Successful interventions—Medication System Failure that is identified and corrected before it reaches the patient.
2. Noted on Successful Interventions Tally Sheet (AT 2951.1) for purposes of trending and performance improvement (AT 2951.1 is faxed to the Pharmacy weekly).
3. Documentation failure—Medication System Failures when errors are made transcribing and/or charting medication on MARs, IDNs, Diabetic Record, Immunization Record, or any other form critical to the documentation of medication administration.
   a. To be corrected, if appropriate
   b. Noted on Successful Interventions Tally Sheet (AT 2951.1) for purposes of trending and performance improvement.

B. Medication System Failures that **DO** reach the patient.

1. All Medication System Failures that reach the patient are reported on AT-2951 according to severity of patient outcome. See TABLE 1 "Procedures for reporting Medication System Failures that reach the Patient."
2. The section of Medication System Failures Report titled "Severity of Patient Outcome" will be rated and filled out on the unit by a Registered Nurse to expedite appropriate patient care and reporting responsibilities.

**DATA ANALYSIS**

A. Hospital Medication System Failures form AT-2951 will be faxed to the Pharmacy when completed and data will be compiled and analyzed.

B. Successful Intervention Tally Sheet AT-2951.1 will be faxed to the Pharmacy every Monday morning.

C. The Pharmacy Medication System Failures Chairperson will:

1. Designate an ORYX Code to all Medication Systems Failure that reach the patient and report to the ORYX System Administrator in Standards and Compliance.
2. Track all Medication System Failures and Successful Interventions and provide a quarterly summary report to the designated Medication Error Report Coordinator in Standards Compliance, Coordinator of Nursing Service and Program Management.
3. Significant trends and recommendations will be reported to Central Nursing Services, Pharmacy Services Manager, Program Management, Standards Compliance Coordinator, Care of the Patient PMT, and others, as needed.

**QUALITY ASSURANCE**

A. A hospitalwide quality assurance team will be formed to analyze the data collected by the Department of Pharmacy Services. The primary purpose of the QAT will be to advance error prevention by analyzing all

*continues*

4–98 continued

**TABLE 1 Procedures for reporting Medication System Failures that reach the patient:**

| **Outcome Severity Level**<br>**1 = Inconsequential**<br>A med error occurred in which the patient experienced no or minimal adverse consequences and no treatment or intervention other than monitoring or observations was required. | **Outcome Severity Level**<br>**2 = Serious**<br>A med error occurred in which the patient experienced short term, reversible adverse consequences and treatment(s) and/or intervention(s) in addition to monitoring or observation was required. | **Outcome Severity Level**<br>**3 = Critical**<br>A med error occurred in which the patient experienced life-threatening and/or permanent adverse consequences. |
|---|---|---|
| **Employee discovering the system failure will:**<br>1. Evaluate the status of the patient by taking vital signs if applicable and recording the vital signs record (*MH-5749*). Pertinent observations of any signs or symptoms the patient is exhibiting should be noted in the IDNs. (NP 312)<br>2. Notify the Shift Lead in charge of the unit.<br>3. Give supportive care and treatment to the patient as indicated by the situation/physician's orders.<br>4. Initiate and Medication System Failures Form (*AT 2951*).<br>5. Route the form to the pharmacy (via FAX) **AND** HSS. | **Employee discovering the system failure will:**<br>1. Evaluate the status of the patient by taking vital signs if applicable and recording the vital signs record (*MH-5749*). Pertinent observations of any signs or symptoms the patient is exhibiting should be noted in the IDNs. (NP 312)<br>2. Notify the Shift Lead in charge of the unit.<br>3. Give supportive care and treatment to the patient as indicated by the situation/physician's orders.<br>4. Initiate and Medication Systems Failure Form (*AT 2951*).<br>5. Route the form to the pharmacy (via FAX) **AND** HSS.<br>6. Complete an SIR (Special Incident Report *MH-2506*). | **Employee discovering the system failure will:**<br>1. Evaluate the status of the patient by taking vital signs if applicable and recording the vital signs record (*MH-5749*). Pertinent observations of any signs or symptoms the patient is exhibiting should be noted in the IDNs. (NP 312)<br>2. Notify the Shift Lead in charge of the unit.<br>3. Give supportive care and treatment to the patient as indicated by the situation/physician's orders.<br>4. Initiate and Medication System Failures Form (*AT 2951*).<br>5. Route the form to the pharmacy (via FAX) **AND** HSS.<br>6. Complete an SIR (Special Incident Report *MH-2506*). |
| **Shift Lead Will Ensure That:**<br>1. The patient is given supportive care and treatment as appropriate.<br>2. The Unit Psychiatrist/Physician and Program HSS are notified as appropriate.<br>3. The Med System Failures report is initiated.<br>4. Ensure Medication System Failures Report is routed appropriately.<br>5. *After hours NOD is notified at the time the Med System Failure is discovered. | **Shift Lead Will Ensure That:**<br>1. The patient is given supportive care and treatment as appropriate.<br>2. The Unit Psychiatrist/Physician and Program HSS are notified as appropriate.<br>3. The Med System Failure report is initiated.<br>4. *After hours NOD is notified at the time the Med System Failure is discovered.<br>5. Medication System Failure Report is routed appropriately.<br>6. The SIR is written. | **Shift Lead Will Ensure That:**<br>1. The patient is given supportive care and treatment as appropriate.<br>2. The Unit Psychiatrist/Physician and Program HSS are notified as appropriate.<br>3. The Med System Failures Report is initiated.<br>4. *After hours NOD is notified at the time the Med System Failure is discovered.<br>5. Medication System Failures Report is routed appropriately.<br>6. The SIR is written. |
| **NOD will:**<br>*Notify PMOD/MOD, if appropriate. | **NOD will:**<br>*Notify PMOD/MOD. | **NOD will:**<br>*Notify PMOD/MOD. |
| **Program HSS Will:**<br>Review Medication System Failures Reports (AT 2951), summarize the findings and make recommendations to program management where applicable. | **Program HSS Will:**<br>Review Medication System Failure Reports (AT 2951), summarize the findings and make recommendations to program management where applicable. | **Program HSS Will:**<br>Review Medication System Failures Reports (AT 2951), summarize the findings and make recommendations to program management where applicable. |
| | **Unit Supervisor Will:**<br>If further investigation is necessary, the US/HSS will forward the report to the Program Director or designee no later than 72 hours following receipt. | **Unit Supervisor Will:**<br>If further investigation is necessary, the US/HSS will forward the report to the Program Director or designee no later than 72 hours following receipt. |
| **Pharmacy Will:**<br>1. Fill out the ORYX Code section of the form.<br>2. Compile data from the reports. | **Pharmacy Will:**<br>1. Fill out the ORYX Code section of the form.<br>2. Compile data from the reports. | **Pharmacy Will:**<br>1. Fill out the ORYX Code section of the form.<br>2. Compile data from the reports. |

continues

**4–98** continued

pertinent data collected in response to a Medication System Failure to assess the cause and factors contributing to the failure. A record of the findings of the QAT will contain at least:

1. The date, location, and participants in the QA review;
2. The pertinent data and other information related to the Medication System Failure reviewed;
3. The findings and determinations generated by the QA review; and
4. Recommended changes to hospital or pharmacy policy, procedures, systems, or processes, if any.

## PHARMACY SPECIFIC QUALITY ASSURANCE

A. Pharmacy Tote Worksheet (V11.01 or current) will be used by the Pharmacist and Pharmacy Technician in the production of each hospital unit's medication tote to track Medication System Failures that occur in the preparation of the ATC unit dose strip, hand picks, and PRNS to be used in the distribution of medication to the patient. Data will be tracked and analyzed so that changes in pharmacy procedures may be implemented that will improve performance, thus, reducing Medication System Failures.

## ATTACHMENTS

AT 2951—Medication System Failures that reach the patient.
AT2951.1—Successful Intervention Tally Sheet
V11.01—Pharmacy Tote Worksheet
GA536.3—Unit Medication Return Record
GA526—Unit/Pharmacy Daily Fax Communication Sheet

Courtesy of Kenneth Lundgren, Pharm.D., Pharmacy Services Manager, Atascadero State Hospital, Atascadero, California.

*continues*

**4–98** continued

## MEDICATION SYSTEM FAILURES AT 2951

System Failures that reach the patient

| **Patient Name:** | | **AT #:** | | **Unit:** |
|---|---|---|---|---|
| **Date or Order & Duration** | **Medication or Treatment Ordered** | **Strength** | **Route** | **Frequency** |
| | | | | |

**Please Describe the Event:**

| ☐ 1 Wrong Dose | ☐ 2 Wrong Dose | ☐ 3 Wrong Route | ☐ 4 Wrong Time | ☐ 5 Dose Omitted | ☐ 6 Wrong Patent |
|---|---|---|---|---|---|

| **Name of employees involved in the system failure:** |
|---|
| |
| |
| |

| **Physician Notified** | |
|---|---|
| Date: | Time: |
| **HCC/NOD Notified** | |
| Date: | Time: |

**Also check any of the boxes below that best describe the event**

| ☐ **PRESCRIBING MD Order Problems** | ☐ **DISPENSING Pharmacy/NL** | ☐ **TRANSCRIPTION** | ☐ **ADMINISTRATION** |
|---|---|---|---|
| ☐ Illegible MD order<br>☐ No MD signature<br>☐ No date noted<br>☐ No time noted<br>☐ Wrong drug for indication<br>☐ Dose/strength<br>☐ Route<br>☐ Frequency/time interval<br>☐ Start date/time<br>☐ No NTE/duration<br>☐ No PRN indication<br>☐ Over guidelines<br>☐ Non-formulary item<br>☐ Order needs consult<br>☐ Verbal Order not signed<br>☐ Allergy indicated<br>☐ Med contraindicated<br>☐ Sig unclear/confusing<br>☐ Drug/drug interaction<br>☐ Drug/food interaction<br>☐ Problem number issue<br>☐ Un-approved/illegible abbrev.<br>☐ Other Specify: | ☐ Wrong patient<br>☐ Wrong drug<br>☐ Wrong strength<br>☐ Wrong quantity<br>☐ Dose omitted<br>☐ Expired product<br>☐ Start/stop miscalculated<br>☐ Titration miscalculated<br>☐ Known allergy<br>☐ Inaccurate labeling<br>☐ Other specify: | ☐ Patient<br>☐ Drug<br>☐ Strength<br>☐ Directions<br>☐ Duration<br>☐ Frequency<br>☐ Doctor<br>☐ DC date<br>☐ Not noted by Licensed, LOC<br>☐ MAR problem<br>☐ Addressograph problem<br>☐ FAX malfunction<br>☐ Dose given but not charted<br>☐ Other specify: | ☐ Dose not given by charted<br>☐ First dose given too soon/too late<br>☐ One time order only<br>☐ Given more frequently than ordered<br>☐ Given less frequently than ordered<br><br>**Reason for system failure**<br><br>☐ Incorrect ID of patient<br>☐ MAR not checked<br>☐ Forgot<br>☐ Distracted<br>☐ Misread MAR<br>☐ DC date not noticed<br>☐ Misread medication label<br>☐ Dosage miscalculated<br>☐ Stop/start time miscalculated<br>☐ Titration schedule miscalculated<br>☐ Patient allergic/allergy not noticed<br>☐ Other specify: |

| **Severity of Patient Outcome** | | | **Treatment Variance** |
|---|---|---|---|
| ☐ **1 = Inconsequential**<br>A med error occurred in which the patient experienced no or minimal adverse consequences and no treatment or intervention other than monitoring or observations was required. | ☐ **2 = Serious**<br>A med error occurred in which the patient experienced short term, reversible adverse consequences and treatment(s) and or intervention(s) in addition to monitoring or observation were required. | ☐ **3 = Critical**<br>A med error occurred in which the patient experienced life-threatening and or permanent adverse consequences. | ***(number of incidence)*** |

| ☐ **Verbal Counseling** | ☐ **Written Counseling** | ☐ **Retraining** |
|---|---|---|
| Report of Action of Shift Lead: | | |
| | | |

| **ORYX Code—Type of Error**<br>**To be identified by entry staff** | | | |
|---|---|---|---|
| ☐ **1**—Prescribing Error | ☐ **2**—Dispensing Error | ☐ **3**—Administration Error | ☐ **4**—Complex Error |

AT-2951 CNS (Rev. 01/02) (pg 1) (Not to be filed in Patient Unit Record)

*continues*

4–98 continued

**HSS/Review Recommendations (within 72 hrs of receipt of report)**

**Signature:** ______________________ **Date:** ______________

**US Review (Within 72 hours of HSS review, if applicable):**

**Signature:** ______________________ **Date:** ______________

**Program Director/Designee review (if applicable):**

**Signature:** ______________________ **Date:** ______________

AT-2951 CNS (Rev. 01/02) (pg 2) (Not to be filed in Patient Unit Record)

*continues*

**4–98** continued

**Successful Intervention Tally Sheet AT 2951.1**

Medication System Failures that do not reach the patient

Medication system failure was identified and corrected before it reached the patient.

| **Date:** | **Unit:** |
|---|---|

| **PRESCRIBING—MD ORDERS** | |
|---|---|
| Allergy indicated | |
| Blanket order | |
| Consent not obtained | |
| Deviates from protocol | |
| Drug/drug interaction | |
| Drug/food interaction | |
| Frequency/time interval | |
| Hold med—specify med | |
| Hold med—time frame | |
| Illegible order | |
| Incorrect dose/strength | |
| "MAY REFUSE" needed | |
| Med contraindicated | |
| No date or time noted | |
| No dose/strength | |
| No MD signature | |
| No NTE/duration | |
| No PRN clarification | |
| Nonformulary item | |
| Nonformulary item | |
| Order confusing | |
| Order needs consult | |
| Over guidelines no consult | |
| Preexisting drug therapy | |
| Problem number issue | |
| Route | |
| Start date/time | |
| Unapproved/illegible abbrev. | |
| **VO/TO**—Order not signed | |
| Wrong drug for indication | |
| | |
| **DISPENSING/PHARMACY** | |
| Dose omitted | |
| Expired product | |
| Known allergy | |
| Label problem | |
| Start/stop miscalculated | |
| Titration miscalculated | |
| Wrong dosage Form | |
| Wrong drug | |
| Wrong patient | |
| Wrong quantity | |
| Wrong strength | |
| | |
| | |
| **ATC Machine Problems** | |
| Crushed Tablet | |
| Missing Tablet | |
| Multiple Tablets | |
| | |
| | |
| | |
| | |
| | |
| | |
| | |

| **PHARMACY AUTOMATION** | |
|---|---|
| Addressograph problem | |
| DC missed | |
| FAX malfunction | |
| Incorrect prescription (directions) | |
| Incorrect titration | |
| NTE missed | |
| Order duplicated | |
| Order omitted | |
| Patient admit | |
| Patient transfer | |
| Wrong DC date | |
| Wrong doctor | |
| Wrong dosage form | |
| Wrong drug | |
| Wrong duration | |
| Wrong frequency | |
| Wrong patient | |
| Wrong route | |
| Wrong start date | |
| Wrong strength | |
| Wrong time | |
| Wrong unit | |
| | |
| **DOSE ADMINISTRATION** | |
| Wrong Patient | |
| Wrong Drug | |
| Wrong Dose | |
| Wrong Route | |
| Wrong Time | |
| Dose Omitted | |
| | |
| **UNIT TRANSCRIPTION** | |
| Alteration (e.g., whiteout, felt pen) | |
| Diet order not faxed | |
| Incorrect DC date | |
| Lab slip not made out | |
| Med/Tx given without an order | |
| Missing blood glucose notation | |
| Missing initial as med given | |
| Missing frequency | |
| No cosign | |
| No MD signature | |
| No NTE | |
| No observed PRN agitation on MAR | |
| No pre/post vital signs | |
| No PRN effectiveness charted | |
| No problem number | |
| No reason for refuse/omit on MAR | |
| No signature at bottom of MAR | |
| No site of injection | |
| No start/stop date or time | |
| Order not noted | |
| Order not signed within 48 hours | |
| PRN missing time intervals | |
| STAT/now orders not chart pg. 2 | |
| Other: | |
| | |

1. **Use Hash marks to indicate number of incidents.**
2. **Begin a new tally sheet each week.**
3. **FAX tally sheet to Pharmacy Monday of every week.**

☐ **FAXED** ______________

Initial & Date—Fax to Pharmacy Weekly

AT-Proposed 2951.1 CNS (New 01/02) (Not to be filed in Patient Unit Record)

*continues*

**4–98** continued

PHARMACY TOTE WORKSHEET V11.01

**UNIT** ______

**EXCHANGE DATES** ______

**START TIME** ______

**FINISH TIME** ______

UNIT CONCERNS

**MISSING PATIENT BAGS** ______

**MISSING PRNS BAGS** ______

**REPLACE SOILED BAGS** ______

**MISSING RETURN TO PHARMACY BAGS** ______

MEDICAL RECORDS CONCERNS

**ANY DOSE CHANGE OR CORRECTIONS** ______

**TRANSFER OR NEW ADMIT CORRECTION** ______

**TECHNICIAN TOTE** ______

**DAYS OF FILL** ______

**TO** ______

**START TIME** ______

**FINISH TIME** ______

ATC CONCERNS

**REPLACE CRUSHED OR BROKEN TABS** ______

**EMPTY POUCHES FILLED** ______

**EXTRA MEDS IN POUCH CORRECTED** ______

**EXTRA EMPTY POUCHES REMOVED** ______

**UTC TAPING** ______

**TECHNICIAN STRAP** ______

**START TIME** ______

**FINISH TIME** ______

UNIT CONCERNS

**MISSING PATIENT BAGS** ______

**MISSING PRNS BAGS** ______

**MISC. (explain)** ______

ATC CONCERNS

**REPLACE CRUSHED OR BROKEN TABS** ______

**EMPTY POUCHES FILLED** ______

**EXTRA MEDS IN POUCH CORRECTED** ______

**EXTRA EMPTY POUCHES REMOVED** ______

**UTC TAPING** ______

**MISC. (explain)** ______

**TOTAL TAG NUMBER** ______

TECH FILLING CONCERNS

**TOO MANY PRN'S** ______

**NOT ENOUGH PRN'S** ______

**TOO MANY HANDPICKS** ______

**NOT ENOUGH HANDPICKS** ______

**WRONG DRUGS (DOSE)** ______

**OUTDATED DRUGS** ______

**MISC. (explain)** ______

MEDICAL RECORDS CONCERNS

**ANY DOSE CHANGE OR CORRECTIONS** ______

**TRANSFER OR NEW ADMIT CORRECTION** ______

**MISC. (explain)** ______

**PHARMACIST** ______

**UNIT SIGNATURE** ______

*continues*

**4–98** continued

Atascadero State Hospital
**Unit Medication Return Record**

Unit:

**Other Return Codes:**

| | | |
|---|---|---|
| 5 Start time miscalculated | 9 Patient off unit | 13 Over sedated or condition being evaluated |
| 6 Stop time miscalculated | 10 Discharged from ASH | 14 Titration schedule changed |
| 7 No existing order/not on med | 11 Patient nauseated | 15 |
| 8 Titration miscalculated | 12 Dose held | 16 |

| Patient Name & AT # | Medication | Date(s) of dose | Which doses? noon dose, am's only, this pm, all remaining doses, etc. | Check Reason for Return | | | | |
|---|---|---|---|---|---|---|---|---|
| | | | | 1 Med DC'd | 2 Dose Change | 3 Dose Refused | 4 NL Used Leftover | Other Code ↓ |
| | | | | | | | | |
| | | | | | | | | |
| | | | | | | | | |
| | | | | | | | | |
| | | | | | | | | |
| | | | | | | | | |
| | | | | | | | | |
| | | | | | | | | |
| | | | | | | | | |
| | | | | | | | | |
| | | | | | | | | |
| | | | | | | | | |
| | | | | | | | | |
| | | | | | | | | |
| | | | | | | | | |
| | | | | | | | | |
| | | | | | | | | |
| | | | | | | | | |

**Return sheet with doses in tote bag on the day of exchange**

GA 536.3 Pharm Rev. 12-11-01

*continues*

4–98 continued

Atascadero State Hospital
Unit/Pharmacy Daily Fax Communication Sheet

| Date: | Unit: |
|---|---|

**FAX to Pharmacy at ext. 3361 ("Disp" Button)**

| | | | | | Pharmacy Use Only | |
|---|---|---|---|---|---|---|
| **Patient Name And AT Number** | **Date of Order** | **Med Name Strength Schedule** | **# of Doses Needed** | **Reason Code See Codes Below** | **Amount Sent** Pharmacy Tech | **Checked By** Pharmacist |
| | | | | | | |
| | | | | | | |
| | | | | | | |
| | | | | | | |
| | | | | | | |
| | | | | | | |
| | | | | | | |
| | | | | | | |
| | | | | | | |
| | | | | | | |
| | | | | | | |

**Reason Codes:**

| | |
|---|---|
| 1—Dose dropped or fell out of strip | 4—Pt spit out or vomited medications |
| 2—Dose changed/recent new order | 5—Missing medication—was picked up from pharmacy |
| 3—Pt refused then changed mind | 6—Missing medication—NOT prepared by pharmacy |

1. **Use FAX sheet 1 time only**
   **(or cross out items when received so pharmacy does not duplicate your request.)**
2. **Save FAX sheets for 30 days**

| Staff Name: Please Print Legibly |
|---|

GA 526 (Rev. 1/09/02)

## 4–99
## Pharmacy Technician Level I Job Description and Performance Appraisal

TITLE: Pharmacy Technician – Level I POSITION NUMBER: ____________

DEPARTMENT: Pharmacy APPROVED BY: ____________

REPORTS TO: Pharmacist DATE: ____________

NAME: ____________ REVIEW DATE: ____________ SCORE: ____________

**JOB SUMMARY:**

Utilizing special knowledge and background of drug terminology, assists pharmacist in the preparation and delivery of medications. Helps maintain records and drug inventories. Maintains dispensing and storeroom areas in neat, clean, and stocked condition for safe and efficient operation of the Pharmacy. Assists pharmacist and the Pharmacy in provision or required services and meeting goals and objectives.

**JOB QUALIFICATIONS:**

Education: Requires high school or equivalent; general knowledge of high school subject matter possibly including sciences, simple medical procedures or terminology or office equipment.

Experience: Requires a minimum of six months but less than one year of experience on this and related jobs.

**PHYSICAL AND MENTAL EFFORTS:**

Physical: Requires light physical effort on a regular basis, as in frequent standing, walking, bending, stooping or reaching, and/or occasional lifting of light items (i.e., up to 20 lbs.). Periodic eye or ear strain included in this level (less than 50% of the time).

Mental: Occasional stress due to periodic or cyclical workload pressures.

**CONTACTS:**

Requires internal and/or external contact on routine matters, supplying or seeking information related to work being done.

**ENVIRONMENTAL AND WORKING CONDITIONS:**

One or a few unpleasant conditions routinely present (cramped working space, drafty area, poor lighting, inadequate equipment or furnishings).

Rev. 8/00

*continues*

4–99 continued

**Pharmacy Technician Level I - Responsibilities and Standards**

**Rating Scale:** **0 = Below Expectations**

1. Prepares medications for dispensing under the direct supervision of the pharmacist, demonstrating accuracy, precision, and consistency relating to selection, packaging, and labeling functions.

1-1 Accurately prepares medication for dispensing from computer fill lists, physician order copies, or other request forms, using approved policies and procedures. Maintains an average bin fill error rate of 1% or less (reported errors divided by number of lines filled) within review year.

**Exceeds:** Maintains an average bin fill error rate of 0.5% or less (reported errors divided by number of lines filled) within review year with no occasion when error leads to medication error as determined by incident reports. 0 3 4

1-2 Fills assigned unit dose cassettes and prepares and labels medications in a timely manner to maintain established delivery schedules, with no more than two (2) occasions per review year when assignment not completed on time, as observed by pharmacist.

**Exceeds:** Always completes assignment as assigned within review year, as observed by pharmacist. 0 2 3

1-3 Accurately prepares stock solutions to maintain appropriate inventory levels, utilizing formula worksheets with no more than two (2) occasions within review year relating to using improper procedures or documentation, and/or allowing inventories to be depleted, as observed by the pharmacist.

**Exceeds:** No more than one occasion within review year relating to using improper procedures or documentation, and/or allowing inventories to be depleted, as observed by pharmacist. **0** **1** 2

1-4 Prepares sterile products according to approved procedures, documentation requirements, and aseptic technique. Meets standard: No more than two (2) instances of documentation/preparation errors, or breakdown in aseptic technique as evidenced by pharmacist inspection or department certification review.

**Exceeds:** No instances of documentation/preparation errors, or breakdown in aseptic technique as evidenced by pharmacist inspection or department certification review. 0 2 3

1-5 According to hospital policies and procedures, recycles injectable premixed sterile products with no more than two (2) lost products due to improper recycling procedure.

**Exceeds:** No loss of product due to improper recycling procedure. 0 1 2

1-6 Repackages medications according to department policies maintaining proper manufacturing documentation and assuring all work is checked by pharmacist. Meets standards: No more than two (2) instances in review year when work must be repeated because of failure to follow proper procedure, or product integrity is not assured.

**Exceeds:** No instances in review year when work must be repeated because of failure to follow proper procedure, or product integrity is not assured. 0 2 3

*continues*

**4–99** continued

1-7 Prepares controlled drugs for substocks on the nursing units. Accurately performs record keeping and prepares documents for use on the nursing units. Resolves all record keeping and inventory discrepancies. Work is spot checked by a pharmacist prior to dispensing. All errors or problems are reported to the Director of Pharmacy.

**Exceeds:** No instances in review year when performed incorrectly. 0 2 3

1-8 Prepares lock boxes for anesthesia and PACU following prescribed department policies and procedures. Resolves record keeping errors and reports to the Director of Pharmacy. No more than two (2) occasions within review year when done incorrectly.

**Exceeds:** No instances in review year when performed incorrectly. 0 2 3

1-9 Screens phone calls and visitors to minimize pharmacist interruptions. Assists the pharmacist by charging for and screening information for missed doses. All complete work is checked and approved by a pharmacist prior to dispensing. No more than two (2) instances of non-compliance.

**Exceeds:** No instances in review year of non-compliance. 0 2 3

1-10 Performs weekly controlled substance inventories, prepares controlled drug orders, receives controlled drug merchandise, accurately maintains all related records reporting any discrepancies immediately to the Director of Pharmacy. This includes weekly safe and Pyxis floor counts as well as return bin procedures. No more than two (2) instances of non-compliance.

**Exceeds:** No instances in review year when not performed or performed incorrectly as assigned. 0 3 4

1-11 Prepares code cart trays and special kits for nursing units. No more than two (2) instances when not done properly.

**Exceeds:** No occasions in review year when performed incorrectly. 0 1 2

CALCULATION OF MERIT INDEX FOR THIS RESPONSIBILITY

| Points Received | / | Total Points |
|---|---|---|
| ______ | / | 32 |

Comments: ______________________________

______________________________

______________________________

2. Distributes medications as required, to all patient care areas of the hospital.

2-1 Accurately and efficiently delivers medications to patient care areas, according to established schedules, assuring timely provision of medications to patients with no more than two (2) incorrect or missed deliveries within review year, as observed by pharmacist.

**Exceeds:** No incorrect or missed deliveries within review year, as observed by pharmacist. 0 1 2

*continues*

**4–99** continued

2-2 Consistently and thoroughly checks patients, medication bins at the time of exchange, to assure all needed medications are transferred to current bin with no occasions within review year when a patient suffers harm because a medication was not transferred to current bin. No more than two (2) occasions within review year when medication error results because medication was not transferred to current bin at exchange time.

**Exceeds:** No occasions within review year of medication error because of failure to transfer a medication to current bin at exchange time. 0 1 2

2-3 Delivers all medications reliably without breakage or spillage with no more than two (2) occasions within review year when additional medication must be prepared and dispensed, as a result of breakage or spillage.

**Exceeds:** No occasions within review year, when additional medication must be prepared and dispensed as a result of breakage or spillage. 0 1 2

2-4 Reviews and monitors night cabinet for outdated medications as assigned. No more than two (2) instances in review year when not performed properly.

**Exceeds:** No instances within review year of non-compliance. 0 1 2

2-5 Prepares Central Supply order properly as assigned. No more than two (2) instances when not done properly.

**Exceeds:** No instances of non-compliance. 0 1 2

2-6 Reviews and restocks night medication cabinet daily as assigned. Charges for medications and replaces stock in the appropriate locations. Meets standards: No more than two (2) occasions in review year when night medication cabinet is improperly restocked or charges are lost.

**Exceeds:** No occasions in review year when night medication cabinet is improperly restocked or charges are lost. 0 1 2

CALCULATION OF MERIT INDEX FOR THIS RESPONSIBILITY

| Points Received | / | Total Points |
|---|---|---|
| ______ | / | 12 |

Comments: ____________________

____________________

____________________

3. Records – Assists in the creation, handling, and maintenance of a variety of pharmacy records, to promote efficient operation of the pharmacy and regulatory compliance.

3-1 As assigned, obtains daily patient census, accurately updates Patient Medication drawers regarding admissions, discharges, and transfers, as observed by pharmacist with no more than two (2) occasions within review year when medication drawers are improperly maintained according to census report.

**Exceeds:** No occasions within review year when profiles are improperly filed, according to census report. 0 1 2

*continues*

**4–99** continued

3-2 Accurately and reliably files medication orders and requests for specific patient, as observed by pharmacist. Orders are filed at least daily and no more than three occasions of omission or improper filing within review year, as observed by pharmacist.

0 1 (NA)

3-3 Accurately, consistently, and legibly records quantities of medications to be charged to patients, on computer lists when filling daily medications with no more than two (2) occasions within review year when quantities are improperly charged.

**Exceeds:** No occasions within review year when quantities are improperly charged.

0 1 2

3-4 Accurately records quantities of medications issued when filling floor stock requests with no more than two (2) occasions within review year when quantities to be issued are omitted or incorrect as determined by review of the requisition.

**Exceeds:** No occasions within review year when quantities to be issued are omitted and incorrect, as determined by review of the requests for items filled, as determined by a review of the request. 0 1 2

CALCULATION OF MERIT INDEX FOR THIS RESPONSIBILITY

| Points Received | / | Total Points |
|---|---|---|
| ______ | / | 7 |

Comments: ____________________________________________

____________________________________________

____________________________________________

4. Assists in maintaining proper inventory and control of drugs and supplies purchased by the Pharmacy.

4-1 Accurately documents quantities of medications received from vendors, and initials receiving document, as observed by direct review, and places price stickers on merchandise with no more than two (2) occasions within review year when required documentation is missing or inaccurate by direct review.

**Exceeds:** No occasions within review year when required documentation is missing or inaccurate. 0 1 2

4-2 Maintains orderly stock levels of all medications in dispensing area, to facilitate the proper and timely filling of medication orders, as observed by pharmacist. Dispensing area and work station are consistently and adequately stocked with medications as observed by pharmacist. This includes IV room stock replenishment as well as customized floor stock replenishment duty as assigned. No more than two (2) occasions when not performed properly.

**Exceeds:** No instances in review year of non-compliance. 0 1 2

4-3 Reliably and accurately records medications in order book when necessary to reorder, as observed by review of the record with no more than two (2) occasions within review year when stock depletion

*continues*

**4–99** continued

is due to individual failure to reorder. No more than two (2) occasions within review year when stock depletion occurs as result of individual error in ordering correct item.

**Exceeds:** No occasions within review year when individual failure to order, or order correctly, results in stock depletion. 0 1 2

4-4 Reviews and places wholesaler orders as required. Anticipates requirements, orders appropriate quantities, and follows up problems with the pharmacy purchasing coordinator. No more than two (2) occasions when not done properly.

**Exceeds:** No occasions in review year when order does not come in or is placed incorrectly. 0 1 2

CALCULATION OF MERIT INDEX FOR THIS RESPONSIBILITY

| Points Received | / | Total Points |
|---|---|---|
| ______ | / | 8 |

Comments: ______________________________

______________________________

______________________________

5. Maintains dispensing area and medication storeroom in neat, orderly, and clean condition, as observed by pharmacist.

5-1 Drugs stored in dispensing area and work stations are maintained in a neat and orderly condition at all times, to reduce potential for errors, as observed by pharmacist. Drugs are not routinely found missing, misplaced, or disorganized in dispensing area and work stations, as observed by pharmacist. 0 1 (NA)

5-2 Removes outdated medications from stock when assigned monthly and properly segregates outdated drugs to prevent issuance, as observed by pharmacist with no more than two (2) occasions within review year when outdated medications are not removed, as observed by pharmacist. This includes main pharmacy and Pyxis stock.

**Exceeds:** No occasions within review year when outdated medication review is not performed when assigned. 0 2 3

5-3 Consistently maintains work station in a neat, clean, and orderly condition. As observed by pharmacist, keeps work station neat, picked-up, and free from debris. 0 1 (NA)

CALCULATION OF MERIT INDEX FOR THIS RESPONSIBILITY

| Points Received | / | Total Points |
|---|---|---|
| ______ | / | 5 |

Comments: ______________________________

______________________________

*continues*

4–99 continued

## GOALS FOR DEVELOPMENT OR PLAN FOR PERFORMANCE IMPROVEMENT

| | GOAL | TARGET DATE | INDIVIDUAL RESPONSIBLE |
|---|---|---|---|
| 1. | | | |
| 2. | | | |
| 3. | | | |
| 4. | | | |

## OVERALL PERFORMANCE RATING

| RESPONSIBILITY | POINTS RECEIVED | POINTS POSSIBLE |
|---|---|---|
| 1. | | 32 |
| 2. | | 12 |
| 3. | | 7 |
| 4. | | 8 |
| 5. | | 5 |
| TOTAL | | 64 |

**EVALUATOR'S COMMENTS:**

**EMPLOYEE'S COMMENTS:**

## ADMINISTRATIVE REVIEW

| | | |
|---|---|---|
| EMPLOYEE'S SIGNATURE | TITLE | DATE |
| EVALUATOR'S SIGNATURE | TITLE | DATE |
| SENIOR EVALUATOR'S SIGNATURE | TITLE | DATE |

Courtesy of Faxton St. Luke's Health Care, New Hartford, New York.

# 4–100
# Pharmacy Technician Level II Job Description and Performance Appraisal

TITLE: Pharmacy Technician – Level II POSITION NUMBER: ____________

DEPARTMENT: Pharmacy APPROVED BY: ____________

REPORTS TO: Pharmacist DATE: ____________

NAME: ____________ REVIEW DATE: ____________ SCORE: ____________

**JOB SUMMARY:**

Utilizing special knowledge and background of drug terminology, assists pharmacist in the preparation and delivery of medications. Helps maintain records and drug inventories. Maintains dispensing and storeroom areas in neat, clean, and stocked condition for safe and efficient operation of the Pharmacy. Assists pharmacist and the Pharmacy in provision or required services and meeting goals and objectives.

**JOB QUALIFICATIONS:**

Education: Requires high school or equivalent; general knowledge of high school subject matter possibly including sciences, simple medical procedures or terminology or office equipment.

Experience: Requires a minimum of six months but less than one year of experience on this and related jobs.

**PHYSICAL AND MENTAL EFFORTS:**

Physical: Requires light physical effort on a regular basis, as in frequent standing, walking, bending, stooping or reaching, and/or occasional lifting of light items (i.e., up to 20 lbs.). Periodic eye or ear strain included in this level (less than 50% of the time).

Mental: Occasional stress due to periodic or cyclical workload pressures.

**CONTACTS:**

Requires internal and/or external contact on routine matters, supplying or seeking information related to work being done.

**ENVIRONMENTAL AND WORKING CONDITIONS:**

One or a few unpleasant conditions routinely present (cramped working space, drafty area, poor lighting, inadequate equipment or furnishings).

Rev. 9/00

*continues*

**4–100** continued

**Pharmacy Technician Level II - Responsibilities and Standards**

**Rating Scale:** **0 = Below Expectations**

1. Prepares medications for dispensing under the direct supervision of the pharmacist, demonstrating accuracy, precision, and consistency relating to selection, packaging, and labeling functions.

1-1 Accurately prepares medication for dispensing from computer fill lists, physician order copies, or other request forms, using approved policies and procedures. Maintains an average bin fill error rate of 1% or less (reported errors divided by number of lines filled) within review year.

**Exceeds:** Maintains an average bin fill error rate of 0.5% or less (reported errors divided by number of lines filled) within review year with no occasion when error leads to medication error as determined by incident reports. 0 1 2

1-2 Fills assigned unit dose cassettes and prepares and labels medications in a timely manner to maintain established delivery schedules, with no more than two (2) occasions per review year when assignment not completed on time, as observed by pharmacist.

**Exceeds:** Always completes assignment as assigned within review year, as observed by pharmacist. 0 1 2

1-3 Accurately prepares stock solutions to maintain appropriate inventory levels, utilizing formula worksheets with no more than two (2) occasions within review year relating to using improper procedures or documentation, and/or allowing inventories to be depleted, as observed by the pharmacist.

**Exceeds:** No more than one occasion within review year relating to using improper procedures or documentation, and/or allowing inventories to be depleted, as observed by pharmacist.

**0** **1** 2

1-4 Prepares enhanced sterile product medications including hyperalimentation, control drug drips, Persantine, Sandostatin, epidurals, IVIG, and primes tubing for chemotherapy products. Follows approved policies and procedures with proper documentation and aseptic technique. Meets standard: No more than two (2) instances of documentation where products need to be remade due to improper mixing technique as evidenced by pharmacist inspection or department review.

**Exceeds:** No instances of documentation where product needs to be remade due to improper mixing technique as evidenced by pharmacist inspection or department review. 0 2 3

1-5 According to hospital policies and procedures, recycles injectable premixed sterile products with no more than two (2) lost products due to improper recycling procedure.

**Exceeds:** No loss of product due to improper recycling procedure. 0 1 2

1-6 Repackages medications according to department policies maintaining proper manufacturing documentation and assuring all work is checked by pharmacist. Meets standards: No more than two (2) instances in review year when work must be repeated because of failure to follow proper procedure, or product integrity is not assured.

**Exceeds:** No instances in review year when work must be repeated because of failure to follow proper procedure, or product integrity is not assured. 0 2 3

1-7 Prepares controlled drugs for substocks on the nursing units. Accurately performs record keeping and prepares documents for use on the nursing units. Resolves all record keeping and inventory

*continues*

**4–100** continued

discrepancies. Work is spot checked by a pharmacist prior to dispensing. All errors or problems are reported to the Director of Pharmacy.

**Exceeds:** No instances in review year when performed incorrectly. 0 2 3

1-8 Prepares lock boxes for anesthesia and PACU following prescribed department policies and procedures. Resolves record keeping errors and reports to the Director of Pharmacy. No more than two (2) occasions within review year when done incorrectly.

**Exceeds:** No instances in review year when performed incorrectly. 0 2 3

1-9 Screens phone calls and visitors to minimize pharmacist interruptions. Assists the pharmacist by charging for and screening information for missed doses. All complete work is checked and approved by a pharmacist prior to dispensing. No more than two (2) instances of non-compliance.

**Exceeds:** No instances in review year of non-compliance. 0 2 3

1-10 Performs weekly controlled substance inventories, prepares controlled drug orders, receives controlled drug merchandise, accurately maintains all related records reporting any discrepancies immediately to the Director of Pharmacy. This includes weekly safe and Pyxis floor counts as well as return bin procedures. No more than two (2) instances of non-compliance.

**Exceeds:** No instances in review year when not performed or performed incorrectly as assigned.

0 3 4

1-11 Prepares code cart trays and special kits for nursing units. No more than two (2) instances when not done properly.

**Exceeds:** No occasions in review year when performed incorrectly. 0 1 2

1-12 Prepares enhanced sterile product medications and performs needed calculations to determine amount of medication to be added in preparing final product. Meets standard: No more than two (2) instances of documentation where final product needs to be remade due to incorrect calculations as evidenced by pharmacist inspection or department review.

**Exceeds:** No instances of documentation where final product needs to be remade due to incorrect calculations as evidenced by pharmacist inspection or department review. 0 1 2

1-13 Prepares enhanced sterile product medications and consistently meets timeliness of preparation within established schedules, policies, and guidelines. Meets standard: No more than two (2) instances of documentation where intervention was needed because technician was unable to meet timeliness of service as evidenced by pharmacist inspection or department review.

**Exceeds:** No instances of documentation where intervention was needed because technician was unable to meet timeliness of service as evidenced by pharmacist inspection or department review.

0 1 2

CALCULATION OF MERIT INDEX FOR THIS RESPONSIBILITY

| Points Received | / | Total Points |
|---|---|---|
| ______ | / | 33 |

Comments: ____________________________________________

____________________________________________

____________________________________________

*continues*

**4–100** continued

2. Distributes medications as required, to all patient care areas of the hospital.

2-1 Accurately and efficiently delivers medications to patient care areas, according to established schedules, assuring timely provision of medications to patients with no more than two (2) incorrect or missed deliveries within review year, as observed by pharmacist.

**Exceeds:** No incorrect or missed deliveries within review year, as observed by pharmacist.

0 1 2

2-2 Consistently and thoroughly checks patients, medication bins at the time of exchange, to assure all needed medications are transferred to current bin with no occasions within review year when a patient suffers harm because a medication was not transferred to current bin. No more than two (2) occasions within review year when medication error results because medication was not transferred to current bin at exchange time.

**Exceeds:** No occasions within review year of medication error because of failure to transfer a medication to current bin at exchange time. 0 1 2

2-3 Delivers all medications reliably without breakage or spillage with no more than two (2) occasions within review year when additional medication must be prepared and dispensed as a result of breakage or spillage.

**Exceeds:** No occasions within review year when additional medication must be prepared and dispensed as result of breakage or spillage. 0 1 2

2-4 Reviews and monitors night cabinet for outdated medications as assigned. No more than two (2) instances in review year when not performed properly.

**Exceeds:** No instances review year of non-compliance. 0 1 2

2-5 Prepares Central Supply order properly as assigned. No more than two (2) instances when not done properly.

**Exceeds:** No instances of non-compliance. 0 1 2

2-6 Reviews and restocks night medication cabinet daily as assigned. Charges for medications and replaces stock in the appropriate locations. Meets standards: No more than two (2) occasions in review year when night medication cabinet is improperly restocked or charges are lost.

**Exceeds:** No occasions in review year when night medication cabinet is improperly restocked or charges are lost. 0 1 2

CALCULATION OF MERIT INDEX FOR THIS RESPONSIBILITY

| Points Received | / | Total Points |
|---|---|---|
| ______ | / | 12 |

Comments: ____________________________________________

____________________________________________

____________________________________________

3. Records – Assists in the creation, handling, and maintenance of a variety of pharmacy records, to promote efficient operation of the pharmacy and regulatory compliance.

*continues*

**4–100** continued

3-1 As assigned, obtains daily patient census, accurately updates Patient Medication drawers regarding admissions, discharges, and transfers, as observed by pharmacist with no more than two (2) occasions within review year, when medication drawers are improperly maintained according to census report.

**Exceeds:** No occasions within review year when profiles are improperly filed, according to census report. 0 1 2

3-2 Accurately and reliably files medication orders and requests for specific patient, as observed by pharmacist. Orders are filed at least daily and no more than three occasions of omission or improper filing, within review year, as observed by pharmacist.

0 1 (NA)

3-3 Accurately, consistently, and legibly records quantities of medications to be charged to patients on computer lists when filling daily medications with no more than two (2) occasions within review year when quantities are improperly charged.

**Exceeds:** No occasions within review year when quantities are improperly charged. 0 1 2

3-4 Accurately records quantities of medications issued when filling floor stock requests with no more than two (2) occasions within review year when quantities to be issued are omitted or incorrect as determined by review of the requisition.

**Exceeds:** No occasions within review year when quantities to be issued are omitted and incorrect, as determined by review of the requests for items filled, as determined by a review of the request.

0 1 2

CALCULATION OF MERIT INDEX FOR THIS RESPONSIBILITY

| Points Received | / | Total Points |
|---|---|---|
| ______ | / | 7 |

Comments: ____________________________________________

____________________________________________

____________________________________________

4. Assists in maintaining proper inventory and control of drugs and supplies purchased by the Pharmacy.

4-1 Accurately documents quantities of medications received from vendors, and initials receiving document, as observed by direct review, and places price stickers on merchandise with no more than two (2) occasions within review year when required documentation is missing or inaccurate by direct review.

**Exceeds:** No occasions within review year when required documentation is missing or inaccurate.

0 1 2

4-2 Maintains orderly stock levels of all medications in dispensing area to facilitate the proper and timely filling of medication orders, as observed by pharmacist. Dispensing area and work station are consistently and adequately stocked with medications as observed by pharmacist. This includes IV room stock replenishment as well as customized floor stock replenishment duty as assigned. No more than two (2) occasions when not performed properly.

**Exceeds:** No instances in review year of non-compliance. 0 1 2

*continues*

**4–100** continued

4-3 Reliably and accurately, records medications in order book when necessary to reorder, as observed by review of the record with no more than two (2) occasions within review year, when stock depletion is due to individual failure to reorder. No more than two (2) occasions within review year, when stock depletion occurs as result of individual error in ordering correct item.

**Exceeds:** No occasions within review year when individual failure to order, or order correctly, results in stock depletion. 0 1 2

4-4 Reviews and places wholesaler orders as required. Anticipates requirements, orders appropriate quantities, and follows up problems with the pharmacy purchasing coordinator. No more than two (2) occasions when not done properly.

**Exceeds:** No occasions in review year when order does not come in or is placed incorrectly. 0 1 2

CALCULATION OF MERIT INDEX FOR THIS RESPONSIBILITY

| Points Received | / | Total Points |
|---|---|---|
| ______ | / | 8 |

Comments: ________________________________________

________________________________________

________________________________________

5. Maintains dispensing area and medication storeroom in neat, orderly, and clean condition, as observed by pharmacist.

5-1 Drugs stored in dispensing area and work stations are maintained in a neat and orderly condition at all times to reduce potential for errors, as observed by pharmacist. Drugs are not routinely found missing, misplaced, or disorganized in dispensing area and work stations, as observed by pharmacist. 0 1 (NA)

5-2 Removes outdated medications from stock when assigned monthly and properly segregates outdated drugs to prevent issuance, as observed by pharmacist with no more than two (2) occasions within review year when outdated medications are not removed, as observed by pharmacist. This includes main pharmacy and Pyxis stock.

**Exceeds:** No occasions within review year, when outdated medication review is not performed when assigned. 0 2 3

5-3 Consistently maintains work station in a neat, clean, and orderly condition. As observed by pharmacist, keeps work station neat, picked-up, and free from debris. 0 1 (NA)

CALCULATION OF MERIT INDEX FOR THIS RESPONSIBILITY

| Points Received | / | Total Points |
|---|---|---|
| ______ | / | 5 |

Comments: ________________________________________

________________________________________

*continues*

4–100 continued

## GOALS FOR DEVELOPMENT OR PLAN FOR PERFORMANCE IMPROVEMENT

| | GOAL | TARGET DATE | INDIVIDUAL RESPONSIBLE |
|---|---|---|---|
| 1. | ________ | ________ | ________ |
| 2. | ________ | ________ | ________ |
| 3. | ________ | ________ | ________ |
| 4. | ________ | ________ | ________ |

## OVERALL PERFORMANCE RATING

| RESPONSIBILITY | POINTS RECEIVED | POINTS POSSIBLE |
|---|---|---|
| 1. | ________ | 33 |
| 2. | ________ | 12 |
| 3. | ________ | 7 |
| 4. | ________ | 8 |
| 5. | ________ | 5 |
| TOTAL | ________ | 65 |

**EVALUATOR'S COMMENTS:**

**EMPLOYEE'S COMMENTS:**

## ADMINISTRATIVE REVIEW

| EMPLOYEE'S SIGNATURE | TITLE | DATE |
|---|---|---|
| EVALUATOR'S SIGNATURE | TITLE | DATE |
| SENIOR EVALUATOR'S SIGNATURE | TITLE | DATE |

Courtesy of Faxton St. Luke's Health Care, New Hartford, New York.

# 4–101
# Pharmacy Technician Level III Job Description and Performance Appraisal

TITLE: Pharmacy Technician – Level III POSITION NUMBER: ____________

DEPARTMENT: Pharmacy APPROVED BY: ____________

REPORTS TO: Pharmacist DATE: ____________

NAME: ____________ REVIEW DATE: ____________ SCORE: ____________

**JOB SUMMARY:**

Utilizing special knowledge and background of drug terminology, assists pharmacist in the preparation and delivery of medications. Helps maintain records and drug inventories. Maintains dispensing and storeroom areas in neat, clean, and stocked condition for safe and efficient operation of the Pharmacy. Assists pharmacist and the Pharmacy in provision or required services and meeting goals and objectives.

**JOB QUALIFICATIONS:**

Education: Requires high school or equivalent; general knowledge of high school subject matter possibly including sciences, simple medical procedures or terminology or office equipment.

Experience: Requires a minimum of six months but less than one year of experience on this and related jobs.

**PHYSICAL AND MENTAL EFFORTS:**

Physical: Requires light physical effort on a regular basis, as in frequent standing, walking, bending, stooping or reaching, and/or occasional lifting of light items (i.e., up to 20 lbs.). Periodic eye or ear strain included in this level (less than 50% of the time).

Mental: Occasional stress due to periodic or cyclical workload pressures.

**CONTACTS:**

Requires internal and/or external contact on routine matters, supplying or seeking information related to work being done.

**ENVIRONMENTAL AND WORKING CONDITIONS:**

One or a few unpleasant conditions routinely present (cramped working space, drafty area, poor lighting, inadequate equipment or furnishings).

Rev. 9/00

*continues*

**4–101** continued

**Pharmacy Technician Level III - Responsibilities and Standards**

**Rating Scale:** **0 = Below Expectations**

1. Prepares medications for dispensing under the direct supervision of the pharmacist, demonstrating accuracy, precision, and consistency relating to selection, packaging, and labeling functions.

   1-1 Accurately prepares medication for dispensing from computer fill lists, physician order copies, or other request forms, using approved policies and procedures. Maintains an average bin fill error rate of 1% or less (reported errors divided by number of lines filled) within review year.

   **Exceeds:** Maintains an average bin fill error rate of 0.5% or less (reported errors divided by number of lines filled) within review year with no occasion when error leads to medication error as determined by incident reports. 0 1 2

   1-2 Fills assigned unit dose cassettes and prepares and labels medications in a timely manner to maintain established delivery schedules, with no more than two (2) occasions per review year when assignment not completed on time, as observed by pharmacist.

   **Exceeds:** Always completes assignment as assigned within review year, as observed by pharmacist. 0 1 2

   1-3 Accurately prepares stock solutions to maintain appropriate inventory levels, utilizing formula worksheets with no more than two (2) occasions within review year relating to using improper procedures or documentation, and/or allowing inventories to be depleted, as observed by the pharmacist.

   **Exceeds:** No more than one occasion within review year relating to using improper procedures or documentation, and/or allowing inventories to be depleted, as observed by pharmacist.

   **0** **1** 2

   1-4 Prepares enhanced sterile product medications including hyperalimentation, control drug drips, Persantine, Sandostatin, epidurals, IVIG, and primes tubing for chemotherapy products. Follows approved policies and procedures with proper documentation and aseptic technique. Meets standard: No more than two (2) instances of documentation where products need to be remade due to improper mixing technique as evidenced by pharmacist inspection or department review.

   **Exceeds:** No instances of documentation where product needs to be remade due to improper mixing technique as evidenced by pharmacist inspection or department review. 0 1 2

   1-5 According to hospital policies and procedures, recycles injectable premixed sterile products with no more than two (2) lost products due to improper recycling procedure.

   **Exceeds:** No loss of product due to improper recycling procedure. 0 1 2

   1-6 Repackages medications according to department policies maintaining proper manufacturing documentation and assuring all work is checked by pharmacist. Meets standards: No more than two (2) instances in review year when work must be repeated because of failure to follow proper procedure, or product integrity is not assured.

   **Exceeds:** No instances in review year when work must be repeated because of failure to follow proper procedure, or product integrity is not assured. 0 1 2

*continues*

**4–101** continued

1-7 Prepares controlled drugs for substocks on the nursing units. Accurately performs record keeping and prepares documents for use on the nursing units. Resolves all record keeping and inventory discrepancies. Work is spot checked by a pharmacist prior to dispensing. All errors or problems are reported to the Director of Pharmacy.

**Exceeds:** No instances in review year when performed incorrectly. 0 1 2

1-8 Prepares lock boxes for anesthesia and PACU following prescribed department policies and procedures. Resolves record keeping errors and reports to the Director of Pharmacy. No more than two (2) occasions within review year when done incorrectly.

**Exceeds:** No instances in review year when performed incorrectly. 0 1 2

1-9 Screens phone calls and visitors to minimize pharmacist interruptions. Assists the pharmacist by charging for and screening information for missed doses. All complete work is checked and approved by a pharmacist prior to dispensing. No more than two (2) instances of non-compliance.

**Exceeds:** No instances in review year of non-compliance. 0 1 2

1-10 Performs weekly controlled substance inventories, prepares controlled drug orders, receives controlled drug merchandise, accurately maintains all related records reporting any discrepancies immediately to the Director of Pharmacy. This includes weekly safe and Pyxis floor counts as well as return bin procedures. No more than two (2) instances of non-compliance.

**Exceeds:** No instances in review year when not performed or performed incorrectly as assigned. 0 1 2

1-11 Prepares code cart trays and special kits for nursing units. No more than two (2) instances when not done properly.

**Exceeds:** No occasions in review year when performed incorrectly. 0 1 2

1-12 Prepares enhanced sterile product medications and performs needed calculations to determine amount of medication to be added in preparing final product. Meets standard: No more than two (2) instances of documentation where final product needs to be remade due to incorrect calculations as evidenced by pharmacist inspection or department review.

**Exceeds:** No instances of documentation where final product needs to be remade due to incorrect calculations as evidenced by pharmacist inspection or department review. 0 1 2

1-13 Prepares enhanced sterile product medications and consistently meets timeliness of preparation within established schedules, policies, and guidelines. Meets standard: No more than two (2) instances of documentation where intervention was needed because technician was unable to meet timeliness of service as evidenced by pharmacist inspection or department review.

**Exceeds:** No instances of documentation where intervention was needed because technician was unable to meet timeliness of service as evidenced by pharmacist inspection or department review.

0 1 2

1-14 Demonstrates an interest in expanding knowledge of pharmacy through continuing education. Meets standard: Documents at least six (6) contact hours of pharmacy related continuing education within review year.

**Exceeds:** Documents a minimum of twelve (12) contact hours of pharmacy related continuing education within review year. 0 1 2

*continues*

**4–101** continued

1-15 Demonstrates knowledge of the Autros order entry system (equivalent) and prepares final check/confirmation of orders for a pharmacist. Meets standard: Maintains an order transcription error rate of 0.6% or less during a review year.

**Exceeds:** Maintains an order transcription error rate of 0.3% or less during the review year.

0 1 2

1-16 Maintains active membership in a pharmacy professional organization. Meets standards: Attends meetings and is involved.

**Exceeds:** Develops and provides an educational program to fellow technicians and/or pharmacists.

0 1 2

CALCULATION OF MERIT INDEX FOR THIS RESPONSIBILITY

| Points Received | / | Total Points |
|---|---|---|
| ______ | / | 32 |

Comments: ______________________________________________

______________________________________________

______________________________________________

2. Distributes medications as required, to all patient care areas of the hospital.

2-1 Accurately and efficiently delivers medications to patient care areas, according to established schedules, assuring timely provision of medications to patients with no more than two (2) incorrect or missed deliveries within review year, as observed by pharmacist.

**Exceeds:** No incorrect or missed deliveries within review year, as observed by pharmacist.

0 1 2

2-2 Consistently and thoroughly checks patients, medication bins at the time of exchange, to assure all needed medications are transferred to current bin with no occasions within review year when a patient suffers harm because a medication was not transferred to current bin. No more than two (2) occasions within review year when medication error results because medication was not transferred to current bin at exchange time.

**Exceeds:** No occasions within review year of medication error because of failure to transfer a medication to current bin at exchange time. 0 1 2

2-3 Delivers all medications reliably without breakage or spillage with no more than two (2) occasions within review year when additional medication must be prepared and dispensed, as a result of breakage or spillage.

**Exceeds:** No occasions within review year, when additional medication must be prepared and dispensed as result of breakage or spillage. 0 1 2

2-4 Reviews and monitors night cabinet for outdated medications as assigned. No more than two (2) instances in review year when not performed properly.

**Exceeds:** No instances review year of non-compliance. 0 1 2

*continues*

**4–101** continued

2-5 Prepares Central Supply order properly as assigned. No more than two (2) instances when not done properly.

**Exceeds:** No instances of non-compliance. 0 1 2

2-6 Reviews and restocks night medication cabinet daily as assigned. Charges for medications and replaces stock in the appropriate locations. Meets standards: No more than two (2) occasions in review year when night medication cabinet is improperly restocked or charges are lost.

**Exceeds:** No occasions in review year when night medication cabinet is improperly restocked or charges are lost. 0 1 2

CALCULATION OF MERIT INDEX FOR THIS RESPONSIBILITY

| Points Received | / | Total Points |
|---|---|---|
| ______ | / | 12 |

Comments: ____________________________________________

____________________________________________

____________________________________________

3. Records – Assists in the creation, handling, and maintenance of a variety of pharmacy records, to promote efficient operation of the pharmacy and regulatory compliance.

3-1 As assigned, obtains daily patient census, accurately updates Patient Medication drawers regarding admissions, discharges, and transfers, as observed by pharmacist with no more than two (2) occasions within review year when medication drawers are improperly maintained according to census report.

**Exceeds:** No occasions within review year when profiles are improperly filed, according to census report. 0 1 2

3-2 Accurately and reliably files medication orders and requests for specific patient, as observed by pharmacist. Orders are filed at least daily and no more than three occasions of omission or improper filing within review year, as observed by pharmacist.

0 1 (NA)

3-3 Accurately, consistently, and legibly records quantities of medications to be charged to patients, on computer lists when filling daily medications with no more than two (2) occasions within review year, when quantities are improperly charged.

**Exceeds:** No occasions within review year when quantities are improperly charged. 0 1 2

3-4 Accurately records quantities of medications issued when filling floor stock requests with no more than two (2) occasions within review year when quantities to be issued are omitted or incorrect as determined by review of the requisition.

**Exceeds:** No occasions within review year when quantities to be issued are omitted and incorrect, as determined by review of the requests for items filled, as determined by a review of the request. 0 1 2

*continues*

**4–101** continued

CALCULATION OF MERIT INDEX FOR THIS RESPONSIBILITY

| Points Received | / | Total Points |
|---|---|---|
| ______ | / | 7 |

Comments: ____________________________________________

____________________________________________

____________________________________________

4. Assists in maintaining proper inventory and control of drugs and supplies purchased by the Pharmacy.

 4-1 Accurately documents quantities of medications received from vendors, and initials receiving document, as observed by direct review, and places price stickers on merchandise with no more than two (2) occasions within review year when required documentation is missing or inaccurate by direct review.

 **Exceeds:** No occasions within review year when required documentation is missing or inaccurate.
 0 1 2

 4-2 Maintains orderly stock levels of all medications in dispensing area to facilitate the proper and timely filling of medication orders, as observed by pharmacist. Dispensing area and work station are consistently and adequately stocked with medications as observed by pharmacist. This includes IV room stock replenishment as well as customized floor stock replenishment duty as assigned. No more than two (2) occasions when not performed properly.

 **Exceeds:** No instances in review year of non-compliance. 0 1 2

 4-3 Reliably and accurately records medications in order book when necessary to reorder, as observed by review of the record with no more than two (2) occasions within review year when stock depletion is due to individual failure to reorder. No more than two (2) occasions within review year when stock depletion occurs as result of individual error in ordering correct item.

 **Exceeds:** No occasions within review year when individual failure to order, or order correctly, results in stock depletion. 0 1 2

 4-4 Reviews and places wholesaler orders as required. Anticipates requirements, orders appropriate quantities, and follows up problems with the pharmacy purchasing coordinator. No more than two (2) occasions when not done properly.

 **Exceeds:** No occasions in review year when order does not come in or is placed incorrectly.
 0 1 2

CALCULATION OF MERIT INDEX FOR THIS RESPONSIBILITY

| Points Received | / | Total Points |
|---|---|---|
| ______ | / | 8 |

Comments: ____________________________________________

____________________________________________

____________________________________________

*continues*

**4–101** continued

5. Maintains dispensing area and medication storeroom in neat, orderly, and clean condition, as observed by pharmacist.

   5-1 Drugs stored in dispensing area and work stations are maintained in a neat and orderly condition at all times, to reduce potential for errors, as observed by pharmacist. Drugs are not routinely found missing, misplaced, or disorganized in dispensing area and work stations, as observed by pharmacist. 0 1 (NA)

   5-2 Removes outdated medications from stock when assigned monthly and properly segregates outdated drugs to prevent issuance, as observed by pharmacist with no more than two (2) occasions within review year when outdated medications are not removed, as observed by pharmacist. This includes main pharmacy and Pyxis stock.

   **Exceeds:** No occasions within review year, when outdated medication review is not performed when assigned. 0 2 3

   5-3 Consistently maintains work station in a neat, clean, and orderly condition. As observed by pharmacist, keeps work station neat, picked-up, and free from debris. 0 1 (NA)

CALCULATION OF MERIT INDEX FOR THIS RESPONSIBILITY

| Points Received | / | Total Points |
|---|---|---|
| ______ | / | 5 |

Comments: ____________________________________________

______________________________________________________

*continues*

4–101 continued

## GOALS FOR DEVELOPMENT OR PLAN FOR PERFORMANCE IMPROVEMENT

| | GOAL | TARGET DATE | INDIVIDUAL RESPONSIBLE |
|---|---|---|---|
| 1. | | | |
| 2. | | | |
| 3. | | | |
| 4. | | | |

## OVERALL PERFORMANCE RATING

| RESPONSIBILITY | POINTS RECEIVED | POINTS POSSIBLE |
|---|---|---|
| 1. | | 32 |
| 2. | | 12 |
| 3. | | 7 |
| 4. | | 8 |
| 5. | | 5 |
| TOTAL | | 64 |

**EVALUATOR'S COMMENTS:**

**EMPLOYEE'S COMMENTS:**

## ADMINISTRATIVE REVIEW

| | | |
|---|---|---|
| EMPLOYEE'S SIGNATURE | TITLE | DATE |
| EVALUATOR'S SIGNATURE | TITLE | DATE |
| SENIOR EVALUATOR'S SIGNATURE | TITLE | DATE |

Courtesy of Faxton St. Luke's Health Care, New Hartford, New York.

# 4–102
# Orientation Checklist for Pharmacy Personnel

EMPLOYEE NAME: ______________________ DATE OF HIRE: ______________

APPROVED BY (Manager's Signature): ______________________

*The employee demonstrates competency in:*

**Department Organization, Functions, and Responsibilities**

______ ________ Organizational chart
______ ________ Position descriptions
______ ________ Department scope of care/responsibilities and functions
______ ________ Location of decentralized and centralized services

**Department Policy and Procedures**

______ ________ Location in the department
______ ________ Policy and procedure pertinent to job description

**Job Responsibilities, Job Description, Performance Appraisal, and Continuing Education**

______ ________ Job description
______ ________ Criteria-based performance appraisal system
______ ________ Continuing education requirements

**Communication Systems**

______ ________ Telephone system
______ ________ Computer system
______ ________ Employee mailbox
______ ________ Pharmacy newsletter
______ ________ Operation meetings
______ ________ General staff meetings
______ ________ Hospital newsletter
______ ________ Department/intradepartmental memos
______ ________ Beeper system
______ ________ Information bulletin board

**Information Management (Computer System)**

______ ________ Hardware: computer/printer/keyboard/light pen
______ ________ Sign on/off
______ ________ Password security
______ ________ Message screen
______ ________ PF keys
______ ________ Other important keys
______ ________ Screen format
______ ________ Pharmacy master menu
______ ________ Technician functions

(Date) (Initials—Instructor and Student)

*continues*

**4–102** continued

**General Pharmacy Laws Affecting Job Responsibilities**

| (Date) | (Initials—Instructor and Student) | |
|---|---|---|
| ________ | ____________ | Classification of drugs |
| ________ | ____________ | Controlled Substances Act |
| ________ | ____________ | Federal Food, Drug and Cosmetic Act |
| ________ | ____________ | State laws pertinent to technicians |
| ________ | ____________ | Generic substitution |

**Pharmaceutical/Medical Terminology, Drug Dosage Forms, Routes of Administration**

________ ____________ Medication dosage forms
________ ____________ Routes of administration
________ ____________ Pharmacy/medical terminology

**Hazardous Drugs/Right to Know**

________ ____________ Hazardous drug file
________ ____________ MSDS
________ ____________ Right to know

**Medication Distribution Systems**

________ ____________ Unit-dose system
________ ____________ Floor stock medications
________ ____________ Medication delivery rounds
________ ____________ Central pharmacy
________ ____________ Decentralized pharmacy satellites

**Operation/Service Time Deadlines**

________ ____________ Medication cassette schedule
________ ____________ Sterile product schedule
________ ____________ Chemotherapy schedule
________ ____________ Controlled substance schedule
________ ____________ Floor stock schedule

**Controlled Substance System**

________ ____________ Computerized inventory program
________ ____________ Issues, returns, purchases, adjustments
________ ____________ Daily reports
________ ____________ Recordkeeping/filing system
________ ____________ Schedule of controlled substances
________ ____________ Prescriptions for Schedule II

**Medication Cassettes/Carts/Exchange**

________ ____________ Fill lists
________ ____________ Admissions, discharges, and transfers
________ ____________ Audits
________ ____________ Acknowledge carts
________ ____________ Exchanges
________ ____________ Cart double-check/documentation

(Date) (Initials—Instructor and Student)

*continues*

**4–102** continued

**Floor Stock Medications**

__________ ____________ Exchange systems
__________ ____________ Floor stock lists per nursing or patient care unit

**Interpreting Physician Medication Orders**

__________ ____________ Prioritizing
__________ ____________ Filling/processing
__________ ____________ Double-check system
__________ ____________ Abbreviations/terminology
__________ ____________ Labeling
__________ ____________ Patient profiles

**Quality Assessment and Improvement Program**

__________ ____________ Department plan
__________ ____________ Scope of care
__________ ____________ Indicators for assessment
__________ ____________ Reporting
__________ ____________ Hospitalwide QA meeting and functions
__________ ____________ Joint Commission standards, survey, and accreditation process
__________ ____________ Board of Pharmacy Regulations
__________ ____________ Department of Health Regulations

**Sterile Product Program**

__________ ____________ IV fill lists
__________ ____________ Credits
__________ ____________ Delivery schedules
__________ ____________ Multitask software/Automix compounder
__________ ____________ Baxa pump
__________ ____________ Preparation of TPN—policies and procedures
__________ ____________ Aseptic technique and training program
__________ ____________ Shaker table
__________ ____________ Laminar flow hoods
__________ ____________ Restocking
__________ ____________ Storage, labeling of medications
__________ ____________ Cardioplegic solutions
__________ ____________ Antibiotic reconstitution
__________ ____________ QA maintenance logs
__________ ____________ Waste disposal

**Chemotherapy Admixture Program**

**Repackaging Medications**

__________ ____________ Repacking log
__________ ____________ Containers and closures
__________ ____________ Labeling
__________ ____________ Computer program for repackaging
__________ ____________ Required documentation
__________ ____________ Double-check system
(Date) (Initials—Instructor and Student)

*continues*

4–102 continued

**Emergency Code Box Replacement System**

__________ ____________ Procedure
__________ ____________ Labeling
__________ ____________ Double-check system
__________ ____________ Type of boxes/locations
__________ ____________ Transport boxes
__________ ____________ Log

**Same-Room Maternity Box Replacement System**

__________ ____________ Procedure
__________ ____________ Double-check system
__________ ____________ Contents

**Purchasing/Inventory Management**

__________ ____________ Purchasing
__________ ____________ Receiving
__________ ____________ Reordering
__________ ____________ Restocking
__________ ____________ Expiration date tracking system
__________ ____________ Borrow/lend
__________ ____________ Drug recalls
__________ ____________ Expired medications/credits

**Equipment Review**

__________ ____________ Laminar flow hood
__________ ____________ Biological safety cabinet
__________ ____________ Computer/printer/keyboard/light pen
__________ ____________ Lab oven
__________ ____________ Compounding equipment
__________ ____________ Automix
__________ ____________ Baxa pump
__________ ____________ TPN computer
__________ ____________ Controlled substances computer

**Nursing Unit/Patient Care Area Medication Inspections/Evaluations**

__________ ____________ Monthly inspection schedule
__________ ____________ Purpose of inspection
__________ ____________ Required documentation
(Date) (Initials—Instructor and Student)

EMPLOYEE SIGNATURE ____________________________ DATE: ____________

ADDITIONAL TRAINING NEEDS: ____________________________________

____________________________________________________________

____________________________________________________________

Source: Adapted from Saint Barnabas Health Care System, Livingston, New Jersey.

# 4–103
# Pharmacy Competencies Checklist

**POSITION: PHARMACIST**

NAME: ______________________________

| Method | I. Knowledge of Meditech | Date | Evaluator | Date Re-Eval |
|---|---|---|---|---|
| | 1. Demonstrates competency inputting medication orders for inpatients and outpatients via order entry. | | | |
| | 2. Demonstrates competency inputting IV medication orders for inpatients and outpatients via order entry. | | | |
| | 3. Demonstrates competency in use of office automation. | | | |
| | 4. Demonstrates competency in use of computer system for retrieval of patient clinical data. | | | |
| | 5. Knows about use of resource personnel for Meditech problems. | | | |
| | 6. Demonstrates competency in printing of Medication Administration Records, IV labels, and routine reports. | | | |
| **Method** | **II. Knowledge of Pyxis** | **Date** | **Evaluator** | **Date Re-Eval** |
| | 1. Knows policies and procedures in Pyxis Policy Book. | | | |
| | 2. Knows narcotic control procedures. | | | |
| | 3. Demonstrates ability to retrieve/return medications. | | | |
| | A. Correctly obtains narcotics for Pyxis technicians. | | | |
| | B. Correctly obtains patient controlled analgesia (PCA) pumps. | | | |
| | C. Correctly returns/refills narcotics. | | | |
| | D. Correctly returns PCA pumps. | | | |
| | E. Correctly returns/refills unused PCA medications. | | | |
| | 4. Knows about use of resource personnel for Pyxis problems. | | | |
| | 5. Knows procedure to follow with controlled drug discrepancy. | | | |
| | 6. Knows procedure to add/delete user. | | | |
| **Method** | **III. PCA** | **Date** | **Evaluator** | **Date Re-Eval** |
| | | | | |
| | | | | |
| | | | | |

*continues*

4–103 continued

| Method | VI. Infectious Materials | Date | Evaluator | Date Re-Eval |
|---|---|---|---|---|
| | 1. Demonstrates correct handwashing techniques. (Minimum time required = 10 seconds.) | | | |
| | 2. Knows what is "Red-Bagged." | | | |
| | 3. Knows location of protective personnel equipment on units (gown, gloves, eyewear, masks, special TB masks). | | | |
| | 4. Demonstrates proper method to dispose of sharps. | | | |
| | 5. Knows Universal Precautions. | | | |
| | 6. Knows isolation techniques, including Acid Fast Bacilli (AFB). | | | |
| **Method** | **IX. Fire, Safety, and Disaster** | **Date** | **Evaluator** | **Date Re-Eval** |
| | 1. Demonstrates action to take in case of fire in patient room (R-A-C-E). | | | |
| | 2. Knows location of fire alarm, extinguisher, and exits. | | | |
| | 3. Knows role in case of disaster. | | | |
| | 4. Knows use of Material Safety Data Sheets (MSDSs), and hazardous materials management. | | | |
| **Method** | **X. Purchasing** | **Date** | **Evaluator** | **Date Re-Eval** |
| | 1. Demonstrates competency in use of purchasing computer. | | | |
| | 2. Knows policies and procedures for issuing purchase orders. | | | |
| | 3. Demonstrates competency in returning medications to wholesaler. | | | |
| | 4. Knows policies and procedures for returning medications for credit. | | | |
| **Method** | **XI. Age-Specific Procedures** | **Date** | **Evaluator** | **Date Re-Eval** |
| | 1. Can prepare age-specific medication doses and dilutions. | | | |
| | A. Infant | | | |
| | B. Pediatric | | | |
| | C. Adolescent | | | |
| | D. Adult | | | |
| | E. Geriatric | | | |

NOTE: The above criteria are designed to ensure that the individual performing this job demonstrates competence to the ages of the patients served. These competencies are demonstrated throughout the Position Description/Evaluation Tool and include but are not limited to the position description's major duties, special requirements, and continuous quality improvement factors. Any negative response on this form will be reflected in the overall performance rating of the individual and established as a goal for improvement through additional training, education, or other form of remediation.

*continues*

**4–103** continued

**GENERAL HOSPITAL**
**Department of Pharmacy Services**
**COMPETENCY ADDENDUM—Age-Specific Standards**

The Competency Addendum is completed for all staff having regular clinical contact with patients in age groups specified and documents the level of success in meeting performance expectations.

Name: ______________________________ Age group served:

| | | |
|---|---|---|
| __________ | Infant | (<1 year) |
| __________ | Pediatric | (1–12 years) |
| __________ | Adolescent | (13–17 years) |
| __________ | Adult | (18–65 years) |
| __________ | Geriatric | (>65 years) |

| Specific Age-Appropriate Care | Verification Method(s) | Verification Level |
|---|---|---|
| *Infant (<1 year)*<br>Recognizes the unique differences that occur in drug absorption, due to pH-dependent passive diffusion and gastric-emptying time; in drug distribution, due to differences in extracellular and total body water and in protein binding of drugs in plasma; in drug metabolism, due to immature metabolic pathways; and in drug elimination, due to underdeveloped renal capacities.<br>1. Familiar with dosage forms and dosages appropriate for this specific age group.<br>2. Provides appropriate medication dose requirements based upon age-specific criteria, such as, but not limited to, patient's age, height, weight, laboratory data. | | |
| *Pediatric (1–12 years)*<br>Recognizes the important pharmacokinetic differences that occur in this age group due to the maturing processes of absorption, distribution, metabolism, and elimination and their effect on drug therapy.<br>1. Familiar with dosage forms and dosages appropriate for this specific age group.<br>2. Provides appropriate medication dose requirements based upon age-specific criteria, such as, but not limited to, patient's age, height, weight, laboratory data. | | |
| *Adolescent (13–17 years)*<br>Recognizes the important pharmacokinetic differences that occur in this age group due to the maturing processes of absorption, distribution, metabolism, and elimination and their effect on drug therapy.<br>1. Familiar with dosage forms and dosages appropriate for this specific age group.<br>2. Provides appropriate medication dose requirements based upon age-specific criteria, such as, but not limited to, patient's age, height, weight, laboratory data. | | |

*continues*

**4–103** continued

| **Specific Age-Appropriate Care** | **Verification Method(s)** | **Verification Level** |
|---|---|---|
| *Adult (18–65 years)*<br>Understands how the absorption, distribution, metabolism, and elimination of medications combine to make drug therapy unique in each individual.<br>1. Familiar with dosage forms and dosages appropriate for this specific age group.<br>2. Provides appropriate medication dose requirements based upon age-specific criteria, such as, but not limited to, patient's age, height, weight, laboratory data. | | |
| *Geriatric (>65 years)*<br>Recognizes the peculiar differences that occur with advanced age in drug absorption, due to such factors as decreased gastric blood flow and decreased GI motility; in drug distribution, due to decreased total body water and increased adipose tissue; in drug metabolism, due to decreased liver blood flow and decreased liver size; and in drug elimination, due to diminished renal blood flow and GFR.<br>1. Familiar with dosage forms and dosages appropriate for this specific age group.<br>2. Provides appropriate medication dose requirements based upon age-specific criteria, such as, but not limited to, patient's age, height, weight, laboratory data. | | |

Verification Method Codes: (use all that apply)

C = Course/class
M = Mandatory review
W = Written materials/policy
S = Standard of care review
O = Observation
AV = Audiovisual
D = Demonstration
I = Inservice
NA = Not applicable to position

Verification Level Codes:

S = Satisfactorily meets
N = Needs improvement

Employee's Signature ____________________ Date ____________

Evaluator's Signature ____________________ Date ____________

## 4–104
## New Hire: Competency Validation, Tech I

EMPLOYEE NAME: ______________________________ DATE OF HIRE: ______________

JOB TITLE: Technician DEPARTMENT: Pharmacy

**Key:** O = Observation; D = Demonstration; C = Cognitive Testing; DP = Developing; P = Proficient; S = Self Assessment

| | Review Date | Validation Method | | | Competency Status | | | |
|---|---|---|---|---|---|---|---|---|
| Critical Element/Competency | | O | D | C | D | P | S | Follow-up Action |
| **1. Pharmaceutical Preparation** | | | | | | | | |
| 1.1 Utilizes proper infection control techniques per hospital policy and procedure. | | | | | | | | |
| 1.2 Fills carts for daily exchange per policy and procedure. | | | | | | | | |
| 1.3 Accurately prepares active orders for delivery of hourly rounds. | | | | | | | | |
| 1.4 Prepares ASU orders and delivers per policy and procedure. | | | | | | | | |
| 1.5 Monitors unit stock levels. | | | | | | | | |
| 1.6 Performs calculations to fulfill desired dosage. | | | | | | | | |
| **2. Pharmaceutical Products** | | | | | | | | |
| 2.1 Handles and stores pharmaceutical preparations per policy and procedure. | | | | | | | | |
| 2.2 Accounts for controlled substances with regard to: regulation, documentation, proper storage, weekly inventories. | | | | | | | | |
| 2.3 Utilizes the Pyxis medication system according to policy and procedure. | | | | | | | | |

This certifies that the above named employee has demonstrated the ability to perform the skills listed above, within the practice guidelines established at the Medical Center.

Date: ______________ Signature of Employee: ______________________________

Signature of person(s) conducting assessment: ______________________________

*continues*

**4–104** continued

EMPLOYEE NAME: ______________________ DATE OF HIRE: ______________

JOB TITLE: Technician DEPARTMENT: Pharmacy

**Key:** O = Observation; D = Demonstration; C = Cognitive Testing; DP = Developing; P = Proficient; S = Self Assessment

| | Review Date | Validation Method | | | Competency Status | | | |
|---|---|---|---|---|---|---|---|---|
| Critical Element/Competency | | O | D | C | D | P | S | Follow-up Action |
| 2.4 Delivers chemotherapy on demand, per hospital policy and procedure. | | | | | | | | |
| 2.5 Accurately fills stock orders for other departments. | | | | | | | | |
| 2.6 Records incoming stock. | | | | | | | | |
| 2.7 Maintains IV room stock. | | | | | | | | |
| 2.8 Maintains night cabinet. | | | | | | | | |
| 2.9 Prepares anesthesia trays. | | | | | | | | |
| 2.10 Prepares narcotic boxes. | | | | | | | | |
| 2.11 Prepares code cart trays. | | | | | | | | |
| **3. Unit Dosing** | | | | | | | | |
| 3.1 Performs unit dosing of products from a bulk container per policy and procedure. | | | | | | | | |
| 3.2 Utilizes Euclid machine, per policy and procedure. | | | | | | | | |
| 3.3 Utilizes the repeater pump, per policy and procedure. | | | | | | | | |

This certifies that the above named employee has demonstrated the ability to perform the skills listed above, within the practice guidelines established at the Medical Center.

Date: ____________ Signature of Employee: ______________________________

Signature of person(s) conducting assessment: ______________________________

*continues*

**4–104** continued

EMPLOYEE NAME: ______________________ DATE OF HIRE: ______________

JOB TITLE: Technician DEPARTMENT: Pharmacy

**Key:** O = Observation; D = Demonstration; C = Cognitive Testing; DP = Developing; P = Proficient; S = Self Assessment

| | Review Date | Validation Method | | | Competency Status | | | |
|---|---|---|---|---|---|---|---|---|
| Critical Element/Competency | | O | D | C | D | P | S | Follow-up Action |
| **4. Sterile Preparations** | | | | | | | | |
| 4.1 Demonstrates proper preparation of sterile pharmaceutical products per policy and procedure. | | | | | | | | |
| 4.2 Prepares oral pharmaceutical agents for unit dosing. | | | | | | | | |
| 4.3 Prepares IV admixtures. | | | | | | | | |
| 4.4 Prepares vaccinations/T.B. tests, etc. | | | | | | | | |
| 4.5 Completes touch contamination kit annually. | | | | | | | | |
| 4.6 Demonstrates aseptic technique using laminar flowhood annually. | | | | | | | | |
| **5. AS/400** | | | | | | | | |
| 5.1 Utilizes AS/400 to complete assigned duties. | | | | | | | | |
| 5.2 Credits and debits patient accounts appropriately. | | | | | | | | |
| 5.3 Calculates expiration dates to unit dose items utilizing PLL program. | | | | | | | | |
| 5.4 Labels pharmaceutical products, utilizing multiple free form labels. | | | | | | | | |

This certifies that the above named employee has demonstrated the ability to perform the skills listed above, within the practice guidelines established at the Medical Center.

Date: ____________ Signature of Employee: ______________________

Signature of person(s) conducting assessment: ______________________

*continues*

4–104 continued

EMPLOYEE NAME: ______________________ DATE OF HIRE: ______________

JOB TITLE: Technician DEPARTMENT: Pharmacy

**Key:** O = Observation; D = Demonstration; C = Cognitive Testing; DP = Developing; P = Proficient; S = Self Assessment

| | Review Date | Validation Method | | | Competency Status | | | |
|---|---|---|---|---|---|---|---|---|
| Critical Element/Competency | | O | D | C | D | P | S | Follow-up Action |
| **6. Medication Station Areas** | | | | | | | | |
| 6.1 Maintains pharmacy/nursing medication stations per hospital policy and procedure. | | | | | | | | |
| 6.2 Maintains medication station in a neat and orderly manner, including: patient bins, pharmacy work station, nursing medication station. | | | | | | | | |
| **7. Quality Improvement** | | | | | | | | |
| 7.1 Participates in quality improvement plan and identifies areas for improvement. | | | | | | | | |
| 7.2 Participates in Quality Improvement work team as designated by director. | | | | | | | | |
| 7.3 Monitors and documents IV waste appropriately. | | | | | | | | |
| **8. Annual Requirements** | | | | | | | | |
| 8.1 Obtains a minimum of 4 recognition points per year. | | | | | | | | |
| 8.2 Handwashing monitor completed annually. | | | | | | | | |
| 8.3 Completes the Annual Technician Re-Credentialing Math Test. | | | | | | | | |

This certifies that the above named employee has demonstrated the ability to perform the skills listed above, within the practice guidelines established at the Medical Center.

Date: ______________ Signature of Employee: ______________________

Signature of person(s) conducting assessment: ______________________

Source: Faxton-St. Luke's Health Care, New Hartford, New York.

## 4–105
## New Hire: Competency Validation, Tech II

EMPLOYEE NAME: ______________________ DATE OF HIRE: ______________

JOB TITLE: Technician Level II-Advanced IV Duties DEPARTMENT: Pharmacy

**Key:** O = Observation; D = Demonstration; C = Cognitive Testing; DP = Developing; P = Proficient; S = Self Assessment

| | Review Date | Validation Method | | | Competency Status | | | |
|---|---|---|---|---|---|---|---|---|
| Critical Element/Competency | | O | D | C | D | P | S | Follow-up Action |
| **1. Aseptic Technique** | | | | | | | | |
| 1.1 Demonstrates aseptic technique. | | | | | | | | |
| **2. Horizontal Laminar Flow Hood** | | | | | | | | |
| 2.1 Demonstrates proper work habits. | | | | | | | | |
| **3. Hyperalimentation** | | | | | | | | |
| 3.1 Demonstrates proper technique in preparing. | | | | | | | | |
| 3.2 Demonstrates knowledge of calculations. | | | | | | | | |
| 3.3 Demonstrates proper labeling. | | | | | | | | |
| 3.4 Prepares final check for Pharmacist. | | | | | | | | |
| **4. Epidurals** | | | | | | | | |
| 4.1 Demonstrates knowledge of calculations. | | | | | | | | |
| 4.2 Demonstrates proper documentation. | | | | | | | | |
| 4.3 Demonstrates proper use of filter needle with ampules. | | | | | | | | |
| 4.4 Demonstrates proper technique with removing excess air from final product. | | | | | | | | |
| 4.5 Prepares final check for Pharmacist. | | | | | | | | |

This certifies that the above named employee has demonstrated the ability to perform the skills listed above, within the practice guidelines established at the Medical Center.

Date: ____________ Signature of Employee: ______________________

Signature of person(s) conducting assessment: ______________________

*continues*

**4–105** continued

EMPLOYEE NAME: ______________________ DATE OF HIRE: ______________

JOB TITLE: Technician Level II-Advanced IV Duties DEPARTMENT: Pharmacy

**Key:** O = Observation; D = Demonstration; C = Cognitive Testing; DP = Developing; P = Proficient; S = Self Assessment

| | Review Date | Validation Method | | | Competency Status | | | |
|---|---|---|---|---|---|---|---|---|
| Critical Element/Competency | | O | D | C | D | P | S | Follow-up Action |
| **5. Narcotic Drips** | | | | | | | | |
| 5.1 Demonstrates proper documentation. | | | | | | | | |
| 5.2 Demonstrates knowledge of calculations/ conversions. | | | | | | | | |
| 5.3 Demonstrates proper labeling/expirations/ paper work. | | | | | | | | |
| 5.4 Demonstrates proper technique in preparing: i.e., 1. Using filter needles with ampules 2. Withdrawing same amount of diluent as drug to be added. | | | | | | | | |
| 5.5 Prepares final check for a Pharmacist. | | | | | | | | |
| **6. Persantine Drips** | | | | | | | | |
| 6.1 Demonstrates knowledge of calculations/ conversions. | | | | | | | | |
| 6.2 Demonstrates knowledge of labeling, i.e., MFFL and preparing labeling. | | | | | | | | |
| 6.3 Demonstrates proper techniques in using filter needles with ampules. | | | | | | | | |
| 6.4 Prepares final check for Pharmacist. | | | | | | | | |
| **7. Sandostatin** | | | | | | | | |
| 7.1 Demonstrates knowledge of protocol reference. | | | | | | | | |
| 7.2 Demonstrates proper technique in preparing. | | | | | | | | |

This certifies that the above named employee has demonstrated the ability to perform the skills listed above, within the practice guidelines established at the Medical Center.

Date: ____________ Signature of Employee: ______________________

Signature of person(s) conducting assessment: ______________________

*continues*

**4–105** continued

EMPLOYEE NAME: ______________________ DATE OF HIRE: ______________

JOB TITLE: Technician Level II-Advanced IV Duties DEPARTMENT: Pharmacy

**Key:** O = Observation; D = Demonstration; C = Cognitive Testing; DP = Developing; P = Proficient; S = Self Assessment

| | Review Date | Validation Method | | | Competency Status | | | |
|---|---|---|---|---|---|---|---|---|
| Critical Element/Competency | | O | D | C | D | P | S | Follow-up Action |
| 7.3 Demonstrates knowledge of calculating rates. | | | | | | | | |
| 7.4 Prepares final check for Pharmacist. | | | | | | | | |
| **8. IV Administration Sets** | | | | | | | | |
| 8.1 Demonstrates knowledge of set description and uses. | | | | | | | | |
| 8.2 Demonstrates proper labeling of administration set. | | | | | | | | |
| 8.3 Demonstrates proper priming of administration sets. | | | | | | | | |
| **9. Documentation** | | | | | | | | |
| 9.1 Preparing log sheet for chemotherapy paperwork. | | | | | | | | |
| 9.2 Preparing hyperal log sheet. | | | | | | | | |
| 9.3 Preparing log sheet for epidurals, narcotic drips, any miscellaneous drips and Persantine drips. | | | | | | | | |
| **10. Videos** | | | | | | | | |
| 10.1 Aseptic Preparation of Parenteral Products. (30 Minutes) | | | | | | | | |
| 10.2 Quality Assurance for Pharmacy—Prepared Sterile Products. (1 Hour) | | | | | | | | |
| 10.3 Reducing Medication Errors. (30 Minutes) | | | | | | | | |

This certifies that the above named employee has demonstrated the ability to perform the skills listed above, within the practice guidelines established at the Medical Center.

Date: ____________ Signature of Employee: ______________________

Signature of person(s) conducting assessment: ______________________

*continues*

**4–105** continued

EMPLOYEE NAME: ______________________ DATE OF HIRE: ______________

JOB TITLE: Technician Level II-Advanced IV Duties DEPARTMENT: Pharmacy

**Key:** O = Observation; D = Demonstration; C = Cognitive Testing; DP = Developing; P = Proficient; S = Self Assessment

| | Review Date | Validation Method | | | Competency Status | | | |
|---|---|---|---|---|---|---|---|---|
| Critical Element/Competency | | O | D | C | D | P | S | Follow-up Action |
| **11. Communication** | | | | | | | | |
| 11.1 Demonstrates professional communication with other health care professionals and co-workers, including verbal, written, and telecommunications. | | | | | | | | |
| **12. Safety** | | | | | | | | |
| 12.1 Employee adheres to established safety and risk management activities while performing all duties. | | | | | | | | |
| 12.2 Complies with hospital policies and procedures regarding Incidents Reporting and notifies supervisor promptly. | | | | | | | | |
| 12.3 Demonstrates proper body mechanics. | | | | | | | | |
| **13. Annual Requirements** | | | | | | | | |
| 13.1 Obtains a minimum of 4 recognition points per year. | | | | | | | | |
| 13.2 Handwashing monitor completed annually. | | | | | | | | |
| 13.3 Completes the Annual Technician Re-Credentialing Math Test. | | | | | | | | |

This certifies that the above named employee has demonstrated the ability to perform the skills listed above, within the practice guidelines established at the Medical Center.

Date: ______________ Signature of Employee: ______________________________

Signature of person(s) conducting assessment: ______________________________

Source: Faxton-St. Luke's Health Care, New Hartford, New York.

# 4–106
# New Hire: Competency Validation, Tech III

EMPLOYEE NAME: ______________________ DATE OF HIRE: ______________

JOB TITLE: Technician Level III DEPARTMENT: Pharmacy

**Key:** O = Observation; D = Demonstration; C = Cognitive Testing; DP = Developing; P = Proficient; S = Self Assessment

| | Review Date | Validation Method | | | Competency Status | | | |
|---|---|---|---|---|---|---|---|---|
| Critical Element/Competency | | O | D | C | D | P | S | Follow-up Action |
| **1. Technician Level III** | | | | | | | | |
| 1.1 Demonstrates knowledge of responsibilities as Level II Technician. | | | | | | | | |
| 1.2 Completes six (6) months of work as Level II Technician. | | | | | | | | |
| **2. Continuing Education** | | | | | | | | |
| 2.1 Maintains at least 6 hours per year of continuing education. | | | | | | | | |
| 2.2 Demonstrates active membership in a professional pharmacy organization. | | | | | | | | |
| **3. Autros Order Entry/Equivalent** | | | | | | | | |
| 3.1 Demonstrates knowledge of order-entry skills. | | | | | | | | |
| 3.2 Prepares final check/confirmation of orders for a pharmacist. | | | | | | | | |
| **4. National Technician Certification** | | | | | | | | |
| 4.1 Achieves National Technician Certification. | | | | | | | | |
| 4.2 Certification displayed in Pharmacy. | | | | | | | | |

This certifies that the above named employee has demonstrated the ability to perform the skills listed above, within the practice guidelines established at the Medical Center.

Date: ____________ Signature of Employee: ______________________

Signature of person(s) conducting assessment: ______________________

*continues*

**4–106** continued

EMPLOYEE NAME: ______________________ DATE OF HIRE: ______________

JOB TITLE: Technician Level III DEPARTMENT: Pharmacy

**Key:** O = Observation; D = Demonstration; C = Cognitive Testing; DP = Developing; P = Proficient; S = Self Assessment

| | Review Date | Validation Method | | | Competency Status | | | |
|---|---|---|---|---|---|---|---|---|
| Critical Element/Competency | | O | D | C | D | P | S | Follow-up Action |
| **5. Annual Requirements**<br>5.1 Handwashing monitor completed annually.<br>5.2 Completes the Annual Technician Re-Credentialing Math Test. | | | | | | | | |

This certifies that the above named employee has demonstrated the ability to perform the skills listed above, within the practice guidelines established at the Medical Center.

Date: ____________ Signature of Employee: ______________________

Signature of person(s) conducting assessment: ______________________

Source: Faxton-St. Luke's Health Care, New Hartford, New York.

# 4–107
# Learning Assessment for Drug Use in the Neonate

The developmental uniqueness of the neonate has tremendous impact on drug therapy. Developmental changes in the newborn affect all aspects of drug action, from absorption and protein binding to receptor interaction and elimination.

## PROTEIN BINDING

In general, only the non–protein-bound or free drug molecules are active. The albumin of newborns, compared to that of adults, binds less warfarin and sulfonamides but similar amounts of diazepam. For most drugs in premature infants, a greater percentage of the total drug in the circulation is unbound because the amount and the binding affinity of circulating proteins are decreased. In the premature neonate, circulating total drug concentrations that are in the therapeutic range for adults or older children may reflect free drug concentrations that are in the toxic range.

## ABSORPTION

The rates of drug absorption are related to several factors, beginning with the route of administration and including the same characteristics that influence transfer of any substance across lipid bilayers: degree of ionization, molecular weight, lipid solubility, and active transport.

## ENTERAL ROUTE

Enteral drug treatment of neonates may not produce reliable and reproducible circulating drug concentrations for a variety of reasons. Rates of drug absorption are much greater from the intestine than from the stomach. Delayed gastric emptying, often as a result of gastroesophageal reflux, slows passage of the drug into the intestine, which prolongs the absorption phase, and may reduce the therapeutic effects of drugs administered orally. In addition, premature neonates malabsorb fat, which may also affect enteral drug absorption.

## INTRAMUSCULAR ROUTE

Intramuscular drug absorption is directly proportional to blood flow and the surface area of the collection of drug in the muscle. The sick or hypothermic neonate often has poor perfusion of the muscle and limited muscle mass. Injections intended for the muscle may enter the subcutaneous tissue as a result of limited muscle mass, and the absorption is slow and unpredictable. Intramuscular injections may also leave sterile abscesses in the neonate. Prolonged intramuscular administration of drugs in neonates should be avoided.

## INTRAVENOUS ROUTE

Intravenous drug administration is most likely to ensure effective drug therapy, but it is not without problems. The infusion rate of IV fluids in neonates is so slow that a drug injected high up in the IV tubing may not reach the circulation for hours. The most reliable method of administering IV drugs in neonates is a separate, small-volume syringe pump.

## DISTRIBUTION

Dramatic developmental changes in body composition of newborns influence the distribution of polar and nonpolar drugs within the body. At 26 weeks of gestation, water makes up 85% of body weight, with less than 1% as fat. By 40 weeks of gestation, the body is about 75% water and 15% fat. The low fat content of the brain of premature newborns may affect the distribution and effects of centrally acting drugs, such as barbiturates and anesthetics.

*continues*

**4–107** continued

## METABOLISM

Many drugs require biotransformation before they can be eliminated from the body. The liver is the primary site for most of this biotransformation, but other organs may be involved. Slow metabolic reactions and decreased elimination function combine to prolong half-life for many drugs in neonates, compared to adults. Factors that may affect biotransformation include organ damage, drug interactions, nutrition, illness, hepatic blood flow, protein binding, and biliary function. Dosages often must be adjusted empirically on the basis of therapeutic drug monitoring.

## ELIMINATION

There are several routes of elimination of drug from the body, including biliary tract, lungs, and kidneys. Both metabolized and unchanged forms of drugs may be excreted. Glomerular and tubular function are decreased at birth. Newborn glomerular filtration averages 30% of adult rate. While the maturation of glomerular filtration accelerates after birth, renal tubular maturation proceeds more slowly. This produces an imbalance in glomerular and tubular function that persists for several months, which may exert a profound influence on the elimination rate for many drugs in the neonate. In addition, renal function of newborns may be altered by hypoxemia, by nephrotoxic drugs, and underperfusion, which prevent accurate prediction of the rates of drug elimination.

*continues*

4–107 continued

**LEARNING ASSESSMENT FOR DRUGS IN THE NEONATE**

______________________________ Pharmacist's Name

______________________________ Date

**Drug Use in the Neonate Post Test**

Name: ______________________________

Date: ______________________________

---

*Read each question carefully, then write T(true) or F(false) on the line next to the question.*

1. ____________ For most drugs in premature babies, a greater percentage of drug is not protein bound.
2. ____________ Rates of drug absorption in premature babies are much greater from the intestine than from the stomach.
3. ____________ Prolonged intramuscular administration of drugs in neonates is not problematic.
4. ____________ The most reliable method of administering IV drugs in neonates is a separate small-volume syringe pump.
5. ____________ The low fat content of premature newborns may affect the distribution and effects of centrally acting drugs such as barbiturates and anesthetics.
6. ____________ Many drugs require biotransformation, primarily by the kidney, to be eliminated from the body.
7. ____________ Elimination half-life is often prolonged in neonates compared to adults.
8. ____________ The development uniqueness of neonates has a tremendous impact on drug therapy.

SCORE: ______________________________ (75% required to pass)

Source: Adapted from Saint Barnabas Health Care System, Livingston, New Jersey.

# 4–108
# Sterile Product Preparation Skills Checklist

Evaluation of technique of ______________________________

Orientation: ________________ Annual Review: __________

Return demonstration (once for annual review, 3 times for orientation). See procedures found in PHAR(2).

| | Met Standards | Did not Meet Standards | Met Standards | Did not Meet Standards | Met Standards | Did not Meet Standards |
|---|---|---|---|---|---|---|
| **Operator preparation** | | | | | | |
| handwashing | | | | | | |
| jewelry, watch removed | | | | | | |
| no gum, food, etc. | | | | | | |
| gloves (if needed) | | | | | | |
| **Horizontal Laminar Flow Hood** | | | | | | |
| cabinet operating > 30 minutes | | | | | | |
| surface prep | | | | | | |
| grills are not covered | | | | | | |
| no paraphernalia at sides | | | | | | |
| clean materials ONLY past six inch line | | | | | | |
| **Work area and organization** | | | | | | |
| components organized | | | | | | |
| horizontal arrangement | | | | | | |
| no obstruction of air to sterile surface | | | | | | |
| no overwraps or other clutter | | | | | | |
| correct equipment/material-size and quantity | | | | | | |
| worksheet/labels in close proximity (worksheets not within cabinet) | | | | | | |
| **Technique** | | | | | | |
| demonstrates laminar flow technique: (no shadowing) | | | | | | |
| demonstrates proper use of syringe: (measuring, vial and ampule entry, hand position) | | | | | | |
| demonstrates aseptic technique | | | | | | |
| thawing procedure/labeling | | | | | | |
| **Dispensing** | | | | | | |
| labeling procedures followed | | | | | | |
| documentation | | | | | | |
| **Clean-up** | | | | | | |
| proper disposal of waste | | | | | | |
| clean-up procedure | | | | | | |
| Signature of Reviewer: | | | | | | |
| Date: | | | | | | |

______________________________
EMPLOYEE SIGNATURE

Comments: ______________________________

______________________________

Source: Courtesy of Mercy Hospital, Wilkes-Barre, Pennsylvania.

## 4–109
## Position Description/Performance Appraisal for Clinical Staff Pharmacist

| | | | |
|---|---|---|---|
| **Title:** | Clinical Staff Pharmacist | **Department:** | Pharmacy Services |
| **Reports to:** | Pharmacy Supervisor | **Revision Date:** | |

**BASIC FUNCTION**

Provides pharmaceutical care to the patients of ____________ , ____________________ .

**EDUCATION AND TRAINING**

Graduate of an accredited college of pharmacy. PharmD preferred. Completion of an ASHP-accredited residency preferred. BPS certification preferred. BLS certificate. At least one of the following required:

- PharmD from ACPE-accredited school of pharmacy
- ASHP-accredited residency
- BPS certification
- Certified Diabetes Educator
- Certified Geriatric Pharmacist
- CE certificates of completion of all 8 ASHP Clinical Skills Modules
- CE certificates of completion of all 16 PSAP-II Pharmacotherapy Self-Assessment Clinical Units

Licensed (or immediately eligible for such) as a Registered Pharmacist by the Commonwealth of Pennsylvania. At least two years of health care system pharmacy experience preferred.

**PHYSICAL DEMANDS**

Potential exposure to hazardous materials such as cytotoxic drugs and bulk chemicals. Prepares cytotoxic drugs in a Class IIA vertical hood. Must possess sufficient manual dexterity to operate equipment. Must be able to communicate effectively with coworkers and the public in person. Must be able to use telephone, computer terminal, and other routine office equipment. Must have visual acuity to differentiate individual products, labeling, and handwriting. Must possess sufficient hearing to respond to verbal requests, including those on the telephone, in person, and via the public address and alarm systems. Prolonged standing or walking. Frequent bending, stretching, and lifting from floor level to seven feet. Frequent travel to other hospital departments including clinical areas. Occasional coverage for other Med Care facilities. Occasional lifting of products weighing up to 40 pounds. Must be able to lift unit dose cassettes and transport unit dose and IV carts. Understands verbal and written instructions.

| Essential Duties | Standards | Performance Level | Comments |
|---|---|---|---|
| Assumes responsibility for patient outcomes | Evaluated orders for appropriateness and drug interactions | | |
| | Intervened with physicians when appropriate in at least 24 instances | | |
| | Documented at least 60 target drug interventions | | |

*continues*

4–109 continued

| Essential Duties | Standards | Performance Level | Comments |
|---|---|---|---|
| | Coordinated DUE for _____ and prepared for presentation to Pharmacy and Therapeutics or other Medical Staff Committee | | |
| | Evaluated at least 12 ADRs | | |
| | Made daily rounds to monitor drug therapy and provided information to other health professionals | | |
| | Determined estimated CrCl for patients 65 years or older and made appropriate dosage adjustments | | |
| | Maintained certification in BLS | | |
| | Had at least one face-to-face conversation each day with a patient, physician, and other member of the health care team | | |
| | Demonstrated the knowledge and skills necessary to provide age-appropriate care to neonatal, pediatric, adolescent, adult, and/or geriatric patients | | |
| Dispenses medications | Accurately compounded, dispensed, and provided pharmaceutical care in accordance with departmental policies and procedures | | |
| | Completed assigned Medication Area Reviews monthly | | |
| | Checked and approved items prepared by pharmacy assistants | | |
| | Maintained control and inventory of Controlled Substances | | |
| | Followed Formulary guidelines | | |
| Prepares sterile products | Aseptically prepared sterile products, including TPNs and specialty products (checklist attached) | | |
| | Aseptically prepared cytotoxic drugs (checklist attached) | | |
| | Provided appropriate compatibility and stability information | | |
| Evaluates pharmacoeconomics | Evaluated the Formulary and made appropriate decisions based on the therapeutic and cost/benefit analysis | | |

*continues*

4–109 continued

| Essential Duties | Standards | Performance Level | Comments |
|---|---|---|---|
| | Dispensed fewer than four non-Formulary drugs (excluding exceptions) | | |
| | Assisted with inventory control and appropriate purchasing practices, in collaboration with the Materials Coordinator | | |
| | Demonstrated knowledge of the organization's cost of therapeutic choices | | |
| Educates | Participated and assisted in educational programs for staff, nursing, medicine, employees, patients, and the community | | |
| | Kept current with progressive pharmacy and therapeutic practices and developments by seeking, reviewing, and attending continuing education programs and reading publications | | |
| | Acted as a preceptor for pharmacy students | | |
| | Provided at least 24 patient education sessions | | |
| | Provided and documented at least six comprehensive DI requests | | |
| | Participated in at least one service, professional or community activity | | |
| Communicates using information technology | Displayed competency in the use of all pharmacy resources, including computer software and hardware and other technology | | |
| | Performed routine resupply, billing, and maintenance functions of Pyxis | | |
| Improves quality | Participated in maintaining quality control of pharmacy products | | |
| | Developed, participated in, and evaluated quality improvement programs in the pharmacy and in related departments | | |
| | Actively participated in hospital or other Med Care committees | | |

*continues*

4–109 continued

| Essential Duties | Standards | Performance Level | Comments |
|---|---|---|---|
| Performs other related duties as necessary | | | |
| Demonstrates the ___________ Core Values in the performance of daily duties | | | |

Supervisor recommendation:

____ Maintain as Clinical Staff Pharmacist

____ Change to Staff Pharmacist

________________________________ Supervisor

________________________ Date

Source: Adapted from Mercy Health Partners, Wilkes-Barre, Pennsylvania.

# 4–110
# Certification Examination: Intravenous Additives (IVADDs)

Name: ______________________________ Date: ____________

This written certification examination encompasses material from your knowledge in aseptic technique, parenteral nutrition, and intravenous solutions admixtures. GOOD LUCK!!!

1. Which solution is considered **hypertonic**?
   a. 0.9% sodium chloride
   b. 10% dextrose in water
   c. $D_5W$/0.45% sodium chloride
   d. 4% sodium chloride
2. What is the **maximum** concentration of dextrose that can be given peripherally? ____________
3. A nurse calls from the SICU and asks you if insulin is compatible with heparin. Which reference can **best** answer this question?
   a. The *Physician's Desk Reference*
   b. The *New York Times*
   c. *Facts and Comparisons*
   d. *Handbook of Injectable Drugs*
4. A ______ μM filter will remove most bacteria and render intravenous solutions sterile.
5. Amphotericin B must be administered in what IV solution? ____________
6. Which of the following is **false** concerning an aseptic environment?
   a. The laminar flow hood may be used immediately after it is turned on.
   b. The presence of cardboard boxes, papers, and pens inside the hood *increases* the risk of bacterial contamination.
   c. All work should be performed **at least** 6 inches inside the hood.
   d. Always use a syringe two times greater than the fluid volume when making intravenous solutions.
7. The **minimum** concentration of isopropyl alcohol that should be used to sterilize the hood is ________ .
8. The pain service asks the IV room to compound a morphine sulfate solution 1 mg/mL for PCA administration. You only have the 10-mg/mL concentration available. What volume of 10-mg/ML morphine sulfate solution is required to make 30 mL of a 1-mg/mL morphine sulfate solution? ____________
9. Which of the following **MUST** be worn when preparing intravenous drugs?
   a. Clean latex gloves
   b. A gown with closed front, long sleeves, and closed cuffs
   c. A face mask covering the mouth and nose
   d. A hair cap (hair covered completely)
   e. All of the above
10. The following affect the compatibility of IV admixture drugs **EXCEPT**:
    a. pH of admixture
    b. Temperature
    c. The drug's pharmacokinetics
    d. The concentration of the drug in the admixture

*continues*

**4–110** continued

## APPENDIX A: PRACTICAL EXAMINATION—GUIDELINES

The practical examination will require the participant to prepare an intravenous admixture. The exam will primarily evaluate aseptic technique. However, some knowledge of intravenous solutions, incompatibilities, and basic departmental policy and procedures will be required.

A supervisor will evaluate the participant on the basis of preset criteria developed from the department's policy and procedure **IS-A-6**, "Aseptic Technique in Laminar Flow Hood" (see below).

**Practical Examination:**

The participant is required to exhibit an understanding of the following to successfully complete the practical exam:

1. The correct use of gowns, gloves, masks, and caps
2. Proper handwashing techniques
3. Thorough preparation of the laminar flow hood and all material within the hood
4. Sufficient aseptic technique when dissolving, reconstituting, and preparing the IV admixture
5. The correct labeling and profiling of the finished product
6. The ability to detect any incompatibilities or drug interactions

The practical examination will be graded on a pass/fail basis.

## PRACTICAL EXAMINATION

Name: ______________________________ Date: ____________

**A. Preparation of Individual and Laminar Flow Hood**

| | Yes | No |
|---|---|---|
| 1. *Proper Attire:* | | |
| Gown | ______ | ______ |
| Hair cap | ______ | ______ |
| Face mask | ______ | ______ |
| Clean latex gloves | ______ | ______ |
| Jewelry removed | ______ | ______ |
| 2. *Laminar Flow Hood* | | |
| Hood is cleaned with sterile water for irrigation, followed by 70% isopropyl alcohol. Hood is wiped in one direction from inside to outside. | ______ | ______ |
| 3. *Hand Washing* | | |
| Hands are thoroughly washed with soap and water before wearing gloves. | ______ | ______ |
| 4. *Preparation of Needed Materials* | | |
| All materials needed for the admixture are placed inside the hood (i.e., syringes, needles, drug vials, etc.). Glassware is wiped before entering the hood. All drugs are removed from their boxes. | ______ | ______ |

**B. Working Inside the Laminar Flow Hood**

| | Yes | No |
|---|---|---|
| All work is performed at least 6 inches inside the hood. | ______ | ______ |
| An open path of air is maintained inside the hood when arranging IV solution bottles, vials, or ampules. | ______ | ______ |

*continues*

4–110 continued

**C. Aseptic Handling/Proper Use of Syringes**

1. *Insertion of Needle*

Needle is correctly placed in syringe. Fingers do not touch the point of attachment. ________ ________

2. *Use of Syringe*

Fingers do not touch the inside part of the plunger. ________ ________

Syringe used is two times the drug volume. ________ ________

**D. Transferring Drugs from Vials/Ampules**

1. *Preparation of Vials*

Vials are swabbed with 70% alcohol. ________ ________

2. *Transferring of Drug*

A volume of air equal to volume of solution is injected into the vial. ________ ________

Fingers do not touch the inside of the syringe plunger. ________ ________

A 0.22-μM filter is used with drugs drawn from ampules. ________ ________

All air bubbles are removed. ________ ________

3. *Preparation of Product for Dispensation*

IV solutions are examined for particulate matter/contamination. ________ ________

IV solutions are properly sealed and labeled. ________ ________

**E. Miscellaneous**

IV admixture solution is evaluated for incompatibilities and drug interactions. ________ ________

**Comments of Supervisor/Manager:** ______________________________________________

______________________________________________

______________________________________________

______________________________________________

Final Grade: Pass ____________

Fail ____________

Supervisor/Manager: ______________________________

Date: ______________

*continues*

4–110 continued

## Department of Pharmacy
## IVADDs Certification Examination

Name: ______________________________

Date: ____________________

The above Associate has successfully taken and passed both the didactic and the practical IVADD certification examination.

Supervisor/Manager: ______________________

Date: ______________

Source: Adapted from Montefiore Medical Center, Bronx, New York.

# 4–111
# Certification in Basic Pharmacotherapy

**Program Goals**

The goal of this program is to ensure that pharmacy practitioners can adequately identify, assess, and maximize pharmacotherapy for patients at the Medical Center. Excellence in pharmaceutical care will hopefully improve patient outcome and reduce the risk of medication misadventures.

**Objectives**

After completing the program, the pharmacist will be able to:

1. Describe the responsibilities of the pharmacist in providing patient-focused care.
2. Identify patient-specific, drug or disease-related problems and identify aspects of therapy that could be enhanced through pharmacotherapy consultation.
3. Identify variables that should be monitored to assess a patient's response to pharmacotherapy.
4. Document all patient-focused care interventions on the clinical information system or the medical record.
5. Effectively utilize all drug information references available at the Medical Center.

**Program Requirements**

To successfully complete this program and obtain certification, the pharmacist must be able to:

1. Demonstrate basic competence in selected areas of pharmacotherapy. These include:

   –Basic laboratory indices and patient assessment

   –Cardiology

   –Endocrinology (Diabetes Mellitus)

   –Respiratory Diseases (Asthma, COPD)

   –Basic Infectious Diseases

   –Basic Pediatrics

   This can be accomplished through completion of self-learning modules provided by the responsible preceptor.
2. Successful completion of a comprehensive examination (minimum passing grade: 70%).
3. Participation in a "hands on" learning experience. This may include patient care rounds, group discussion, journal club, or case presentation. The type and length will be determined by the responsible preceptor.

**Text (optional):** Pharmacotherapy: A Pathophysiologic Approach. JT DiPiro, RL Talbert, PE Hayes, GC Yee and LM Posey, 4th ed.

*continues*

**4–111** continued

**Learning Experience/Overall Evaluation**

Preceptor: ____________________ Pharmacist: ____________________

Type of Experience: (circle one)
Patient Care Rounds
Case Presentation/Discussion
Journal Club
Other: ____________________

| *Learning Objectives* | *Score* |
|---|---|
| 1. Understands the basic pathophysiology behind the disease state being discussed. | /10 pts |
| 2. Understands the rationale behind the therapeutic options/interventions discussed. | /10 pts |
| 3. Able to identify the pharmacologic options (i.e., drug, dosage form, frequency, etc.) available as per Formulary | /10 pts |
| 4. Understands the overall goals or outcome of therapy. | /10 pts |
| 5. Ability to develop a pharmaceutical plan of care as it's related to the disease state being discussed. | /10 pts |
| 6. Recognizes potential adverse drug reactions of recommended pharmacotherapy. | /10 pts |
| 7. Uses sound judgment when recommending pharmaceutical care plan. | /10 pts |
| 8. Attendance is satisfactory. | /10 pts |
| 9. Individual is prepared for case discussion/patient care rounds. | /10 pts |
| 10. Actively participates in learning experience. | /10 pts |

Pharmacist comments: ____________________

Preceptor comments: ____________________

Pharmacist Signature: ____________________ Date: __________
Preceptor Signature: ____________________ Date: __________

**Pharmacist Certification**

Name: ____________________

Date: ____________________

The above Associate has successfully taken and passed both the didactic and practical Basic Pharmacotherapy certification program.

Supervisor/Manager: ____________________

Date: ____________________

Courtesy of Montefiore Medical Center, Bronx, New York.

# 4–112 Reconsidering Cultural Values, Ethics, Religious Beliefs, and Patient Care Policy and Procedure

**Subject:** Reconsidering Cultural Values, Ethics, Religious Beliefs, and Patient Care Policy and Procedure

**Policy Number:** PAGE ___ OF ___

**Date Approved:** **Date Issued:** **Date Revised:**

## GENERAL POLICY

The Medical Center acknowledges that there are aspects of patient care that may conflict with an associate's cultural values, ethics, and religious beliefs. This policy establishes a formal mechanism to address general concerns and specific requests without compromising our organizational commitment to providing quality patient care, regardless of disability, race, creed, color, gender, national origin, life style, or ability to pay. Associates are encouraged to state their concern or make a request not to participate in any aspect of patient care based on their cultural values, ethics, and religious beliefs.

## ELIGIBILITY

All associates.

## PROCEDURE

**Associates**—Associates are encouraged to discuss general concerns or specific requests with their respective supervisor. Associates are required to submit a written request within forty-eight (48) hours of an assignment to their supervisor for excuse from any aspect of patient care or treatment because of conscientious objection based on a conflict with their religious, cultural, or ethical values. Urgent request(s), due to an immediate presentation of an unplanned assignment, must be verbally presented to their supervisor with a follow-up request in writing. All verbal and written requests should include a description of the duties objected to and an explanation of why they are objectionable to the associate based on religious, cultural, or ethical grounds.

**Supervisor**—The supervisor is responsible for evaluating the request and granting it if it is meritorious. The disposition of the request will be communicated to the associate both verbally and in writing and documented in the associate's files. In the event the supervisor denies the request or determines the request is without merit or is questionable, he/she should consult with the respective Human Resources representative supporting his/her area. In an effort to address the interest of all parties, the Human Resources Department may consult with the Division of Bioethics, Risk Management, and legal counsel. The final decision regarding the questionable request will be made by the Human Resources Department.

In the event of an emergency situation, if granting the request would significantly compromise patient care and there is no immediately available alternative that would ensure patient care, the supervisor may deny the request. An associate's refusal to provide the necessary patient care may result in disciplinary action up to and including termination.

If the supervisor determines the request to be an ongoing accommodation prohibiting the associate from performing the major functions of his/her job, the supervisor will refer the case to the Human Resources Department. The Human Resources Department will consider medical center-wide vacancies in attempting to accommodate requests for associate transfer or reassignment.

*continues*

**4–112** continued

## PREEMPLOYMENT

During the preemployment screening process, the job for which a candidate is being considered should be fully described so that the prospective associate can determine whether there are aspects of the job that might present a conflict with his/her cultural values, ethics, or religious beliefs. When considering a candidate's suitability for a position, interviewers should assess whether any objections to participating in any activities of the job can be reasonably accommodated.

All Medical Center Human Resources policies and practices are guidelines and may be changed, modified, or discontinued at any time by the Vice-President, Human Resources, or designee, with or without notice. Exceptions do not invalidate the basic policy.

Source: Adapted from Montefiore Medical Center, Bronx, New York.

# 4–113
# National Standards for Culturally and Linguistically Appropriate Services (CLAS)

The U.S. Department of Health and Human Services Office of Minority Health (OMH) has developed a set of 14 standards intended to assure cultural competence in health care; i.e., "that all people entering the health care system receive equitable and effective treatment in a culturally and linguistically appropriate manner."

The standards are intended to be inclusive of all cultures and not limited to any particular population group or sets of groups; however, they are especially designed to address the needs of racial, ethnic, and linguistic population groups that experience unequal access to health services. Ultimately, the aim of the standards is to contribute to the elimination of racial and ethnic health disparities and to improve the health of all Americans.

The CLAS standards are primarily directed at health care organizations; however, individual providers are also encouraged to use the standards to make their practices more culturally and linguistically accessible. The principles and activities of culturally and linguistically appropriate services should be integrated throughout an organization and undertaken in partnership with the communities being served.

**How are the Standards Organized?**

The 14 standards are organized by themes: Culturally Competent Care (Standards 1–3), Language Access Services (Standards 4–7), and Organizational Supports for Cultural Competence (Standards 8–14). Within this framework, there are three types of standards of varying stringency: mandates, guidelines, and recommendations as follows:

- CLAS mandates are current federal requirements for all recipients of federal funds (Standards 4, 5, 6, and 7).
- CLAS guidelines are activities recommended by OMH for adoption as mandates by Federal, State, and national accrediting agencies (Standards 1, 2, 3, 8, 9, 10, 11, 12, and 13).
- CLAS recommendations are suggested by OMH for voluntary adoption by health care organizations (Standard 14).

**The 14 Standards**

1. Health care organizations should ensure that patients/consumers receive from all staff members effective, understandable, and respectful care that is provided in a manner compatible with their cultural health beliefs and practices and preferred language.
2. Health care organizations should implement strategies to recruit, retain, and promote at all levels of the organization a diverse staff and leadership that are representative of the demographic characteristics of the service area.
3. Health care organizations should ensure that staff at all levels and across all receive ongoing education and training in culturally and linguistically appropriate service delivery.
4. Health care organizations must offer and provide language assistance services, including bilingual staff and interpreter services, at no cost to each patient/consumer with limited English proficiency at all points of contact, in a timely manner during all hours of operation.
5. Health care organizations must provide to patients/consumers in their preferred language both verbal offers and written notices informing them of their right to receive language assistance services.

*continues*

**4–113** continued

6. Health care organizations must assure the competence of language assistance provided to limited English proficient patients/consumers by interpreters and bilingual staff. Family and friends should not be used to provide interpretation services (except on request by the patient/consumer).
7. Health care organizations must make available easily understood patient-related materials and post signage in the languages of the commonly encountered groups and/or groups represented in the service area.
8. Health care organizations should develop, implement, and promote a written strategic plan that outlines clear goals, policies, operational plans, and management accountability/oversight mechanisms to provide culturally and linguistically appropriate services.
9. Health care organizations should conduct initial and ongoing organizational self-assessments of CLAS-related activities and are encouraged to integrate cultural and linguistic competence-related measures into their internal audits, performance improvement programs, patient satisfaction assessments, and outcomes-based evaluations.
10. Health care organizations should ensure that data on the individual patient's/consumer's race, ethnicity, and spoken and written language are collected in health records, integrated into the organization's management information systems, and periodically updated.
11. Health care organizations should maintain a current demographic, cultural, and epidemiological profile of the community as well as a needs assessment to accurately plan for and implement services that respond to the cultural and linguistic characteristics of the service area.
12. Health care organizations should develop participatory, collaborative partnerships with communities and utilize a variety of formal and informal mechanisms to facilitate community and patient/consumer involvement in designing and implementing CLAS-related activities.
13. Health care organizations should ensure that conflict and grievance resolution processes are culturally and linguistically sensitive and capable of identifying, preventing, and resolving cross-cultural conflicts or complaints by patients/consumers.
14. Health care organizations are encouraged to regularly make available to the public information about their progress and successful innovations in implementing the CLAS Standards and to provide public notice in their communities about the availability of this information.

The complete report, along with supporting material, is available online at www.OMHRC.gov/CLAS.

Source: U.S. Department of Health and Human Services' (HHS) Office of Minority Health (OMH) Web site: http://www.omhrc.gov/clas/finalcultural1a.htm.

# 4–114
# Request for Password to Clinical Information System User Registration Form

DEPARTMENT HEAD: COMPLETE SECTIONS A & B. HAVE EMPLOYEE READ AND SIGN STATEMENT ON THE BACK OF THIS FORM. SEND FORM TO MIS SECURITY ADMINISTRATION.

**REGISTRATION INFORMATION (SECTION A)**

Last Name: ______________________________ Date of Birth: ______________________________

First Name: ______________________________ Department: ______________________________

Middle Initial: __________ Sex: __________ Job Title: ______________________________

SS #: ______________________________ Office Phone/Beeper: ______________________________

Type: ______________________________ Facility: ______________________________
(Physician/Nonphysician)

Office/Floor: ______________________________

**SECURITY AUTHORIZATION (SECTION B)**

Assign New ID (New Hire) ______________ Assign New ID (Transfer/Promotion) ______________

Inactivate ID __________ Reactivate ID __________ Change Registration Information ________

Job Title ____________________________________________________________

______________________________ ______________________________
Authorizing Supervisor/Manager Date Security Administrator (or Rep) Date

**MIS SECURITY ADMINISTRATION ONLY (SECTION C)**

Copy of Signed Confidentiality Agreement on back of this form ______________________________

Access Code Assigned ______________________________ Date __________ Initials __________

Source: Adapted from Montefiore Medical Center, Bronx, New York.

# 4–115
# Patient Information Confidentiality Agreement

**Name:** ______________________________ **Position:** ______________________

**Confidentiality Agreement**

I recognize that, in the course of performing services at the Medical Center, I may gain access to patient information that is required by law and by Administrative Policy and Procedure to be kept confidential and that may be disclosed only under limited conditions. I agree that

- I will keep confidential all patient information to which I gain access whether in the direct provision of care or otherwise.
- I will access and use patient information only on a "need to know" basis.
- I will disclose patient information only to the extent authorized and necessary to provide patient care.
- I will not discuss patient information in public places or outside of work.

I understand that it is my obligation and responsibility to ensure the confidentiality of all patient information. Improper disclosure or misuse of patient information, whether intentional or due to neglect on my part, is a breach of organizational policy which will result in disciplinary action and could result in dismissal.

**Signature:** ______________________________ **Date:** ______________________

**Computer Access Agreement**

During the course of my work at the Medical Center, I may be assigned a computer identification number and instructed to develop a personal password. In order to maintain confidentiality of patient information stored in the computer systems, I agree that

- I will keep my computer identification number and passwords confidential and will not share them with anyone for any reason.
- I will not leave a computer terminal unattended without first logging off.
- I will contact security administration immediately if I have reason to believe that my computer identification number or password has been revealed.
- I will report immediately to security administration any suspected unauthorized access to patient information.

I understand that it is my obligation and responsibility to protect my computer identification number and password from improper use, and not to do so is a breach of organizational policy that will result in disciplinary action and could result in dismissal.

**Signature:** ______________________________ **Date:** ______________________

Source: Adapted from Montefiore Medical Center, Bronx, New York.

# 4–116
# Infection Control Policy and Procedure
## DEPARTMENT OF PHARMACY

**Subject:** Infection Control, Pharmacy

**Manual Code:**

**Date Issued:**

**Date Revised:**

**Approved by:** Director of Pharmacy ______________________________

**Reviewed by/Date Reviewed:** _________ _________ _________ _________

1. **Purpose**
   The Pharmacy Department participates in carrying out the hospital's overall responsibility for the effective assessment, prevention, and control of infection. The objectives of the pharmacy's infection control program are to maintain a sanitary environment, prevent cross-infection between patients and personnel, and observe operational practices that prevent the dispensation of contaminated products issued to patients.

   Crucial to the department's initiative are the mandated OSHA guidelines for training on occupational exposure to bloodborne pathogens.

   Barriers will be used for *all* patient care activities where there is a risk of exposure to blood, any body fluids, nonintact skin, and mucous membrane–lined areas. This practice was referred to as Universal Precautions, but is now known as Standard Precautions. The Standard Precautions emphasize the need for health care workers to consider *all* pathogens and to adhere rigorously to infection control procedures for minimizing the risk of transmission and exposure to blood and body fluids of all patients.

2. **Patient Care Activities**
   The Pharmacy Department is directly involved in the following patient care activities that involve the use of barriers:

   2.1 Dispense drugs and provide drug counseling directly to patients on an outpatient basis.

   2.2 Dispense drugs directly or provide patient monitoring or education services on an inpatient basis.

   2.3 Prepare intravenous medications.

   2.4 Extemporaneously compound sterile products.

   2.5 Repackage medications for individual patient use.

3. **Standard Precaution Practices**
   Standard precaution practices employed by pharmacy personnel include:

   3.1 *Handwashing*
   Hands should be washed by all personnel before and after starting work in the pharmacy.

   Personnel involved in repackaging, dispensing, and preparation of sterile medications should maintain scrupulous handwashing techniques. Refer to the Infection Control Handwashing Policy.

   3.2 *Aseptic Technique*
   Aseptic techniques are practices carried out to maintain the sterility of products that are manufactured or compounded under a sterile laminar air flow hood. These include but are not limited to the following:

   - Hands and forearms scrubbed with germicidal soap (Chlorhexidine) prior to the preparation of sterile products; repeated when returning from any absence from the area
   - Sterile latex gloves, masks, gowns, and protective head coverings worn when preparing sterile products

*continues*

**4–116** continued

- On a daily basis, counter tops wiped with 70% alcohol, floors washed with a germicidal soap, and all trash removed; no cardboard boxes permitted in this area.
- Staff with upper respiratory infections or sores on their hands restricted from working in the IV admixture areas

  Refer to Pharmacy Policy and Procedure “Aseptic Technique in a Laminar Air Flow Hood.”

  3.2.1 A signature record of daily hood cleaning activity is maintained.

  3.2.2 To maintain the efficiency of laminar flow hoods, air filters should be changed monthly, and air flow inspections should be performed biannually as required.

  3.2.3 Aseptic techniques should be used when:

  - Preparing total parenteral nutrition solutions
  - Preparing all extemporaneously prepared parenteral admixtures and irrigating solutions
  - Preparing ophthalmic preparations
  - Prepackaging any of the above

3.3 *Handling of Needles and Sharps*

All health care workers should take precautions to prevent any injuries by needles, scalpels, and other sharp instruments.

3.3.1 Needles should not be recapped, purposely bent, or broken by hand.

3.3.2 All needles, syringes, and other disposable sharp instruments should be immediately disposed of in puncture-resistant containers.

3.3.3 Needlestick injuries should be handled as specified in the Infection Control Needlestick Injury Policy.

3.4 *Attire*

Each employee should wear a clean, white lab coat when actively on duty in the pharmacy.

3.4.1 Employees assigned to the IV Room should:

- Wear a freshly laundered protective outer apron daily. Aprons should be removed and properly stored away upon leaving the IV Room. At the end of the day, all aprons should be collected and laundered.
- Wear gloves when preparing intravenous and total parenteral nutrition admixtures, irrigating solutions, and sterile compounding products. Gloves should be changed frequently, ideally after each contact with items outside of the sterile hood environment.
- Wear masks and protective head covers when preparing sterile or intravenous products in a laminar air flow hood.

3.4.2 Gloves, hats, and masks should be disposed of upon leaving the IV Room and replaced with new ones when resuming work.

3.4.3 In outpatient dispensing areas, counting trays are used to count all tablets and capsules and are wiped clean after each use. Bare hands do not come into contact with medications.

4. **Environmental Practices**

4.1 Entry to the pharmacy is not permitted to patients or other unauthorized personnel.

4.2 Entry to the IV Room is limited to properly attired personnel assigned to the area and/or authorized personnel.

4.3 In conjunction with Environmental Services, a cleaning schedule is implemented in all pharmacy areas.

4.4 Each employee has the responsibility of maintaining his or her work area in a clean and orderly condition.

4.5 All drug spills should be cleaned up immediately. Try to limit contamination to other areas. Environmental services should be notified to assist in the cleanup if the spill is nontoxic.

*continues*

**4–116** continued

4.6 Spills of antineoplastic agents should be handled as specified in Pharmacy Policy and Procedure "Antineoplastic Parenteral Drugs: Safe Preparation and Disposal."

4.7 Refrigerators for storing drugs and pharmaceuticals should not be used to store food. Refrigerators should also be routinely defrosted and cleaned as needed.

4.8 Workstations must be kept free of exposed food and garbage. Eating and drinking are not allowed in the IV Room, Manufacturing/Packaging, or any dispensing areas of the pharmacy.

4.9 Smoking is not permitted in the pharmacy or in any area of the hospital.

5. **Operational Practices**

5.1 *Purchasing*

The pharmacy purchases drugs from pharmaceutical manufacturers who meet the following good manufacturing criteria:

5.1.1 Upon request from the Pharmacy Department, the supplier should furnish analytical control, sterility testing and bioavailability data, descriptions of testing procedures for raw materials and finished products, or any other information that may be indicative of the quality of a given finished drug product.

5.1.2 There should be no history of recurring product recalls indicative of deficient quality control procedures.

5.1.3 A representative of the Pharmacy Department should be able to visit pharmaceutical companies to inspect their manufacturing and quality control procedures.

5.1.4 All drug products shipped to the hospital should conform to the requirements of the most recent United States Pharmacopeia–National Formulary (USP-NF) unless otherwise specified by the pharmacist. Items not recognized by the USP-NF should meet the specifications set forth by the Pharmacy Department.

5.1.5 All single-unit packages of drugs should conform to the Guidelines for Single-Unit Packages of Drugs of the American Society of Health-System Pharmacists.

5.1.6 The name and address of the manufacturer of the final dosage form should be present on the product labeling.

5.1.7 Expiration dates should be clearly indicated on the package label.

5.2 *Storage*

All merchandise ordered by the pharmacy is received and processed by the department.

5.2.1 Each item placed into inventory is given a week of receipt date sticker.

5.2.2 For outdated pharmaceuticals, the Pharmacy Procedure and Information on Expiration Date is followed. Expired items are removed from stock and returned to the pharmaceutical company for credit.

5.2.3 Each product should be stored under the recommended environmental conditions stated on the individual label. In the absence of specific instructions, the product should be stored at room temperature and protected from moisture, freezing, and excessive heat.

5.2.4 In the event of a drug recall, the Recalled Drug Procedure is followed.

5.3 *Repackaging*

When single-dose packages are not commercially or economically available, repackaging of bulk medication is done following the departmental procedure on the repackaging. All repackaged pharmaceuticals are held in quarantine until released by responsible personnel.

5.3.1 Sterile products undergo sterility testing according to the procedure on the subject.

*continues*

**4–116** continued

5.4 *Dispensing*
The pharmacist should observe the following in the process of dispensing:

5.4.1 Whenever possible, single-dose or single-use packages are to be dispensed.

5.4.2 Unused medications from patient units are returned to stock only if the original package or seal is intact. This will minimize the possibility of contamination from patient to patient or from staff to patient.

5.4.3 Proper stock rotation and observance of expiration dates is necessary to ensure the dispensing of suitable products. A product dispensed on an infrequent basis should be observed for evidence of chemical, physical, and microbiological stability.

Examples: Microbial growth in liquid dosage forms may be accompanied by discoloration, turbidity, or gas formation. For sterile liquids, the presence of microbial contamination usually cannot be detected visually, but any haze, color change, cloudiness, surface file, particulate or flocculent matter, or gas formation is sufficient reason to suspect contamination.

5.4.4 The pharmacy will maintain necessary records, including lot numbers and expiration dates, of drugs dispensed in accordance with the federal, state, and local regulations and Pharmacy Department procedures.

5.5 *Quality Improvement Practices Regarding Infection Control*
To ensure that the department's standards for infection control are being met, the Pharmacy Department routinely monitors the following:

- Needles returned in cassettes
- Sterile technique
- IV Additive Certification

6. **Vaccines**
The Pharmacy Department is also responsible for the purchasing, storage, and availability of vaccines, serums, and other biological therapeutic materials.

6.1 In certain circumstances, when these drugs are not supplied by the pharmacy, information as to their availability shall be issued.

6.2 In the event that there is an outbreak of a contagious disease in any location of the hospital, the pharmacy should be notified immediately so that an adequate supply of vaccine or immunological products is available.

7. **Work-Related Accidents**
Work-related accidents or illnesses should be handled as specified in the Administrative Procedure.

8. **Isolation Precautions**
Occasionally, pharmacy personnel will need to enter the room of a patient on isolation precautions to deliver drug therapy or provide patient monitoring or education. Before entering a room of a patient on isolation, they must consult with the nurse to receive the appropriate precaution requirements. Pharmacy personnel must observe standard precautions and careful handwashing practices.

9. **Infection Control Administrative Protocol**
The Pharmacy Department has a commitment to education and training in Infection Control and Universal Safeguard programs.

9.1 Annual attendance at housewide educational programs is mandated for all department personnel.

9.2 The pharmacy also participates in the Antibiotic Surveillance and Infection Control Committees of the hospital.

Source: Adapted from Montefiore Medical Center, Bronx, New York.

# 4–117
# Record of Laminar Flow Hood Cleaning

**Hood** ______________ **Location** ______________ **Month** ______________ **Year** ______________

| Date | 7:30 | 8:00 | 8:30 | 9:00 | 9:30 | 10:00 | 10:30 | 11:00 | 11:30 | 12:00 | 1:00 | 2:00 | 3:00 | 4:00 | Other |
|---|---|---|---|---|---|---|---|---|---|---|---|---|---|---|---|
| 1 | | | | | | | | | | | | | | | |
| 2 | | | | | | | | | | | | | | | |
| 3 | | | | | | | | | | | | | | | |
| 4 | | | | | | | | | | | | | | | |
| 5 | | | | | | | | | | | | | | | |
| 6 | | | | | | | | | | | | | | | |
| 7 | | | | | | | | | | | | | | | |
| 8 | | | | | | | | | | | | | | | |
| 9 | | | | | | | | | | | | | | | |
| 10 | | | | | | | | | | | | | | | |
| 11 | | | | | | | | | | | | | | | |
| 12 | | | | | | | | | | | | | | | |
| 13 | | | | | | | | | | | | | | | |
| 14 | | | | | | | | | | | | | | | |
| 15 | | | | | | | | | | | | | | | |
| 16 | | | | | | | | | | | | | | | |
| 17 | | | | | | | | | | | | | | | |
| 18 | | | | | | | | | | | | | | | |
| 19 | | | | | | | | | | | | | | | |
| 20 | | | | | | | | | | | | | | | |
| 21 | | | | | | | | | | | | | | | |
| 22 | | | | | | | | | | | | | | | |
| 23 | | | | | | | | | | | | | | | |
| 24 | | | | | | | | | | | | | | | |
| 25 | | | | | | | | | | | | | | | |
| 26 | | | | | | | | | | | | | | | |
| 27 | | | | | | | | | | | | | | | |
| 28 | | | | | | | | | | | | | | | |
| 29 | | | | | | | | | | | | | | | |
| 30 | | | | | | | | | | | | | | | |
| 31 | | | | | | | | | | | | | | | |

Source: Adapted from Mercy Health Partners, Wilkes-Barre, Pennsylvania.

# 4–118
# Temperature, Medication Storage

**Policy Number:** ______________
**Date Originated:** ______________
**Date Revised:** ______________
**Page:** ______________

## Pharmacy Services Policy Subject: Temperature, Medication Storage

### I. POLICY

A. Proper storage temperatures for medications will include the following:

1. **Freezer**—a cold place in which the temperature is maintained at –4 to 14°F *(–20 to –10°C)*
2. **Refrigerator**—a cold place in which the temperature is maintained at 36 to 46°F *(2 to 8°C)*
3. **Cold Place**—any temperature not exceeding 46°F *(8°C)*
4. **Cool Place**—any temperature between 46 and 59°F *(8 to 15°C)*
5. **Room Temperature**—"the temperature prevailing in a working area"
6. **Controlled Room Temperature**—maintained at 59 to 86°F *(15 to 30°C)*
7. **Warm Place**—any temperature between 86 and 104°F *(30 to 40°C)*
8. **Excessive Heat**—as in "Protect from excessive heat"—any temperature above 104°F *(40°C)*

B. Freezer and refrigerator temperatures must be monitored with a functional thermometer and documented daily on a temperature log. Adjustments and actions to correct variations in temperatures shall also be documented. Logs are maintained in the pharmacy area.

### II. REFERENCE OF AUTHORIZATION

USP/NF XXII

Source: Adapted from Long Beach Memorial Medical Center, Long Beach, California.

## 4–119
## Refrigerator Temperature Log

**Location:** ______________________________

**Month/Year:** ______________________________

Temperature (Fahrenheit)

| | | | | | | | | | | | | | | | | | | | | | | | | | | | | | | |
|---|---|---|---|---|---|---|---|---|---|---|---|---|---|---|---|---|---|---|---|---|---|---|---|---|---|---|---|---|---|---|
| 42 | | | | | | | | | | | | | | | | | | | | | | | | | | | | | | |
| 41 | | | | | | | | | | | | | | | | | | | | | | | | | | | | | | |
| 40 | | | | | | | | | | | | | | | | | | | | | | | | | | | | | | |
| 39 | | | | | | | | | | | | | | | | | | | | | | | | | | | | | | |
| 38 | | | | | | | | | | | | | | | | | | | | | | | | | | | | | | |
| 37 | | | | | | | | | | | | | | | | | | | | | | | | | | | | | | |
| 36 | | | | | | | | | | | | | | | | | | | | | | | | | | | | | | |
| 35 | | | | | | | | | | | | | | | | | | | | | | | | | | | | | | |
| 34 | | | | | | | | | | | | | | | | | | | | | | | | | | | | | | |
| 33 | | | | | | | | | | | | | | | | | | | | | | | | | | | | | | |
| 32 | | | | | | | | | | | | | | | | | | | | | | | | | | | | | | |
| | 1 | 2 | 3 | 4 | 5 | 6 | 7 | 8 | 9 | 10 | 11 | 12 | 13 | 14 | 15 | 16 | 17 | 18 | 19 | 20 | 21 | 22 | 23 | 24 | 25 | 26 | 27 | 28 | 29 | 30/31 |

Day of the Month

**Note:** Temperatures above/below white range in graph are unacceptable.
If temperature cannot be corrected by adjusting the thermostat, notify Facilities (x: ###).
Completed forms should be filed on the unit and kept for 12 months.

Source: Adapted from Hamot Medical Center, Erie, Pennsylvania.

# 4–120
# Post-HIV Exposure Prophylaxis
## DEPARTMENT OF PHARMACY

**Subject:** Post-HIV Exposure Prophylaxis

**Manual Code:**

**Date Issued:**

**Date Revised:**

**Approved by:** Director of Pharmacy ______________________________

**Reviewed by/Date:** ________ ________ ________ ________

## POLICY

### Post-HIV Exposure Prophylaxis

Any Associate who has been exposed to any body fluid, whether through a needlestick, cut, splash exposure, or human bite, must go to the Occupational Health Service (OHS) immediately to be evaluated. If the OHS is closed, the Associate must be evaluated in the Emergency Department. Time is of the essence. Postexposure prophylaxis should be started as soon as possible, preferably within 1–2 hours of exposure. Current CDC guidelines indicate that upon evaluation, a protease inhibitor may or may not be added to AZT +/– lamivudine therapy.

## PROCEDURES

### Associates Evaluated in the Emergency Department

Associates should receive the initial doses of HIV prophylaxis drugs in the Emergency Department. The Emergency Department physician will write follow-up prescriptions for the patient that will provide enough medication until the patient can be seen and evaluated in the OHS office. This could be a 1–3-day supply, depending upon the day of the week and when OHS is next open. "Post-HIV Exposure Prophylaxis" should be written on the prescription. The follow-up prescriptions for the 1–3-day supply of prophylactic medication will be filled by the inpatient pharmacy. Departmental prescription filling policies and procedures should be followed.

Associates should be directed to the inpatient pharmacy to have these prescriptions filled Monday–Friday 5 PM to 9 AM, on weekends, and on hospital holidays. All other times (9 AM–5 PM Monday–Friday), these patients should be directed to the outpatient Pharmacy.

The follow-up prescriptions will be provided free of charge.

The OHS will evaluate the Associate as soon as possible after the exposure. Any prescriptions for the duration of the prophylactic regimen will be written by the OHS. The medication will either be provided directly by the OHS, or the patient will be directed to the Pharmacy, and the prescriptions will be filled at no charge.

Source: Adapted from Montefiore Medical Center, Bronx, New York.

# 4–121
# Surgical Antibiotic Prophylaxis

**GUIDELINES ON ANTIMICROBIAL PROPHYLAXIS IN SURGERY**

**REVISED JANUARY 2000**

**Single Dose Before Surgery**

| Nature of Operation | Recommended Drug(s) and Dose (Adult - A); (Pediatric - P) | Recommended Drug(s) for Patients with a History of Severe Penicillin Allergy Dose (Adult - A); (Pediatric - P) |
|---|---|---|
| **CLEAN** | | |
| **Cardiac**<br>Prosthetic valve, coronary artery bypass, other open-heart surgery, pacemaker implant | Cefazolin 1 gram IV (A), 209 mg/kg IV (P) | Vancomycin 1 gram IV (A), 20 mg/kg IV (P) |
| **Non-Cardiac Thoracic** | Cefazolin 1 gram IV (A), 20 mg/kg IV (P) | Vancomycin 1 gram IV (A), 20 mg/kg IV (P) |
| **Vascular**<br>Arterial surgery involving the abdominal aorta, a prosthesis, or a groin incision | Cefazolin 1 gram IV (A), 20 mg/kg IV (P) | Vancomycin 1 gram IV (A), 20 mg/kg IV (P) |
| Lower extremity amputation for ischemia | | |
| **Neurosurgery**<br>Craniotomy, spinal surgery, other (i.e., CSF shunt) | Nafcillin 1-2 gram IV (A), 20 mg/kg IV (P) | Vancomycin 1 gram IV (A), 20 mg/kg IV (P) |
| **Orthopaedic**<br>Total joint replacement, internal fixation of fractures | Cefazolin 1 gram IV (A), 20 mg/kg IV (P) | Vancomycin 1 gram IV (A), 20 mg/kg (P) |

*continues*

**4–121** continued

| Nature of Operation | Recommended Drug(s) and Dose (Adult - A); (Pediatric - P) | Recommended Drug(s) for Patients with a History of Severe Penicillin Allergy Dose (Adult - A); (Pediatric - P) |
|---|---|---|
| **Urology**<br>Transurethral resection of prostate (TURP) with presence of bacteremia | Cefazolin 1 gram IV (A) or Oral cephalexin 500 mg (A) | Trimethoprim-Sulfamethoxazole Oral: 1 DS × 1 (A) |
| **CLEAN—CONTAMINATED** | | |
| **Plastic**<br>Implantation of permanent prosthetic material, entering oral cavity or pharynx | Cefazolin 1 gram IV (A), 20 mg/kg IV (P) | Clindamycin 600 mg IV (A), 5 mg/kg IV (P) plus Gentamicin 1.5 mg/kg (A), 2 mg/kg (P) |
| **Head and Neck**<br>Entering oral cavity or pharynx | Cefazolin 1 gram IV (A), 20 mg/kg IV (P) | Clindamycin 600 mg IV (A), 5 mg/kg IV (P) plus Gentamicin 1.5 mg/kg (A), 2 mg/kg (P) |
| **Abdominal**<br>Gastroduodenal | High risk only: Cefazolin 1 gram IV (A), 20 mg/kg IV (P) | Flagyl 500 mg IV (A) plus Gentamicin 1.5 mg/kg IV (A)<br>Gentamicin 2 mg/kg IV (P) plus Clindamycin 5 mg/kg IV (P) |
| **Biliary Tract** | High risk only: Cefazolin 1 gram IV (A), 20 mg/kg IV (P) | Flagyl 500 mg IV (A) plus Gentamicin 1.5 mg/kg IV (A)<br>Gentamicin 2 mg/kg IV (P) plus Clindamycin 5 mg/kg IV (P) |
| **Colorectal** | Oral: Kanamycin (A)* plus Erythromycin (A) or<br>Parenteral: Cefoxitin 1 gram IV (A), 20 mg/kg (P) | Flagyl 500 mg IV (A) plus Gentamicin 1.5 mg/kg IV (A)<br>Gentamicin 2 mg/kg IV (P) plus Clindamycin 5 mg/kg IV (P) |
| **Appendectomy** | Cefoxitin 1 gram IV (A), 20 mg/kg IV (P) | Flagyl 500 mg IV (A) plus Gentamicin 1.5 mg/kg IV (A)<br>Gentamicin 2 mg/kg IV (P) plus Clindamycin 5 mg/kg IV (P) |

*After appropriate diet and catharsis, one gram of each at 1 PM, 2 PM, and 11 PM the day before an 8 AM operation.

**Biliary Tract Surgery:** High risk is defined as those more than 70 years old and those with acute cholecystitis, a non-functioning gallbladder, obstructive jaundice or common duct stones.

**Gastroduodenal:** The risk of infection after gastroduodenal surgery is high when gastric acidity and gastrointestinal motility are diminished by obstruction, hemorrhage, gastric ulcer or malignancy, or by therapy with an H2-blocker such as ranitidine (*Zantac*) or a proton pump inhibitor such as omeprazole (*Prilosec*), and is also high in patients with morbid obesity.

When surgery is delayed or prolonged beyond 4 hours, a second dose is recommended.

*continues*

**4–121** continued

To facilitate the administration of the preop dose in the O.R., the following steps are being taken:

1. The night before surgery, the physician shall write the order for the antibiotic TO BE GIVEN IN THE O.R.
2. The drug order shall be processed at the patient unit in the usual manner, i.e., nursing copy shall be affixed to the medication administration record, the chart shall be flagged, and the pharmacy copy shall be sent to the Pharmacy (tube #21).
3. Pharmacy will not send the drug to the patient unit since the drug shall be obtained by the anesthesiologist from the O.R.
4. Anesthesiologist shall administer the drug 30 minutes–1 hour before surgery and chart the dose given in the medication administration record.

Recent studies document that post operative antimicrobial administration is not necessary.

**References**

Dellinger EP. Quality standard for antimicrobial prophylaxis in surgical procedures. *Clin Infect Dis* 1994; 18:422–7.

ASHP therapeutic guidelines on antimicrobial prophylaxis in surgery. *Clin Pharm* 1992; 11:483–513.

Anonymous. Antimicrobial prophylaxis in surgery. 1995; 37:79–82.

Source: Montefiore Medical Center, Bronx, New York.

## 4–122
## Practice Recommendations for Health Care Facilities Implementing the U.S. Public Health Service Guidelines for Management of Occupational Exposures to Bloodborne Pathogens

| Practice recommendation | Implementation checklist |
|---|---|
| Establish a bloodborne pathogen policy. | All institutions where health care personnel (HCP) might experience exposures should have a written policy for management of exposures. |
| | The policy should be based on the U.S. Public Health Service (PHS) guidelines. |
| | The policy should be reviewed periodically to ensure that it is consistent with PHS recommendations. |
| Implement management policies. | Health care facilities (HCF) should provide appropriate training to all personnel on the prevention of and response to occupational exposures. |
| | HCF should establish hepatitis B vaccination programs. |
| | HCF should establish exposure-reporting systems. |
| | HCF should have personnel who can manage an exposure readily available at all hours of the day. |
| | HCF should have ready access to postexposure prophylaxis (PEP) for use by exposed personnel as necessary. |
| Establish laboratory capacity for bloodborne pathogen testing. | HCF should provide prompt processing of exposed person and source person specimens to guide management of occupational exposures. |
| | Testing should be performed with appropriate counseling and consent. |
| Select and use appropriate PEP regimens. | HCF should develop a policy for the selection and use of PEP antiretroviral regimens for HIV exposures within their institution. |
| | Hepatitis B vaccine and HBIG should be available for timely administration. |
| | HCF should have access to resources with expertise in the selection and use of PEP. |
| Provide access to counseling for exposed HCP. | HCF should provide counseling for HCP who might need help dealing with the emotional effect of an exposure. |
| | HCF should provide medication adherence counsel ing to assist HCP in completing HIV PEP as necessary. |

*continues*

4–122 continued

| Practice recommendation | Implementation checklist |
|---|---|
| Monitor for adverse effects of PEP. | HCP taking antiretroviral PEP should be monitored periodically for adverse effects of PEP through baseline and testing (every 2 weeks) and clinical evaluation. |
| Monitor for seroconversion. | HCF should develop a system to encourage exposed HCP to return for follow-up testing.<br><br>Exposed HCP should be tested for HCV and HIV. |
| Monitor exposure management programs. | HCF should develop a system to monitor reporting and management of occupational exposures to ensure timely and appropriate response.<br><br>**Evaluate**<br>• exposure reports for completeness and accuracy,<br>• access to care (i.e., the time of exposure to the time of evaluation), and<br>• laboratory result reporting time.<br><br>**Review**<br>• exposures to ensure that HCP exposed to sources not infected with bloodborne pathogens do not receive PEP or that PEP is stopped.<br><br>**Monitor**<br>• completion rates of HBV vaccination and HIV PEP and<br>• completion of exposure follow-up. |

Source: Centers for Disease Control *MMWR Reports & Recommendations,* June 29, 2001 / 50(RR11);43-4. http://www.cdc.gov/mmwr/preview/mmwrhtml/rr5011a2.htm.

## 4–123
## Management of Occupational Blood Exposures

**Provide immediate care to the exposure site.**

- Wash wounds and skin with soap and water.
- Flush mucous membranes with water.

**Determine risk associated with exposure by**

- type of fluid (e.g., blood, visibly bloody fluid, other potentially infectious fluid or tissue, and concentrated virus) and
- type of exposure (i.e., percutaneous injury, mucous membrane or nonintact skin exposure, and bites resulting in blood exposure).

**Evaluate exposure source.**

- Assess the risk of infection using available information.
- Test known sources for HBsAg, anti-HCV, and HIV antibody (consider using rapid testing).
- For unknown sources, assess risk of exposure to HBV, HCV, or HIV infection.
- Do not test discarded needles or syringes for virus contamination.

**Evaluate the exposed person.**

- Assess immune status for HBV infection (i.e., by history of hepatitis B vaccination and vaccine response).

**Give PEP for exposures posing risk of infection transmission.**

- HBV
- HCV: PEP not recommended.
- HIV
  - Initiate PEP as soon as possible, preferably within hours of exposure.
  - Offer pregnancy testing to all women of childbearing age not known to be pregnant.
  - Seek expert consultation if viral resistance is suspected.
  - Administer PEP for four weeks if tolerated.

**Perform follow-up testing and provide counseling.**

- Advise exposed persons to seek medical evaluation for any acute illness occurring during follow-up.

*continues*

4–123 continued

**HBV exposures**

- Perform follow-up anti-HBs testing in persons who receive hepatitis B vaccine.
  - Test for anti-HBs one to two months after last dose of vaccine.
  - Anti-HBs response to vaccine cannot be ascertained if HBIG was received in the previous three to four months.

**HCV exposures**

- Perform baseline and follow-up testing for anti-HCV and alanine amino-transferase (ALT) four to six months after exposures.
- Perform HCV RNA at four to six weeks if earlier diagnosis of HCV infection desired.
- Confirm repeatedly reactive anti-HCV enzyme immunoassays (EIAs) with supplemental tests.

**HIV exposures**

- Perform HIV-antibody testing for at least 6 months postexposure (e.g., at baseline, six weeks, three months, and six months).
- Perform HIV antibody testing if illness compatible with an acute retroviral syndrome occurs.
- Advise exposed persons to use precautions to prevent secondary transmission during the follow-up period.
- Evaluate exposed persons taking PEP within 72 hours after exposure and monitor for drug toxicity for at least two weeks.

Source: Centers for Disease Control *MMWR Reports & Recommendations*, June 29, 2001 / 50(RR11);43-4. http://www.cdc.gov/mmwr/preview/mmwrhtml/rr5011a2.htm.

# 4–124
# CDC Guidelines for Hand Hygiene in Health Care Settings

## Recommendations of the Health Care Infection Control Practices Advisory Committee and the HICPAC/SHEA/APIC/IDSA Hand Hygiene Task Force

Prepared by
John M. Boyce, M.D.1
Didier Pittet, M.D.2
*1 Hospital of Saint Raphael*
*New Haven, Connecticut*
*2 University of Geneva*
Geneva, Switzerland

### Summary

*The Guideline for Hand Hygiene in Health Care Settings provides health-care workers (HCWs) with a review of data regarding handwashing and hand antisepsis in health-care settings. In addition, it provides specific recommendations to promote improved hand hygiene practices and reduce transmission of pathogenic microorganisms to patients and personnel in health care settings. This report reviews studies published since the 1985 CDC guideline (Garner JS, Favero MS. CDC guideline for handwashing and hospital environmental control, 1985. Infect Control 1986;7:231–43) and the 1995 APIC guideline (Larson EL, APIC Guidelines Committee. APIC guideline for handwashing and hand antisepsis in health care settings. Am J Infect Control 1995;23:251–69) were issued and provides an in-depth review of hand hygiene practices of HCWs, levels of adherence of personnel to recommended handwashing practices, and factors adversely affecting adherence. New studies of the in vivo efficacy of alcohol-based hand rubs and the low incidence of dermatitis associated with their use are reviewed. Recent studies demonstrating the value of multidisciplinary hand hygiene promotion programs and the potential role of alcohol-based hand rub in improving hand hygiene practices are summarized. Recommendations concerning related issues (e.g., the use of surgical hand antiseptics, hand lotions or creams, and wearing of artificial fingernails) are also included.*

### Recommendations

#### Categories

These recommendations are designed to improve hand hygiene practices of HCWs and to reduce transmission of pathogenic microorganisms to patients and personnel in health care settings. This guideline and its recommendations are not intended for use in food processing or food-service establishments, and are not meant to replace guidance provided by FDA's Model Food Code.

As in previous CDC/HICPAC guidelines, each recommendation is categorized on the basis of existing scientific data, theoretical rationale, applicability, and economic impact. The CDC/HICPAC system for categorizing recommendations is as follows:

*Category IA.* Strongly recommended for implementation and strongly supported by well-designed experimental, clinical, or epidemiologic studies.

*Category IB.* Strongly recommended for implementation and supported by certain experimental, clinical, or epidemiologic studies and a strong theoretical rationale.

*Category IC.* Required for implementation, as mandated by federal or state regulation or standard.

*Category II.* Suggested for implementation and supported by suggestive clinical or epidemiologic studies or a theoretical rationale.

*continues*

**4–124** continued

*No recommendation.* Unresolved issue. Practices for which insufficient evidence or no consensus regarding efficacy exist.

**Recommendations:**

1. Indications for handwashing and hand antisepsis
   - A. When hands are visibly dirty or contaminated with proteinaceous material or are visibly soiled with blood or other body fluids, wash hands with either a non-antimicrobial soap and water or an antimicrobial soap and water (IA) .
   - B. If hands are not visibly soiled, use an alcohol-based hand rub for routinely decontaminating hands in all other clinical situations described in items 1C–J (IA). Alternatively, wash hands with an antimicrobial soap and water in all clinical situations described in items 1C–J (IB).
   - C. Decontaminate hands before having direct contact with patients (IB).
   - D. Decontaminate hands before donning sterile gloves when inserting a central intravascular catheter (IB).
   - E. Decontaminate hands before inserting indwelling urinary catheters, peripheral vascular catheters, or other invasive devices that do not require a surgical procedure (IB).
   - F. Decontaminate hands after contact with a patient's intact skin (e.g., when taking a pulse or blood pressure, and lifting a patient) (IB).
   - G. Decontaminate hands after contact with body fluids or excretions, mucous membranes, non-intact skin, and wound dressings if hands are not visibly soiled (IA).
   - H. Decontaminate hands if moving from a contaminated body site to a clean body site during patient care (II).
   - I. Decontaminate hands after contact with inanimate objects (including medical equipment) in the immediate vicinity of the patient (II).
   - J. Decontaminate hands after removing gloves (IB).
   - K. Before eating and after using a restroom, wash hands with a non-antimicrobial soap and water or with an antimicrobial soap and water (IB).
   - L. Antimicrobial-impregnated wipes (i.e., towelettes) may be considered as an alternative to washing hands with non-antimicrobial soap and water. Because they are not as effective as alcohol-based hand rubs or washing hands with an antimicrobial soap and water for reducing bacterial counts on the hands of HCWs, they are not a substitute for using an alcohol-based hand rub or antimicrobial soap (IB).
   - M. Wash hands with non-antimicrobial soap and water or with antimicrobial soap and water if exposure to *Bacillus anthracis* is suspected or proven. The physical action of washing and rinsing hands under such circumstances is recommended because alcohols, chlorhexidine, iodophors, and other antiseptic agents have poor activity against spores (II).
   - N. No recommendation can be made regarding the routine use of non-alcohol-based hand rubs for hand hygiene in health care settings. Unresolved issue.
2. Hand-hygiene technique
   - A. When decontaminating hands with an alcohol-based hand rub, apply product to palm of one hand and rub hands together, covering all surfaces of hands and fingers, until hands are dry (IB). Follow the manufacturer's recommendations regarding the volume of product to use.

*continues*

**4–124** continued

B. When washing hands with soap and water, wet hands first with water, apply an amount of product recommended by the manufacturer to hands, and rub hands together vigorously for at least 15 seconds, covering all surfaces of the hands and fingers. Rinse hands with water and dry thoroughly with a disposable towel. Use towel to turn off the faucet (IB). Avoid using hot water, because repeated exposure to hot water may increase the risk of dermatitis (IB).

C. Liquid, bar, leaflet or powdered forms of plain soap are acceptable when washing hands with a non-antimicrobial soap and water. When bar soap is used, soap racks that facilitate drainage and small bars of soap should be used (II).

D. Multiple-use cloth towels of the hanging or roll type are not recommended for use in health care settings (II).

3. Surgical hand antisepsis

   A. Remove rings, watches, and bracelets before beginning the surgical hand scrub (II).

   B. Remove debris from underneath fingernails using a nail cleaner under running water (II).

   C. Surgical hand antisepsis using either an antimicrobial soap or an alcohol-based hand rub with persistent activity is recommended before donning sterile gloves when performing surgical procedures (IB).

   D. When performing surgical hand antisepsis using an antimicrobial soap, scrub hands and forearms for the length of time recommended by the manufacturer, usually 2–6 minutes. Long scrub times (e.g., 10 minutes) are not necessary (IB).

   E. When using an alcohol-based surgical hand-scrub product with persistent activity, follow the manufacturer's instructions. Before applying the alcohol solution, prewash hands and forearms with a non-antimicrobial soap and dry hands and forearms completely. After application of the alcohol-based product as recommended, allow hands and forearms to dry thoroughly before donning sterile gloves (IB).

4. Selection of hand hygiene agents

   A. Provide personnel with efficacious hand-hygiene products that have low irritancy potential, particularly when these products are used multiple times per shift (IB). This recommendation applies to products used for hand antisepsis before and after patient care in clinical areas and to products used for surgical hand antisepsis by surgical personnel.

   B. To maximize acceptance of hand hygiene products by HCWs, solicit input from these employees regarding the feel, fragrance, and skin tolerance of any products under consideration. The cost of hand hygiene products should not be the primary factor influencing product selection (IB).

   C. When selecting non-antimicrobial soaps, antimicrobial soaps, or alcohol-based hand rubs, solicit information from manufacturers regarding any known interactions between products used to clean hands, skin care products, and the types of gloves used in the institution (II).

   D. Before making purchasing decisions, evaluate the dispenser systems of various product manufacturers or distributors to ensure that dispensers function adequately and deliver an appropriate volume of product (II).

   E. Do not add soap to a partially empty soap dispenser. This practice of "topping off" dispensers can lead to bacterial contamination of soap (IA).

5. Skin care

   A. Provide HCWs with hand lotions or creams to minimize the occurrence of irritant contact dermatitis associated with hand antisepsis or handwashing (IA).

   B. Solicit information from manufacturers regarding any effects that hand lotions, creams, or alcohol-based hand antiseptics may have on the persistent effects of antimicrobial soaps being used in the institution (IB).

*continues*

**4–124** continued

6. Other Aspects of Hand Hygiene
   A. Do not wear artificial fingernails or extenders when having direct contact with patients at high risk (e.g., those in intensive care units or operating rooms) (IA).
   B. Keep natural nails tips less than 1/4-inch long (II).
   C. Wear gloves when contact with blood or other potentially infectious materials, mucous membranes, and non-intact skin could occur (IC).
   D. Remove gloves after caring for a patient. Do not wear the same pair of gloves for the care of more than one patient, and do not wash gloves between uses with different patients (IB).
   E. Change gloves during patient care if moving from a contaminated body site to a clean body site (II).
   F. No recommendation can be made regarding wearing rings in health care settings. Unresolved issue.
7. Health-care worker educational and motivational programs
   A. As part of an overall program to improve hand hygiene practices of HCWs, educate personnel regarding the types of patient care activities that can result in hand contamination and the advantages and disadvantages of various methods used to clean their hands (II).
   B. Monitor HCWs' adherence with recommended hand hygiene practices and provide personnel with information regarding their performance (IA).
   C. Encourage patients and their families to remind HCWs to decontaminate their hands (II).
8. Administrative measures
   A. Make improved hand hygiene adherence an institutional priority and provide appropriate administrative support and financial resources (IB).
   B. Implement a multidisciplinary program designed to improve adherence of health personnel to recommended hand hygiene practices (IB).
   C. As part of a multidisciplinary program to improve hand hygiene adherence, provide HCWs with a readily accessible alcohol-based hand rub product (IA).
   D. To improve hand-hygiene adherence among personnel who work in areas in which high workloads and high intensity of patient care are anticipated, make an alcohol-based hand rub available at the entrance to the patient's room or at the bedside, in other convenient locations, and in individual pocket-sized containers to be carried by HCWs (IA).
   E. Store supplies of alcohol-based hand rubs in cabinets or areas approved for flammable materials (IC).

**Performance Indicators**

1. The following performance indicators are recommended for measuring improvements in HCWs' hand hygiene adherence:
   A. Periodically monitor and record adherence as the number of hand-hygiene episodes performed by personnel/number of hand-hygiene opportunities, by ward or by service. Provide feedback to personnel regarding their performance.
   B. Monitor the volume of alcohol-based hand rub (or detergent used for handwashing or hand antisepsis) used per 1,000 patient-days.
   C. Monitor adherence to policies dealing with wearing of artificial nails.
   D. When outbreaks of infection occur, assess the adequacy of health care worker hand hygiene.

Source: Centers for Disease Control and Prevention. Guideline for Hand Hygiene in Health-Care Settings: Recommendations of the Healthcare Infection Control Practices Advisory Committee and the HICPAC/SHEA/APIC/IDSA Hand Hygiene Task Force. *MMWR* 2002;51(No. RR-16):31–34, 45.

# 4–125
# Infection Control

## POLICY

The pharmacy compounds and dispenses parenteral admixtures, topical preparations, and oral medications. Procedures will be followed to prevent the preparation and dispensing of contaminated or outdated medications that could be hazardous for patients, resulting in hospital-acquired infections.

## PROCEDURES:

A. **EQUIPMENT AND SUPPLIES**

1. Utensils, counting trays, spatulas, and packaging equipment should be washed with detergent when used.
2. Any medications dropped on the floor or contaminated in any way are to be discarded in the proper medication destruction box.
3. When pouring liquid medications, care should be taken that lips of bottles do not touch. Liquid spilled on the side of the bottle or counter surfaces should be wiped off. If an excess amount of liquid medication is poured, it is NOT to be returned to the original stock bottle.
4. The dispensing area should be kept clean and uncluttered at all times.
5. Single-dose vials should be used when possible and discarded after use. Multiple-dose vials should be discarded at the manufacturer's expiration date. Within the period of use, vials will be visually inspected for contamination (i.e., cloudy solution or particulates). If the vial is contaminated, it will be thrown away immediately. (TB skin test solution will be dated and discarded 30 days after opening.)
6. Aseptic technique will be used when compounding sterile preparations.
7. All sterile preparations will be prepared under laminar flow unit.
8. Only sterile water for irrigation is used to reconstitute medications for oral use.
9. Only sterile water or normal saline for injection is used to reconstitute medication for parenteral use.
10. Needles must never be reused and must be disposed of in a sharps container.

B. **ENVIRONMENTAL SERVICE**

1. Countertops should be wiped down with detergent germicide daily by environmental services.
2. Floors and horizontal surfaces should be cleaned daily by environmental services.
3. Shelves should be dust free.
4. Trash is removed from the department daily.

C. **PERSONNEL**

Employee Health

1. All personnel will adhere to policies on standard precautions, bloodborne pathogens, handwashing, and employee health policies.
2. Hygiene
   a. Employees should wear clean clothing (which adheres to dress code), surgery scrubs, or lab coats to work.

*continues*

**4–125** continued

b. Hands should be washed thoroughly before handling medications and frequently while at work.

c. There will not be any food or drink in the IV room.

3. Education

a. New employees participate in infection control during orientation.

b. The handling of sterile antineoplastic products requires a comprehensive knowledge of aseptic technique, and no person should attempt to work with such products until he or she has been properly trained. All persons working with sterile products must be familiar with all products, procedures, techniques, equipment, and facilities required and available, so as to prepare the most sterile product.

c. Inservice education will be provided to all personnel involved in the preparation of administration of sterile parenteral products including incompatibility.

D. **MEDICATIONS**

1. Whenever possible, unit dose meds are purchased. This decreases the possibility of infections transmitted through the handling of medications. Those meds that are purchased in bulk are repackaged in unit dose bubbles.

2. All medication charged and dispensed to a patient in multiple-dose containers are to be used on that one patient only.

E. **GUIDELINES FOR PREPARATION OF IV ADMIXTURES AND OTHER STERILE PRODUCTS**

1. Laminar Flow Hood

a. The laminar flow hood should remain on continuously. If the hood is turned off for any period of time, it is to run for 30 minutes and be cleaned with Osyl/Isopropyl alcohol prior to use.

b. Prefilters are changed quarterly by maintenance. Maintenance maintains a log for the purpose of recording each time the filters are changed.

c. The laminar flow hoods (including HEPA filter) and biological safety cabinet are inspected and certified twice a year by a laminar hood certification service.

d. All intravenous admixtures are prepared in the laminar flow hood. All operations or manipulations are carried out in such a manner as to minimize the possibility of contamination of the admixture.

e. To further reduce the potential for error, only one type of IV solution should be prepared at a time in the hood. Only those materials necessary for the preparation of a given sterile product are permitted in the functional area of the laminar hood. The hood should be kept free of any unnecessary bottles, vials, etc.

f. The laminar flow hood will be cleaned at least twice daily with Osyl and Isopropyl alcohol. A cleaning log will be maintained.

g. Traffic in the IV room will be kept to a minimum.

h. All work in the hood should be performed at least six inches back from the front edge of the laminar flow hood.

i. Do not store objects against the HEPA filter screen.

j. When working in the hood, all manipulations should be performed in a manner which will not allow anything to come between the HEPA filter and surfaces meant to be kept sterile.

*continues*

**4–125** continued

k. If the IV product is contaminated, the product will be discarded.

l. The IV room is to be maintained in an orderly and neat manner. Countertops are to be wiped down daily with 70% alcohol. Trash is to be removed at least twice daily by environmental services. There is to be no cardboard in the IV room.

m. A notebook containing the following logs will be maintained: hood cleaning; and professional hood inspection.

n. Stability:

1. For those IVs that are compounded and stored at room temperature, the product expires at midnight following the day it was compounded unless otherwise specified by product literature.
2. For those IVs that are compounded and stored under refrigeration, the product expires at midnight three days following compounding unless otherwise specified by product literature.

2. Aseptic Technique

F. **SAMPLING OF IVs: QUALITY CONTROL**

1. IV sampling will be done every weekday by the designated pharmacy technician.
2. An IV bag returned for credit that it not premade by the manufacturer or an antibiotic will be sampled.
3. Using secondary venoset, and IVEX filter and an evacuated bottle of appropriate size, draw the IV in question through the IVEX filter. Aseptic technique is to be used and no liquid is to be left in the filter set. The manufacturer's protective caps should be put on both ends of the filter set.
4. On a preprinted pharmacy label, note the contents, date filtered, and initials of the technician preparing the filter.
5. An IV filter log will be kept in the IV room and the person doing the sampling will note the following:
   - Date filtered;
   - Initial of tech who prepared the IV;
   - Initial of tech who filtered the IV; and
   - Contents of the IV.
6. The labeled filter should be sent to microbiology.
7. After microbiology furnishes the pharmacy with a copy of the report form, the results will be noted in the IV filter log. Positive culture results are shared with the person(s) responsible and, followed for trends. If the same person's initials are identified on a positive culture result more than once, more intensive IV technique training will result.

**Signed by** ______________________________

**Effective** ______________________________

Courtesy of Judy Sikes, PhD, CPHQ, Director of Accreditation/Medical Staff Services, Parkview Medical Center, Pueblo, Colorado.

# 4–126
# Parenteral Nutrition: Infection Control

## POLICY

Strict adherence to stringent aseptic technique is critical in the prevention of infection during the administration of parenteral nutrition. Digression may lead to patient complication and sepsis.

## PROCEDURE

1. Parenteral nutrition tubing is never used for any other procedures, i.e., piggyback infusions, administering or draining blood, central venous pressure determinations.
2. Parenteral nutrition is prepared in the pharmacy using proper sterile technique.
3. Parenteral nutrition is carefully handled during storage and administration to avoid bacterial contamination.
4. Prepared solutions are dated and may be refrigerated.
   a. A TPN must never be warmed in a microwave.
   b. Regardless of the storage method, solutions expire at midnight following the day of preparation.
5. Macronutrients attached to the parenteral nutrition pump (i.e., Amino Acid, Dextrose and Lipids) are to be changed every morning by the IV room pharmacy technician. Anytime a new bag is added to the parenteral nutrition pump, labels are to be placed on each bag with the initials of the technician, date hung, date of expiration, and the initials of the pharmacist checking the bag.
6. When checking a TPN bag the pharmacist must verify that each macronutrient stock bag on the compounder has been checked as described in #5.
7. Each bag or bottle of macronutrient hung on the compounding machine is carefully inspected for cracks or leaks. Any defective product will be discarded.
8. Every bag of TPN is closely inspected for leaks, particular matter, and when possible, precipitate formation before being dispensed. This inspection is intended to prevent phlebitis and bacterial and/or fungal contamination. Any bag not passing the visual inspection will be discarded.
9. Bags are labeled clearly including a patient's name, location, room number, time due, date of expiration, parenteral nutrition contents, and initials of the person preparing and checking the solution.

**Signed by** ______________________________

**Effective** ______________________________

Courtesy of Judy Sikes, PhD, CPHQ, Director of Accreditation/Medical Staff Services, Parkview Medical Center, Pueblo, Colorado.

# 4–127
# Injectable Vial Stability

## POLICY

Injectable solution withdrawn from vials will be contaminant free.

## PROCEDURE

I. Multidose Vials for Injection (Multidose vials contain a preservative.)

   A. Multidose vials will be discarded at the manufacturer's expiration date, with the exception of TB skin test solution, which will be dated and discarded 30 days after opening.

   B. Insulin will be stored under refrigeration and therefore will be treated as any other multiple-dose vial.

   C. Within the period of use, vials will be visually inspected for contamination (i.e., cloudy solution or particulates). If the vial is contaminated, it will be thrown away immediately.

II. Single-Dose Vials

   A. Single-dose vials do not contain a preservative.

   B. Use of single-dose vials

      1. Laminar Flow Hood

         a. Aseptic technique is observed in laminar flow hoods.

         b. If the entire vial is not used, the vial may be used up to midnight of the day it is open.

      2. No Laminar Flow Hood

         a. Vial is to be thrown away immediately after use, even if not completely used.

**Signed by** ______________________________

**Effective** ______________________________

Courtesy of Judy Sikes, PhD, CPHQ, Director of Accreditation/Medical Staff Services, Parkview Medical Center, Pueblo, Colorado.

# 4–128
# 2000 JCAHO Preparedness Sessions

**Describe the role of the Pharmacy and Therapeutics Committee at the Medical Center.**

The Pharmacy and Therapeutics (P&T) Committee is a Committee of the Medical Staff and is responsible for the development and surveillance of all medication use policies and practices to assure optimum clinical results and a minimum potential for hazard to patients. The P&T Committee reports to the Medical Staff Governing Body, the Division Councils.

The P&T Committee has three primary functions: Formulary Maintenance; Safe Medication Prescribing, Administration, and Dispensing; and Medication Usage Evaluation.

*Formulary Maintenance*

The Formulary is a continually revised compilation of pharmaceuticals that reflects the current clinical judgment of the Medical Staff. The P&T Committee is responsible for the maintenance of the Formulary and the evaluation of new drugs to determine their clinical value and safety at the Medical Center. The P&T Committee reviews requests for the addition of drugs to the Formulary and periodically reviews therapeutic classes of drugs to ensure that the most safe, efficacious, and cost-effective drugs are available for patients in the Medical Center. The Medical Staff, through the P&T Committee, has authorized the Pharmacy Department to dispense all medications under the generic name when prescribed under the brand name. The P&T Committee is also responsible for the development of all drug distribution and administration policies and procedures within the Medical Center.

*Medication Improvement Committee*

The second functional responsibility of the P&T Committee is the safe prescribing, administration, and dispensing of medications. The Medication Improvement Committee (MIC) is a committee of the P&T Committee responsible for continuous evaluation and performance improvement of the medication use system. The MIC accomplishes this through the routine monitoring of Adverse Drug Reaction reporting, Medication Error reporting, and Pharmacist Intervention Documentation. Additionally, the MIC monitors compliance with Medical Center policies and procedures regarding the safe and effective prescribing, dispensing, administration, and monitoring of medications to patients.

*Medication Usage Evaluation*

Medication Usage Evaluation is the third functional responsibility of the P&T Committee. The P&T Committee is responsible for improving the quality of therapeutic drug outcomes in our patients by evaluating the appropriateness, safety, and efficacy of therapeutic agents utilized at the Medical Center. Medication Usage Evaluation is a planned, systematic, and ongoing evaluation of the use of target drugs or drug classes. The MUE process is conducted as a criteria based, ongoing, planned, and systematic means of monitoring and evaluating drug use. The therapeutic, empiric, and prophylactic use of selected drugs are addressed. The process is designed to identify opportunities to improve the use of drugs and resolve problems in their use.

**How is the Medical Staff involved in the selection of drugs for the Formulary? How are drugs added to the Formulary? What is the review process?**

Additions to the Formulary are made by physicians who would like to use the new drug in patients at the Medical Center. The P&T Committee reviews objective data prepared by the Pharmacy Department regarding the drug and any Formulary or therapeutic alternatives to determine the cost-effective value of adding the drug to the Medical Center Formulary.

*continues*

**4–128** continued

The Committee meets 4–6 times per year to evaluate these requests and reviews the drugs on the Formulary. The physician(s) requesting the new drug presents to the Committee why the new drug is a valuable addition to current Formulary agents. By majority vote, the Committee determines the Formulary status of newly requested drugs.

**What role does Nursing play in the Formulary process?**

The Department of Nursing is a voting member of the P&T Committee. Additionally, this individual is a member of the MIC. This Nursing "expert" also provides guidance regarding practical drug therapy and medication administration issues. Medication administration and monitoring policies and procedures are routinely developed by the Department of Nursing in collaboration with other disciplines and presented to the P&T Committee for review and approval. Nurses in collaboration with pharmacists and physicians discuss individual patient requests for non-formulary drugs to determine whether or not a Formulary alternative can be prescribed.

**What happens if an MD orders a drug that is not on the Formulary?**

Occasionally patients require medications that are not on the Formulary. In these cases, a pharmacist consults with the prescribing physician to determine the therapeutic need for the non-formulary medication and to identify any Formulary alternatives appropriate for the patient and the clinical situation. Many times physicians change the non-formulary medication order to a Formulary alternative. When the pharmacist and physician determine that the non-formulary medication is the most clinically appropriate choice, the pharmacist will dispense the medication and record the discussion in the medication profile. If the medication is not readily available, the Pharmacy Department will usually procure the non-formulary medication within 24 hours.

**How are hospital staff made aware of drugs that are added/included in the Formulary?**

A Medical Center Formulary is published every two years by the Pharmacy Department. In between publications, a supplement is prepared. The Formulary is available at each patient care area. Copies are also available to attending and house staff physicians as well as other health care professionals requesting a personal copy. Information regarding Formulary changes and revisions is also published 4 times per year in the *Pharmacy Bulletin* and *P&T Notes*, publications sent to all full time and house staff physicians, the Nursing department, and other health care professionals throughout the Medical Center.

**Can certain drugs be prescribed only by specific physicians?**

Three basic categories of drugs can only be prescribed by or must be authorized by physicians approved by the P&T Committee.

*Restricted Antibiotics*: The P&T Committee may restrict the use of certain antibiotics by requiring approval of a member of the Division of Infectious Diseases.

*Chemotherapeutic Agents*: A list of chemotherapeutic agents that can only be prescribed for by authorized physicians in the Departments of Oncology or Hematology is approved by the P&T Committee.

*Select Hematologic Agents*: A list of select hematologic agents and physicians authorized by the Hematology Department to prescribe these agents is approved by the P&T Committee. Physicians other than those appearing on this list may prescribe these hematology agents upon review by a pharmacist.

The Medical Staff Office confirms that attending physicians are privileged to order medications. The Pharmacy Department receives a signature card for each privileged physician. Signature cards have the attending physicians' signatures and DEA numbers. These signature cards authorize the Pharmacy Department to dispense therapeutically equivalent generic medications and inform pharmacists that the physician is privileged to order medications at the Medical Center. Signature cards are kept on file in the Pharmacy Department.

*continues*

4–128 continued

**How do prescribers know that certain drugs are restricted?**

**How do pharmacists know that a prescriber is authorized to use these drugs?**

The lists of restricted antibiotics, chemotherapeutic, and hematologic medications are published in the Medical Center Formulary. When new drugs are added to these lists, the information is included in the *Pharmacy Bulletin* and *P&T Notes* and distributed to the medical, nursing, pharmacy, and health care staffs. Lists of these restricted drugs and the physicians authorized to prescribe them are posted in every pharmacy satellite area. The lists are updated annually.

**What is the Medical Center's definition of a medication error?**

A medication error is defined in the Nursing Medication Administration Policy and Procedure as any of the following:

Inappropriate prescribing by a physician or other authorized health care prescriber. This includes:

- Incorrect indication for the prescribed medication
- Incorrect or missing drug dosage, route of administration, frequency, dosage form
- Prescribing a medication to a patient allergic to the drug
- Use of an unapproved or inappropriate abbreviation
- The medication order is illegible.

Inappropriate administration by nursing staff or other authorized health care provider. This includes:

- Administration of a medication without a physician's order
- Omission of an ordered medication when there are no circumstances to warrant omission
- Administration of the wrong medication, administration of a medication in the wrong dosage, by the wrong route, or to the wrong patient
- Administration of the medication at the wrong time (more than one hour before or after the designated time). There may be exceptions to this depending on individual patient circumstances, i.e., off unit, delivery of medications, etc. The time of a "stat" order is that time when the nurse is notified of the need for the medication.
- Infusion of the wrong IV solution/blood product or infusion at the wrong rate.

Inappropriate dispensing of a medication. This can include:

- Missing doses/delayed doses
- Incorrect reconstitution or preparation
- Incorrect label information.

**How are medication errors/occurrences monitored and tracked? What is the role of the P&T Committee in monitoring medication errors and what corrective actions or improvements have been implemented to decrease the numbers of errors?**

When a medication error is identified, the responsible physician is informed immediately and any urgent care is rendered. The individual noting the medication error completes the Medical Center's Occurrence Report and submits the report to his or her immediate supervisor. Actions taken and patient outcome are documented directly onto this report. These reports are submitted to the Pharmacy Department for input into the Medical Center's medication error database. The severity of a medication error will depend on the potential or actual harm is caused the patient and how it may have affected overall patient outcome. The Medication Improvement

*continues*

**4–128** continued

Committee will rank medication errors on a scale from 0 to 7 to assess their severity and impact on patient care, and if possible, to identify any prescribing, administration or dispensing error trends that may be occurring within the institution. Any recommended actions to improve the medication use system in an effort to prevent future medication errors are presented to the P&T Committee for approval and implementation.

**What is the Medical Center's definition of an adverse drug reaction?**

The P&T Committee has adopted both the FDA and the World Health Organization's definitions of an Adverse Drug Reaction.

*FDA's Definition:*

> "An 'adverse drug experience' is any adverse event associated with the use of a drug in humans, whether or not considered drug related, including the following:
>
> - an adverse event occurring in the course of a drug in professional practice;
> - an adverse event occurring from drug overdose, whether accidental or intentional;
> - an adverse event occurring from drug abuse;
> - an adverse event occurring from drug withdrawal; and
> - any significant failure of expected pharmacological action."

*WHO's Definition:*

> "An adverse drug reaction is a reaction which is noxious and unintended, and which occurs at doses normally used in man for the prophylaxis, diagnosis, or therapy of disease, or for the modification of physiological function."

**What is the system for monitoring adverse drug reactions?**

The P&T Committee oversees the Medical Staff's ADR surveillance at the Medical Center. The Pharmacy Department through the Medication Improvement Committee acts as the clearing house for all ADRs reported and provides statistical and clinical information regarding ADRs to the P&T Committee at least quarterly. ADR surveillance is primarily conducted in a retrospective and concurrent fashion. Information on ADR Surveillance and reporting is included in the Hospital Formulary, is presented as part of the House Staff orientation annually, and is referenced in the Nursing orientation program.

**Who is involved in the ADR reporting process? How are ADRs reported?**

All health care professionals are urged to contribute and participate in ADR surveillance. There are a variety of ways in which Adverse Drug Reactions are reported to the Pharmacy Department.

*Adverse Drug Reaction Reporting Form.* Adverse Drug Reaction Notice Cards shall be available on every patient unit and in the Pharmacy. Completed cards should be sent to the Pharmacy Office. Each report is individually reviewed and screened by the Pharmacy Department.

*ADR Hotline.* Via a voice mail system, any health care provider can report an ADR in less than one minute, by dialing extension _____ and selecting option #2, as follows:

*continues*

**4–128** continued

TO REPORT AN ADVERSE DRUG REACTION, PLEASE RESPOND TO THE FOLLOWING QUESTIONS AND PRESS THE POUND (#) KEY AFTER EACH OF YOUR RESPONSES.

- INDICATE THE PATIENT'S NAME, THEN PRESS THE POUND (#) KEY.
- INDICATE WHERE THE PATIENT IS, WHICH FLOOR, ROOM NUMBER, ETC., THEN PRESS THE POUND (#) KEY.
- INDICATE THE MEDICAL RECORD NUMBER, THEN PRESS THE POUND (#) KEY.
- INDICATE THE DATE OF THE ADVERSE DRUG REACTION, THEN PRESS THE POUND (#) KEY.
- INDICATE WHAT TYPE OF REACTION THE PATIENT IS HAVING, THEN PRESS THE POUND (#) KEY.
- INDICATE THE SUSPECTED DRUG, THEN PRESS THE POUND (#) KEY.
- INDICATE YOUR NAME AND PHONE NUMBER.
- HANG UP. YOUR ADR MESSAGE WILL BE PICKED UP BY THE PHARMACY AND REVIEWED.

These reports are individually reviewed and screened by the Pharmacy Department.

*Medical Records.* Cases are identified in medical records based on ICD-9 codes defined for adverse drug reactions. These reports are sent to both Pharmacy offices monthly by the MIS Department (Data Management Group) and represent the bulk of the retrospective surveillance. Each of these cases is reviewed by the Pharmacy.

*Utilization Management/Quality Improvement Department.* Cases identified by UM personnel throughout the institution should be reported to the Pharmacy Department via the UM/QI reporting process, the ADR Reporting Cards, or the ADR Hotline. Cases are individually reviewed and screened by the Pharmacy Department.

*Radiology & Cardiac Catheterization Reports.* Cases are identified by these departments as quality improvement indicators and forwarded to the Pharmacy Department. Since these cases are reviewed at the Radiology and Cardiac Cath QI Committee meetings, the reports are not reviewed any further by the Pharmacy Department.

Once a report is received in the Pharmacy from any source (except Radiology and Cardiac Cath), it is screened and thoroughly evaluated by a pharmacist for a variety of data elements.

In addition to the patient demographics, suspected drug, type of ADR, and whether or not the reaction caused the patient to be admitted, ADR cases are assigned a Probability Rating (Remote, Possible, Probable, Highly Probable) based upon the Jones Algorithm, the process used by the FDA's MedWatch surveillance system. ADRs are also rated by severity (minor, mild, moderate, severe, or serious) based upon the FDA definition of a "serious" reaction and the UM/QI severity classifications (from HCFA guidelines to the PRO). As well, dose related versus non-dose related reactions are noted and the type of health care personnel reporting the ADR is identified. Documentation of adverse reactions in the patient medical records is ensured by the Department of Pharmacy.

**What is the role of the P&T Committee in the ADR Program?**

Reports of ADR surveillance are reviewed by the Medication Improvement Committee and summary reports are presented to the P&T Committee members for review of trends and any necessary action. Information from these summary reports is used to identify educational materials for the *P&T* Notes and the *Pharmacy Bulletin* and/or the *Pharmacy Weekly Bulletin*. The Medication Improvement Committee may recommend to the P&T Committee for approval and implementation systems or policy changes based on ADR surveillance data to improve the quality of care rendered to patients. To help prevent future adverse drug reactions, the P&T Committee has approved a process whereby the Pharmacy alerts physicians by mail that their patients may have experienced an adverse drug reaction while they were in the hospital.

*continues*

4–128 continued

**Do you report ADRs to the FDA and manufacturer? What types get reported to the FDA?**

Cases requiring physician review and/or submission to the FDA's MedWatch program (cases that are unusual or are identified as severe or serious) are presented to the Medication Improvement Committee. Reports to the FDA are completed by the Pharmacy Department. Reports of significant or severe ADRs are also reported to the Department of Health by the UM/QI staff and Risk Management.

**How are medications monitored by nurses, pharmacists, and physicians?**

**How does the Medical Center document monitoring for medication effectiveness?**

The effects of medications are monitored in a variety of ways by many health care disciplines.

Pharmacists routinely evaluate medication effects and outcomes through the drug distribution and dispensing system. Additionally, more intensive drug therapy monitoring is done in targeted patient populations throughout the medical center. These populations are targeted because the Pharmacy Department, in collaboration with the Medical Staff, has determined these patients to be at a high risk for developing a drug related problem either because of their disease state, therapeutic drug regimen, or age related complications. These patient types include, but are not limited to, pediatric patients, infectious disease patients, family medicine patients, critical care patients, cardiology patients, AIDS patients, and patients on investigational drug protocols.

Nurses and physicians routinely review the effects and outcomes of medications in their day to day treatment of the patient. Drug therapy is reviewed daily, and revisions in therapy made based on objective laboratory and clinical information. Documentation of these therapeutic decisions are noted in the patient's medical record.

Various projects conducted by the Medication Improvement Committee continuously monitor the medication use system to identify areas for improvement. The outcome of medication use is the focus of these evaluations.

The Medical Center's Medication Usage Evaluation program is responsible for improving the quality of therapeutic drug outcomes in our patients by evaluating the appropriateness, safety, and efficacy of therapeutic agents utilized at the Medical Center. This planned, systematic, and ongoing evaluation of the use of target drugs or drug classes is conducted as a criteria-based means of monitoring and evaluating drug use. The therapeutic, empiric, and prophylactic uses of selected drugs are addressed. The process is designed to identify opportunities to improve individualized drug therapy for patients as well as improving the entire medication use system.

**How are investigational drugs handled in the hospital?**

The Investigational Drug Service of the Pharmacy Department and the Oncology Investigational Drug Service ensure that investigational drugs are prescribed, dispensed, and administered in a safe, effective, and efficient manner. The Investigational Drug Service helps assure that investigational drug studies are carried out scientifically and comply with all applicable guidelines as required by the Food and Drug Administration, this institution, and any other appropriate regulatory agency. All investigational drugs, unless otherwise authorized by the Pharmacy Department, are stored and dispensed by the Pharmacy Department either through the inpatient pharmacy service or the Oncology pharmacy service.

The Pharmacy Department is required to review each investigational drug protocol before it is approved for use within the Medical Center. After Pharmacy Department approval, the investigational drug protocol will not commence until approved by the Institutional Review Board. A member of the Pharmacy Department sits on the Institutional Review Board as deputy chair and is a member of the IRB Executive Committee.

**How is informed consent obtained?**

Informed consent is obtained by the Principal Investigator or designee on the Medical Center authorized Investigational Drug Informed Consent form. The Informed Consent form is inserted into the patient's medical record.

*continues*

**4–128** continued

**Is information about each investigational drug available to the staff?**

Information about each investigational drug is available in the patient's medical record. The appropriate pages of the Institutional Review Board application outlining the medication effects, dosage, and administration are located in the patient's medical record.

Pharmacy personnel prepare guidelines, policies and procedures for the pharmacy department component of any pharmacy-involved investigational protocol. These highlight the purpose of the study, randomization procedures, drug preparation, dispensing and labeling, investigators authorized to prescribe, and drug information for health care personnel. This information is available to all Pharmacy Department personnel.

**What about emergency use of non-IRB approved investigational drugs?**

Emergency use of an investigational drug is defined by the following criteria:

1. There is no standard acceptable treatment available for a patient's condition.
2. The patient does not meet inclusion criteria of a protocol or requires an investigational agent not under study at this institution.
3. There is not sufficient time to obtain Investigational Review Board approval.

The responsible physician will decide that such a situation exists based upon predetermined criteria. Permission to use the medication must be obtained from the physician's department chair. The physician then contacts the Office for Research and Sponsored Programs who designates an Investigational Review Board member to review the request. If deemed appropriate, the responsible physician or designee will make contact with the FDA or drug sponsor to get the drug released. The responsible physician will then contact the Pharmacy with the appropriate drug information, the patient's name and location, and when the drug will be available from the FDA or drug sponsor. Written approval from the Investigational Review Board to the Pharmacy will follow.

Emergency use of a drug is limited to one time use. If a physician desires to use the drug in more than one patient, an Investigational Review Board protocol and application must be submitted and approved. An Investigational New Drug application through the FDA also may be required.

As with any investigational drug, informed consent must be obtained prior to drug administration. Emergency-use investigational agents are intended for a specific patient and are stored separately from other investigational drugs. Storage, inventory, and dispensing of the drug must be done through the Pharmacy Department.

**Name a few investigational drugs that are being currently used at the Division.**

Rapimmune, Ultraset, A-Z Study Drug, and ERLB-302.

**Is the pharmacy medication profile available to individuals outside the Pharmacy Department?**

The Pharmacy patient medication profiles are located in *IDX* and are available for review by all health care professionals.

**What information resources are available for pharmacists, nurses, and physicians?**

All health care professionals have access at each patient care area to the Medical Center Formulary and the American Hospital Formulary Service, a publication of the American Society of Hospital Pharmacists. Pharmacy satellite locations have a variety of drug therapy references and texts. Each Pharmacy satellite location also contains the *United States Pharmacopeia Drug Information Patient Education Sheets* either in the pharmacy computer or as a hard copy on file. Additional drug information is available from Pharmacists in decentralized satellite locations. These areas can be contacted via telephone or in person.

*continues*

4–128 continued

**What happens if a patient wants to use his or her own medications?**

Per Medical Center policy, patients are strongly encouraged not to bring their own medications to the Medical Center upon admission. Patients are urged to send personal medications home with a friend or relative. Patients are only permitted to receive medications dispensed by the Pharmacy Department and are not to be allowed to take their own medications. In unusual circumstances, the Pharmacist and Physician may agree that the patient may use his or her own supply. In these cases, the physician must write a medication order indicating that the patient may take his or her own medication. The Pharmacy Department must receive the patient's supply and relabel it in a fashion compatible with the unit dose system and dispense a daily supply.

**Has the Medical Center defined the most clinically important drug-food interactions? How is a drug with potential for drug-food interaction identified? Who counsels patients on drug-food interactions at discharge?**

The Departments of Pharmacy, Nutrition, and Nursing in collaboration with the Patient and Family Education Task Force have identified 6 drug-food interactions that are most clinically important in the patient population at the Medical Center. These are:

1. Monoamine Oxidase Inhibitors

   Interaction: Ingestion of monoamine oxidase inhibitors with foods that have a high tyramine or histamine content, such as aged cheeses, red wine, beer (including alcohol-free or reduced alcohol beverages), certain types of fish (skipjack, tuna, tropical) and foods that contain a large amount of caffeine may precipitate a hypertensive crisis. Patients should be counseled to avoid or limit their intake of these foods while on MAOIs and for 4 weeks after discontinuing a MAOI.
   Severity: Major
   Prevalence: Low

2. Warfarin

   Interaction: Changes in Vitamin K intake may lead to changes in anticoagulation parameters and may necessitate increased or decreased warfarin requirements. Patients should be counseled to eat a normal, balanced diet while on warfarin, and not to make any substantial changes in dietary intake of green, leafy vegetables or vegetables containing large amounts of Vitamin K.
   Severity: Moderate
   Prevalence: High

3. Tetracyclines (Tetracycline Hydrochloride, Demeclocycline)

   Interaction: Ingestion of milk, milk-containing, or other dairy products within 1 to 2 hours of taking certain tetracycline antibiotics can reduce the absorption of the antibiotic by 50% or more, decreasing its clinical efficacy. Patients should be counseled to take tetracycline or demeclocycline one hour before or two hours after ingesting a dairy product. Doxycycline and minocycline, two other tetracycline antibiotics, are not affected by this interaction.
   Severity: Moderate
   Prevalence: Low

4. Low Diuretics (Furosemide, Ethacrynic Acid, Bumetanide)

   Interaction: Loop diuretics can cause hypokalemia. Dietary supplementation with foods having a high potassium content may be indicated. Also, hypertensive patients and congestive heart failure patients may need to follow a low sodium diet. Patient education may be required on sodium content of foods.
   Severity: Moderate
   Prevalence: High

*continues*

**4–128** continued

5. Thiazide Diuretics

   Interaction: Thiazide diuretics can cause hypokalemia. Dietary supplementation with foods having a high potassium content may be indicated. Also, hypertensive patients and congestive heart failure patients may need to follow a low sodium diet. Patient education may be required on sodium content of foods.
   Severity: Major
   Prevalence: High

6. Isoniazid

   Interaction: Ingestion of isoniazid, an antituberculosis drug having monoamine oxidase inhibition activity, with foods that contain large amounts of the pressor amines tyramine and histamine may lead to their accumulation and result in a hypertensive crisis.
   Severity: Major
   Prevalence: High

When a patient is receiving one (or more) of these 6 drugs during the admission, a pharmacist, nurse, or dietician obtains the appropriate USPDI Patient Education sheets from the Pharmacy Satellite and discusses the information with the patient and/or the patient's family. This information is reinforced by the pharmacist, nurse, or dietitian upon discharge of the patient.

**Where/How is potential food-drug interaction patient education documented?**

This process should be documented in the patient's medical record in the progress notes section by the individual(s) who provides the patient with the information/education.

**What is the process for identifying and managing drug interactions?**

Pharmacists are the most prominent health professionals that identify and manage drug interactions. During the profiling of new drugs, a drug interaction may be identified. The Pharmacist gathers any necessary information regarding the patient from the medical record and/or the patient and uses professional judgment to evaluate the clinical significance of any identified drug interaction. If the drug interaction is deemed clinically significant, the pharmacist collaborates with the responsible physician to evaluate the risk versus benefit of continuing the agents that are interacting. The pharmacist may recommend to discontinue one or more of the interacting agents or to continue the medications with appropriate monitoring for therapeutic or adverse effects.

**Who educates patients at the Division about their medications and potential drug-drug and food-drug interactions?**

All health care professionals educate patients and/or their families about medications. Pharmacists provide educational support for patients and families regarding medications and medication use. The primary purpose of this education is consistent with the Pharmaceutical Care mission of the Department of Pharmacy.

Pharmacists at the Medical Center promote rational, patient-oriented drug therapy through the responsible provision of drug therapy and medication education for the purpose of achieving definite outcomes that improve a patient's quality of life. These outcomes are:

- Cure of a disease
- Elimination or reduction of a patient's symptomatology
- Arresting or slowing of a disease process
- Preventing a disease or symptomatology

The ultimate purpose of patient and family education activities by the Department of Pharmacy is to ensure that patients and their families are receiving adequate, accurate education about the medications being used for

*continues*

4–128 continued

their clinical condition during admission and upon discharge. This includes education relating to food-drug interactions as well.

Once educational needs have been assessed, pharmacists are available to educate all patients and families upon request.

Medication education materials are available for pharmacists and any other health care professional providing medication education from each pharmacy area throughout the Medical Center and the Patient/Health Education Department. The Medical Center utilizes a personal-computer based medication education database available from the *United States Pharmacopeia - Drug Information for Patients*.

Clinical Pharmacy Managers provide additional patient and family pharmaceutical education as the foundation of the department's Pharmaceutical Care initiatives for specifically defined patient populations within the medical center. These populations are targeted because the Pharmacy Department, in collaboration with the Medical Staff, has determined these patients to be at a high risk for developing a drug-related problem either because of their disease state, therapeutic drug regimen, or age-related complications.

These patient types include, but are not limited to, pediatric patients, infectious disease patients, family medicine patients, neurology patients, critical care patients, adult medicine and cardiology patients, AIDS patients, and patients on investigational drug protocols.

The Pharmacy Department also provides a variety of organized group, patient and family education sessions for assorted patient groups coordinated through the Social Service and Patient/Health Education Departments.

**How does the Medication Usage Evaluation (MUE) program work in the Medical Center?**

Medication Usage Evaluation is the responsibility of the P&T Committee. The P&T Committee is responsible for improving the quality of therapeutic drug outcomes in our patients by evaluating the appropriateness, safety, and efficacy of therapeutic agents utilized at the institution. Medication Usage Evaluation is a planned, systematic, and ongoing evaluation of the use of target drugs or drug classes. The MUE process is conducted as a criteria based, ongoing, planned, and systematic means of monitoring and evaluating drug use. The therapeutic, empiric, and prophylactic uses of selected drugs are addressed. The process is designed to identify opportunities to improve the use of drugs and resolve problems with their use.

MUE criteria are objective, written elements addressing the appropriate, safe, and effective use of the target drug or drug class. The criteria include the prophylactic, empiric, and therapeutic uses of the target drug or drug class. The criteria are developed by the Department of Pharmacy in collaboration with a representative of the Medical Staff considered to be an "expert" in the therapeutic use of the target drug.

Data collection is retrospective and/or concurrent and conducted by the Pharmacy Department. Variant usage is discussed with responsible physicians during the data collection period in an attempt to initiate positive outcomes during the patient's treatment course. Data collection continues until an appropriate number of cases are evaluated. Once data collection is complete, a report is generated by the Department of Pharmacy and presented to the P&T Committee for analysis.

The P&T Committee analyzes the MUE data comparing the results with the established criteria and determines if the identified problems are real. The P&T Committee develops a performance improvement plan that includes continued data collection to determine if corrective actions have resulted in an improvement in the use of the drug.

**Where/How does the Medical Center communicate MUE information?**

The findings, recommendations, and follow-up actions of the P&T Committee are shared with the Medical Staff, hospital administration, the Quality Improvement/Utilization Management Department, the Pharmacy Department, and other health professionals practicing within the institution at least quarterly via the *Pharmacy Bulletin* or *P&T Notes* and the clinical departments or divisions. When appropriate, individualized department-specific follow-up plans are developed by the involved departments and initiated by the Medical Staff.

*continues*

**4–128** continued

**How does the P&T Committee decide on which drugs to do MUEs?**

Drugs or drug classes evaluated in the MUE process include representatives of all drug classes used at the Medical Center and fall into one or more of the following categories:

- Drugs that are known or suspected to cause adverse reactions or interact with another drug (or drugs) in a manner that presents a significant health risk;
- Drugs used in the treatment of patients who may be at high risk for adverse drug reactions because of age, disability, or unique metabolic characteristics;
- Drugs that have been designated, through the Medical Center's Quality Assurance and Infection Control activities, for monitoring and evaluation; and
- Drugs that are frequently prescribed by the Medical Staff.

Additionally, the P&T Committee may add a drug to the Formulary with a follow-up MUE after 6–12 months to measure and ensure that the drug is being used at the Medical Center in the manner in which the P&T Committee intended.

In 1998, 1999, and 2000, the MUE program evaluated the use of the following medications:

| | |
|---|---|
| Therapeutic substitution with simvastatin | Use of fosphenytoin |
| Pharmacist-coordinated vaccination program | Use of levalbuterol |
| Adherence to change order clarification forms | Focused evaluation of ciprofloxacin |
| Compliance with Non-Formulary documentation | Informed consent documentation |
| Use of immediate release nifedipine | Medication Error initiative |

**What is your drug recall system?**

The Pharmacy Department has an extensive drug recall policy. Drug recall information may be obtained from a variety of sources including, but not limited to, the pharmaceutical manufacturer, wholesaler, the pharmaceutical buying group, the Materials Management Department, or the FDA. The responsible Pharmacy personnel inspect all areas where the recalled drug may be within the department, the pharmacy satellites, other departments, and patient care areas to retrieve any recalled medication. Physicians caring for patients who are receiving any of the recalled medications are consulted by the Pharmacy to initiate alternative therapy.

The Pharmacy contacts designated individuals in the Pharmacy Departments in the Medical Center-affiliated institutions informing them of the recall. The Pharmacy also contacts designated individuals at each of the outreach programs where pharmaceuticals are provided by the Pharmacy to inform them of the recalled drug.

These actions take place 7 days a week, 24 hours a day.

If the recalled drug is not purchased by the Pharmacy, a note to this effect is entered into the drug recall file kept in the Pharmacy Department.

All collected recalled drugs are sent to the Pharmacy Department from all of the areas that had the drug, and are sequestered from other drugs in containers marked "recall" until arrangements are made for their return to the pharmaceutical manufacturer.

*continues*

**4–128** continued

**How are drug orders verified when questions develop in the dispensing of medications?**

Pharmacists intervene on behalf of patients when medication orders require clarification, when drug therapy dosages and regimens require adjustments based upon individual patient or disease characteristics, when clinically significant drug-drug and/or drug-food interactions are present, when potential ADRs or medication errors may occur, and when the selection of drug therapy may not be optimal. Pharmacists collaborate with physicians and nurses on behalf of patients hundreds of times each month and document these interventions in the Department's Intervention Documentation database. Many of these interventions result in changes in drug therapy designed for more optimal outcomes. Either physicians rewrite medication orders or a Change Order/ Clarification Form is initiated by the Pharmacy for inclusion in the Medical Record.

Reports from the Intervention Documentation database are used to identify trends and serve as an important tool in identifying and targeting drug therapy monitoring, MUE, and performance improvement initiatives. Educational and training programs for the Pharmacy and other disciplines are based upon drug therapy issues requiring the most number of interventions.

**How are emergency drugs controlled in the Medical Center?**

Emergency medication kits are prepared, issued, restocked, and controlled by the Department of Pharmacy. The emergency medication kits contain drugs and supplies for use during cardiac arrests. Four types of emergency medication kits are available. The CAC Emergency Kit is intended for use in inpatient areas where emergency supplies other than drugs are available and not included in the kit. The regular Emergency Kit is intended for use in inpatient areas or off-site clinic areas where emergency supplies and drugs are not available and therefore included in the kit. The Pediatric CAC Emergency Kit contains drugs for use during cardiac arrests that occur in pediatric units. In designated stepdown areas, critical care areas, the emergency department and the post anesthesia care units, some emergency medications are required during transport of critically ill patients.

When emergency kits are used, a **yellow** lock provided inside the box must be used to secure the box until it is returned to the Pharmacy. The control number of these locks should be recorded on the crash cart checklist. These locks are controlled by the Pharmacy Department. For off-site kits, the messenger service returns the used/expired kits to the Pharmacy for replacement.

Restocking of the emergency kits is conducted by the Pharmacy Department technical staff and checked by a pharmacist. After pharmacist verification for accuracy, the kits are locked with **red** breakaway locks. These locks are also controlled by the Pharmacy Department.

Emergency medications are not to be stored in crash carts.

The CAC Committee of the Medical Center is responsible for approving changes in the emergency kits. Major changes to the kits are made annually by the Pharmacy.

**How is the use of sample medication controlled in the Medical Center?**

The distribution of medication samples for patients unable to obtain prescribed medications is an ethical responsibility of the Medical Center. In the interest of effective control and patient safety, the use of medication samples in the Medical Center is under the control of the Pharmacy Department in collaboration with the Ambulatory Care Center at the Medical Center and the Medical Group. The Medical Center allows for the use of medication samples in designated outpatient locations only. Distribution of medication samples directly to inpatient care areas by medical service representatives is not permitted.

*Medication samples in authorized locations must be* ***locked, labeled, and logged*** *in accordance with the Medical Center policy and state law. Sample medications may only be dispensed by physicians or other practitioners authorized to prescribe medications in* **the state.**

*continues*

**4–128** continued

**Locked**: *All medication samples must be secured in a locked cabinet.* Any samples not secured should be appropriately discarded (destroyed, crushed). **Note:** because of their hazardous or toxic nature, the Environmental Protection Agency has determined that warfarin, nicotine patches, nitroglycerin, epinephrine, phenol, lindane, and diethylstilbestrol cannot be discarded as regular trash and therefore should be returned to the pharmacy. Chemotherapy waste should be discarded in chemotherapy waste containers.

**Labeled:** *All medication samples must be labeled* in accordance with state law governing prescriptions. In addition to the manufacturer's labeling, a label affixed to the sample container should contain, at minimum, the date of dispensing, patient's name and address, name of the prescriber and directions for appropriate use. The pharmacy can provide preprinted "generic" labels upon request.

**Logged**: *A separate inventory/dispensing record* for each strength of each sample must be kept at the sample cabinet. This record should include the name and quantities of each lot number of sample medication, the date of dispensation, the quantity dispensed, the name of the prescribing physician or authorized prescriber, and the name or initials of the individual authorized to dispense sample medications. The pharmacy can provide those log sheets upon request. These records should be kept for at least 5 years.

It is the responsibility of the clinical units to routinely inspect their areas for adherence to the Medical Center's legal and regulatory medication related policies.

Source: Montefiore Medical Center, Bronx, New York.

# 4–129
# Joint Commission Update

The Joint Commission on Accreditation of Healthcare Organizations (Joint Commission) is the not-for-profit safety and quality evaluator of nearly 5,000 hospitals. In promoting the need for new patient safety standards, the Joint Commission cited a 1999 Institute of Medicine report that estimated medical errors kill between 44,000 and 98,000 hospital patients annually.

The Joint Commission's new safety standards went into effect July 1, 2001. These policies required hospitals to initiate specific efforts to prevent medical errors and to tell patients when they have been harmed during their treatment. The Joint Commission has reported that, overall, implementation of the new standards has gone smoothly and without too many problems. It has put out literature over the past several months regarding frequently asked questions, and its Web site, jcaho.org, has a section on compliance issues that will guide an institution through the procedure of implementation.

The new standards underscore the importance of strong organization leadership in building what the Joint Commission refers to as a "culture of safety." The Joint Commission policies state that a culture should "strongly encourage the internal reporting of medical errors, and actively engage clinicians and other staff in the design of remedial steps to prevent future occurrences of these errors." According to a recent Joint Commission media release, "the additional emphasis on effective communication, appropriate training, and teamwork found in the standards language draw heavily upon lessons learned in both the aviation and health care industries."

A second major focus of the new standards is on the prevention of medical errors through the "prospective analysis and redesign of vulnerable patient care systems" (e.g., the ordering, preparation, and dispensing of medications). Potentially vulnerable systems can readily be identified through relevant national databases such as the Joint Commission's Sentinel Event Database or through the hospital's own risk management experience. Finally, the standards make clear the hospital's responsibility to tell a patient if he or she has been harmed by the care provided.

When the new standards are implemented, over 50 percent of all of the Joint Commission's hospital standards will relate directly to patient safety. The Joint Commission has been publishing standards for quality in health care for 50 years. However, the new standards are based on the Joint Commission's six-year experience in overseeing the management of sentinel (adverse) events in accredited organizations, and on the opinions of a special panel that included patient safety experts as well as leaders from government, hospitals, insurance companies, universities, and consumer advocacy groups. Broad field input was also solicited in finalizing the standards.

Similar standards also are being developed for the nearly 14,000 Joint Commission-accredited nursing homes, behavioral health facilities, outpatient clinics, laboratories, managed care organizations, and home health agencies. Those standards have not been formally issued yet, but are sure to come in the near future. New standards now being required include:

- Designating one or more qualified individuals or an interdisciplinary group to manage the organizationwide patient safety program—typically these individuals may include directors of performance improvement, safety officers, risk managers, and clinical leaders;
- Defining the scope of the program activities, that is the types of occurrences to be addressed—typically ranging from "no harm," frequently occurring "slips" to sentinel events with serious adverse outcomes;
- Defining procedures for immediate response to medical/health care errors, including care of the affected patient(s), containment of risk to others, and preservation of factual information for subsequent analysis;
- Clearing systems for internal and external reporting of medical/health care errors;
- Defining mechanisms for support of staff involved in a sentinel event;

*continues*

4–129 continued

- At least annually, reporting to the governing body on the occurrence of medical/health care errors and actions taken to improve patient safety, both in response to actual occurrences and proactively;
- At least annually, selecting at least one high-risk process for proactive risk assessment; such selection is to be based, in part, on information published periodically by the Joint Commission that identifies the most frequently occurring types of sentinel events and patient safety risk factors;
- Assessing the intended and actual implementation of the process to identify the steps where there is, or may be, undesirable variation (i.e., what engineers call potential "failure modes");
- For each identified "failure mode," identifying the possible effects on patients (what engineers call the "effect"), and how serious the possible effect on the patient;
- For the most critical effects, conducting a root cause analysis to determine why the variation (the failure mode) leading to that effect may occur;
- Redesigning the process and/or underlying systems to minimize the risk of that failure mode or to protect patients from the effects of that failure mode;
- Testing and implementing the redesigned process;
- Identifying and implementing measures of the effectiveness of the redesigned process; and
- Implementing a strategy for maintaining the effectiveness of the redesigned process over time.

Courtesy of Julia J. Dodd, R.Ph., J.D., Cowles & Thompson, P.C., Dallas, Texas.

**Part 5**

# CMS and Joint Commission Standards Checklist

The following materials serve as examples. Hospitals should consult with counsel or other appropriate advisors before adapting the materials in this part to suit particular purposes.

## Part 5 Contents

## INTRODUCTION

"Hospital Checklist: CMS and Joint Commission Standards" is a tool designed to reference similarities and differences between CMS regulations and Joint Commission accreditation standards for hospital compliance. It is an invaluable tool for quality assurance nurses, directors of nursing, infection control nurses, medical records personnel, risk managers, and hospital administrators.

CMS regulations are cited in the Code of Federal Regulations (C.F.R.). The Hospital Conditions of Participation (COPs) at 42 C.F.R. Subpart E is cited as 42 C.F.R. 482. CMS expects the hospital, as part of its participation agreement, to implement a demonstrable process and system to produce the desired outcome for compliance with the regulations. Citations or Statements of Deficiency (SODs) are written when the hospital fails to maintain a system to produce the desired outcome or when the hospital fails to monitor and correct undesirable outcomes. CMS can take termination actions if the intent of the regulation is not objectively met by the hospital.

"Hospital Checklist: CMS and Joint Commission Standards" compares CMS regulations to Joint Commission accreditation standards in a table format. The table contains a section for the user to enter applicable state laws for a complete reference guide. **Remember**, the hospital's policies, procedures, and protocols (PPPs) must reflect the requirements of CMS, the Joint Commission, and the state to be in compliance, so it makes sense to include all of the requirements in one easy-to-use checklist.

This checklist **is intended** for use as a reference guide to aid the user in determining the most stringent requirements for compliance, so the user can formulate PPPs that meet or exceed the most restrictive requirement. It **is not intended** to be utilized as a complete set of regulations, conditions, standards, or laws governing hospitals or compliance.

Denise Casaubon, RN, Paralegal
a teeny tiny corporation
dba DNR Medical-Legal Consultants

Rose Sparks, RN, BA
a Wildcat Corporation
dba DNR Medical-Legal Consultants

## AREAS OF RISK

| Requirement | CMS | | Joint Commission | State |
|---|---|---|---|---|
| ***Compliance Federal, State, Local Laws*** | **482.11(a)**<br>**482.11(c)** | | **MA.2**—Compliance with law/regulation<br>**MA.2.1**—CEO responds to agencies' reports and recommendations.<br>**GO.2.4**—Compliance with law/regulation | |
| ***Governing Body [GB] Administration*** | **482.12** | Legally responsible for the conduct of the hospital<br>**(a)** Appoint medical staff [MS].<br>**(a)(4)** Approve MS bylaws and rules/regulations.<br>**(a)(5)** Ensure MS is accountable to the GB for quality of care provided.<br><br>**(b)** Appoint a CEO.<br><br>**(c)** Patients under the care of a physician<br>**(c)(2)** Patient admissions<br>**(c)(5)** Written protocols for organ donation<br>**(d)** Plan and budget<br><br>**(d)(6)** Revised/updated annually<br>**(d)(7)** Plan prepared under the direction of the GB<br>**(e)** Responsible for contracted services<br>**(f)** Emergency services | **MA.1**—CEO responsible for operating the hospital according to GB.<br><br>**GO.2.1**—Adopt bylaws addressing legal responsibilities.<br><br>**GO.2.2**—MS participation in governance<br>**MS.1**—MS responsibility for quality of professional services provided and accountability to the GB.<br><br>**GO.2.3**—Select qualified CEO.<br>**MA.1.1**—CEO education/experience<br>**MS.6.1**—Privileges granted to admit patients to inpatient services<br><br>**RI.2**—Policies for procurement and donation of organs/ other tissues<br>**LD.1.5**—Approves annual budget.<br>**LD.1.5.3**—Annual audit by an accountant<br>**LD.1.5.2**—Budget review process<br><br>**LD.2.10**—Selecting outside resources for needed services<br><br>**GO.2.5**—Developing, reviewing, and revising policies and procedures<br><br>**GO.2.6**—GB provides for conflict resolution.<br>**LD.1.7**—Each department's scope of services is defined in writing. | |

*continues*

**Areas of Risk** continued

| Requirement | CMS | | Joint Commission | State |
|---|---|---|---|---|
| ***Patients' Rights [PR]*** | **482.13** | Hospital must promote and protect each PR. | **RI.1**—Hospital addresses ethical issues in patient care. | |
| | | **(a)(1)** Inform patient or representative of PR before furnishing or discontinuing care. | **RI.1.4**—Each patient receives written patient's rights. | |
| | | **(a)(2)** Establish a patient grievance process that includes referral to utilization review (UR) and quality assurance (QA). | **RI.1.2.4**—Patients involved in resolving care decision dilemmas<br>**RI.1.3.4**—Resolution of complaints | |
| | | **(b)** Patients have the right to participate in plan of care. | **RI.1.2**—Patients are involved in care. | |
| | | **(b)(2)** Patient or representative has the right to make informed decisions for care. | **RI.1.2.1**—Informed consent obtained<br>**RI.4.3**—Address right to perform or refuse to perform taskswith longer length of stay. | |
| | | **(b)(3)** Patient has the right to formulate advance directives. | **RI.1.2.5**—Hospital addresses advanced directives.<br>**RI.1.2.6–1.2.8**—Resuscitation, life sustaining treatment, end of life | |
| | | **(c)(1)** Right to personal privacy | **RI.1.3.2**—Privacy | |
| | | **(c)(2)** Right to receive safe care | **RI.1.3.3**—Security | |
| | | **(c)(3)** Right to be free from abuse or harassment | | |
| | | **(d)(1)** Right to confidentiality of medical records (MR) | **RI.1.3.1**—*Confidentiality* | |
| | | **(d)(2)** Right to access information contained in MR in reasonable amount of time | | |
| | | **(e)(1)** Right to be free from restraints (physical or chemical) not medically necessary | **TX.7.1**—Restraint or seclusion use<br>**TX.7.1.4.1**— Restaint and seclusion limited to emergencies where patient is at risk to hurt self or others. | |
| | | **(e)(2)** Restraint used only to improve the patient's well-being | | |
| | | **(e)(3)** Use of a restraint must be | | |
| | | **(e)(3)(i)** used when less restrictive measures ineffective | **TX.7.1.4**—Non physical techniques are preferred | |
| | | **(e)(3)(ii)** in accordance with a physician's order. The order must | **TX.7.1.5**—Restraint or seclusion use ordered by licensed practitioner | |
| | | **(e)(3)(ii)(A)** never be written as a standing or as needed order | **TX.7.1.6**—A licensed practitioner evaluates the patient in person. | |

*continues*

**Areas of Risk** continued

| Requirement | CMS | Joint Commission | State |
|---|---|---|---|
| | **(e)(3)(iii)** according to written changes to patient's plan of care<br>**(e)(3)(iv)** implemented in the least restrictive manner<br>**(e)(3)(v)** in accordance with safe restraint techniques<br>**(e)(3)(vi)** ended at earliest time.<br>**(e)(4)** Patient must be continually assessed, monitored, reevaluated.<br>**(e)(5)** Direct patient care staff must have ongoing education and training in safe use of restraints.<br>**(f)(1)** Patient has the right to be free from seclusion and restraint imposed as coercion or discipline.<br>**(f)(2)** Only used in emergency situations to protect patient/ others<br>**(f)(3)(ii)(C)** Practitioner must see and evaluate restraint/ seclusion within 1 hour of intervention<br>**(f)(3)(ii)(D)** Restraint or seclusion orders max: 4 hours adults, 2 hours age 9–17, 1 hour if under 9—for a total of 24 hours<br>**(f)(4)(i)** Restraint *and* seclusion require continual face-to-face monitoring *OR*<br>**(f)(4)(ii)** continuous video and audio monitoring.<br>**(f)(7)** Hospital must report to CMS any death that occurs while a patient is restrained or secluded. | **TX.7.4**—Use of behavior management conforms to patient's treatment plan<br><br>**TX.7.1.2**—Used correctly by trained staff<br><br>**TX.7.1.11**—Restrained patients are monitored.<br><br>**TX.7.1.7**—Written or verbal orders for use of restraint and seclusion are time limited.<br>**TX.7.1.8**—Restrained or secluded patients are regularly reevaluated.<br><br>**TX.7.1.15**—Collect data on use of restraints and seclusion to monitor and improve performance. | |

*continues*

**Areas of Risk** continued

| Requirement | CMS | | Joint Commission | State |
|---|---|---|---|---|
| ***Quality Assurance [QA]***<br>***Continuous Quality Improvement [CQI]***<br>***Performance Improvement [PI]*** | **482.21** | GB ensures there is an effective hospitalwide program.<br>**(a)** Written plan, ongoing activities<br>**(a)(1)** Evaluation of contracted services<br>**(a)(2)** Evaluation of infections and medication therapy<br>**(a)(3)** Evaluation of medical and surgical services<br>**(b)** Services meet medically related needs of patients.<br>**(c)** Implementation of program and documentation of remedial actions and outcomes | **PI.1**—Organization wide approach to performance measurement, analysis and improvement (not scored at this standard)<br>**PI.4–PI.4.4**—Aggregation and analysis of data and sentinel events<br>**PI.3–PI.3.1.3**—Collection of data to monitor performance<br>**PI.5**—Improved performance is achieved and sustained.<br>**NR.4**—Nursing and PI activities (not scored at this standard).<br>**HR.4.3**—Collect data on competence patterns and trends of staff.<br><br>**TX.7.5.1**—PI identifies opportunities to reduce risks of restraint use.<br>**LD.1.4**—PI organization priorities in response to unusual events.<br>**LD.2.7**—Directors maintain quality control programs.<br>**LD.4–LD.4.5**—Leadership's role in PI<br>**MS.3.1.6.1.5**—MS's participation in PI<br>**MS.8–MS.8.4**—MS's role in PI<br>**IM.8**—Hospital collects and aggregates data/information to support care and service delivery/operations.<br><br>**ORYX specific requirements are not included in the scope of this manual.** | |

*continues*

**Areas of Risk** continued

| Requirement | CMS | | Joint Commission | State |
|---|---|---|---|---|
| ***Medical Staff [MS]*** | **482.22** | Organized MS responsible for the care of patients | **MS.6–MS.6.8**—Care of the patient | |
| | | **(a)** Composition of MS | **MS.1.1.1**—MS includes licensed physicians and licensed independent practitioners. | |
| | | **(a)(1)** Periodic peer review | | |
| | | **(a)(2)** Credentialing | **MS.5–MS.5.15.7**—Credentialing | |
| | | **(b)** Accountable to the GB | **GO.2.2.1**—MS at GB meetings | |
| | | **(b)(2)** If MS has executive committee, majority of members are MDs or DOs. | **MS.3.1**—There is an executive committee of MS.<br>**MS.3.1.4**—The majority of voting members are licensed physicians. | |
| | | **(b)(3)** Responsibility for the organization and conduct of MS assigned to an MD or DO | **MS.4–MS.4.2.1.15**—Department leadership | |
| | | **(c)** Medical staff bylaws adopted and enforced | **MS.2.2**—MS bylaws/rules/regulations | |
| | | **(c)(1)** Approved by the GB | **MS.2.1**—Approved by the GB | |
| | | **(c)(2)** Statement of privileges of each category of MS | **MS.1.1.3**—Delineated clinical privileges | |
| | | **(c)(3)** Describe MS organization | **MS.2.3.4**—Description MS organization | |
| | | **(c)(4)** Describe qualifications for MS appointment | **MS.5.4.3**—Professional criteria | |
| | | **(c)(5)** History and physical [H&P] are completed 7 days before or 48 hours after admission by an MD, DO, or oromaxillofacial surgeon. | **PE.1.7.1**—H&P completed in 24 hours<br>**PE.1.7.1.1**—H&P within last 30 days in MR with recorded changes<br>**MS.6.2.1**—Oral and maxillofacial surgeons | |
| | | **(c)(6)** Criteria for determining privileges | **MS.3.1.6.1.2 and MS.3.1.6.1.4**—Clinical privileges<br>**MS.5.11**—Appointment for no more than 2 years | |
| | | **(d)** Autopsies: securing and notification | **MS.8.5–MS.8.5.3**—Autopsies: securing, defining, and performing<br>**PE.2–PE.2.4**—Patient reassessments<br>**PE.4.2**—Practitioner with clinical privileges determines scope of assessment and care of patients in need of Emergency Care.<br>**MS.2.3.2, MS.3.1.6.1.7, MS.5.2, MS.5.4.4.1**—Fair hearing processes<br>**MS.2.3.3**—Mechanism for corrective action | |

*continues*

**Areas of Risk** continued

| Requirement | CMS | | Joint Commission | State |
|---|---|---|---|---|
| ***Nursing Services [NS]*** | **482.23** | Organized, 24 hour NS under the supervision of an RN<br>**(a)** Plan of administrative authority and delineation of responsibilities for patient care Director of Nursing (DON) must be an RN.<br>**(b)** Staffing and delivery of care ensures immediate availability of an RN for patient care.<br>**(b)(2)** Nurses must have valid, current licenses.<br>**(b)(3)** RN supervises/evaluates care for each patient.<br>**(b)(4)** Current Nursing Care Plans for each patient<br>**(b)(5)** RN makes patient care assignments.<br>**(b)(6)** Responsibility for nonemployee nurses (registry)<br>**(c)** Preparation and administration of drugs and biologicals<br>**(c)(2)** Orders for drugs and biologicals must be in writing and signed by the practitioner responsible for the patient's care.<br>**(c)(2)(i)** Telephone orders PPP<br>**(c)(3)** Blood transfusions are administered per approved MS policies and procedures.<br>**(c)(4)** Reporting transfusion and adverse drug reactions and errors in administration of drugs | **LD.2.11**—Department directed by qualified professional<br><br>**NR.1**—Nursing services directed by RN executive<br>**NR.2**—Nurse executive establishes standards of nursing practices.<br><br>**LD.2.4**—Sufficient number qualified/competent persons to provide care<br>**HR.2**—Adequate number of qualified staff<br><br>**PE.4.3**—RN assesses the patient's need for nursing care.<br>**PE.3–PE.3.1**—Patient care needs and care decisions<br><br>**TX.3.6**—Orders are verified and patients identified before medication given.<br>**TX.3.3**—Policies for medication orders<br><br>**IM.7.7**—Protocols for verbal orders<br>**MS.8.1.3**—Use of blood/blood components<br><br>**TX.3.9**—Medication effects on patients are monitored.<br><br>**PE.1.7.1**—Nursing assessment in 24 hours<br>**PE.2–PE.2.4**—Patient reassessments<br>**NR.3**—Policies, standards of patient care, and nursing practice are approved by nurse executive. | |

*continues*

**Areas of Risk** continued

| Requirement | CMS | | Joint Commission | State |
|---|---|---|---|---|
| ***Medical Records Services [MR]/ Information Management*** | **482.24** | MR must be maintained for every person evaluated or treated.<br>**(a)** Must employ personnel to ensure prompt completion, filing, and retrieval of records<br>**(b)** Form and retention of MR: accurate, promptly filed, retained, and accessible and system of author identification that protects security of entries<br>**(b)(1)** Retained at least 5 years<br>**(b)(2)** Coding and indexing system<br>**(b)(3)** Procedures for ensuring confidentiality and release<br>**(c)** Content of MR: reason for admission, patient's progress, and response to treatment<br>**(c)(1)** Legible, complete, and authenticated (name and discipline) and dated promptly<br>**(c)(1)(ii)** Authentication: signatures, written initials, or computer entry<br>**(c)(2)** MR must document the following:<br>**(c)(2)(i)** H&P 7 days before or 48 hours after admission<br>**(c)(2)(ii)** Admitting diagnosis<br>**(c)(2)(iii)** Results of evaluations and findings<br>**(c)(2)(v)** Properly executed informed consent forms<br>**(c)(2)(vi)** Information necessary to monitor the patient's condition<br>**(c)(2)(vii)** Discharge summary, outcome, and follow-up care<br>**(c)(2)(viii)** MR completed in 30 days after discharge. | **IM.7.1.**—Hospital maintains MR for every individual assessed or treated.<br>**IM.2**—Confidentiality, security, and integrity of data/ information are maintained.<br>**IM.7.1.1**—Entries made in MR by authorized individuals<br>**IM.7.6**—MR data are managed in a timely manner.<br>**IM.7.1.2**—MR retention based on law and regulation<br>**IM.2.1**—Protect MR against destruction, loss, tampering, and unauthorized use.<br>**IM.7.2**—Information to identify patient, support diagnosis, justify treatment, course, and results<br>**IM.7.8**—Entries are dated, author identified, and authenticated (when necessary).<br>**PE.1.7.1**—H&P completed in 24 hours<br>**IM.7.2**—As noted above<br>**PE.1.5.1**—Test reports require clinical interpretation.<br>**RI.3.1**—Consent forms address information in RI.1.2.1.1–RI.1.2.1.5.<br>**IM.7.2**—As noted above<br>**IM.5**—Transmission of data is timely and accurate. | |

*continues*

**Areas of Risk** continued

| Requirement | CMS | | Joint Commission | State |
|---|---|---|---|---|
| ***Pharmaceutical Services [PS]*** | **482.25** | PS to meet the needs of patients. MS is responsible for developing PPP that minimize drug errors.<br>**(a)** Pharmacy or drug storage is administered in accordance with professional principles/state law.<br>**(a)(1)** Full-time, part-time, or consulting pharmacist is responsible for developing, supervising, and coordinating activities of PS.<br>**(a)(2)** Adequate number of personnel to ensure quality of PS<br>**(a)(3)** Current, accurate records on receipt and disposition of all scheduled drugs<br>**(b)(1)** Compounding, packaging, and dispensing under the supervision of a pharmacist<br>**(b)(2)** Drugs and biologicals must be kept in a locked storage area.<br>**(b)(3)** Outdated, mislabeled, or unusable drugs and biologicals must not be available for patient use.<br>**(b)(4)** PPP for removing drugs when pharmacist is not available<br>**(b)(5)** Protocol for automatic stop orders determined by the MS<br>**(b)(6)** Drug administration errors, drug reactions, and incompatibilities reported immediately to physician<br>**(b)(7)** Reporting of abuse and loss of controlled substances<br>**(b)(8)** Drug information available to professional staff<br>**(b)(9)** Established formulary | **TX.3.5.2**—Pharmacists review all prescriptions or orders.<br>**TX.3.4**—Medications prepared/administered per law, regulation, licensure, and standard of practice<br>**LD.2.11**—Department directed by qualified professional<br>**TX.3.5**—Preparation/dispensing medications appropriately controlled<br>**TX.3.5.5**—Emergency medications are available/secure in pharmacy and patient care areas.<br>**TX.3.5.6**—System for retrieval and safe disposition for discontinued and recalled medications<br>**TX.3.5.4**—Services are available when department is closed.<br>**TX.3.1**—Identified selection of medications<br>**TX.3.5.1**—A patient medication dose system is implemented | |

*continues*

**Areas of Risk** continued

| Requirement | CMS | | Joint Commission | State |
|---|---|---|---|---|
| ***Radiologic Services [RS]*** | **482.26** | **(a)** Hospitals must maintain, or have available, diagnostic RS.<br>**(b)** Must be free from hazards for patients and personnel<br>**(b)(2)** Periodic equipment inspections must be done.<br>**(b)(3)** Use of exposure meters or badge tests<br>**(b)(4)** Provided only on the order of practitioners with privileges<br>**(c)(1)** Personnel: full-time, part-time, or consulting radiologist<br>**(d)** Record of RS must be maintained.<br>**(d)(1)** Signed reports of interpretations<br>**(d)(2)** Retained at least 5 years | **LD.2.11**—Department directed by qualified professional<br>**PE.1.5**—Diagnostic testing to determine patient's health care needs | |

continues

**Areas of Risk** continued

| Requirement | CMS | Joint Commission | State |
|---|---|---|---|
| ***Laboratory Services [LS]*** | **482.27** **(a)** Hospitals must maintain, or have available, adequate LS.<br>**(b)(1)** Emergency LS must be available 24 hours a day.<br>**(b)(2)** Written description of LS must be available to the MS.<br>**(b)(4)** MS and a pathologist must determine tissue specimens that require macroscopic or macroscopic and microscopic examinations.<br>**(c)(1)** Potentially HIV infectious blood and blood products<br>**(c)(2)** Services furnished by an outside blood bank<br>**(c)(3)** Quarantine of blood and blood products pending completion of testing<br>**(c)(4)** Patient notification of administration of potentially HIV infectious blood or blood products<br>**(c)(5)** Timeframe for notification<br>**(c)(6)** Content of notification<br>**(c)(7)** Policies and procedures for notification<br><br>**CLIA (waived testing) specific requirements are not included in the scope of this manual. They can be found at 42 CFR 493, Subpart P.** | **PE.1.10**—LS and consultation readily available to meet patient needs<br><br>**PE.1.10.1**—Hospital provides for prompt performance of examinations in pathology/clinical LS.<br><br>**PE.1.5**—Diagnostic testing to determine patient's health care needs<br>**PE.1.10.2–PE.1.10.2.2**—Laboratory testing by hospital or approved reference or contract laboratories<br>**PE.1.11–PE.1.15.2**—Waived testing under federal law and regulation | |

*continues*

| Requirement | CMS | | Joint Commission | State |
|---|---|---|---|---|
| ***Food and Dietetic Services [FDS] and Nutrition Care*** | **482.28** | Must have an organized FDS that is directed and staffed by adequate personnel<br>**(a)(1)** Must have a full-time employee who<br>**(a)(1)(i)** serves as the director<br>**(a)(1)(ii)** is responsible for the daily management of FDS<br>**(a)(2)** There must be qualified dietitian, full-time, part-time, or consulting.<br>**(b)(1)** Therapeutic diets must be prescribed by the practitioner(s) responsible for the care of the patient.<br>**(b)(2)** Nutritional needs must be met in accordance with recognized dietary practices.<br>**(b)(3)** Therapeutic diet manual approved by the MS and dietitian and available to staff | **LD.2.11**—Department directed by qualified professional<br>**TX.4.3**—Responsibilities for all activities are assigned.<br>**TX.4.2**—Authorized individuals prescribe food/nutrition products in a timely manner.<br>**TX.4.5**—Each patient's response to nutrition care is monitored.<br>**PF.3.2**—Patient is educated about nutrition interventions and modified diets.<br>**PE.1.2**—Nutritional status is assessed when appropriate to patient needs.<br>**TX.4**—Each patient's nutrition care is planned.<br>**TX.4.1**—Interdisciplinary nutrition therapy plan is developed and updated.<br>**TX.4.1.1**—Meals/snacks support program goals.<br>**TX.4.4**—Food/nutrition distribution and administration<br>**TX.4.6**—Nutrition meets patients' needs for special diets and altered diet schedules.<br>**TX.4.7**—Nutrition care standardized throughout the hospital | |

*continues*

**Areas of Risk** continued

| Requirement | CMS | | Joint Commission | State |
|---|---|---|---|---|
| ***Utilization Review [UR] or Continuum of Care*** | **482.30** | **(a)** This section applies except in the following circumstances:<br>**(a)(1)** A PRO has assumed binding review for the hospital.<br>**(a)(2)** HCFA has determined the UR procedures by the state under Title XIX of the Act are superior to the procedures required in this section.<br>**(b)** UR committee composition<br>**(c)** Scope/frequency of review<br>**(d)** Determination regarding admissions or continued stays<br>**(e)** Extended stay review<br>**(f)** Review of professional services | **CC.1**—Patients have access to appropriate level of care and services.<br>**CC.2.1**—Criteria define patient information necessary for appropriate care.<br>**CC.3**— Continuity of care and services provided to patient.<br>**CC.4**— Hospital provides for referral, transfer, or discharge of the patient based on patient needs and hospital capacity to provide care**CC.5**— Hospital ensures clinical information is exchanged when patients are admitted, referred, transferred, or discharged.**CC.6**— Established procedures used to resolve denial-of-care conflicts. | |
| | **These sections are compared for total content only. DO NOT compare line by line.** | | **These sections are compared for total content only. DO NOT compare line by line.** | |

*continues*

**Areas of Risk** continued

| Requirement | CMS | Joint Commission | State |
|---|---|---|---|
| ***Physical Environment [PE]*** | **"Life Safety Code"**<br>**482.41** **(a)** PE must be developed and maintained to ensure safety of patients.<br>**(a)(1)** There must be emergency power and lighting.<br>**(a)(2)** There must be facilities for emergency gas and water.<br>**(b)** Life safety from fire<br>**(b)(2)** Must have procedures for the storage and disposal of trash<br>**(b)(3)** Must have a written fire control plan<br>**(b)(4)** Must maintain written evidence of inspection and approval of fire control agencies<br>**(c)(2)** Facilities, supplies, and equipment must be maintained to ensure safety and quality.<br>**(c)(4)** Must be proper ventilation, light, and temperature controls in PS and FDS | **EC.1.5.1**—Compliance with Life Safety Code<br>**EC.1**—*Hospital plans for environment of care consistent with mission, services, law, and regulation (not scored at this standard).*<br>**EC.1.7.1**—Provides reliable emergency power source<br>**EC.1.7**—Plans for managing utilities.<br>**EC.1.3**—Hazardous materials and waste management plan<br>**EC.1.5**—Plans for fire prevention<br>**EC.1.2**—Plans for secure environment<br>**EC.1.6**—Plans for managing medical equipment<br>**EC.1.1.1**—Plans for worker safety<br>**EC.1.1.2**—Develop policy re: smoking.<br>**EC.2**—*Hospital provides for environment of care consistent with mission, services, law, and regulation (not scored at this standard).*<br>**EC.2.1–EC.2.10.4.1**—Implementation<br>**EC.3–EC.3.4**—Plans and provides for other environmental concerns<br>**EC.4–EC.4.3**—Measures outcomes of implementation | |

*continues*

**Areas of Risk** continued

| Requirement | CMS | | Joint Commission | State |
|---|---|---|---|---|
| ***Infection Control [IC]*** | **482.42** | The hospital must have an active program for the prevention, control, and investigation of infections and communicable diseases. | **IC.1**—The organization uses a coordinated process to reduce risks of nosocomial infections in patients and health care workers. | |
| | | **(a)** Have designated infection control officer(s) develop and implement policies. | **IC.1.1**—IC process is managed by one or more qualified individuals. | |
| | | **(a)(1)** Infection control officer(s) must develop a system for identifying, reporting, investigating, and controlling infections and communicable diseases. | **IC.2**—Provide surveillance data.<br>**IC.3**—Report IC information internally and to public health agencies.<br>**IC.5**—Take action to control outbreaks.<br>**IC.6.2**—IC process includes at least 1 activity to prevent spread of infection. | |
| | | **(a)(2)** Must maintain a log of incidents related to infections and communicable diseases<br>**(b)** The CEO, MS, and DON must | **IC.6.1**—Management systems support the IC process. | |
| | | **(b)(1)** ensure hospitalwide quality assurance and training programs address problems identified by infection control officer(s) | **IC.4**—Take action to prevent or reduce the risk of nosocomial infections. | |
| | | **(b)(2)** be responsible for implementation of successful corrective action plans | **IC.6**—IC process is designed to lower the risks and improve the rates or trends of epidemiologically significant infections. | |

*continues*

**Areas of Risk** continued

| Requirement | CMS | | Joint Commission | State |
|---|---|---|---|---|
| ***Discharge Planning [DP]*** | **482.43** | Must have DP policies and procedures that apply to all patients<br>**(a)** Must identify all patients who are likely to suffer adverse health consequences on discharge if there is no DP<br>**(b)(2)** An RN, social worker, or other qualified personnel must develop or supervise the DP evaluation.<br>**(b)(3)** Evaluation must include patient's need for post-hospital services and availability of services.<br><br>**(b)(4)** Evaluation must include patient's capacity for self-care or care in the environment from which they entered the hospital.<br>**(b)(5)** Evaluation must be completed in a timely manner, to avoid delays in discharge.<br>**(b)(6)** Evaluation must include discussion of the plan with the patient or the individual acting on the patient's behalf and must be in the MR.<br>**(c)(3)** Hospital must arrange for the initial implementation of the DP.<br>**(c)(4)** Hospital must re-assess DP if needs change. | **PE.1.6**—Need for DP assessment is determined.<br><br>**PF.3.6**—Patient is educated about resources, care, services, or treatment to meet needs.<br><br>**PF.3.8**—Education includes self-care activities.<br><br>**PE.1.7.1**—Patient's screening assessment completed in 24 hours of inpatient admission.<br><br>**IM.7.3.4.1**—Compliance with discharge criteria is documented in the patient's MR.<br><br>**PF.3.3**—Hospital assures patient is educated to safely use medical equipment or supplies.<br><br>**TX.6.1.1**—DP from rehabilitation services is integrated into the functional assessment.<br>**PF.3.9**—Discharge instructions are given to patient and those responsible for providing continuing care. | |

*continues*

**Areas of Risk** continued

| Requirement | CMS | | Joint Commission | State |
|---|---|---|---|---|
| ***Organ, Tissue, and Eye Procurement [OTEP]*** | **482.45** | **(a)** Must have and implement written protocols<br>**(a)(1)** Agreement with a designated organ procurement organization [OPO], which the hospital must notify in a timely manner of all deaths<br>**(a)(2)** Agreement with at least one tissue bank and one eye bank<br>**(a)(3)** Ensures families of potential donors are informed of donation options<br>**(a)(4)** Use discretion and sensitivity with respect to potential donors<br>**(a)(5)** Ensure that staff is educated on donation issues, death records are reviewed to improve identification of potential donors, and potential donors are maintained while testing and placement of organs is done<br>**(b)(1)** A hospital where transplants are performed must be a member of the Organ Procurement and Transplantation Network [OPTN] the United Network for Organ Sharing [UNOS] and abide by its rules.<br>**(b)(2)** "Organ" means human kidney, liver, heart, lung or pancreas.<br>**(b)(3)** A transplanting hospital must provide data to OPTN [UNOS], the Scientific Registry, and the OPOs. | **RI.2**—Implement policies and procedures, developed with MS participation, for procuring and donation of organs and tissues<br>**Intent of RI.2**—The OPO is identified and hospital has procedures for notifying OPO in a timely manner.<br><br>The OPO determines medical suitability for organ donation.<br><br>Hospital has procedures for family notification of each potential donor.<br><br>Notification is made by the hospital's designated requestor or organ procurement representative.<br><br>Written documentation by designated requester for acceptance or denial of organ donation<br><br>Hospital staff exercises discretion and sensitivity to the beliefs and desires of the families of potential donors.<br><br>Hospital maintains records of potential donors.<br><br>Hospital works with OPO, tissue and eye banks in reviewing death records to improve potential donor identification.<br><br>Hospital works with OPO, tissue and eye banks in educating staff on donation issues. | |
| | **These sections are compared for total content only. DO NOT compare line by line.** | | **These sections are compared for total content only. DO NOT compare line by line.** | |

*continues*

**Areas of Risk** continued

| Requirement | CMS | | Joint Commission | State |
|---|---|---|---|---|
| | **Optional CMS Services** | | | |
| ***Surgical Services [SS]*** | **482.51** | SS must be well organized and provided in accordance with acceptable standards of practice. | **TX.5**—MS defines the scope of assessment for operative and other procedures. | |
| | | **(a)(1)** OR must be supervised by RN, MD, or DO.<br>**(a)(2)** LPNs and scrub techs work under the supervision of an RN.<br>**(a)(3)** RNs perform circulating duties. | **LD.2.11**—Department directed by qualified professional | |
| | | **(a)(4)** SS must maintain a roster specifying surgical privileges.<br>**(b)** Must develop policies governing surgical care | **MS.6.4**—Individuals perform surgical procedures in the scope of their delineated privileges. | |
| | | **(b)(1)** Must be an H&P in every patient's chart before surgery (except in emergencies)<br>**(b)(2)** Properly executed informed consent form for the operation must be in every patient's chart before surgery (except in emergencies).<br>**(b)(3)** Must have the following equipment: call system, cardiac monitor, resuscitator, defibrillator, aspirator and tracheotomy set | **PE.1.8**—Before surgery H&P, diagnostic tests and preoperative diagnosis must be completed/recorded in MR.<br>**TX.5.2**—*Before obtaining informed consent, risks, benefits, potential complications discussed with patient/family (not scored in this standard).* | |
| | | **(b)(4)** Must have provisions for postoperative care<br>**(b)(5)** OR register complete and must be up-to-date | **TX.5.4**—Patient is monitored postprocedure. | |
| | | **(b)(6)** Operative report written or dictated immediately following surgery and signed by surgeon | **IM.7.3.2**—Operative report is dictated or written immediately after surgery.<br>**IM.7.3.2.1**—Operative report is authenticated by the surgeon.<br>**IM.7.3.2.2**—If operative report is not placed immediately in MR after surgery, progress note entered.<br>**IM.7.3.3**—Postop documentation<br>**IM.7.3.5**—Postop documentation for DC | |

continues

**Areas of Risk** continued

| Requirement | CMS | | Joint Commission | State |
|---|---|---|---|---|
| ***Anesthesia Services [AS]*** | **482.52** | Must be provided in a well-organized manner under the supervision of a physician.<br>**(a)** Organization of AS must be appropriate to scope of services anesthesia administered by<br>**(a)(1)** A qualified anesthesiologist<br>**(a)(2)** Doctor of medicine or osteopathy<br>**(a)(4)** Certified RN anesthetist under the supervision of the operating practitioner or anesthesiologist who is immediately available<br>**(a)(5)** Anesthesiology assistant who completed a 6-year program<br>**(b)** Policies on anesthesia procedures must include delineation of pre-anesthesia responsibilities. The policies must ensure the following are provided:<br>**(b)(1)** Pre-anesthesia evaluation performed within 48 hours prior to surgery by an individual qualified to administer anesthesiology<br>**(b)(2)** Intraoperative record<br>**(b)(3)** Post-anesthesia follow-up report written within 48 hours after surgery for inpatients<br>**(b)(4)** Post-anesthesia follow-up evaluation for anesthesia recovery in accordance with PPP approved by MS for outpatient | **LD.2.11**—Department directed by qualified professional<br>**TX.2**—Moderate or deep sedation and anesthesia provided by qualified individuals.<br>**TX.2.1.1**—Moderate or deep sedation and anesthesia care is planned.<br><br>**TX.2.4.1**—Patients are discharged by a qualified practitioner according to criteria approved by the MS.<br><br>**PE.1.8.1**—Pre-sedation or pre-anesthesia assessment<br>**PE.1.8.3**—Patient re-evaluated immediately before induction<br><br>**TX.2.3**—Patient's physiological status is monitored during sedation or anesthesia.<br><br>**PE.1.8.4**—Post-operative status is assessed on admit to/discharge from recovery area.<br><br>**TX.2.2**—Sedation and anesthesia options/risks are discussed with patient/family. | |

*continues*

**Areas of Risk** continued

| Requirement | CMS | | Joint Commission | State |
|---|---|---|---|---|
| ***Nuclear Medicine Services [NMS]*** | **482.53** | **(a)** Organization of NMS must be appropriate to scope of services.<br>**(a)(1)** Director must be a doctor of medicine or osteopathy qualified in nuclear medicine.<br>**(a)(2)** Qualifications, training, and responsibilities of NMS personnel must be approved by NMS director and MS.<br>**(b)** Radioactive materials are handled in accordance with acceptable standards of practice.<br>**(b)(1)** In-house preparation<br>**(b)(2)** Storage and disposal<br>**(b)(3)** Laboratory tests and quality control<br>**(c)** The equipment must be<br>**(c)(1)** maintained in safe operating condition<br>**(c)(2)** inspected, tested, and calibrated at least annually by qualified personnel<br>**(d)(1)** NMS reports must be maintained for at least 5 years.<br>**(d)(2)** The practitioner approved by the MS to interpret diagnostic procedures must sign and date test interpretations.<br>**(d)(3)** Must maintain records of receipt and disposition of radiopharmaceuticals<br>**(d)(4)** NMS is ordered only by a practitioner whose scope of licensure and defined privileges allow such referrals. | **PE.1.10.1**—Hospital provides prompt performance of examinations in nuclear medicine.<br><br>**LD.2.11**—Department is directed by qualified professional. | |

continues

**Areas of Risk** continued

| Requirement | CMS | | Joint Commission | State |
|---|---|---|---|---|
| ***Outpatient Services [OS]*** | **482.54** | **(a)** Must be organized and integrated with inpatient services<br>**(b)(1)** Assign an individual to be responsible for the OS.<br>**(b)(2)** Have appropriate professional and nonprofessional personnel available. | **LD.1.3.4.2**—MS approves sources of patient care provided outside the hospital.<br><br>**LD.2.11**—Department is directed by qualified professional.<br><br>**MS.6.3**—MS determines non-inpatient services for which a patient must have an H&P. | |
| ***Emergency Services [ES]*** | **482.55** | **(a)(1)** Must be organized and under the direction of a qualified member of the MS and<br>**(a)(2)** Services must be integrated with other hospital departments<br>**(a)(3)** PPP governing medical care are established by and a continuing responsibility of the MS<br>**(b)(2)** Must be adequate medical and nursing personnel qualified in emergency care to meet the needs of the facility<br><br>**NOTE: THESE ARE NOT THE REQUIREMENTS FOR EMTALA. EMTALA is found at 42 C.F.R. § 489.20 and 489.24.** | **LD.2.11**—Department is directed by qualified professional.<br><br>**PE.4.2**—Practitioner with clinical privileges determines scope of assessment and care of patients in need of ES.<br>**IM.7.5**—When ES are provided, time and means of arrival documented in MR.<br>**IM.7.5.1**—MR notes if patients receiving ES left against medical advice.<br>**IM.7.5.2**—MR of patient receiving ES notes termination of treatment, final disposition, condition at discharge, and instructions for follow-up. | |

*continues*

**Areas of Risk** continued

| Requirement | CMS | | Joint Commission | State |
|---|---|---|---|---|
| ***Rehabilitation Services [RS]*** | **482.56** | **(a)** Organization of the RS must be appropriate to the scope of services offered.<br>**(a)(1)** The director of RS must have knowledge, experience, and capabilities to properly supervise and administer RS.<br>**(a)(2)** RS must be provided by staff who meet the qualifications specified by the MS consistent with state law.<br>**(b)** Services must be furnished in accordance with a written plan of treatment. RS must be given in accordance with medical staff orders, and the orders must be incorporated in the patient's record. | | |
| ***Respiratory Care Services [RCS]*** | **482.57** | **(a)** Organization of RCS must be appropriate to the scope and complexity of services offered.<br>**(a)(1)** Director of RCS must be a doctor of medicine or osteopathy. The director may be full- or part-time.<br>**(b)** Services are delivered in accordance with MS directives.<br>**(b)(1)** Written procedures for personnel and supervision<br>**(b)(2)** Blood gases or other clinical laboratory tests<br>**(b)(3)** Services must be provided in accordance with doctor's orders. | | |

*continues*

**Areas of Risk** continued

| Requirement | CMS | Joint Commission | State |
|---|---|---|---|
| ***Personnel Records [PR]/Human Resources*** | No COP titled "Personnel" | **HR.1**—Defined qualifications and performance expectations for all staff positions<br><br>**HR.4**—Orientation process<br><br>**HR.4.2**—Ongoing inservice and education training<br><br>**HR.5**—Assess each staff member's performance expectations stated in their job description.<br><br>**LD.2.8**—Directors provide orientation, inservices, and continuing education for all persons in department. | |
| ***Disaster Preparedness [DP]*** | No COP titled "Disaster Preparedness" | **EC.1.4**—A plan addresses emergency management. | |

Source: Copyright © 2003, Denise Casaubon and Rose Sparks.

## DEEMED STATUS

### Background

The Social Security Act § 1861(e) and § 1865(a) permit for deemed status of hospitals. Deemed status means that institutions accredited as hospitals by the Joint Commission or the American Osteopathic Association (AOA) are deemed to meet all of the Medicare Conditions of Participation, except:

- the requirement for utilization review as specified in section 1861(e)(6) of the Act and in 42 C.F.R. 482.30;
- the additional special requirements necessary for the provision of active treatment in psychiatric hospitals section 1861 (f) of the Act and 42 C.F.R. 482.60; and
- any requirements under section 1861(e) of the Act and implementing regulations that CMS, after consulting with the Joint Commission or AOA, identifies as being higher or more precise than the requirements for accreditation in section 1865(a)(4) of the Act.

### Procedure

A hospital deemed to meet program requirements must authorize the accreditation organization to release to CMS, or the state agency responsible for licensing, a copy of the most current accreditation survey. The hospital must furnish the accreditation survey report to the government agency that processes the deemed status requests (CMS or the state agency).

### Determination

CMS or the state agency will review the survey and related survey information and make a determination to grant or deny deemed status to the hospital.

If deemed status is granted, the hospital is considered in compliance with the Medicare Conditions of Participation for the period of time the accreditation is valid (usually a period of three years).

CMS may use a validation survey (42 C.F.R. 488.7) or an accreditation survey or any other survey information (such as Life Safety Code requirements) to determine that a hospital does not meet the Medicare Conditions of Participation. In this case, the hospital is not granted deemed status, and may be required to submit a Plan of Correction to CMS to maintain Medicare certification.

## PROVIDER-BASED DESIGNATION

### Background

Provider-based, or integral-component, designation is granted by CMS for a hospital's services that receive Medicare reimbursement under the hospital's Medicare number. These services may not be provided in the actual hospital, but may be provided by the same organization that governs the hospital, such as a hospital-based outpatient diagnostic center that is located on the hospital's campus. The hospital should request provider-based designation to accommodate the correct allocation of costs and reimbursement where there is more than one type of service being given within the same organization. If the request for a provider-based designation is approved by CMS, there is an increase in the portion of the facility's general and administration costs.

Medicare is under statutory and regulatory mandates to operate as a prudent purchaser of services that will enhance the services and care to its beneficiaries. Medicare must comply with the intent of section 1861 (v)(1)(A) of the Social Security Act that requires reimbursement for services that are both cost effective and advantageous to its beneficiaries.

### Policy

Changes to the provider-based status or designation have been proposed. The final regulations for determining provider-based status were published in August 2002. If a hospital or facility would like to obtain a provider-based status, it is recommended to contact your regional CMS office for assistance at this time.

### Determination

CMS will determine if the entity will be granted a provider-based status or designation with the assistance of the state agency and the fiscal intermediary. The hospital will receive written approval or denial of the provider-based designation status.

## ADDITIONAL RESOURCES

www.jcaho.org
www.cms.hhs.gov
www.acreditinfo.com
http://access.gpo.gov
www.cdc.gov

# Index

## Q



## R



## S